Dār al-islām / dār al-ḥarb

Studies in Islamic Law and Society

VOLUME 40

The titles published in this series are listed at *brill.com/sils*

Dār al-islām / dār al-ḥarb

Territories, People, Identities

Edited by

Giovanna Calasso and Giuliano Lancioni

BRILL

LEIDEN | BOSTON

Library of Congress Cataloging-in-Publication Data

Names: Calasso, Giovanna, editor. | Lancioni, Giuliano, editor.
Title: Dar al-Islam — Dar al-ḥarb : territories, people, identities /
edited by Giovanna Calasso and Giuliano Lancioni.
Description: Leiden ; Boston : Brill, [2017] | Series: Studies In islamic law
and society ; v. 40 | Includes bibliographical references and index.
Identifiers: LCCN 2017017583 (print) | LCCN 2017019739 (ebook) | ISBN
9789004331037 (E-book) | ISBN 9789004328686 (hardback : alk. paper)
Subjects: LCSH: Islam—Relations. | Dar al-ḥarb. | Islam | Dhimmis (Islamic
law) | Islam and world politics.
Classification: LCC BP171 (ebook) | LCC BP171 .D37 2017 (print) | DDC
297.2/72—dc23
LC record available at https://lccn.loc.gov/2017017583

Typeface for the Latin, Greek, and Cyrillic scripts: "Brill". See and download: brill.com/brill-typeface.

ISSN 1384-1130
ISBN 978-90-04-32868-6 (hardback)
ISBN 978-90-04-33103-7 (e-book)

This book is printed on acid-free paper and produced in a sustainable manner.

Contents

Editorial Note

The editorial conventions in this volume follow the 16th edition of the *Chicago Manual of Style*, with some adaptations in the articles written in French.

Transcribed terms are always written in lower case italics (e.g., *dār al-islām*), except proper names (Rūm, not derived adjectives, e.g. *rūmī*), which have a first capital and are written in Roman, unless they are referred to as terms (e.g., "the name *Muḥammad*").

Arabic terms for which a lexicalized English (or French) form exists are written in that form, according to the preferred spelling in the 3rd edition of the *Oxford Dictionary of English* (e.g., Qur'an, fatwa, Hadith, imam, Islam, jihad, Maghrib(i), Mashriq(i), mufti, shah, sharia, sheikh, Shi'a, ulema, umma).

Introduction: Concepts, Words, Historical Realities of a "Classical" Dichotomy

Giovanna Calasso

1 Investigating Absences

Why a book about *dār al-islām / dār al-ḥarb*? Because this terminological pair—"the abode of Islam" and "the abode of war"—has never really been the focus of research specifically devoted to it, despite its being currently referred to in studies as if it were widely known and representative of "the Islamic vision" of the world. So far, in fact, no analysis aimed at reconstructing its historical and conceptual origins has been attempted, exploring its articulations and also its reception within the different genres of Islamic literature, other than juridical texts. When, some years ago, the issue was raised in an article,[1] the topic appeared in all its complexity, and from there the idea of drawing other scholars' attention to the theme originated.

This book actually stems from the International Colloquium entitled "*Dār al-islam/dār al-ḥarb*: territories, people, identities", held at Sapienza University of Rome on 5–6 December 2012, whose purpose was to start providing some answers by exploring a territory which used to be considered familiar but was in fact relatively unexplored. Moreover, although it is true that *dār al-islām / dar al-ḥarb* is a categorization coined by Muslim jurists, the tendency in studies to emphasize the primary role of law, especially in Sunni Islam, has until now narrowed down the field of research almost exclusively to juridical texts. Thus, it is essentially within juridico-political studies, mainly in the sections concerning jihad, that the two notions are dealt with (e.g., in Khadduri, Lambton, Crone, Hallaq),[2] still without being themselves the object of a thorough analysis. However, as Éric Chaumont observes in his article, "le rapport à l'autre

1 Giovanna Calasso, "Alla ricerca di *dār al-islām*. Una ricognizione nei testi di giuristi e tradizionisti, lessicografi, geografi e viaggiatori," *Rivista degli Studi Orientali* 83 (2010): 271–96.

2 Majid Khadduri, *War and Peace in the Law of Islam* (Baltimore: The Johns Hopkins Press, 1955); Majid Khadduri, ed., *The Islamic Law of Nations: Shaybānī's Siyar*. Translated with an Introduction, Notes and Appendices (Baltimore: The Johns Hopkins Press, 1966); Ann K. S. Lambton, *State and Government in Medieval Islam: An Introduction to the Study of Islamic Political Theory: The Jurists*, London Oriental Series, v. 36 (Oxford: Oxford University Press, 1981); Patricia Crone, *Medieval Islamic Political Thought* (Edinburgh: Edinburgh Univ. Press, 2004); Wael B. Hallaq, *Sharīʿa: Theory, Practice, Transformations* (Cambridge: Cambridge University Press, 2009).

 | DOI 10.1163/9789004331037_002

en islam ne s'épuise pas dans la doctrine du jihad [...]: ce rapport belliqueux s'impose dans les cadres du droit musulman et, malgré l'importance du *fiqh* en son sein, l'islam ne se réduit pas à son droit."[3]

It should also be pointed out that not even the jurists who coined these terms and used them widely in their writings gave a definition or dealt with them in a separate section. And this could explain the scant attention that the two categories themselves have received, while in our view even this absence in medieval sources should be given some reflection. Actually, it is something which might be compared with the way Muslim jurists dealt with conversion to Islam, an eminently religious event and yet entailing a change of juridical status, which as such must have been a significant issue for Islamic law in its formative period. However, Muslim scholars did not provide a separate heading for it, scattering the whole matter and its rich casuistry in different sections of their treatises, above all in their chapters on marriage.[4]

Thus, a closer study of this dual categorization and its terminology requires that we reconsider more generally a different way of thinking, with its own characteristics, which should be explored rather than observed through the prism of other ways of thinking[5] which makes us see an absence as something "lacking" rather than something that ought to be interpreted. For instance, what can be drawn from medieval Arabic lexicons, so far never systematically analyzed with reference to the two expressions at issue? And yet, dictionaries "have an important role in revealing clues to the way a culture organizes its conceptual categories, its *episteme*."[6] Actually, going through the main classical Arabic dictionaries dating from between the third/ninth and eighth/fourteenth centuries, the *dār al-islām* collocation is not found either under the entry *dār* or *islām*; but investigating this absence enables us now to consider how Arabic lexicographers treated the two phrases which are the object of our collective exploration, to have an insight into their categories and to read them within the more general framework of the different Islamic genres.

It is the prism of other ways of thinking which has also led scholars to constrain into a rigid conceptual pattern what appears to have been, for Muslim jurists, first and foremost a categorization of the world devised as a useful instrument in defining rules governing the relations between Muslims and

3 Éric Chaumont, present volume, p. 157.

4 See Maya Shatzmiller, "Marriage, Family, and the Faith: Women's Conversion To Islam," *Journal of Family History* 21, no. 3 (1996): 239–40.

5 An essential point of reference in this direction is Wael Hallaq's reflections in his "Introduction" to *Sharīʿa*.

6 Lancioni, present volume, p. 48.

non-Muslims of the outside world, to bring order to an extremely mobile reality, made of continuous exchanges as well as conflicts. In fact, judging from the success of the expression *dār al-islām* among western scholars, we could almost say that they made it their own because it seemed to correspond to *their* idea of "*the* Muslim world," in the singular. But the way Muslim authors used this expression, alongside an array of other similar ones, to identify their own world—*dārunā*, our *dār*— and how they used its converse—*dār al-ḥarb* / *al-kufr*—still has not received the attention it deserves.

And yet *dār al-islām* and *dār al-ḥarb*, apart from their use in juridical texts, are a pair of terms which have to do with the crucial issue of how to conceive oneself and others and translate this idea into words—words which at a certain point crystallized into two conventional formulas, constituting an oppositional pair. This is therefore something which should be related to the Islamization process, intended as the process which led Islam to become the doctrinal, juridical and institutional system, and Muslim society to become the kind of society, that they were both far from being at the time of the great military expansion outside the Arabian Peninsula. This is what Alessandro Bausani meant when he stated that Muhammad's Islam was only "a possibility of Islam,"[7] or what Richard Bulliet highlighted stressing the "fundamental relationship between conversion to Islam and the development of what may be called an Islamic society. When in the second half of the first/ seventh century the Arabs conquered the Persian empire and half of the Byzantine empire, they did not bring with them the religion that is described in general books on Islam. They brought with them ... a mere germ of later developments."[8] Well known but often overlooked facts.

In the present volume, a relationship between this process and the *dār al-islām* / *dār al-ḥarb* binomial is in fact established, showing firstly how the crystallization of this dichotomy in certain words cannot be dated before the fourth/tenth century, and also that behind the permanence of words and conceptual references—that of *hijra*, in its varying association with that of jihad—lies a flexible thought, which in time has produced different, or even contrasting positions, facing the change of historical circumstances. The

7 Alessandro Bausani, "'Sopravvivenze pagane nell'Islam' o integrazione islamica?," *Studi e Materiali di Storia delle Religioni* 36 (1966): 191.

8 Richard W. Bulliet, *Conversion to Islam in the Medieval Period: An Essay in Quantitative History* (Cambridge: Harvard University Press, 1979), 1; see also Houari Touati, *Islam et voyage au Moyen Âge: histoire et anthropologie d'une pratique lettrée*, L'univers historique (Paris: Seuil, 2000); and, more recently, Fred M. Donner, "Qur'ânicization of Religio-Political Discourse in the Umayyad Period," *Revue Des Mondes Musulmans et de La Méditerranée* 129 (2011): 79–92.

transitions from a ruling minority living among a majority of other religious communities to a ruling majority, then to a majority ruled by a non-Muslim foreign power, and eventually to minorities living in foreign non-Muslim countries are in fact major changes to be considered.

Therefore, the issue of how "self" and "others" have been conceived by Muslim authors needs to be further defined: conceived by whom, starting from what time, with which contents and implications? It is such questions to which we have tried to find answers.

2 Between *hijra* and jihad

Of course, like every collection of studies, this book does not systematically meet the various questions raised by this type of research, but it fills in some blanks and offers new perspectives. For example, an analysis of the occurrences of *dār al-islām* and *dār al-ḥarb* and similar expressions in the literary genre of Qur'anic commentaries—until now never surveyed in relation to these notions—is presented in two contributions, one addressing the topic in an exhaustive way for what concerns Ṭabarī's *Tafsīr* (Roberto Tottoli), the other investigating it within a wider time frame with reference to the Qur'anic verses in which the notion of "emigrating"(*hājara*) occurs (Raoul Villano).

The conceptual significance of the notion of *hijra* (emigration)—a pivotal event in Muhammad's biography, but also a highly recommended and praiseworthy action for the members of the early Muslim community—in the construction of an idea of boundary and the relating opposition between *dār al-islām* and *dār al-ḥarb* is actually highlighted in different ways (Calasso, Villano, Tottoli, Zappa): as a historical event—the Prophet's *hijra*—perceived by Islamic tradition as a symbolic watershed, and as such put forward by several reformist movements until the modern age, but also as an action charged with a high ethical value in the Qur'an itself. In fact, while the term *hijra* is not found in the sacred book of Islam, the Qur'anic occurrences of the verb *hājara* are significant. As for the commentaries to the verses about "emigrating," the expressions *dār al-islām* and *dār al-ḥarb* start occurring frequently only with Ṭabarī's *Tafsīr* (fourth/tenth century), which proves to be a real turning point in this literary domain, not to be overlooked when outlining the phases of the "canonization" process of the binomial and their becoming sort of "technical terms." If the commentaries of the second/eighth and early third/ninth century never used the word *dār* associated with *islām* or *ḥarb*, nor the expressions *dār al-islām* / *dār al-ḥarb*, it means that this conceptual and linguistic dichotomy was still not so established as to be exported into Qur'anic exegesis.

In Tottoli's view, the recurring, close connection between emigrating and the *dār al-islām / dār al-ḥarb* oppositional pair found in Ṭabarī's *Tafsīr* represents a further stage in the development of this dual concept, which originated around the first conquest wars and then was made its own by *siyar* juridical literature: "the combination of the real relations between the two abodes and of the ideal confrontation between the realm of faith and that of unbelief,"[9] which reflects a more self-confident attitude dating back to the time when Islam was beginning to gain a majority in spite of the break-up of its political unity. The fact that for far more than three centuries Muslims were not the majority within the countries under Muslim rule is indeed not to be underestimated.

Or is the origin of the *dār al-islām / dār al-ḥarb* dichotomy and its connection with the notion of *hijra* to be traced back to the Qur'an itself?

Swimming against the tide, although going off in different directions, two studies in the present volume credit the Qur'an itself with a decisive role in the conceptual genesis of this oppositional pair, although it is not explicitly found there, one focusing on the notion of *hijra* (Villano), the other on that of jihad (Chaumont). And these are in fact the pillars on which—alternately—the dichotomy has rested through time. The Qur'an points indeed to the act of emigrating as the symbol of one's loyalty to God and his Messenger—instead of his own tribe—a horizontal displacement establishing "a temporal dichotomy [which] lastly turns into an ethical or moral dichotomy."[10] Therefore, as Raoul Villano maintains, it is in the Qur'anic notion of "emigrating" that the origin of the *dār al-islām / dār al-ḥarb* dichotomy should be identified. And this would perfectly suit Gianroberto Scarcia's thesis[11]—referred to also by other contributors to this volume—according to which the very meaning of *dār al-ḥarb*, as opposed to *dār al-islām*, should be interpreted, based on some Qur'anic passages, as the *dār* of those who wage war against God, and not of those against whom war must be waged, in opposition to the *dār* of those who submit themselves to God.

Things are seen very differently by Éric Chaumont, who focuses on the chapter about *al-siyar wa 'l-jihād* of the *Kitāb al-Muhaḏḏab* by the outstanding fifth/

9 Present volume, p. 122.

10 See Villano, p. 144.

11 See Gianroberto Scarcia, "*Islām* e *Ḥarb*, *ʿArab* e *ʿAjam*: nota a due celeberrime dicotomie islamiche," in *Azhàr: studi arabo-islamici in memoria di Umberto Rizzitano (1913–1980)*, ed. Antonino Pellitteri and Giovanni Montaina, Annali della Facoltà di lettere e filosofia dell'Università di Palermo. Studi e ricerche 23 (Palermo: Facoltà di lettere e filosofia dell'Università di Palermo, 1995), 205–10.

eleventh century Shafi'i legist Šīrāzī. Actually the first section of the chapter opens with the issue of *hijra*. Does this mean that in Šīrāzī's mind emigration is a form of jihad, perhaps even its most valuable form?

Chaumont, however, maintains that it is on the notion of jihad as "community obligation" (*farḍ ʿalā ʾl-kifāya*) that the dual theologico-political geography of classical Islam, opposing *dār al-islām* to *dār al-ḥarb*, rests. The way *al-mušrikūn*—*all* non-Muslims, according to *tafsīr* literature—are viewed in the Qur'an not as mere impurity but as filth (*najas*), and the duty imperatively prescribed by God to take up arms against them, would in itself be sufficient to explain the existence of the oppositional pair and its wording, as well as to explain why all classical *fiqh* treatises include a chapter on jihad. In any case, in Šīrāzī's mind, *hijra* and jihad undeniably seem to share a common root and the different stress put on each of them by the two authors only confirms the existence of a complex web of connections between the two notions and the relevance they both have in originating the *dār al-islām / dār al-ḥarb* dichotomy.

As for early treatises on jihad, Roberta Denaro's analysis highlights the difference between juridical works produced in the caliph's court environment for the benefit of political power and those written by authors residing in areas bordering on the Byzantine empire, the *ṯuġūr*—"the frontier" *par excellence*—and who preach and practice jihad themselves. The emphasis on the *dār al-ḥarb / dār al-islām* opposition is confirmed as the product of court jurists, who are committed to turning jihad into an instrument of power legitimation, while in treatises on jihad written by authors residing on the periphery of the empire, all engaged in a spiritual fight, the two expressions never occur and Baghdad's court—in theory the center of *dār al-islām*—does not appear to be a point of reference, nor does the jihad promoted by caliphs and their jurists represent a kind of struggle in which these authors can identify.

3 Mapping the Occurrences

A most interesting outcome of this collection of studies is their mapping—albeit still a partial one—of the occurrences of *dār al-islām* and *dār al-ḥarb* and of an array of similar expressions in a wide range of texts of different kinds, geographical provenance and ages, spanning the second/eighth and ninth/fifteenth centuries: lexicons, Qur'anic commentaries, Hadith, treatises on jihad, texts on *siyar* and other juridical works, geographical and historical writings, as well as archival documents. Moreover, other types of texts are analyzed with reference to the early modern and modern age, such as fatwas, international agreements, capitulation treatises, *inšāʾ* works.

This mapping highlights the fact that the division of the world into the two *dārs* is not, at its core, a "historical" categorization, and indeed Muslim historians hardly ever make use of it. It is a categorization based on the exclusive and exclusionary vision of the religions of the Book[12] which, in Islam, however, combined with a juridical theory that recognized an institutional status to internal differences (*ḏimmī, musta'min*), does not necessarily establish a boundary between an Islamic domain exclusively made of Muslims and an external domain belonging to other religions (Calasso).

Of course mapping the occurrences can be misleading, and the study of the phrases used in texts to denominate the others does not necessarily make us understand how they were conceived and how well-known they were: terminology tends to be more rigid and schematic than reality, and often schematic and reductive or rather generic expressions are used, even when one is aware of the internal differences found in "the other" reality and knows its varieties (Lev, Rhoné).

In Yaacov Lev's analysis, the term *rūm*—one of the most frequent terms to indicate non-Muslims in Arabic sources between the fourth/tenth and sixth/twelfth centuries, as well as in Geniza letters—is shown to be an idiomatic expression conveying a very broad meaning, its use being "loose and instrumental." Frequently terminology "serves as the lowest common denominator of convenience," the author concludes, and "what seems strange to us was satisfactory to and well understood by twelfth-century contemporaries," a remark which leads us back to the initial reflections on the need to be responsive to other ways of thinking, expressed through words—and sometimes through silence—which is at the basis of our research.

And yet, however misleading terminology may be, the comparison between terminological usages in different textual domains and in different ages—including the presence or absence of the expressions *dār al-islām* and *dār al-ḥarb*, or the choice of referring to people by loose geographical or ethnical terms—allows a series of observations which will eventually enable us to get a more nuanced picture of the central theme of the volume (Lancioni, *Concluding remarks*).

---

12 The close relationship between world religions and writing, and "the boundaries the written word creates, or rather defines," are explored, in an anthropological perspective, by Jack Goody, in *The Logic of Writing and the Organization of Society*, Studies in Literacy, Family, Culture, and the State (Cambridge: Cambridge University Press, 1986); for a rich and insightful reflection on the conceptual issue of monotheism, to be traced back to the crucial "Mosaic distinction," in which "the discriminating element is not unicity, but exclusion," see Jan Assmann, *Die Mosaische Unterscheidung oder der Preis des Monotheismus* (München: Hanser, 2003).

Most of the contributions refer to Sunni Islam, while Scarcia Amoretti's work introduces into the picture the point of view of Imami Shi'ism, a community which, until the Safavid period, did not have a defined territory governed by a legitimate ruler, and lived within a context of Sunni hegemony practicing *taqiyya*—"legitimate dissimulation", according to the current definition, although, for the author, something much more substantial in a *bāṭin* (esoteric) perspective. In fact, in Imami texts, a further expression occurs to indicate this community without its own territory, that of *dār al-īmān*, "the abode of faith," which is used in contrast not only to *dār al-ḥarb/kufr*, but also—which is more significant—to *dār al-islām*: this raises the question of the theological, even more than juridical, nature of the opposition, and highlights, in Shi'i context, a question of "alterity" mainly internal to Islam. From a chronological point of view, the author's references to the Imami theologian Ibn Bābawayh, (311/923–381/991–2), confirm that the fourth/tenth century was a crucial moment in the conceptual history of the binomial which is the object of our research, in both Shi'i and Sunni contexts.

The theme is also covered, with reference to medieval Shi'ism in the first part of Alessandro Cancian's contribution, significantly titled "Faith as territory" and dedicated in particular to the *dār al-islām / dār al-ḥarb* binomial in texts by authors of the Gunabadi branch of the modern Shi'i Sufi order of Niʿmat-Allāhiyya. In the words of Hamid Algar, quoted by Cancian, "the concept of *dār al-ḥarb* was not developed in any special way in Shi'ite jurisprudence.... Shi'ite jurists did, however, establish a third category of territory, *dār al-īmān* (the realm of faith), defined by prevailing acceptance of the imams among its people. Greater theoretical importance was given to the opposition between this realm and *dār al-islām* than to that between *dār al-islām* and *dār al-ḥarb*,"[13] the latter terms occurring in Shi'i juridical literature without significant differences from the Sunni texts, but clearly without having the same importance and meaning as in Sunni thinking. The prevalence of the inner dimension of faith over the "outer" one, related to juridical and territorial belonging, is intertwined in Shi'i context with the relevance of another dichotomy: the one establishing a frontier between the imam's followers and all other Muslims.

---

13 Hamid Algar, "Dār al-ḥarb," *Encyclopaedia Iranica, Vol. VI, Coffeehouse–Dārā* (London: Routledge & Kegan Paul, 1993). See Cancian, present volume, 298.

4 The Notion of Frontier and Frontier Case Studies

The notions of border and boundaries, implicitly at the center of the *dār al-islām / dār al-ḥarb* dichotomy, and studies dealing with these notions—theory and practices—within the Islamic medieval world, are the object of reflections (Calasso), and some "frontier" contexts are presented in the volume as case studies: Spain, Anatolia and the border regions of north-eastern Iran through the analysis of medieval texts, the *bilād al-sūdān* with reference to a long period of time spanning the fourth/tenth to the thirteenth/nineteenth centuries.

Fierro and Molina present the results of research on medieval historiographical and legal sources on al-Andalus and show that the expression *dār al-ḥarb* is never used in narratives about the conquest of Spain; that, where found, it is alone and not used in opposition to *dār al-islām*; and that the occurrences of *dār al-islām* are in general extremely rare. Moreover, some northern regions such as the western Basque country—Alaba in chronicles—unlike the "classic" narrative of the Muslim conquest of al-Andalus, from the beginning seem to have had an intermediate status, that of *dār amān*, despite being inhabited not by Christians but by *majūs*, pagans. Therefore, the notion of *dār al-islām* is almost totally absent in the historiography *of* al-Andalus and *on* al-Andalus, in contrast with the presence, however limited, of *dār al-ḥarb*, in any case always with reference to Christian enemies in the centuries following the conquest, when a frontier in the north was almost established.

While Roberta Denaro focuses on early texts dealing with jihad at the frontier with the Byzantine empire, Camille Rhoné's study is centered on the north-eastern border regions of Iran between the third/ninth and the fifth/eleventh centuries, where the enemy is not an empire, a state structure, but nomadic tribes, and where frontiers are therefore moving. In the historical sources taken into consideration, the enemy is mainly described using ethnic terms, rather than with reference to the *dār al-islām / dār al-ḥarb* opposition. Nevertheless, the way in which it is represented is stereotyped, tending to give the idea that the enemy is one, united, homogeneous people; and yet the diversity of the ethnical components of the inhabitants of the regions beyond the frontier was well known to Muslim authors, for instance to geographers. Moreover, although the diffusion of Islam among the people of the steppes contradicts the global image of the Turks as infidels, and in spite of commercial exchanges and the presence of Muslim merchants in the region, the lords of the local dynasties are surrounded by ulema who represent them as defensive ramparts against barbarians, as heroes of a perpetual frontier war. Therefore, in this context, the rhetorical discourse opposing *dār al-islām* to *dār al-ḥarb*, elaborated in Baghdad by jurists at the service of the central power, seems to function, according to Rhoné's reading of the sources, as the implicit model of reference.

As for Anatolia, which became part of the territories under Muslim rule at the end of the fifth/eleventh century, the idea of belonging to the Roman world lives on for a long time, overpowering the idea of *dār al-islām* (Michel Balivet): chronicles and administrative documents between the fifth/eleventh and the seventh/thirteenth centuries keep referring to *bilād al-rūm, diyār-ı rūm, sulṭān-ı rūm*. To the eyes of external Muslim observers, the fact that a large number of people of the Book still reside there is influential; the leading Turkish elite is accused of tolerating customs not in keeping with Islam's prescriptions and thirteenth century Arabic historiographical sources consider even the Seljuk sultans' orthodoxy to be suspect. All in all, among the areas which were part of the Roman empire and were then subjected to Muslim rule in medieval times, this vast region seems to have been the most difficult to conceptualize by Muslim authors as belonging to Islam.

The relevance of a study dedicated to a frontier area such as *bilād al-sūdān* (Francesco Zappa) lies mainly in the fact that this context, peripheral to the historic core of Islam, has never been the focus of research connected to the conceptualization of the notions we are investigating. It is true that, for obvious reasons, sources about *bilād al-sūdān* cannot be expected to provide information about the emergence and elaboration of such "classical" notions; at best they can tell us about their different applications, appropriations and interpretations. However, as Alessandro Bausani maintained, "borders" (be they geographical, chronological, doctrinal, linguistic or other) can help us identify and highlight certain phenomena which are also present in the center, although sometimes less visible.

In the context of *bilād al-sūdān* the *dār al-islām* / *dār al-ḥarb* binomial rarely occurs in the sources, mainly juridical, and in the earliest period of contact until the twelfth-thirteenth century, sub-Saharan Africa appears in its entirety as *dār al-kufr*. The central juridical problem which emerges is then the lawfulness of commerce with misbelievers. But the importance of trans-Saharan commerce for Maghrib's economy will lead to the contriving of juridical tricks and narrative stratagems in geographical and historical texts. The space Muslim merchants have in *bilād al-sūdān* is represented as a network of enclaves within *dār al-kufr*, and sources constantly hint at an imaginary frontier delimiting Muslim colonies and protecting them from a contaminating contact. Then the reality of multiethnic Muslim empires starting from the seventh/thirteenth century makes the image of Muslim enclaves in *dār al-kufr* obsolete. After having taken new forms, the debate on the definition of the frontier between the two *dār*s will come back to the forefront with the reform movements which will result in the great jihads of the eleventh/seventeenth and twelfth/eighteenth centuries. These movements will once again question the Muslim identity of the populations and the states of the region, whose sovereigns are accused of practicing a kind of syncretism with local cults. In the rich polemical and apologetical literature produced and promoted by Usman dan Fodio, the presence of the *dār al-islām* / *dār al-ḥarb* binomial becomes much more frequent than in previous sources and acquires all its significance and its dynamic potential in relation to the idea of *hijra*. In conclusion, in the sub-Saharan African context, the frontier between the two *dār*s appears to have an extremely fluid and changing character according to authors and historical period, and the question of belonging to *dār al-islām* is the object of a debate and an issue whose importance seems to be increasing in time.

5 Theory and Practice in Mediterranean Intersection Territories and in Ottoman Sources

Moving to the Mediterranean, on the threshold of the modern age, Francisco Apellániz's research focuses on the area of Cyprus, which he defines as "a normative crossroads between *dār al-ḥarb* and *dār al-islām*," an intersection territory where Islamic and non-Islamic religious and legal concepts and norms frequently overlap. Investigating the category of the so-called Fazolati—as they are called in Venetian archival documents of the fifteenth century—the author also raises the question of whether people perceived the implications of the Islamic scholars' division of the world. If for fourteenth century jurists *dār al-ḥarb* and *dār al-islām* remained two necessary analytical categories, allowing them to differentiate between *ḏimmī*s and *ḥarbī*s, "what was the real significance of this division in the Islamic borderlands, as the cities of commerce of the late Middle Ages? … The Fazolati dispute illustrates that not only rulers but other social actors were aware of this theoretical divide [between *dār al-ḥarb* and *dār al-islām*] and manipulated it at their own advantage", for instance Venetian merchants who tried to have the status of Fazolati recognized by Mamluk authorities in order to avoid expulsion from Egypt. This issue also "shows the ability of Mediterranean peoples to navigate through the loopholes of legal concepts and doctrines."[14]

As for Ottoman sources—archival documents, texts of international agreements, chronicles, fatwas, *inšā'* works and miscellanies—Nicola Melis's study shows how misleading it would be to cling to the categories of classic Hanafi

14 Apellániz, present volume, pp. 159, 175.

law, which never admitted the existence of anything but *dār al-islām* and *dār al-ḥarb*, including in *dār al-islām* the territories which, according to Mawardī's Shafi'i view, would belong to *dār al-ʿahd*. But, Melis maintains, the territorial dimension, in terms of *dār*s, is never mentioned in Ottoman sources when dealing with truces. Thus, as Alexander de Groot writes "[t]he usual theoretical notion of Islamic scholars that the world was divided in two.... is not useful for our understanding of the historical development of Ottoman foreign relations" as well as their territorial conception. "The very strict Islamic legal terminology about territoriality in Ottoman texts is contrasted by a very rich literary and administrative terminology about world division that includes several subcategories of territory."[15] Some fatwas by Ebüssuʿūd Efendi (1567) about the renovation of capitulation treaties with Venice and Genoa, show for instance that the status granted by the *ʿahdnāme*s did guarantee to *mustaʾmin*s—foreigners provided with a safe-conduct—certain elements of extraterritoriality and quasi-immunity which were usually unavailable to Ottoman non-Muslims. In other words, the discourse focused on the group or individual status, rather than on a territorial conception (p. 191).

Sources from the Ottoman period are also at the center of Antonino Pellitteri's analysis, although in the context of the western Mediterranean area and from a different perspective. The author focuses on some passages from the chronicles of two Maghribi historians and *fuqahāʾ* who lived in the eighteenth and the nineteenth centuries, concerning the Norman expansion in northern Africa in the sixth/twelfth century. Yet, he also looks back on the terminology found in a document related to Sicily—a Mediterranean *ṯaġr*-land *par excellence*—at the time of the Fatimid victory (fourth/tenth century), stretching the picture on to a further comparison with the terms used by other tenth/sixteenth–eleventh/seventeenth century Muslim historians referring to different geographical and political contexts. The objective is to stress the idea of otherness as self-mirroring, which can be perceived in these authors' representation of *dār al-ḥarb*: an idea more suitably expressed by the term *barr al-ʿaduww* (the enemy's mainland), hinting at a contact zone instead of a closed divide.

Also dating from the Ottoman period, the *Risāla fī dār al-ḥarb wa-suknāhā* by the Tunisian reformer Muḥammad Bayram V (1256/1840–1307/1889) presents us with the adaptation of classical Hanafi jurisprudence to the changing needs of a new international scenario, thanks to the author's masterful ability in the use of analogical reasoning (Francesca Romana Romani and Eleonora Di Vincenzo). Far from being a uniform reality *dār al-ḥarb* includes different

---

15 See Melis, present volume, 185–86.

types of countries—duly classified by the author—and thanks to analogical reasoning, the emigration of a Muslim to the "territory of war" can be qualified, depending on conditions and perspective, as a prohibited or reprehensible, but also as a recommendable and even mandatory action, in order to protect oneself from the injustices suffered in one's own Islamic country. On the other hand, when referring to the author's time, "the abode of Islam" is no more called *dār al-islām*, nor *bilād al-islām*, but *bilād al-muslimīn*, Muslims' lands, thus highlighting that a major change occurred: Islam is now narrowed down to the sole religious sphere of Muslim individuals.

6 The Use of the Categories of *dār al-islām* and *dār al-ḥarb* in the Colonial Age: India and Indonesia

An exhaustive picture of the presence and use of the two categories in Indian Islamic thought is presented by Yohanan Friedmann, starting from the *Fatāwā-yi ʿĀlamgīrī*, the earliest legal work written in India in the second half of the eleventh/seventeenth century, where a reference to *dār al-islām* and *dār al-ḥarb* is found. Retracing in the first pages the classifications of medieval Muslim authors and in particular the theme of the permanent and obligatory state of war between *dār al-islām* and *dār al-ḥarb*, as maintained by authors such as Lewis and Crone, Friedmann observes: "In the classical legal sources I have not come across an explicit statement according to which *dār al-ḥarb* is so called because it should be incorporated into *dār al-islām* by means of war."[16] Friedmann rather points out that Muslim jurists are mainly interested in how Muslims should behave in *dār al-ḥarb* and non-Muslims *mustaʾmin* in *dār al-islām*. Besides intermittent battles there are also economic transactions between the two areas, which can be gauged from the extensive discussion of types of goods which may or may not be exported into *dār al-ḥarb*. On the basis of these premises, the discussions which took place in nineteenth century British India are analyzed. In this context, the definition of the legal status of this area as *dār al-ḥarb* appears crucial in relation to the lawfulness of interest transactions with the Hindus and the British.

At the end of the 1930s the problem of India's legal status was once again at the center of discussions, and the two antithetical positions by Aḥsan Gīlānī and Mawdūdī are analyzed. While Gīlānī wants to establish an analogy between Mecca before the Muslim conquest and India under British domination, thus viewing British India as *dār al-ḥarb*, according to Mawdūdī's criteria, it is next

16 Present volume, 344.

to impossible for an area to be transformed from *dār al-islām* into *dār al-ḥarb* or *dār al-kufr*. Moreover, he maintains that *dār al-kufr* is merely "foreign territory:" only countries at war with Muslims are *dār al-ḥarb* (p. 367). Thus India, which, in Mawdūdī's view, was without any doubt *dār al-islām* before the British entered the subcontinent, at the beginning of the nineteenth century became *dār al-ḥarb* because the British were fighting against the Muslim government. However in the 1930s, Mawdūdī maintains, India should be considered *dār al-kufr* because Muslim laws are not in effect, and, at the same time, *dār al-ṣulḥ* (land of covenant) because it is not at war with a Muslim country: a possible convergence, that between *dār al-kufr* and *dār al-ʿahd* which is not found in classical sources. Unlike Gīlānī, and in keeping with Shafi'i thought, Mawdūdī however maintains that Islamic law is universally valid. Therefore, interest transactions which are unlawful between Muslims cannot be lawful between Muslims and infidels, even in *dār al-kufr* (pp. 370–71).

The views of two other eminent scholars—of Deobandi formation—are also analyzed, that of Ḥusayn Aḥmad Madanī (1879–1957) and that of Saʿīd Aḥmad Akbarābādī, who discuss what determines the juridical status of a territory, the first maintaining that it is the religious affiliation of the sovereign, the other the freedom to practice their religion enjoyed by its Muslim inhabitants. As for the *šarʿī* status of India after Partition, according to Akbarābādī it cannot be *dār al-ḥarb,* or *dār al-islām*, because it is a secular, democratic state. Classical concepts can no longer be applied to the modern situation: India has to be considered by its Muslim inhabitants as their *national home,* a category which Akbarābādī, despite being an *ʿālim* of traditional formation, does not hesitate to describe as *šarʿī*:. an example, Friedmann observes, which shows that when historical reality requires it, "Muslim law may develop in rather unexpected directions" (p. 375).

Therefore, the contributions by Francesco Zappa, Francisco Apellániz and Yohanan Friedmann show how, in different contexts and times, the definitions of the two *dār*s and their application to a certain domain have been perceived as crucial in relation to very concrete economic realities: trans-Saharan commerce in the Middle Ages, the fiscal situation of European merchants in the eastern Mediterranean in the Mamluk age, the possibility of making interest transactions dealing with non-Muslims in colonial India. But, while in the case of India the definition of its areas under British rule as *dār al-ḥarb,* far from implicating a call for jihad, was mainly aimed at allowing Muslims to carry out otherwise prohibited commercial operations, in the case of western Africa in Usman dan Fodio's times, the qualification of the whole *bilād al-sūdān* as *dār al-kufr* was meant to authorize jihad against its population as well as to affirm the necessity of emigration—*hijra*—revitalising the founding event of Muhammad's Islam.

As in India, the issue of the legal *šarʿī* status of territories under colonial domination arose in Indonesia, and Chiara Formichi's study analyses the political currency gained by the *dār al-islām* concept in fourteenth/twentieth century Indonesia between the two wars. As in Usman dan Fodio's Nigeria, we find again, in the mid-twentieth century, the founding notion of *hijra* following the Prophet's model, deserting an Indonesian Mecca (under colonial domination) and creating an Indonesian Medina. Ancient words, such as *hijra* and *jāhiliyya,* still circulate in modern Indonesian contexts, but curiously *dār al-ḥarb* does not appear. Instead, the relation between *dār al-islām* and the Qur'anic otherworldly *dār al-salām,* with the implicit suggestion of an equivalence between *islām* and *salām,* "peace"—also mentioned in Scarcia Amoretti's and Villano's contributions—is found more than once. As for the different and even contrasting theoretical orientations of medieval Muslim jurists—who viewed the notion of *dār al-islām* in terms either of personality or territoriality of law—they do not seem to be significant in this new framework of political relations. *Dār al-islām* is now used as a synonym for the Islamic state and Darul Islam is the name of a political movement opposing colonial power.

7 Concluding Reflections

In contrast to the fixed and permanent categories they are currently identified with, *dār al-islām* and *dār al-ḥarb* appear as two notions which have been given different meanings and functions according to authors, times and contexts, but which kept on existing through time, crystallized in certain words and, with their very existence, affected the way Muslims scholars rationalized how to react to changing and challenging historical circumstances. In particular, *dār al-ḥarb* appears through time as the object of a process of distinction which has almost resulted, in the modern age, in the reversal of its traditional definition. And yet Hanafi jurists, and occasionally Muslim geographers as well, already used the plural form, *dūr al-ḥarb / al-kufr*, testifying to the fact that, also in the Middle Ages, the others' world could be perceived as a reality, not just as an abstraction.

As for *dār al-islām,* supposedly an even more fixed notion, the studies collected in this volume converge on contrasting the image of a monochrome and unitary "Islamic world" also with reference to the "classic" Islamic Age, sharing a trend which has characterized Islamic studies in recent decades:

two collective works—both published in 2013—are a case in point. The one, edited by Maribel Fierro and John Tolan, dedicated to the legal status of *ḏimmīs* in the Muslim west, shows that in confronting juridical texts from Mashriq and Maghrib, "there is little evidence for a standard, uniform *ḏimmī* system, but rather a wide variety of local adaptations."[17] The other one, *Defining Boundaries in al-Andalus* by Janina Safran, aims to demonstrate that a clear distinction between the spheres of Muslims and non-Muslims—within the Muslim domain of al-Andalus—was an ideal, while "the evidence of ninth-tenth-century Maliki legal texts reveals a discursive negotiation of principles of difference and separation in contingent circumstances of social interaction:"[18] "Jurists invoked Qur'anic verses of separation but, through the casuistry of exception-making, accommodated close social relationships."[19] Even more compelling is the outcome of Christian Müller's in-depth analysis—presented in the volume edited by Fierro and Tolan—of a fifth/eleventh-century Andalusi law manual, showing a legal reasoning that includes *ḏimmīs* at all levels, thus proving that medieval Islamic law considered non-Muslim subjects as members of Muslim society.[20] Although no specific chapter in *fiqh* manuals deals with *ḏimmī*-related issues, yet they can be found in almost every section.[21]

And still, the idea of an internal frontier—between Muslims and non-Muslims within Islamic territory—as well as that of an external one, subsumed under the dichotomy *dār al-islām* / *dār al-ḥarb*, seem to be unchangeable in their conceptual core.

Or is it rather a question of unchanging words? In Mathieu Tillier's article which opens the 2014 special issue of the *Bulletin d'Etudes Orientales* dedicated to the theme "Le pluralisme judiciaire dans l'Islam prémoderne," the author states: "Les transformations constantes qui affectèrent les institutions judiciaires islamiques sont en décalage avec une terminologie qui, de son côté, reste stable le plus souvent." "Bien que les réalités évoluent sans cesse, les références demeurent en général inchangées: les auteurs arabes musulmans

17 John Tolan, "Concluding Remarks," in *The legal status of ḏimmī-s in the Islamic West: second/eighth-ninth/fifteenth centuries*, ed. Maribel Fierro and John Tolan, Religion and law in medieval Christian and Muslim societies 1 (Turnhout: Brepols, 2013), 367.

18 Janina M. Safran, *Defining Boundaries in al-Andalus: Muslims, Christians, and Jews in Islamic Iberia.* (Ithaca: Cornell University Press, 2013), 17.

19 Ibid., 216.

20 Christian Müller, "Non-Muslims as part of Islamic law: Juridical casuistry in a fifth/eleventh-century law manual," in *The legal status of ḏimmī-s*, 60.

21 Maribel Fierro, "Introduction," in *The legal status of ḏimmī-s*, 11.

tendent à évoquer les institutions dans des termes consacrés par la tradition." Is it what happened with *dār al-islām* and *dār al-ḥarb*? If until the fourth/tenth century—in the period when Muslims continued to be a minority, however growing, governing a non-Muslim majority—textual sources give evidence of a variety of expressions used to convey the same concepts even within the same genre (see Tottoli's and Villano's contributions on *tafsīr* literature), starting from this period mentions of *dār al-islām / dār al-ḥarb* become ubiquitous and their assumed (canonized) meaning indicates the abode where Islam rules and that where it does not. A permanence of words, however, which would cover a wide range of meanings from the time Muslims found themselves experiencing the condition of a minority under non-Muslim rule, meanings which would almost come to be reversed in the new international scenario of the nineteenth century, up to the contemporary one.

References

Algar, Hamid. "Dār al-ḥarb." *Encyclopaedia Iranica, Vol. VI, Coffeehouse–Dārā*. London: Routledge & Kegan Paul, 1993.

Assmann, Jan. *Die Mosaische Unterscheidung oder der Preis des Monotheismus*. München: Hanser, 2003.

Bausani, Alessandro. "'Sopravvivenze pagane nell'Islam' o integrazione islamica?" *Studi e Materiali di Storia delle Religioni* 36 (1966): 189–209.

Bulliet, Richard W. *Conversion to Islam in the Medieval Period: An Essay in Quantitative History*. Cambridge: Harvard University Press, 1979.

Calasso, Giovanna. "Alla ricerca di *dār al-islām*. Una ricognizione nei testi di giuristi e tradizionisti, lessicografi, geografi e viaggiatori." *Rivista degli Studi Orientali* 83 (2010): 271–96.

Crone, Patricia. *Medieval Islamic Political Thought*. Edinburgh: Edinburgh Univ. Press, 2004.

Donner, Fred M. "Qur'ânicization of Religio-Political Discourse in the Umayyad Period." *Revue Des Mondes Musulmans et de La Méditerranée* 129 (2011): 79–92.

Fierro, Maribel. "Introduction." In *The legal status of ḏimmī-s in the Islamic West: second/eighth-ninth/fifteenth centuries*, edited by Maribel Fierro and John Tolan, 9–18. Religion and law in medieval Christian and Muslim societies 1. Turnhout: Brepols, 2013.

Goody, Jack. *The Logic of Writing and the Organization of Society*. Studies in Literacy, Family, Culture, and the State. Cambridge: Cambridge University Press, 1986.

Hallaq, Wael B. *Sharīʿa: Theory, Practice, Transformations*. Cambridge: Cambridge University Press, 2009.

Khadduri, Majid. *War and Peace in the Law of Islam*. Baltimore: The Johns Hopkins Press, 1955.

Khadduri, Majid, ed. *The Islamic Law of Nations: Shaybānī's Siyar*. Translated with an Introduction, Notes and Appendices. Baltimore: The Johns Hopkins Press, 1966.

Lambton, Ann K. S. *State and Government in Medieval Islam: An Introduction to the Study of Islamic Political Theory: The Jurists*. London Oriental Series, v. 36. Oxford: Oxford University Press, 1981.

Müller, Christian. "Non-Muslims as part of Islamic law: Juridical casuistry in a fifth/eleventh-century law manual." In *The legal status of ḏimmī-s in the Islamic West: second/eighth-ninth/fifteenth centuries*, edited by Maribel Fierro and John Tolan, 21–63. Religion and law in medieval Christian and Muslim societies 1. Turnhout: Brepols, 2013.

Safran, Janina M. *Defining Boundaries in al-Andalus: Muslims, Christians, and Jews in Islamic Iberia*. Ithaca: Cornell University Press, 2013.

Scarcia, Gianroberto. "*Islām* e *Ḥarb*, *'Arab* e *'Ajam*: nota a due celeberrime dicotomie islamiche." In *Azhàr: studi arabo-islamici in memoria di Umberto Rizzitano (1913–1980)*, edited by Antonino Pellitteri and Giovanni Montaina, 205–10. Annali della Facoltà di lettere e filosofia dell'Università di Palermo. Studi e ricerche 23. Palermo: Facoltà di lettere e filosofia dell'Università di Palermo, 1995.

Shatzmiller, Maya. "Marriage, Family, and the Faith: Women's Conversion To Islam." *Journal of Family History* 21, no. 3 (1996): 235–66.

Tolan, John. "Concluding Remarks." In *The legal status of ḏimmī-s in the Islamic West: second/eighth-ninth/fifteenth centuries*, edited by Maribel Fierro and John Tolan, 365–71. Religion and law in medieval Christian and Muslim societies 1. Turnhout: Brepols, 2013.

Touati, Houari. *Islam et voyage au Moyen Âge: histoire et anthropologie d'une pratique lettrée*. L'univers historique. Paris: Seuil, 2000.

PART 1

Concepts and Terminology

CHAPTER 1

Constructing and Deconstructing the *dār al-islām* / *dār al-ḥarb* Opposition

Between Sources and Studies

Giovanna Calasso

Behind the construction of the world vision expressed in the *dār al-islām / dār al-ḥarb* dichotomy there is a historical path which is worth briefly returning to.

The foundation of garrison cities by the Arabs during their military conquests was the initial way in which they left their mark on the newly conquered territories, seized from other political powers, removed from other laws, long before Islamic law had become a new well-defined legal system: as described by Muslim historians and geographers, they were cities without walls, having "mimetic" names just referring—as the Arab lexicographers explained them[1]—to certain features of the ground where they were located—Basra, Kufa—or referring to their military function, as in the case of Fusṭāṭ. Although they had no walls, these garrison cities functioned as fortresses for the new faith, not yet firmly established, that of an army mostly composed of nomads, insofar as they protected them from being exposed to contact with local populations, at a time when Islamic identity was in the making, as we would now say.

Then, for centuries after the conquests, the Islamization process followed, and with it the slow and lengthy movement of crossing the frontier between different religious belongings. An Arabic equivalent of the word "conversion" actually doesn't exist in sources such as Ibn Saʿd *Ṭabaqāt*—recording biographical notes about individuals of the earliest Muslim generations—where the concept is only expressed by the verbal forms *aslama* or *daḫala fī 'l-islām*, "to enter Islam,"[2] an action which entails crossing a threshold, be it into a physical space or a community. As documented in the *Jamharat ansāb al-ʿarab* by

1 See Giovanna Calasso, "Les remparts et la loi, les talismans et les saints. La protection de la ville dans les sources musulmanes médiévales," *Bulletin d'Etudes Orientales* 44 (1993): 93–104, in particular p. 92–93 and relating bibliography.

2 Giovanna Calasso, "Récits de conversion, zèle dévotionnel et instruction religieuse dans les biographies des 'gens de Basra' du *Kitāb al-Ṭabaqāt* d'Ibn Saʿd," in *Conversions islamiques*, ed. Mercedes García Arenal (Paris: Maisonneuve et Larose, 2001), 19–47.

 | DOI 10.1163/9789004331037_003

Ibn Ḥazm, the expression *daḫala fī* is commonly used in genealogist terminology to indicate the "entrance" into a clan (*baṭn*) of external elements, usually belonging to a lesser clan.[3] A rather significant linguistic detail, not only for understanding the way in which conversion to Islam was thought of by Arab authors whose accounts constitute our most ancient sources, but also for understanding how, in the idea of frontier implied in the *dār al-islām / dār al-ḥarb* dichotomy, the person- or community-related element conceptually precedes the territorial one, entering the religious community being set on the model of joining a clan.

1 Terminology

My interest in the notion of *dār al-islām* and its opposition with *dār al-ḥarb* stemmed from Muslim travelers' travelogues, relating their travels beyond or within or at the frontiers of Islamic territories, insofar as I noticed the scant relevance of this opposition in these writings, even though all their authors were involved, to different extents, in crossing the boundaries between the world of Islam and other people's worlds: the unknown author of the *Aḫbār al-Ṣīn wa'l-Hind*, Ibn Faḍlān, Ibn Jubayr and Ibn Baṭṭūṭa, as well as the Persian Ismaili author of the *Safar-nāma* Nāṣir-i Ḫusraw (d. ca. 465/1072). And sometimes, as in this last case, the boundaries they crossed were within the world of Islam itself, between the Sunni territories of the Seljuk empire and those of the Ismaili Fatimid caliphate.

Ibn Faḍlān, who describes in his travelogue a journey from Baghdad to the northern regions of Bulġār (309–10/921–22), never mentions the two *dār*s, and

3 See Ibn Ḥazm, *Jamharat ansāb al-ʿarab* (Cairo: Dār al-maʿārif, 1382/1962), 222, to which Khalid Yahya Blankinship refers in *The End of the Jihād State: The Reign of Hishām Ibn ʿAbd al-Malik and the Collapse of the Umayyads*, SUNY Series in Medieval Middle East History (Albany: State University of New York Press, 1994), 43. As for the historical connection between belonging to Muslim society and affiliation to an Arab tribe, see Clément Onimus, "Les *mawālī* en Egypte dans la documentation papyrologique," *Annales Islamologiques* 39 (2005): 81–106. On the basis of papyrologycal documentation, the author states that until the fourth/tenth century belonging to Muslim society didn't necessarily entail belonging to the Muslim religious community, the essential element for integration being affiliation to a tribe, a clan, a family, an individual, in other words being part of a genealogy (p. 83–84). See also Yaacov Lev, "Coptic Rebellions and the Islamization of Medieval Egypt (8th–10th Century): Medieval and Modern Perceptions," *Jerusalem Studies in Arabic and Islam* 39 (2012): 320–23.

balad al-kuffār just once.[4] However, a turning point can be perceived when he first begins to measure the distances covered from place to place only after leaving Bukhara, as if from Baghdad to Bukhara distances did not matter: Jurjāniyya, a ghost city as he depicts it, marks the moment when he is crossing the boundary between what in his mind is the world he belongs to and the others' world. Nāṣir-i Ḫusraw makes reference in his *Safar-nāma* to the opposition between the two domains just once, when, using the common terminology of Muslim geographers, he explains the name of the river Orontes, al-ʿĀṣī, "the rebellious:" "so called because when it flows (in its last stretch) from the land of Islam to the lands of the infidels (*čūn az bilād-i islām bi-bilād-i kufr mi-ravad*) it becomes rebellious."[5] No mention of the two *dār*s is found here, and yet the passage is revealing as it defines moving from *bilād-i islām* to *bilād-i kufr* as an act of rebellion. As for Ibn Jubayr, about to board a ship in Acre to sail back home (580/1184), stopping over in Norman Sicily, he feels compelled to warn Muslims—when free to move around Islamic lands (*fī bilād al-muslimīn*)—against even just passing through an infidel country (*balda min bilād al-kufr*), because of the sufferings they would experience: "Beware, beware of entering their lands!".[6] Thus, even if a mental map of *dār al-islām*, as a notion of collective identity, emerges from all these texts, this map has moving or even blurred boundaries, according to the historical period and the political environment, the authors' geographical place of origin and religious allegiance within the Islamic community, as well as subjective perception.[7]

---

4 Aḥmad Ibn Faḍlān, *Risālat Ibn Faḍlān*, ed. Sāmī Dahhān (Dimašq: Maṭbūʿāt al-Majmaʿ al-ʿilmī al-ʿarabī bi-Dimašq, 1379/1960), 80–81. It is also worth noting that it is not Ibn Faḍlān himself who mentions the *balad al-kuffār*, but the Ḫwārizm-šah, Muḥammad b.ʿIrāq: "He (meaning the Turk Tekın) was formerly with us as an ironsmith and he is well acquainted with the selling of iron in the land of the infidels."

5 Nāṣir-i Ḫusraw, *Safar-nāma*, ed. Muḥammad Dabīr-Siyāqī (Teheran: Kitābfurūš Zawwād, 1354SH), 19.

6 Abū 'l-Ḥusayn Muḥammad Ibn Jubayr, *Riḥlat Ibn Jubayr*, 2nd ed. (Beirut: Dār wa-maktabat al-Hilāl, 1986). Ibn Jubayr mentions *bilād al-muslimīn* also in another passage, when stating that mount Lebanon marks the boundary between Muslim territories and those under Franks' control (*bayna bilād al-muslimīn wa 'l-Ifranj*) (ibid., 206), while Damascus is defined by him as *ḫātima bilād al-islām* (p. 211).

7 Giovanna Calasso, "Partire: l'incipit delle relazioni di viaggio di Nāṣer-e Khosrow, Ibn Jubayr e Ibn Baṭṭūṭa," in *In memoria di Francesco Gabrieli*, suppl. no. 2 to *Rivista degli Studi Orientali* 71 (Roma: Bardi, 1997), 81–98, and Calasso, "Les multiples départs des voyageurs musulmans du moyen âge et les contours mouvants du *dār al-islām*," *Annali di Ca' Foscari* 48, no. 3 (s. or. 40) (2009): 79–96.

The next step in my research into the central issue to which the December 2012 Colloquium was later devoted[8] was to carry out a survey of sources of different kinds, not only juridical texts, but also Hadiths and, besides travelogues, geographical and historiographical works as well as Arabic lexicons.[9] This approach was sparked by the perception that this dual classification of the world elaborated by medieval Muslim jurists, yet still in use in modern times, should be reconsidered, leaving out some stereotypes resulting from an oversimplified reading, so as to let new questions arise, choosing new vantage points.

Of course the terminological research, that is looking into the occurrence of these expressions in written texts, can only give a general insight and may also be misleading.[10] And yet it is an indicator which is worth reflecting on. Perhaps it may seem pointless to look for the presence of these two terms, created by a jurist's mind, in geographical texts, and predictable to find that they rarely occur, but it is interesting to compare their terminology with that of jurists, particularly when the works considered are those of tenth-century Muslim geographers, who deliberately limited themselves to describing Islamic lands,[11] accurately defining their boundaries. The expression *dār al-islām* in fact rarely occurs in these texts,[12] although their authors make use of other equally

---

8 See Calasso, "Introduction", this volume, 1.

9 Giovanna Calasso, "Alla ricerca di *dār al-islām*. Una ricognizione nei testi di giuristi e tradizionisti, lessicografi, geografi e viaggiatori," *Rivista degli Studi Orientali* 83 (2010): 271–96.

10 See also Yaacov Lev, present volume, 86.

11 Muqaddasī explicitly states that he will focus on the "kingdom of Islam" (*mamlakat al-islām*), ignoring "the kingdoms of the infidels" (*mamālik al-kuffār*), for neither did he travel to those regions, nor does he believe they are worth talking about (Muḥammad b. Aḥmad al-Muqaddasī, *Aḥsan al-taqāsīm fī maʿrifat al-aqālīm*, ed. Michael Johan de Goeje, 2nd ed. [Leiden: Brill, 1906], 9).

12 In Iṣṭaḫrī's *Masālik wa'l-mamālik*, as noted by Friedmann in the present volume (342n4), we can find some rare occurrence of *dār al-islām* (Abū Isḥāq Ibrāhīm al-Iṣṭaḫrī, *Kitāb Masālik al-mamālik*, ed. Michael Johan de Goeje, 2nd ed. [Leiden: Brill, 1927], 281, 291) and of *dār al-ḥarb* (p. 35–36 and p. 290, 291); likewise in Ibn Ḥawqal's *Ṣūrat al-arḍ* (*Kitāb Ṣūrat al-arḍ*, ed. M. J. de Goeje and J. H. Kramers [Leiden: Brill, 1938], 14, 340, 467). I have here the occasion to correct what I stated in Calasso, "Alla ricerca di *dār al-islām*," 286. An expression whose interpretation is uncertain occurs in Muqaddasī's work, in a passage where the author draws up a list of everything which can be found in the region of Syria: *mafraq al-dārayn*, "the separation between the two territories". According to Miquel it is likely to refer to the separation between *dār al-islām* and *dār al-ḥarb* "la limite passant au nord du Šām, vers les places frontières (*ṯuġūr*), enjeu traditionnel des luttes entre Byzantins et musulmans" (Muḥammad b. Aḥmad al-Muqaddasī, *Aḥsan al-taqāsīm fī maʿrifat al-aqālīm*

general and all-embracing expressions such as *bilād al-islām* or *mamlakat al-islām*, as well as, which is more noteworthy, the word *islām* itself to indicate the same concept. So we find *fī 'l-islām, fī ḥudūd al-islām, rāji'an ilā 'l-islām,*[13] and even, rather curiously, *ṭūl al-islām,* to indicate the total extent of Islamic lands.[14] Thus geographers give a concrete, spatial meaning to the word *islām*, while jurists cannot dispense with the term *dār*, which, however, does not necessarily have a territorial meaning. In their representation, the two *dār*s appear as sharply separate realms; however, juridical casuistry mainly deals with what happens when leaving one and entering the other, since it is this crossing the frontier—whether material, that is territorial, or else immaterial, that is referring to a community—which has juridical consequences, but also because these crossings, in peace as well as in war, are a reality which cannot be ignored.

Fourth/tenth-century geographers share a common lexicon which, on average, shows a clear preference for expressions which are not *dār al-islām* and *dār al-ḥarb*, which randomly occur in their works just as one of the possible ways to design two sets of countries, *bilād*: they can happen to be found in a passage on the mineral riches of a region of the Islamic lands, as well as in a description of the natural boundaries separating the territories inhabited by Muslims from those inhabited by the *kuffār*.[15] And in their writings we may even run into the expression *dār al-ḥarb*—or its correspondent *dār al-kufr*—in the plural form: for instance in a passage by Ibn Ḥawqal[16] where the author, describing the Ṭuḫāristān region, after mentioning the cities of Munk and Hulbuk, states: "Beyond these places, in the lands of unbelief (*fī dūr al-kufr*) we find Waḫḫān and Karrān." The variant *dūr al-ḥarb* occurs further on, in the context of an overall evaluation of the Transoxiana region: "As for energy and courage there isn't *fī 'l-islām* a more useful region to jihad. The reason lies in the fact that the boundaries of Transoxiana are the nearest to the lands of war (*dūr al-ḥarb*)"[17] But, on the whole, although the two conventional expressions, *dār*

(*La meilleure répartition pour la connaissances des provinces*). Traduction partielle, annotée par André Miquel (Damas: Institut français de Damas, 1963), 152.

13 Besides the occurrences already mentioned in Ibn Ḥawqal and Muqaddasī (Calasso, "Alla ricerca di *dār al-islām*," 287–88), some examples can be found also in Iṣṭaḫrī, *Masālik*, 59, 70, 140, 180, 290, 291.

14 Calasso, "Alla ricerca di *dār al-islām*," 289.

15 See for example Iṣṭaḫrī, *Masālik*, 281, l. 1 and l. 10.

16 Ibn Ḥawqal, *Ṣūrat al-arḍ*, 449; transl. *Configuration de la terre* (*Kitāb Ṣūrat al-arḍ*). Introduction et traduction, avec index, par J. H. Kramers et G. Wiet [Beirut: Commission internationale pour la traduction des chefs-d'oeuvre, 1964], 434. The passage has been already pointed out by Yohanan Friedmann in the present volume (342n4).

17 Ibn Ḥawqal, *Ṣūrat al-arḍ*, 467 (transl. 449).

al-islām and *dār al-ḥarb,* rarely occur, the perception of the existence of two distinct sets, one of which is identified by the reference to Islam, is similar to the one emerging from juridical texts.

As for early medieval historiographical sources, for instance Balāḏurī and Ṭabarī, instead of using such all-embracing and oppositional terms, even when describing the head-on collision which took place during the wars of conquest, simply named territories after their inhabitants: *bilād al-rūm* for the Byzantine land, rarely *arḍ al-rūm.*[18] There is generally no mention of *mušrikūn* or *dār al-ḥarb*, nor of *dār al-islām.* Just *muslimūn* and *rūm*, Muslims and Greeks, the latter meaning Christians without mentioning Christianity. And the case of Ṭabarī is particularly worthy of interest, since *dār al-islām* and *dār al-ḥarb* frequently occur in some of his other works, such as the *Kitāb iḫtilāf al-fuqahā'*,[19] as well as his *Tafsīr.*[20] And this not only has to do with the notions we are dealing with as an expression of the mental categories of a medieval Muslim scholar, but also with the mental boundaries he establishes between different territories of knowledge and literary genres. And if, as Tarif Khalidi points out, Ṭabarī's *Tafsīr* "is indeed the meeting place of his major areas of scholarly interest,"[21] the presence of the two expressions in his *Tafsīr*, as well as in his juridical writings, and their absence in his historical work are in themselves significant of the boundaries he perceives between the fields of knowledge to which they pertain and the one to which they do not. Indeed the conceptualization of the two *dār*s, which was devised by Muslim jurists as a necessary instrument in dealing with rules governing the relations between Muslims and non-Muslims of the "outside", is almost completely ignored by early Muslim historians, whose aim is to record in chronological order military and dynastic events which pertain to the political sphere.

In later historiographical works, such as Ibn al-Aṯīr's (d. 630/1233) *Kāmil*, the expression *dār al-ḥarb* occurs only twice, one of them referring to al-Andalus, while in Ibn Ḫaldūn's (d. 784/1382) *Kitāb al-ʿibar*, as noted by Fierro and Molina, "there are forty-two passages where *dār al-ḥarb* is mentioned: five refer to the

---

18 Aḥmad b. Yaḥyā al-Balāḏurī, *Kitāb Futūḥ al-buldān*, ed. Ṣalāh al-dīn al-Munajjid (Cairo, 1956), 194, l. 6, 13; 199, l. 12, 14; 200, l. 1, 5, 8; 201, l. 14; 218; 221; 224. As for Ṭabarī, see Calasso, "Alla ricerca di *dār al-islām*," 278–79.

19 Calasso, "Alla ricerca di *dār al-islām*," 281–82.

20 See the contributions by Roberto Tottoli and Raoul Villano to the present volume.

21 Tarif Khalidi, "Al-Ṭabarī: An Introduction," in *Al-Ṭabarī: A Medieval Muslim Historian and His Work*, ed. Hugh Kennedy, Studies in Late Antiquity and Early Islam 15 (Princeton, NJ: The Darwin Press, 2008), 2.

East, two to the Maghrib or Ifrīqiya, and thirty-five to al-Andalus."[22] In a passage relating to the Banū Marīn's jihad in al-Andalus, *dār al-ḥarb* is paired with *arḍ al-islām*.[23] As for the expression *dār al-islām*, apparently it only occurs in a reference to the pair *dār al-islām / dār al-ḥarb*: in this passage[24] Ibn Ḫaldūn, remembering the role the Mamluks played in the defense of Islamic territories after the violent demise of Baghdad's caliphate at the hand of the Mongols, states that in that moment God came to rescue the Muslims "by sending to them out of the Turkish people and out of its mighty and numerous tribes, guardian amirs and devoted defenders who are imported as slaves from the land of war to the lands of Islam (*min dār al-ḥarb ilā dār al-islām*)."[25] Without drawing conclusions from these mere quantitative data, we can still observe that the passage in which Ibn Ḫaldūn uses the *dār al-islām* / *dār al-ḥarb* binomial is legally relevant as it refers to Muslims purchasing slaves, which, from a juridical point of view, can only take place from the outside, from that "outside" designated as *dār al-ḥarb*, Islamic law forbidding the enslavement of Muslims as well as *ḏimmīs*.

2 Constructing Boundaries

As for *how* the *dār al-islām* / *dār al-ḥarb* binomial took form, since we cannot exactly date its first appearance—even if it is reasonable to place it in the second half of the eighth century[26]—it seems to me that it should be traced back, even more than to the concept of jihad, which is usually assumed to have been at the very origin of the elaboration of the two notions, to that of *hijra*, the founding event of Islamic identity, the moving away from idolatry and oppression representing "the watershed in the Islamic self-narratives of

22 See Fierro and Molina in the present volume, 241.

23 Ibn Ḫaldūn, *Kitāb al-ʿIbar* (Būlāq, 1284/1867), 7:260.

24 Ibid., 5:371.

25 This is a slightly modified translation of David Ayalon, "*Mamlūkiyyāt* (B) Ibn Khaldūn's View of the Mamlūk Phenomenon," *Jerusalem Studies in Arabic and Islam* 2 (1980): 340.

26 In a recent article, Fred Donner ("Qur'ânicization of Religio-Political Discourse in the Umayyad Period," *Revue des Mondes Musulmans et de la Méditerranée* 129 [2011]: 79–92) considers the formulation, around the mid-eighth century, of the expression *dār al-islām*, and its converse *dār al-ḥarb*, as "an interesting side development related to the shift from 'Believers' to 'Muslims' and the enthronement of the concept of *islām* as the new designator for the community," which in his view developed in the court circles of the Umayyad caliphs of Syria (p. 85).

its own origins".[27] A connection which can also be perceived in a passage of Abū Yūsuf's (d. 182/798) *Kitāb al-Ḫarāj*, where the author, dealing with the issue of *jizya*, reports the decisions of Ḫālid b. al-Walīd concerning the inhabitants of al-Ḥīra, and uses the expressions *dār al-hijra* and *dār al-islām* apparently with a very similar meaning. This would seem to suggest that the concept of *dār al-islām* was an extension of what was conceived as *dār al-hijra*.[28]

Also the term *hijra*, like the expressions *dār al-islām* and *dār al-ḥarb* or *al-kufr*, is not found in the Qur'an, but the numerous occurrences of the verb *hājara* in the sacred book of Islam—not necessarily associated to *jihād fī sabīl Allāh*—make emigration the founding gesture of separation for the believer. Perhaps it is to this original journey, the emigration from Mecca of the Prophet and his early followers, that we should return to find the source of the representation of the two *dārs*, which at the very beginning were none other than Mecca and Medina. The latter was made the first abode of the Muslim community by the Prophet and thus—in later jurists' mind—the first *dār al-islām*, as it appears in the words of the fifth/eleventh century Hanafi jurist Saraḫsī: *"fa'l- madīna innamā kāna lahā ḥukm dār al-islām ḏālika 'l-waqt ḥīna kāna rasūlu 'llāh ma'a 'l-muslimīn fihā,"* "only the city of Medina had indeed the legal status of *dār al-islām* when the Messenger of God was there with the Muslims".[29] The statement is found in the context of a discussion about the sharing of war booty, aiming to demonstrate—in contrast to other opinions, such as Šāfiʿī's—that the Prophet clearly indicated that it could not take place while still in *dār al-ḥarb*, postponing on several occasions the division of *ġanīma*, in spite of insistent pressures, until the return to *dār al-islām*. Therefore, after the victory of Ḥunayn, the Prophet delayed the division until he was back in Jaʿrāna—near the recently conquered Mecca—at the time *dār al-islām*'s frontier land: *"fa-innahu aḫḫara al-qisma hattā intahā ilā 'l-Jaʿrāna wa kānat ḥudūd dār al-islām fī ḏālika 'l waqt."*[30]

---

27 Caterina Bori, "'All We Know Is What We Have Been Told': Reflections on Emigration and Land as Divine Heritage in the Qur'ān," in *The Coming of the Comforter: When, Where, and to Whom?: Studies on the Rise of Islam and Various Other Topics in Memory of John Wansbrough*, ed. Carlos A. Segovia and Basil Lourié, Orientalia Judaica Christiana 3 (Piscataway, NJ: Gorgias Press, 2012), 310.

28 The issue has been looked into more extensively in Calasso, "Alla ricerca di *dār al-islām*," 276–79.

29 Muḥammad b. Aḥmad al-Saraḫsī, *Kitāb al-Mabṣūṭ* (Beirut: Dār al-Fikr, 1421/2000), 10:16.

30 Ibid. The disagreement between Saraḫsī and Sāfiʿī, even more than about where the booty division should take place, revolves around the issue of what turns an enemy territory into *dār al-islām*, whether the mere conquest or, as Saraḫsī maintains, the fact that Islamic laws are enforced there (ibid., 10:20).

We should also consider the possibility that the two notions did not originate simultaneously, and that the idea of *dār al-kufr* or *dār al-ḥarb* could have preceded that of *dār al-islām*, understood in its global and all-embracing meaning, as found in second/eighth–third/ninth-century legal texts. As for the different ways Muslim jurists conceived the two notions, depending on their personality—or territoriality of law orientation,[31] they necessarily also affected the way the boundary which ideally lies between the two *dār*s was construed. Is it a frontier based on religious belonging, as would appear from the choice of the word *Islam* as the identifying element of one of the two entities? Is it a boundary between spheres of political and juridical dominion, which as such cannot be stepped over by Islamic laws, or a boundary which can be crossed—and thus in some way ignored—by virtue of their personal character?[32] Actually, if frontiers and frontier lands are explicitly mentioned by geographers—*āfāq, ḥudūd, tuḫūm, ṯuġūr*—[33]as well as in treatises on the merits of jihad, in juridical texts they are mainly evoked through the verbs *daḫala* and *ḫaraja*, "to go in" and "to go out"—with reference to *dār al-islām* and *dār al-ḥarb*—which draw a close web of movements across the frontier between an "inside" and an "outside", having legal consequences which, evaluated and regulated in a different way according to the jurist's orientation, lies at the basis of juridical casuistry.

The concepts of frontier and boundaries have long been at the center of anthropologists' and historians' reflections,[34] a theme that has had growing

31 Calasso, "Alla ricerca di *dār al-islām*," 282ff.

32 David Santillana, *Istituzioni di diritto musulmano malichita, con riguardo anche al sistema sciafiita*, vol. 1 (Rome: Anonima Romana Editoriale, 1921), 97; Giovanna Calasso, "Alla ricerca di *dār al-islām*," 282–83.

33 See Michael Bonner, "The Naming of the Frontier: ʿAwāṣim, Thughūr, and the Arab Geographers," *Bulletin of the School of Oriental and African Studies* 57, no. 1 (1994): 17–24, and, for a more extensive treatment of the topic, Ralph W. Brauer, "Boundaries and Frontiers in Medieval Muslim Geography," *Transactions of the American Philosophical Society* 85, no. 6 (1995): 1–73. A section of this work is dedicated to internal frontiers: despite the breakup of the caliphal empire and the formation of numerous independent states "that in turn entailed the establishment between them of numerous 'internal boundaries'" (p. 9), the author points out that in travelers' writings he has encountered "no reports of borders control in connection with overland travel anywhere within the Islamic realm" (p. 34).

34 Boundaries and frontiers are strictly related to the concept of identity. To quote just some significant studies starting from the late 1960s: Fredrik Barth, ed., *Ethnic Groups and Boundaries. The Social Organization of Culture Difference* (Oslo: Universitetsforlaget, 1969); Jean-Loup Amselle, *Logiques métisses: anthropologie de l'identité en Afrique et ailleurs* (Paris: Payot & Rivages, 1999); and Jean-Loup Amselle, "I fondamenti antropologici

success since the 1950s. Frontier lines or areas, places of separation and exclusion, or interaction and exchange, external or internal frontiers, physical or mental, have been at the center of a large number of research works, also with reference to the Muslim world.[35] As an example I would like to quote two studies focusing on Spain, by Jean Gautier-Dalché[36] and by Ann Christys, published respectively in 1959 and in 2002. Inquiring into the construction process of the notion of frontier in Spain, Gautier-Dalché pointed out how in the sixth/twelfth century this notion was still very vague in Latin texts (in Gautier-Dalché's words "la frontière est encore quelque chose de vague, de plastique, de mouvant"), and how the actual frontier was in any case more an area than a line, an unstable frontier area, a march, which widened or narrowed according to the changes in the local power balance. Only between the sixth/twelfth and the seventh/thirteenth centuries "ce qui était flottant, imprecis, est devenu net."

Ann Christys came to similar conclusions in her study *Crossing the frontier of ninth century Hispania*—a contribution to the volume *Medieval Frontiers: Concepts and Practices*[37]—where a comparative analysis of Latin and Arabic sources concerning the rebellion of Maḥmūd Ibn ʿAbd al-Jabbār of Mérida (d. ca. 845) highlighted that both the concept and the vocabulary of frontier—a frontier which separates and opposes Muslims and Christians—became apparent in the sources only after the fifth/eleventh century. "Until the advances made by the northern kingdoms in this century … the opposition which both the Latin and the Arabic chronicles perceived between the groups

---

della costruzione delle identità," in *Identità collettive tra medioevo e età moderna*, ed. P. Prodi and W. Reinhard (Bologna: CLUEB, 2002), 31–42. Hastings Donnan and Thomas M. Wilson, eds., *Border Approaches: Anthropological Perspectives on Frontiers* (Lanham: Univ. Press of America, 1994); Ugo Fabietti, *Etnografia della frontiera: antropologia e storia in Baluchistan*, Gli argonauti 22 (Roma: Meltemi, 1997).

35 Among the most recent studies, see Travis E. Zadeh, *Mapping Frontiers across Medieval Islam: Geography, Translation, and the ʿAbbāsid Empire*, Library of Middle East History 27 (London: I. B. Tauris, 2011), who centers his work on the theme of the fabled barrier built by Alexander the Great against the apocalyptic nations of Gog and Magog, and dedicates a part of his analysis to the perspective on the frontier, as well as its terminology, found in Arabic and Persian geographical writings (chapter 4, "A geography of neighbors," 67–96).

36 Jean Gautier-Dalché, "Islam et chrétienté en Espagne au XIIe siècle: contribution à l'étude de la notion de frontière," *Hespéris* 47 (1959): 183–217.

37 "Crossing the Frontier of Ninth Century Hispania," in *Medieval Frontiers: Concepts and Practices*, ed. David Abulafia and Nora Berend (Aldershot, Hants, England: Ashgate, 2002), 35–53. In David Abulafia's rich introduction to the volume—"Seven Types of Ambiguity, C. 1100–C. 1500," 1–33—several possible approaches to the issue of frontier are examined as well as related to the wider study of medieval societies, referring to Latin Christendom, Byzantium and the Islamic lands.

within their own immediate spheres were greater than those between Muslim and Christian." Thus, "until the rhetoric of crusade began to colour the vocabulary used to describe Maḥmūd's journey—Ann Christys maintains—in both Latin and the Arabic chronicles, he remained the enemy equally of Cordoba and of Oviedo, and didn't notice the frontier he was later said to have crossed."[38]

In the same volume Ronnie Ellenblum, starting from the analysis of an Oriental case, the Latin kingdom of Jerusalem, questions the validity of the modern 'linear model' for the notion of boundary in the Middle Ages. In his opinion "behind the very assumption that medieval states had fixed borders, there are hidden assumptions of concepts of sovereignty, of responsibility for the fate of subjects and of geographical and even cartographical knowledge on the part of the rulers ..." Therefore in Ellenblum's view, "the development of well demarcated borderlines is closely related to the development of modern states." For the Middle Ages Ellenblum suggests a different approach in which the center replaces the borders as a point of reference. Medieval political communities were in fact more characterized by their centers or by their common association to a sovereign, rather than by their physical space. "Kings in turn were more often identified not through the lands which they ruled but through the people who owed them loyalty ... usually referring to their ethnic identity;"[39] and the same applies to Muslim rulers.

Thus, while the territorial boundaries of a medieval state were much more fluid than a modern state border, and, concerning religious frontiers, recent and less recent studies point out that their perception becomes apparent in Latin or Arabic historiographical sources only after the end of the fifth/eleventh century, in recent times it is the very *dār al-islām / dār al-ḥarb* dichotomy found in Islamic juridical sources since the early Abbasid period that has been the object of a deconstructive analysis. This concerns both the word *islām*, which inevitably gives a religious connotation to the first *dār*, and the word *ḥarb*, which also inevitably casts its shadow of hostility on the second *dār*. And it is the jurisdictional interpretation of the Hanafi school—very different from the Shafi'i one, according to which the laws of Islam apply to Muslims even beyond the borders of *dār al-islām*—to be the point of reference for all these studies.

As for the most recent ones, their authors clearly seem to be spurred by the concern—connected to modern international political relations—to

38 "Crossing the Frontier of Ninth Century Hispania," 53.

39 Ronnie Ellenblum, "Were There Borders and Borderlines in the Middle Ages? The Example of the Latin Kingdom of Jerusalem," in *Medieval Frontiers: Concepts and Practices*, ed. David Abulafia and Nora Berend (Aldershot, Hants, England: Ashgate, 2002), 108.

demonstrate that the very existence of this pair of notions does not entail that hostility should inform the relations between *dār al-islām* and all other political entities, or to demonstrate that the opposition between *dār al-islām* and *dār al-ḥarb* has nothing to do with religious belonging. But besides evaluating their contribution to the issue, it is worth considering some references to medieval juridical texts which are found in these studies, being relevant to our discussion.

3 The Existence of More than One *dār al-ḥarb* Facing a *dār al-islām* Not Only Made of Muslims

Let us consider the allegedly interchangeable meaning of the expressions *dār al-ḥarb* and *dār al-kufr*: as suggested by Mushtaq Muhammad Ahmad, some passages by Hanafi jurists such as Saraḫsī (fifth/eleventh century) show not only that *dār al-kufr* does not necessarily correspond to *dār al-ḥarb*, but also that there can be more than one *dār al-ḥarb*. This idea can be deduced, for example, from the case in which Muslims entered *dār al-ḥarb* with a safe-conduct and in the meantime another *dār al-ḥarb* attacked the aforementioned *dār al-ḥarb*. In such case—this is the point Saraḫsī is interested in—it would not be lawful for these Muslims to take part in war, unless for self-defense.[40] What is worth highlighting is that in this passage we find an explicit distinction between different non-Muslim political entities, a concept in the plural of the non-Muslim *dār*. Moreover Saraḫsī, as well as other Hanafi jurists, made a difference within the latter, according to whether their inhabitants had a hostile attitude towards Muslims; only in that case are they to be considered *dār al-ḥarb*. And in Saraḫsī, Kāsānī and Marġīnānī we can also find occurrences of, and even a preference for, the plural form, *dūr al-ḥarb*, as noted by Baber Johansen.[41]

---

40 Saraḫsī, *al-Mabṣūṭ*, 10:79.

41 Baber Johansen, “Entre révélation et tyrannie: le droit des non-musulmans d’après les juristes musulmans,” in *Identité et droit de l’autre: a Robbins Collection publication, University of California at Berkeley*, ed. Laurent Mayali, Studies in comparative legal history (Berkeley, CA: University of California at Berkeley, 1994), 127–46; (republished in: Baber Johansen, *Contingency in a Sacred Law: Legal and Ethical Norms in the Muslim Fiqh*, Studies in Islamic Law and Society, v. 7 [Leiden: Brill, 1999], 228n48). For the occurrence of the plural forms *dūr al-ḥarb* and *dūr al-kufr* in Ibn Ḥawqal’s geographical work, see supra p. 45. As for Muqaddasī, he states at the very beginning of his work that he will focus on the “kingdom of Islam” (*mamlakat al-islām*), ignoring “the kingdoms of the infidels” (*mamālik al-kuffār*: see note 11 above).

Mushtaq Muhammad Ahmad's is the study of a contemporary Indian Muslim author who, like other contemporary Muslim authors, aims at demonstrating that "the doctrine of *dār* has nothing to do with the theory that the Islamic state and other political entities will normally be engaged in hostility. Rather, it denotes political jurisdiction".[42] According to the author "the majority of the *fuqahā'* declared that the *ratio* of war (*'illat al-qitāl*) in Islamic law is not disbelief but *muḥārabah* (waging war against Islam or Muslims)".[43] The same is stated by Samy Ayoub in his article "Territorial jurisprudence, *ikhtilaf al-darayn:* political boundaries and legal jurisdiction".[44] Also in his view Hanafi juridical documentation demonstrates that the notions of *dār al-islām* and *dār al-ḥarb* are but jurisdictional concepts: Islamic law does not apply in *dār al-ḥarb* and Muslims committing crimes in that *dār*—even against other Muslims—when going back to *dār al-islām* cannot be prosecuted by Islamic courts. As for Qur'anic passages explicitly inviting Muslims to perpetual warfare against *kāfirūn*, until their submission, they should be considered in reference to the specific space-time context of the origins.

---

42 Mushtaq Muhammad Ahmad, "The notions of *dār al-ḥarb* and *dār al-Islām* in Islamic jurisprudence with special reference to the Ḥanafī school," *Islamic Studies* 47 (2008): 18.

43 Ibid., 24. Ridwan al-Sayyid instead points out that "from the texts of Imam al-Shafi'i ... infidelity is the sole valid reason for war", adding: "In fact, al-Shafi'i's view laid the foundation for the concept of *dār al-islām* and *dār al-ḥarb*" (Ridwan al-Sayyid, "*Dār al-Ḥarb* and *Dār al-Islām*: traditions and interpretations," in *Religion between violence and reconciliation*, ed. Thomas Scheffler, Beiruter Texte und Studien, Bd. 76 [Beirut: Orient-Institut–Ergon Verlag in Kommission, 2002], 126). On the understanding of jihad as obligatory aggressive war by Syrian jurists and on how "the more general acceptation of the Syrian school reached its peak in the thought of al-Shafi'i, who elevates the destruction of unbelief to be the primary justification for jihad," see also Roy Parviz Mottahedeh and Ridwan al-Sayyid, "The Idea of the *Jihād* in Islam before the Crusades," in *The Crusades from the Perspective of Byzantium and the Muslim World*, ed. Angeliki E. Laiou and Roy Parviz Mottahedeh (Washington, D.C.: Dumbarton Oaks Research Library and Collection, 2001), 26–27; and Majid Khadduri, ed., *The Islamic Law of Nations: Shaybānī's Siyar.* Translated with an Introduction, Notes and Appendices (Baltimore: The Johns Hopkins Press, 1966), 58.

44 "Territorial jurisprudence, *ikhtilaf al-darayn*: Political boundaries & legal jurisdiction," *Contemporary Islamic Studies*, no. 2012 (April 2012): 2. A well-structured synthesis of the Hanafi *iḫtilāf al-dārayn* doctrine is found in Carlo Alfonso Nallino's study dedicated to the prominent thirteenth/nineteenth century jurist Ibn 'Ābidīn and the way he conceives the insurances issue: Carlo Alfonso Nallino, "Delle assicurazioni in diritto musulmano hanafita," *Oriente moderno* 7 (1927): 446–52. Significantly, Nallino observes that insurances are dealt with in Ibn 'Ābidīn treatise *al-Radd al-muḫtār*, in the chapter on jihad "where a European jurist would never imagine to go looking for it": a further example of differences in classifying things in different cultural contexts.

Classic statements found in western Islamic studies, such as Ann Lambton's, "the only proper relationship to the non-Islamic world is one of perpetual warfare," or similar statements by Patricia Crone like "the relationship between them was deemed to be one of war, whether latent or actively pursued," as well as "Muslims were legally obliged to wage holy war against *dār al-ḥarb* until it ceased to exist," would then be sharply denied.[45] The same applies to the statements we find in Bernard Lewis' influential work *The political language of Islam*: "There is a morally necessary, legally and religiously obligatory state of war, until the final and inevitable triumph of Islam over unbelief."[46] Of course these statements take into account only *one* of the different points of view of medieval Muslim jurists, representing it *tout court* as *the* Muslim point of view; which is in fact the same approach as that of the authors of the previously mentioned articles referring almost exclusively to texts of the Hanafi school.

A juridical concept strictly connected with the conceptualization of the notion of *dār al-islām* and which was the object of specific elaboration by Hanafi authors is in fact that of *ʿiṣma*, the theme of a study by Baber Johansen—originally published in the proceedings of the eighth UEAI Congress in 1978—constituting to this day its most in-depth analysis.[47] A concept which is emphasized in both Mushtaq Muhammad Ahmad's and Samy Ayoub's articles, as already done by Khaled Abou El Fadl in his substantial essay "Islamic Law and Muslim minorities."[48]

While for most Muslim jurists *dār al-islām* is the domain in which the law of Islam prevails, for Hanafi scholars the essential characteristic of *dār al-islām* is the safety of its inhabitants. This safety, as Johansen explains, is conceived by Hanafi scholars as a consequence of the juridical bond existing between sovereign and subjects, which ensures the inviolability (*ʿiṣma*: protection) of the person, freedom and properties of each subject (Muslim but also *d̠immī*

45 Ann K. S. Lambton, *State and Government in Medieval Islam: An Introduction to the Study of Islamic Political Theory: The Jurists*, London Oriental Series, v. 36 (Oxford: Oxford University Press, 1981), 201; Patricia Crone, *Medieval Islamic Political Thought* (Edinburgh: Edinburgh Univ. Press, 2004), 359, 363.

46 *The Political Language of Islam* (Chicago: University of Chicago Press, 1988), 73.

47 Baber Johansen, "Der *ʿiṣma*-Begriff im hanafitischen Recht," in *Actes du 8me Congrès de l'Union Européenne des Arabisants et Islamisants, Aix-en-Provence, septembre 1976* (Aix-en-Provence: Edisud, 1978), 89–108, republished in his collection of essays *Contingency in a Sacred Law*, 238–62.

48 Khaled Abou El Fadl, "Islamic Law and Muslim Minorities: The Juristic Discourse on Muslim Minorities from the Second/Eighth to the Eleventh/Seventeenth Centuries," *Islamic Law and Society* 1, no. 2 (1994): 161.

and *musta'min*). In fact this protection gives the subject the right to appeal to a Muslim court against a third party liable for harm or damage to his person or property;[49] on the contrary, there is no responsibility for acts perpetrated against people who are not "protected", whose blood is *hadr* or *hadar* (the opposite of *maʿṣūm*), as in the case of a *ḥarbī*.[50] In spite of the existence of this thorough study of the concept, also dealt with by Johansen in his more recent essay *Entre révélation et tyrannie. Le droit des non-musulmans d'après les juristes musulmans*,[51] the notion of *ʿiṣma* is currently referred to only in its meaning of impeccability and infallibility of the imam or of the Prophet, or else as a technical juridical term for the marriage bond or the marital authority. The relevance to the notion of *dār al-islām* of the aforementioned meaning of *ʿiṣma* has not usually been considered at all.

It is on the basis of this concept of a juridical bond existing between the sovereign and his subjects and ensuring them protection—Muslim and non-Muslim alike, significantly—that Samy Ayoub, in his article about *iḫtilāf al-dārayn* asserted that for Hanafi scholars "the individuals' religious affiliation was never a factor in the Hanafi legal structure of the concept of *dār*."[52] In fact, it is by stressing the distinction between Islamic law and the religious identity of the individuals submitted to it, that is, highlighting the religiously plural character of societies to which Islamic law was historically applied, that the idea of an exclusively Islamic belonging, commonly considered to be at the core of the idea of *dār al-islām*, can be challenged.

---

49 Johansen, "Der *ʿiṣma*-Begriff im hanafitischen Recht," 89.

50 Joseph Schacht, *An Introduction to Islamic Law* (Oxford: Clarendon Press, 1982), 184. It is the only indirect hint at the juridical notion of *ʿiṣma* to be found in Schacht's text. Concerning the validity of a *ḏimmī*'s testimony, also without an explicit reference to the notion of *ʿiṣma*, Ahmed Oulddali states: "Ces droits qui lui confère son appartenance au *dār al-islām* le mettent a priori en position de force ou de superiorité par rapport à celui qui vient d'ailleurs [...] Il existe donc une unité judiciaire à l'intérieur du *dār al-islām* permettant de protéger tous les sujets qu'ils soient musulmans ou non, meme s'ils ne sont pas égaux entre eux" ("Recevabilité du témoignage du ḏimmī d'après les juristes mālikites d'Afrique du Nord," in *The legal status of ḏimmī-s in the Islamic West: second/eighth-ninth/fifteenth centuries*, ed. Maribel Fierro and John Tolan, Religion and law in medieval Christian and Muslim societies 1 [Turnhout: Brepols, 2013], 279). On the theme, see also N. J. Coulson, "The State and the Individual in Islamic Law," *International and Comparative Law Quarterly* 6, no. 1 (1957): 49–60.

51 Johansen, "Entre révélation et tyrannie", republished in Johansen, *Contingency in a Sacred Law*, 219–37.

52 Ayoub, "Territorial jurisprudence, *ikhtilaf al-darayn*," 3.

Thus, recent studies carried out by authors such as Mushtaq Muhammad Ahmad and Samy Ayoub explicitly aim to deconstruct the *dār al-islām* / *dār al-ḥarb* opposition both in relation to the word *islām*—stressing that religious affiliation is not relevant in the juridical concept of *dār*—and in relation to the word *ḥarb*, emphasizing the distinction between *dār al-kufr* and *dār al-ḥarb* or envisioning the existence of more than one *dār al-ḥarb*—and in so doing calling into question the supposedly unitary nature of the latter.

4 Self-Representation and Representation by Western Scholars: From the Singular to the Plural

This shift from the singular to the plural is intended to dismantle a dichotomy which, although it has so far hardly been questioned or even really looked into, was nevertheless made their own by western scholars. This was perhaps because the first term, *dār al-islām*, in the singular and centered on the word *islām*, besides providing a convenient synthetic expression for a geopolitical concept, corresponded to their idea of "the Islamic world," while the second, *dār al-ḥarb*, referring to "the Other," also in the singular and centered on the word *war*, confirmed the representation of an Islam spreading by force of arms, moreover conceived by Muslims themselves. Thus a simplified and simplifying image has imposed itself and has kept on circulating in studies, either in its original Arabic form or translated as the "abode of Islam" and the "abode of war," making any discussion seem superfluous.

It is true that, while within the array of casuistic analysis provided by medieval juridical texts it is possible to find some hints at the existence of more than one *dār al-ḥarb* (*dūr al-ḥarb*), as well as at possible hostile relations between different *dār al-ḥarb*, or to the existence of more *dār al-kufr* which only according to their hostile attitude towards Muslims become *dār al-ḥarb*, apparently we cannot find any evidence of a distinction within the notion of *dār al-islām*, at least in Sunni sources. *Dār al-islām* is conceived by medieval Sunni authors only in the singular: *dārunā*, our *dār*. And this calls into question even further the idea of a symmetrical opposition between the two *dārs*, although this is the image suggested by the *dār al-islām* / *dār al-ḥarb* pair.

At this point it is not devoid of interest to confront this Islamic self-representation, the fact that, in Lambton's words "all Islamic lands are looked upon as a unity"[53] by the subjects belonging to the realm defined by the expression *dār al-islām*, with the critical reflections which, in recent decades, have been

53 Lambton, *State and Government in Medieval Islam*, 201.

dedicated to the western notion of "the Muslim world," in the singular, causing, for example, the "Revue du monde musulman et de la Méditerranée" to change its name to "Revue *des* mondes musulmans et de la Méditerranée" in 1996. In the editorial which announced the change of name of the review Pierre Robert Baduel and Sylvie Denoix[54] made reference for some reflections to two emblematic publications from the time of the great masters of orientalism, the *Revue du monde musulman* (published by the Mission Scientifique du Maroc between 1906 and 1926) and the *Annuaire du monde musulman*, both strictly connected with the name of Louis Massignon and in whose titles the "Muslim world" appears in the singular. It is in fact the "invariants" of Muslim thought which are the center of interest, in a unitary vision filtered through an essentially religious prism which also seems to find support "in the field:" "*Anā muslim*—writes Massignon—me répondait en 1907 un petit débardeur d'Aden à qui je cherchais de faire dire s'il était yémenite ou somali, et qui me répondait son *civis romanus sum.*"[55] Even more than the primacy of religious allegiance, Massignon rightly perceived in this answer a sense of supernational—and thus unitary—community belonging, and yet, as the authors observe highlighting the relative and situational nature of identity, "Il est évident qu'à la même question sur son identité posée par un autochtone il eût fait une réponse différente qu'à l'européen Massignon."[56]

Today, "the Muslim world", in the singular, as a subject of research is thought to express a globalizing, essentialist vision which turns this world into a unitary and basically immutable reality, the religious phenomenon being overestimated and used as an explicative factor in every field, to the disadvantage of history, that is, the possibility of changing. Moreover, the only religious phenomenon which is given prominence is Islam, while the world in question has always included a considerable non-Muslim population. In short, the expression "the Muslim world" does not account for its plurality.[57]

A significant gap divides the perspective underlying the name change of the *Revue des mondes musulmans et de la Méditerranée* from that of the miscellaneous volume *Unity and Variety in Muslim Civilization*, edited by Gustave von Grunebaum in the 1950s. At the core of the volume lay the idea that "the unity of Muslim civilization ... is a compound of the official "great tradition" and of

54 Pierre-Robert Baduel and Sylvie Denoix, "Vers une *Revue des mondes musulmans* ou de la difficulté de nommer," *Revue du monde musulman et de la Méditerranée* 77–78 (1995): 7–18.

55 Ibid., 8.

56 Ibid., 10.

57 Sylvie Denoix, "Des culs-de-sacs heuristiques aux garde-fous épistémologiques ou comment aborder l'aire culturelle du « monde musulman »," *Revue des mondes musulmans et de la Méditerranée* 103–4 (2004): 9, 11.

the local and national traditions of different countries to which it travelled."[58] What the studies collected in this volume address is therefore "conflict, coexistence and interaction of the Islamic and the local patterns."[59] "In the *dār al-islām*—as stated in the foreword—the Islamic pattern is in general in the position of the great tradition. In contrast, the little tradition is the catchment of the popular undercurrent."[60] As we can see, "the Islamic pattern"—which is thought to characterize *dār al-islām*—is, without hesitation, seen in the singular. For example, referring to what Ibn Ḫaldūn says about the different methods of elementary teaching used in the various regions of the Islamic world, Grunebaum observes: "it is obvious that Ibn Khaldun, in accordance with Islamic erudites of all times, views the different systems of instruction but as relatively insignificant variants of one and the same universally accepted education which mirrors the ideal unity of the *dār al-islām*."[61] It is this "ideal unity," unanimously attributed to the world of Islam throughout history, postulating as a common denominator and explanatory factor the religious phenomenon, which is being questioned today, while the plurality which is put in the forefront cuts across the "great tradition" no less than local traditions.

Thus the singular, in the Muslim conception of *dār al-islām* and in the western idea of "the Muslim world," has different meanings. In the Muslim Sunni view of *dār al-islām* the singular originated as a reference to the unitary juridical system of Islam; however, thanks to the existence of a plurality of orientations, which later became officially recognized schools, it entailed a variety of interpretations concerning the dynamics of Muslim relations with the rest of the world, without necessarily implying a denial of the diversities within its own world. Functioning from within as a protective casing made of a flexible material, from without it has been stiffened into a hard shell, a kind of armor, from which recent scholarship is trying to free its subject of study, in order to let its complexities emerge.

---

58 Robert Redfield and Milton Singer, "Foreword," in *Unity and Variety in Muslim Civilization*, ed. Gustave Edmund von Grunebaum, Comparative Studies of Cultures and Civilizations 7 (Chicago: University of Chicago Press, 1955), V.

59 Gustave Edmund von Grunebaum, "The Problem: Unity in Diversity," in *Unity and Variety in Muslim Civilization*, ed. Gustave Edmund von Grunebaum, Comparative Studies of Cultures and Civilizations 7 (Chicago: University of Chicago Press, 1955), 27.

60 Ibid., 28.

61 Ibid., 26–27.

5 Law, Ethics, Identity

It is rather the overlapping of a notion of collective identity with the juridical concept of *dār* that, in the Sunni medieval context, has turned the *dār al-islām / dār al-ḥarb* binomial into a dichotomy. By constrast, in the Shi'ite context, that of a minority which has always represented an oppositional movement, the distinction between *dār al-islām* and *dār al-īmān*, "the abode of Islam" and "the abode of faith," shifts the focus from law to ethics: thus a formally Islamic land—theoretically *dār al-islām*—where sin and corruption thrive is to be considered *dār al-kufr*.[62]

After the seventh/thirteenth century, when—following the Mongol invasion in the east and the Reconquista in the west—considerable Muslim communities find themselves under non-Muslim domination, the issue of *hijra* once again becomes significant. And, inextricably linked to the juridical issue of whether it would be necessary for Muslims living in that condition to emigrate, the question of what *dār al-islām* is inevitably arises. Khaled Abou El Fadl's article, reviewing the positions of the four law schools on the matter, presents us with answers ranging from extreme pragmatism to an obstinate denial of reality and often deliberately ambiguous, so rich and varied that they could hardly correspond to the current stereotype of a classification of the world divided into two symmetrically opposed entities.[63] And above all, what in my view deserves attention is how the casuistic juridical methodology may result in the dismantling and overlapping of the two entities, which in theory are so sharply separated.

The complexities surrounding the invocation of the *dār al-islām* and *dār al-ḥarb* dichotomy, even within a single *maḏhab*, in connection with the problem of Muslim minorities, have been recently highlighted also in the long article by Basheer Nafi, "Fatwā and war: on the allegiance of the American Muslim soldiers in the aftermath of September 11,"[64] which thoroughly analyzes the collective fatwa, about "the permissibility of the participation of Muslim military personnel in the US armed forces in the war operations in Afghanistan and

62 Abou El Fadl, "Islamic Law and Muslim Minorities," 152.

63 Ibid., 161.

64 Basheer Nafi, "Fatwā and War: On the Allegiance of the American Muslim Soldiers in the Aftermath of September 11," *Islamic Law and Society* 11, no. 1 (2004): 78–116. I am grateful to Caterina Bori for pointing it out to me.

elsewhere in other Muslim countries", signed by sheikh Yūsuf al-Qaraḍāwī[65] and other four specialists in Islamic law.

Before commenting on the fatwa which is centered around "the complexity of the Muslim's allegiance to the nation state," the author analyzes some other cases in which "Muslim *ʿulamāʾ* in different historical periods and under different circumstances, dealt with legal problems arising from the residing of Muslims in non-Muslim lands," in order to explore the intricate relationship between *fiqh* and history, illustrated by the broad variations between the main Sunni *maḏhab*s as well as within each *maḏhab*. The historical antecedents considered here firstly concern the positions of Maliki jurists who, in the Maghrib and Granada after the Reconquista, became increasingly rigid and came to reject any form of Muslim residence under non-Muslim rule, as expressed in several fatwas included in Wanšarīsī's *Miʿyār*.[66] For Maliki jurists, residence in non-Muslim lands was becoming "a religious and ethical decision as much as a political one," as Abou El Fadl pointed out.[67] The strict Maliki demarcation between *dār al-islām* and *dār al-ḥarb* was invoked again during the jihad movement of Shaykh Usman dan Fodio, at the beginning of the thirteenth/nineteenth century, and aroused a heated debate among his successors, showing, in Bashir Nafi's view, how "the concept of *dār al-ḥarb* has been a vital *sharʿī* instrument for legitimating *hijra* and subsequent *jihād*."[68] As for the pragmatic attitude—and its limits—of the Shafi'i mufti of Mecca, when asked by the Muslim minority of Malabar in the tenth/sixteenth century whether it was legitimate for Muslims to return a Malabari converted to Islam to unbelievers, who could otherwise force Muslims to leave their homeland, it reveals, in Nafi's view, "the tension between the desire to sanction a level of normalcy in the life of Muslim minorities and the safeguarding of their Islamic identity." Instead, in the twelfth/eighteenth century, the determining factor in the Ottoman ulema and statesmen's attitude to the Muslims of Crimea after its annexation by the Russians, was their pledge of religious allegiance to the Ottoman sultan in his capacity as caliph, rather than political affiliation.

In addressing the position of Muslim minorities living in a modern state, and the nature of the relationship between the Muslim individual and the non-Islamic state, Qaraḍāwī's and his associates' fatwa goes beyond the Ottoman

---

65 On the various dimensions of the controversial figure of this authoritative Sunni religious scholar, Islamist activist and media star, see Bettina Gräf and Jakob Skovgaard-Petersen, *Global Mufti. The Phenomenon of Yūsuf al-Qaraḍāwī* (London: Hurst & Company, 2009).

66 Ibid., 85.

67 Abou El Fadl, "Islamic Law and Muslim Minorities," 163.

68 Nafi, "Fatwā and War," 87.

acceptance of the fact that the Muslim community will remain under the jurisdiction of a non-Muslim state. It is based on a new understanding of what constitutes the abode of Islam (*dār al-islām*), which no longer adheres to the traditional dichotomous *fiqh* construct: the contemporary world is defined as one world of *ʿahd* (covenant), the pursuit of the Islamic way of life should not be contingent upon living in a country that applies the sharia, and countries that historically were regarded as "abode of war" (*dār al-ḥarb*) are no longer regarded as such. "This new Islamic worldview—Nafi concludes—implies the deconstruction of the theological and political barriers that the traditional Muslim jurists constructed between *dār al-islām* and what lay beyond," while "the unprecedented movement of peoples across the globe has made the geographical bases of *dār al-islām* obsolete."[69]

Before concluding, I would like to draw attention to one last question. One of the main arguments of jurists, who maintained the necessity for Muslims to emigrate from territories under non-Muslim domination, was the risk of becoming subject to the laws of unbelievers. Saḥnūn reports that, for this very reason, Mālik strongly disapproved even of Muslims traveling in the lands of non-believers solely for trade purposes. But, to what extent can the rules of the other *dār*—rules that Hanafi jurists used to call *aḥkām al-širk*—be considered "law," in their view? Johansen answers the question this way: "En tant qu'organisation politique et étatique, le 'territoire de guerre' crée des relations de droit qui forcent les musulmans à les prendre en compte dans la réalité politique et dans leurs constructions juridiques. Le princes non-musulmans exercent des formes de pouvoir qui ne sont ni légales—parce que le droit musulman ne les reconnait pas—ni légitimes—parce qu'elles sont utilisés contre le 'territoire de l'islam.' Mais elles ont des effets politiques et juridiques sur les musulmans…. Le droit des non-musulmans du territoire de guerre est une fonction de leur force politico-militaire. En tant que tel … le territoire de la guerre restreint la sphère de l'applicabilité du droit musulman au 'territoire d'islam.' L'identité juridique des musulmans se forge sous l'influence des droits des non-musulmans…."[70]

Once again the theme of identity returns, a word which occurs so often today to appear inescapable, "a myth of our time"[71]. In principle, identity refers to the idea of a stable and permanent core, something non-negotiable, which

---

69 Ibid., 107, 115.

70 Johansen, "Entre révélation et tyrannie," 234.

71 Francesco Remotti, *L'ossessione identitaria*, Anticorpi 9 (Roma: Laterza, 2010), xii. In the author's view, "if the myth of race has officially declined, the myth of identity has triumphed instead" (my translation, Ibid., xiv.).

escapes change. But this permanent core is a representation, "un foyer virtuel auquel il nous est indispensable de nous référer … mais sans qu'il ait jamais d'existence réelle,"[72] a construction which involves a will to enhance differences, and as such entails in some way the use of force: bonds are broken, connections are interrupted to give rise to the construction of identity.[73] In fact, identity requires boundaries which are meant to be clear-cut and unquestionable, even though the porousness, weakness and provisionality of real boundaries might indicate that otherness is not without but within "us."[74]

Only at a macro level can the *dār al-islām / dār al-ḥarb* binomial be seen as an example of identity representation, being the crystallization into conventional formulas of a collective, all-embracing self/other representation[75]. The joining of the first term of this binomial to the word *Islam* confirms the fact that religion was, and is, a powerful tool for the construction of identity,[76] and that, in this sense, monotheisms—religions of the Scripture—hold a privileged position. Conversely, the term *dār al-ḥarb*, in its formally incongruous reference to war,[77] evokes the violence implied in the exclusive and exclusionary vision of the religions of the Book, the violence of Scripture, and of writing itself.[78]

Muslim jurists, who devised the *dār al-islām / dār al-ḥarb* binomial for their own use, managed to face up to the challenges of history, adapting, in different ways according to their orientation, the meaning of the notion of *dār al-islām*—and consequently *dār al-ḥarb*—to contingent situations, defining and redefining it, and therefore playing a dynamic role in an apparently static

72 Claude Lévi-Strauss, ed., *L'identité*. Séminaire interdisciplinare dirigé par Claude Lévi-Strauss (Paris: Grasset, 1977), 332.

73 Francesco Remotti, *Contro l'identità*, 1st ed., Sagittari Laterza 99 (Roma: Laterza, 1996), 9–10.

74 Remotti, *L'ossessione identitaria*, xix.

75 At a micro level, the issue of identity (or identities) manifests itself above all within historical and social contexts characterized by a plurality of groups, a multiplicity of social subjects, producing perceptions-categorizations of—real or imaginary—significant differences between each other.

76 Remotti, *Contro l'identità*, 38.

77 Gianroberto Scarcia, "*Islām* e *Ḥarb*, *ʿArab* e *ʿAjam*: nota a due celeberrime dicotomie islamiche," in *Azhàr: studi arabo-islamici in memoria di Umberto Rizzitano (1913–1980)*, ed. Antonino Pellitteri and Giovanni Montaina, Annali della Facoltà di lettere e filosofia dell'Università di Palermo. Studi e ricerche 23 (Palermo: Facoltà di lettere e filosofia dell'Università di Palermo, 1995), 205–10.

78 Jack Goody, *The Logic of Writing and the Organization of Society*, Studies in Literacy, Family, Culture, and the State (Cambridge: Cambridge University Press, 1986), 1–44.

conceptual framework. What they never wanted indeed, was to dispense with the words expressing that dual opposition which was their own creation.

References

Abou El Fadl, Khaled. "Islamic Law and Muslim Minorities: The Juristic Discourse on Muslim Minorities from the Second/Eighth to the Eleventh/Seventeenth Centuries." *Islamic Law and Society* 1, no. 2 (1994): 141–87.

Abulafia, David. "Seven Types of Ambiguity, C. 1100–C. 1500." In *Medieval Frontiers: Concepts and Practices*, edited by David Abulafia and Nora Berend, 1–33. Aldershot, Hants, England: Ashgate, 2002.

Ahmad, Mushtaq Muhammad. "The notions of *dār al-ḥarb* and *dār al-Islām* in Islamic jurisprudence with special reference to the Ḥanafī school." *Islamic Studies* 47 (2008): 5–37.

Amselle, Jean-Loup. *Logiques métisses: anthropologie de l'identité en Afrique et ailleurs*. Paris: Payot & Rivages, 1999.

Amselle, Jean-Loup. "I fondamenti antropologici della costruzione delle identità." In *Identità collettive tra medioevo e età moderna*, edited by P. Prodi and W. Reinhard, 31–42. Bologna: CLUEB, 2002.

Ayalon, David. "*Mamlūkiyyāt* (B) Ibn Khaldūn's View of the Mamlūk Phenomenon." *Jerusalem Studies in Arabic and Islam* 2 (1980): 340–49.

Ayoub, Samy. "Territorial jurisprudence, *ikhtilaf al-darayn*: Political boundaries & legal jurisdiction." *Contemporary Islamic Studies*, no. 2012 (April 2012): 2.

Baduel, Pierre-Robert, and Sylvie Denoix. "Vers une *Revue des mondes musulmans* ou de la difficulté de nommer." *Revue du monde musulman et de la Méditerranée* 77–78 (1995): 7–18.

Balāḏurī, Aḥmad b. Yaḥyā al-. *Kitāb Futūḥ al-buldān*. Edited by Ṣalāh al-dīn al-Munajjid. Cairo, 1956.

Barth, Fredrik, ed. *Ethnic Groups and Boundaries. The Social Organization of Culture Difference*. Oslo: Universitetsforlaget, 1969.

Blankinship, Khalid Yahya. *The End of the Jihād State: The Reign of Hishām Ibn 'Abd al-Malik and the Collapse of the Umayyads*. SUNY Series in Medieval Middle East History. Albany: State University of New York Press, 1994.

Bonner, Michael. "The Naming of the Frontier: 'Awāṣim, Thughūr, and the Arab Geographers." *Bulletin of the School of Oriental and African Studies* 57, no. 1 (1994): 17–24.

Bori, Caterina. "'All We Know Is What We Have Been Told': Reflections on Emigration and Land as Divine Heritage in the Qur'ān." In *The Coming of the Comforter: When, Where, and to Whom?: Studies on the Rise of Islam and Various Other Topics in*

Memory of John Wansbrough, edited by Carlos A. Segovia and Basil Lourié, 303–42. Orientalia Judaica Christiana 3. Piscataway, NJ: Gorgias Press, 2012.

Brauer, Ralph W. "Boundaries and Frontiers in Medieval Muslim Geography." *Transactions of the American Philosophical Society* 85, no. 6 (1995): 1–73.

Calasso, Giovanna. "Les remparts et la loi, les talismans et les saints. La protection de la ville dans les sources musulmanes médiévales." *Bulletin d'Etudes Orientales* 44 (1993): 93–104.

Calasso, Giovanna. "Partire: l'incipit delle relazioni di viaggio di Nāṣer-e Khosrow, Ibn Jubayr e Ibn Baṭṭūṭa." In *In memoria di Francesco Gabrieli*, suppl. no. 2 to *Rivista degli Studi Orientali* 71, 81–98. Roma: Bardi, 1997.

Calasso, Giovanna. "Récits de conversion, zèle dévotionnel et instruction religieuse dans les biographies des 'gens de Basra' du *Kitāb al-Ṭabaqāt* d'Ibn Sa'd." In *Conversions islamiques*, edited by Mercedes García Arenal, 19–47. Paris: Maisonneuve et Larose, 2001.

Calasso, Giovanna. "Les multiples départs des voyageurs musulmans du moyen âge et les contours mouvants du *dār al-islām*." *Annali di Ca' Foscari* 48, no. 3 (s. or. 40) (2009): 79–96.

Calasso, Giovanna. "Alla ricerca di *dār al-islām*. Una ricognizione nei testi di giuristi e tradizionisti, lessicografi, geografi e viaggiatori." *Rivista degli Studi Orientali* 83 (2010): 271–96.

Christys, Ann. "Crossing the Frontier of Ninth Century Hispania." In *Medieval Frontiers: Concepts and Practices*, edited by David Abulafia and Nora Berend, 35–53. Aldershot, Hants, England: Ashgate, 2002.

Coulson, N. J. "The State and the Individual in Islamic Law." *International and Comparative Law Quarterly* 6, no. 1 (1957): 49–60.

Crone, Patricia. *Medieval Islamic Political Thought*. Edinburgh: Edinburgh Univ. Press, 2004.

Denoix, Sylvie. "Des culs-de-sacs heuristiques aux garde-fous épistémologiques ou comment aborder l'aire culturelle du « monde musulman »." *Revue des mondes musulmans et de la Méditerranée* 103–4 (2004): 7–26.

Donnan, Hastings, and Thomas M. Wilson, eds. *Border Approaches: Anthropological Perspectives on Frontiers*. Lanham: Univ. Press of America, 1994.

Donner, Fred M. "Qur'ânicization of Religio-Political Discourse in the Umayyad Period." *Revue Des Mondes Musulmans et de La Méditerranée* 129 (2011): 79–92.

Ellenblum, Ronnie. "Were There Borders and Borderlines in the Middle Ages? The Example of the Latin Kingdom of Jerusalem." In *Medieval Frontiers: Concepts and Practices*, edited by David Abulafia and Nora Berend, 105–19. Aldershot, Hants, England: Ashgate, 2002.

Fabietti, Ugo. *Etnografia della frontiera: antropologia e storia in Baluchistan*. Gli argonauti 22. Roma: Meltemi, 1997.

Gautier-Dalché, Jean. "Islam et chrétienté en Espagne au XIIe siècle: contribution à l'étude de la notion de frontière." *Hespéris* 47 (1959): 183–217.

Goody, Jack. *The Logic of Writing and the Organization of Society*. Studies in Literacy, Family, Culture, and the State. Cambridge: Cambridge University Press, 1986.

Gräf, Bettina, and Jakob Skovgaard-Petersen. *Global Mufti. The Phenomenon of Yūsuf al-Qaraḍāwī*. London: Hurst & Company, 2009.

Grunebaum, Gustave Edmund von. "The Problem: Unity in Diversity." In *Unity and Variety in Muslim Civilization*, edited by Gustave E. von Grunebaum, 17–37. Comparative Studies of Cultures and Civilizations 7. Chicago: University of Chicago Press, 1955.

Ibn Faḍlān, Aḥmad. *Risālat Ibn Faḍlān*. Edited by Sāmī Dahhān. Dimašq: Maṭbūʿāt al-Majmaʿ al-ʿilmī al-ʿarabī bi-Dimašq, 1379/1960.

Ibn Ḫaldūn, Walī 'l-dīn. *Kitāb al-ʿIbar*. Būlāq, 1284/1867.

Ibn Hauqal [Ḥawqal], Muḥammad. *Configuration de la terre* (*Kitāb Ṣūrat al-arḍ*). Introduction et traduction, avec index, par J. H. Kramers et G. Wiet. 2 vols. Beirut: Commission internationale pour la traduction des chefs-d'oeuvre, 1964.

Ibn Ḥawqal, Abū 'l-Qāsim al-Naṣībī. *Kitāb Ṣūrat al-arḍ*. Edited by M. J. de Goeje and J. H. Kramers. Leiden: Brill, 1938.

Ibn Ḥazm, Abū Muḥammad ʿAlī. *Jamharat ansāb al-ʿarab*. Cairo: Dār al-maʿārif, 1382/1962.

Ibn Jubayr, Abū 'l-Ḥusayn Muḥammad. *Riḥlat Ibn Jubayr*. 2nd ed. Beirut: Dār wa-maktabat al-Hilāl, 1986.

Iṣṭaḫrī, Abū Isḥāq Ibrāhīm al-. *Kitāb Masālik al-mamālik*. Edited by Michael Johan de Goeje. 2nd ed. Leiden: Brill, 1927.

Johansen, Baber. "Der *ʿiṣma*-Begriff im hanafitischen Recht." In *Actes du 8me Congrès de l'Union Européenne des Arabisants et Islamisants, Aix-en-Provence, septembre 1976*, 89–108. Aix-en-Provence: Edisud, 1978.

Johansen, Baber. "Entre révélation et tyrannie: le droit des non-musulmans d'après les juristes musulmans." In *Identité et droit de l'autre: a Robbins Collection publication, University of California at Berkeley*, edited by Laurent Mayali, 127–46. Studies in comparative legal history. Berkeley, CA: University of California at Berkeley, 1994.

Johansen, Baber. *Contingency in a Sacred Law: Legal and Ethical Norms in the Muslim Fiqh*. Studies in Islamic Law and Society, v. 7. Leiden: Brill, 1999.

Khadduri, Majid, ed. *The Islamic Law of Nations: Shaybānī's Siyar.* Translated with an Introduction, Notes and Appendices. Baltimore: The Johns Hopkins Press, 1966.

Khalidi, Tarif. "Al-Ṭabarī: An Introduction." In *Al-Ṭabarī: A Medieval Muslim Historian and His Work*, edited by Hugh Kennedy, 1–10. Studies in Late Antiquity and Early Islam 15. Princeton, NJ: The Darwin Press, 2008.

Lambton, Ann K. S. *State and Government in Medieval Islam: An Introduction to the Study of Islamic Political Theory: The Jurists*. London Oriental Series, v. 36. Oxford: Oxford University Press, 1981.

Lev, Yaacov. "Coptic Rebellions and the Islamization of Medieval Egypt (8th–10th Century): Medieval and Modern Perceptions." *Jerusalem Studies in Arabic and Islam* 39 (2012): 303–44.

Lévi-Strauss, Claude, ed. *L'identité*. Séminaire interdisciplinare dirigé par Claude Lévi-Strauss. Paris: Grasset, 1977.

Lewis, Bernard. *The Political Language of Islam*. Chicago: University of Chicago Press, 1988.

Mottahedeh, Roy Parviz, and Ridwan al-Sayyid. "The Idea of the *Jihād* in Islam before the Crusades." In *The Crusades from the Perspective of Byzantium and the Muslim World*, edited by Angeliki E. Laiou and Roy Parviz Mottahedeh, 23–29. Washington, D.C.: Dumbarton Oaks Research Library and Collection, 2001.

Muqaddasī, Muḥammad b. Aḥmad al-. *Aḥsan al-taqāsīm fī maʿrifat al-aqālīm*. Edited by Michael Johan de Goeje. 2nd ed. Leiden: Brill, 1906.

Muqaddasī, Muḥammad b. Aḥmad al-. *Aḥsan al-taqāsīm fī maʿrifat al-aqālīm* (*La meilleure répartition pour la connaissances des provinces*). Traduction partielle, annotée par André Miquel. Damas: Institut français de Damas, 1963.

Nafi, Basheer. "Fatwā and War: On the Allegiance of the American Muslim Soldiers in the Aftermath of September 11." *Islamic Law and Society* 11, no. 1 (2004): 78–116.

Nallino, Carlo Alfonso. "Delle assicurazioni in diritto musulmano hanafita." *Oriente moderno* 7 (1927): 446–61.

Nāṣir-i Ḫusraw. *Safar-nāma*. Edited by Muḥammad Dabīr-Siyāqī. Teheran: Kitābfurūš Zawwād, 1354SH.

Onimus, Clément. "Les *mawālī* en Egypte dans la documentation papyrologique." *Annales Islamologiques* 39 (2005): 81–106.

Oulddali, Ahmed. "Recevabilité du témoignage du ḏimmī d'après les juristes mālikites d'Afrique du Nord." In *The legal status of ḏimmī-s in the Islamic West: second/eighth–ninth/fifteenth centuries*, edited by Maribel Fierro and John Tolan. Religion and law in medieval Christian and Muslim societies 1. Turnhout: Brepols, 2013.

Redfield, Robert, and Milton Singer. "Foreword." In *Unity and Variety in Muslim Civilization*, edited by Gustave E. von Grunebaum. Comparative Studies of Cultures and Civilizations 7. Chicago: University of Chicago Press, 1955.

Remotti, Francesco. *Contro l'identità*. 1st ed. Sagittari Laterza 99. Roma: Laterza, 1996.

Remotti, Francesco. *L'ossessione identitaria*. Anticorpi 9. Roma: Laterza, 2010.

Santillana, David. *Istituzioni di diritto musulmano malichita, con riguardo anche al sistema sciafiita*. Vol. 1. Rome: Anonima Romana Editoriale, 1921.

Saraḫsī, Muḥammad b. Aḥmad al-. *Kitāb al-Mabṣūṭ*. Beirut: Dār al-Fikr, 1421/2000.

Sayyid, Ridwan al-. "*Dār al-Ḥarb* and *Dār al-Islām*: traditions and interpretations." In *Religion between violence and reconciliation*, edited by Thomas Scheffler, 123–33. Beiruter Texte und Studien, Bd. 76. Beirut: Orient-Institut–Ergon Verlag in Kommission, 2002.

Scarcia, Gianroberto. "*Islām* e *Ḥarb*, *'Arab* e *'Ajam*: nota a due celeberrime dicotomie islamiche." In *Azhàr: studi arabo-islamici in memoria di Umberto Rizzitano (1913–1980)*, edited by Antonino Pellitteri and Giovanni Montaina, 205–10. Annali della Facoltà di lettere e filosofia dell'Università di Palermo. Studi e ricerche 23. Palermo: Facoltà di lettere e filosofia dell'Università di Palermo, 1995.

Schacht, Joseph. *An Introduction to Islamic Law*. Oxford: Clarendon Press, 1982.

Zadeh, Travis E. *Mapping Frontiers across Medieval Islam: Geography, Translation, and the 'Abbāsid Empire*. Library of Middle East History 27. London: I. B. Tauris, 2011.

CHAPTER 2

The Missing *dār*

On Collocations in Classical Arabic Dictionaries

Giuliano Lancioni

1 Introduction

All-purpose dictionaries have an important role in revealing clues to the way a culture organizes its conceptual categories, its *episteme* in Michel Foucault's terms.[1] While scientific works or specialized lexicons can give more accurate definitions, it is general dictionaries which show most clearly which technical concepts have made their way into ordinary discourse and can be regarded as a record of shared knowledge in a given culture in a particular time span.

In the case of the classical Arabic-Islamic culture, dictionaries play a special role, since lexicographical works written for the general (learned) public appeared much earlier, and with much greater scope, than in European culture. In particular, the "alphabetical revolution" heralded by the Encyclopédie—which arguably introduced a formal, as opposed to a conceptual, sorting method for knowledge—happened much earlier, at least from the fourth/tenth century.[2]

Specifically, as far as the *dār al-islām* / *dār al-ḥarb* and related dichotomies are concerned, while legal literature might add many subtleties and technicalities to the picture, the presence of relevant terms in dictionaries sheds light on how the Arabic-Islamic culture conceptualized them and how these words

1 Michel Foucault, *The Archaeology of Knowledge* (translation of *L'archeologie du savoir*) (New York, NY: Pantheon Books, 1982), 191, (transl. of Michel Foucault, *L'archeologie du savoir* [Paris: Gallimard, 1969]): "The episteme is not a form of knowledge (*connaissance*) or type of rationality which, crossing the boundaries of the most varied sciences, manifests the sovereign unity of a subject, a spirit, or a period; it is the totality of relations that can be discovered, for a given period, between the sciences when one analyses them at the level of discursive regularities."

2 I have identified elsewhere (Giuliano Lancioni, "Sull'ordinamento dei dizionari arabi classici," in *In memoria di Francesco Gabrieli*, suppl. no. 2 to *Rivista degli Studi Orientali* 71 [Rome: Bardi, 1997], 113–27) the appearence of Jawharī's (d. 400/1009) *Ṣiḥāḥ*, the first dictionary that employs the so-called "rhyme order" (i.e., the alphabetical sorting of roots according to the last letter, than the first and the other ones), as the watershed in this alphabetization of reality.

 | DOI 10.1163/9789004331037_004

ceased to be purely technical words and became a part of the shared lexicon of the learned public.

As the discussion will show, the presence or absence of a word or a fixed sequence of words (a collocation in contemporary lexicographical parlance) does not lead to an automatic interpretation: reasons that lead a specific lexicographer to include a word or a collocation in a work vary, and the absence of very common items, especially of very common sequences, does not mean the absence of those items from the common speech of learned people. Sometimes the reverse clearly holds: as some clues clearly hint (e.g., the marking of a number of common words as *maʿrūf* "known"), often a lexicographer does not bother to define something that he deems common enough to be commonplace for the dictionary user.

This contribution is organized as follows: first (2) a description is provided of lexicographical works that are included as sources in the sample, then (3) relevant passages in these sources are analyzed and discussed. A discussion follows (4) on the status of collocations of the type found in the sources within contemporary lexicography, together with an analysis (5) of terminology and technical terms in the context of Medieval Arabic-Islamic culture. The last section (6) provides some provisional conclusions about data provided by sources and how they might be interpreted.

2 The Sample

Arabic lexicography produced an enormous quantity of works, witness to what I called elsewhere the hypertext-like nature of the classical Arabic-Islamic written culture.[3] This large body of literature, together with the huge dimension of many dictionaries, made virtually impossible until recently a thorough search for the presence, or absence, of words and set expressions and a comparison of their definitions.

This state of affairs has changed dramatically in the last few years with the increasing availability of many classical sources in electronic form. The ability to exploit both digitally reproduced and encoded texts not only sped up research (a scholar can quite easily query for a given expression without even bothering to go to a library), but allowed research that was simply not possible before: in the case of lexicography, a researcher had to limit him/herself to

3 Cf. Giuliano Lancioni, "Variants, Links, and Quotations: Classical Arabic Texts As Hypertexts," in *Scritti in onore di Biancamaria Scarcia Amoretti*, ed. Daniela Bredi et al., vol. 2, 3 vols. (Roma: Edizioni Q, 2008), 245–65.

look for specific words in the root arrangement, without having any practical possibility of finding occurrences of the same words elsewhere in sometimes really huge works.

Complaints occasionally found, even if rarely written down, about bad research practices arising from the usage of classical sources in electronic form are simply not well-founded: while it is true that electronic sources in text form are often far from perfect (a natural downside of the understandably frequent practice of editing documents automatically produced by OCRs—optical character recognition software—rather than inputting them by hand), one should remember that queries are only a preliminary stage to access to the original text, in paper or digitally reproduced form. This stage enormously increases the possibility of finding relevant passages, after which everything goes on as was usual before the Information Technology era.

This latter, often not well understood feature of digitally-oriented research makes it as necessary as it was before to sample dictionaries, rather than exhaustively analyze works available in electronic form: while preliminary queries would allow researchers relatively quickly to find relevant passages in a large body of works, the subsequent task of reading, analyzing and comparing the query results is as impractical as it used to be: even more so, since the ability to search for queried expressions in the full text of sources increases the number of passages to be scrutinized.

The aim of this article makes it reasonable to limit the sample to some of the most relevant and most widely circulated classical dictionaries. Since the stated goal is to detect how expressions linked to the *dār al-islām* / *dār al-ḥarb* dichotomy were categorized in the shared knowledge of classical Arabic-Islamic culture, the more a work was employed and widespread the more important it becomes. *Al-Qāmūs al-muḥīṭ* which, according to Haywood, is still extant in more than 8,000 manuscripts (which makes it perhaps *the* lexicographical best-seller before the age of print)[4] is much more relevant in this respect than a possibly much more accurate dictionary with a much more limited diffusion.

On the other hand, since this contribution serves as a lexical introduction to a number of further discussions in this volume about the historical development of concepts, it is important to analyze a number of representative works across the history of Arabic lexicography. Representativeness and the need for historical coverage do sometimes collide, yet overall a reasonable sample of lexicographical works does arise quite naturally.

4 Cf. John A. Haywood, *Arabic Lexicography: Its History, and Its Place in the General History of Lexicography* (Leiden: Brill, 1965), 85, who quotes Ṣiddīq Ḥasan Ḫān.

Here is a list of dictionaries selected according to these criteria in chronological arrangement according to the date of death of their authors:

1. *Kitāb al-ʿAyn* by (the pseudo-)al-Ḫalīl b. Aḥmad (d. 175/791);
2. *Jamharat al-luġa* by Ibn Durayd (d. 321/933);
3. *Majmal al-luġa* by Ibn Fāris (d. 395/1004);
4. *al-Ṣiḥāḥ* by Jawharī, (d. 400/1009);
5. *al-Muḥkam* by Ibn Sīda (d. 458/1066);
6. *Lisān al-ʿArab* by Ibn Manẓūr (d. 711/1311);
7. *al-Qāmūs al-Muḥīṭ* by Fīrūzābādī (d. 817/1415).

3 The Relevant Passages in the Sources

3.1 *The* Kitāb al-ʿAyn

The *Kitāb al-ʿAyn* is the oldest Arabic dictionary; while tradition tends to question the attribution of its final version to Ḫalīl (in favor of his much despised nephew Layṯ), it is nevertheless a work from not later than the beginning of third/ninth century, which gives it an extraordinary importance. Another interesting element is that, contrary to what is sometimes stated, the *Kitāb al-ʿAyn* is not an exhaustive dictionary: its primary scholarly aim is to list the full set of Arabic roots according to an ingenious permutation principle set up by Ḫalīl, rather than to include all words in the language.

This feature enhances, rather than limiting, its interest for our research: in selecting words to illustrate roots, the author of the works is likely to have chosen among the very shared lexical thesaurus which we are to investigate. In other words, the selection operated by the lexicographer(s) is in itself illuminating of what was commonplace at the age of its composition.

The *dār al-ḥarb* pole of the dichotomy is well-represented in the *Kitāb al-ʿAyn*; the *dār al-ḥarb* collocation is recognized and gets a fairly technical definition: *bilād al-mušrikīn allaḏīna lā ṣulḥa baynahum wa-bayna ʾl-muslimīn* "country of the *mušrikūn* between whom and the Muslims there is no pact."[5] This definition implies the common domain status of such legal terms as *mušrik* "associator, he who associates other divinities to God" and *ṣulḥ* "capitulation pact between Muslims and the population of a conquered territory."

Moreover, the definiendum here is deemed clear enough to be used as part of a definition elsewhere, one of the clearest signs of a well-established meaning:

5 Al-Ḫalīl b. Aḥmad al-Farāhīdī, *Kitāb al-ʿAyn*, ed. al-Maḫzūmī and al-Samarrāʾī (Dār wa-maktabat al-Hilāl, n.d.), 3:213, s.v. *ḥrb*.

in glossing the word *fatḥ*, the text says (by using, slightly circularly, the *maṣdar* of a derived form from the same root) *iftitāḥ dār al-ḥarb* "the opening [i.e., the conquest] of *dār al-ḥarb*."[6] And elsewhere, in the clarification of the meaning of *taġr* in the sense of *taġr al-ʿaduww* "the enemy's border," we find *mā yalī dār al-ḥarb* "what is contiguous to *dār al-ḥarb*."[7] Finally, in the definition of *kafara*, *dār al-ḥarb* is introduced as a reference domain: *wa-yaqūlu li-ahl dār al-ḥarb: qad kafarū, ay: ʿaṣaw wa-'mtanaʿū* "it is told of the people of *dār al-ḥarb: kafarū*, that is 'they are rebellious and resist'."[8]

What is more surprising is that the *Kitāb al-ʿAyn* not only lacks a definition of *dār al-islām*, but even feels it necessary to define Islam itself as *al-istislām li-amr Allāh taʿālā wa-huwa 'l-inqiyād li-ṭāʿatihi wa'l-qabūl li-amrihi* "the submission [as usual, with another form of the same root] to the Order of God Almighty, that is the yielding to His power and the acceptation of His order." The need for a definition in this case seems rather puzzling, because it is reasonable to think that no learned person (and no person in general) at the epoch of the redaction of the *Kitāb al-ʿAyn* could have any doubt about what Islam was. However, it could be inferred that the author of the dictionary felt the need to give a more accurate definition, perhaps because the legal-theological debate about basic tenets of the still relatively new religion was alive.

3.2 *Two Surprising Cases:* **Jamharat al-luġa** *and* **Majmal al-luġa**

The lack, errors excepted, of any reference to the poles of the dichotomy in two important dictionaries of the fourth/tenth century such as Ibn Durayd's *Jamharat al-luġa* and Ibn Fāris's *Majmal al-luġa* is somewhat surprising. However, this striking feature can be partly explained with the nature and scope of each dictionary.

Ibn Durayd has a specific aim of including words missing in other dictionaries (which makes it such an interesting source for lexicography), and is a landmark work in the trend towards widening and deepening the scope of dictionaries through exploration of the language of the Bedouin: in such a context, it is quite obvious that collocations deemed relatively well-established by now do not get much attention.

On the other hand, Ibn Fāris—as his importance as a teacher of Ibn Jinnī's clearly shows—inaugurates the age of lexicographers more interested in the demonstration of some theoretical view, specifically the unity of meaning of

6 Ibid., 3:194, s.v. *ftḥ*.

7 Ibid., 4:400, s.v. *tġr*.

8 Ibid., 5:356, s.v. *kfr*.

all derivatives of the same root, rather than in giving the reader a complete coverage of the language.

3.3 Ṣiḥāḥ

In the fourth/tenth century, lexicography, like other language sciences, branches into two different approaches: while Ibn Fāris, by paralleling Ibn Jinnī's approach, is more interested in issues of philosophy of language, Jawharī, as happens with grammatical works such as the *Kitāb al-uṣūl* by Ibn al-Sarrāj, devotes its work to providing learned readers with more practical information. This shifts the focus of the work towards shorter, more concise definitions, where synonymy is often the main strategy.

One should not forget in this regard that Jawharī's stated goal is to include all correct words of the language, a project which makes *Ṣiḥāḥ* the first exhaustive dictionary, or at least the first dictionary which aims at exhaustiveness, in the history of Arab lexicography.

A consequence of this new approach is a reduction of the presence of collocations in favor of the inclusion of single words, a reduction which later dictionaries based (like the *Lisān* itself) on Jawharī will largely overcome. However, the presence of both *bilād al-islām* and *bilād al-ʿajam* in the same definition shows somehow the presence of the basic concepts: *talīd* is defined as *allaḏī wulida bi-bilād al-ʿajam ṯumma ḥumila ṣaġīran fa-nabata fī bilād al-islām* "he who was born in the country of *ʿajam* and later was transferred as a child so that he grew up in the country of Islam."

3.4 Muḥkam

Ibn Sīda's large dictionary—the twin work to his perhaps better-known thesaurus *al-Muḫaṣṣaṣ*—is an interesting case, because it shows how complex the evaluation of lexical material in general dictionaries can be. While Ibn Sīda is half a century later than Jawharī, he prefers, according to a general archaicizing attitude very typical of al-Andalus, especially in the fifth/eleventh and sixth/twelfth centuries, to take the *Kitāb al-ʿAyn* as his model work, and to quote it as much as possible if a definition is found there.[9]

In three cases, definitions from the *Kitāb al-ʿAyn* are repeated almost verbatim: *ṯaġr*, without the qualification *al-ʿaduww*, is literally repeated as *mā yalī dār al-ḥarb*, which is in itself re-defined verbatim as *bilād al-mušrikīn allaḏīna*

9 This utmost respect for the principle of authority is an original character of Arab lexicography through the ages: the *Lisān* quotes extensively from Jawharī, and even contemporary dictionaries, such as the *Munjid*, tend to quote classical works, especially the *Qāmūs*, whenever a definition can be found.

lā ṣulḥa baynahum wa-bayna 'l-muslimīn. In the definition of *fatḥ*, only the information about the broken plural form *futūḥ* is added.

However, an addition from Ṯaʿlab, probably a source common to *Muḥkam* and *Ṣiḥāḥ*, as the similarity with Jawharī's definition for *talīd* shows, is the gloss for *ḥamīl*, defined as *allaḏī yuḥmalu min bilād al-širk ilā bilād al-islām* "he who is brought from the country of *širk* to the country of Islam," where the comparison with Jawharī shows the practical equivalence of *bilād al-širk* and *bilād al-ʿajam*.

3.5 Lisān al-ʿArab

One striking element in Ibn Manẓūr's treatment of terms in the *dār al-islām* / *dār al-ḥarb* dichotomy is the frequency of reference to one or the other collocation outside their specific lexical entries: we find a number of matter-of-fact quotations, where the terms are used as common domain lexical items, without any need for definition.

We do find definitions, usually transferred verbatim from previous dictionaries: that is the case of *dār al-ḥarb*, whose definition repeats literally what is first found in the *Kitāb al-ʿAyn*.[10] However, what are most frequently, and interestingly, found are uses of the terms in definitions, or wider explanations, of meanings of other words.

Dār al-islām, while not being explicitly defined, is mentioned sub voce *ʿhd* in explaining the meaning of the Hadith *lā yuqtal mu'min bi-kāfir wa-lā ḏu ʿahd fī ʿahdihi* "a believer shall not be killed by an unbeliever nor the owner of a pact [will be killed] during [the validity of] his pact." Ibn Manẓūr quotes Ibn al-Aṯīr's paraphrase in *Nihāya: wa-lā ḏū ḏimma fī ḏimmatihi wa-lā mušrik uʿṭiya amānan fa-daḫala dār al-islām, fa-lā yuqtal ḥattā yaʿūdu ilā ma'manihi* "nor the owner of protection [will be killed] during [the validity of] his protection, nor a *mušrik* to whom a safe-conduct has been granted and entered *dār al-islām*: he will not be killed until he comes back to his origin of safe-conduct (*ma'man*)."[11]

The close synonym *bilād al-islām* can be found in the verbatim reproduction of Jawharī's definition of *talīd*, and, in the same locus, for the rarer *tilād*.[12]

---

10 Ibn Manẓūr, *Lisān al-ʿArab*, 3rd ed. (Beirut: Dār Ṣādir, 1414AH), 1:303a, s.v. *ḥrb*. The same happens with *ṯaġr*, Ibid., 4:103, s.v. *ṯġr*.

11 Ibn Manẓūr, *Lisān al-ʿArab*, 3:312b, s.v. *ʿhd*. The quotation is from Ibn al-Aṯīr, *al-Nihāya fī ġarīb al-ḥadīṯ wa'l-aṯar*, ed. al-Zāwī and al-Ṭanāḥī (al-Maktaba al-islāmiyya, n.d.), 3:325, s.v. *ʿahida*.

12 Ibn Manẓūr, *Lisān al-ʿArab*, 3:100b, s.v. *tld*. The same word gets a feminine definition, Ibid., 469b, s.v. *wld*.

Interestingly, a very incidental quotation of *dār al-salām* can be found under the root √byt, where, in order to explain, or rather to put in context, Ibn Sīda‘s identification of *bayt Allāh ta‘ālā* "God's house" as the Ka‘ba: in quoting (Abū ‘Alī) al-Fārisī, Ibn Manẓūr adds as parallel metaphors *‘abd Allāh* "God's slave" for the Prophet and *dār al-salām* "the abode of peace" for the paradise (*janna*).[13]

Dār al-salām is quoted more directly in the entry *dār*, where *dār al-fanā’* "the abode of annihilation," metaphor for *al-dunyā* "the lower (world)" is opposed to *dār al-salām* (together with *dār al-qarār*), for *al-āḫira* "the other (world)."[14]

3.6 Qāmūs

Fīrūzābādī's *Qāmūs* is probably the most influent dictionary in the history of Arabic lexicography, if diffusion and number of translations and commentaries are taken into account. The deliberately concise character of its entries makes it closer to the contemporary concept of a dictionary (while such works as the *Lisān* stay halfway between what nowadays would be considered as a dictionary proper and an encyclopedia) and strengthens its value as the condensation of the episteme of a specific culture, the classical Arabic-Islamic culture.

The need for terseness leads Fīrūzābādī strongly to prefer synonymy to definition, with some resulting circularity. When no synonym is at hand, the author often resorts to the strategy of marking the word, entirely or with a qualifying noun, as *ma‘rūf* "known" (abbreviated with a *mīm*). This is the case for *ḥarb*, that is marked as a known word; also the default irregular feminine is unmarked, since Fīrūzābādī limits itself to adding *wa-qad tuḏakkaru* "it may be masculine," by assuming that the reader already knows the default gender.

However, the *Qāmūs* deems it necessary to define *dār al-ḥarb*; the definition of the *Kitāb al-‘Ayn* is reproduced with a most interesting variant: instead than *bilād al-mušrikīn allaḏīna lā ṣulḥa baynahum wa bayna ’l-muslimīn* "country of the *mušrikūn* between whom and the Muslims there is no pact," Fīrūzābādī has *baynanā wa-baynahum* "between us and them," an opposition between "us" and "them" that is probably beyond conciseness and testifies to a more entrenched vision of Islam as the pervasive, de facto religion of "our" world.[15]

---

13 Ibn Manẓūr, *Lisān al-‘Arab*, 2:15a, s.v. *byt*. The same applies to Jerusalem in the explanation of the etymology of the Arabic transcription of the Hebrew form of the place name, *Ūrā Šallam*, Ibid., 4:35b, s.v. *’wr*, which is paraphrased as *bayt al-salām* or *dār al-salām* and equated to "paradise" (because of a direct relation between the "seventh paradise" [*al-janna al-sābi‘a*] and Jerusalem established in a quotation by Ka‘b).

14 Ibn Manẓūr, *Lisān al-‘Arab*, 2:15a, s.v. *byt*.

15 Fīrūzābādī, *al-Qāmūs al-muḥīṭ*, ed. Muḥammad Na‘īm al-‘Irqsūsī, 8th ed. (Beirut: Mu’assasat al-Risāla, 1426/2005), 73, s.v. *ḥrb*.

Previous definitions repeated in the *Qāmūs* include *fatḥ*, which is glossed, in a string of relatively unrelated meanings that includes *al-mā' al-jārī* "running water" and *al-naṣr* "victory" (in which meaning *fatāḥa* is declared as a synonym), as *iftitāḥ dār al-ḥarb*.[16] In the case of *dār al-salām* "the abode of peace," labeled as usual as a metaphor for *janna* "paradise," it is in a string with *nahr al-salām* "the river of peace," epithet for the *Dajla* "Tigris," and *madīnat al-salām*, of course Baghdad.[17]

The need and desire for conciseness probably determines an interesting variant in the definition of *talīd* (declared synonym of *talad*): we find *man wulida bi'l-ʿajam fa-ḥumila ṣaġīran fa-nabata bi-bilād al-islām* "who was born in ʿAjam and was brought as a child so that he grew up in the lands of Islam," where *bilād al-islām* "the countries of Islam" is opposed to *ʿajam* rather than *bilād al-ʿajam*, as if the term were something like "land of the barbarians" in a human-geographical sense.[18]

A final reference which testifies to the high level of structuring within the Islamic world and the stable status of religious minorities is given by the surprisingly accurate definition of *jāṯalīq* "Catholicos" and of the organizational hierarchy of the Eastern churches: *ra'īs li'l-naṣārā fī bilād al-islām bi-madīnat al-salām, wa-yakūnu taḥta yad biṭrīq Anṭākiya, ṯumma 'l-miṭrān tahta yadihi, ṯumma 'l-usquff yakūnu fī kull balad min taḥt al-miṭrān, ṯumma 'l-qissīs, ṯumma 'l-šammās* "head of the Christians in the lands of Islam in Baghdad (*madīnat al-salām*), under the authority of the Patriarch (*biṭrīq*) of Antiochia; then, the metropolitan (*miṭrān*) is under his power, the bishop (*usquff*) of any place is under the authority of the metropolitan, then the priest (*qissīs*), then the deacon (*šammās*)."[19]

This hierarchy strongly resembles other familiar hierarchies in lexicographical definitions (whose archetype is probably the hierarchy of tribal categories) and shows most clearly the common sense established status of such a category as *bilād al-islām*.

16 Ibid., 232b, s.v. *fth*. Analogously, *ṯaġr* is paraphrased—within the usual, rather haphazard sequence of meanings—*mā yalī dār al-ḥarb*, Ibid., 359a, s.v. *ṯġr*.

17 Fīrūzābādī, *Qāmūs*, 1122b, s.v. *slm*.

18 Ibid., 270a, s.v. *tld*.

19 Ibid., 871a, s.v. *jṯlq*. The hierarchy is repeated in slightly different terms in dealing with *usquff*, Ibid., 820a, s.v. *sqf*.

4 On Collocations

Dār al-ḥarb, dār al-islām and other more or less synonymic phrasal terms would be defined as collocations in contemporary lexicography.

An informal definition: two or more words form a collocation if the frequency of their co-occurrence is significantly higher than a random distribution (difficult to say how much higher). A more formal definition refers to "sequences of lexical items which habitually co-occur, but which are nonetheless fully transparent in the sense that each lexical constituent is also a semantic constituent".[20]

Collocations are distinguished from idioms in that the meaning of the sequence can be somehow inferred by the meaning of individual constituents, while the meaning of idioms is less compositional and is somewhat arbitrary.

Therefore, *it is raining cats and dogs* is an idiom (because there is no way to infer the meaning of the whole from the meaning of individual words), while *heavy rain* is a collocation, since the meaning of the sequence derives from the meaning of each word: *heavy* and *rain* do mean what allows one to understand the meaning of *heavy rain*, even if "the meaning carried by one (or more) of its constituent elements is highly restricted contextually, different from its meaning in more neutral contexts":[21] In this case, *heavy* gets a highly restricted meaning, and cannot be interpreted as, for instance, something having a specific weight.

Idioms, collocations and free sequences of words are placed along a continuum where it is difficult to draw a clear border: a free sequence becomes a collocation if the words that composes it happen to be together in a statistically significant way, which tends to specialize the meaning of the sequence and to produce metaphorical or metonymic meanings; when the original meaning of the metaphor or metonymy gets lost, we have an idiom.

Both *dār al-islām* and *dār al-ḥarb* (and most of the other forms of the dichotomy we find in classical dictionaries) are sequences frequent enough to be deemed collocations; however, their meaning is still linked enough to the meaning of *dār* and *islām* vs *ḥarb* to rule out their being regarded as idioms.

Along the continuum that has casual co-occurrence of words at one end (where meaning is entirely compositional) and pure idioms at the other end, where meaning has no relations with individual words, *dār al-islām* can be regarded as more compositional than *dār al-ḥarb*: i.e., a literal interpretation

20 D. A. Cruse, *Lexical Semantics*, Cambridge Textbooks in Linguistics (Cambridge: Cambridge University Press, 1986), 40.

21 Ibid.

of "the abode of Islam" is more interpretable than "abode of war," which can be difficult to understand without some grasp of Islamic law.

This different degree of compositionality might be a reason, as we shall see in section 6, to explain why lexicographers choose to, or not to, explicitly include a collocation in a dictionary.

5 Technical Terms and the Issue of Terminology

Dār al-islām and *dār al-ḥarb* (and perhaps some of the variants found in Arabic dictionaries) would ordinarily be labeled as "technical terms:" words or (as in these cases) collocations that acquire a specific, more precise meaning within the specialized vocabulary of a given discipline.

However obvious it may seem to us, the concept of technical term is extremely difficult to specify before the scientific revolution: it is with the growing formalization of science and of scientific research that terms tended to acquire a specific, not ad hoc meaning distinguished from other possible meanings a word or a collocation might have in ordinary speech.

On the other hand, not unlike collocations and idioms, technical terms are not a category with a clear-cut yes-or-no membership: some terms are used in a relatively consistent way across a number of authors in a discipline without matching all the criteria that identify technical terms (among others, precision, standardization, lack of ambiguity), and can therefore be called quasi-technical terms.

More specifically, in the Arabic-Islamic Middle Ages many disciplines did doubtless develop sets of (quasi-)technical terms, since they are found consistently in a corpus of a technical discipline, with few, if any, doubts about their meanings in a given context.

A very clear example of this process of technicalization of the language in the Arabic-Islamic Middle Ages can be found in grammar. Already at the end of the second/eighth century, the early extant work of grammar, the *Kitāb* of Sībawayhi, shows a relatively clear usage of terms to refer to linguistic categories. However, Sībawayhi rarely, if ever, bothers to define these terms in a way clear enough to let us speak of technical terms proper.

In the context of early Arabic grammar, a very fruitful concept is the idea of quasi-definitions (the term is mine) originally proposed by Jonathan Owens under the heading *When is terminology terminology?*:

> A question that looms especially prominent in a consideration of early Arabic theory is what constitutes technical terminology. The early Arabic

> grammarians tend to be unhelpful here, rather rarely giving explicit definitions for the terms they use ... The basic criteria for establishing whether or not a given linguist was using a given term as a fixed concept are clear. When a term is consistently used to represent a constant extensional class or a fixed process it can be taken as a technical term.[22]

What makes the usage of grammatical terminology properly technical in later grammatical treatises is the appearance of "books of definitions", the first instance of which is the *Kitāb al-Ḥudūd fī 'l-naḥw* "Book of definitions on grammar" by Rummānī (d. 384/994). Even if the *Kitāb al-Ḥudud* is very sketchy (it contains only 88 short definitions of technical terms), it marks a watershed, by introducing the idea of devoting a work to an explicit definition of the *iṣṭilāḥ*, the conventional language of a specific discipline.[23]

No specific tradition of "book of definitions" arose in the classical juridical literature. Several reasons can account for this state of affairs: the relation with sources, differences between law schools (a domain in which law was a model to grammar, as the late appearance of the grammatical *ḫilāfāt* "divergences" literature shows), a lesser degree of formalization of theory. However, the method proposed by Owens for early grammarians might be fruitfully applied to juridical texts, although "extracting paradigms from syntagms" is a notoriously painstaking—and sometimes plainly impossible—task.

6 Conclusions

Coming back to Classical dictionaries, a review of terms directly or indirectly related to the *dār al islām* / *dār al-ḥarb* dichotomy allows us to make a few provisional conclusions about the relations between terms and explanations for the "missing" (or latent) part of the dichotomy, *dār al-islām*.

First, in classical dictionaries *dār al-ḥarb* seems to be much more an established term than *dār al-islām*: the former can be found virtually everywhere, with a clearly technical definition, which includes crucially—alongside the presence of *mušrikūn*—the absence of a *ṣulḥ*; the latter is never explicitly defined.

22 Jonathan Owens, *Early Arabic Grammatical Theory: Heterogeneity and Standardization*, Amsterdam Studies in the Theory and History of Linguistic Science, v. 53 (Amsterdam: Benjamins, 1990), 11.

23 Rummānī, "Kitāb al-Ḥudūd fī 'l-naḥw," in *Rasāʾil fī 'l-naḥw wa'l-luġa*, ed. Jawād and Maskūnī (Baghdad: Wizārat al-Iʿlām, 1388/1989), 37–50.

On the other hand, both terms have alternatives, some of which, even for *dār al-ḥarb*, have a clearly non-technical character, one obvious example being (*bilād al-*)*ʿajam*, which refers to an ethnical, rather than a religious, category, sometimes opposed to a pretty religious one such as *bilād al-islām*.

Interestingly, the two terms never seem to be felt as components of a true dichotomy: otherwise, the common strategy of defining, for instance, *dār al-ḥarb* as *ḍidd* "opposite" of *dār al-islām*, would be employed.[24]

However, *dār al-islām* and related terms (such as *bilād al-islām*) are often used cursorily, as an item of common sense or matter-of-fact knowledge. Therefore, the lack of explicit definition could only mean that they are well-established terms that nobody would need to define; since they are not single words, calling them *maʿrūf* would not be fine (since the *maʿrūf* strategy is always applied to single words and never to collocations).

One should not forget that, actually, collocations have always been included in dictionaries in a more or less haphazard way: lexicographers have until very recently felt their primary task to be collecting all individual words in a language (perhaps excluding words deemed incorrect or dialectal) and have traditionally assigned collocations a secondary role, if only because they are difficult to arrange once alphabetical order becomes *the* sorting strategy in dictionaries.[25]

I will conclude these notes with a couple of considerations on the different treatment of the two poles of this dichotomy by Arab lexicographers, considerations that may give some clue to a possible explanation for their different status in Classical dictionaries.

A first point is that the lack of an explicit definition for *dār al-islām* and its presence for *dār al-ḥarb* is perphaps linked to the different degree of compositionality of the two collocations. In fact, the meaning of *dār al-islām* can be more or less precisely inferred from the meaning of the words that compose the collocation: *dār al-islām* is the "house" or "abode" (*dār*) of Islam, that is the area where Islam dwells; everybody is more or less able to understand the term

---

24 This argument is admittedly somewhat weakened by the fact that *ḍidd* is never used to oppose collocations as antonyms and is always applied to single words. However, other, similar strategies could have been used provided the lexicographers felt it convenient to describe *dār al-ḥarb* in terms of *dār al-islām* or the other way round.

25 This problem has not been overridden even in contemporary dictionaries that include a large number of collocations: in many cases, they are either listed separately, usually as if they were written as a single word (a choice that makes their research difficult for most users, at least if the dictionary is consulted in paper form), or included in the entry for the word deemed the central or most significant one. See, for an example, Chris Fox, *Longman Dictionary of Contemporary English* (Harlow: Longman, 2004).

without a detailed definition, which should moreover substantially repeat the definiendum.

On the other hand, *dār al-ḥarb* "deserves" a definition more than *dār al-islām*: i.e., the meaning of the collocation is more difficult to determine from the meanings of its components. In fact, the literal meaning "abode" or "house of war" does not closely amount to the actual meaning of the collocation: without a legal explanation, which lexicographers provide in an accurate way, it is hard to figure out what the expression really means.[26]

Another possible clue capitalizes on Fīrūzābādī's revised definition of *dār al-ḥarb*: if the separation is between "them" and "us," a fundamental point in much anthropological research is that it is much more difficult to define what is "us" and groups often find it much easier to try to define the other in opposition to themselves. This helps explain why what lexicographers really need to define is who the others are.

References

Cruse, D. A. *Lexical Semantics*. Cambridge Textbooks in Linguistics. Cambridge: Cambridge University Press, 1986.

Fīrūzābādī, Abū 'l-Ṭāhir Muḥammad al-. *Al-Qāmūs al-muḥīṭ*. Edited by Muḥammad Na'īm al-'Irqsūsī. 8th ed. Beirut: Mu'assasat al-Risāla, 1426/2005.

Foucault, Michel. *L'archeologie du savoir*. Paris: Gallimard, 1969.

Foucault, Michel. *The Archaeology of Knowledge* (translation of *L'archeologie du savoir*). New York, NY: Pantheon Books, 1982.

Fox, Chris. *Longman Dictionary of Contemporary English*. Harlow: Longman, 2004.

Ḫalīl b. Aḥmad al-Farāhīdī, al-. *Kitāb al-'Ayn*. Edited by al-Maḫzūmī and al-Samarrā'ī. Dār wa-maktabat al-Hilāl, n.d.

Haywood, John A. *Arabic Lexicography: Its History, and Its Place in the General History of Lexicography*. Leiden: Brill, 1965.

Ibn al-Aṯīr. *Al-Nihāya fī ġarīb al-ḥadīṯ wa'l-aṯar*. Edited by al-Zāwī and al-Ṭanāḥī. Al-Maktaba al-islāmiyya, n.d.

Ibn Manẓūr, Muḥammad b. Mukarram. *Lisān al-'Arab*. 3rd ed. Beirut: Dār Ṣādir, 1414AH.

26 This would explain why alternative collocations for *dār al-ḥarb*, such as *dār al-širk* or *dār al-'ajam* are never explicitly defined: they are more compositional than *dār al-ḥarb* (the "abode or politeism" or "abode of the non-Arabs" is much easier to figure out), besides being probably a less stable sequence—that is, individual words happen together more rarely than *dār al-ḥarb*—which does not push lexicographers to give them an explicit definition, even if they use them in glossing other definienda.

Lancioni, Giuliano. "Sull'ordinamento dei dizionari arabi classici." In *In memoria di Francesco Gabrieli*, suppl. no. 2 to *Rivista degli Studi Orientali* 71, 113–27. Roma: Bardi, 1997.

Lancioni, Giuliano. "Variants, Links, and Quotations: Classical Arabic Texts As Hypertexts." In *Scritti in onore di Biancamaria Scarcia Amoretti*, edited by Daniela Bredi, Leonardo Capezzone, Lucia Rostagno, and Wasim Dahmash, 2:245–65. Roma: Edizioni Q, 2008.

Owens, Jonathan. *Early Arabic Grammatical Theory: Heterogeneity and Standardization*. Amsterdam Studies in the Theory and History of Linguistic Science, v. 53. Amsterdam: Benjamins, 1990.

Rummānī, Abū 'l-Ḥasan 'Alī al-. "Kitāb al-Ḥudūd fī 'l-naḥw." In *Rasā'il fī 'l-naḥw wa'l-luġa*, edited by Jawād and Maskūnī, 37–50. Baghdad: Wizārat al-I'lām, 1388/1989.

CHAPTER 3

The Perception of the Others

Rūm and Franks (Tenth–Twelfth Centuries)

Yaacov Lev

1

In the Muslim perception the world is divided into *dār al-islām* (the abode of Islam) and *dār al-ḥarb/kufr* (the abode of war/unbelief), but the historical development of this division has not yet been studied. Recently, Fred M. Donner has suggested that this dichotomy reflects the evolution from the early community of Believers into a fully-fledged Muslim identity separated from Christianity and Judaism and, in political terms, the crystallization of a Muslim state—a process that took place during the Umayyad period.[1]

The terms *dār al-islām* and *dār al-ḥarb/kufr* dominate legal writings, but in other writings the most frequent term referring to Byzantium/Europe and Byzantines/Europeans is *Rūm/rūmī*. The term *Rūm* is mentioned once in the Qur'an (Q 30:2) where it alludes to the military vicissitudes of the Rūm who have been defeated but will, eventually, prevail.[2] The Qur'an continues by saying that the Believers will rejoice at the future victory of the Rūm, which is understood as referring to Byzantium (or Greeks) and its wars with the Persians.

This non-Arabic foreign term came to dominate medieval Arabic geographical and historical writings and the way it was used is well illustrated by two fourth/tenth century works listing the excellences of Egypt.[3] The first text is by ʿUmar b. Muḥammad Yūsuf al-Kindī (d. after 350/961) who devotes two paragraphs to Egypt's sea borne trade and begins with its Asian dimension. He states that Egypt is the entrepôt (*furḍa*, port) of Mecca and Medina as well

1 Fred M. Donner, "Qur'ânicization of Religio-Political Discourse in the Umayyad Period," *Revue Des Mondes Musulmans et de La Méditerranée* 129 (2011): 79–92. For a wider treatment of the *dār al-islām*/*dār al-ḥarb/kufr* division, including additional sources and literature, see Giovanna Calasso, "Alla ricerca di *dār al-islām*. Una ricognizione nei testi di giuristi e tradizionisti, lessicografi, geografi e viaggiatori," *Rivista degli Studi Orientali* 83 (2010): 271–96; Michael Bonner and Gottfried Hagen, "Muslim Accounts of the dār al-islām," in *The New Cambridge History of Islam*, ed. Robert Irwin, vol. 4 (Cambridge, 2010), 474–94.

2 Arthur Jeffery, *The Foreign Vocabulary of the Qur'ān* (Leiden: Brill, 2007), 146–47.

3 For a broad discussion of the Qur'anic text and exegeses, see Nadia Maria El Cheikh, *Byzantium Viewed by the Arabs* (Cambridge, Mass.: Harvard University Press, 2004), 25–34.

 | DOI 10.1163/9789004331037_005

as of Ṣanaʿa, Aden, Oman and Šiḥr (a port in Ḥaḍramawt). Beyond the Arab Peninsula Egypt's maritime trade also involved Sind, India, Goa (Sindābūr, misspelled as Sir.ndīb), and China. The Egyptian port that served this trade was Qulzum (on the Gulf of Suez).

This straightforward account, which mentions no seas, is followed by a more complex and vaguer, not to say simplistic, description of Egypt's Mediterranean trade that begins by stating that Egypt is the entrepôt of the Sea of Rūm "from Syria and the Land of Rūm from Antioch to beyond Constantinople, Rome and the Land of the Franks (*Ifranjiyya*)." The section dealing with the southern shores of the Mediterranean begins with Anṭāblus and also refers to Tripoli, Qayrawān, Tāhart, Sijilmāsa, Sūsa, Ṭanja and Andalus. The Mediterranean islands of Sicily, Crete, Cyprus and Rhodes are also mentioned. It seems that the author's knowledge of the southern Mediterranean was more detailed and precise than that of the northern Mediterranean or, to put it differently, his knowledge of the Christian world was limited to two terms: Rūm and Franks. However, the account of Egypt's Mediterranean trade is far more detailed than that of the India Ocean trade.[4]

Another account of Egypt's excellences was written by Ibn Zūlāq, the fourth/tenth century's most renowned Egyptian historian, who describes the port towns of Damietta and Farma as the entrepôts of the Land of Rūm, Ifranja and Cyprus, while Alexandria is referred to as the entrepôt of Crete, Sicily, the Land of Rūm and Maghrib. At first glance Ibn Zūlāq's account can be interpreted as alluding to the division of the Christian Mediterranean world into Byzantium (Rūm) and Latin Christendom (Ifranja). However, the term Rūm lacks precision since it has a wide meaning, also alluding to Italy and Italians.[5]

Ibn Zūlāq's use of the terms Rūm and Ifranja is congruous with the way these terms were used in the Jewish context (merchants' letters of the Cairo Geniza), and Shelomo Dov Goitein has called attention to the wide geographic meaning of terms such as Maghrib, comprising all the Muslim Mediterranean world west of Egypt (North Africa, Andalus and Sicily) and Rūm, designating both Byzantium and Christian Europe in general. Goitein points out that the term Franks (*Ifranj*) "… already appears in the oldest Geniza papers …", but is sparingly used during the fourth/tenth century.[6] He also states that

---

4 ʿUmar b. Muḥammad Yūsuf al-Kindī, *Faḍāʾil Miṣr*, ed. Ibrahīm Aḥmad al-ʿAdawī and ʿAlī Muḥammad ʿUmar (Cairo, 1971), 70–71.

5 Ibn Zūlāq, "Faḍāʾil Miṣr" (MS, Dublin), fol. 13A, Chester Beatty Library 4683.

6 Shelomo Dov Goitein, *A Mediterranean Society* (Berkeley: University of California Press, 1967–93), vol. 1, p. 43.

> Terminology betrays the existence of a deep barrier between the Muslim East and the Muslim West and between both and Europe (including Byzantine Asia Minor). When a person describes another as a Rūmī or a Maghribi, without specifying his city or country, he shows lack of familiarity with, or interest in, the latter's permanent or original domicile.[7]

Goitein's reference to "a deep barrier" between the Muslim Mediterranean and Europe poses a serious question: did Muslim traders go to Italy and Byzantium on trade expeditions, something the Jewish traders refrained from doing? In the Geniza documents studied by Goitein there are only two letters by Jewish merchants who visited European ports, the first from the fifth/eleventh century which concerns business in Amalfi and the other from the thirteenth century which gives an account of a business trip to Genoa and Marseilles. Another letter from 1060 tells us about an unsuccessful business trip from Palermo to the Land of Rūm where the merchant in question sustained losses in trying to sell pepper and ginger.[8]

The issue of "a deep barrier" between the Muslim and Christian Mediterranean has been much elaborated and emphasized by Jessica L. Goldberg, who states:

> Every scholar studying Geniza commercial materials has had to conclude, sometimes with surprise, that the writers of these documents operated in an almost exclusive Islamic milieu.

She goes on saying that merchants studied by her "... almost never traveled to Christian realms or entered into business relationships with inhabitants of such realms".[9] The discussion of terminology that follows must take into account Goitein's and Goldberg's references to "a deep barrier" and might be considered as its reflection.

7 Ibid., 13–4.

8 Shelomo Dov Goitein, *Letters of Medieval Jewish Traders* (Princeton: Princeton University Press, 1973), 8, 42–45, 57–61; Menahem Ben-Sasson, *The Jews of Sicily 825–1068. Documents and Sources* (Jerusalem: Ben-Zvi Institute, 1991), 71, ll. 5–9, 72, ll. 16–17; 80, ll. 5–9, 81, ll. 16–17 (texts and Hebrew transl.).

9 Jessica L. Goldberg, *Trade and Institutions in the Medieval Mediterranean. The Geniza Merchants and Their Business World* (Cambridge: Cambridge University Press, 2012), 25, 306, 307–8, 333–6.

2

The presence of Europeans in Egypt prior to the Fatimid period, especially in the fourth/tenth century, is poorly attested to by contemporary sources. In a 959 Jewish legal document there is a casual reference to the Market of the Greeks in Fusṭāṭ but there are no accounts testifying to the presence of Greek/Byzantine traders in Egypt at that time and the information about trade relations between the two countries is limited. It must be pointed out that in the army created by Aḥmad Ibn Ṭūlūn, the quasi-independent ruler of Egypt (r. 254/868–270/884), there were white-skinned slaves referred to as *rūm* whose ethnic and/or geographic identity is poorly attested to. The largest component in this army were, however, black slaves (*ʿabīd*). This type of army also characterized the Ikhshidid period in Egypt (323/935–358/969) and one of its better known emirs was Fātik al-Rūmī, who as a young child was captured with his brother and sister along the Muslim-Byzantine border in northern Syria and, eventually, was owned and manumitted by a resident of Ramla. He rose to eminence in the service of Muḥammad Ibn Ṭuġj, the ruler of Egypt (r. 323/935–334/946) and was eulogized by the poet Mutanabbī during his stay in Egypt. People referred to as *Rūm* also served in the armies of the third/ninth–fourth/tenth century Aghlabid and Fatimid rulers of Tunisia, and these references must be understood as alluding to white-skinned servile military manpower most probably brought from, or captured in, Italy. In Cairo, founded by the Fatimids, there was a Rūm quarter and references to unidentified Rūm slaves (*ġilmān al-Rūm*), in military and non-military contexts, appear in eleventh-century Egyptian sources. Another group whose presence in the courts of third/ninth–fourth/tenth century rulers of Tunisia and Egypt is widely referred to are the Ṣaqāliba. They were white-skinned slaves (mostly eunuchs) whose geographic and ethnic origin escapes precise identification.[10]

The Fatimid conquest of Egypt brought in its wake the extension of a local ninth-tenth century commercial network that connected Fatimid Tunisia, Sicily and southern Italy, in which Amalfi was prominent, to Egypt. The presence of over one hundred Amalfitan merchants in May 996 in Cairo is mentioned by contemporary chroniclers. They are referred to as *Rūm* and as Amalfitans and were victims of riots that broke out following a disastrous fire that had struck the Fatimid navy at the Cairo arsenal. The way the Fatimid regime dealt

10 Maqrīzī's information about the Rūm quarter in Cairo is quite enigmatic. See *Musawwadat kitāb al-Mawāʿiẓ wa'l-iʿtibār*, ed. Ayman Fu'ād Sayyid (London, 1995), 350. For the ethnic composition of the Fatimid army, see Yaacov Lev, "Army, Regime, and Society in Fatimid Egypt, 358–487/968–1094," *International Journal of Middle East Studies* 19 (1987): 337–66.

with the event convinced the Amalfitans and other European trading nations (Byzantines and Italians) that what had happened was an exception to the rule and the Fatimid regime sent a message that it would continue to protect foreign merchants visiting the country.[11]

The growing number of European merchants in Alexandria and Cairo exposed the local society to the great variety of the Christian Mediterranean world, while the basic terminology referring to them as *Rūm* and *Ifranj* remained unchanged but was flexible enough to express geographical nuances. This simultaneous terminological rigidity and flexibility is neatly illustrated by an early twelfth century Geniza letter recently published and studied by Miriam Frenkel. The letter describes the trade situation in Alexandria and the demand for products such as alum and pepper, and refers to traders from Rūm, Venice (Banādiqa), and Constantinople, whose absence that year was regretfully alluded to. Actually, the identity of the Rūm merchants cannot be established, and one is tempted to conclude that, in this context, the term should be understood as meaning Christians in general. The writer seems to inform his reader that at the time of writing the Christian (Rūm) merchants were sluggish in conducting their business, while the Venetians traded in pepper and one could expect a supply of only foodstuffs such as wine, cheese, honey and olive oil from Constantinople that year. The broad and general term *Rūm* is echoed by another sweeping reference to *marākib maġribiyya*, Maghribi ships, with no precise geographical identification of these ships. What seems strange to us was satisfactory to and well understood by sixth/twelfth century contemporaries.[12]

This general use of the term Rūm for Christian traders is widely attested to in Geniza letters and examples are legion. One of the more vivid is provided by a letter written between 1061 and 1062 in al-Mahdiyya in which the author describes some of his trade dealings and provides his reader in Alexandria with commercial and financial information on rates of exchange between different currencies. He mentions two groups of traders with whom he did business: *ahl al-Andalus / al-Andalusiyyūn* and Rūm.[13]

---

11 For sources and literature, see Yaacov Lev, "A Mediterranean Encounter: The Fatimids and Europe, Tenth to Twelfth Centuries," in *Shipping, Trade and Crusade in the Medieval Mediterranean*, Studies in Honour of John Pryor, ed. Ruthy Gertwagens and Elizabeth Jeffrey (Farnham, 2012), 141–42.

12 Miriam Frenkel, *"The Compassionate and Benevolent". The Leading Elite in the Jewish Community of Alexandria in the Middle Ages* (Jerusalem, 2006), doc. 14, ll. 12, 14, 16, 18, 22 (text and Hebrew transl.).

13 Ben-Sasson, *The Jews of Sicily*, doc. 72, ll. 6, 8, 14 (text and Hebrew transl.).

This letter puts the appellation Rūm in its proper context, since it indicates that referring to people by a loose geographical term was the norm.

Ahl al-Andalus/al-Andalusiyyūn could mean Jews, Muslims or Christians coming from Muslim Spain for business to al-Mahdiyya. Consequently, the term *Rūm* seems to be an idiomatic expression conveying a general meaning. In this case, as in many others, the term was thought to need no further elaboration. Its use was loose and instrumental. Furthermore, in specific circumstances, in the Geniza documents Christians were alluded to as such using Arabic and Hebrew expressions such as *naṣrānī* and *edom/ʿarelīm.*

The terms *Rūm/rūmī* were also used to allude to foreign textiles and products, and their usage in the sphere of material culture conveys the same ambiguity as in the geographic and religious contexts. Jewish marriage documents from the Geniza are a fascinating source for the history of medieval Middle Eastern clothing and items referred to as *rūmī* are mentioned when the bridal dowry is detailed. In a Karaite marriage document (*ketubba*) from Jerusalem of 1028, for example, the personal belongings (jewelry and clothing) of the bride are meticulously listed, including a *rūmī minšafa*. Whether *minšafa* refers to a garment or fabric is still a debated issue and the country of origin of this textile remains obscure. However, given the fact that this document was written in Jerusalem, the term *Rūm* most likely refers to Byzantium and not to Italy. Furthermore, textiles were alluded to by way either of their function, which is not always clear, or their town/country of production. Both ways of referring to textiles are illustrated by this document which also mentions a Sicilian *ṯawb*, tunic or dress.[14] Karaite marriage documents have been edited and studied by Judith Olszowy-Schlanger and many references to clothing as *rūmī* in these documents indicate Byzantine silk. This usage falls within a broader pattern and is similar to the way the term *maġribī* was used to indicate silk items made in the Muslim west.[15]

Similar broad meanings of the terms *Rūm* and *Maġrib* in the context of trade and state purchases are attested to in Maqrīzī's list of the purchases of the Fatimid vizier al-Ma'mūn al-Baṭā'iḥī (515/1122–519/1126), which refers to a period between 1122 and 1124. The vizier used to purchase textiles and other products on an annual basis for the state and massive purchases were made

14 Shelomo Dov Goitein, *Palestinian Jewry in Early Islamic and Crusader Times* (Jerusalem: Ben-Zvi Institute, 1980), 197, l. 21 (text and Hebrew transl.).

15 Judith Olszowy-Schlanger, *Karaite Marriage Documents from the Cairo Geniza* (Leiden, 1998), doc. 23, ll. 35–36; doc. 36, ll. 7, 9; doc. 37, ll. 18–20; doc. 39, l. 21 (texts and English transl.).

in Alexandria from *maġribī* and Rūm merchants, while other products were bought from (or in) Andalus, Mahdiyya, Sicily and *bilād al-rūm*.

Maqrīzī (766/1364–845/1442) is a late author, but this text reflects earlier sixth/twelfth century contemporary sources, most likely the history of the vizier written by his son, the historian Ibn al-Ma'mūn (d. 586/1190), which, apparently, was part of a larger work dealing with the history of Egypt and is known today only through quotations by later authorities. The purchases from *bilād al-rūm* included pure silver, precious stones, atlas brocades, timber, pitch, anchors, hemp, copper and lead. This account confirms Goitein's findings about the importation of materials such as lead, wax, and silver to Egypt and supports David Jacoby's argument about Egypt's dependence throughout the centuries on its European trading partners for naval and military supplies. Although the term *bilād al-rūm* leaves the precise identity of Egypt's European trading partners vague, it can be argued that materials could have been brought from both Italy and Byzantium and, from a Muslim point of view, the term Rūm clearly reflected their foreign European/Christian origin.[16]

While Ibn al-Ma'mūn's text quoted by Maqrīzī throws some light on the way Fatimid state purchases worked, Maḫzūmī's sixth/twelfth century administrative manual provides rich detail on Fatimid taxation in Alexandria and purchases from foreign traders. The term *rūm* appears frequently in the text in a general meaning and in collocations such as Christian/European merchants and ships (*tujjār al-rūm, al-marākib al-rūmiyya*). This undifferentiated usage should not mislead us as to the way the Fatimid tax collectors gathered information on the Rūm for taxation purposes. The names of individual Christian/European merchants were registered as well as the names of ships and nations. The term referring to nation (in modern parlance) is *jins* (pl. *ajnās*) and the idea of division into nations is expressed by phrases such as *wa-kull jins min ajnās al-rūm* and *ajnās tujjār al-rūm*. From a Muslim perspective, for the purpose of trade and taxation the world of the Rūm was divided into nations, while in the religious context Christians are referred to as *naṣārā*. This is the term applied to Christian pilgrims who went to Jerusalem via Egyptian ports

16 Maqrīzī, *Kitāb al-Muqaffā al-kabīr*, ed. Mohammed Yalaoui (Beirut, 1991), VI, 488–89; David Jacoby, "Byzantine Trade with Egypt from the Mid-Tenth Century to the Fourth Crusade," *Thesaurismata* 30 (2000): 25–77; "The Supply of War Materials to Egypt in the Crusader Period," *Jerusalem Studies in Arabic and Islam*, David Ayalon in Memoriam 25 (2001): 102–32. Both reprinted in Jacoby's *Commercial Exchanges Across the Mediterranean* (Aldershot, 2005).

and were individually taxed.[17] Undoubtedly, certain professional groups within the state administration had comprehensive knowledge of the composition of the Christian/European world. This knowledge, although only partially reflected by the source material, was also shared by the Muslim and Jewish mercantile classes.

3

The First Crusade and the subsequent wars of the Crusades were a historical watershed and cast a long shadow on the Muslim Eastern Mediterranean for two centuries. Muslim lands were conquered by the enemy, whose presence became entrenched and warfare in the region endemic. The identification of the Franks as infidels and the perceived division between the abode of Islam and the abode of war/infidelity came to dominate Arabic terminology referring to the Franks/Crusades and their deeds. Arabic and Judeo-Arabic texts contemporary with the First Crusade reflect an early stage of this terminological shift, and the evidence is rather surprising. Six years after the conquest of Jerusalem by the armies of the First Crusade, ʿAlī b. Ṭāhir al-Sulamī (d. 500/1106) expounded his views about holy war and contemporary events to people at the Great Mosque of Damascus. His knowledge, or vision, of the Christian/European world was shaped by the Hadith (traditions/Prophetic tradition) and he quoted one saying according to which the Muslims would conquer both Constantinople and Rome. He also quoted another tradition saying that the Rūm would conquer Jerusalem but would be repulsed by the Muslim who would eventually conquer Constantinople.[18]

When discussing the duty of conducting holy war in his own time he refers to the contemporary situation by describing it as "… the time in which we live now when this group (*al-firqa*) is attacking the lands of Islam."[19] He sets the events of the First Crusade in the wider historical perspective of a war between Islam and its enemies which, rather surprisingly, are left unidentified. When referring to the wider historical context of the First Crusade and the conquest of Jerusalem, he asserts that the enemies of Islam coveted Muslim lands and "… a nation (*ṭāʾifa*) of them ascended on the island of Sicily, at the

17 Maḫzūmī, *Kitāb al-Minhāj fī ʿilm ḫarāj Miṣr*, ed. Claude Cahen and Yūsuf Rāġib (Cairo, 1986), esp. 28, 46, see also 9, 10, 12, 25, 29, 34, 47, 55.

18 ʿAlī b. Ṭāhir al-Sulamī, *Kitāb al-Jihād*, under the title *Arbaʿa kutub fī ʾl-jihād*, ed. Suhayl Zakkār (Damascus, 2007), 54–55.

19 Ibid., 46.

time when its people were in a state of internal rivalry and division, and in a similar way they took possession of town after town in Andalus …".[20]

Sulamī explains the Muslim failure to face the onslaught of the enemy as the result of internal divisions but leaves the religious and national identity of the enemy unclear. One can argue that this obfuscation of the enemy added to the dramatic appeal of both his sermons and the written text, especially as the ultimate goal of the enemy—Jerusalem—and the religious nature of the war waged on the Muslims—holy war—are clearly spelt out. In any case, an orator preaching in the early 1010s at the Grand Mosque of Damascus on the duty of jihad could safely assume that his audience perfectly well knew the identity of the enemy being alluded to.

The rhetorical tricks employed by Sulamī were unique to him, and other people who dealt with the human consequences of the First Crusade clearly identified the aggressors as Franks. Some Jews and Muslim survived the slaughter committed by the Crusading army during the conquest of Jerusalem in 1099. The ransoming of captives was a sacred duty in Judaism and the monotheistic tradition, and Jewish communities in Palestine and Egypt began frantic efforts to ransom captured Jews. Their main concern was to raise the necessary funds to pay the ransom and provide for the destitute captives to be set free. The letters exchanged between the Jewish communities were written immediately after the conquest of Jerusalem and the Crusaders are referred to as Franks (*Ifranj*).[21] Between the early and late Middle Ages this term came to be used as a general designation for Christians/Europeans of western Europe in contrast to Rūm, which was used when referring to Byzantium/Byzantines.

4 Conclusions

Terminology is both inductive and misleading. It reflects and offers an insight into the mind set behind it, but terminology tends to be rigid and, frequently, serves as the lowest common denominator of convenience. While important

20 Ibid., 45. Sulamī's text is much referred to and translated in recent scholarship but the terms *al-firqa* and *ṭā'ifa* are glossed over. See, for example, Niall Christie, "Jerusalem in the Kitāb Al-Jihād of 'Alī Ibn Ṭāhir Al-Sulamī," *Medieval Encounters* 13 (2007): 209–21; "Motivating Listeners in the Kitāb al-Jihād of 'Alī Ibn Ṭāhir al-Sulamī (1106)," *Crusades* 6 (2007): 1–14; Paul E. Chevedden, "The View of the Crusades from Rome and Damascus," *Oriens* 39 (2011): esp. 290, 298–99. Both scholars, however, address a much wider range of topics than those dealt with in this article, which focuses on terminology.

21 Goitein, *Palestinian Jewry*, 242, l. 9; 243, l. 27; 252, l. 26 (texts and Hebrew transl.).

and a prerequisite for any study of perceptions, terminology in itself cannot serve as a gauge for Muslim perception and understanding of the Christian world. Furthermore, the basic terminology designating the Christian world was also used by Jews living in Muslim lands.

References

Ben-Sasson, Menahem. *The Jews of Sicily 825–1068. Documents and Sources*. Jerusalem: Ben-Zvi Institute, 1991.

Bonner, Michael, and Gottfried Hagen. "Muslim Accounts of the dār al-islām." In *The New Cambridge History of Islam*, edited by Robert Irwin, 4:474–94. Cambridge, 2010.

Calasso, Giovanna. "Alla ricerca di *dār al-islām*. Una ricognizione nei testi di giuristi e tradizionisti, lessicografi, geografi e viaggiatori." *Rivista degli Studi Orientali* 83 (2010): 271–96.

Chevedden, Paul E. "The View of the Crusades from Rome and Damascus." *Oriens* 39 (2011): 257–329.

Christie, Niall. "Jerusalem in the Kitāb al-Jihād of 'Alī Ibn Ṭāhir al-Sulamī." *Medieval Encounters* 13 (2007): 209–21.

Christie, Niall. "Motivating Listeners in the Kitāb al-Jihād of 'Alī Ibn Ṭāhir al-Sulamī (1106)." *Crusades* 6 (2007): 1–14.

Donner, Fred M. "Qur'ânicization of Religio-Political Discourse in the Umayyad Period." *Revue Des Mondes Musulmans et de La Méditerranée* 129 (2011): 79–92.

El Cheikh, Nadia Maria. *Byzantium Viewed by the Arabs*. Cambridge, Mass.: Harvard University Press, 2004.

Frenkel, Miriam. *"The Compassionate and Benevolent". The Leading Elite in the Jewish Community of Alexandria in the Middle Ages*. Jerusalem, 2006.

Goitein, Shelomo Dov. *A Mediterranean Society*. Berkeley: University of California Press, 1967–1993.

Goitein, Shelomo Dov. *Letters of Medieval Jewish Traders*. Princeton: Princeton University Press, 1973.

Goitein, Shelomo Dov. *Palestinian Jewry in Early Islamic and Crusader Times*. Jerusalem: Ben-Zvi Institute, 1980.

Goldberg, Jessica L. *Trade and Institutions in the Medieval Mediterranean. The Geniza Merchants and Their Business World*. Cambridge: Cambridge University Press, 2012.

Ibn Zūlāq, Abū Muḥammad al-Ḥasan. "Faḍā'il Miṣr." MS. Dublin, Chester Beatty Library 4683.

Jacoby, David. "Byzantine Trade with Egypt from the Mid-Tenth Century to the Fourth Crusade." *Thesaurismata* 30 (2000): 25–77.

Jacoby, David. "The Supply of War Materials to Egypt in the Crusader Period." *Jerusalem Studies in Arabic and Islam*, David Ayalon in Memoriam 25 (2001): 102–32.

Jacoby, David. *Commercial Exchanges Across the Mediterranean*. Aldershot, 2005.

Jeffery, Arthur. *The Foreign Vocabulary of the Qurʾān*. Leiden: Brill, 2007.

Kindī, ʿUmar b. Muḥammad Yūsuf al-. *Faḍāʾil Miṣr*. Edited by Ibrahīm Aḥmad al-ʿAdawī and ʿAlī Muḥammad ʿUmar. Cairo, 1971.

Lev, Yaacov. "Army, Regime, and Society in Fatimid Egypt, 358–487/968–1094." *International Journal of Middle East Studies* 19 (1987): 337–66.

Lev, Yaacov. "A Mediterranean Encounter: The Fatimids and Europe, Tenth to Twelfth Centuries." In *Shipping, Trade and Crusade in the Medieval Mediterranean*, Studies in Honour of John Pryor, edited by Ruthy Gertwagens and Elizabeth Jeffrey, 141–42. Farnham, 2012.

Maḫzūmī, Abū ʾl-Ḥasan ʿAlī al-. *Kitāb al-Minhāj fī ʿilm ḫarāj Miṣr*. Edited by Claude Cahen and Yūsuf Rāġib. Cairo, 1986.

Maqrīzī, Taqī ʾl-dīn Abū ʾl-ʿAbbās al-. *Kitāb al-Muqaffā al-kabīr*. Edited by Mohammed Yalaoui. Beirut, 1991.

Maqrīzī, Taqī ʾl-dīn Abū ʾl-ʿAbbās al-. *Musawwadat kitāb al-Mawāʾiẓ wa'l-iʿtibār*. Edited by Ayman Fu'ād Sayyid. London, 1995.

Olszowy-Schlanger, Judith. *Karaite Marriage Documents from the Cairo Geniza*. Leiden, 1998.

Sulamī, ʿAlī b. Ṭāhir al-. *Kitāb al-Jihād*, under the title *Arbaʿa kutub fī ʾl-jihād*. Edited by Suhayl Zakkār. Damascus, 2007.

CHAPTER 4

Some Observations on *dār al-ḥarb / dār al-islām* in the Imami Context

Biancamaria Scarcia Amoretti

1 Premise

As the collection of studies including this contribution* shows, a convincing "history" of the meaning of the binomial pair *dār al-ḥarb/dār al-islām* (or more often, *dār al-kufr* and equivalents / *dār al-islām* and equivalents) is still lacking. This binomial pair, paradoxically, is widely used to represent what is considered to be the "Islamic vision" *par excellence* of the relationship between *itself* and *other than itself*: a world in which peace reigns—*islām* = *salām*—and another world seen as the "enemy" that Islam battles against, where the meaning of *ḥarb*, war, is loaded with an ideological value that the term does not necessarily contain.[1] Starting from the Qur'an, war in itself is, indeed, seen as an inevitable "structural" phenomenon of imperfect human societies, and so needs to be managed.

Ḥarb (and/or *qitāl*) on the other hand takes on a specific connotation in the legal texts dedicated to the jihad: in this context, obviously, it is the starting point for the existence of an objective contrast.[2]

---

* I would like to thank G. Tecchiato, J. Karimi, S. Curzu, G. Scarcia, R. Mauriello and the Embassy of the Islamic Republic of Iran at the Holy See for their generous and valuable assistance.

1 Cf. Gianroberto Scarcia, "*Islām* e *Ḥarb*, *ʿArab* e *ʿAjam*: nota a due celeberrime dicotomie islamiche," in *Azhàr: studi arabo-islamici in memoria di Umberto Rizzitano (1913–1980)*, ed. Antonino Pellitteri and Giovanni Montaina, Annali della Facoltà di lettere e filosofia dell'Università di Palermo. Studi e ricerche 23 (Palermo: Facoltà di lettere e filosofia dell'Università di Palermo, 1995), 205–10. The primariness of the idea of a *rejected* Islam rather than a *belligerent* Islam (with the extension of the concept of hostility towards Muslims also to intimidation) upheld there is confirmed by the Iranian scholar Dāniš-Pažūh (more precisely by the sources he cites) s.v. "Dār al-islām/1," ed. Ġulām ʿAlī Ḥaddād ʿĀdil, *Dānišnāma-ʾi Jahān-i Islām* (Tehran: Bunyād-i Dāʾirat al-Maʿārif-i Islāmī, 1391SH/2012), 684.

2 Cfr. Biancamaria Scarcia Amoretti, "*Jihād*: encore à propos de définitions et de leurs implications," in *Politique et religion en Méditerranée: Moyen Âge et époque contemporaine*, ed. Henri Bresc, Georges Dagher, and Christiane Veauvy (Saint-Denis: Bouchène, 2008), 87–105.

 | DOI 10.1163/9789004331037_006

Some progress in the analysis of the above-mentioned binomial pair has been made above all regarding Sunni thought.[3] Through examples, I shall try to show some conceptual and legal issues relating to this question in an Imami Shi'ite, or Twelver, environment, which is not intended to fill the gap, but simply to launch some reflection on it.

The medieval period—which is rightly given pride of place by most of the contributions to this volume—must be distinguished, at least in a few words, from the modern and contemporary one. Indeed, in the last two centuries at least, regardless of the terminology used and the traditional organization of the texts of *fiqh*, it seems to me that in the perception of those concerned the binomial pair *dār al-ḥarb* (*kufr*) / *dār al-islām*, is no longer able to take into account the infinity of conflicts in a world that is increasingly globalized and marked by mobility, especially in theoretical terms. The subordinate position of the Muslim world, determined by the various modalities and phases of colonialism, is very important. The examples presented here are, of course, merely indicative, but some observations, even if obvious, may help to explain why the question deserves further study. These examples regarding the Middle Ages have been chosen according to whether they contain doctrinal "peculiarities" that in turn may imply certain legal considerations and allow a comparison with what other authors discuss in this volume concerning the Sunni world. Regarding the most recent history of Imamism, some limited observations are intended to account for how the changed contexts and the shifting balance of power are also incisive at an ideological level.

2 The Question

Today, the most common definition of *dār al-islām*, when referring to the Middle Ages, focuses on the role of the Law: where Islamic Law rules, there is, at least theoretically, *dār al-Islām / salām*. If the Law (*šarīʿa*) is the conclusive element, this implies that the ruler must be a Muslim. Conquest, loss or a temporary handing over of power interferes with this. As is well known, Islam, however, has experienced internal divisions, with specific theological and legal repercussions, since the very first decades of its history. This implies that the type of Islam practiced by the ruler became an essential factor in the definition of *dār al-islām* to be collocated in a precise time and place. In fact, only a limited or episodic number of cases in which the Islam professed by the

3 See Giovanna Calasso, "Alla ricerca di *dār al-islām*. Una ricognizione nei testi di giuristi e tradizionisti, lessicografi, geografi e viaggiatori," *Rivista degli Studi Orientali* 83 (2010): 271–96.

ruler was Imamism has been recorded. When this happened, it took place in peripheral areas of the Islamic ecumene. The most notable, which had a great impact,[4] was late. Indeed, with the conquest of Iran by Shah Ismāʿīl in 1501, the Safavid dynasty was installed there. The new ruler "converted" to Imamism and his successors were Imami. The Safavids were responsible for starting the irreversible conversion of the majority of the population of the Iranian plateau to Imamism, and even more for having shared the management of religious matters (and others) with the scholars (*ʿulamāʾ*). Historically, Safavid Iran marks the dividing line between *before* and *after*: a *before* that can be called the Middle Ages and an *after* that has lasted until now.

The first centuries of the history of Imamism are marked by the need to find an alternative to the dominant adversary, namely Sunnism, which was the Islam practiced by the caliphs, an alternative which should implement the "exemplary model" that lies at the basis of Imami history. According to those concerned—the Imamis, obviously—this model was placed at the origin of Islam: personified in the figure of ʿAlī, considered to be the *alter ego* of the Prophet, and to a certain extent even superior to him as possessing a hidden science that assured him the understanding of the Truth underlying the Revelation. In this view, which is of course not shared by the majority of Muslims, the most complete expression of a "just rule," and thus the existence of a true *dār al-islām*, would coincide with the caliphate of ʿAlī (35/656–40/661), the fourth caliph. ʿAlī, as caliph, ruled the whole Islamic ecumene of the time. His defeat would determine the irreversibility of the Sunni hegemony. Imamism theorizes that ʿAlī transmitted his prerogatives to some of his descendants. These are the imams. Historically speaking, they would become the only true heirs of the prophetic role and consequently, at least in theory, the only lawmakers for the Imami community. However, the imams ruled their community/ies, but not an Islamic state. This led to the common use of the expression *dār al-īmān* to refer to a community that could not be located in a precise, delimited area. This identification did not necessarily contrast with the all-encompassing one of *dār al-islām*.

Twelve imams can be counted. The last would disappear in 260/874 in Samarra to return only at the end of time. This led to the beginning of *ġayba*, namely "absence." It was believed that for some decades afterwards, the imam communicated with a few scholars: this was the "lesser *ġayba*". However, from

4 Cfr. Biancamaria Scarcia Amoretti, "Rethinking the *Šīʿe* Role in Early Safavid Iran: Two Questions," ed. Michele Bernardini, Masashi Haneda, and Maria Szuppe, *Eurasian Studies* 5, no. 1–2: special volume *Liber Amicorum. Études sur l'Iran médiéval et moderne offertes à Jean Calmard* (2006): 307–17.

329/941, this mysterious communication would be interrupted or suspended at the very least. Imamism would enter the "greater *ġayba*". The question which would emerge concerned which authority would be entrusted with the interpretation of the sources or, better, the implementation of the method or indicated system lying at the basis of *dār al-islām*.[5] The legal experts (*ʿulamāʾ/ fuqahāʾ*) would now enter the scene, especially the great interpreters of the tradition (*sunna*) that the imams had left to their community, to complete the prophetic Sunna. It can be noted that here the principle of *ijmāʿ* is not overlooked, but only considered a sort of *presumption*.

3 Theology Versus Law

A doctrinal element that marked medieval Shi'ism: *taqiyya*, is the starting-point, usually defined as the Occultation motivated by one's own religious faith that is considered legitimate, or rather right and proper, if the relative declaration represents a danger for the individual and/or the community. This is even theorized in the same way as a duty, almost equal to *arkān*, by one of the first and most important medieval Twelver scholars in both theological and legal terms: Ibn Babawayh. Born in Qum, probably around 311/923, he died in Rayy in 381/991–2; he experienced the passage from the "lesser *ġayba*" to the "greater *ġayba*" that will be concluded, as has been said, only with the return of the twelfth imam to earth. The physical absence of the imam in this world meant, at least for a certain arc of time and according to some schools,[6] the impossibility of announcing jihad, and applying the *ḥudūd* punishments, like the death penalty, contemplated in the Qur'an for certain sins. In general, in the Shi'a system, centrality is attributed to the scholar as both theologian (*ʿālim*) and jurist (*faqīh*), the necessary principled interpreter of the Law for the common believer. These are two competences that are nearly always interwoven in a scholar's production, but not necessarily in a complementary fashion.

5 It can be noted that the other important branch of Shi'ism, namely the Ismaili sect, would resolve the problem at source, proclaiming the need for the physical presence of an imam at any time, as the absolute Lawmaker on the basis of his prerogative of knowing the real sense of the Revelation that lies beneath the common sense of texts, starting from the Qur'an.

6 It should be noted that I have in mind in particular a specific Twelver school, Uṣūliyya, which was a majority and long lasting: cfr. the entry, supplemented by an exhaustive bibliography, by J. J. G. Jansen, "Uṣūliyya 2. In Modern Islamic Theologico-Political Parlance," *Encyclopaedia of Islam, Vol. X, T-U* (Leiden: Brill, 2000), where the rival current is also illustrated, the Aḫbāriyya.

Concerning *taqiyya*, the apparently most explicit definition is given by Ibn Bābawayh in his "Creed," *Risālat al-Iʿtiqādāt*.[7] It begins with this statement: "Our belief concerning *taqiyya* (permissible dissimulation) is that it is obligatory, and he who forsakes it is in the same position as he who forsakes prayer." The author invokes the authority of the sixth imam, Jaʿfar al-Ṣādiq, who would legitimize it on the basis of the verse (Q 6:108, transl. Pickthall), "Revile not those who invoke (deities) other than Allah, lest wrongfully they revile Allah through ignorance." This leads to a rule not open to appeal:

> Now until the Imām al-Qā'im appears *taqīya* is obligatory and it is not permissible to dispense with it. He, who abandons it before the appearance of al-Qā'im, has verily gone out of the religion of Allah, Exalted is He, and the religion of the imams, and disobeys Allah and His Messenger and the Imams. Imam Jaʿfar was asked concerning the Word of Allah, Mighty and Glorious is He: "Verily the noblest among you, in the sight of Allah is the most pious (*atqākum*)" (Q 49:13). He said: (It means) he who adheres most scrupulously to the practice of *taqīya*. And Allah, the Blessed and Exalted has described the showing of friendship to unbelievers as being (possible only) in the state of *taqīya*..... And furthermore, on the authority of Jaʿfar al-Ṣādiq: Mix with the people ... outwardly, but oppose them inwardly, so long as Amirate (*imratun*) is a matter of opinion ...

It is clear that a *taqiyya* that shares its root with *pietas* cannot be translated as "permissible dissimulation" (apart from anything else, it is something ethically positive, and not merely *permissible*). Clearly, this is primarily a theological question. Its eventual legal repercussions cannot be taken for granted from the moment that the exercise of *taqiyya*, in itself does not imply, for the Imami believer, a different "law" to follow in public: on the contrary, it is precisely acquiescence with the "Law" of the majority that allows the *dissimulation* referred to above. All this shows that, when considering a legal text, we get the impression of a hiatus between the theological-doctrinal elaboration and the legal theory. The legal texts all follow an identical pattern—at least formally. The *iḫtilāf* adheres to the usual nitpicking case law and opinions are not

7 The commonly accepted English translation used here is by Asaf Ali Asghar Fyzee, *A Shiʿite Creed: A Translation of Risālatu'l Iʿtiqādāt of Muḥammad B. ʿAli Ibn Bābawayhi Al-Qummī Known as Shaykh Ṣadūq*, Islamic Research Association Series 9 (London: Oxford University Press, 1942), 110–12. See, for a different approach to the question, Mohammad Ali Amir-Moezzi, "Dissimulation tactique (*taqiyya*) et scellement de la prophétie (*khatm al-nubuwwa*)," *Journal Asiatique* 302, no. 2 (2014): 411–38.

distinguished according to *maḏhab*. The pattern is a framework where each and every norm can be collocated. The consequence is that the specificity of the context—Imamism in this case—never emerges.

Ibn Bābawayh was no exception. As an Imami theologian, he could only leave open, for example, the question of the possibility of a *bāṭin* meaning of the term *taqiyya* in the affirmations of Ja'far al-Ṣādiq and his reading of the Qur'anic text. As a jurist he could, without contradicting himself, align himself with a tried and tested pattern that did not see highlighting differences as a priority. As partial proof, a survey of the occurrence of the two expressions discussed here, *dār al-ḥarb / dār al-islām,* in his most famous legal work, a sort of "Vademecum" for the common believer, *Man lā yaḥḍaruhu al-faqīh,* does not reveal anything different. One example is the prohibition on killing women and children in *dār al-ḥarb*, which would be repeated often in every Sunni legal manual, and which would also appear in almost the same words, for example, in another fundamental Imami work, namely Kulaynī's *Kāfī* (m. 939–940).[8]

The uniformity of the legal treatments that share a common language and frame which is at issue here emerges clearly in an important, although not recent, study by Khaled Abou El Fadl, which is particularly convincing given the number of sources cited, entitled *Islamic Law and Muslim Minorities: the Juristic Discourse on Muslim Minorities from the Second/Eighth to the Eleventh/Seventeenth Centuries.*[9] With reference to the impossibility of placing the Shi'i presence in a set place, quite correctly, the author notes that "... early Shi'i jurists representing an oppositional movement were more interested in substantive questions of justice, corruption and knowledge than in formal categorization of the territory" and that Ja'far al-Ṣādiq (d. 148/765) "suggested that the believer might be in fact able to better serve Islam in non-Muslim territory" [p. 148]. Moreover, he specifies that in the Shi'i perspective—and this is his only, however indirect, reference to *taqiyya*—besides the distinction between *dār al-islām* and *dār al-īmān*, "qualitatively, *dār al-islām* could be equivalent to *dār al-kufr* if corrupt beliefs and practices are widespread, but in the absence of the abode of the true faith, Muslims may continue to

8 Abū Ja'far Muḥammad Ibn Bābawayh, *Man lā yaḥḍaruhu al-faqīh*, ed. 'Alī Akbar al-Ġifārī, vol. 2 (Qum: Mu'assasat al-našr al-Islāmī, n.d.), 52–53, "bāb al-ḫarāj wa'l-jizya" (consulted on line); Abū Ja'far Muḥammad al-Kulaynī, *Al-Kāfī*, 4th ed., vol. 5 (Qum: Dār al Kutub al-Islāmiyya, n.d.), 28–29, "Kitāb al-jihād.". The already cited work by Dāniš-Pažūh (cf. note 1 above) confirms what is said.

9 Khaled Abou El Fadl, "Islamic Law and Muslim Minorities: The Juristic Discourse on Muslim Minorities from the Second/Eighth to the Eleventh/Seventeenth Centuries," *Islamic Law and Society* 1, no. 2 (1994): 141–87. I would like to thank Giovanna Calasso for this reference.

reside in corrupt territories as long as they can practice their religion" and that, consequently, "a just life is not necessarily achieved in a territory that formally espouses Islam" (pp. 152–153). However, there is an opening in the idea some have that the mere impediment to openly proclaiming one's faith can be sufficient to determine *dār al-kufr* (or *ḥarb*).

In the rest of his work, the author concentrates on emphasizing the points of convergence with other legal schools on the legitimacy and the opportunity of living in *dār al-islām* in opposition to *dār al-kufr* with particular reference to the question of which law must be applied in *dār al-kufr* regarding "the person," "property," and religious freedom. Yet this convincing and important legal discourse in the above-mentioned work largely evades two questions correlated to Imamism. The Sunni believer has a state ruled by a Sunni ruler as the reference and possible alternative to *dār al-kufr / dār al-ḥarb*, even after the formal end of the caliphate (1258), while for the Imami believer, at least until the Safavids, this is an exceptional fact that can by no means be taken for granted. Moreover, the recognition of the Shi'i representatives as a specifically Imami "legal school" would happen only from the late Ottoman period onwards.[10] Also in law, the Imami believer could—and often had to—practice *taqiyya* in its most literal sense. At the same time, Imamism, as a minority current, would not escape from the commonplace that as a minority, (*ḫāṣṣ* vs. *ʿāmm*) it would have the privilege of knowing the dominant thought, while the contrary was by no means the case.

The exceptional nature of what is described above determined an apparently anomalous situation, since in practice it gave continuity to Shi'ism.[11] The body of *ʿulamāʾ* became the "voice" of the imam in *ġayba*. It is not a single, uniform voice. Each scholar used the ancient prerogative—of law and duty—to give a personal interpretation (*ijtihād*)[12] as the solution of any case presented

10 There is some basic information in Robert Gleaves, "Jaʿfar al-Ṣādeq ii. Teachings," *Encyclopaedia Iranica, Vol. XIV, Isfahan ix–Jobbāʾi* (London; Boston: Routledge & Kegan Paul, 2008).

11 See note 6 above.

12 The introduction and use of the technical term *ijtihād* to indicate the prerogative of the scholar (*mujtahid*) to give a legal response to the "common believer" (*muqallid*) in the Imami environment are controversial (cf. J. Calmard, "Mardjaʿ-i Taḳlīd," *Encyclopaedia of Islam, Vol. VI, Mahk-Mid* (Leiden: Brill, 1991), 548–49). In this case, the use seems plausible in the context of the present paper, given that it refers to works and authors subsequent to the third/ninth century when it was accredited as the prerogative of the lawmakers (cf. D. B. Macdonald, "Idjtihād II," *Encyclopaedia of Islam, Vol. III, H-Iram* [Leiden: Brill, 1971]). For an overview, cf. Wilferd Madelung, "Authority in Twelver Shiism in the absence of the Imam," in *La notion d'autorité au Moyen Age: Islam, Byzance, Occident: Colloques*

freely by a believer to *that* particular scholar. The fact that the scholar in question worked on a set of legal texts that, as has been seen, are the expression of an evidently interiorized homogeneous model becomes of secondary importance.

Collective identity was represented mainly by communities that lived in the largest Sunni environment:[13] the emblematic case is Qom.[14] What is of interest here is the fact that the idea of a single centre of reference would take hold late, as an effect of the Safavid presence in Iran. And this is the case even if the symbolic value of the sacred places is undisputed, starting from Najaf, the seat of ʿAlī's tomb, a place of pilgrimage, a burial ground desired by the common believer and so on.[15] In practice, the "scholar," every scholar with the right credentials—doctrine and faith—has as his "territory" the believer that turns freely to him as Interpreter of the Law. Such a relationship between believer and scholar is the same as creating a sort of *dār al-imān* each time, which is necessary to keep alive the hypothesis that in a precise time and place the real *dār al-islām* will occur. And the persistent Imami quasi-vocation for insurrection, motivated by their frustration at living—or being under the impression of living—in a situation of permanent precariousness, is to some extent complementary, however much in apparent contradiction. The question of *taqiyya* should perhaps be reconsidered.

A passage from *Biḥār al-anwār*, finished in 1694, is significant. The author, Muḥammad Bāqir Majlisī (1037/1627–1110/1698), retraced the history of Shi'a

internationaux de La Napoule, session des 23–26 octobre 1978, ed. George Makdisi, Dominique Sourdel, and Janine Sourdel-Thomine, 1re éd. (Paris: Presses universitaires de France, 1982), 163–73.

13 The case of the so-called "Republic of the Sarbadārs" (eight/fourteenth century), with its centre in Sabzavar (Khorasan), is typical: cf. H. R. Roemer, "The Jalayirids, Muzaffarids and Sarbadārs," in *The Cambridge History of Iran. Vol. 6: The Timurid and Safavid Periods*, ed. Peter Jackson, Laurence Lockhart, and Arthur John Arberry (Cambridge: Cambridge Univ. Press, 1986), 16–39; and Shivan Mahendarajah, "The Sarbadar of Sabzavar. Re-Examining Their Shi'a Roots and Alleged Goal to 'Destroy Khurasanian Sunnism,'" *Journal of Shi'a Islamic Studies*, no. 4 (2012): 379–402.

14 Biancamaria Scarcia Amoretti, "L'imamismo in Iran nell'epoca selgiuchide: A proposito del problema della 'comunità,'" in *La bisaccia dello sheikh. Omaggio ad Alessandro Bausani islamista nel sessantesimo compleanno*, ed. Gianroberto Scarcia, Quaderni del seminario di iranistica, uralo-altaistica e caucasologia dell'Università degli Studi di Venezia 19 (Venezia, 1981), 127–39.

15 Cf. Pierre-Jean Luizard, *La formation de l'Irak contemporain: le rôle politique des ulémas chiites à la fin de la domination ottomane et au moment de la construction de l'Etat irakien*, Nouv. éd. (Paris: CNRS Ed, 1991).

from its beginnings to reconstruct it accurately through the texts and testimony of the scholars of the past and show their internal coherence and development. He worked at the court of two Safavid shahs, when there was a state, Iran, which, since Imamism was the religion of the ruler, was also a territorial point of reference, as it was in fact for the Shi'ites dispersed through the Islamic ecumene.[16] The text in question is taken from a letter that the eighth imam, ʿAlī al-Riḍā (d. 203/818), wrote to the caliph Ma'mūn, to clarify some doctrinal points which the caliph found unclear and on which he had asked for an interpretation.[17]

The text is a sort of mini-dictionary designed to place the meaning of *dār al-islām* in a specific doctrinal context: it does not seem appropriate to try to translate the technical terms. It ends with a reference to the precept *al-amr bi'l-maʿrūf wa'l-nahy ʿan al-munkar* which seems to be a necessary addition, that is anyway essential for this discussion:

> Islam is something other than *īmān*. Each *muʾmin* is a Muslim, but not every Muslim is a *muʾmin*. The thief when he steals is not *muʾmin* at that moment, and the fornicator is not *muʾmin* when he fornicates. Those who follow and carry out the *ḥudūd* imposed on them are Muslim, not *muʾmin*, nor *kāfir*. And God, the Sublime and Exalted, would never allow a *muʾmin* to whom He has already promised Paradise to go to Hell and He would not allow a *kāfir* to whom He has already promised the fire of Hell for eternity to escape. God does not pardon those who associate someone with Him, but He pardons everything else to whom He wishes. Sinners among the people of *tawḥīd* will go to Hell, but they will leave and intercession will be a reward for them. Today the *dār* is *dār* of *taqiyya*, that is *dār al-Islām*, it is not *dār* of *kufr* nor *dār* of *īmān*.

16 An important example is that of the formation of the Shi'i dynasties in Deccan: cf. Biancamaria Scarcia Amoretti, ed., *Sguardi sulla cultura sciita nel Deccan*, Rivista degli Studi Orientali 64/1–2 (Roma: Bardi, 1991).

17 The text is in Muḥammad Bāqir Majlisī, *Biḥar al-anwār*, 3rd edition, vol. 10 (Beirut: Mu'assasat al-Wafā', 1983), *Kitāb al-Iḥtijāj, bāb* 20, 357. It should be noted that ʿAlī al-Riḍā is the imam linked par excellence to Iran. He was called by the caliph of the time, Ma'mūn, while he was in Marw, in Khorasan, to confirm his nomination as "presumed heir to the throne", which happened in 816. The imam prevaricated for some time and when he finally decided, two years later, the situation had radically changed. He died while travelling (818): according to Imami tradition, he was poisoned on the orders of the caliph himself. He is buried near the tomb of Hārūn al-Rašīd. The site, today Mashhad, would soon become a pilgrimage destination for the devout, as it remains to this day.

Until this point, it is quite clear. The question lies inside the Islamic ecumene. Once the destiny of those who will be saved and those who will be condemned is pronounced, there is no longer any point in speaking of *dār al-ḥarb* or, all the more so, of *dār al-kufr*, as categories that would in any way interest the theological world. On the other hand, it did interest the "legal" world, as has been noted: consequently, the different legal manuals, including modern ones and those of the "Jaʿfarī school," contain a *bāb al-jihād*, basically identical to what was theorized by Sunnism.[18] Yet this does not seem to be the case in our text, which continues: "and *al-amr bi'l-maʿrūf wa'l-nahy ʿan al-munkar* are two duties to be respected if you fear something for yourself and *īmān* is the expression of sincere faith, abstention from serious sins, it is intimate knowledge and explicit pronouncing and fulfilment of *arkān*."

At first reading, this statement from the imam would seem to give permission for the common believer to act in a state of *taqiyya*, that is to say "dissemblance:" that dissemblance/dissimulation which the very same imam was showing towards the caliph who asked him and which he could by no means in his heart consider "legitimate." However, if examined more carefully, the whole text can be interpreted quite differently, as a theological affirmation, not a catechesis, where *taqiyya* = true Islam. This is, of course, a hypothesis still to be confirmed, but to be noted as an example of how the approach to the analysis of the possible meanings of *dār al-islām* and its "opposite" is still in its infancy; the latter has been much too simplistically identified mainly as *dār al-ḥarb* alone, in the sense of "the homeland of non-Muslims" and so a synonym for a *dār al kufr* that today is instead used more easily to indicate above all a "deviance" within Islam itself.

4 *Authority/Territoriality*

The modern period—it should be stressed again—is the time in which Shi'ism obtained state-level visibility and the Safavid rulers (1501–1732) were the protagonists. After a confused interval, there was a handover to the Qajar dynasty (1779–1924) which would rule Iran until the threshold of the contemporary age. It is important to note that, starting from the Safavids, as already remarked,

18 Cf., as an example, a text significantly entitled: *Fiqh al-imām Jaʿfar al-Ṣādiq*, by a scholar of Jabal ʿĀmil, Muḥammad Jawād Muġniya (1904–1979), 6 books in 3 volumes. The discussion of jihad in the edition referred to here is in Muḥammad Jawād Muġniya, *Fiqh al-imām Jaʿfar al-Ṣādiq*, vol. 1/2 (Beirut: Dār al-ʿilm li'l-malāyīn, 1960), 259–69, followed coherently by *bābs* dedicated to *qitāl*, *ġanā'im*, etc.

Shi'ism had an impact on the whole Islamic ecumene. In particular, the Shi'ite communities present outside Iran, in Iraq above all, but also in India and in the south of Lebanon, would become more visible and at the same time—even if in different forms—recognize more or less publicly the Safavid/Iranian leadership.[19] It appears more pertinent in the logic of this note to indicate changes at a conceptual level, since they indicate a peculiar modernizing journey in Shi'ism, and are preparatory to the acquired meaning of the *dār al-Islām / dār al-ḥarb* binomial in the contemporary world.

The great "cultural revolution" of Shi'ism that began with Safavids can be dated back to the institution of the *marjaʿ-i taqlīd*. This designated the *mujtahid/faqīh* as an "exemplary model" that the common believer must "imitate", regarding both the articles of faith and the application of the law.[20] There are two processes at its base: the establishment of a hierarchy in the body of scholars and the beginning of its clericalization. Both processes can be collocated in the context of a new conception of the state and the function of the ruler: a conception that tends to give the ruler control (through nominations and benefices) of the religious establishment, which in turn conditions the action of the ruler through his legal-religious authority over the common people. The balance between the two powers led to something similar to the relationship between State and Church formalized in England under Henry VIII (r. 1509–1547). Here a distinction—although in an embryonic stage—can be identified between "lay" institutions and religious authorities that was probably not perceived as such by those directly involved, but was seen as such by the West. It was not by chance that the Western powers of the time were interested in Iran as a possible ally against the Ottoman enemy considering this religious fact as a connecting element.[21]

Obviously, if there is a body of scholars and its members must have specific requisites and obey precise rules, then hierarchy is inevitable. It is equally inevitable that at first glance this would appear to be an undeniable act of modernization in "our" terms. What impact did this have in terms of *dār al-ḥarb / dār al-islām*? The first effect was predictable: jihad can be announced even

19 Cf., as an example, *La Shīʿa nell'Impero Ottomano, Atti del Convegno (Roma, 15 aprile 1991)* (Roma: Fondazione Caetani, 1993).

20 The already cited entry by Calmard, "Mardjaʿ-i Taḳlīd." (see note 12 above) is so complete and up to date bibliographically that I refer to it for the structure of the institution and its history.

21 Cf. Palmira Brummet, "The Myth of Shah Ismail Safavi: Political Rhetoric and 'Divine' Kingship," in *Medieval Christian Perceptions of Islam: A Book of Essays*, ed. John Tolan, Garland's Medieval Casebooks 10 (New York, NY: Garland, 1996), 331–59.

in the absence of the Prophet by the ruler as his regent (*nāʾib*).[22] A second concerned the legitimacy of the recognized religious authority in sanctioning the action of the ruler and political power in general. For this to happen, the action must enter into the category of *kufr*, a category which is interpreted not in abstract theological terms but as an action that has repercussions in practice. Therefore, *kufr* is whatever damages "the community of believers," which in this way is considered a "political actor". A paradigmatic example is the clash between the *marjaʿ-i taqlīd*, Mirzā Muḥammad Ḥasan Šīrāzī (d. 1312/1895) and the Qājār shah, Nāṣir al-dīn (r. 1264/1848–1313/1896). The shah was accused of having conceded the exploitation of all tobacco production to a British company: a treasonable act towards the country—the "nation," it is tempting to say—given that it alienated a good which God had entrusted to the community. The shah was considered guilty by the *mujtahid* who issued a fatwa of condemnation in December 1881. The latter's authority was not only never questioned, but it was upheld by the "people/community of believers" that stood solidly behind him and forced the ruler to revoke the concession.[23] Therefore, it is hardly surprising that in Iran between 1905 and 1911 there was a "constitutional revolution", starting before that of the Young Turks in 1908. This gave rise to a Parliament where a "constitutional monarchy" was experimented with, a "division of powers" was discussed openly and, above all as far as the question in hand is concerned, a "clerical" presence was seen both among the supporters of constitutionalism and those that contested it.[24] The failure of this experiment should not diminish its significance. It would remain a precedent to look to.

5 The Contemporary World

Sketching the discussion on the question of war and peace in the contemporary context and updating thoroughly the meaning to be given to the *dār al-ḥarb / dār al-Islām* binomial pair is too challenging, at least for the author of

22 The already cited *Fiqh al-imām Jaʿfar al-Ṣādiq* (see note 18 above), in the chapter on jihad dedicated a full and detailed section to the question: "Iḏn al-imām aw nāʾibihi," Muġniya, *Fiqh al-imām Jaʿfar al-Ṣādiq*, 1/2:261–63.

23 Cf. Nikki R. Keddie, *Religion and Rebellion in Iran: The Tobacco Protest of 1891–1892* (London: Frank Cass, 1966).

24 Cf. the accurate account of facts by E.G. Browne, *The Persian Revolution of 1905–1909* (London: Frank Cass, 1966); and the entry "Constitutional Revolution," *Encyclopaedia Iranica, Vol. VI, Coffeehouse–Dārā* (London; Boston: Routledge & Kegan Paul, 1992).

this note. Indeed, today it is no longer possible to hypothesize, as we did in the previous section, that there are autonomous developments that are not significantly influenced by a hegemonic model, even if they are not structurally peripheral as in the case of Iran: this is "globalization," as already mentioned. The repercussions of the various nineteenth-century forms of colonialism continue to be felt, despite the formal independence of each country. Trying to update the legal discussions is not the only complex issue. In this context, where global travel has become easy and often essential, discussion on what is negative in the choice of Muslims to live in *dār al-ḥarb* has become only a sort of "rhetorical exercise." While it is certainly the case that today, more than in the past, whoever emigrates is in a sort of "exile" and risks losing his own identity, especially in those cases where religion is an essential element, it is also true that, where there is complete freedom of movement, the risk is no longer there, precisely due to the ease of travel and the ability to organize a community outside one's country of origin. Technology can be the solution, as it has been in the Shi'ite context. The *mujtahid* can be questioned using the internet and in the same way communicate his fatwas to the believer who has asked him. In this way, a virtual *dār al-imān* is recreated. *Dār al-ḥarb* can be invoked in some specific cases, for example towards the State of Israel. In general, the attention of those concerned has concentrated on what happens in the Islamic ecumene, and more precisely in their own country. It is the enemy within that counts. *Dār al-islām* has been corrupted by the presence of *dār al-kufr*, a "house of misbelief" to be confronted. The problem affects both the Sunni and the Shi'ite worlds. The representative of power is singled out and, if appropriate, judged to be guilty. A case in point is the assassination of Sadat (October 1981) by a member of a group called, by no means coincidentally, *Takfīr wa'l-hijra*, and the legitimacy of this action had some support in Egypt, motivated by Egypt's unjustifiable recognition of Israel.

Another example, formally different but perhaps not so much in substance, where it was the representative of power who took on the role of indicating the "right way," was Khomeini's official statement on the legitimacy of an armed response to the Iraqi attack—which, it should be remembered, gave rise to a war that lasted nearly a decade (1980–1988). The duty of the good believer is to commit himself to a *jihād-i muqaddas*, "holy war/crusade."[25] The choice of the

25 The title of the discourse in question is *Farmān-i āmadabāš bi millat-i Īrān barāyi rafʿ-i tajāwuz-i baʿṯī* (Proclamation of alarm to the Iranian nation to neutralize the attack by the Baʿathist enemy), and can be found in the collection entitled "Ṣaḥīfa-yi imām Ḫumaynī": Rūḥ Allāh Ḫumaynī, *Ṣaḥīfa-yi imām: Majmūʿa-yi āṯār-i imām Ḫumaynī* (Tehran, 1999), 13:271.

phrase is certainly well-thought: *jihād* does not need the attribute *muqaddas*, and yet this is not a *bidʿa*, an innovation.[26] Even though Khomeini addressed his compatriots in the symbolic location of Jamārān, where he lived, the imam wanted to be understood by the West: a "positive acculturation"[27] that implies the full awareness of a by now irreversible globalization process and of the right to be part of it.

Does (or does not) the undeniable fact that the situations are alike mean that the two cases are comparable? The exceptional nature of the Iranian example is a fact, as is the importance of Egypt in all the Islamic world. The mass of documentation and analysis on both cases is such that any conclusion here would be partial and rash. However, I would like to point out that the questions tackled here, without any doubt an eccentric starting point, could be of some use once they were further researched.

References

Abou El Fadl, Khaled. "Islamic Law and Muslim Minorities: The Juristic Discourse on Muslim Minorities from the Second/Eighth to the Eleventh/Seventeenth Centuries." *Islamic Law and Society* 1, no. 2 (1994): 141–87.

Amir-Moezzi, Mohammad Ali. "Dissimulation tactique (*taqiyya*) et scellement de la prophétie (*khatm al-nubuwwa*)." *Journal Asiatique* 302, no. 2 (2014): 411–38.

---

26 This is shown in the most significant passages where the term *jihād* appears in the most famous work of Khomeini: *Wilāyat al-faqīh*. The approach is purely legal, even when the eventual political repercussions are made explicit. Use has been made of the annotated translation by Hamid Algar, Ruhollah Khomeini, *Islamic Government*, trans. Hamid Algar (Teheran: The Institute for Compilation and Publication of Imam Khomeini's Works International Affairs Division; no date is given, but it was probably published for the first time in 1980). Here is the list of the most relevant uses of the term for the discussion in this article in my opinion: 23–24, 41–42, 66, 76, 82, 93–94. It can be noted that Khomeini also dedicated a work to the "greater *jihād*", Rūh Allāh Ḫumaynī, *Mubāraza bā nafs yā jihād akbar* (Tehran: Mu'assasa-yi intišārati-i Amīr Kabīr, 1979). For an alternative reading of his work and character, see Yahya Christian Bonaud, *L'Imam Khomeyni, un gnostique méconnu du XXe siècle: métaphysique et théologie dans les œuvres philosophiques et spirituelles de l'Imam Khomeyni*, [Les éditions Albouraq Héritage spirituel 5] (Beyrouth: Les Editions Al-Bouraq, 1997).

27 On the idea of "positive acculturation", see Raffaele Mauriello, *Descendants of the Family of the Prophet in Contemporary History: A Case Study, the Šīʿī Religious Establishment of Al-Naǧaf (Iraq)*, Supplementi alla "Rivista degli Studi Orientali" 83/1 (Pisa: Fabrizio Serra, 2011).

Bonaud, Yahya Christian. *L'Imam Khomeyni, un gnostique méconnu du XXe siècle: métaphysique et théologie dans les œuvres philosophiques et spirituelles de l'Imam Khomeyni.* [Les éditions Albouraq Héritage spirituel 5]. Beyrouth: Les Editions Al-Bouraq, 1997.

Browne, E. G. *The Persian Revolution of 1905–1909*. London: Frank Cass, 1966.

Brummet, Palmira. "The Myth of Shah Ismail Safavi: Political Rhetoric and 'Divine' Kingship." In *Medieval Christian Perceptions of Islam: A Book of Essays*, edited by John Tolan, 331–59. Garland's Medieval Casebooks 10. New York, NY: Garland, 1996.

Calasso, Giovanna. "Alla ricerca di *dār al-islām*. Una ricognizione nei testi di giuristi e tradizionisti, lessicografi, geografi e viaggiatori." *Rivista degli Studi Orientali* 83 (2010): 271–96.

Calmard, J. "Mardja'-i Taḳlīd." *Encyclopaedia of Islam, Vol. VI, Mahk-Mid.* Leiden: Brill, 1991.

"Constitutional Revolution." *Encyclopaedia Iranica, Vol. VI, Coffeehouse–Dārā.* London; Boston: Routledge & Kegan Paul, 1992.

Dāniš-Pažuh, Muḥammad Taqī. "Dār al-islām/1." Edited by Ġulām 'Alī Ḥaddād 'Ādil. *Dānišnāma-'i Jahān-i Islām*. Tehran: Bunyād-i Dā'irat al-Ma'ārif-i Islāmī, 1391/2012.

Fyzee, Asaf Ali Asghar. *A Shi'ite Creed: A Translation of Risālatu'l I'tiqādāt of Muḥammad B. 'Ali Ibn Bābawayhi Al-Qummī Known as Shaykh Ṣadūq*. Islamic Research Association Series 9. London: Oxford University Press, 1942.

Gleaves, Robert. "Ja'far al-Ṣādeq ii. Teachings." *Encyclopaedia Iranica, Vol. XIV, Isfahan ix – Jobbā'ī*. London; Boston: Routledge & Kegan Paul, 2008.

Ḫumaynī, Rūh Allāh. *Mubāraza bā nafs yā jihād akbar*. Tehran: Mu'assasa-yi intišārati-i Amīr Kabīr, 1979.

Ḫumaynī, Rūh Allāh. *Ṣaḥīfa-yi imām: Majmū'a-yi āṯār-i Imām Ḫumaynī*. Tehran, 1999.

Ibn Bābawayh, Abū Ja'far Muḥammad. *Man lā yaḥḍaruhu al-faqīh*. Edited by 'Alī Akbar al-Ġifārī. Vol. 2. Qum: Mu'assasat al-našr al-Islāmī, n.d.

Jansen, J. J. G. "Uṣūliyya 2. In Modern Islamic Theologico-Political Parlance." *Encyclopaedia of Islam, Vol. X, T-U*. Leiden: Brill, 2000.

Keddie, Nikki R. *Religion and Rebellion in Iran: The Tobacco Protest of 1891–1892*. London: Frank Cass, 1966.

Khomeini, Ruhollah. *Islamic Government*. Translated by Hamid Algar. Teheran: The Institute for Compilation and Publication of Imam Khomeini's Works (International Affairs Division), n.d.

Kulaynī, Abū Ja'far Muḥammad al-. *Al-Kāfī*. 4th ed. Vol. 5. Qum: Dār al Kutub al-Islāmiyya, n.d.

La Shī'a nell'Impero Ottomano, Atti del Convegno (Roma, 15 aprile 1991). Roma: Fondazione Caetani, 1993.

Luizard, Pierre-Jean. *La formation de l'Irak contemporain: le rôle politique des ulémas chiites à la fin de la domination ottomane et au moment de la construction de l'Etat irakien*. Nouv. éd. Paris: CNRS Ed, 1991.

Macdonald, D. B. “Idjtihād II.” *Encyclopaedia of Islam, Vol. III, H-Iram*. Leiden: Brill, 1971.

Madelung, Wilferd. “Authority in Twelver Shiism in the absence of the Imam.” In *La notion d'autorité au Moyen Age: Islam, Byzance, Occident: Colloques internationaux de La Napoule, session des 23–26 octobre 1978*, edited by George Makdisi, Dominique Sourdel, and Janine Sourdel-Thomine, 1re éd., 163–73. Paris: Presses universitaires de France, 1982.

Mahendarajah, Shivan. “The Sarbadar of Sabzavar. Re-Examining Their Shi'a Roots and Alleged Goal to ‘Destroy Khurasanian Sunnism.’” *Journal of Shi'a Islamic Studies*, no. 4 (2012): 379–402.

Majlisī, Muḥammad Bāqir. *Biḥar al-anwār*. 3rd edition. Vol. 10. Beirut: Mu'assasat al-Wafā', 1983.

Mauriello, Raffaele. *Descendants of the Family of the Prophet in Contemporary History: A Case Study, the Šīʿī Religious Establishment of Al-Naǧaf (Iraq)*. Supplementi alla “Rivista degli Studi Orientali” 83/1. Pisa: Fabrizio Serra, 2011.

Muġniya, Muḥammad Jawād. *Fiqh al-imām Jaʿfar al-Ṣādiq*. Vol. 1/2. 6 vols. Beirut: Dār al-ʿilm li'l-malāyīn, 1960.

Roemer, H. R. “The Jalayirids, Muzaffarids and Sarbadārs.” In *The Cambridge History of Iran. Vol. 6: The Timurid and Safavid Periods*, edited by Peter Jackson, Laurence Lockhart, and Arthur John Arberry, 1–40. Cambridge: Cambridge Univ. Press, 1986.

Scarcia Amoretti, Biancamaria. “L'imamismo in Iran nell'epoca selgiuchide: A proposito del problema della ‘comunità.’” In *La bisaccia dello sheikh. Omaggio ad Alessandro Bausani islamista nel sessantesimo compleanno*, edited by Gianroberto Scarcia, 127–39. Quaderni del seminario di iranistica, uralo-altaistica e caucasologia dell'Università degli Studi di Venezia 19. Venezia, 1981.

Scarcia Amoretti, Biancamaria, ed. *Sguardi sulla cultura sciita nel Deccan*. Rivista degli Studi Orientali 64/1–2. Roma: Bardi, 1991.

Scarcia Amoretti, Biancamaria. “Rethinking the *Šīʿe* Role in Early Safavid Iran: Two Questions.” Edited by Michele Bernardini, Masashi Haneda, and Maria Szuppe. *Eurasian Studies* 5, no. 1–2: special volume *Liber Amicorum. Études sur l'Iran médiéval et moderne offertes à Jean Calmard* (2006): 307–17.

Scarcia Amoretti, Biancamaria. “*Jihād*: encore à propos de définitions et de leurs implications.” In *Politique et religion en Méditerranée: Moyen Âge et époque contemporaine*, edited by Henri Bresc, Georges Dagher, and Christiane Veauvy, 87–105. Saint-Denis: Bouchène, 2008.

Scarcia, Gianroberto. “*Islām* e *Ḥarb*, *ʿArab* e *ʿAjam*: nota a due celeberrime dicotomie islamiche.” In *Azhàr: studi arabo-islamici in memoria di Umberto Rizzitano (1913–1980)*, edited by Antonino Pellitteri and Giovanni Montaina, 205–10. Annali della Facoltà di lettere e filosofia dell'Università di Palermo. Studi e ricerche 23. Palermo: Facoltà di lettere e filosofia dell'Università di Palermo, 1995.

PART 2

Early Texts

CHAPTER 5

Naming the Enemy's Land

Definitions of dār al-ḥarb *in Ibn al-Mubārak's* Kitāb al-Jihād

Roberta Denaro

1

> Like all binary opposites, the distinction between Romans and Barbarians has a function, or rather a series of functions depending on the intention of the author, ancient or modern, who employs it. When the distinction and the contexts in which it is used are placed under the microscope inevitably something very much more complicated than the initial polarity appears.[1]

Such observations on the Roman/Barbarian basic polarity in the definition of territories and identities in Late Antiquity might also in my view well apply to the *dār al-islām / dar al-ḥarb* dichotomy.

From the seventh century CE, the *dār al-islām / dār al-ḥarb* dichotomy, in a great part of the Mediterranean area, came to replace—or perhaps to be superimposed on—the Roman/Barbarian opposition between interior and exterior, between friend and foe, to be understood (in a somewhat Schmittian sense) as categories reciprocally determined by a profound otherness, which could only be evened out through conflict (i.e., the jihad). And just as for the Roman/Barbarian polarity, so also for the *dār al-ḥarb / dār al-islām* opposition, closer scrutiny of the distinction and the contexts in which it is used (or not used) inevitably shows a far more complex and richly nuanced situation.

The aim of this study is, then, to contribute to a preliminary "mapping" of the use of the *dār al-islām / dār al-ḥarb* dichotomy, rescuing it from the meta-historical realm to which it was relegated by the orientalist tradition on the one hand, and Islamic tradition on the other, thereby taking on board some issues recently raised by Giovanna Calasso.[2]

1 Ian Wood, "Conclusion: Strategies of Distinction," in *Strategies of Distinction: The Construction of Ethnic Communities, 300–800*, ed. Walter Pohl and Helmut Reimitz, The Transformation of the Roman World, v. 2 (Leiden: Brill, 1998), 297.

2 Giovanna Calasso, "Alla ricerca di *dār al-islām*. Una ricognizione nei testi di giuristi e tradizionisti, lessicografi, geografi e viaggiatori," *Rivista degli Studi Orientali* 83 (2010): 271–96.

 | DOI 10.1163/9789004331037_007

The issue is, therefore, to reconnect this dichotomy with its own history, marking out its path, the areas where it emerges and those where it makes no appearance or remains under the surface. My attention focuses on those texts that have sought to define, regulate (and in some cases narrate)[3] the jihad between the second/eighth and third/ninth centuries. What we have is a corpus of texts (more or less autonomous collections of traditions on jihad, *siyar*, *maġāzī*) belonging to Hadith literature, and therefore showing uniformity both in the arrangement of the material (based on the *isnād* system) and in the thematic ordering. Amidst this set of texts, the *Kitāb al-jihād*[4] by Ibn al-Mubārak (d. 181/797) stands out as a fundamental reference point for a number of reasons. In fact the *Kitāb al-jihād* (henceforth KJ) is one of the first independent texts on the subject, and takes on a central importance in reconstructing a specific perspective of the early Abbasid period on jihad, martyrdom and umma.[5] For our purposes, therefore, it represents a major touchstone to verify whether the *dār al-islām / dār al-ḥarb* dichotomy had already been codified and played an active part in representing territories that were at the same time real and spiritual. This is also due to the particular genesis of the KJ, "child of the frontier" if there ever was one, composed by an author whose—real or alleged—biography is dominated by jihad

3 For a general view of the fictional and narrative nature of some apparently non-fictional texts, see Stefan Leder, ed., *Story-Telling in the Framework of Non-Fictional Arabic Literature* (Wiesbaden: Harrassowitz, 1998); on the literary topoi featuring in some traditions on *jihād* and *maġāzī*, see Albrecht Noth, *The Early Arabic Historical Tradition: A Source-Critical Study*, 2nd ed., Studies in Late Antiquity and Early Islam; 3 (Princeton: Darwin Press, 1994), 145–67; and Roberta Denaro, "The Narratives of Jihād in Early Islamic Historiography," in Ghāzī *and* Ghazw *in Muslim Historiography and Literature*, ed. Michele Bernardini and Francesca Bellino, forthcoming.

4 Ibn al-Mubārak, *Kitāb al-jihād*, ed. Nazīh Ḥammād (Tunis: al-Dār al-tūnisiyya li'l-našr, 1972).

5 On the Arab-Byzantine frontier as the place where a peculiar concept of umma, closely related to the ideology of jihad, emerged, see Michael Bonner's seminal studies ("Some Observations Concerning the Early Development of Jihad on the Arab-Byzantine Frontier," *Studia Islamica*, no. 75 (1992): 5–31, and *Aristocratic Violence and Holy War*, Studies in the Jihad and the Arab-Byzantine Frontier, 81, New Haven, Connecticut: American Oriental Society, 1996); for a different approach to Ibn al-Mubārak's biography and works see Christopher Melchert, "Ibn al-Mubārak's *Kitāb al-Jihād* and Early Renunciant Literature," in *Violence in Islamic Thought from the Qur'ān to the Mongols*, ed. Robert Gleave and István Kristó-Nagy (Edinburgh: Edinburgh University Press, 2015), 49–69. On the KJ see also Roberta Denaro, *Dal martire allo šahīd: fonti, problemi e confronti per una martirografia islamica*, 1. ed, Centro alti studi in scienze religiose 4 (Roma: Edizioni di storia e letteratura, 2006), 106–16, and Asma Afsaruddin, *Striving in the Path of God: Jihād and Martyrdom in Islamic Thought* (Oxford: Oxford University Press, 2013), 149–57.

and *ṯuġūr*.[6] Moreover, it was in fact on the very border—one of the various armed borders of Islam against the *dār al-ḥarb*—that the text enjoyed wide circulation.[7] However, we will return to the peripheral, borderland nature of the KJ and the "centrifugal" features emerging from the author's biography later on.

On the basis of the evidence presented above, we might therefore expect to find the *dār al-islām / dār al-ḥarb* dichotomy already firmly established in the KJ—the work of an author who was both a *muḥaddiṯ* and a *mujāhid*—and, significantly, characterized by a strong emphasis on jihad as a supremely meritorious activity and indeed a means of spiritual salvation.[8]

And yet, on examining the traditions referred to in the KJ, a different spiritual geography emerges, constructed on other antinomies. In fact, neither in the Hadiths dealing with specific jihad and *ġazawāt* episodes, nor in the other, non-narrative Hadiths where the aim is to define the nature and limits of jihad, are the enemy and its territory ever described as *ḥarbī* or *dār al-ḥarb*, as the following table briefly outlines:

TABLE 5.1 *Naming the enemy and its territory in* KJ

Hadith	
n. 32, 44	*nasīru bi-arḍ al-rūm fī ṣā'ifa*
n. 33, 45	*ġazawnā* [...] *arḍ al-rūm*

6 Cf. Bonner, *Aristocratic Violence and Holy War*, 119–22, and Roberta Denaro, "From Marw to the *ṯuġūr*. Ibn al-Mubārak and the shaping of a biographical tradition," *Eurasian Studies* 7, no. 1–2 (2009): 125–44.

7 On its fortune in Andalusia, where it circulated together with the *siyar*s of Awzāʿī and Fazārī, see Cristina De la Puente, "El ŷihād en el califato omeya de al-Andalus y su culminación bajo Hišām II," in *Almanzor y los terrores del milenio*, ed. Fernando Valdés Fernández, La Península Ibérica y el Mediterráneo entre los siglos XI y XII 2 (Aguilar de Campo, Palencia [Spain]: Fundación Santa María La Real, Centro Estudios del Románico, Monasterio de Santa María la Real, 1999), 28; and Michael Bonner, *Jihad in Islamic History: Doctrines and Practice* (Princeton: Princeton University Press, 2006), 111–12. It is no coincidence that such a trio of works, along with local production on the topic of jihad, enjoyed uninterrupted popularity in Muslim Spain, another very ideologically charged frontier of Islam. On the role played by Ibn al-Mubārak as founding figure of the *mutaṭawwiʿa* movement along the eastern borderlands, see Deborah G. Tor, *Violent Order: Religious Warfare, Chivalry, and the ʿAyyār Phenomenon in the Medieval Islamic World*, Istanbuler Texte und Studien 11 (Würzburg: Ergon-Verl, 2007), 53–62.

8 These kinds of traditions have been examined in Bonner, *Aristocratic Violence and Holy War*, 123–25; cf. also Afsaruddin, *Striving in the Path of God*, 150–56, and those specifically related with martyrdom in Denaro, *Dal martire allo šahīd*, 106–12.

TABLE 5.1 *Naming the enemy and its territory in KJ* (cont.)

Hadith	
n. 71, 65	*man aḥabba an yalḥaqa bi'l-Šām, [...] bi'l-ʿIrāq, bi'l-Miṣr*
n. 100, 86	*fa-laḥiqa bi'l-Šām*
n. 101, 87	*fa-tawajjaha ġāziyyan ilā 'l-Šām*
n. 102, 87	*tajahhaza Bilāl li'l-ḫurūj ilā 'l-Šām*
n. 143, 117	*naḥnu nasīru bi-arḍ al-rūm*
n. 145, 119	*fa-ġazawnā Siqilliya min arḍ al-rūm*
n. 146, 121	*rajul min Bakr marra bi-arḍ al-rūm*
n. 150, 124	*ġazawnā [...] arḍ al-rūm*
n. 182, 146	*kāna murābiṭan bi-arḍ Fāris*
n. 190, 151	*fa-inna Allāh [...] takaffala lī bi'l-Šām wa-ahli-hā*
n. 212, 161	*ra'ā [...] bi-arḍ al-rūm*
n. 217, 164	*ḥuṣira bi'l-Šām*
n. 261, 184	*sariyya daḫalat arḍ al-rūm*

As emerges clearly from these data, the term *dār al-ḥarb* does not occur in descriptions of enemy territory, which is in fact usually referred to by its specific geographical name (Sicily, Iraq, Syria, etc.) or the name of its inhabitants (*arḍ al-rūm* or *arḍ Fāris*).

When not specified ethnically, the enemy is simply *al-ʿaduww*, as opposed to Muslims, as indeed we also read elsewhere in a Hadith stating that "the best of all the people is a man who, having sold a herd of camels, transforms the proceeds into an equipment (for the jihad) and mornings and evenings stays [on the front line] between the Muslims and their enemies (*bayna yaday al-muslimīn wa bayna ʿaduwwihim*)".[9]

It would, however, be misleading to suggest that the lack of the later "classical" terminology (opposing territory under Islamic rule to lands with which no relations other than war can be contemplated) implies a non-dichotomous view of the issue at stake. In this respect, conflict is seen as fundamental in the KJ, and is conceived in terms no less clear-cut than in the *dār al-islām / dār al-ḥarb* antithesis. Here jihad is surrounded by the aura of the absolute, and, as emerges clearly in the following dialogue, ascribed to Ibn al-Mubārak and Fazārī (d. 188/804), the jihad along the Arab-Byzantine frontier is presented as preferable to all the others:

9 *KJ*, n. 164, 135–36.

> Abū Isḥāq al-Fazārī said to Ibn al-Mubārak: "You left the frontiers of Khurasan, al-Washajird and Qazwīn, when God most high said: 'Fight those unbelievers near you' (Q 9:123)." And he said : "O Abū Isḥāq, I have found a verse more certain [or more relevant, *awkad*] than that: 'Fight those who do not believe in God and the Last Day, and [who] do not forbid what God and His Messenger have forbidden' (Q 9:29)." Then he said: "Those are fighting about our world [in other words, worldly domination], meaning the Turks and the Daylam, whereas these are waging war against us about our faith, meaning the Byzantines. So which is the more worthy of defense: our world or our faith?." He [Abū Isḥāq] said: "Nay, our faith."[10]

Traditions of this kind, which undoubtedly served decades earlier to legitimate the Omayyad dynasty and its military campaigns,[11] are included in the *KJ*, revealing an eschatological inclination which would subsequently underlie the *Kitāb al-fitan* of Nuʿaym b. Ḥammād (d. 228/843)—significantly enough a pupil of Ibn al-Mubārak.[12]

For the *KJ*, as indeed for the *Kitāb al-fitan*, jihad is an option for the individual believer, a choice between this and the other world (*al-dunyā* and

10 Ibn al-ʿAdīm, *Taʾrīḫ Ḥalab*: I, 203 (quoted in David Cook, "Muslim Apocalyptic and *jihād*," *Jerusalem Studies in Arabic and Islam* 20 [1996]: 98). On the literary and ideological representations of jihad against the Byzantines see Ahmad Shboul, "Byzantium and the Arabs. The Image of Byzantines as Mirrored in Arabic Literature," in *Byzantine Papers: Proceedings of the First Australian Byzantine Studies Conference, Canberra, 17–19 May 1978*, ed. Ann Moffatt, Michael Jeffreys, and Elizabeth Jeffreys, Byzantina Australiensia (Canberra: Humanities Research Centre, Australian National University, 1981), 43–68; Nadia Maria El Cheikh, *Byzantium Viewed by the Arabs* (Cambridge, Mass.: Harvard University Press, 2004), 60–71, and Thomas Sizgorich, "'Do Prophets Come with a Sword?' Conquest, Empire, and Historical Narrative in the Early Islamic World," *The American Historical Review* 112, no. 4 (October 1, 2007): 993–1015; Suliman Bashear, "Apocalyptic and Other Materials on Early Muslim-Byzantine Wars: A Review of Arabic Sources," *Journal of the Royal Asiatic Society* 1, no. 02 (July 1991): 173–207, and Cook, "Muslim Apocalyptic and *jihād*."

11 Cf. Afsaruddin, *Striving in the Path of God*, 154–55 and 122–25.

12 Cf. Hayrettin Yücesoy, *Messianic Beliefs and Imperial Politics in Medieval Islam: The ʿAbbāsid Caliphate in the Early Ninth Century*, Studies in Comparative Religion (Columbia, S.C.: University of South Carolina Press, 2009), 106–15 on the subject of missionary activity and Byzantine raids. For apocalyptic traditions transmitted by Ibn al-Mubārak, see Ibn al-Munādī, *Kitāb al-Malāḥim*, ed. ʿAbd al-Karīm al-ʿUqaylī (Qum: Dār al-Sīra, 1998), 155, 196.

al-āḫira)[13], and only secondarily a means to extend Islamic territory, a means requiring a juridical regulation.

Thus, the *dār al-islām / dār al-ḥarb* association does not appear significant in the lexicon of the KJ, which uses other dichotomies in constructing a model of "holy war" and a model for the community of believers based on the *Ṣaḥāba*—dichotomies such as *nār/janna*, or *al-dunyā/al-āḫira*.[14] When the aim is to evoke two different, opposed religious and territorial spheres, reference is made to *muslimūn* and *ʿaduwwuhum*, calling the non-Muslims countries *arḍ* (and not *dār*) *al-ʿaduww*.

2

The absence of the "classical" terminology does not, however, appear to be peculiar to Ibn al-Mubārak. Further evidence of how rarely the *dār al-islām / dār al-ḥarb* binomial is referred to can be found in texts that, like the KJ, are focused on jihad/*siyar*. If, in fact, the work by Ibn al-Mubārak is the earliest extant *independent* text dedicated to jihad, we must also bear in mind that, between the second half of the second/eighth century and the first half of the third/ninth, Hadith literature had seen the emergence of a specific subgenre dedicated to the *siyar*, variously translated as "Muslim laws of nations", "Islamic international law" or "war law".[15]

On examining the lexicon of these *siyar*/jihad/*maġāzī* works, contemporary with or subsequent to the KJ, *arḍ/bilād al-ʿaduww* appear in almost all cases to be preferred to *dār al-ḥarb*, with a general tendency to specify the name of the territory through reference to its inhabitants (thus we may find reference to *arḍ al-rūm, arḍ al-turk*, etc.). Incidentally, it is worth noting that that lexical feature also seems to be shared with texts of Arab historiography referring to the territory of enemy states. For example, Ibn Saʿd (d. 230/845), narrating the death of the legendary Companion Abū Ayyūb al-Anṣārī, reports that he asked

---

13 See for example KJ, n. 219, 165; n. 227, 169; n. 229 and 230, 180–81.

14 See, for example, the various kinds of *mujāhid*s listed in ibid., n. 10, 33, comparing those who fight aspiring to this world (*ibtiġāʾan al-dunyā*) with those who fight aspiring to the face of God (*ibtiġāʾan wajh Allāh*), or the many traditions stating that one day spent on the path of God is "better than this world and everything it contains" (as in n. 18, 37; n. 23, 39–40; n. 24, 40 *passim*).

15 For the meaning of *siyar* cf. Majid Khadduri, ed., *The Islamic Law of Nations: Shaybānī's Siyar.* Translated with an Introduction, Notes and Appendices (Baltimore: The Johns Hopkins Press, 1966), 38–41; and Muhammad Munir, "Islamic International Law (Siyar): An Introduction," *SSRN Electronic Journal*, 2007, 3–11.

to be buried in enemy territory, using the expression *arḍ al-ʿaduww*, not *dār al-ḥarb*.[16]

A complete record of this literature, consisting of both independent texts and specific chapters within more extensive collections, would have to begin with the *maġāzī* text attributed to Makḥūl (d. 116/734), a Syrian scholar and *mujāhid* who not only fought in the Omayyad campaigns against the Byzantines, but also seems to have taken an interest in the juridical issue of the obligatory nature of jihad.[17] Mention must also be made of the *Kitāb al-Siyar* of Awzāʿī (d. 157/774), now lost but still extant in the eleventh century, confuted by Abū Yūsuf (d. 182/798) in his *Kitāb al-Radd ʿalā Siyar al-Awzāʿī*.[18] The first truly significant text, however, remains the *kitāb al-jihād* of the *Muwaṭṭaʾ* by Mālik b. Anas (d. 179/796), passed down with variants relevant to the object of our debate here. In fact, the two versions in which it circulated, one by Yaḥyā b. Yaḥyā al-Maṣmūdī (d. 234/848), and the other by Šaybānī (d. 189/805), show significant differences precisely in the chapter dedicated to jihad.[19]

In Šaybānī's version, apart from a small *bāb* on *faḍl al-jihād*,[20] the chapter on jihad does not exist (or has not been included) and the short section on *siyar* deals with juridical issues (in particular war booty and the taxation involved) without any particular emphasis on jihad *per se*.[21] Yaḥyā's version is more extended, also featuring some non-juridical sections, such as two *bāb al-tarġīb fī 'l-jihād*[22] and a *bāb al-šuhadāʾ fī sabīli 'llāh*;[23] here too *arḍ al-muslimīn* and

16 Ibn Saʿd, *Ṭabaqāt*, ed. Josef Horovitz, vol. 3/2 (Leiden: Brill, 1904), 49–50. On the (almost non-existent) use of the dichotomy in geographical texts, cf. Calasso, "Alla ricerca di *dār al-islām*," 286–90.

17 Cf. Afsaruddin, *Striving in the Path of God*, 119.

18 Cf. Anke Bouzenita, *'Abdarraḥmān al-Auzāʿī, ein Rechtsgelehrter des 2. Jahrhunderts d.H. und sein Beitrag zu den Siyar: Erarbeitet auf der Grundlage des K. ar-Radd ʿalā Siyar al-Auzāʿī*, Islamkundliche Untersuchungen, Bd. 240 (Berlin: K. Schwarz, 2001).

19 Bonner, *Jihad in Islamic History*, 102–4, and Ridwan al-Sayyid, "*Dār al-Ḥarb* and *Dār al-Islām*: Traditions and Interpretations," in *Religion between Violence and Reconciliation*, ed. Thomas Scheffler, Beiruter Texte und Studien, Bd. 76 (Beirut: Orient-Institut–Ergon Verlag in Kommission, 2002), 123–28.

20 Mālik b. Anas, *Al-Muwaṭṭaʾ. Riwāyat Muḥammad b. al-Ḥasan al-Šaybānī*, ed. ʿAbd al-Wahhāb ʿAbd al-Laṭīf (Cairo: Wizārat al-Awqāf 1994), *bāb* 101, 101.

21 Ibid., 201.

22 Mālik b. Anas, *Al-Muwaṭṭaʾ: Riwāyat Yaḥyā b. Yaḥyā b. Kaṯīr al-Layṯī al-Andalusī al-Qurṭubī*, ed. Ṣidqī Ǧamīl al-ʿAṭṭār (Beirut: Dār al-Fikr, 2002), *bāb* 1, 271–72 and *bāb* 18, 283–85.

23 Ibid., *bāb* 14, 281–82.

arḍ al-ʿaduww are the standard expressions to refer to Islamic territory and enemy states.[24]

The *Kitāb al-Siyar*[25] by Fazārī, a contemporary and friend of Ibn al-Mubārak, and, like him, active along the Arab-Byzantine *ṯuġūr*,[26] is another "borderland" text. With respect to KJ, it combines elements of a treatise on juridical points of war law, such as the sharing of spoils, the treatment of prisoners, etc., with rhetorical jihad apologetics, i.e. *tarġīb al-jihād*. A systematic comparison of the language used in the two texts is yet to be made and would certainly prove interesting, as already suggested by the clear difference in the use of the terms jihad and *ribāṭ*.[27] Also in describing enemy territory the *Kitāb al-Siyar* differs from KJ in that it provides a wider range of expressions to define it: reference is made to *bilād al-ʿaduww*,[28] to which *bilād al-muslimīn*[29] or *arḍ al-muslimīn* corresponds,[30] but, more importantly, we find here—as far as I can tell—the first occurrence of the couple *dār al-islām* and *dār al-ḥarb*.[31] Unlike KJ, this book examines specifically legal points, such as whether an individual can be considered war booty (*fay*ʾ) if he converted to Islam in enemy territory (*aslama fī dār al-ḥarb*),[32] or the case of someone leaving Islamic territory (*dār al-islām*) to enter enemy territory (*dār al-ḥarb*) without the permission of the imam,[33] or, again, whether there exists a right to the spoils of an ally (*muʿāhid*) who goes forth from Islamic territory into enemy territory and returns bearing goods plundered from the enemy.[34]

---

24 See, for example, ibid., n. 979, 272; [nos. 988], 275.

25 Abū Isḥāq al-Fazārī, *Kitāb al-Siyar. Riwāyat Muḥammad b. Waḍḍāḥ al-Qurṭūbī*, ed. Farūq Ḥammāda (Beirut: Muʾassasat al-risāla, 1987).

26 On Fazārī and his *Siyar* see Miklos Muranyi, "Das *Kitāb al-Siyar* von Abū Isḥāq al-Fazārī. Das Manuskript der Qarawiyyīn Bibliothek zu Fās," *Jerusalem Studies in Arabic and Islam* 6 (1985): 63–97, and Bonner, *Aristocratic Violence and Holy War*, 109–19.

27 Bonner, *Jihad in Islamic History*, 100.

28 *Siyar*, n. 177, 164 and nos. 180–82, 165.

29 Ibid., n. 183, 165.

30 Ibid., n. 10, 106.

31 It looks very likely that such early use of the *dār al-islām* / *dār al-ḥarb* dichotomy by Fazārī may be dated back to his teacher Abū Ḥanīfa, whose lectures at Kūfa were attended by Fazārī, Šaybānī and many others. It is also worth noting how this confirms the role of the Hanafis in popularizing the legal term of *siyar* (cf. Khadduri, *The Islamic Law of Nations*, 39).

32 *Siyar*, n. 199, 170.

33 Ibid., n. 203, 171.

34 Ibid., n. 207, 172.

These are the first occurrences of the two terms in reciprocal relation and opposition; however, it is also to be noted that these are the *only occurrences* in the entire *Kitāb al-Siyar*, and that the language of the texts makes more frequent use of *arḍ* or *bilād al-ʿaduww*, which are the standard expressions to define territory inhabited by Muslims and by their enemies.

And yet the greatest effort to codify Islamic international law with the related terminology is represented by the work of Šaybānī, a disciple of Abū Ḥanīfa (d. 150/767) and Abū Yūsuf (d. 182/798), and, like the latter, active at the Abbasid court with the function of *qāḍī*. It is to Šaybānī that we owe the major works on the subject, *al-Siyar al-kabīr* and *al-Siyar al-ṣaġīr*, and it was he who brought in the technical use of the term *siyar* previously used as synonymous of jihad. In Saraḫsī's commentary on *Siyar*,[35] on which Khadduri based his reconstruction of Šaybānī's *Siyar*, *dār al-ḥarb* and *dār al-islām* seem to have achieved their status of standard terms, as can be seen for example in the case of an enemy (*rajul min ahl al-ḥarb*), converted to Islam and killed by a Muslim before entering Islamic territory (*dār al-islām*).[36]

Finally, from the generation following upon Šaybānī we have the *Muṣannaf* by ʿAbd al-Razzāq al-Ṣanʿānī (d. 211/827), another fundamental text in establishing terminology and law on the *siyar*/jihad issue prior to the great Hadith compilations, brought together in the canonical *Six Books*.

In the section dedicated to war law the *dār al-islām* / *dār al-ḥarb* dichotomy is once again absent, but what we do find is an equivalent couple referring not to the territory but to the populations inhabiting it: in fact, *ahl al-ḥarb* vs *ahl al-islām*.[37] In this case, too, the term most used to refer to enemy territory remains *arḍ al-ʿaduww*.[38] Interestingly enough, however, we also have terminology connoting it in religious terms as *dār al-širk*.[39] The *Muṣannaf* also contains another juridical category that defines a territorial typology departing from the *dār al-islām* / *dār al-ḥarb* polarization, the *arḍ al-ṣulḥ*, which indicates non-Muslim territory with which peace had been made (temporarily, as indicated by the term which can also be translated as "armistice").[40] A contrast

---

35 Muḥammad b. Aḥmad al-Saraḫsī, *Šarḥ al-Siyar al-kabīr li-Muḥammad b. al-Ḥasan al-Šaybānī*, ed. al-Munajjid (Cairo: Maṭbaʿat Miṣr, 1957).

36 Ibid., n. 117, 126; see also nos. 483, 336; 485, 337; 489, 338; 499, 342; 502, 343 *passim*.

37 ʿAbd al-Razzāq al-Ṣanʿānī, *Al-Muṣannaf*, ed. Ḥabīb al-Raḥmān al-ʿAẓamī, vol. 5 (Beirut: al-Maktab al-Islāmī, 1983), n. 9680, 300.

38 See, for example, ibid., 5:nos. 9297 and 9298, 179; n. 9327, 188.

39 Ibid., vol. 5, n. 9366, 196.

40 On this third temporary division of the Islamic territory and the semantic meaning of the term *ṣulḥ*, see also Majid Khadduri, "Ṣulḥ," *Encyclopaedia of Islam, Vol. IX, San-Sze* (Leiden: Brill, 1998); cf. also Khadduri, *The Islamic Law of Nations*, 12–13, and Bernard Lewis, *The*

is drawn between this enemy territory where fighting has temporarily been suspended and territory inhabited by Muslims (again *arḍ al-muslimīn*).[41]

3

What emerges from this rapid overview is, in the first place, a feature of lexicon that belies the current idea of the *dār al-islām / dār al-ḥarb* contraposition as the original polarization (upon which international Islamic law was founded), as a standard and undisputed expression in Islamic representations of territories and identities. The traditions on jihad that define a juridical and religious otherness which, unlike *ḏimma*, cannot be integrated, as being in religious, territorial and military opposition to umma and its territory, show in the early stages a wide range of expressions, the most frequent—from a purely statistical point of view, at least—being *arḍ al-ʿaduww*. Similarly, *arḍ* (or *bilād*) *al-muslimīn* occurs far more frequently than *dār al-islām*.

This feature, already observed in KJ, is also borne out by the later texts and, moreover, in the output following after Šaybānī this multiplicity of synonymous terms is maintained. For example, a fourth/tenth-century jihad treatise includes *balad al-islām*, *arḍ al-islām*, and *balad al-muslimīn* as well as *dār al-islām*, and without any apparent distinction alternates between *arḍ al-ʿaduww*, *balad al-ḥarb*, *arḍ al-ḥarb*, *arḍ al-kufr* and *dār al-ḥarb*.[42] In other words, at least lexically the *dār al-ḥarb / dār al-islām* antinomy is not the only one used to express the contraposition between Islam and non-Islam.

The specifically juridical nature of this terminology is thus confirmed and made clear: from this point of view, comparison between the KJ and the *Kitāb al-Siyar* proves illuminating. While the former represents an approach to the theme of jihad wholly focusing on holy war as individual action reiterating the example of the Companions of the Prophet, the latter combines a juridical approach with this perspective: the first use of the *dār al-islām / dār al-ḥarb* dichotomy occurs in the context of a Hadith of relevance to war law rather than to topics of spiritual edification.

Political Language of Islam, paperback ed., 4. [Nachdr.], Middle Eastern Studies: Political Science (Chicago: Univ. of Chicago Press, 1991), 78.

41 ʿAbd al-Razzāq al-Ṣanʿānī, *Muṣannaf*, vol. 5, n. 9326, 188.

42 Cf. s. v. "dār al-ḥarb" and "dār al-islām" in the index to Abū Muḥammad ʿAbdallāh Ibn Abī Zayd al-Qayrawānī, *Der Heilige Krieg (Ǧihād) aus der Sicht der mālikitischen Rechtsschule*, ed. Mathias von Bredow, Beiruter Texte und Studien 44 (Stuttgart: Steiner, 1994).

And in fact the sense of territory in the *KJ* appears to be based on another dichotomy, entirely internal to *dār al-islām*, contrasting center with periphery, the Baghdad of the caliph and his court with the borderland inhabited by *murābiṭūn* and scholar-ascetics. From this perspective the biographies of Ibn al-Mubārak and Šaybānī seem to reflect each other virtually in reverse.

Their biographies seem to follow lines that run parallel in many parts. Both Ibn al-Mubārak and Šaybānī (15 years his junior) lived between the end of the Omayyad period and the beginning of the Abbasid caliphate, and came from families of *mawālī*. In their education they had some teachers in common, such as Mālik b. Anas, Awzāʿī and Abū Ḥanīfa, leading figures in the period. On the death of Abū Ḥanīfa, Šaybānī followed his principal pupil, Abū Yūsuf, and took up teaching in Baghdad, where he achieved considerable prestige, succeeding Abū Yūsuf as Chief *qāḍī*.[43] Ibn al-Mubārak, on the other hand, had among his teachers Sufyān al-Ṯawrī (d. 161/778), Mālik and various others, but despite his fame as *muḥaddiṯ* and expert in law, he lived on his activity as a tradesman, alternating jihad and pilgrimage.

These parallel lines diverge in the relations with the Abbasid power, and in particular on the question of whether or not to take on public office. From this point of view, the biographies of Ibn al-Mubārak and Šaybānī[44] embody two different paradigms. This contrast in attitudes towards the central power, often reflected in acceptance or refusal of the office of judge, was soon to take the form of a contraposition between Hanbalis (claiming Ibn al-Mubārak as their founding father) and Hanafis.[45] In the case of these two scholars, it was reflected in their allegedly different attitudes towards Hārūn al-Rašīd. Šaybānī, a brilliant jurist well integrated in the caliph's entourage, had a long career as *qāḍī* and died at Rayy, on the way back from an expedition to Samarkand, on which he had accompanied the caliph.

On the other hand, the sources describe Ibn al-Mubārak as extremely cautious, taking a low profile vis-à-vis the central power, if not actually in open opposition to Hārūn al-Rašīd.[46] Various passages in his biography, which clearly reflect the well-established biographical topos "pious man vs. ruler", nevertheless reveal a spirit of detachment from the central power, its attractions, and

43 On the dignity of *qāḍī al-quḍāt*, created by the early Abbasids, and on Abū Yūsuf's role as counsellor of Hārūn al-Rašīd cf. Joseph Schacht, *An Introduction to Islamic Law* (Oxford: Clarendon Press, 1982), 50–51.

44 On Šaybānī's life and writings cf. Khadduri, *The Islamic Law of Nations*, 26–38.

45 Cf. Nimrod Hurvitz, *The Formation of Hanbalism: Piety into Power*, Culture and Civilization in the Middle East (London: Routledge, 2002), 85.

46 Cf. Denaro, "From Marw to the *ṯuġūr*," 133–34.

above all its capital, Baghdad[47], which is certainly not the heart of *dār al-islām* in Ibn al-Mubārak's verse, but rather an insidious place, a trap for the true Muslim:

> Baghdad is not a place for those who want to adore God/ to the kings Baghdad is abode and seat, but is a trap for he who reads the Qur'an.[48]

The geographical conception on which the KJ is based lies in this dichotomy between center and periphery, between Baghdad and the borderland, between places made for kings and places fit for pious ascetics and *mujāhids*. And it may well be significant that this text, central to the construction of jihad ideology but of little importance to its juridical regulation, shows no trace of the "renowned albeit ill-known dichotomy" *dār al-islām* / *dār al-ḥarb*.[49]

References

ʿAbd al-Razzāq al-Ṣanʿānī. *Al-Muṣannaf*. Vol. 5. Edited by Ḥabīb al-Raḥmān al-ʿAẓamī. Beirut: al-Maktab al-Islāmī, 1983.

Afsaruddin, Asma. *Striving in the Path of God: Jihād and Martyrdom in Islamic Thought*. Oxford: Oxford University Press, 2013.

Bashear, Suliman. "Apocalyptic and Other Materials on Early Muslim-Byzantine Wars: A Review of Arabic Sources." *Journal of the Royal Asiatic Society* 1, no. 02 (July 1991): 173–207.

Bonner, Michael. "Some Observations Concerning the Early Development of Jihad on the Arab-Byzantine Frontier." *Studia Islamica*, no. 75 (1992): 5–31.

Bonner, Michael. *Aristocratic Violence and Holy War*. Studies in the Jihad and the Arab-Byzantine Frontier, 81. New Haven, Connecticut: American Oriental Society, 1996.

Bonner, Michael. *Jihad in Islamic History: Doctrines and Practice*. Princeton: Princeton University Press, 2006.

---

47 On the diverging representations of Baghdad see Michael Cooperson, "Baghdad in Rhetoric and Narrative," *Muqarnas* 13 (1996): 99–113.

48 ʿIyāḍ b. Mūsā al-Qāḍī, *Tartīb al-madārik*, vol. 1 (Beirut: Dār Maktabat al-Ḥayāt, n.d.), 307.

49 Gianroberto Scarcia, "*Islām* e *Ḥarb*, *ʿArab* e *ʿAjam*: nota a due celeberrime dicotomie islamiche," in *Azhàr: studi arabo-islamici in memoria di Umberto Rizzitano (1913–1980)*, ed. Antonino Pellitteri and Giovanni Montaina, Annali della Facoltà di lettere e filosofia dell'Università di Palermo. Studi e ricerche 23 (Palermo: Facoltà di lettere e filosofia dell'Università di Palermo, 1995), 208, quoted in Calasso, "Alla ricerca di *dār al-islām*," 275.

Bouzenita, Anke. *'Abdarraḥmān al-Auzā'ī, ein Rechtsgelehrter des 2. Jahrhunderts d.H. und sein Beitrag zu den Siyar: Erarbeitet auf der Grundlage des K. ar-Radd 'alā Siyar al-Auzā'ī*. Islamkundliche Untersuchungen, Bd. 240. Berlin: K. Schwarz, 2001.

Calasso, Giovanna. "Alla ricerca di *dār al-islām*. Una ricognizione nei testi di giuristi e tradizionisti, lessicografi, geografi e viaggiatori." *Rivista degli Studi Orientali* 83 (2010): 271–96.

Cook, David. "Muslim Apocalyptic and *jihād*." *Jerusalem Studies in Arabic and Islam* 20 (1996): 66–104.

Cooperson, Michael. "Baghdad in Rhetoric and Narrative." *Muqarnas* 13 (1996): 99–113.

De la Puente, Cristina. "El ŷihād en el califato omeya de al-Andalus y su culminación bajo Hišām II." In *Almanzor y los terrores del milenio*, edited by Fernando Valdés Fernández, 23–38. La Península Ibérica y el Mediterráneo entre los siglos XI y XII 2. Aguilar de Campo, Palencia [Spain]: Fundación Santa María La Real, Centro Estudios del Románico, Monasterio de Santa María la Real, 1999.

Denaro, Roberta. *Dal martire allo šahīd: fonti, problemi e confronti per una martirografia islamica*. 1. ed. Centro alti studi in scienze religiose 4. Roma: Edizioni di storia e letteratura, 2006.

Denaro, Roberta. "From Marw to the *ṯuġūr*. Ibn al-Mubārak and the shaping of a biographical tradition." *Eurasian Studies* 7, no. 1–2 (2009): 125–41.

Denaro, Roberta. "The Narratives of Jihād in Early Islamic Historiography." In Ghāzī *and* Ghazw *in Muslim Historiography and Literature*, edited by Michele Bernardini and Francesca Bellino, forthcoming.

El Cheikh, Nadia Maria. *Byzantium Viewed by the Arabs*. Cambridge, Mass.: Harvard University Press, 2004.

Fazārī, Abū Isḥāq al-. *Kitāb al-Siyar. Riwāyat Muḥammad b. Waḍḍāḥ al-Qurṭūbī*. Edited by Farūq Ḥammāda. Beirut: Mu'assasat al-risāla, 1987.

Hurvitz, Nimrod. *The Formation of Hanbalism: Piety into Power*. Culture and Civilization in the Middle East. London: Routledge, 2002.

Ibn Abī Zayd al-Qayrawānī, Abū Muḥammad 'Abdallāh. *Der Heilige Krieg (Ǧihād) aus der Sicht der mālikitischen Rechtsschule*. Edited by Mathias von Bredow. Beiruter Texte und Studien 44. Stuttgart: Steiner, 1994.

Ibn al-Mubārak, 'Abd Allāh b. 'Abd al-Raḥmān. *Kitāb al-jihād*. Edited by Nazīh Ḥammād. Tunis: al-Dār al-tūnisiyya li'l-našr, 1972.

Ibn al-Munādī, Abū 'l-Ḥusayn Aḥmad. *Kitāb al-Malāḥim*. Edited by 'Abd al-Karīm al-'Uqaylī. Qum: Dār al-Sīra, 1998.

Ibn Sa'd, Abū 'Abd Allāh Muḥammad. *Kitāb al-Ṭabaqāt al-kabīr*. Edited by Josef Horovitz. Vol. 3/2. Leiden: Brill, 1904.

'Iyāḍ b. Mūsā al-Qāḍī. *Tartīb al-madārik*. Vol. 1. Beirut: Dār Maktabat al-Ḥayāt, n.d.

Khadduri, Majid, ed. *The Islamic Law of Nations: Shaybānī's Siyar.* Translated with an Introduction, Notes and Appendices. Baltimore: The Johns Hopkins Press, 1966.

Khadduri, Majid. "Ṣulḥ." *Encyclopaedia of Islam, Vol. IX, San-Sze*. Leiden: Brill, 1998.

Leder, Stefan, ed. *Story-Telling in the Framework of Non-Fictional Arabic Literature*. Wiesbaden: Harrassowitz, 1998.

Lewis, Bernard. *The Political Language of Islam*. Paperback ed., 4. Middle Eastern Studies: Political Science. Chicago: Univ. of Chicago Press, 1991.

Mālik b. Anas. *Al-Muwaṭṭa'. Riwāyat Muḥammad b. al-Ḥasan al-Šaybānī*. Edited by ʿAbd al-Wahhāb ʿAbd al-Laṭīf. Cairo: Wizārat al-Awqāf, 1994.

Mālik b. Anas. *Al-Muwaṭṭa': Riwāyat Yaḥyā b. Yaḥyā b. Kaṯīr al-Layṯī al-Andalusī al-Qurṭubī*. Edited by Ṣidqī Ǧamīl al-ʿAṭṭār. Beirut: Dār al-Fikr, 2002.

Melchert, Christopher. "Ibn al-Mubārak's *Kitāb al-Jihād* and Early Renunciant Literature." In *Violence in Islamic Thought from the Qur'ān to the Mongols*, edited by Robert Gleave and István Kristó-Nagy, 49–69. Edinburgh: Edinburgh University Press, 2015.

Munir, Muhammad. "Islamic International Law (Siyar): An Introduction." *SSRN Electronic Journal*, 2007.

Muranyi, Miklos. "Das *Kitāb al-Siyar* von Abū Isḥāq al-Fazārī. Das Manuskript der Qarawiyyīn Bibliothek zu Fās." *Jerusalem Studies in Arabic and Islam* 6 (1985): 63–97.

Noth, Albrecht. *The Early Arabic Historical Tradition: A Source-Critical Study*. 2nd ed. Studies in Late Antiquity and Early Islam; 3. Princeton, N.J.: Darwin Press, 1994.

Saraḫsī Muḥammad b. Aḥmad al-. *Šarḥ al-Siyar al-kabīr li-Muḥammad b. al-Ḥasan al-Šaybānī*. Edited by al-Munajjid. Cairo: Maṭbaʿat Miṣr, 1957.

Sayyid, Ridwan al-. "*Dār al-Ḥarb* and *Dār al-Islām*: Traditions and Interpretations." In *Religion between Violence and Reconciliation*, edited by Thomas Scheffler, 123–28. Beiruter Texte und Studien, Bd. 76. Beirut: Orient-Institut–Ergon Verlag in Kommission, 2002.

Scarcia, Gianroberto. "*Islām* e *Ḥarb, ʿArab* e *ʿAjam*: nota a due celeberrime dicotomie islamiche." In *Azhàr: studi arabo-islamici in memoria di Umberto Rizzitano (1913–1980)*, edited by Antonino Pellitteri and Giovanni Montaina, 205–10. Annali della Facoltà di lettere e filosofia dell'Università di Palermo. Studi e ricerche 23. Palermo: Facoltà di lettere e filosofia dell'Università di Palermo, 1995.

Schacht, Joseph. *An Introduction to Islamic Law*. Oxford: Clarendon Press, 1982.

Shboul, Ahmad. "Byzantium and the Arabs. The Image of Byzantines as Mirrored in Arabic Literature." In *Byzantine Papers: Proceedings of the First Australian Byzantine Studies Conference, Canberra, 17–19 May 1978*, edited by Ann Moffatt, Michael Jeffreys, and Elizabeth Jeffreys, 43–68. Byzantina Australiensia. Canberra: Humanities Research Centre, Australian National University, 1981.

Sizgorich, Thomas. "'Do Prophets Come with a Sword?' Conquest, Empire, and Historical Narrative in the Early Islamic World." *The American Historical Review* 112, no. 4 (October 1, 2007): 993–1015.

Tor, Deborah G. *Violent Order: Religious Warfare, Chivalry, and the 'Ayyār Phenomenon in the Medieval Islamic World.* Istanbuler Texte und Studien 11. Würzburg: Ergon-Verl, 2007.

Wood, Ian. "Conclusion: Strategies of Distinction." In *Strategies of Distinction: The Construction of Ethnic Communities, 300–800*, ed. Walter Pohl and Helmut Reimitz, 297–303. The Transformation of the Roman World, v. 2. Leiden: Brill, 1998.

Yücesoy, Hayrettin. *Messianic Beliefs and Imperial Politics in Medieval Islam: The 'Abbāsid Caliphate in the Early Ninth Century*. Studies in Comparative Religion. Columbia, S.C: University of South Carolina Press, 2009.

CHAPTER 6

Dār al-islām / *dār al-ḥarb* in the *Tafsīr* by Ibn Jarīr al-Ṭabarī and in Early Traditions

Roberto Tottoli

1

The study of key concepts and of the technical terms that came into use for them is fundamental to knowing when they emerged and found their way into Muslim literature, on the one hand, and into scholarly research on the other. Terms and expressions assume a technical meaning through the ages and come to be considered as pointing to a specific concept long after the time when they were thought to originate. Many examples could be given from various religious cultures and also from Islamic history. The emergence of the so-called *bāb al-ijtihād*, whose closing is subject to debate, as well as the early formulation of the *waḥdat al-wujūd* in Ibn ʿArabī's and his followers' works, or further questions such as the early relation between the terms *ḥadīṯ* and *ḫabar*, and the emergence in different fields of technical terms such as *isrāʾīliyyāt*, *nahḍa* or *salafī* etc. are all examples of this.[1]

All these questions and perspectives of research also emerge in connection with the concept of *dār al-islām* and *dār al-ḥarb*. It was Giovanna Calasso in a recent article who shed new light on the origin of the terms and of the concepts related to them.[2] The expressions, or rather the dichotomy between the two terms, constitute the classical and referential terms to express what is inside and what is outside the Muslim world, and as such usually appear together

1 In this regard, see, for example, Roberto Tottoli, "Origin and Use of the Term *isrāʾīliyyāt* in Muslim Literature," *Arabica* 46 (1999): 193–210; on the early meaning and use of *ḫabar* see Roberto Tottoli, "G. H. A. Juynboll and the Meaningfulness of *ḥadīth* and *ḥadīth*-Related Technical Terminology: The Term *khabar* in Western and Early Muslim Literature" (Conference in memory of Gautier H. A. Juynboll (1935–2010), LUCIS, Leiden University, 2011). Research projects of this kind are today improved and further prompted thanks to the diffusion of electronic databases and new tools for research. For all of those who, like most of us, have long been accustomed to the painful job of reading volume after volume of the major works in the various literary genres, this is new and revolutionary.

2 Giovanna Calasso, "Alla ricerca di *dār al-islām*. Una ricognizione nei testi di giuristi e tradizionisti, lessicografi, geografi e viaggiatori," *Rivista degli Studi Orientali* 83 (2010): 271–96.

 | DOI 10.1163/9789004331037_008

as a founding concept in the early relation between what is Islamic and what is not. It has thus been used as a theological concept in describing the realm of Islam and the realm of unbelief, largely corresponding to the geographical borders between Islam and the Western and surrounding worlds in the Middle Ages, at least until recent times. Calasso underlined how this concept is taken for granted in handbooks on Islam,[3] books on jihad and other Western essays, though the situation is rather complicated in Muslim literary attestations. In fact, the Qur'an does not mention the expressions, nor do the major Hadith collections and other works include them: they sometimes appear only in chapter titles. So, in general, as regards attestations of the expression *dār al-islām*, though it appears as a widespread concept in fourth/tenth century literature, before this period the situation appears rather complicated and with differing attestations and uses according to the different literary genres and contexts.[4]

2

In studying the early attitudes to these terms and their adoption, an interesting test is to check the use and quotation of these expressions or of related concepts in the work of Ibn Jarīr al-Ṭabarī (d. 310/923). A number of reasons suggest this. Though this may not have been the case at the time he wrote and in the subsequent Muslim evaluations, Ṭabarī is usually considered a turning point in the exegetical and historical literary activity and his work summarizes the early three centuries of traditional and literary activities.[5] The period in

3 Calasso pointed out how, for example, in the entry "Dār al-islām," *Encyclopaedia of Islam, Vol. II, C–G* (Leiden: Brill, 1965), by Armand Abel, no author from the classical period is quoted in bibliographical references and the history of the binomial *dār al-Islām / dār al-ḥarb* is yet to be written; see Calasso, "Alla ricerca di *dār al-islām*," 274.

4 Further, the other point to be underlined is the nearly complete absence of the expressions—not mentioned or only in rare occurrences in some works—in geographical literature, suggesting that the terms of the question fall outside the scope of the geographical literature: see Calasso, "Alla ricerca di *dār al-islām*," 286–89. However, this should be treated with caution, as the author herself states, see ibid., 280.

5 On his works and activity, see Hugh Kennedy, ed., *Al-Ṭabarī: A Medieval Muslim Historian and His Work*, Studies in Late Antiquity and Early Islam 15 (Princeton, NJ: The Darwin Press, 2008). For a general outline and further bibliography, see also Clifford E. Bosworth, "al-Ṭabarī," *Encyclopaedia of Islam, Vol. X, T–U* (Leiden: Brill, 2000). The fundamental studies on his life, education and works are still those by Franz Rosenthal and Claude Gilliot: Franz Rosenthal, ed., *General introduction and from the Creation to the Flood*, The History of al-Ṭabarī, v. 1 (Albany: State University of New York Press, 1989); Claude Gilliot, "La

which Ṭabarī wrote his works was thus at the crossroads of the emergence and diffusion of religious concepts and expressions such as these. Irrespective of his role and position as regards this specific question, there is in fact no doubt that from the fourth/tenth century onwards all literary genres attest to the circulation of the "classical" *dār al-islām* / *dār al-ḥarb* dichotomy. Further, the variety of Ṭabarī's literary activity is also important in order to see the dynamics of occurrences in relation to genres. In this regard, Ṭabarī's biography can be of some help. As is well-known, he thought of himself as a jurist and thus dedicated more space to his juridical interests also in his other works. Fate decided differently and his activity in the field of law went almost unnoticed and was very soon forgotten, while his works on history and exegesis were those where he left the most important mark on the history of Islam and of its literatures.

Ṭabarī makes use of the expressions or of related concepts above all in a number of passages of his Qur'anic commentary, also displaying some significant features clearly reflecting specific thematic concerns. Most of these passages show a number of meanings connected to the concept of *hijra*, i.e., migration, and among these, there is also the connection of *hijra* to jihad and the confrontation with misbelievers and enemies.[6] Most probably the Qur'an reflects early confrontations of Muslims with Meccan and Medinan environments, while early traditions enhance the merit of *hijra* and jihad mostly connected to Syrian borders, with a clear superposition between physical and direct participation and the moral intent connected to these activities. The strict connection between *hijra* and the *dār al-Islām* / *dār al-ḥarb* expressions appears in Ṭabarī's comments on related verses and passages though *hijra* occurrences attest to some difference in topic and meaning. First of all, the physical abodes and the moral categories somehow overlap. For instance, in the comment on Q 4:100, the expression *dār al-islām* appears close to others (*arḍ al-širk*, *arḍ al-islām*, *dār al-hijra*), apparently denoting the same concepts in connection with the person who sets out to make *hijra*, but death prevents

---

formation intellectuelle de Tabari," *Journal Asiatique* 276, no. 3 (December 1, 1988): 203–44; Claude Gilliot, "Les œuvres de Tabari (m. 310/923)," *Mélanges de l'Institut Dominicain d'Études Orientales (MIDEO)* 19 (1989): p. 49–90, index; and on his Qur'an commentary Claude Gilliot, *Exégèse, langue, et théologie en Islam: l'exégèse coranique de Tabari (m. 311/923)*, Etudes musulmanes 32 (Paris: Libr. J. Vrin, 1990); and the recent Mustafa Shah, "Al-Ṭabarī and the Dynamics of *tafsīr* : Theological Dimensions of a Legacy," *Journal of Qur'anic Studies* 15, no. 2 (June 2013): 83–139.

6 See on this question, for example, Khalil Athamina, "*Aʿrāb* and *Muhājirūn* in the Environment of *Amṣār*," *Studia Islamica*, no. 66 (1987): 5–25; Wilferd Madelung, "Has the Hijra Come to an End?," *Revue des Études Islamiques* 54 (1991): 225–37; Patricia Crone, "The First-Century Concept of Hiǧra," *Arabica* 41, no. 3 (1994): 352–87.

him from fulfilling it; God takes care of his reward.[7] All the expressions quoted attest to their later widespread use in explaining the concepts of *dār al-islām* and *dār al-ḥarb*. As further stated later on when commenting on Q 8:72, those who believe should not remain amongst those who do not (*ahl al-širk*), but rather they should migrate from *dār al-širk*.[8] Migration is departure from the enemies' and misbelievers' abodes.

In other cases of this conceptual framework the meaning is neither geographical nor inter-communal borders, but rather the faith/un-faith dichotomy. Thus, following this line, in relation to the occurrence of the concept of *hijra* mentioned in Q 4:97 with the expression *fa-tuhājirūna*, Ṭabarī again quotes the *dār al-islām* in connection with the *dār al-kufr*, i.e., using a different expression than *dār al-širk*. Ṭabarī further explains that this verse would refer to the converts to Islam who were still in Mecca at the time of the Prophet and who refrained from emigrating along with Muhammad so that some of them left Islam and even joined the *mušrikūn* in the war against the Muslims.[9] The terms in this case refer to Mecca and Medina as the realms of faith and unbelief in the confrontation at the time of Muhammad. Other passages are similar to this. For instance, when commenting on Q 8:72 about those who believed and migrated "struggling with their possessions and their selves" on the path of God and those who did not, the terms are explained by Ṭabarī himself in his commentary as referring to leaving the *dār al-kufr* or *dār* (or *arḍ*) *al-ḥarb* which is the realm of *kuffār* towards *dār al-islām*.[10] Further, also in connection with Q 60:10, about believing women, i.e. the *muhājirāt*, the term is glossed as referring to migrating from *dār al-kufr* to *dār al-islām* and points to the time of the Prophet.[11] The same concept appears in verse Q 8:75 where migration is mentioned and the explanation is that this refers to migration from *dār al-kufr* to *dār al-islām*.[12] Though not mentioned directly in the Qur'anic passages, it is Ṭabarī himself who introduces the expression when commenting on Q 9:22–24 about the question of following parents and relatives instead of joining God, and thus preferring *kufr* above *īmān*. Here the

---

7 Abū Jaʿfar Muḥammad b. Jarīr al-Ṭabarī, *Jāmiʿ al-bayān ʿan tafsīr āy al-Qurʾān* (Beirut: Muʾassasat al-Risāla, 2000), 9:113. See also ibid., 8:29 (comm. on Q 4:91) upon leaving the *dār al-širk*.

8 Ṭabarī, *Jāmiʿ al-bayān*, 14:89.

9 Ibid., 9:102; cf. also, on similar concepts, ibid., 18:645.

10 Ṭabarī, *Jāmiʿ al-bayān*, 14:81–82.

11 Ibid., 23:325; see also ibid., 23:334; and cf. Ibid., 23:330: about the believers who have wives in the *dār al-ḥarb*.

12 Ṭabarī, *Jāmiʿ al-bayān*, 14:89.

text prompts Ṭabarī to explain that this refers to those who refused the *hijra* and preferred to stay with their families in the *dār al-širk* instead of migrating to the *dār al-islām* and to the Messenger of God.[13] In this direction there are also the exegetical explanations given when the term *al-muhājirīn* occurs, referring to migration to the *dār al-islām* from the *dār al-ḥarb* (on Q 9:100),[14] or from their proper homes and tribes (on Q 9:117).[15] The exegesis here points to the overlapping of the concepts of *dār al-ḥarb* and "homes and tribes", thus representing the double reference to the Muhammad-Meccans rivalry and confrontation and an extension to a more general meaning of the abodes of faith and unbelief.

A few occurrences of the expressions combine mention of the *hijra* with an explicit thematic concern for hypocrites and in particular the temptations constituted by hypocrites' example and in relation to believers. For instance, commenting on Q 4:89, Ṭabarī explains that it is recommended not to take protectors from among *munāfiqūn* unless they "migrate on the path of God" (*yuhājirūna fī sabīl Allāh*) but, instead, if they do not act accordingly, to kill them. It is in one of his final comments usually following the list of traditions that Ṭabarī glosses this part of the verse, stating that it means leaving the *dār al-širk*, i.e. leaving the abode where people associate something else with God, and joining/going to the *dār al-islām wa-ahlihi*, striving for the religion of God.[16] The expressions are here used in accordance with the meaning of *hijra*, i.e. the 'emigration' from paganism to true belief, following the *hijra* of Muḥammad and the early community, but also denoting a moral intent drawing a line between faith and unbelief, where unbelief is expressed by the concept of *širk*. This is made clear by Ṭabarī himself when he states that making the *hijra min dār al-širk ilā dār al-islām* means *min al-kufr ilā 'l-islām* ('from misbelief to Islam').[17] In another passage (Q 29:11) the text mentions the hypocrites alone, and it is Ṭabarī who explains the extent of the meaning of the verse by stating that in order to distinguish between the two parties (i.e. hypocrites and believers), there is also the migration from *dār al-širk* to *dār al-islām*.[18]

A few passages do not mention any *hijra* but instead connect the expressions to confrontation with enemies and adversaries of the Muslim community. In Q 4:92, a believer is prohibited from killing another believer, and some specific

13 Ibid., 14:175–7, *dār al-širk* is mentioned in 14:177.
14 Ibid., 14:434.
15 Ibid., 14:539.
16 Ibid., 8:17.
17 Ibid., 8:18.
18 Ibid., 20:14.

cases are mentioned, one of which relates to the situation of someone killing a believer (*mu'min*), though amongst an enemy people (*qawm ʿaduww*). In discussing the particulars of the Qur'anic contents Ṭabarī explains that an example of this is the man from the *ahl al-ḥarb* who proceeds to the *dār al-islām*, converts to Islam and then goes back to the *dār al-ḥarb* etc.[19] The meaning here is slightly different and goes back to the juridical implications of what took place on the borders between Islamic and the outer world, which indirectly goes back to the frontier and jihad activities in Muslim times. The case of the expressions used in relation to the inner enemies is similar. Commenting on the meaning of *yunfaw* in Q 5:33 connected to the destiny of those combating God and his Messenger, the exegetical note adds that the term properly means that someone acting in this way, along with the other punishments listed, will be looked for and captured unless he escapes the *dār al-islām*, thus pointing to the realm of the community of Islam, first of all as a geographical abode (*arḍ al-muslimīn* as it is explained later on) but also as an indication of exclusivity. The reports stating that the term in this passage means to leave *dār al-islām* for *dār al-ḥarb* according to Ibn ʿAbbās or from *dār al-islām* to *dār al-širk wa'l-ḥarb* according to Layṯ b. Saʿd point in this direction.[20] The significance of this passage is to attest—according to the exegetical parts by Ṭabarī and to the reports ascribed to previous transmitters—to a use of different terms and expressions to convey the same concepts. Later on, for instance, commenting upon the following verse (Q 5: 34) about the possibilities for those combating against the believers for repenting and being saved, Ṭabarī includes reports quoting *dār al-islām* and *dar al-kufr*.[21]

This is all as regards his commentary, but Ṭabarī quotes the expressions in some of his other works. These other quotations are not so numerous as those appearing in the commentary, but they attest to his further use of the terms and, along with this, better qualify the variety of uses emerging from the commentary quotations. Calasso has already noted that Ṭabarī does not mention the expression *dār al-islām* in his *Ta'rīḫ*.[22] Further, we find only a

19 Ibid., 9:40; see also ibid., 9:39, 14: 87, where there is mention of *dār al-ḥarb* and *dār al-kufr* which appear in different reports; and ibid., 18:645, and 22:250, quoting the expression *dār al-ḥarb* only. See also ibid., 24:97 on Q 76:8 where the term *asīran* is glossed as referring to the *ḥarbī* of the people of *dār al-ḥarb*.

20 Ṭabarī, *Jāmiʿ al-bayān*, 10:268–9 and nos. 11857, 11859–60. In this last report it is discussed if the Muslims must follow him when he is in the *dār al-širk* or not. On the migration from *dār al-širk* to *dār al-islām*, see also Ibid., 21:269.

21 Ṭabarī, *Jāmiʿ al-bayān*, 10:285–6: see also in part. 10:286: *sulṭān al-muslimīn*.

22 Calasso, "Alla ricerca di *dār al-islām*," 278.

couple of chapters in his other work *Kitāb Iḫtilāf al-fuqahāʾ* where the expression appears. Calasso has already discussed one of these occurrences about the situation of the *ḥarbī* converting to Islam and committing sins or crimes before entering *dār al-islām*. The juridical point at issue is whether or not he is to be punished, but what is more important is that the expressions appear in the context of relations with the outer world, i.e. on the borders.[23] It is the same meaning that is attested to, as we shall see, in the earlier juridical literature, and the concept is related to human communities and to a situation where the Muslim communities must be defended from external perils and dangers.[24] Another occurrence is instead related to trade and to what it is possible for a Muslim to make outside the *dār al-islām* and for the *ḥarbī* inside *dār al-islām* when he is trading in a way forbidden by Muslim law. The expressions used here are *dār al-ḥarb* and *dār al-islām*.[25] Along with these occurrences, two further quotations are attested to in the surviving part of Ṭabarī's *Tahḏīb al-āṯār*. One mentions *dār al-islām* in a report going back through ʿUmar b. al-Ḫaṭṭāb to the Prophet in relation to the Christian Banū Taġlib and the question of the *jizya*. The expression occurs in a passage discussing the attitude of Muslims accepting them amongst themselves inside *dār al-islām*.[26] The terms point to early Islam and the definition of the abode of early Muslims in the peninsula. The other occurrence states after a long discussion that the preferred choice is to make *hijra* from *dār al-širk* to the *dār al-islām*, putting a distance between Muslims and the religion of the unbelievers.[27] The setting refers back to the Prophet's time, but the concepts, cited along with the *hijra*, point to the imagery discussed in the occurrences in the commentary.

All the attestations in Ṭabarī, and above all the most numerous in his commentary, constitute a significant amount of evidence for a number of reasons. First of all it must be remarked that his is the first *tafsīr* to include the expressions.[28] Though in general later Qur'anic commentaries do not include

23 Ibid., 281–82.

24 Ibid., 282–83. See Abū Jaʿfar Muḥammad b. Jarīr al-Ṭabarī, *Kitāb Iḫtilāf al-fuqahāʾ* (Beirut: Dār al-kutub al-ʿilmiyya, 2002), 1:272–73.

25 Ṭabarī, *Kitāb Iḫtilāf al-fuqahāʾ*, 1:82–83.

26 Abū Jaʿfar Muḥammad b. Jarīr al-Ṭabarī, *Tahḏīb al-āṯār* (Cairo: Maṭbaʿat al-Madanī, n.d.), 3:224 no. 356.

27 Ibid., 2:787.

28 The statement refers to verse-by-verse commentaries. In fact, among Qur'anic sciences, see in connection with Q 5:33 how Abū ʿUbayd b. Sallām al-Harawī explains the contents of the Qur'anic passage as indicating those leaving the *dār al-islām* and being directed to *dār al-ḥarb*/*dār al-širk*: Abū ʿUbayd al-Harawī, *al-Nāsiḫ wa'l-mansūḫ fī 'l-Qur'ān al-ʿazīz wa-mā fīhi min al-farāʾiḍ wa-l-sunan* (Riyadh: Maktabat al-Rušd, 1997), 1:142 no. 285.

numerous occurrences of them, all those written after Ṭabarī include the terms, thus attesting to how after the beginning of the fourth/tenth century the *dār al-islām*/*dār al-ḥarb* dichotomy had become a sort of technical expression. Ṭabarī for some reason is at a crossroads as regards the exegetical literary genre. Further, and more important, the occurrences of the expressions in his *tafsīr* attest to a strong connection to the *hijra* concept and to the confrontation with enemies, thus clearly pointing to the liminal situation of a condition in which Muslims had to face this and even warfare with misbelievers. The context is the battlefield, with the juridical implications given by confrontations and the questions originated by the crossing of the borders, as well as a moral injunction bearing on the concept that a believer must join the other Muslims in their abode, the *dār al-islām*, making *hijra*, migration. The reference to the time of Muhammad overlaps with the injunction set down for early Muslim generations, probably referring above all to the places of traditional definition of apocalyptic, jihadist and confrontational religious imagery, i.e. the frontier dividing believers from unbelievers and thus traditions originating from there.

3

A better insight into the significance and meaning of the use by Ṭabarī of these expressions can be obtained by discussing their occurrences and meaning before Ṭabarī and also what took place after him. After him the situation is simple and clear: the terms appear in all the following Qur'anic commentaries such as that of Māturidī (d. 333/944) or Jaṣṣāṣ's (d. 370/981) *Aḥkām al-Qur'ān* onwards, and above all in law handbooks such as, for instance, *al-Ḥāwī al-kabīr* by Māwardī (d. 450/1058) or the *Muḥallā* by Ibn Ḥazm (d. 456/1064), the *Mabsūṭ* or the *Šarḥ al-Siyar al-kabīr* by Saraḫsī (d. ca. 483/1090), the *Muġnī* by Ibn Qudāma (d. 620/1223). In these law books, quotations of *dār al-islām* / *dār al-ḥarb* are ubiquitous and the terms appear in full context of their use in later sources when their meaning became assumed to indicate the realms and abodes where Islam rules and those where it does not. A look at the occurrences of the term before Ṭabarī, however, highlights a different situation. In any case what is essential is knowing Ṭabarī's sources better and better understanding

---

As regards the Shi'i side, the expressions appear in ʿAyyāšī (d. 320/932), *Tafsīr* (Beirut: Mu'assasat al-Aʿlamī li-l-maṭbūʿāt, 1991), 1:345, 2:91; al-Qummī, *Tafsīr* (Najaf: Maktabat al-Najaf, 1387), 2:320; cf. also Kulaynī who, in his *Kāfī*, quotes the expressions in a few passages with no novelty as regards subjects and images: *Al-Kāfī* (Tehran: Dār al Kutub al-Islāmiyya, 1367), 5:10, 29, 211, 358; 7:245.

his use and the meanings reflected in his usage of the terms, and, if possible, seeing how and why he decided to insert them in a Qur'anic commentary for the first time.

The most significant and numerous quotations prior to Ṭabarī's *Tafsīr* come from *siyar* literature (law or conduct of war), works collecting early traditions and discussing condition in warfare recalling, notwithstanding the typical doubts on the soundness of their contents, early conquest times.[29] What is more important in this regard is that these and the related expressions appear in quite a considerable number of passages in such works, as early as in the *Kitāb al-Siyar* by Fazārī (d. 188/804) and above all in the one by Šaybānī (d. 189/805), who several times mentions *dār al-islām* and *dār al-ḥarb* in relation to various different cases, but all concerning the definition of controversial juridical points connected to the frontiers and the relations between the abode of Islam on the one hand and the abode of war and of the enemy on the other. We consequently find in their works a clear expression of one place ruled by Muslims and another by the enemy and the related questions about prisoners, booties, warfare, personal relations between the two sides, etc.[30] The expressions clearly point to this setting and reflect the need to regulate the condition of persons moving between places under Islamic control and places controlled by non-Muslims, so that the most common verbs connected to the expression are 'to enter', 'to leave' or 'to stay' in *dār al-islām* and *dār al-ḥarb*.

The terms appear so often that they already constitute a sort of reference term to define this specific condition. Close to this usage is the one in the coeval *Kitāb al-Ḫarāj* by Abū Yūsuf (d. 182/798) who quotes both *dār al-islām* and *dār al-ḥarb* in relation to economic questions connected to what was taking place in this specific setting: *ḏimma*, slaves, buying goods, booties[31] or in the reports about situations where there is mention of entering and exiting

29 On this literature, its meaning and its early features, see Michael Bonner, *Jihad in Islamic History: Doctrines and Practice* (Princeton: Princeton University Press, 2006), 99–100.

30 Abū Iṣḥāq al-Fazārī, *Kitāb al-Siyar. Riwāyat Muḥammad b. Waḍḍāḥ al-Qurṭubī*, ed. Fārūq Ḥammāda (Beirut: Mu'assasat al-risāla, 1987), 1:111 n. 26, 171 nos. 203, 205, 172 no. 207, 183 no. 249, 228 no. 370, 251 no. 433, 254 no. 467; Muḥammad b. al-Ḥasan al-Šaybānī, *Šarḥ al-Siyar al-kabīr*, Dār al-muttaḥida li'l-našr (Beirut, 1975), 1:109–10 nos. 60–64, 113–14 nos. 74–75 84 and 86, 118, 121, 129 no. 106, 130 no. 109, 132–33 nos. 111 and 114, 137 (in a chapter title), 139–40 no. 122, 145, 146, 159 no. 183, 166, 168 no. 198, 169–70 nos. 201–205, 173–74 nos. 206–8 and 210, 176 no. 211, 177–82 nos. 215–27, 184 nos. 238–40, 185–87 no. 244–49, 189–90 no. 259–61, 191 no. 264, 192 nos. 267–68, 193–94 nos. 273–74, 197–98, 200, 205, 206, 211, 213–14 no. 335, 215 no. 340, 217, 218–19 nos. 345–50, 247, 249–50, 256.

31 Abū Yūsuf, *Kitāb al-Ḫarāj* (Cairo: al-Maktaba al-azhariyya li'l-turāṯ, n.d.), 1:32, 145, 198–99, 206, 214, 215.

from one *dār* to the other.[32] The specificity given by the topic of the work and thus dictated by a genre consideration appears clearly if we go back to the work of Abū Yūsuf discussing the *Siyar* by Awzāʿī (d. 157/774). Abū Yūsuf quotes the expressions extensively, mainly in connection with the ways in which they appear in the works of *siyar* quoted above: the image of exiting from and entering *dār al-islām* is the most frequent,[33] along with other connections with warfare, and related topics such as booty, prisoners, etc.[34]

From here the terms in their first meaning and framework reference also entered some significant works. For instance Šāfiʿī (d. 204/820) already quotes them extensively, pointing to the relations on the border and thus to a strict connection between *dār al-islām* and *dār al-ḥarb*.[35] His *Kitāb al-Umm* clearly includes these subjects with the expressions in use in the *siyar* literature. Thus *dār al-islām* and *dār al-ḥarb* appear one close to the other to describe alternate conditions while being on one or the other side;[36] or as in the traditions quoted above, again the verbs used clearly indicate the relation to entering,[37] exiting from[38] or staying[39] in the *dār al-islām* or *dār al-ḥarb*; some significant passages mention, instead, migration from one abode to the other,[40] or the situation in which the *dār al-ḥarb* becomes (*ṣāra*) *dār al-islām*, i.e. through military conquest.[41] In these occurrences, in general, as is also attested to in the terminology of some passages, *dār* appears to be synonymous with *arḍ*, or of *bilād* which is a term that even appears as an alternative in some passages (see for ex. *bilād al-islām* / *al-ḥarb*).[42]

32 Ibid., 1:205 cf. 1:207.

33 Abū Yūsuf, *al-Radd ʿalā Siyar al-Awzāʿī* (Ḥaydarābād, n.d.), 1:1, 5, 7, 34, 47, 55, 61, 62, 63, 73–75, 80, 98, 99, 103, 129, 131–133.

34 Ibid., 1:1, 2–3, 47, 48, 55, 75, 80, 83, 89, 94.

35 As mentioned by Yohanan Friedmann, *Tolerance and Coercion in Islam. Interfaith Relations in the Muslim Tradition* (Cambridge: Cambridge University Press, 2003), 55–56, the juridical literature also makes use of other expressions for the same concepts.

36 Abū ʿAbd Allāh Muḥammad al-Šāfiʿī, *Kitāb al-Umm* (Beirut: Dār al-kutub al-ʿilmiyya, 1993), 1:298.

37 Ibid., 4:291, 293, 295, 296, 309; cf. also 7:160; cf. 7:352, 8:25.

38 Ibid., 4:241, 277, 288, 289, 293, 305, 5:163, 7:360, 366–368, 370–372, 374, 379, 381, 388.

39 Ibid., 4:198, 214, 223, 287, 301, 307, 5:59, 6:47, 49, 7:229, 380; on situations or conditions taking place in one of the *dār*, see 4:219, 261, 262, 298, 308, 312, 5:47 (about the conversion to Islam by Sufyān b. Ḥarb, at the time when his wife was still a *kāfira* in Mecca, since Mecca was *dār al-ḥarb*), 51, 6:39, 182, 187, 7:34, 353, 364, 375, 377, 378, 383, 8:41.

40 Ibid., 4:205.

41 Ibid., 4:279, 5:48, 7:352.

42 Ibid., 3:243, 4:241, 260, 301, 309; cf. 4:277: *bilād al-ʿaduww*; see also 4:272: *dār al-islām* / *dār ʿahd*.

Among early attestations in juridical literature, it is quite interesting that though Mālik's *Muwaṭṭa'* in the version by Yaḥyā b. Yaḥyā (d. 234/848) does not include the expression, Šaybānī's version has it in a report on a legal point about the believing woman married to an unbeliever living in the abode of Islam: *kāfir fī dār al-islām.*[43] Šaybānī also uses the expressions in other works, though not to the same extent as in his *Siyar*, with the same meaning and in related questions, thus attesting on the one hand to the meaning of the terms in his time and on the other hand to the inner connections of all the works attributed to him.[44] The alternation of terms expressing the same meaning and usage such as in Šāfiʿī also appears in the *Mudawwana* by Saḥnūn (d. 240/855). In the discussion of juridical concern implicating personal condition or properties when crossing the borders from/to *dār al-islām* to/from *dār al-ḥarb*, along with these terms which appear as the favorite ones, we find in the same passages *ahl/arḍ/bilād + al-islām/al-ḥarb/al-širk.*[45] Further, the problems generated by warfare imply the use of the terms also in the books on *amwāl* of the third century AH.[46] All these occurrences as a whole attest to how the terms, originating in reference to *siyar* and jihad, entered into use in relation to this subject, but from here they acquired a specific meaning to be used also in connection with other topics.

Other literature prior to Ṭabarī includes mention of the terms but not to the extent that it appeared in *siyar* literature and in some juridical works. They are nevertheless important attestations. However, as they are not systematic quotations, it is not always easy to understand the proper meaning in relation to the works as a whole.

The attestations in Hadith collections appear scanty and reduced. Tirmiḏī, for instance, is the only one among the so-called canonical collections to

---

43 Mālik b. Anas, *Al-Muwaṭṭa'. Riwāyat Muḥammad b. al-Ḥasan al-Šaybānī*, ed. ʿAbd al-Wahhāb ʿAbd al-Laṭīf (Cairo, 1994), 1:204.

44 Muḥammad b. al-Ḥasan al-Šaybānī, *al-Ḥujja ʿalā ahl al-Madīna* (Beirut: ʿĀlam al-kutub, 1403), 3:360, 4:70; Muḥammad b. al-Ḥasan al-Šaybānī, *al-Jāmiʿ al-ṣaġīr* (Beirut: ʿĀlam al-kutub, 1406), 1:524.

45 Saḥnūn, *Al-Mudawwana al-kubrā* (Beirut: Dār Iḥyā' al-turāṯ al-ʿarabī, n.d.), 2:18–23, 38, 302–3, 314, 323–24.

46 Abū ʿUbayd (d. 224/838), *al-Amwāl* (Beirut: Dār al-fikr, n.d.), 1:179 no. 364; Ibn Zanjawayh (d. 251/865), *al-Amwāl* (Markaz al-Malik Fayṣal li'l-buʿūṯ wa'l-dirāsāt al-islāmiyya, n.d.), 1:337, 352, 2:579. Other works may quote the expressions for specific concerns, but in connection with juridical questions, see for instance Ḫallāl (d. 311/923), quoting them in relation to births, marriages and "family" questions crossing the *dār al-islām*, *Aḥkām ahl al-milal wa'l-ridda min al-jāmiʿ li-masā'il al-imām Aḥmad b. Ḥanbal* (Beirut: Dār al-kutub al-ʿilmiyya, 1994), 1:25, 27, 29, 178, 239, 274, 285.

mention it in a passage on the battle (*ġazw*) with the enemy and the applicability of the *ḥadd* penalty of cutting off the hands in this situation; here there is mention of the imam who comes out of the *arḍ al-ḥarb* and returns to the *dār al-islām*.[47] This tradition seems to point to the theme of the situation on the borders, like the other rare mentions in Hadith collections, namely in the *Sunan* by Saʿīd b. Manṣūr (d. 227/842) regarding the man who comes from the people of the war and enters *dār al-islām* with an *amān*.[48] One Hadith attributed to Ibn Abī Šayba (d. 235/849) but only attested to in later sources and ascribed to ʿUmar b. ʿAbd al-ʿAzīz (r. 99/717–101/720) includes quotation of *dār al-islām* in connection with repentance and expulsion.[49] Hadith-related literature bears some further occurrence. In this regard great importance attaches to the mention of the terms also adding an eschatological trait, such as it can be perceived in an early occurrence in the *Fitan* by Nuʿaym b. Ḥammād (d. 228/843), where it is stated that the center (*ʿaqr*) of the *dār al-islām* is in Syria (*bi'l-Šām*) with a following list of benefits for the place and the people there. Nuʿaym's tradition, also quoted by Ibn Saʿd (d. 230/845), is significant since it points to the use of the term in connection with the early rich eschatological and apocalyptical traditions that originated on the Byzantine frontier, which was also the place where the connection of these themes to jihad and asceticism in the related *zuhd* traditions most probably emerged and was diffused.[50]

It is no less important with regard to the occurrences of the terms that early historical literature, usually including many reports about conquest, generally does not mention them. The few instances attested to in fact are not connected to warfare. A couple of early occurrences of the expressions are found in the works of Wāqidī (d. 207/822). In one passage of his *Kitāb al-maġāzī* dealing with the raid of Usāma b. Zayd to Mu'ta, *dār al-islām* is quoted to indicate the land of Islam to be reached or not by converts to Islam, with the aim of receiving

47 Abū ʿĪsā Muḥammad al-Tirmiḏī, *al-Jāmiʿ al-kabīr* (Beirut: Dār al-ġarb al-islāmī, 1998), 4:53.

48 Saʿīd b. Manṣūr, *Sunan* (Hyderabad: al-Dār al-salafiyya, 1982), 2:344 no. 2829.

49 *Yustatābū fa-in tābū wa-illā nufū min dār al-islām*: al- Firyābī, *Kitāb al-qadar* (Aḍwā' al-salaf, 1997), 1:222 no. 396, 258.

50 Nuʿaym b. Ḥammād, *Kitāb al-Fitan* (Cairo: Maktabat al-tawḥīd, 1412), 1:253; cf. version quoted in Ibn Saʿd, *al-Ṭabaqāt al-kubrā* (Beirut: Dār Ṣādir, 1968), 7:747; and Abū 'l-Qāsim al-Ṭabarānī, *al-Muʿjam al-kabīr* (Cairo: Maktabat Ibn Taymiyya, 1415/1994), 7:53 no. 6359. The expression is probably recalled in the connection of *hijra*—*dār al-islām* which is further underlined by the quotation in Ṭabarī of a statement from Qatāda that al-Šām, i.e. Syria, was named the support (*ʿimād*) of the *dār al-hijra*: Ṭabarī, *Jāmiʿ al-bayān*, 18:469.

what the *muhājirūn* have, according to the advice of the Prophet Muhammad.[51] The other mention is in the problematic *Kitāb al-ridda* where the expression is used in relation to the return of Ṭulayḥa b. Ḫuwaylid to Medina after the death of Abū Bakr and when ʿUmar became caliph.[52] The occurrences appear neither in connection with the complex concept of *hijra* nor along with *dār al-ḥarb* or related expressions. Amongst other works, Yaʿqūbī (d. 284/897), in reference to India, mentions a place as being now in *dār al-islām*, and Ibn Aʿṯam al-Kūfī (d. 314/926) inserts the terms in a report going back to Ibn ʿAbbās.[53] Finally, we refer here to a couple of quotations in Jāḥiẓ (d. 255/868) which cannot constitute clear evidence of a wider use of the terms, but nevertheless attest to their circulation in the third/ninth century. Jāḥiẓ mentions *dār al-islām* in a couple of his books, in one passage of his *Ḥayawān* and in a few more in *ʿUṯmāniyya*, all of them bearing no juridical implications but simply indicating the abode of Islam and contrasting it with the other realms mentioned as *dār al-kufr* and *dār al-širk*.[54]

The brief review of some of the literature attested to before Ṭabarī's works contains sufficient information to draw some brief conclusions on the probable early origin and occurrences of the terms. The strict early connection between *siyar* literature and the *dār al-islām* / *dār al-ḥarb* binomial has been analyzed and brought to attention in some previous studies, as for instance by Armand Abel who connected them to the concept of jihad.[55] The terms thus seem to have emerged in connection with a corpus of rules regulating the relations with the outer world, the "other side", in the times after the first conquests. But *siyar* and early juridical literature, given the number of occurrences and the stable concepts they refer to, must have exercised an action of

51 Muḥammad b. ʿUmar al-Wāqidī, *Kitāb al-Maġāzī*, ed. M. Jones (London: Oxford University Press, 1966), 3:1123; English translation, Muḥammad b. ʿUmar al-Wāqidī, *The Life of Muḥammad: Al-Wāqidī's Kitāb Al-Maghāzī*, ed. Rizwi Faizer, trans. Rizwi Faizer, Amal Ismail, and Abdulkader Tayob, Routledge Studies in Classical Islam (Abingdon: Routledge, 2011), 548.

52 Muḥammad b. ʿUmar al-Wāqidī, *Kitāb al-Ridda* (Beirut: Dār al-ġarb al-islāmī, 1990), 1:111.

53 Abū ʾl-ʿAbbās Aḥmad al-Yaʿqūbī, *Taʾrīḫ* (Beirut: Dār Ṣādir, 2000), 1:94; Abū Muḥammad Aḥmad Ibn Aʿṯam al-Kūfī, *Kitāb al-Futūḥ* (Hyderabad: Dāʾirat al-maʿārif al-ʿuṯmāniyya, 1968), 4:253.

54 Abū ʿUṯmān al-Jāḥiẓ, *Kitāb al-Ḥayawān* (Beirut: Dār al-kutub al-ʿilmiyya, 2002), 4:273; *al-ʿUṯmāniyya* (Cairo: Dār al-Kutub al-ʿArabī, 1955), 244–45 on Islam in *dār al-islām* and *kufr* in *dār al-kufr*; 305 (here the expression *dār al-islām* indicates under the rule of Islam, when Islam was diffused, thus not at the time of early revelations in Mecca), stating that ʿAlī was not born in *dār al-islām* but—cf. p. 299—in *dār al-širk*.

55 See Armand Abel, "Dār al-ḥarb," *Encyclopaedia of Islam, Vol. II, C–G* (Leiden: Brill, 1965).

systematization on concepts and terms which no doubt had emerged before. This preceding situation probably refers to early conquests and warfare on the borders where most probably *dār al-islām* and *dār al-ḥarb* emerged to mark the division on the field of the first wave of jihad, and in relation to space in the armed confrontation. If it is so, it was very probably there that the concepts were developed, combining practical uses and real confrontation along with the rhetoric of religious and moral intents, so that the concepts denote not only a strict war-like language but also a confrontation between religious realms. The first wave of jihad then gave way to the juridical discussion of the *siyar*.[56] The subsequent juridical evolution in the *fiqh* works thus seems to be the result of the further later developments of these concepts occurring during the Abbasid imperial activities and pointing to a progressive definitions of the two expressions as pointing to two different abodes.[57]

4 Conclusion

In the light of the previous attestations of the *dār al-islām* / *dār al-ḥarb* dichotomy and related expressions, Ṭabarī's attestations in his Qur'anic commentaries seem to follow two lines. First of all they bear testimony to the juridical development around the early meaning connecting them to borders warfare, enemies and warlike confrontation, similar to *siyar* attestations. But what is more significant is the strict connection of the expression to *hijra* and related concepts. Ṭabarī recalls the migration of the Prophet and connects it to the duty of all Muslims to reach the abode of Islam to escape the insidious abode of war/unbelief/or polytheism. The abodes are thus Mecca and Medina as well as the Islamic community and the outside world. Ṭabarī was not the first to introduce this connection,[58] but no doubt he made of it the major concern in his quotations of the terms above all in his commentary.

Most probably after the first emergence of the terms, their introduction and use in juridical literature, they began to circulate and to be diffused during the third/ninth century. The emergence of the expressions thus took place with the stabilization of a frontier and when the question entered juridical discussion on how to deal with the confrontation on the more or less broadly fixed borders. The connection to *hijra*, given this situation and the definition of terms and their meaning, followed closely. As attested to so clearly in Ṭabarī

56 Calasso, "Alla ricerca di *dār al-islām*," 275–6: see sources quoted.

57 See ibid., 284–85.

58 Ibid., 277.

this connection is a step further in the enrichment of the concept, since it represents the combination of the real relations between the two abodes and of the ideal confrontation between the realm of faith and that of unbelief.

We can add some hypotheses as to why such an evolution in meaning and usage of the expressions and related terms took place. One possible reason for this could be connected to the peculiar condition of the Muslim community, at least for the first three centuries of Islam, namely that of being a minority within the conquered countries and regions. Yohanan Friedmann has already perfectly discussed the issues involved in the relation of Islam to other communities in various traditional reports. I suggest that, though Friedmann does not push his discussion so far, many aspects of early Islamic juridical discussions and traditions about the relation with the other reflect this dynamic rather than a self-confident attitude from the beginning. The origin of this attitude is thus not only the product of an aggressive and conquering attitude towards the surrounding world and communities, but also includes the need of a minority community, living among a majority of other religious communities, to draw frontier lines on the ground. This is a factor which is usually underestimated, since it is forgotten that for well over three centuries Muslims were not the majority within countries under Muslim rule. This could well explain the reason why a concept like this will assume geographical connotations only in later re-interpretations and usage.

Further, when Ṭabarī was writing, in the abode of Islam the process that led to the end of its political unity had already started. If *dār al-islām* in its first occurrences referred mainly to the small community of believers in the warlike confrontation with enemies, in his time it was a realm where Muslims were beginning to become a majority and thus *dār al-islām* was to become a useful concept to designate the regions under Muslim rule, notwithstanding the growing political divisions. In this case too, Ṭabarī's work is at the crossroads of the emerging of the classical theory but also the one that closes the various early meanings of the expressions, in the middle of political changes which prompted his introduction of the terms in the genre of *tafsīr*, in line with the diffusion that the *dār al-islām* and *dār al-ḥarb* concepts were gaining in his time.

References

Abel, Armand. "Dār al-ḥarb." *Encyclopaedia of Islam, Vol. II, C–G*. Leiden: Brill, 1965.
Abel, Armand. "Dār al-islām." *Encyclopaedia of Islam, Vol. II, C–G*. Leiden: Brill, 1965.
Abū ʿUbayd al-Qāsim b. Sallām al-Harawī. *Al-Amwāl*. Beirut: Dār al-fikr, n.d.

Abū ʿUbayd al-Qāsim b. Sallām al-Harawī. *Al-Nāsiḫ wa'l-mansūḫ fī 'l-Qur'ān al-ʿazīz wa-mā fīhi min al-farā'iḍ wa'l-sunan*. Riyadh: Maktabat al-Rušd, 1997.

Abū Yūsuf, Yaʿqūb b. Ibrāhīm. *Al-Radd ʿalā Siyar al-Awzāʿī*. Hyderabad, n.d.

Abū Yūsuf, Yaʿqūb b. Ibrāhīm. *Kitāb al-Ḫarāj*. Cairo: al-Maktaba al-azhariyya li'l-turāṯ, n.d.

Athamina, Khalil. "*Aʿrāb* and *Muhājirūn* in the Environment of *Amṣār*." *Studia Islamica*, no. 66 (1987): 5–25.

ʿAyyāšī, Muḥammad b. Masʿūd al-. *Tafsīr*. Beirut: Mu'assasat al-Aʿlamī li-l-maṭbūʿāt, 1991.

Bonner, Michael. *Jihad in Islamic History: Doctrines and Practice*. Princeton: Princeton University Press, 2006.

Bosworth, Clifford E. "al-Ṭabarī." *Encyclopaedia of Islam, Vol. X, T–U*. Leiden: Brill, 2000.

Calasso, Giovanna. "Alla ricerca di *dār al-islām*. Una ricognizione nei testi di giuristi e tradizionisti, lessicografi, geografi e viaggiatori." *Rivista degli Studi Orientali* 83 (2010): 271–96.

Crone, Patricia. "The First-Century Concept of Hiğra." *Arabica* 41, no. 3 (1994): 352–87.

Fazārī, Abū Iṣḥāq al-. *Kitāb al-Siyar. Riwāyat Muḥammad b. Waḍḍāḥ al-Qurṭubī*. Edited by Fārūq Ḥammāda. Beirut: Mu'assasat al-risāla, 1987.

Firyābī, al-. *Kitāb al-qadar*. Aḍwā' al-salaf, 1997.

Friedmann, Yohanan. *Tolerance and Coercion in Islam. Interfaith Relations in the Muslim Tradition*. Cambridge: Cambridge University Press, 2003.

Gilliot, Claude. *Exégèse, langue, et théologie en Islam: l'exégèse coranique de Tabari (m. 311/923)*. Etudes musulmanes 32. Paris: Libr. J. Vrin, 1990.

Gilliot, Claude. "La formation intellectuelle de Tabari." *Journal Asiatique* 276, no. 3 (December 1, 1988): 203–44.

Gilliot, Claude. "Les œuvres de Tabari (m. 310/923)." *Mélanges de l'Institut Dominicain d'Etudes Orientales (MIDEO)* 19 (1989): p. 49–90, index.

Ḫallāl, Abū Bakr al-. *Aḥkām ahl al-milal wa'l-ridda min al-jāmiʿ li-masā'il al-imām Aḥmad b. Ḥanbal*. Beirut: Dār al-kutub al-ʿilmiyya, 1994.

Ibn Aʿṯam al-Kūfī, Abū Muḥammad Aḥmad. *Kitāb al-Futūḥ*. Hyderabad: Dā'irat al-maʿārif al-ʿuṯmāniyya, 1968.

Ibn Saʿd, Abū ʿAbd Allāh Muḥammad. *Al-Ṭabaqāt al-kubrā*. Beirut: Dār Ṣādir, 1968.

Ibn Zanjawayh, Abū Aḥmad Ḥamīd. *Al-Amwāl*. Markaz al-Malik Fayṣal li'l-buʿūṯ wa'l-dirāsāt al-islāmiyya, n.d.

Jāḥiẓ, Abū ʿUṯmān al-. *Al-ʿUṯmāniyya*. Cairo: Dār al-kutub al-ʿarabī, 1955.

Jāḥiẓ, Abū ʿUṯmān al-. *Kitāb al-Ḥayawān*. Beirut: Dār al-kutub al-ʿilmiyya, 2002.

Kennedy, Hugh, ed. *Al-Ṭabarī: A Medieval Muslim Historian and His Work*. Studies in Late Antiquity and Early Islam 15. Princeton, NJ: The Darwin Press, 2008.

Kulaynī, Abū Jaʿfar Muḥammad al-. *Al-Kāfī*. Tehran: Dār al Kutub al-Islāmiyya, 1367.

Madelung, Wilferd. "Has the Hijra Come to an End?" *Revue des Études Islamiques* 54 (1991): 225–37.

Mālik b. Anas. *Al-Muwaṭṭaʾ. Riwāyat Muḥammad b. al-Ḥasan al-Šaybānī*. Edited by ʿAbd al-Wahhāb ʿAbd al-Laṭīf. Cairo, 1994.

Nuʿaym b. Ḥammād. *Kitāb al-Fitan*. Cairo: Maktabat al-tawḥīd, 1412AH.

Qummī, al-. *Tafsīr*. Najaf: Maktabat al-Najaf, 1387AH.

Rosenthal, Franz, ed. *General introduction and from the Creation to the Flood*. The History of al-Ṭabarī, v. 1. Albany: State University of New York Press, 1989.

Šāfiʿī, Abū ʿAbd Allāh Muḥammad al-. *Kitāb al-Umm*. Beirut: Dār al-kutub al-ʿilmiyya, 1993.

Saḥnūn, Abū ʾl-Saʿīd ʿAbd al-Salām. *Al-Mudawwana al-kubrā*. Beirut: Dār iḥyāʾ al-turāṯ al-ʿarabī, n.d.

Saʿīd b. Mansūr. *Sunan*. Hyderabad: al-Dār al-salafiyya, 1982.

Šaybānī, Muḥammad b. al-Ḥasan al-. *Al-Ḥujja ʿalā ahl al-Madīna*. Beirut: ʿĀlam al-kutub, 1403AH.

Šaybānī, Muḥammad b. al-Ḥasan al-. *Al-Jāmiʿ al-ṣaġīr*. Beirut: ʿĀlam al-kutub, 1406.

Šaybānī, Muḥammad b. al-Ḥasan al-. *Šarḥ al-Siyar al-kabīr*. Beirut: Dār al-muttaḥida li'l-našr, 1975.

Shah, Mustafa. "Al-Ṭabarī and the Dynamics of *tafsīr*: Theological Dimensions of a Legacy." *Journal of Qur'anic Studies* 15, no. 2 (June 2013): 83–139.

Ṭabarānī, Abū ʾl-Qāsim al-. *Al-Muʿjam al-kabīr*. Cairo: Maktabat Ibn Taymiyya, 1415/1994.

Ṭabarī, Abū Jaʿfar Muḥammad b. Jarīr b. Yazīd al-. *Jāmiʿ al-bayān ʿan tafsīr āy al-Qurʾān*. Beirut: Mu'assasat al-Risala, 2000.

Ṭabarī, Abū Jaʿfar Muḥammad b. Jarīr b. Yazīd al-. *Kitāb Iḫtilāf al-fuqahāʾ*. Beirut: Dār al-kutub al-ʿilmiyya, 2002.

Ṭabarī, Abū Jaʿfar Muḥammad b. Jarīr b. Yazīd al-. *Tahḏīb al-āṯār*. Cairo: Maṭbaʿat al-Madanī, n.d.

Tirmiḏī, Abū ʿĪsā Muḥammad al-. *Al-Jāmiʿ al-kabīr*. Beirut: Dār al-ġarb al-islāmī, 1998.

Tottoli, Roberto. "G. H. A. Juynboll and the Meaningfulness of *ḥadīth* and *ḥadīth*-Related Technical Terminology: The Term *khabar* in Western and Early Muslim Literature." Conference in memory of Gautier H. A. Juynboll (1935–2010), LUCIS, Leiden University, 2011.

Tottoli, Roberto. "Origin and Use of the Term *isrāʾīliyyāt* in Muslim Literature." *Arabica* 46 (1999): 193–210.

Wāqidī, Muḥammad b. ʿUmar al-. *Kitāb al-Maġāzī*. Edited by M. Jones. London: Oxford University Press, 1966.

Wāqidī, Muḥammad b. ʿUmar al-. *Kitāb al-Ridda*. Beirut: Dār al-ġarb al-islāmī, 1990.

Wāqidī, Muḥammad b. ʿUmar al-. *The Life of Muḥammad: Al-Wāqidī's Kitāb Al-Maghāzī*. Edited by Rizwi Faizer. Translated by Rizwi Faizer, Amal Ismail, and Abdulkader Tayob. Routledge Studies in Classical Islam. Abingdon, Oxon: Routledge, 2011.

Yaʿqūbī, Abū ʾl-ʿAbbās Aḥmad al-. *Taʾrīḫ*. Beirut: Dār Ṣādir, 2000.

CHAPTER 7

The Qur'anic Foundations of the *dār al-islām* / *dār al-ḥarb* Dichotomy

An Unusual Hypothesis

Raoul Villano

> Oltretutto, è logico in sé che si dia, nelle due espressioni, un preciso parallelismo: per cui, se *islām* indica un atteggiamento (di quiescenza positiva) nei confronti di Dio, è ovvio che *ḥarb* indichi anch'esso un atteggiamento (nel caso negativo, di ribellione) dell'uomo nei confronti del medesimo Dio. E dal momento che *ḥarb* si rifà a radice attestata nella precisa accezione tecnica (coranica) di "rifiuto di Dio", non si vede perché debba esser nel caso prescelta la sua accezione *non tecnica* di "menar le mani", con un soggetto e un oggetto dell'azione evocata non omogenei a quelli dell'azione cui allude *Dār al-islām*[1]

∴

1 Preamble

It is a generally recognized fact that the *dār al islām* / *dār al-ḥarb* dichotomy does not originate in the Qur'an. As a matter of fact the dichotomy itself is still totally absent from the Qur'anic lexicon, while it is possible to find it in the Hadith—actually, only in the titles of the books[2]—like, by way of example, in the second *bāb* of the *kitāb al-wakāla* (The Book of Representation) in

1 Gianroberto Scarcia, "*Islām* e *Ḥarb*, *ʿArab* e *ʿAjam*: nota a due celeberrime dicotomie islamiche," in *Azhàr: studi arabo-islamici in memoria di Umberto Rizzitano* (1913–1980), ed. Antonino Pellitteri and Giovanni Montaina, Annali della Facoltà di lettere e filosofia dell'Università di Palermo. Studi e ricerche 23 (Palermo: Facoltà di lettere e filosofia dell'Università di Palermo, 1995), 208.

2 For a survey of Buḫārī's text, see Giovanna Calasso, "Alla ricerca di *dār al-islām*. Una ricognizione nei testi di giuristi e tradizionisti, lessicografi, geografi e viaggiatori," *Rivista degli Studi Orientali* 83 (2010): 279–281.

 | DOI 10.1163/9789004331037_009

Buḫārī's *al-Jāmiʿ al-ṣaḥīḥ*: *Iḏa wakkala al-muslim ḥarbiyyan fī dār al-ḥarb aw fī dār al-Islām jāza* (If a Muslim deputizes a non-Muslim either in the *dār al-ḥarb* or in the *dār al-islām*).[3]

Even from a conceptual point of view, indeed, the *dār al-islām* / *dār al-ḥarb* dichotomy is generally traced back to the Hadith and to the biographical material contained in the *sīra*/*maġāzī* literature, as can be seen in the *dār al-ḥarb* entry of the *Encyclopaedia of Islam*, which clearly states that "the Qur'an does not as yet divide the world into territories where peace and the faith of Islam reign (*dār al-islām*) and territories under perpetual threat of a missionary war (*dār al-ḥarb*)"[4] and traces this idea back to the prophet who invited Caesar and Chosroes (and the Jews) to be converted, citing Buḫārī's *Kitāb al-Jihād* and the *Kitāb al-Maġāzī*.[5] By doing so, on the one hand, the interpretation according to which the expression *dār al-ḥarb* has to be understood as "enemy territory object of a missionary war"[6] is explicitly taken for granted; on the other, since in this alleged vision of the world the *dār al-islām* is obviously understood as the "territory of peace", the debatable idea according to which some kind of analogy should be assumed between *islām* and *salām* is implicitly fed.

To be clear, this article will not address the way in which the *dār al-islām* / *dār al-ḥarb* dichotomy is actually treated in classical juridical texts.[7] It merely aims to propose a rather unusual hypothesis on the conceptual genesis of the dichotomy itself, namely that the conceptual framework that underlies the *dār al-islām* / *dār al-ḥarb* dichotomous opposition is basically Qur'anic and should be traced back precisely to the Qur'anic treatment of the notion of *hijra*.[8]

3 Muḥammad b. Ismāʿīl al-Buḫārī, *al-Jāmiʿ al-ṣaḥīḥ*, ed. Muḥibb al-Dīn al-Ḫaṭīb and Muḥammad Fu'ād ʿAbd al-Bāqī (Cairo: Al-Maṭbaʿa al-salafiyya, 1400AH), 2: 145 (XL, 2); cf. Calasso, "Alla ricerca di *dār al-islām*," 281.

4 Armand Abel, "Dār al-ḥarb," *Encyclopaedia of Islam, Vol. II, C–G* (Leiden: Brill, 1965); cf. also Hamid Algar, "Dār al-ḥarb," *Encyclopaedia Iranica. Vol. 6: Coffeehouse–Dārā* (New York, NY: Bibliotheca Persica Press, 2002), 668, who traces the idea of *dār al-ḥarb* back to the Hadith referring to Mecca and clearly states that the technical legal meaning is a later development of Hanafi jurisprudence.

5 Abel, "Dār al-ḥarb."

6 For a different interpretation of the semantic value of *ḥarb* in this context, see Scarcia, "*Islām* e *ḥarb*," 208.

7 A survey and a critical reflection is in Calasso, "Alla ricerca di *dār al-islām*."

8 The very fact that *hijra* could be the conceptual source of the *dār al-islām* / *dār al-ḥarb* binary opposition has already been pointed out (see, e.g., ibid., 276–279). What is new in our hypothesis is the idea that it could have been precisely in the Qur'anic *milieu* that *hijra* itself assumed those special characteristics that would make it the starting point for all later developments.

Moreover, in this framework, it will become clearer how the original meaning of the expression *dār al-ḥarb* is by no means "enemy territory object of missionary war," but rather the "land of those who wage war against God."[9]

Now, one of the most striking aspects we encounter when studying early Islam is the fact that, while in the first two centuries sources in almost every field do not yet appear structured and codified, during the third/ninth century everything becomes formalized, organized, perfectly structured and codified. Roughly the same applies also to Qur'anic exegesis: while for the first two or three centuries we can find only some rather fragmentary (if not contradictory) sources[10] between the end of the third and the beginning of the fourth centuries, suddenly, exegetical traditions appear fully stabilized and even perfectly traced back to their mythical and probably utopic genesis.[11] This work of rearrangement and revision of exegetical traditions will continue, of course, even much later, during the fourth, fifth and sixth centuries AH, but the late third century really gives an impressive feeling of discontinuity between previous and later exegetical works.[12]

Also the *dār al-islām* / *dār al-ḥarb* dichotomy never occurs in commentaries of the second and early third centuries AH; then, suddenly, at the end of the third century, and particularly in Ṭabarī's *Jāmiʿ al-bayān ʿan taʾwīl āy al-Qurʾān*, the dichotomous formula *dār al islām* / *dār al-ḥarb* [*al-kufr*] appears fully operative and is also traced back, as we shall see, to several mythical ancestors of Qur'anic exegesis. It is quite clear, at least in this case, that the lexical formalization took place elsewhere and was then superimposed, more or less consistently, over autonomous, and probably slightly different, traditions.

The question of the greater or lesser authenticity of the traditions reported in the great exegetical collections of the late third and early fourth centuries compared to the traditions of *tafsīr* manuscripts allegedly dating to the

9 Cf. Scarcia, "*Islām* e *ḥarb*," 208.

10 On the fragmentary nature of the first two centuries of Qur'anic exegesis, see, e.g., Claude Gilliot, "Les débuts de l'exégèse coranique," *Revue du Monde Musulman et de la Méditerranée* 58, no. 1: Les premières écritures islamiques (1990): 82–100.

11 For an example, see Claude Gilliot, "Portrait 'Mythique' d'Ibn 'Abbās," *Arabica* 32, no. 2 (1985): 127–84.

12 See, e.g., Claude Gilliot, *Exégèse, langue, et théologie en Islam: l'exégèse coranique de Tabari (m. 311/923)*, Etudes musulmanes 32 (Paris: Libr. J. Vrin, 1990); and Norman Calder, "*Tafsīr* from Ṭabarī to Ibn Kathīr: Problems in the Description of a Genre, Illustrated with Reference to the Story of Abraham," in *Approaches to the Qur'ān*, ed. Gerald R. Hawting and Abdul-Kader A. Shareef (London: Routledge, 1993), 101–40; a slightly different view in Walid Saleh, *The Formation of the Classical* Tafsīr *Tradition. The Qur'ān Commentary of al-Thaʿlabī (d. 427/1035)*, Brill (Leiden, 2004).

second and early third centuries AH, or even of the Qur'an itself as a historical source, has been discussed at length and cannot certainly be addressed in a few words.[13] It is a fact that has long puzzled scholars who, in some cases, even went so far as to suggest that the whole history of the first two centuries of Islam could be only a later invention artificially reconstructed to fit the needs of the groups who held power precisely during the third century.[14] It is interesting in this connection to remember also the provocative point of view of John Burton who, right on the basis of the spurious character of all traditions concerning the collection of the Qur'an, paradoxically ends up claiming that the only reliable historical source that we have in our hands today is the Qur'an itself.[15] There is a middle ground: while giving some degree of confidence to early exegetical tradition, it is possible to investigate the history and evolution of a given concept during the first centuries of Islam through a critical, but not ideologically biased, use of sources.

2 The *dār al-islām* / *dār al-ḥarb* Dichotomy and the Qur'an

As already said, the *dār al-islām* / *dār al-ḥarb* dichotomy is never found in the Qur'an; indeed, on closer inspection, it can be noted that even the word *dār*/*diyār* (or *dūr*) can never be found with the technical meaning of "territory" which is typical of the later usage of the dichotomy in the classical literature on the subject.

The word *dār*/*diyār* (or *dūr*) is used in the Qur'an in three different meanings. The first is its primary meaning, namely "home", "house", to say "an enclosed space, surrounded by walls, buildings or nomadic tents, placed more or less in a circle"[16]. This first basic meaning is used very extensively throughout the Qur'an, both in its singular (*dār*) form, as, by way of example, in the case of *sūrat Hūd* (Q 11:65): *fa-qāla tamattaʿū fī dārikum ṯalāṯata ayyāmin* (so he said: "continue to live in your homes for another three days")[17], as in its plural (*diyār*) form, like, again by way of example, in the case of *sūrat al-ḥajj*

---

13 A good survey is in Herbert Berg, *The Development of Exegesis in Early Islam: The Authenticity of Muslim Literature from the Formative Period*, Curzon (Richmond, 2000); cf. also Harald Motzki, "The Collection of the Qur'ān. A Reconsideration of Western Views in Light of Recent Methodological Developments," *Der Islam* 78 (2001): 1–34.

14 See, as paradigmatic of this attitude, John Wansbrough, *Quranic Studies: Sources and Methods of Scriptural Interpretation* (Oxford, United Kingdom, 1977).

15 John Burton, *The Collection of the Qur'ān* (Cambridge, 1977), 239–240.

16 Georges Marçais, "Dār," *Encyclopaedia of Islam, Vol. II, C–G* (Leiden: Brill, 1965), 113.

17 The English translations of the Qur'an are taken from Muhammad Abdel Haleem, *The Qur'an. A New Translation* (Oxford: Oxford University Press, 2004). See also Q 7:78; 7:91;

(Q 22:40): *allaḏīna uḫriǧū min diyārihim bi-ġayri ḥaqqin* (those who have been driven unjustly from their homes)[18].

The second meaning of *dār/diyār* (or *dūr*) in the Qur'an is a kind of extended meaning in which the singular form *dār* stands for Medina. It is possible to find this specific meaning only in a single case, which is *sūrat al-ḥašr* (Q 59:9): *wa'llaḏīna tabawwa'ū 'l-dāra wa'l-īmāna min qablihim* (Those who were already firmly established in their homes [in Medina, here: *al-dār*], and firmly rooted in faith). This meaning is found only once in the whole Qur'an, but it is quite relevant to our discussion since the word *dār* is used for the first time with the meaning of Medina and is already made a symbol of faith.

The third and last meaning of *dār* in the Qur'an is a kind of even more widely extended meaning: the concepts of totality, in the Qur'an, will inevitably end up including the Hereafter, and so the reference in these cases is always to the Abode of the Hereafter, usually called *al-dār al-āḫira* as in *sūrat al-anʿām* (Q 6:32): *wa-la'l-dāru 'l-āḫiratu ḫayrun li'llaḏīna yattaqūna* (the Home in the Hereafter is best for those who are aware of God)[19], but also merely *dār*, as in *sūrat ṣād* (Q 38:46: *innā aḫlaṣnāhum bi-ḫāliṣatin ḏikrā 'l-dāri* (We caused them to be devoted to Us through their sincere remembrance of the Final Home), or again the lasting home (*dār al-qarār*), as in *sūrat ġāfir* (Q 40:39): [...] *wa inna 'l-āḫirata hiya dāru 'l-qarāri* (it is the Hereafter that is the lasting home).

Still within this third meaning, in the Qur'an the *dār al-salām* is the Abode of Peace in the Gardens of Heaven, as in *sūrat al-anʿām* (Q 6:127): *lahum dāru 'l-salāmi ʿinda rabbihim* (They shall have the Home of Peace with their Lord), or in *sūrat yūnus* (Q 10:25): *wa-'llāhu yadʿū ilā dāri 'l-salāmi* (And Allah summoneth to the Abode of Peace). Sometimes the Gardens of Heaven are called the happy homecoming, or the reward of the home (*ʿāqibat / ʿuqbā al-dār*), like in *sūrat al-anʿām* (Q 6:135): *fa-sawfa taʿlamūna man takūnu lahu ʿāqibatu 'l-dāri* (you will come to realize who will have a happy homecoming in the Hereafter),[20] or in *sūrat al-raʿd* (Q 13:22): *ulā'ika lahum ʿuqbā 'l-dāri* (These will have the reward of the [true] home).[21] At other times the Gardens are said to be the Home of the righteous, as in *sūrat al-naḥl* (Q 16:30): *wa-la-dāru 'l-āḫiratu ḫayrun wa-la-niʿma dāru 'l-muttaqīna* (and the Home of the Hereafter is even

---

13:31; 28:81; 29:37; cf. Muḥammad Fu'ād ʿAbd al-Bāqī, *al-Muʿjam al-mufahras li-alfāẓ al-Qur'ān al-karīm* (Cairo, 1945), 264–65.

18 See also Q 2:84; 2:85; 2:243; 2:246; 3:195; 4:22; 8:47; 11:67; 11:94; 17:5; 33:27; 59:2; 59:8; 60:8; 60:9.

19 See also Q. 2:94; 7:169; 12:109; 16:30; 28:77; 28: 83; 29:64; 33:29.

20 See also Q 28:37.

21 See also Q 13:24; 13:42.

better. And excellent indeed is the Home of the righteous), or, finally, the everlasting Home, as in *sūrat fāṭir* (Q 35:35): *allaḏī aḥalla-nā dāra 'l-muqāmati min faḍlihi* (He has, in His bounty, settled us in the everlasting Home).

Conversely, the abode of evil-doers (*dār al-fāsiqīn*) or the abode of ruin (*dār al-bawār*) will consistently be Hell, as in *sūrat al-aʿrāf* (Q 7:145) *sa-ūrīkum dāra 'l-fāsiqīna* (I will show you the abode of evil-doers) or in *sūrat Ibrāhīm* (Q 14:28): *wa-aḥallū qawmahum dāra 'l-bawāri* (and made their people end up in the home of ruin). Another name for Hell is the dreadful home (*sūʾ al-dār*), as in *sūrat al-raʿd* (Q 13:25) *wa-lahum sūʾu 'l-dāri* (theirs is the dreadful home),[22] or, finally, even in the case of evil-doers Hell can surely be called the lasting home (*dār al-ḫuld*), as in *sūrat fuṣṣilat* (Q 41:28): *ḏālika jazāʾu aʿdāʾi 'llāhi 'l-nāru lahum fīhā dāru 'l-ḫuldi* (that is the reward of the enemies of God—the Fire will be their lasting home).

Therefore, summarizing, it can be said that in the Qur'an it is possible to find three main meanings for the word *dār / diyār*: (1) the basic meaning: home, house, a space surrounded by walls, buildings or nomadic tents; (2) the extended meaning: the new home or the house of believers, Medina; (3) the even more widely extended meaning: the everlasting home, the Abode of the Hereafter. The technical meaning of "territory" which will later be typical of classical texts on this subject is still totally absent from the Qur'anic lexicon. At first glance, everything seems to confirm the idea that the lexical and conceptual genesis of the *dār al-islām* / *dār al-ḥarb* dichotomy should be sought elsewhere.

As for the oppositional pair *islām* / *ḥarb*, it is true that, if it is legitimate to understand *islām* as the set of those who surrender to the will of God, it is not clear why, conversely, one cannot understand *ḥarb* as the set of those who wage war against the same God,[23] consistently with what happens, by way of example, in the case of the *dār al-islām* / *dār al-kufr* dichotomy. In all cases, and despite the presence of some Qur'anic occurrence of the word *ḥarb* in an objectively warlike meaning, as in the case of *sūrat al-anfāl* (Q 8:57): *fa-immā taṯqafannahum fī 'l-ḥarbi fa-šarrid bihim man ḫalfahum laʿallahum yaḏḏakkarūna* (If you meet them in a battle, make a fearsome example of them to those who come after them, so that they may take heed) it is fair to point out right away even the presence of other Qur'anic occurrences in which the *muḥārib* may well be the one who wages war against God, given the unavoidable consequences for him, as in the case of *sūrat al-māʾida* (Q 5:33): *inna-mā jazāʾa 'llaḏīna yuḥāribūna 'llāha wa-rasūlahu wa-yasʿawna fī 'l-arḍi fasādan*

22 See also Q 40:52.

23 Cf. Scarcia, "*Islām* e *ḥarb*," 208.

an yuqattalū aw yuṣallabū aw tuqaṭṭaʿa aydīhim wa-arjuluhum min ḫilāfin aw yunfaʿū min al-arḍi (Those who wage war against God and His Messenger and strive to spread corruption in the land should be punished by death, crucifixion, the amputation of an alternate hand and foot, or banishment from the land).

3 The *dār al-islām* / *dār al-ḥarb* Dichotomy and the Commentaries: A Quantitative Approach

Be that as it may, the *dār al-islām* / *dār al-ḥarb* dichotomy is undoubtedly missing in the lexical repertoire of the Qur'an. Consistently with this absence on the lexical level, and not surprisingly at all, early *tafsīr* works also never use the *dār al-islām* / *dār al-ḥarb* dichotomy to explain a text which itself never uses such expressions. Actually, the commentaries of the second and early third centuries never use even the word *dār* in the later technical meaning of "territory"; nevertheless, there are several logical synonyms, or perhaps equivalent expressions, that can be considered relevant for the purposes of this research.

First of all, the expression *dār al-īmān* (the abode of faith) can be considered equivalent to *dār al-islām*, while the two expressions *dār al-kufr* (the abode of unbelief) and *dār al-širk* (the abode of idolatry) can be considered equivalent to *dār al-ḥarb*. Moreover, as for the word *dār* itself, the two words *arḍ* (land) and *ahl* (people) can loosely be considered synonyms, if not properly equivalent.

There are, in fact, several reasons why these expressions could be regarded as equivalent or, at least, relevant to our discussion; however, for the purposes of this research at least two reasons are especially noteworthy: first, Ṭabarī's treatment of such expressions shows clearly that he considered them to be more or less interchangeable terms; second, as we shall see, the verses where expressions such as *arḍ al-islām* / *arḍ al-ḥarb* or *ahl al-islām* / *ahl al-ḥarb* appear in the commentaries of the second and early third centuries are to a large extent the same verses where the expressions *dār al-islām* / *dār al-ḥarb* [*al-kufr*] will appear in the commentaries of the late third and early fourth centuries, and notably in Ṭabarī's *Jāmiʿ al-bayān*.

Now, this fact already suggests that the commentaries of the second/eighth and early third/ninth centuries never use the *dār al-islām* / *dār al-ḥarb* dichotomy because in those centuries the same dichotomy—while perhaps already developed in other kinds of texts—was still not established enough, at a lexical and conceptual level, to be adopted by Qur'anic exegesis. Moreover, the path along which these expressions tend to emerge also suggests that, in their classical technical meanings, they must have originated in other fields and then, only later, been adopted by Qur'anic exegesis. Furthermore, in some specific cases, the presence or absence of such clearly datable expressions can be marginally useful also as a specific marker of the true antiquity of a given text, or at least of the concrete shape in which such text has been transmitted: this is the case of the *Tanwīr al-miqbās min Tafsīr Ibn ʿAbbās*[24] whose attribution and dating are still uncertain and have been widely discussed.[25] Now the very fact that in this text we find the earliest complete attestation of the *dār al-islām / dār al-ḥarb* (actually *dār al-kufr*) dichotomy in the field of Qur'anic exegesis already suggests that it was composed between the second half of the third/ninth century and the beginning of the fourth/tenth century, which is, by the way, the same dating already proposed, although with different arguments, by Andrew Rippin.[26]

Now, as may be seen even through a quick general overview, the difference between the number of occurrences in early *tafsīr* texts and in Ṭabarī's *Jāmiʿ al-bayān* is nothing short of impressive.

In the *Tafsīr* of Mujāhid b. Jabr al-Makkī (d. 102/720)[27] transmitted by Ādam b. Iyās (d. 220/835), through Warqā' b. ʿUmar (d. 160/776), on the authority of Mujāhid's disciple Ibn Abī Najīḥ (d. 131/749)[28] there are two occurrences of the expression *ahl al-širk*[29] and one single occurrence for the expressions *ahl al-islām*[30] and *ahl al-ḥarb*.[31]

In the *Tafsīr* of Muqātil b. Sulaymān (d. 150/767)[32] there are three occurrences of the expression *ahl al-kufr*,[33] two of *ahl al-širk*,[34] one of *ahl al-islām*,[35]

---

24 *Tanwīr al-miqbās min Tafsīr Ibn ʿAbbās* (s. l., s. d.).

25 Many, very different, attributions, ranging no less than from the first/seventh to the ninth/fifteenth centuries, have been proposed for this controversial text: ʿAbd Allāh Ibn ʿAbbās (d. ca. 68/687), Muḥammad b. al-Sā'ib al-Kalbī (d. 146/763), Abū Muḥammad ʿAbd Allāh b. Muḥammad b. Wahb al-Dīnawarī (d. 308/920), Abū 'l-Ṭāhir Muḥammad al-Fīrūzābādī (d. 817/1415). See Andrew Rippin, "Tafsīr Ibn ʿAbbās and Criteria for Dating Early Tafsīr Text," *Jerusalem Studies in Arabic and Islam* 19 (1994): 38–83.

26 Ibid., 47–50; cf. Gilliot, "Les débuts," 87–88.

27 Mujāhid b. Jabr al-Makkī, *Tafsīr*, ed. Muḥammad ʿAbd al-Salām Abū al-Nīl (Madīnat Naṣr, Egypt, 1410).

28 On the transmission of the *Tafsīr* of Mujāhid see Gilliot, "Les débuts," 88–89.

29 Mujāhid b. Jabr al-Makkī, *Tafsīr*, 320 (Q 6:23).

30 Ibid., 482 (Q 20:40).

31 Ibid., 536 (Q 29:46).

32 Muqātil b. Sulaymān, *Tafsīr*, ed. ʿAbd Allāh Maḥmūd Šiḥāta, 5 vols. (Beirut, 2002).

33 Ibid., 1:380 (Q 4:55); 2:245 (Q 10:81); 2:383 (Q 13:41).

34 Ibid., 2:117 (Q 8:44); 2:300 (Q 11:113).

35 Ibid., 2:129 (Q 9:71).

one of *ahl al-ḥarb*,[36] and one first occurrence of the dichotomic formula *ahl al-kufr / ahl al-īmān*.[37]

In the *Tafsīr* of Sufyān al-Ṯawrī (d. 161/778)[38] none of these expressions is attested to at all.

In the *Tafsīr al-Qur'ān* of ʿAbd al-Razzāq al-Ṣanʿānī (d. 211/827),[39] the pupil and transmitter of the exegesis of Maʿmar b. Rāšid (d. 154/770), there are two occurrences of *ahl al-islām*,[40] two of *ahl al-širk*,[41] one of *arḍ al–širk*,[42] and one of *dār al-islām*—still used in the meaning of Heaven,[43] consistently with the Qur'anic usage.

In the *Tafsīr* of Furāt b. Furāt al-Kūfī (d. 309/922)[44] there are only two occurrences of the expression *ahl al-širk*.[45]

In the *Tanwīr al-miqbās min Tafsīr Ibn ʿAbbās*,[46] whose attribution and dating, as already stated, are still very uncertain, but which should probably be ascribed to ʿAbd Allāh b. Muḥammad b. Wahb al-Dīnawarī (d. 308/920) and which transmits exegetical materials attributed by their *isnād*s to Ibn ʿAbbās (d. ca. 68/687), but probably dating to the generation prior to that of Dīnawarī (i.e. the late third/ninth century),[47] there is one first occurrence of *dār al-ḥarb*,[48] then one single occurrence for the expression *ahl al-kufr*,[49] and, finally, also what could well be the earliest complete dichotomous occurrence of the expression *dār al-kufr / dār al-islām* in the alleged history of Qur'anic exegesis.[50]

Finally, in the *Jāmiʿ al-bayān ʿan ta'wīl āy al-Qur'ān* of Abū Jaʿfar Muḥammad b. Jarīr al-Ṭabarī (d. 310/923)[51] it is possible to find a very large number of occurrences of all the expressions searched. Two things should be immediately remarked upon: the widespread use of *dār* instead of *ahl* or *arḍ*, and the

36 Ibid., 1:397 (Q 4:92).
37 Ibid., 1:318 (Q 3:179).
38 Abū ʿAbdallāh b. Saʿīd Sufyān al-Ṯawrī, *Tafsīr*, ed. Imtiyāz ʿAlī ʿAršī (Beirut, 1983).
39 ʿAbd al-Razzāq al-Ṣanʿānī, *Tafsīr al-Qur'ān*, 3 vols. (Riyadh, 1989).
40 Ibid., 1:161 (Q 4:42); 1:362 (Q 16:89).
41 Ibid., 1:137 (Q 3:154); 1:188 (Q 5:34).
42 Ibid., 1:172 (Q 4:107).
43 Ibid., 1:294 (Q 10:25).
44 Abū al-Qāsim Furāt b. Furāt al-Kūfī, *Tafsīr*, ed. Muḥammad al-Kāẓim (Beirut, 2011).
45 Ibid., 1:163 (Q 9:6); 2:528 (Q 76, 8).
46 *Tanwīr al-miqbās*.
47 Rippin, "Tafsīr Ibn ʿAbbās," 47–50; cf. Gilliot, "Les débuts," 87–88.
48 *Tanwīr al-miqbās*, 68 (Q 4:24).
49 Ibid., 205 (Q 13:5).
50 Ibid., 155 (Q 9:23).
51 Abū Jaʿfar Muḥammad b. Jarīr al-Ṭabarī, *Jāmiʿ al-bayān ʿan ta'wīl āy al-Qur'ān*, ed. ʿAbd Allāh b. ʿAbd al-Muḥsin al-Turkī, 24 vols. (Beirut, 1997).

definitive acquisition of the dichotomous formalization so that the two expressions now appear regularly paired.

The occurrences of the expressions searched in Ṭabarī—isolated or paired—are as follows: *dār al-ḥarb* (11),[52] *dār al-islām* (8),[53] *dār al-islām* / *dār al-ḥarb* [or vice versa] (5),[54] *dār al-kufr* / *dār al-islām* [or vice versa] (5),[55] *dār al–širk* / *dār al-islām* [or vice versa] (4),[56] *dār al–širk* (4),[57] *arḍ al–širk* / *dār al-islām* (3),[58] *ahl al-širk* (2);[59] *ahl al-islām* (2),[60] *arḍ al-ḥarb* (1),[61] *ahl al-īmān* / *ahl al–širk*, (1)[62] *dār al-ḥarb* / *bilād al-islām* (1),[63] *arḍ al–širk* / *arḍ al-islām wa-dār al-hijra* (1),[64] *dār al-islām* / *dār al–širk wa'l-ḥarb* (1),[65] *arḍ al–širk wa-ahluhā* / *arḍ al-islām wa-ahluhā* (1),[66] *dār al-islām* / *Makka* (1),[67] making a total of 51 occurrences overall.

Therefore, as these first results already show, towards the end of the third century, and notably in Ṭabarī's *Jāmiʿ al-bayān*, the number of occurrences of the expressions searched for is greatly increased; moreover the technical term *dār* tends gradually to replace earlier expressions such as *ahl* and *arḍ*. Furthermore the dichotomous formalization made by combining the two opposite concepts *islām* and *ḥarb*, whatever their real and original meaning might have been, appears definitely established: it is clear that the *dār al-islām* / *dār al-ḥarb* dichotomy has by now entered the lexicon of the commentators and is openly used to explain Qur'anic verses in which it does not appear at all. This is partly due to the ability of the commentators, notably

52 Ibid., 7:315 (Q 4:92) [2]; 8:393 (Q 5:34); 8:396 (Q 5:34); 8:397 (Q 5:34); 11:296 (Q 8:73); 11:299 (Q 8:73); 16:575 (Q 22:39); 21:306 (Q 48:25); 22:582 (Q 60:10); 23:543 (Q 76:8).

53 Ibid., 7:392 (Q 4:100); 8:384 (Q 5:33); 8:399 (Q 5:34); 11:383 (Q 9:23) [2]; 12:49 (Q 9:117); 12:154 (Q 10:25); 12:155 (Q 10:25).

54 Ibid., 7:317 (Q 4:92); 8:384 (Q 5:33); 8:400 (Q 5:34); 11:294 (Q 8:72); 11:637 (Q 9:100).

55 Ibid., 7:380 (Q 4:98); 8:398 (Q 5:34); 8:399 (Q 5:34); 11:293 (Q 8:72); 22:575 (Q 60:10).

56 Ibid., 7:290 (Q 4:89); 7:291 (Q 4:89); 11:384 (Q 9:24); 18:367 (Q 29:11).

57 Ibid., 7:304 (Q 4:91); 8:385 (Q 5:33); 11:299 (Q 8:74); 11:384 (Q 9:24).

58 Ibid., 7:380 (Q 4:98); 11:384 (Q 9:23); 20:179 (Q 39:10).

59 Ibid., 8:393 (Q 5:34) [2].

60 Ibid., 7:317 (Q 4:92); 8:393 (Q 5:34).

61 Ibid., 11:293 (Q 8:72).

62 Ibid., 11:299 (Q 8:74).

63 Ibid., 8:396 (Q 5:34).

64 Ibid., 7:392 (Q 4:100).

65 Ibid., 8:385 (Q 5:33).

66 Ibid., 7:391 (Q 4:100).

67 Ibid., 22:586 (Q 60:10) (quoted in this form being clearly Mecca the first meaning of *dār al-ḥarb*).

Ṭabarī, and partly, as we shall see, to the very fact that the conceptual framework in which the *dār al-islām* / *dār al-ḥarb* dichotomy originated is basically Qur'anic.

A last noteworthy thing about Ṭabarī's revision of early exegetical traditions is that, despite the fact that no commentaries of the second and early third centuries in any way mention the *dār al-islām* / *dār al-ḥarb* dichotomy, Ṭabarī curiously pretends to trace a large number of interpretative traditions in which the *dār al-islām* / *dār al-ḥarb* dichotomy is overtly used back to the authority of several companions (*ṣaḥāba*) and successors (*tābiʿūn*).[68] Among the authorities to whom Ṭabarī brings these traditions back we find, indeed, Muġīra [b. Šuʿba] (d. between 48/668 and 51/671), [Abd Allāh] Ibn ʿAbbās (d. 68/687), Ibrāhīm [al-Naḫāʿī] (d. 74/693), ʿUrwa b. al-Zubayr (d. ca. 93–94/711–713), ʿIkrima [al-Barbarī] (d. 105/723–4), [Ismāʿīl] al-Suddī (d. 127/745), al-Layṯ b. Saʿd (d. 175/791), and Mālik b. Anas (d. 179/796).

4 How the *dār al-islām* / *dār al-ḥarb* Dichotomy Entered the Commentaries: Some Cases in Point

1. The first occurrence that will be discussed here is a very early instance of the expression *ahl al-ḥarb*. It is reported in the *Tafsīr* of Mujāhid b. Jabr al-Makkī.[69] As already said, in these early commentaries we cannot find the complete *dār al-islām* / *dār al-ḥarb* dichotomy or even the single term *dār* associated with *islām* or *ḥarb*. In these early texts it is only possible to find collocations with such terms as *ahl* or *arḍ*; as we shall see, indeed, the technical term *dār* will later incorporate the meaning of both.

In this case Mujāhid is commenting on verse 46 of *sūrat al-ʿankabūt* (Q 29): "[Believers] argue only in the best way with People of the Book, except with those of them who act unjustly (*illā 'llaḏīna ẓalamū minhum*)."

After the opinion of Mujāhid himself, as it was transmitted by his disciple Ibn Abī Najīḥ, "they are those who have associated something to God and are not People of the Book anymore (*fa'ntaṣarū minhum*)"; the *Tafsīr* also mentions, on the authority of Ibn ʿAbbās's disciple Saʿīd b. Jubayr (d. 95/714), another interpretation according to which "except with those of them who act

68 About the backward growth of *isnāds* see Joseph Schacht, *The Origins of Muhammadan Jurisprudence* (Oxford: Clarendon Press, 1979), 163–175; on the relationship between Ṭabari's *isnāds* and early commentaries see Gilliot, "Les débuts," 88.

69 Mujāhid b. Jabr al-Makkī, *Tafsīr*.

unjustly" means, "they are the people of war (*hum ahl al-ḥarb*) and those with whom you have not made a pact (*man lā ʿahda lahu*), saying 'fight them with the sword (*jāhidūhum bi'l-sayf*)!'"[70]

It is quite clear that the way in which Mujāhid uses the expression *ahl al-ḥarb* might be interchanged with something like "they are the people from *dār al-ḥarb*," although this did not happen: probably because when the fixation of this exegetical tradition took place, the later technical meaning of *dār*, incorporating land and people into the single concept of territory, was still not established enough as to be taken by Qur'anic exegesis, otherwise the total absence of such a technical term from all early commentaries would be not so easy to explain.

Moreover, it is worth noting that Mujāhid already introduces the word *ḥarb* (and the *jihād bi'l-sayf*) in his commentary to a Qur'anic verse in which—as we have just seen—both war and jihad with the sword are totally absent. Furthermore, it is clear that, at least for Mujāhid, the meaning of *ḥarb* is, quite simply, the "war with the sword."

2. The second occurrence that is worth dwelling on here is in the *Tafsīr* of Muqātil b. Sulaymān. In his commentary to verse 179 of *sūrat āl-ʿImrān* (Q 3): "Nor was it God's aim to leave you as you were with no separation between the bad and good (*ḥattā yamīza al-ḫabīṯa min aṭ–ṭayyibi*)," Muqātil says: "in His knowledge, until He separates the people of the unbelief from the people of faith (*ḥattā yamīza ahl al-kufr min ahl al-īmān*)."[71]

This is the very first occurrence in which we find two of the expressions searched for in a dichotomous formulation. Actually, Muqātil says "people" (*ahl*), not "territories" (*dār*), but it is clear from this very early occurrence that the first, original, dichotomous opposition was between *īmān* and *kufr*, "faith" and "unbelief", "believers" (*mu'minūn*) and "unbelievers" (*kāfirūn*), "people who surrender to God" (*muslimūn*/*islām*) and "people who wage war against God" (*muḥāribūn*/*ḥarb*), not else.

3. Even the first dichotomous occurrence in Ṭabarī's *Jāmiʿ al-bayān*, indeed, opposes *dār al-širk* to *dār al-islām*. It is to be found in Ṭabarī's exegesis of verse 89 of *sūrat al-nisā'* (Q 4):

> They would dearly like you to reject faith, as they themselves have done, to be like them. So do not take them as allies until they migrate (*fa-lā tattaḫiḏū minhum awliyā'a ḥattā yuhājirū*) [to Medina] for God's cause. If they turn [on you], then seize and kill them wherever you encounter

70 Ibid., 536.

71 Muqātil b. Sulaymān, *Tafsīr*, 1: 318.

them (*fa-in tawallaw fa-ḫuḏūhum wa'qtulūhum ḥayṯu wajadtumūhum*). Take none of them as an ally or supporter.

Ṭabarī glosses:

> *fa-lā tattaḫiḏū minhum awliyā'a ḥattā yuhājirū* (So do not take them as allies until they migrate), it means "until they get out from *dār al-širk* (*ḥattā yaḫrujū min dār al-širk*), separating themselves from their own people, who are polytheists (*wa-yufāriqū ahlahā 'llaḏīna hum bi'llāhi mušrikūna*), [to enter] *dār al-islām* and [join] his people (*ilā dār al-islām wa-ahlihā*)."[72]

It is quite clear that for Ṭabarī the *dār al-islām / dār al-širk* dichotomy is, primarily, a kind of projection of the core concept of *hijra*: *dār al-širk* is Mecca and its people, whereas *dār al-islām* is Medina and the new umma.[73]

Then, shortly afterwards, commenting on the second part of the same verse *fa-in tawallaw fa-ḫuḏūhum ḥayṯu wajadtumūhum* (If they turn [on you], then seize and kill them wherever you encounter them), he adds:

> and if those hypocrites turn away from their acknowledgment of God and His Messenger and back out of their *hijra* from *dār al-širk* to *dār al-islām* (*wa-tawallaw 'an al-hijra min dār al-širk ilā dār al-islām*), and of their separation from unbelievers [to enter] Islam (*wa 'an mufāraqat ahl al-kufr ilā al-islām*), then "seize them," o Believers, "and kill them wherever you find them," means both in their lands and out of their lands (*min bilādihim wa ġayr bilādihim*).[74]

Here the original Qur'anic Mecca/Medina opposition is doubly extended: first of all the strictly territorial meaning of the Qur'anic obligation to emigrate (*ḥattā yuḥājirū*) is expanded by the wider meaning of *dār* including both land and people (*mufāraqat ahl al-kufr*); immediately afterwards, Ṭabarī calls upon the strong relationship between the spatial (*dār al-širk / dār al-islām*)

---

72 Ṭabarī, *Jāmi' al-bayān*, 7: 290.

73 And right for this same reason, other times, as in his commentary on v. 10 of *sūrat al-mumtaḥana* (Q. LX), Ṭabarī will overtly make a dichotomous opposition between *dār al-Islām* and Mecca (ibid., 22: 586).

74 Ibid., 7: 291; note that shortly afterwards Ṭabarī will add that these same interpretative opinions (*wa-bi-naḥwi 'llaḏī qulnā fī ta'wīl ḏālika*) were reported also on the authority of ['Abd Allāh] Ibn 'Abbās and [Ismā'īl] al-Suddī, see ibid., 7: 291–92.

dichotomy and the basic ethical or moral dichotomy (*kufr/islām*), by so doing definitely connecting the territorial meaning of *dār* with its symbolic usage which denotes the faith. As regards the legitimacy of waging war on the hypocrites, finally, Ṭabarī claims that the Qur'an states that it is necessary to fight them wherever they are, which means both in their lands and out of their lands, further discarding, by doing so, the idea according to which, in an alleged Islamic worldview, there would be a basic division between territories where peace reigns (*dār al-islām*) and territories under the perpetual threat of a missionary war (*dār al-ḥarb*).

4. The next occurrence of the *dār al-islām / dār al-ḥarb* dichotomy in Ṭabarī's *Jāmiʿ al-bayān* is to be found in his exegesis of verse 92 of the same *sūrat al-nisāʾ* (Q 4), which says:

> Never should a believer kill another believer, except by mistake. If anyone kills a believer by mistake he must free one Muslim slave and pay compensation to the victim's relatives, unless they charitably forgo it; if [the victim] belonged to a people at war with you but is a believer, then the compensation is only to free a believing slave (*fa-in kāna min qawmin ʿaduwwin lakum wa-huwa muʾminun fa-taḥrīru raqabatin muʾminatin*); if he belonged to a people with whom you have a treaty, then compensation should be handed over to his relatives, and a believing slave set free. Anyone who lacks the means to do this must fast for two consecutive months by way of repentance to God: God is all knowing, all wise.

In this case, it is interesting to compare the commentary of Muqātil with that of Ṭabarī. The exegesis of Muqātil is very straightforward:

> "And if" this victim "belongs to an enemy people," it means, is from the people of war (*min ahl al-ḥarb*) "and he," the victim, "is a believer, then the compensation is only to free a believing slave:" it was revealed—explains Muqātil—for the case of Mardās b. ʿUmar al-Qaysī, and there was no blood money for him.[75]

Here, also, it would clearly be possible to exchange Muqātil's expression *min ahl al–ḥarb* for something like *min dār al-ḥarb*, and, in fact, this is exactly what Ṭabarī will do, at least in some of the traditions reported.

Ṭabarī, as usual, starts his exegesis stating that there is no agreement between the interpreters on the meaning of this verse, but what is noteworthy

75 Muqātil b. Sulaymān, *Tafsīr*, 1: 397.

is that he makes extensive use of the *dār al-islām* / *dār al-ḥarb* dichotomy in the explanation of this verse, quoting a number of different authorities, but avoiding to mention solely and exclusively Muqātil, possibly due to the fact that his name was notoriously associated with sectarian movements and deviant theological positions, such as extreme anthropomorphism.[76]

Ṭabarī's exegesis goes on like this:

> "if [the victim] belonged to a people at war with you but is a believer, then the compensation is only to free a believing slave" (*fa-in kāna min qawmin ʿaduwwin lakum wa-huwa muʾminun fa-taḥrīru raqabatin muʾminatin*) there is no agreement between the interpreters on the meaning of that, some of them would say: "if the victim belongs to a people who is enemy to you, but he is a believer" (*min qawmin hum ʿaduwwin lakum wa-huwa muʾminun*), that is "he did not migrate with you" (*ay bayna aẓhurikum lam yuhājir*), and "he was killed by a Muslim" (*fa-qatalahu Muslim*) there is no blood money for him, but the compensation is only to free a believing slave.[77]

Then he starts to mention the chains of transmitters of the interpretative traditions in agreement with this opinion (*ḏikr man qāla ḏālika*):

> ʿIkrima [al-Barbarī] and Muġīra [b. Šuʿba], on the authority of Ibrāhīm [al-Naḫāʿī] would have said: *fa-in kāna min qawmin ʿaduwwin la-kum wa-huwa muʾminun*, "he" is the man who converts to Islam in *dār al-ḥarb* (*huwa al-rajul yuslimu fī dār al-ḥarb*), then is killed (*fa-yuqtalu*): there is no blood price for him, and for him there is [only] a reparative alms (*kaffāra*).[78] The opinion of [Ismāʿīl] al-Suddī was instead: *fa-in kāna min qawmin ʿaduwwin lakum wa-huwa muʾminun* in the *dār al-ḥarb* (*fī dār al-ḥarb* [in another manuscript: *al–kufr*]),[79] he says: the compensation is only to free a believing slave, and there is no blood price for him).[80]

Finally Ṭabarī also reports the opinion of [ʿAbd Allāh] b. ʿAbbās who said: *fa-in kāna min qawmin ʿaduwwin lakum wa-huwa muʿminun* "and if he was between

76 Cf. Claude Gilliot, "Muqātil, Grand Exégète, Traditionniste, et Théologien Maudit," *Journal Asiatique* 279 (1991): 39–92.

77 Ṭabarī, *Jāmiʿ al-bayān*, 7: 314.

78 Ibid., 7: 315.

79 See ibid. (footnote 7).

80 Ibid.

an enemy people, but he was a believer" (*fa-in kāna fī ahl al-ḥarb wa-huwa mu'min*) and he has been killed by mistake, it is the duty of the killer to atone by freeing a believing slave, or by fasting for two consecutive months. No blood money is expected for that.[81]

5. Generally speaking, it is clear that Ṭabarī prefers the new term *dār* which seems to encapsulate the meaning of both earlier equivalents *ahl* and *arḍ*. Yet sometimes it happens that Ṭabarī still uses the expressions *ahl/arḍ al-širk / ahl/arḍ al-Islām*, but combines them, as in the case of his comment to v. 100 of *sūrat an- nisā'* (Q 4):

> "and if anyone leaves home as a migrant towards God [and His Messenger]" (*wa-man yuhājir fī sabīli 'llāhi*) and is then overtaken by death, his reward from God is sure. "God is most forgiving" and most merciful, about which Ṭabarī glosses: *wa-man yuhājir fī sabīli 'llāhi* means "and who separates himself from the land of *širk* and its people," (*wa-man yufāriqu arḍ al-širk wa-ahlahā*) "running away from it and from them to the land of Islam and its people, the believers, because of his religion" (*harban bi-dīnihi minhā wa-minhum ilā arḍ al-Islām wa-ahlihā al-mu'minīna*).[82]

6. In any case, the close and direct connection between the emergence of the *dār al-islām / dār al-ḥarb* dichotomy and the *hijra* is in Ṭabarī very clear. This fact becomes very explicit in his commentary to the following verse of *sūrat al-anfāl* (Q 8:72):

> Those who believed and emigrated [to Medina] and struggled for God's cause with their possessions and persons, and those who gave refuge and help, are all allies of one another. As for those who believed but did not emigrate, you are not responsible for their protection until they have done so (*wa'llaḏīna āmanū wa-lam yuhājirū mā lakum min walāyatihim min šay'in ḥattā yuhājirū*). But if they seek help from you against persecution, it is your duty to assist them, except against people with whom you have a treaty: God sees all that you do.

Ṭabarī's opinion on the interpretation of this verse is as follows:

> *wa-'llaḏīna āmanū wa-lam yuhājirū mā lakum min walāyatihim min šay'in ḥattā yuhājirū* means: "and those who believe" in God and His Messenger,

81 Ibid., 7: 317.

82 Ibid., 7: 391.

> "and did not migrate" from their people of unbelievers (*qawmahum al-kuffār*) and did not separate themselves from the *dār al-kufr* to reach the *dār al-islām* (*wa-lam yufāriqū dār al-kufr ilā dār al-Islām*). "You are not," o believers in God and His Messenger, who migrated from their people of polytheists and the land of war (*al-muhājirūna qawma-hum al-mušrikīna wa-arḍ al-ḥarb*), "responsible for their protection until they have done so" means until they migrate from their people and from their homes [moving] from *dār al-ḥarb* to *dār al-islām* (*ḥattā yuhājirū qawma-hum wa-dūrahum min dār al-ḥarb ilā dār al-islām*).[83]

He then concludes his explanation by reporting the opinion of some interpreters according to whom the meaning of this verse is that certainly unbelievers help each other and certainly cannot be a [true] believer the one who is resident in the *dār al-ḥarb* and did not migrate (*inna al-kuffāra baʿḍu-hum anṣāru baʿḍin wa innahu lā yakūnu muʾminan man kāna muqīman bi-dār al-ḥarb wa-lam yuhājir*),[84] therefore making the *hijra* a clear symbol of anybody's personal faith and loyalty to Muhammad and to the Muslim community.

7. The last occurrence that will be discussed here is also likely to be the earliest complete attestation of the *dār al-islām / dār al-ḥarb* (actually *al-kufr*) dichotomy in the history of Qur'anic exegesis. It is to be found in the controversial *Tanwīr al-miqbās min Tafsīr Ibn ʿAbbās*, a very popular commentary whose suggested attributions to Ibn ʿAbbās (d. 68/687) or Fīrūzābādī (d. 817/1415) have been demonstrated to be certainly erroneous.[85] As it has been shown by Andrew Rippin, in reality it is very likely that the work should be ascribed to ʿAbd Allāh b. Muḥammad b. Wahb al-Dīnawarī (d. 308/920), or, as its multiple transmission could suggest, dated generally at the time of itinerant preachers of the generation before Dīnawarī, that is around the second half of the third/ninth century.[86]

The exegesis of the *Tanwīr al-miqbās* on verse 23 of *sūrat al-tawba* (Q 9):

> Believers, do not take your fathers and brothers as allies if they prefer disbelief to faith: those of you who do so are doing wrong (*yā ayyuhā 'llaḏīna āmanū lā tattaḫiḏū ābāʾakum wa-iḫwānakum awliyāʾa in istaḥabbū 'l-kufra ʿalā 'l-īmāni wa-man yatawallahum minkum fa-ulāʾika humu 'l-ẓālimūna*),

83 Ibid., 11: 293–94.

84 Ibid., 11: 296.

85 *Tanwīr al-miqbās*; cf. Rippin, "Tafsīr Ibn ʿAbbās."

86 Rippin, "Tafsīr Ibn ʿAbbās," 49–50; cf. Gilliot, "Les débuts," 87–88.

goes this way:

> Believers, do not take your fathers and brothers who are in Mecca among the unbelievers (*allaḏīna bi-Makka min al-kuffār*) as allies in the religion if they prefer disbelief to faith (*in istaḥabbū 'l-kufra 'alā 'l-īmān*): they chose disbelief over faith (*iḫtārū 'l-kufra 'alā al-īmān*) and those of you who do so, taking them as allies in religion, are doing wrong.

Then he adds:

> "if they prefer disbelief to faith" means that they chose *dār al-kufr*, that is Mecca, over the faith in *dar al-islām*, that is Medina (*iḫtārū dār al-kufr ya'nī Makka 'alā al-īmān 'alā dār al-islām ya'nī Madīna*).[87]

Here, in this controversial commentary, the connection between *dār al-islām* = Medina → faith and *dār al-kufr* = Mecca → unbelief is, finally, quite explicit, also because in this case the *dār al-islām / dār al-kufr* dichotomy is used precisely to bring back to *hijra* a verse in which *hijra* was not even mentioned, and therefore the whole Qur'anic and Islamic ethics. Moreover, even in this case, the logical, chronological and conceptual priority of the dichotomous opposition *dār al-islām / dār al-kufr* over the most famous and controversial *dār al-islām / dār al-ḥarb* seems to be confirmed and confirms as well that the very first and real meaning of *ḥarb* in the expression *dār al-ḥarb* should be "the war that the unbelievers wage against God" by refusing to submit themselves to His will.

In the end, with the exception of this case, which could possibly precede somewhat the elaboration of the *Jāmi' al-bayān*, it is clearly al-Ṭabarī who is the first commentator who introduces in Qur'anic exegesis both the single term *dār* with its new wider and symbolic meaning and the whole *dār al-islām / dār al-ḥarb* [*al-kufr*] dichotomy, clearly connecting it to, and rooting it within, the theme of *hijra*.

5 Conclusions: the Qur'an and Islamic Societies

As we have seen, most of the cases analyzed revolve around the theme of *hijra*. In this sense I would like to conclude with a short reflection on a remark by the late Giorgio Vercellin:

87 *Tanwīr al-miqbās*, 155.

> Con *dār* ci troviamo dunque subito all'interno delle metafore orizzontali così peculiari del mondo musulmano, dove lo spostamento, il movimento, la rivolta anche sociale e politica avvengono tra un «dentro» e un «fuori» piuttosto che tra un «basso» e un «alto» come nel mondo cristiano occidentale. Nel mondo musulmano infatti i ribelli si distaccano, si allontanano, fuoriescono dall'ordine esistente piuttosto che sollevarsi contro di esso. Lo stesso Profeta quando compie nel 622 la sua *hijra* («migrazione») in realtà esce da uno spazio (la Mecca) per entrare dentro un altro (Medina).[88]

Vercellin's insight contains at least two suggestions that are worth pointing out: first, that with *dār* we are immediately in the field of Islamic spatial, horizontal metaphors, which are, after all, the Islamic way of translating a moral dichotomy; second, Vercellin's highlighting that it was indeed the Prophet himself who, by performing the *hijra*, came out of a space, to enter another. But that is exactly the point: it is the Qur'an itself, even before other sources, such as Hadith, *sīra* and *maġāzī*, that gives absolute importance to *hijra*, making it, de facto, the first Islamic spatial metaphor of an ethical or moral dichotomy.

All this appears quite clearly in verses such as the following from *sūrat al-nisā'* (Q 4:89): "They would dearly like you to reject faith, as they themselves have done, to be like them. *So do not take them as allies until they migrate* [*to Medina*] for God's cause," or, later in the same *sūra* (Q 4:97–100):

> [97]When the angels take the souls of those who have wronged themselves, they ask them, 'What circumstances were you in?' They reply, 'We were oppressed in this land,' and the angels say, '*But was God's earth not spacious enough for you to migrate to some other place?*' These people will have Hell as their refuge, an evil destination, [98]but not so the truly helpless men, women, and children who have no means in their power nor any way to leave—[99]God may well pardon these, for He is most pardoning and most forgiving. Anyone who migrates for God's cause will find many a refuge and great plenty in the earth, [100]and if anyone leaves home as a migrant towards God and His Messenger and is then overtaken by death, his reward from God is sure. God is most forgiving and most merciful."

Or, finally, in *sūrat al-anfāl* (Q 8:72–75):

88 Giorgio Vercellin, *Istituzioni del mondo musulmano* (Torino: Einaudi, 1996), 22.

> [72]Those who believed and emigrated [to Medina] and struggled for God's cause with their possessions and persons, and those who gave refuge and help, are all allies of one another. *As for those who believed but did not emigrate, you are not responsible for their protection until they have done so.* But if they seek help from you against persecution, it is your duty to assist them, except against people with whom you have a treaty: God sees all that you do. [73]The disbelievers support one another. If you do not do the same, there will be persecution in the land and great corruption. [74]Those who believed and emigrated, and struggled for God's cause, and those who gave refuge and help—they are the true believers and they will have forgiveness and generous provision. [75]*And those who came to believe afterwards, and emigrated and struggled alongside you, they are part of you,* but relatives still have prior claim over one another in God's Scripture: God has full knowledge of all things.

So, it is not at all surprising to find that early commentators and Qur'anic scholars acknowledged from the very beginning the importance of *hijra:* the *sūra*s of the Qur'an themselves are, in fact, primarily distinguished as Meccan or Medinan and both their content and style are clearly distinguishable on that base.[89] The *hijra,* in the Qur'an, is the watershed that splits both the text and the community, and it is the Qur'an itself that points to *hijra* as the real borderline between believers and unbelievers: the horizontal displacement is immediately understood as the symbol of one's loyalty to God and His Messenger, as opposed to loyalty to one's own tribe. *Hijra,* in the Qur'an, is the first paradigmatic example of a spatial dichotomy that becomes a temporal dichotomy and lastly turns into an ethical or moral dichotomy.

This very fact, namely the transformation of space into time, and again into a metaphor for a moral dichotomy, is already fully established in the Qur'an, and will be paradigmatic for the whole of Islamic history, making way for the development of all those horizontal metaphors and of those dichotomous conceptions of the world so peculiar to Islamic societies, among which the *dār al-islām* / *dār al-ḥarb* dichotomy is only one of the earliest and most controversial examples. That said, the question remains whether it is the text that generates the vision of the world underlying a given society or if it is rather the society itself that generates the text that will underlie its same vision of the world.

89 See Faruque, "Emigration," 22.

References

ʿAbd al-Bāqī, Muḥammad Fuʾād. *Al-Muʿjam al-mufahras li-alfāẓ al-Qurʾān al-karīm.* Cairo, 1945.

ʿAbd al-Razzāq al-Ṣanʿānī. *Tafsīr al-Qurʾān.* 3 vols. Riyadh, 1989.

Abdel Haleem, Muhammad. *The Qur'an. A New Translation.* Oxford: Oxford University Press, 2004.

Abel, Armand. "Dār al-ḥarb." *Encyclopaedia of Islam, Vol. II, C–G.* Leiden: Brill, 1965.

Algar, Hamid. "Dār al-ḥarb." *Encyclopaedia Iranica. Vol. 6: Coffeehouse—Dārā.* New York, NY: Bibliotheca Persica Press, 2002.

Berg, Herbert. *The Development of Exegesis in Early Islam: The Authenticity of Muslim Literature from the Formative Period.* Curzon. Richmond, 2000.

Buḫārī, Muḥammad b. Ismāʿīl al-. *Al-Jāmiʿ al-ṣaḥīḥ.* Edited by Muḥibb al-Dīn al-Ḫaṭīb and Muḥammad Fuʾād ʿAbd al-Bāqī. 4 vols. Cairo: Al-Maṭbaʿa al-salafiyya, 1400AH.

Burton, John. *The Collection of the Qurʾān.* Cambridge, 1977.

Calasso, Giovanna. "Alla ricerca di *dār al-islām.* Una ricognizione nei testi di giuristi e tradizionisti, lessicografi, geografi e viaggiatori." *Rivista degli Studi Orientali* 83 (2010): 271–96.

Calder, Norman. "*Tafsīr* from Ṭabarī to Ibn Kathīr: Problems in the Description of a Genre, Illustrated with Reference to the Story of Abraham." In *Approaches to the Qurʾān*, edited by Gerald R. Hawting and Abdul-Kader A. Shareef, 101–40. London: Routledge, 1993.

Faruque, Muhammad al-. "Emigration." *Encyclopaedia of the Qurʾān.* Leiden-Boston, 2002.

Furāt b. Furāt al-Kūfī, Abū al-Qāsim. *Tafsīr.* Edited by Muḥammad al-Kāẓim. Beirut, 2011.

Gilliot, Claude. "Portrait 'Mythique' d'Ibn ʿAbbās." *Arabica* 32, no. 2 (1985): 127–84.

Gilliot, Claude. *Exégèse, langue, et théologie en Islam: l'exégèse coranique de Tabari (m. 311/923).* Etudes musulmanes 32. Paris: Libr. J. Vrin, 1990.

Gilliot, Claude. "Les débuts de l'exégèse coranique." *Revue du Monde Musulman et de la Méditerranée* 58, no. 1: Les premières écritures islamiques (1990): 82–100.

Gilliot, Claude. "Muqātil, Grand Exégète, Traditionniste, et Théologien Maudit." *Journal Asiatique* 279 (1991): 39–92.

Marçais, Georges. "Dār." *Encyclopaedia of Islam, Vol. II, C–G.* Leiden: Brill, 1965.

Motzki, Harald. "The Collection of the Qurʾān. A Reconsideration of Western Views in Light of Recent Methodological Developments." *Der Islam* 78 (2001): 1–34.

Mujāhid b. Jabr al-Makkī. *Tafsīr.* Edited by Muḥammad ʿAbd al-Salām Abū al-Nīl. Madīnat Naṣr, Egypt, 1410AH.

Muqātil b. Sulaymān. *Tafsīr.* Edited by ʿAbd Allāh Maḥmūd Šiḥāta. 5 vols. Beirut, 2002.

Rippin, Andrew. "Tafsīr Ibn 'Abbās and the Criteria for Dating Early Tafsīr Texts." *Jerusalem Studies in Arabic and Islam* 19 (1994): 38–83.
Saleh, Walid. *The Formation of the Classical* Tafsīr *Tradition. The Qur'ān Commentary of al-Tha'labī (d. 427/1035)*. Brill. Leiden, 2004.
Scarcia, Gianroberto. "*Islām* e *Ḥarb, 'Arab* e *'Ajam*: nota a due celeberrime dicotomie islamiche." In *Azhàr: studi arabo-islamici in memoria di Umberto Rizzitano (1913–1980)*, edited by Antonino Pellitteri and Giovanni Montaina, 205–10. Annali della Facoltà di lettere e filosofia dell'Università di Palermo. Studi e ricerche 23. Palermo: Facoltà di lettere e filosofia dell'Università di Palermo, 1995.
Schacht, Joseph. *The Origins of Muhammadan Jurisprudence*. Oxford: Clarendon Press, 1979.
Sufyān al-Ṯawrī, Abū 'Abd Allāh b. Sa'īd. *Tafsīr*. Edited by Imtiyāz 'Alī 'Aršī. Beirut, 1983.
Ṭabarī, Abū Ja'far Muḥammad b. Jarīr al-. *Jāmi' al-bayān 'an ta'wīl āy al-Qur'ān*. Edited by 'Abd Allāh b. 'Abd al-Muḥsin al-Turkī. 24 vols. Beirut, 1997.
Tanwīr al-miqbās min Tafsīr Ibn 'Abbās. s. l., s. d.
Vercellin, Giorgio. *Istituzioni del mondo musulmano*. Torino: Einaudi, 1996.
Wansbrough, John. *Quranic Studies : Sources and Methods of Scriptural Interpretation*. Oxford, United Kingdom, 1977.

PART 3

Law: Theory and Practice

CHAPTER 8

Dār al-islām et *dār al-ḥarb* : Quelques réflexions à propos de la géographie théologico-politique sunnite classique, en regard du *Kitāb al-Muhaḏḏab* d'Abū Isḥāq al-Šīrāzī (m. 476/1083)

Éric Chaumont

al-jār qabla 'l-dār

1 Introduction

À priori, le thème de ce travail, selon son intitulé, devait mener à s'intéresser à la lecture des premiers textes proprement politiques de la littérature musulmane, soit les deux *aḥkām sulṭāniyya*, le premier de l'ašʿaro-šāfiʿite muʿtazilant Māwardī (m. 450/1058) et le second du ḥanbalite également muʿtazilant Abū Yaʿlā (m. 458/1066), et le *Ġiyāṯ al-umam* du pur ašʿarite Juwaynī (m. 478/1085)[1]. En réalité, cette piste n'est pas la bonne pour la raison simple que cette littérature s'intéresse principalement aux affaires politiques *intérieures* de la communauté musulmane. Cette littérature concerne l'imamat en tant qu'institution politique et a pour seule finalité de décrire, de manière normative, ce que doit être le fonctionnement d'une entité politique réputée "musulmane". Aussi bien, les questions liées à la délimitation des territoires *dār al-islām*, *dār*

1 À propos de ces textes, voir Éric Chaumont, "Aux origines du droit constitutionnel musulman : les débuts (tardifs) de la *siyâsa sharʿiyya*," in *Droit, pouvoir et religion: actes du colloque international, Tunis, 5, 6 et 7 mars 2009* ([Tunis]: Association tunisienne de droit constitutionnel, 2010), 39-46; Éric Chaumont, "Al-Mâwardî (m. 450/1058), le Qâḍî Abû Yaʿlâ (m. 458/1066) et *les statuts du gouvernement* (*al-aḥkâm al-sulṭâniyya*)," *Rives méditerranéennes*, no. 19 (October 10, 2004): 75-96; et Nimrod Hurvitz, *Competing Texts: The Relationship Betweeen Al-Mawardi's and Abu Yaʿla's* al-Ahkam al-Sultaniyya, Occasional Publications 8 (Cambridge, MA: ILSP, Harvard Law School, 2007).

 | DOI 10.1163/9789004331037_010

al-ṣulḥ et *dār al-ḥarb* ne sont envisagées que sous un angle étroit dans cette littérature. Elle n'est abordée que parce que c'est en principe – ce n'est pas obligatoirement le cas[2] – à l'imam qu'il appartient au cas échéant de déclarer un jihad et de lever une armée pour ce faire. Les "relations extérieures" de la communauté musulmane n'y sont pas plus envisagées.

En réalité, le lieu naturel où il est question des *dār al-islām*, *dār al-ṣulḥ* et *dār al-ḥarb* est et a toujours été le *fiqh*, le droit positif en tant que le jihad est une obligation sharaïque "communautaire" [*farḍ ʿalā 'l-kifāya*] et que c'est bien autour de cette notion que se définit la géographie théologico-politique musulmane classique.

2 Les origines coraniques de la géographie théologico-politique musulmane

Stricto sensu, la dichotomie *dār al-islām / dār al-ḥarb* pour qualifier l'ensemble de la terre n'est pas coranique. Il semble pourtant que les légistes se sont directement inspirés du Coran pour l'établir.

Comment, tout d'abord, l'"autre", le non-musulman, est-il considéré dans le Coran ? Il ne l'est pas toujours de la même manière mais la doctrine du jihad se fonde sur Coran 9 (*al-Tawba*), 28 : *Les associateurs ne sont que souillure*. Les "associateurs" [*mušrikūn*], selon le *tafsīr*, ce sont *tous* les non-musulmans et Māwardī s'étonne, tout en l'admettant parce que le verset suivant est clair sur ce point, que "les gens du Livre" [*ahl al-kitāb*] – juifs, chrétiens et sabéens – en fassent partie[3]. On sait en effet que le droit musulman leur reconnaît un statut particulier, appelé *ḏimma*, lorsqu'ils vivent en terre d'islam, un statut vexatoire de "protégé" au prix d'un impôt spécifique appelé *jizya*. Ceux-là ne sont donc pas concernés par le verset suivant de la même sourate qui enjoint les Musulmans à les combattre sur le mode de l'impératif [*qātilū* ...] : il s'agit donc bien d'un ordre, d'une obligation. Le verset 5 de la même sourate est encore plus clair : *Combattez les associateurs où que vous les trouviez*. Ces versets sont médinois et traduisent sans doute, d'une part, la rapide dégradation des

---

2 Voir Abū Isḥāq Ibrāhīm b. ʿAlī al-Šīrāzī, *al-Muhaḏḏab fī fiqh al-imām al-Šāfiʿī*, ed. Muḥammad al-Zuḥaylī (Damas: Dār al-Qalam / Beyrouth: al-Dār al-Šāmiyya, 1417), 5:236. Šīrāzī précise que s'il est souhaitable qu'un jihad soit autorisé par l'imam ou le vizir parce que celui-ci est réputé être mieux au courant des affaires de la communauté et de ses intérêts, un jihad « d'initiative privée » rendu nécessaire par la situation reste valide. En toute hypothèse, le jihad garde toujours quelque chose de privé, voir plus bas, p. 154-55.

3 Abū 'l-Ḥasan ʿAlī al-Māwardī, *Al-nukat wa'l-ʿuyūn. Tafsīr al-Māwardī* (Beirut: Dār al-Kutub al-ʿIlmiyya / Muʾassasat al-Kutub al-Ṯaqāfiyya, n.d.), 2:350-52.

rapports entre les tribus juives de Yaṯrib et la jeune communauté musulmane qui s'y était fraîchement installée, et, d'autre part, le refus persistant du plus grand nombre des tribus de La Mecque et du Ḥijāz de reconnaître le prophétat de Muhammad et sa nouvelle religion.

La racine √qtl apparaît 170 fois dans le Coran, 31 occurrences sont mecquoises et 139 médinoises. La racine √jhd, le plus souvent *ʿalā wazn fāʿala* (*jāhada* qui a *jihād et mujāhada* pour noms verbaux), est attestée 41 fois, 8 occurrences sont mecquoises et 33 médinoises. La racine √ḥrb est plus rare. Elle n'est attestée que 11 fois : 8 occurrences sont médinoises et 3 mecquoises. Dans le Coran, la notion de "combat" dirigé contre les non-musulmans se conjugue principalement autour des racines √qtl et √jhd et elle se conjugue à Médine beaucoup plus qu'à La Mecque et l'on sait que c'est à Yaṯrib/Médine qu'un embryon de "nation" musulmane est né pour se développer de manière fulgurante en un "empire", le *dār al-islām* dont il est question dans les traités de *fiqh*.

Il serait absolument absurde de nier, par bien-pensance, la dimension franchement belliqueuse du Coran à l'endroit, de manière générale, des non-musulmans. Si de nombreux musulmans contemporains se disent et se montrent très sincèrement pacifistes vis-à-vis des communautés non-musulmanes, il paraît difficile qu'ils ne se livrent pas à une relecture très critique des sources scripturaires de l'islam.

En résumé, d'une part, le non-musulman considéré comme une "souillure" (*najas*), pas seulement comme une "impureté", et, d'autre part, l'obligation de les combattre de manière guerrière, cela suffit à expliquer pourquoi, premièrement, l'existence d'une géographie légalo-politique bipolaire opposant *dār al-islām* et *dār al-ḥarb*, et, secondement, pourquoi tous les traités de droit musulman comptent un chapitre concernant le jihad en le présentant telle une obligation dont la finalité est d'agrandir le territoire de l'islam. Il ne faut pas s'y méprendre, c'est bien le jihad offensif – il s'agit de pénétrer dans le territoire de l'ennemi de le conquérir ou de le racketter –, pas seulement défensif, que prescrivent le Coran, la sunna et la littérature sharaïque classique.

On entend souvent, invariablement, dire, toujours par bien-pensance, qu'en islam le "vrai" jihad, le "grand" jihad, c'est l'effort spirituel que le musulman doit exercer sur lui-même pour combattre ses propres passions et se conformer intérieurement aux enseignements de l'islam. C'est exact mais cet autre jihad, c'est la *mujāhada* de la littérature soufie, c'est la pratique du soufisme et le respect d'une certaine éthique. En outre, l'existence de ce "grand" jihad n'oblitère pas celle de l'autre, fut-il "petit", ni le fait que ce dernier reste une obligation sharaïque de l'avis de tous les légistes musulmans d'hier à aujourd'hui. Certes, la compréhension de cette obligation a changé tout au long de l'histoire – nous le verrons avec Šīrāzī – mais nous nous situons ici sur le plan des principes tels qu'ils apparaissent dans les textes normatifs de l'islam, au risque, pleinement assumé, d'apparaître "essentialiste", affreusement "orientaliste." Il convient ici de se rappeler que c'est le rappel de ces mêmes principes réputés a-historiques et intangibles qui permet aujourd'hui à des Ẓawāhirī ou à des Qaraḍāwī d'appeler leur communauté au jihad ici ou ailleurs, et, surtout, qu'une partie militante de cette communauté soit sensible à ce rappel.

Par ailleurs, la guerre est une chose qui existe partout et depuis toujours et on peut juger positivement le fait que les sciences sharaïques l'aient prise comme l'un de ses objets à l'instigation du Coran et de la sunna. En effet, la guerre est ainsi régulée : tout n'est pas permis en temps de guerre et c'est grâce à l'existence d'un droit de la guerre.

Il faut encore signaler un trait du droit musulman de la guerre : en ses principes, il est incontestablement triomphaliste en ce sens qu'il sous-entend que la terre entière est appelée à devenir le *dār al-islām*. Cela, l'histoire l'explique aussi : on a rarement vu un Empire pérenne aussi étendu s'établir aussi rapidement avec autant de facilité. C'est dans ce contexte que les théories qui nous occuperont ici sont nées et se sont développées, soit dans un contexte fait de victoires fulgurantes ; d'où des doctrines de dominants qui ignorent ou qui ont pour le moins difficile à se mettre dans la situation inverse, celle de dominés.

3 Le *Kitāb al-Siyar* [*wa'l-jihād*] du *Muhaḏḏab fī fiqh al-imām al-Šāfiʿī* d'Abū Isḥāq al-Šīrāzī (m. 476/1083)

Le *Muhaḏḏab fī fiqh al-imām al-Šāfiʿī*[4] est l'oeuvre majeure d'un légiste bagdadien plus qu'important du onzième siècle[5]. À ce titre, on y trouve un état très représentatif de la question du jihad et des notions de "Territoire de l'islam" et de "Territoire de la guerre" au temps de sa rédaction. Le *Muhaḏḏab*, tout comme le *Tanbīh* – autre texte important mais beaucoup plus bref, il s'agit d'un *muḫtaṣar*, du même auteur –[6] présente l'intérêt d'être présenté par son auteur comme un « retour aux sources » [*uṣūl*] de la doctrine de Šāfiʿī alors que

4 Voir note 2 ci-dessus. Le *Kitāb al-Siyar* se trouve dans Šīrāzī, *Muhaḏḏab*, 5:225-87.

5 À son propos, voir Éric Chaumont, "al-Sh͟īrāzī, Abū Isḥāḳ Ibrāhīm b. ʿAlī," *Encyclopédie de l'Islam, Vol. IX, San-Sze* (Leiden: Brill, 1997). J'ai présenté son œuvre plus en détails dans Éric Chaumont, "*Kitāb al-Lumaʿ fī Uṣūl al-fiqh* d'Abû Isḥâq al-Šîrâzî (m. 476-1083), Introduction, édition critique et index," *Mélanges de l'Université Saint Joseph* 53 (1993-1994): 9-249. Voir aussi Muḥammad Ḥasan Hītū, *Al-imām al-Šīrāzī ḥayātuhu wa-arāʾuhu al-uṣūliyya* (Dimašq, 1980).

6 Le *Tanbīh* a été traduit en français : *Kitâb et-Tanbîh ou Le Livre de l'Admonition...*, Traduction française annotée par G.-H. Bousquet, 4 vols. Le chapitre concernant le jihad se trouve en Abū Isḥāq Ibrāhīm b. ʿAlī al-Šīrāzī, *Kitâb et-Tanbîh, ou le Livre de l'admonition touchant la*

jusqu'alors, la littérature šāfi'ite se réclamait le plus souvent du *Muḫtaṣar* de Muzanī. Il n'est pas bien sûr que les textes de *fiqh* de Šīrāzī représentent réellement un retour aux sources de la doctrine de Šāfi'ī mais il est néanmoins certain que lorsque Šīrāzī émet cette revendication qui est peut-être artificielle, il a, au moins, l'intention de « rafraîchir » la doctrine de son École, dont celle du jihad.

La première section du *Kitāb al-Siyar wa'l-jihād* du *Muhaḏḏab* de Šīrāzī concerne étonnamment l'émigration, *hijra*, dont l'archétype est évidemment celle de Muḥammad et de la jeune et petite communauté musulmane de La Mecque à Yaṯrib, la future Médine. L'émigration qu'évoque ici Šīrāzī est celle de la personne s'étant convertie à l'islam et vivant en « territoire de mécréance » (*dār al-kufr*) où il ne peut « manifester » [*iẓhār*] sa religion et la vivre librement. S'il en a les moyens, en raison de Q 4, 97, obligation lui est faite d'émigrer en terre d'islam. Šīrāzī précise que même si le converti à l'islam est libre de vivre sa religion en dehors du territoire de l'islam sans avoir à craindre la moindre « épreuve » [*fitna*], il reste préférable qu'il émigre parce que le risque existe que ses enfants soient séduits par la mécréance locale. L'idéal, pour lui, c'est « chacun chez soi et les moutons seront bien gardés ».

Le fait que Šīrāzī inaugure le *Kitāb al-Siyar wa'l-jihād* par la question de la *hijra* signifie-t-il que dans son esprit, l'émigration constitue une forme de jihad, sa forme privilégiée ? En toute hypothèse, *hijra* et jihad participent, dans l'esprit de Šīrāzī, d'une même problématique. Cela se comprend dans la mesure où *hijra* et jihad sont l'un et l'autre des déplacements physiques d'un territoire à l'autre. La *hijra* mène dans celui de l'islam, le jihad, plus violent, pénètre dans celui des mécréants.

4 Le jihad comme devoir communautaire

Les fondements de l'obligation du jihad énumérés par Šīrāzī sont classiques (Q 2:216 et 9:41). Ces deux versets, ayant une portée générale (*'āmm*), semblent s'adresser à chacun des membres de la communauté. À priori, il s'agit d'un *farḍ 'ayn*, d'un devoir "personnel" et non "communautaire".

Mais Šīrāzī procède à une particularisation (*taḫṣīṣ*) de la leçon de ces versets et cela en arguant de Q 4:95 et en argumentant "par le pragmatisme" : on ne saurait imaginer de vie dans une communauté dont *tous* les membres auraient à partir au jihad, il faut aussi des cultivateurs, des menuisiers, des

loi musulmane selon le rite de l'imâm Ech-Châféî. 4e partie. Droit pénal et public. Procédure. Preuves., ed. Georges H. Bousquet, vol. 4 (Alger: La Maison des livres, n.d.), 35-41.

commerçants, etc[7]. Šīrāzī invoque implicitement la *maṣlaḥa* : l'"avantage" de la communauté. C'est exactement le même argument qu'il avance ailleurs pour établir que l'*ijtihād* – l'effort de compréhension de la sharia – est lui aussi un devoir communautaire et non pas personnel[8]. Pourtant, sous la plume de ce légiste, cet argument a de quoi étonner. Sur le plan théologico-sharaïque, Šīrāzī s'affirme en effet aš'arite or, selon cette perspective, la *maṣlaḥa* n'a aucune valeur probante en matière sharaïque. La notion de *maṣlaḥa* appartient à l'appareil conceptuel des mu'tazilites. Cela contribue à montrer l'impossibilité d'être purement aš'arite sur le plan sharaïque en ne voyant, derrière la sharia, que la volonté arbitraire de Dieu.

Il convient de bien saisir ce que signifie précisément l'expression *farḍ 'alā 'l-kifāya* si l'on veut comprendre la doctrine shirazienne de "l'effort guerrier sur la voie de Dieu" (*al-jihād fī sabīl Allāh*) et qu'il soutient que c'est un devoir de cette nature. L'islamologie juridique traduit le plus souvent ce concept par "devoir communautaire" mais en réalité l'expression arabe signifie "devoir de suffisance". Qu'est-ce à dire ? Lorsqu'un nombre "suffisant" de membres de la communauté s'en acquitte, il n'incombe plus aux autres ? C'est ainsi que l'islamologie comprend le plus souvent les choses en proposant "devoir communautaire" comme traduction. En réalité, le sens est différent : un devoir est qualifié de *kifāya* lorsque sa finalité est "suffisamment" satisfaite et, s'il n'est pas nécessaire pour cela que tous les membres de la communauté le prenne en charge – chose, on l'a vu, que Šīrāzī estime en plus impensable s'agissant du jihad –, alors les autres en sont dispensés.

Certaines personnes en sont par principe dispensées : la femme, l'esclave, l'enfant, l'insensé, l'aveugle, le handicapé, le malade, le pauvre et la personne endetée (à moins que son créancier ne l'y autorise)[9]. Enfin, tout candidat au jihad doit obtenir l'autorisation de ses parents parce que le respect des parents est une obligation prioritaire par rapport au devoir de combattre les mécréants[10]. Il est intéressant de remarquer que si ni le pauvre ni la personne endetée ne sont pas concernés, c'est parce qu'ils n'ont pas les ressources pécuniaires nécessaires pour financer leur jihad. Cela laisse clairement entendre que le jihad conserve une dimension privée dans la mesure où chaque

---

7 Šīrāzī, *Muhaḏḏab*, 5:227.

8 Voir Abū Isḥāq Ibrāhīm b. 'Alī al-Šīrāzī, *Kitāb al-Luma' fī uṣūl al-fiqh. Le livre des rais illuminant les fondements de la compréhension de la Loi, Traité de théorie légale musulmane*, Introduction, traduction annotée et index par É. Chaumont, Studies in comparative legal history (Berkeley, CA: Robbins Collection, 1999), 337.

9 Šīrāzī, *Muhaḏḏab*, 5:229-34.

10 Ibid., 5:235-36.

combattant est tenu de subventionner les frais liés à sa participation au jihad (monture, armement, etc.) En principe, il ne s'agit pas d'une guerre organisée et financée par l'État. Mais, à lire Māwardī, le jihad est bel et bien une guerre d'État au sens commun dont l'armée est constituée, à côtés de volontaires, de soldats réguliers – "inscrits dans les régistres" –, et rétribués sur le butin remporté[11].

La "suffisance" est quantifiable en ce qui regarde sa fréquence. Le jihad est un devoir qui s'impose et qui s'imposera toujours – il n'est pas "particularisé" dans le temps –, mais à quel rythme ? Selon Šīrāzī, un jihad l'an suffit pour que la finalité de l'obligation le concernant soit satisfaite[12]. Encore ce jihad annuel – qui peut prendre la forme d'une courte razzia – peut-il être différé en raison de circonstances mitigeantes, dont, notamment, l'état de "faiblesse des musulmans" (*ḍuʿf al-muslimīn*)[13]. En outre, une trêve (*hudna*) d'une durée indéterminée avec l'ennemi est licite et permet de n'exercer aucun jihad.

Le principe pourtant est qu'il est souhaitable que la communauté fasse montre de "zèle" et multiplie (*iktār*) les actes jihâdistes, à l'exemple du prophète – modèle incontestable – qui, rapporte-t-on, mena personnellement 27 razzias et ordonna 35 campagnes militaires à ses proches. En réponse à la question d'Abū Hurayra : *Quel est le meilleur des actes ?* Muhammad répondit : *La foi en Dieu et en son messager et le* jihad *sur la voie de Dieu*[14]. La doctrine de Šīrāzī indique pourtant à l'évidence qu'il était très conscient que le modèle prophétique n'était plus sur ce point d'actualité, que le zèle jihadiste du prophète et de ses compagnons n'était indiqué que durant le tout premier âge de l'islam alors qu'un "territoire de l'islam" n'existait pas encore ou à peine et que des conquêtes étaient nécessaires. C'est une chose que, comme telle, Šīrāzī ne pouvait pas écrire ; il n'aurait pas pu écrire non plus que le jihad du prophète n'est plus exemplaire s'il avait vécu à notre époque, au XXIe siècle. Mais il lui restait la possibilité de "bricoler" la doctrine du jihad imposée par le Coran et la sunna et travailler ainsi, au regard des circonstances de son temps, il ne s'en prive pas en s'aidant de ses grands talents de spécialiste de théorie légale. Il est clair que le qualificatif *kifāya* qualifiant le jihad n'a plus pour lui le même sens qu'auparavant pour la bonne et simple raison que la finalité à

11 Abū 'l-Ḥasan ʿAlī al-Māwardī, *Les Statuts gouvernementaux ou règles de droit public et administratif*, trad. Edmond Fagnan. Reproduction de l'edition d'Alger 1915 (Paris: le Sycomore, 1982), 72.

12 Šīrāzī procède par analogie avec la *jizya* dont le payement est annuel, voir Šīrāzī, *Muhaḏḏab*, 5:228.

13 Ibid., 5:229.

14 Ce Hadith est rapporté sous différentes formes par la plupart des traditionnistes, voir ibid., 5:227n3.

satisfaire de ce devoir n'était plus la même dans la péninsule arabique du VIIe siècle et à Bagdad au Ve/XIe siècle. Pourtant, l'obédience théologique qui était la sienne – l'Aš'arisme – et du plus grand nombre de ses coreligionnaires, lui interdit d'écrire cela explicitement.

Le jihad, sous l'une ou l'autre de ses formes, n'est légitime que s'il a pour cible un territoire occupé par une communauté non-musulmane qui sait l'existence de l'islam ; une population "que l'Appel n'a pas atteint" doit tout d'abord être invitée à la conversion, elle ne peut être agressée inopinément. Si elle se refuse à la conversion, le jihad est légitime[15]. Mais cette clause a quelque chose d'abstrait et d'inutile car, comme le précise Abū Ya'lā, rares sont ceux qui, au XIe siècle, ignoraient l'existence de l'islam. En outre, Šīrāzī ajoute qu'un tel jihad peu glorieux reste néanmoins valide en se fondant sur l'exemple du prophète quand, en l'an 6/627, il attaqua inopinément les Banū Muṣṭaliq, tribu polythéiste alliée aux Qurayš mecquois, sans les avoir auparavant invités à embrasser l'islam.

5 Pour conclure

Toute la casuistique développée par Šīrāzī dans son *Kitāb al-Siyar* à propos du jihad – nous n'en avons pas rendu compte ici dans le détail : c'eut été fastidieux – ne semble pas répondre à des situations concrètes actuelles en son temps, à l'inverse de ce qu'on lit dans le *Kitāb al-Siyar* du hanafite Šaybānī (m. 189/805), écrit plus de deux siècles et demi plus tôt[16]. Certes, il faut tenir compte aussi du fait que l'écriture du *fiqh* a toujours été différente chez les šāfi'ites et chez les hanafites, ces derniers restant toujours plus rivés au réel que les seconds, plus enclins à une approche théorique des choses. Et, à cet

15 Ibid., 5:242.. Si le territoire conquis est habité par des « Gens du livre », leur conversion à l'islam n'est pas impérative ; ils peuvent conserver leur confession mais sont alors soumis aux statuts de la *ḏimma*. Si ce n'est pas le cas, le seul choix des habitants est la conversion à l'islam ou la mise à mort (à l'exception des enfants et des femmes qui sont alors réduits en esclavage).

16 Muḥammad b. al-Ḥasan al-Šaybānī fut un disciple direct d'Abū Ḥanīfa. À son propos, voir Éric Chaumont, "al-Shaybānī, Abū 'Abd Allāh Muḥammad b. al-Ḥasan," *Encyclopédie de l'Islam, Vol. IX, San-Sze* (Leiden: Brill, 1997). Il est difficile de savoir ce qui de l'œuvre monumentale qui lui est attribuée est authentique. En toute hypothèse, au sein de l'École hanafite, son œuvre est fondatrice, bien plus importante que celle d'Abū Ḥanīfa lui-même. Son *Kitāb al-Siyar*, extrait de son volumineux *Kitāb al-Aṣl*, a été traduit en anglais et très bien introduit par le traducteur : Majid Khadduri, ed., *The Islamic Law of Nations: Shaybānī's Siyar.* Translated with an Introduction, Notes and Appendices (Baltimore: The Johns Hopkins Press, 1966).

égard, le shafi'ite Šīrāzī est plus que représentatif et cela dans l'ensemble de son œuvre, pas seulement quand il traite du jihad.

Mais les différences de ton et de contenu entre l'un et l'autre ouvrage traduisent sans doute aussi le fait que la question du jihad dirigé contre le "territoire de la guerre" n'avait plus les mêmes enjeux au Vᵉ/XIᵉ siècle.

Pourtant, le texte de Šīrāzī ne rompt pas avec la tradition – l'aurait-il souhaité, ce qui est plus que douteux, qu'il n'aurait pas pu le faire sans que sa pensée ne soit disqualifiée – considérant que le *jihād fī sabīl Allāh* est un devoir "de suffisance" incombant à toutes les générations de musulmans de tout temps. Cette tradition, à vrai dire, est ininterrompue dans le droit musulman, jusqu'à la période contemporaine. Mais il est certain que l'importance accordée au jihad et peut-être surtout la compréhension de la notion de "suffisance" (*kifāya*) qui l'accompagne ont considérablement varié au cours de l'histoire, selon les situations dans lesquelles les communautés musulmanes se sont trouvées par rapport au monde non-musulman. Ce n'est certainement pas pour rien, par exemple, qu'Ibn Rušd (m. 595/1198), vivant dans l'Andalousie des Almohades en y assumant la fonction officielle de "chef de la propagande" (*ra'īs al-ṭalaba*), ajoute le jihad à la liste des cinq actes de dévotion (*ʿibādāt*) dans son traité de droit *Bidāyat al-mūjtahid wa nihāyat al-muqtaṣid*[17]. Le mot "ennemi", l'autre menaçant, et le jihad avaient un sens bien plus concret pour Ibn Rušd que pour Šīrāzī.

Il reste que, malgré la variabilité de sa compréhension, le jihad, parce que devoir pérenne, fait en sorte que la communauté musulmane résidant dans le *dār al-islām* sera toujours, d'une manière ou l'autre, de manière plus ou moins belliqueuse, en guerre, plus ou moins froide, avec le reste du monde. Il est bien certain que le phénomène ici décrit reste très théorique mais les principes qui le sous-tendent sont et seront toujours susceptibles d'être actualisés.

Pour terminer, rappelons avec insistance que le rapport à l'autre en islam ne s'épuise pas dans la doctrine du jihad ici décrite : ce rapport belliqueux s'impose dans les cadres du droit musulman et, malgré l'importance du *fiqh* en son sein, l'islam ne se réduit pas à son droit.

References

Chaumont, Éric. "Al-Mâwardî (m. 450/1058), le Qâḍî Abû Yaʿlâ (m. 458/1066) et *les statuts du gouvernement* (*al-aḥkâm al-sulṭâniyya*)." *Rives méditerranéennes*, no. 19 (October 10, 2004): 75-96.

17 Abū 'l-Walīd Ibn Rušd [Averroès], *Bidāyat al-mujtahid wa-nihāyat al-muqtaṣid*, 2 vols. (Beirut, 1409AH).

Chaumont, Éric. "al-S̲h̲aybānī, Abū ʿAbd Allāh Muḥammad b. al-Ḥasan." *Encyclopédie de l'Islam, Vol. IX, San-Sze*. Leiden: Brill, 1997.

Chaumont, Éric. "al-S̲h̲īrāzī, Abū Isḥāḳ Ibrāhīm b. ʿAlī." *Encyclopédie de l'Islam, Vol. IX, San-Sze*. Leiden: Brill, 1997.

Chaumont, Éric. "Aux origines du droit constitutionnel musulman : les débuts (tardifs) de la *siyâsa sharʿiyya*." In *Droit, pouvoir et religion: actes du colloque international, Tunis, 5, 6 et 7 mars 2009*, 39-46. [Tunis]: Association tunisienne de droit constitutionnel, 2010.

Chaumont, Éric. "*Kitāb al-Lumaʿ fī Uṣûl al-fiqh* d'Abû Isḥâq al-Šîrâzî (m. 476-1083), Introduction, édition critique et index." *Mélanges de l'Université Saint Joseph* 53 (1993-1994): 9-249.

Hītū, Muḥammad Ḥasan. *Al-imām al-Šīrāzī ḥayātuhu wa arā'uhu al-uṣūliyya*. Dimašq, 1980.

Hurvitz, Nimrod. *Competing Texts: The Relationship Betweeen Al-Mawardi's and Abu Yaʿla's* al-Ahkam al-Sultaniyya. Occasional Publications 8. Cambridge, MA: ILSP, Harvard Law School, 2007.

Ibn Rušd, Abū 'l-Walīd [Averroès]. *Bidāyat al-mujtahid wa-nihāyat al-muqtaṣid*. 2 vols. Beirut, 1409AH.

Khadduri, Majid, ed. *The Islamic Law of Nations: Shaybānī's Siyar.* Translated with an Introduction, Notes and Appendices. Baltimore: The Johns Hopkins Press, 1966.

Māwardī, Abū 'l-Ḥasan ʿAlī al-. *Les Statuts gouvernementaux ou règles de droit public et administratif.* Trad. Edmond Fagnan. Reproduction de l'edition d'Alger 1915. Paris: le Sycomore, 1982.

Māwardī, Abū 'l-Ḥasan ʿAlī al-. *Al-nukat wa'l-ʿuyūn. Tafsīr al-Māwardī*. 6 vols. Beirut: Dār al-Kutub al-ʿIlmiyya / Mu'assasat al-Kutub al-Ṯaqāfiyya, n.d.

Šīrāzī, Abū Isḥāq Ibrāhīm b. ʿAli al-. *Al-Muhaḏḏab fī fiqh al-imām al-Šāfiʿī*. Edited by Muḥammad al-Zuḥaylī. 6 vols. Damas Dār al-Qalam / Beyrouth: al-Dār al-Šāmiyya, 1417AH.

Šīrāzī, Abū Isḥāq Ibrāhīm b. ʿAli al-. *Kitāb al-Lumaʿ fī uṣūl al-fiqh. Le livre des rais illuminant les fondements de la compréhension de la Loi, Traité de théorie légale musulmane*, Introduction, traduction annotée et index par É. Chaumont. Studies in comparative legal history. Berkeley, CA: Robbins Collection, 1999.

Šīrāzī, Abū Isḥāq Ibrāhīm b. ʿAli al-. *Kitâb et-Tanbîh, ou le Livre de l'admonition touchant la loi musulmane selon le rite de l'imâm Ech-Châféʿî. 4e partie. Droit pénal et public. Procédure. Preuves.* Edited by Georges H. Bousquet. Vol. 4. Alger: La Maison des livres, n.d.

CHAPTER 9

An Unknown Minority between the *dār al-ḥarb* and the *dār al-islām*

Francisco Apellániz

1 Introduction

All too often, Islamic notions such as *dār al-ḥarb* and *dār al-islām* have served the purposes of deepening the apparent historical divide between Christians and Muslims in the Mediterranean. In this article, I wish to exploit this opposition to point out one of the region's salient characteristics: the persistence of ample areas of intersection, where knowledge of Islamic and non-Islamic religious and legal concepts and norms was required of everyone. More specifically, I will address the issue of how Mediterranean peoples dealt with Islamic notions of legal status, belonging and extraterritoriality. The present volume deals with the boundaries of the Islamic community from a variety of viewpoints, and, in particular, tackles the use of *dār al-ḥarb* and *dār al-islām* in normative, juridical and literary texts. Did people perceive the implications of the Islamic division of the world? What was the real significance of this division in the Islamic borderlands, as the cities of commerce of the late Middle Ages? What was meant by it at a time when the *dār al-ḥarb ceased* to be an abstract space for the spreading of Islam and the fighting of jihad to incarnate specific political realities and exchanges?[1] To answer these questions, I will examine a minority involved in the commercial and cultural crossroads of the Eastern Mediterranean, a place where linguistic and religious groups frequently stepped over political borders. I will be referring to a group of people designated in fifteenth-century Venetian sources as *Fazolati* and by Genoese ones as *Faiholati*. The term's precise meaning is obscure and has long resisted identification by specialists, yet my focus will be on a jurisdictional conflict in

1 For an analysis of the binomial opposition as the result of historical changes, see Khaled Abou El Fadl, "Islamic Law and Muslim Minorities: The Juristic Discourse on Muslim Minorities from the Second/Eighth to the Eleventh/Seventeenth Centuries," *Islamic Law and Society* 1, no. 2 (1994): 141–87; and more recently Giovanna Calasso, "Alla ricerca di *dār al-islām*. Una ricognizione nei testi di giuristi e tradizionisti, lessicografi, geografi e viaggiatori," *Rivista degli Studi Orientali* 83 (2010): 271–96.

 | DOI 10.1163/9789004331037_011

1421, triggered by the sultan's attempt to expel all foreigners infringing Islamic rules of extraterritoriality. The role played by the Fazolati during this episode can help us understand, I argue, how Mediterranean peoples dealt with the *dār al-ḥarb* / *dār al-islām* divide in their daily contacts at marketplaces and in courts.

The Fazolati entered scholarly discussion thanks to two isolated references by the Venetian Senate in 1421. The senators complained about them to the Mamluk sultan of Egypt, regretting that an unspecified number of Venetian subjects had assumed this status (or, literally, had become Fazolati). As a direct consequence, the senators argued, the Venetians involved were now pledging allegiance to a different authority (presumably that of the sultan). The context of these first references deserves some attention. After the accession to the throne of a new sultan, al-Ẓāḥir Sayf al-dīn Ṭaṭar, regulations concerning the presence of Venetian merchants in Egypt underwent important changes. The sultan had just decreed that the legal duration of the Venetians' sojourn must not exceed four months.[2] Although the episode was unanimously labeled by both contemporaries and modern historians as a sign of Mamluk "injustice", at stake was the legal status of Frankish merchants, whose presence in the *dār al-islām* was regulated by the so-called "treaties of commerce", or, from the Islamic viewpoint, the *amān* or safe-conduct. According to *amān* theory, European Christians, legally enemies of Islam, could enter the realm of Islam for trading purposes upon acceptance of this obligation of pre-Islamic origin. The basic legal issue addressed by the new decree was that a foreign merchant in Islamic lands could benefit from a safe-conduct protecting his life and property for a more limited period. Once it expired, the *amān* holder lost any fiscal

2 "Et quia fertur quod aliqui nostri mercatores fecerunt se fazolatos, occasione breuis termini standi deinde, qui est mensium quator, quod nobis ualde displicet, propter multos respectus qui considerari possunt, volumus, et sic vobis mandamus, quod, si inuenietis aliquos se fecisse fazolatos, vel se submisisse alteri seruituti que esset contra concessiones nostras, debeatis dictam concessionem et mandatum revocari facere, et prouidere, et nullo modo assentire quod mercatores, subditi et fideles nostri, post complementum alicuius termini qui constitueretur, tractentur nec abeantur, nisi secundum nostras concessiones. Verum, quia habemus multum cordi factum illorum nostrorum mercatorum qui dicuntur se fecisse fazolatos, volumus quod, si inuenietis aliquos nostros mercatores vel subditos se fecisse fazolatos, vel alteri seruituti se submisisse, debeatis esse cum consule Alexandrie, et ei dicerequod dictos tale somnino licentiat de Alexandria [...] aliquos nostros mercatores vel subditos [...] non debeant se facere fazolatos nec alteri seruituti se submittere", Archivio di Stato di Venezia (hereinafter ASV), Senato, Deliberazioni, Misti, reg. 53, f. 204v, December 23, 1421, published in G. M. Thomas and R. Predelli, eds., *Diplomatarium veneto-levantinum sive acta et diplomata res venetas graecas atque levantis illustrantia*, vol. 2 (1880–1889; repr., Venice, 1880), doc. 176.

or extraterritorial privileges, such as consular jurisdiction. The Senate proceedings suggest that Venetian subjects had taken this step so they would not have to leave Egypt.[3] By December 1421, the matter was on the diplomatic agenda, as the Senate wanted transgressors to be punished and sent back to Venice. The sultan, instead, left the issue out of the bilateral negotiations.[4]

The abovementioned discussions in the Senate have led to a number of interpretations. Ranging from nineteenth-century orientalism to modern economics, all appear to be wrong and sometimes even fantastic, yet these explanations deserve to be mentioned, if only because they evoke the changing approaches of scholars to the Islamic past. Wilhelm Heyd (1823–1906) interpreted the term as "a kind of semi-naturalization," by virtue of which merchants "could become the sultan's subjects without nonetheless enjoying the same rights as the *nationals*." A historian of the Latin trading colonies in the East, Heyd was probably projecting Western legal conceptions onto the Islamic system of governance.[5] Indeed, nothing in the Islamic theory of obligation towards minorities or protected foreigners resembles the "semi-naturalization" evoked here. Perhaps more interestingly, though the decree was interpreted by Heyd and other commentators as arbitrary, the decision was in fact following some legal doctrines of governance that established the duration of *amān* at four months.[6]

3 Joseph Schacht, "Amān," *Encyclopaedia of Islam, Vol. I, A–B* (Leiden: Brill, 1960); Gladys Frantz-Murphy, "Identity and Security in the Mediterranean World Ca. AD 640–Ca. 1517," in *Proceedings of the 25th International Congress of Papyrology: Ann Arbor, July 29–August 4, 2007*, ed. Traianos Gagos and Adam Hyatt, American Studies in Papyrology, Special Edition (Ann Arbor: Scholarly Publishing Office, The University of Michigan Library, 2010), 253–64; John Wansbrough, "The Safe-Conduct in Muslim Chancery Practice," *Bulletin of the School of Oriental and African Studies* 34, no. 1 (1971): 20–35; Philippe Gourdin, "Les marchands étrangers ont-ils un statut de dhimmi?," in *Migrations et diasporas méditerranéennes: Xe–XVIe siècles : actes du colloque de Conques, octobre 1999*, ed. Michel Balard and Alain Ducellier (Paris: Publications de la Sorbonne, 2002), 435–46.

4 Nicolae Iorga, "Notes et extraits pour servir à l'histoire des croisades au XVe siècle. IV. Documents politiques (suite)," *Revue de l'Orient Latin* 5 (1897): 121, ASV, Libri Commemoriali, reg, 11, fol. 75–78, 04/30/1422.

5 "Il existait en Egypte une sorte de demi-naturalisation, par laquelle on devenait sujet du sultan, sans pourtant jouir des droits des nationaux : pour échapper à l'application du décret, certains membres de la colonie Vénitienne s'étaient fait admettre dans cette classe d'individus", Wilhelm von Heyd, *Histoire du commerce du Levant au moyen âge.* (1885; repr., Amsterdam: A. M. Hakkert, 1967), 2:473.

6 Māwardī in particular, see Anver M. Emon, *Religious Pluralism and Islamic Law: "Dhimmīs" and Others in the Empire of Law*, Oxford Islamic Legal Studies (Oxford, United Kingdom: Oxford University Press, 2012), 89.

Perhaps due to his Marxist beginnings, the Romanian historian Nicolae Iorga (1871–1940) proposed reading the word as a derivation of *Francomati*—a form of freed servants in Cyprus.[7] Suggested by the orientalist Albert Socin (1844–1899) and later followed by no less than John Wansbrough, a more legalistic interpretation placed the origin of the term in the Arabic word *fuḍūlī*, a technical designation out of Islamic contract law indicating a person disqualified from participating in commercial transactions.[8] These two explanations rely on vague phonetic resemblances with the Venetian version of the term, though no further arguments are advanced to show in what ways those freed Cypriots or these ineligible partners may correspond with the individuals mentioned by the senators. In his *Levant Trade in the Later Middle Ages* (1983), Eliyahu Ashtor proposed a reading of his own, combining linguistic elements with legal conjectures not directly related to the senators' complaint. According to Ashtor, the word evokes a kerchief supposedly worn by some Easterners, following a linear linguistic trail (*faciola* was a term widely documented for cloth strips, like those used in turbans).[9] The Fazolati were, according to Ashtor, *European* merchants who applied to the Mamluk authorities to be considered as *ḏimmīs*, or local Christians, promising to fulfill their obligations towards the sultan such as paying the poll tax (*jizya*). He expanded this particular interpretation by suggesting that the merchants in question "applied to the Moslem authorities for the status of permanent residents, but without becoming subjects of the sultan". By paying the poll tax voluntarily, Ashtor speculates, they would have escaped the onerous taxes Frankish merchants supposedly were compelled to pay. The unfair economic competition represented by these "converts" would have provoked the reaction in the Venetian Senate. Ashtor's digression on the *jizya*, it should be noted, is not based on the Venetian text, which makes no reference to the issue. Lastly, his speculation on a hybrid status is inconsistent with the legal treatment of non-Muslim subjects, as the payment of the *jizya* is material proof of the *ḏimmīs*' subjection to the Islamic ruler.[10] Ashtor's argument probably echoes the right by Islamic rulers to either ban foreign merchants after the expiration of their legal sojourn, or to consider them as *ḏimmīs* and therefore to request the poll tax from them. Ṭaṭar was not the only Mamluk sultan to reclaim that Frankish merchants respect the

7 Nicolae [Jorga] Iorga, "Notes et extraits pour servir à l'histoire des croisades au XVe siècle. I–III. Comptes des colonies," *Revue de l'Orient Latin* 4 (1896): 112.

8 Heyd, *Histoire du commerce*, II, 2:473n7; Wansbrough, "The Safe-Conduct," 32.

9 Stefano Lusignano, *Chorograffia, et breue historia vniuersale dell'isola de Cipro principiando al tempo di Noè per in fino al 1572* (Bologna, 1573), 35.

10 Claude Cahen, "Dj̲izya I," *Encyclopaedia of Islam, Vol. II, C–G* (Leiden: Brill, 1965).

temporary character of their sojourn. His pious successor Sayf al-Dīn Jaqmaq (1438–1453) "did not want any merchant to stay longer than six months".[11] Be that as it may, for Ashtor, it was the despotic character of Mamluk rule that provoked the opportunistic move by the Venetians, and the word was the term used to designate this particular kind of "convert".[12] Yet Ashtor's explanation fits into a broader narrative regarding Islamic societies in the Middle Ages. In the second half of the twentieth century, social and economic historians such as Ashtor were responsible for a historiographical construct: the myth of a tolerant and industrious Venetian Republic as opposed to a despotic Muslim sultanate, namely, the Mamluks. While the former epitomized the well-governed polity, the sultanate was depicted as fundamentally ignorant of the market economy, disrespectful of property rights and responsible for restrictive policies on Christians and Jews. According to this narrative, the Mamluk sultans brought about the ebb of Middle Eastern entrepreneurs and fostered the general economic decline of the sultanate.[13]

In recent times scholars from other disciplines have not hesitated to add their own economic interpretations of the term. Further elaborating on Ashtor's explanation, for Sheilagh Ogilvie the Fazolati were none other than "Europeans that applied for the status of permanent residents with individual commercial privileges ... which they found preferable to joining a merchant guild".[14] As a scholar of economic development, Ogilvie took up the cudgels for medieval trade to illustrate her thesis on the role and function of merchant

11 Marino Sanudo, *Le vite dei dogi (1474–1494)*, ed. Angela Caracciolo Aricò, vol. 1, Biblioteca veneta 8 (Padova: Antenore, 2002), 228.

12 "Moslem merchants and the Mamluk officials harassed the Europeans ... European merchants tried to find individual solutions for the difficulty of living and trading in the Moslem Levant: they applied to the Moslem authorities for the status of permanent residents, but without becoming subjects of the sultan", Eliyahu Ashtor, *Levant Trade in the Later Middle Ages*, 1983, 400–1 and note 242.

13 For Ashtor's historiography, see Robert Irwin, "Under Western Eyes: A History of Mamluk Studies," *Mamluk Studies Review* 4 (2000): 27–51. As for the "Mamluk decline" depicted by economic writers, Maya Shatzmiller, "A misconstrued link: Europe and the economic history of Islamic trade," in *Relazioni economiche tra Europa e mondo islamico, secc. XIII–XVIII: atti della "trentottesima settimana di studi" 1–5 maggio 2006 = Europe's economic relations with the Islamic world, 13th–18th centuries*, ed. Simonetta Cavaciocchi, Serie II—Atti delle "settimane di studi" e altri convegni 38 (Grassina, Italy: Le Monnier, 2007), 387–413. A well-known example of this construct is the work by Ahmad Darrag, *L'Égypte sous le règne de Barsbay, 825–841/1422–1438* (Damas: Institut français de Damas, 1961).

14 Sheilagh Ogilvie, *Institutions and European Trade: Merchant Guilds, 1000–1800*, Cambridge Studies in Economic History. Second Series (Cambridge: Cambridge University Press, 2011), 212.

guilds. According to her reasoning, the Fazolati were supporters of individual freedom and opposed to corporations. Yet how Ogilvie infers her definition from the abovementioned piece of evidence alone we do not know, as the senators do not mention overseas merchant guilds or trading nations in their complaint. The explanation by Ashtor, taken further by Ogilvie, has at least the merit of taking into account the second issue raised by the senators, that is, the change pursuant to the embrace of Fazolati status. Whoever these merchants were, they had become different from rank-and-file Venetian subjects. As time went on, new pieces of evidence referring to the Fazolati surfaced. A document produced by the notary of the Venetian consul in Damascus, referring to the misdeeds caused by pirates, numbered among the losses some goods belonging to "Moors and Fazolati", for which "the Franks" were held responsible. The text suggests that the Fazolati were a category of merchants different from both the Moors (i.e. the Muslims) and the Franks (Latin Christians), therefore presumably Eastern and non-Muslim. The eminent historian Charles Verlinden—who used overseas notarial documents for their intriguing multicultural character—found it more useful to interpret the category in strictly religious terms. Verlinden read Fazolati as "Copts", following a commonsense reasoning that has Fazolati numbered besides Western Christians and Muslims.[15] Still, one might ask, assuming they were Eastern Christians, why not Melkites, Nestorians or Jacobites? Verlinden's interpretation is inconsistent with the tradition of Venetian notaries to designate Eastern Christians as "Christians of the girdle". In fact, the same notary distinguishes between Christians of the Girdle and Fazolati and, as we will see, contemporary Genoese clerks discerned between Copts (*coffti*) and Fazolati. Apart from common sense, Verlinden advances no further elements in defense of his interpretation and does not explain why the term suddenly appeared in a particular time and place.

As I said earlier, this article does not aim to propose a definite interpretation of the term. Yet a few new elements have arisen lately from Venetian and Genoese sources, substantially enlarging the map on which the question should be framed. In a way, these references remit the question back to the *dār al-ḥarb / dār al-islām* divide, as they point to individuals moving across Muslim and Christian lands in the Eastern Mediterranean. These new references come from two series of documents preserved in Genoa's state archives. Both were produced by the administration of the city of Famagusta, in Eastern

15 "In su laqual nave iera haver de mori e fazolati per i quali franchi, zoe Zenoexi, Veneziani e de molte nazion ano habudo de grande strazo per mori e fazollati", Charles Verlinden, "Marchands chrétiens et juifs dans l'Etat mamelouk au début du XVe siècle d'après un notaire vénitien," *Bulletin de l'Institut historique belge de Rome* 51 (1981): 46.

Cyprus, for nearly a century after the city came under Genoese authority, in 1373. As happened in other Genoese territories, the municipality kept detailed accounts, called *Massaria,* some of whose large volumes have come down to us.[16] A second series is constituted by court proceedings issued by a judicial magistrate known as the *Capitano of Famagusta.*[17] Although some references to the Fazolati from the Massaria's accounts have been mentioned by scholars, my focus will be on the five surviving ledgers of the Capitano's tribunal, mainly covering the years between the late 1430s to the mid-1450s.[18] They contain petitions of justice addressed to the court, sometimes followed by witnesses' depositions as well as legal decisions. Other records are concerned with sundry matters, ranging from the taking of oaths by plyers of different trades to the delivering of safe-conducts.

References from both series present the Fazolati as dwellers of Cyprus, itself a much disputed jurisdictional crossroads where authorities, languages and religions intermingled. They are mentioned together with Copts, Armenians, what seems to be a nurtured Jewish community, migrants from the former crusader territories known as "white Genoese," and former Jewish and Muslim renegades.[19] If we trust how frequently the Fazolati were mentioned by the court scribes, they must have been numerous, at least in Famagusta and Nicosia. Most were city dwellers, sometimes designated as *burgenses*, although some fishermen and Fazolati living in the countryside are also mentioned. In Famagusta the Fazolati owned warehouses, were involved in commerce, and

16 Michel Balard, "La massaria génoise de Famagouste," in *Diplomatics in the eastern Mediterranean 1000–1500: aspects of cross-cultural communication*, ed. Alexander Daniel Beihammer, Maria G. Parani, and Christopher David Schabel, The Medieval Mediterranean 74 (Leiden: Brill, 2008), 235–50.

17 Cathérine Otten, "Le registre de la Curia du capitaine Génois de Famagouste au Milieu du XV siècle: Une source pour l'étude d'une société multiculturelle," in *Diplomatics in the eastern Mediterranean 1000–1500: aspects of cross-cultural communication*, ed. Alexander Daniel Beihammer, Maria G. Parani, and Christopher David Schabel, The Medieval Mediterranean 74 (Leiden: Brill, 2008), 251–74.

18 For mentions of the Fazolati in these records see: Archivio di Stato di Genova, San Giorgio (hereinafter ASG SG), 590/1288, 5r, 24r, 78r, ASG SG 590/1289, 38r, 143r, ASG SG 590/1290, 1v, 3r, 48v, 57r, ASG SG 590/1291, 14r, 62(2), 181v, 199r, ASG SG 590/1292, 20r, 27r, 47r, 51r, 52v, 60r, 64v, 65v, 67v, 70v, 72v, 77v, 79r, 79v, 81r, 83r, 90r, 90v, 198v. The register numbered ASG SG 590/1288 contains a few records dated 1388, where the first mention to the Fazolati can be found, 5r, dated Feb. 10th, 1388, *Aissa faiolatus*.

19 For a Muslim renegade, ASG SG, 590/1288, 114v, for Jews, Otten, "Le registre de la Curia," 273. Copts (*coffti* or *coffiti*) are mentioned in ASG SG 590/1292, 53r, 60r, ASG SG 590/1290, 50r, ASG SG 590/1291, f. 181r.

worked in the markets as plyers of several trades (*bazariotus, censarius*). The documents refer to women married to Fazolati, whilst in one case a certain Maria is described as being "of Fazolato descent". Massaria records from the 1440s and 1450s inform us that some Fazolati were migrants from Beirut, Tripoli or, more vaguely, Syria.

Laura Balletto reported several annotations from the Massaria accounts mentioning Fazolati families taken from Syria, at the expense of the Genoese of Famagusta, to take up residence in the city. These accounts mention foodstuffs—including wine—offered to the Fazolati migrants. Therefore, Balletto concludes, these people were linked together "by something which made them a community or a particular category of persons, but it is not yet possible to define this exactly". By the same token, the court records refer to Fazolati as organizers of maritime links with Beirut or Damietta. In December 1456, a complaint was brought before by the Capitano concerning the trip of some Fazolati to Beirut. According to the deed, Abram and his Fazolati associates failed to embark on time in Beirut, hence causing some losses to the master.[20] Similarly, a Fazolato named Abrayno de Cairo was the object of a trial concerning a trip to Damietta.[21] In December 1447 Joxef and Jacob of Tripoli registered at the court before embarking on a Muslim ship (*ituros super gripariam maurorum*).[22]

In addition, these records provide us with some glimpses of Fazolati onomastics: most first names of people described as Fazolati in the Cypriot-Genoese documents are clearly Semitic and most probably Arabic (Nasar, Cana Semeas, Botros, Monsor, Aissa, Abraynus, Daut, Jacop, Chelel, Semas, Braino, Brachinus, Isach, Nasari, Aissa Safer), followed by others compatible with Arabic-Christian onomastics (Giorgio de Cario [i.e., Cairo], Marion de Tripoli, Sayte de Tripoli). Lastly, there is one name of Greek origin (Teodoro di Tripoli) and a few instances of first names of Latin origin (Pietro di Tripoli, Rolando di Beirut, Augustinus), together with common names such as Jani and others more difficult to trace (Etel, Abet). One item refers to the son of a Fazolato from Tripoli who changed his name from Mose to Giovanni.[23] Lastly,

20 ASG SG 590/1291, 199r.

21 ASG SG 590/1292, 70v.

22 ASG SG 590/1289, 143r.

23 Laura Balletto, "Note sull'Isola di Cipro nel secolo XV," in *La storia dei Genovesi; Atti del Convegno di studi sui ceti dirigenti nelle istituzioni della Repubblica di Genova, Genova, 11–14 giugno 1991*, vol. 12 (Genova, 1994), 122, 140n63; Laura Balletto, "Ethnic Groups, Cross-Social and Cross-Cultural Contacts on Fifteenth-Century Cyprus," in *Intercultural Contacts in the Medieval Mediterranean*, ed. Benjamin Arbel and David Jacoby (Portland, OR: F. Cass, 1996), 43–44; Otten, "Le registre de la Curia," 271–72.

and perhaps more importantly, the Genoese spelling slightly differs from that used in Venice; here the word is spelled *faiholato* or *fayolato* (and, depending on the scribe, also *faiulato* and *fachiolato*).

Genoese evidence contradicts previous interpretations in many respects. First, it blurs any plausible origin from an Arabic word. Any attempt to interpret the term as a possible derivation from a triconsonantal Arabic root should take into account the incompatibilities between the Venetian spelling (*fazala*) and the Genoese one (*fayala*). Second, the Fazolati were not just merchants; rather, the term seems to designate more broadly a category of belonging. Genoese data also undermine the "merchant guild theory": there were Fazolato women, Fazolati lived for generations under Christian rule without being involved with the overseas trade guilds, and if they had once been assimilated *ḏimmīs* unwilling to pay taxes, there is no reason why their kin should still be called Fazolati after their departure from Islamic lands. The idea that Fazolato is merely a *cognomen*, or surname, should also be discarded. In contemporary designations such as in *Giorgio de Cario faiolato or Abrayno de Cairo faiolato* it is implied that the last term is an epithet (usually a collective demonym) and not a cognomen.

The broader cultural implications of the term emerge, again, in a Venetian notarial act, drawn up in Alexandria in 1404. The document refers to one of these Fazolati, a certain Cypriot merchant called Salem (*Salem façolato*). The document sheds light on the linguistic and ethnic background of the group, particularly in the context of the early fifteenth century, when it first appeared in the sources. According to the deed, Salem had a freight contract with a ship owner, himself a Cypriot, according to which the latter should carry his goods to Alexandria. Once in Egypt, a dispute had arisen between the two parties. The document refers to an attempt to settle this dispute by the two Cypriots. We are informed that the original contract was underwritten in Cyprus and styled in Arabic. The deed therefore suggests that Arabic was still spoken in Cyprus as late as in the fifteenth century. Salem, however, needed translation, as he was not able to understand what was going on during the arbitration.[24] The deed is consistent with Genoese information, presenting the Fazolati as dwellers of Cyprus and Arabic-speaking, engaged in trading networks operating in Islamic lands. In a Genoese document dated 1456, we find a *Giorgio de Cario faiolato*, inhabitant of Beirut, underwriting a power of attorney with a certain Barsom de Cario, a dweller of Famagusta.[25]

24 Archivio di Stato di Venezia, Cancelleria Inferiore, Notai, B. 222, Notary A. Vactaciis, f. 80r, Dec., 3, 1404.

25 Balletto, "Note sull'Isola di Cipro," 122.

It seems reasonable at this stage to speculate that the term may have originated in the Near-Eastern Christian milieu in the aftermath of the crusading period. Between 1099 and 1291, Christians belonging to many Eastern churches found themselves under the umbrella of the different crusader states. Needless to say, some of these sects did not obey Rome, but followed their own patriarchs in the East and in some cases were considered heretics by their new Latin masters. As historians of the crusades have pointed out, followers of the monophysite creed, considered not only schismatics but heretics pure and simple, paradoxically were favored by the crusaders in their quest for support by the native population.[26] The progressive fall of the crusader states was accompanied by a migration of these Christians to Cyprus. To be sure, not all the Christian minorities that found their way to Cyprus were "Syrians": Armenians, Copts and Ethiopians, of monophysite creed, were not. Syrians in a proper sense, and therefore expected to have maintained Arabic as the community language, were the Nestorians and the Jacobites (again, monophysites), together with the Maronites—in union with the Roman Church—and, finally, Melkite Syrians faithful to the Byzantine church of the Patriarch of Antioch. In Cyprus, Syrian Christians coexisted with other non-Arabic- speaking communities, particularly in Nicosia and Famagusta. Migrants from Acre flocked in large numbers to Famagusta, where they could still be noticed a century after the Muslim conquest of the city in 1291. As the abovementioned references to the Fazolati suggest, Syrians continued to settle on the island even a century and a half after the fall of the last crusader dominion.[27]

Their new host society was fundamentally different from that where their communities had originated in late antiquity as confessional groups. Progressive conversion to Islam had led to the fragmentation of these

26 Joshua Prawer, "Social Classes in the Crusader States: The 'Minorities,'" in *The Impact of the Crusades on the Near East*, ed. Kenneth M. Setton, Norman P. Zacour, and Harry W. Hazard, A History of the Crusades, Kenneth M. Setton; [...] (Madison: the University of Wisconsin Press, 1985), 72.

27 Gilles Grivaud, "Les minorités orientales à Chypre aux époques médiévale et moderne," in *Chypre et la méditerranée orientale: formations identitaires: perspectives historiques et enjeux contemporains: actes du colloque tenu à Lyon, 1997*, ed. Yannis Ioannou, F. Métral, and Marguerite Yon, Travaux de la Maison de l'Orient méditerranéen 31 (Lyon : Paris: Maison de l'Orient méditerranéen–Diffusion de Boccard, 2000), 43–70; Jean Richard, "La cour des Syriens de Famagouste d'après un texte de 1448," in *Croisades et états latins d'Orient: points de vue et documents*, Collected studies series CS383 (Aldershot: Ashgate, 1992), 383–98; Otten, "Le registre de la Curia," 251; Marwan Nader, *Burgesses and Burgess Law in the Latin Kingdoms of Jerusalem and Cyprus, 1099–1325* (Aldershot: Ashgate, 2006), 137.

confessional groups, which came to be perceived as scattered ethnic communities rather than churches.[28] Eastern Christians later found their place as *ḏimmīs* under the umbrella of cosmopolitan Islamic rulers. In Islamic lands, ethnic and religious differences among these Christians were flattened out by their universal categorization as *ḏimmīs*. Instead, in Christian societies such as those of Cyprus, different legal statuses proliferated, the result of privilege and hereditary right. *Vasmuli, archontes, parèques, francomati, burgenses,* "white" and "black" Venetian and Genoese were just some of the labels used to designate forms of status in the Eastern Mediterranean, a place where Byzantine and feudal legal concepts intermingled with those of the Italian city-states. According to the predominant juridical view in the West that everyone had his own place in society, it was natural that each one of these groups was granted a different legal status. In the case of the Syrians, this legal status was the result of previous concessions and privileges by the crusader rulers, who fashioned different fiscal and citizenship rights for each community.

2 Cyprus: A Normative Crossroads between *dār al-ḥarb* and *dār al-islām*

Fifteenth-century Cyprus can broadly be defined as an epigone crusader state ruled by a French king of the house of Lusignan who was surrounded by a chivalric elite—his vassals, according to feudal law—followed by servile peasants.[29] Yet other jurisdictions overlapped with the king's in the late Middle Ages. Famagusta had come under Genoese rule in 1373; the city then became a commercial melting pot ruled by Genoese institutions and laws, where foreigners could swear allegiance to the Commune.[30] In addition to being subject

28 Marshall G. S. Hodgson, *The Classical Age of Islam*, The Venture of Islam, conscience and history in a world civilization; Vol. 1 (Chicago: Univ. of Chicago Press, 1974), 306.

29 For the general legal framework and the weight of feudal law in Cyprus, see Nader, *Burgesses and Burgess Law*.

30 On the Status of Famagusta under Genoese rule, see Michel Balard, "Note sull'amministrazione Genovese di Cipro nel Quattrocento," in *La storia dei Genovesi; Atti del Convegno di studi sui ceti dirigenti nelle istituzioni della Repubblica di Genova, Genova, 11–14 Giugno 1991*, vol. 12/2 (Genova, 1994), 83–93; David Jacoby, "Citoyens, sujets et protégés de Venise et de Gênes en Chypre du XIIIe au XVe siècle," in *Recherches sur la Méditerranée orientale du XIIe au XVe siécle: peuples, sociétés, économies* (London: Variorum Reprints, 1979); Cathérine Otten, "Les institutions génoises et les affaires de Chypre," in *Etat et colonisation au Moyen Age et à la Renaissance*, ed. Michel Balard, Collection L'Histoire partagée (Lyon: La Manufacture, 1989), 167–78; Benjamin Arbel, "L'eredità Genovese a Cipro,

to feudal law or the Communal dominion of Genoa, a third situation was possible. Families of alleged Venetian and Genoese descent had long since migrated to the new kingdom. These migrants claimed to be the old Genoese and Venetian subjects in the Holy Land, formerly free inhabitants of crusader cities such as Tyre, partially under Venetian jurisdiction.[31] Once transplanted into Cyprus, they came to be known as "white Venetian" and "white Genoese", and they kept their panoply of juridical privileges awarded by the crusader kings. There remains ample evidence that some "white" Venetian and Genoese families continued to use Arabic in Cyprus for generations.[32] In addition, by the fifteenth century, the Lusignan king awarded new trading privileges to the cities of Genoa and Venice, and citizens of these maritime republics enjoyed supplementary tax exemptions and other prerogatives. These circumstances favored the proliferation of people on the island who claimed to be "original" Venetians and Genoese and who forged genealogies for that purpose, to the point that the royal government was forced to implement dissuasive measures and strengthen control procedures.[33] As a result, it was possible to be considered the king's vassal according to feudal law whilst at the same time enjoying alien citizenship and its resulting privileges (most of them concerning, in practice, trading rights). This seems to have been the case even at court. The same murkiness can be noted as regards the religious status of Syrian Christians in Cyprus. The pope labored to make these churches obey Rome, but in practice adherence to Roman Catholicism was limited to some Nestorian, Ethiopian and Armenian groups in Cyprus. Furthermore, confessional boundaries were often transgressed even within the limits of single family groups.[34]

It was in this context of overlapping legal traditions that Eastern Christians found their way into the social world of their Western masters. They were granted a privileged status as compared to the other minority groups, and most

---

1464–1571," ed. Laura Balletto, vol. 1, 2 vols., Collana di fonti e studi / Università degli studi di Genova, sede di Acqui Terme 1 (Genova: G. Brigati, 1997), 21–40.

31 Jean Richard, "Le peuplement latin et syrien en Chypre au XIIIe siècle," *Byzantinische Forschungen* 7 (1979): 157–73.

32 Jean Richard, "Une famille de Vénitiens blancs dans le Royaume de Chypre au milieu du XV siècle: Les Audeth et la seigneurie de Marethasse," *Rivista di Studi Bizantini e Slavi* 1, no. Miscellanea Agostino Pertusi (1981): 89–131.

33 For these legal statuses and the attempts by individuals to obtain them, see Jacoby, "Citoyens, sujets et protégés," among others, 169, 181, 182; and Balard, "La massaria génoise de Famagouste," 244. On the king's reaction towards fraudulent claims of potential "white" Venetians, Louis de Mas Latrie, *Histoire de l'île de Chypre sous le règne des princes de la maison de Lusignan*, vol. 2 (Paris: Imprimerie impériale, 1852), 234.

34 Richard, "Une famille de Vénitiens blancs," 90.

particularly the Greeks. They succeeded in keeping the privileges granted to them by the crusader lords in the Middle East but had these rights supplemented. After the fall of Acre, Henry II allowed the Syrians to keep their laws and Institutions, of which the *Courts of the Raïs* in Famagusta and Nicosia are the best known examples.[35] Perhaps more important, Syrians were declared free and therefore exempt from the personal taxes imposed upon Greeks. As for their commercial operations, they were liable for half the taxes paid by Greek merchants.[36] This particular point, as we will see, has its own importance not only in economic terms but because it implies a striking parallel to the treatment of similar groups under Islamic law.

All this leads us away from our initial concern with the *dār al-ḥarb / dār al-islām* divide. Yet a fact that has received strikingly little attention is the transformation of Cyprus from *dār al-ḥarb* into *dār al-ṣulḥ* during the period under study. It is well known that the Mamluks intervened in Cyprus in 1424–1427 and made the island a tributary state, augmenting the jurisdictional paradoxes of the Lusignan kingdom. The Cypriots signed a treaty with the Mamluks recognizing the sultan as their overlord. An annual tribute was levied until the end of the Mamluk sultanate and later on by its Ottoman successors.[37] The current state of research and the lack of interest by researchers in Cypriot history does not allow us to fully grasp the significance of this fact, and the practical modalities of Mamluk sovereignty over the Island.[38] When the city of Famagusta was reintegrated into the Lusignan kingdom in 1464, the king made it explicit that city rulers should be Christians and not "Mamluks, moors and other infidels".[39] Be that as it may, for most of the fifteenth century, Cyprus hosted Mamluk

35 Richard, "La cour des Syriens de Famagouste"; Nader, *Burgesses and Burgess Law*, 129–79.

36 Grivaud, "Les minorités orientales à Chypre," 63.

37 Coureas, Nicholas, "The Tribute Paid to the Mamluk Sultanate, 1426–1517: The Perspective from Lusignan and Venetian Cyprus," in *Egypt and Syria in the Fatimid, Ayyubid, and Mamluk Eras: Proceedings of the 1st, 2nd, and 3rd International Colloquium Organized at the Katholieke Universiteit Leuven in May 1992, 1993, and 1994*, ed. Urbain Vermeulen and K. d'Hulster, vol. 7, Orientalia Lovaniensia Analecta 223 (Leuven: Peeters, 2013), 363–80.

38 Exceptions to this silence in historiography can be found in Fuess, Albrecht, "Was Cyprus a Mamluk Protectorate? Mamluk Policies toward Cyprus between 1426 and 1517," *Journal of Cyprus Studies* 11, no. 28/29 (2005): 11–28; and Coureas, Nicholas, "Losing the War but Winning the Peace: Cyprus and Mamluk Egypt and Syria in the Fifteenth Century," in *Egypt and Syria in the Fatimid, Ayyubid, and Mamluk Eras: Proceedings of the 1st, 2nd, and 3rd International Colloquium Organized at the Katholieke Universiteit Leuven in May 1992, 1993, and 1994*, ed. Urbain Vermeulen and K. d'Hulster, vol. 7, Orientalia Lovaniensia Analecta 223 (Leuven: Peeters, 2013), 351–62.

39 Arbel, "L'eredità Genovese a Cipro," 22.

contingents and their emirs in a kingdom whose political destinies were determined by Cairo and where Arabic was not only spoken by chancery secretaries, but, seemingly, by the king himself.[40]

3 Mediterranean Border-Crossing : *dār al-ḥarb* and *dār al-islām* in Practice

Syrian Christians were not confined within the narrow boundaries of Western laws and regulations. Within limits, they accommodated themselves to the range of institutional choices available. Nothing prevented an Arabic-speaking Syrian from presenting himself as a former subject of the Italian city-states. There were, therefore, *Syrian* "white" Venetian and "white" Genoese (and, according to some, even Jews and Armenians). Syrian families such as the Bibi, Urry, Goneme, Mistahel, Salah, Sheba and Audeth worked at the king's chancery, where documents were produced in Latin, French, Italian and Arabic.[41] The ambiguity of Cypriot sources, which never distinguish them clearly, highlights what has been called the "assimilation strategy" by these Syrians in the *dār al-ḥarb*. From a cultural, religious and linguistic viewpoint, they played their ambivalent status to their own advantage. On this score, Jean Richard reports how members of Jacobite families managed to obtain benefices in the Latin church.[42] Among the latecomers to the Lusignan kingdom were the Melkites, generally referred to as "Suriens" by the sources. Lacking their own ecclesiastical hierarchy on the island, they were placed under the protection of the Greek bishop. Often considered as part of the white Genoese and Venetian groups, they assimilated into both Greek and Latin society. As we have seen, besides Arabic names, Fazolati onomastics feature Greek and even Latin names.

Though the precise confessional group to which the Fazolati should be assigned cannot be determined, some Eastern Christians took advantage of their own ambivalent religious and linguistic background, and, probably, of the controversial political status of Cyprus. It was in this context of intersecting jurisdictions and overlapping legal layers that some Fazolati and other Syrian-origin merchants became involved in trade with the Middle East. Anecdotes

40 Boustron, Florio, *Chronique de l'Île de Chypre. Publiée par René de Mas Latrie,* Mélanges historiques, choix de documents 5 (Paris: Imprimerie Nationale, 1886), 365.

41 Richard, "Une famille de Vénitiens blancs," 91; Grivaud, "Les minorités orientales à Chypre," 53.

42 Richard, "Une famille de Vénitiens blancs," 90.

of the proverbial wealth of the Nestorian Lakhan family illustrate the weight of Cypriot Nestorians as financiers and the mechanics of their trading networks between Cyprus and Syria.[43] Connections between Jacobites from Syria and Egypt with their coreligionists in the Greek islands are constantly mentioned in the ledgers of the Venetian notaries of Alexandria and Damascus.[44] Moreover, Nestorians, Melkites and Jacobites were all Eastern Christians who could circumvent the major obstacle limiting their Latin colleagues: the papal embargo on trade with Islamic lands.[45]

How did the new state of affairs affect these Arabic-speaking communities, whose churches were led by the patriarchs of Antioch or elsewhere in the *dār al-islām*? From an Islamic viewpoint, these Christians seem to be considered as *ḏimmīs*, irrespective of the places they actually inhabited. This is suggested by a digression on *ḏimmī* sects included in a manual for Mamluk secretaries. The author, al-Saḥmāwī al-Qāhirī (d. 868/1464), described the different Jewish and Christian communities of his time; his main goal was to define where their leaders were (where these churches had their *kursī*). Melkites had their seat in Antioch, Jacobites in Alexandria and Nestorians in Jerusalem, all under Mamluk sovereignty. For Saḥmāwī, it did not matter where a Christian resided but whether he was a follower of an Eastern sect and therefore subject to the sultan's authority.[46] This is consistent with the personal—not territorial—character of Islamic law.[47]

The practical ways Fazolati commercial activities developed in the two *dār*s offer striking similarities. As Ibn Taymiyya noted in his work on governance, Islamic practice had since the times of the caliph ʿUmar levied merchants from the *dār al-ḥarb* with a duty of ten percent—the Islamic *ʿušr*—of their

43 Grivaud, "Les minorités orientales à Chypre," 51; Richard, "Une famille de Vénitiens blancs," 91–92.

44 ASV, CI, N, B. 222, Notary A. Vactaciis, October 20th, 1404, f. 74v, idem, July 29th, 1405, f. 183v. A later deed drawn up in Alexandria is more specific: mention is made of a *Jacobite Christian* from Syria who gives power of attorney to other Syrian Christians living in Rhodes, ASV, CI, N, B. 211, Notary N. Turiano, f. 59v, October 4th, 1455.

45 Richard, "La cour des Syriens de Famagouste," 384.

46 The MS Arabic 4439 of the Bibliothèque Nationale de France, recently attributed to Šams al-dīn Muḥammad b. Muḥammad al-Saḥmāwī al-Qāhirī, *al-Ṯaġr al-bāsim fī ṣināʿat al-kātib wa'l-kātim*, ed. Ašraf Muḥammad Anas Mursī (Cairo, 2009), f. 138–141. On the territoriality of the law, Calasso, "Alla ricerca di *dār al-islām*," 282; and Abou El Fadl, "Islamic Law and Muslim Minorities," 165.

47 Abou El Fadl, "Islamic Law and Muslim Minorities," 165.

goods. But travelling *ḏimmīs* were charged half this amount.[48] This scheme, though subject to minor changes, was still in use in Mamluk times, when there were many foreign merchants in the sultanate. We may assume, therefore, that these *Syrians* could, paradoxically, enjoy a privileged fiscal status on both sides.

The status of Syrian Christians in both the sultanate and Cyprus was the result of very different legal and juridical backgrounds and principles. The privileges granted to Syrians in Cyprus were the result of contingency, as previous alliances with the crusader rulers.[49] In Islamic lands they were instead subject to the general pact (*ʿaqd al-ḏimma*) deriving from their exclusion from the Islamic community. In both cases, their juridical position was one of inferiority. They could not appeal to their own legal institutions when a Frank was concerned, and they could not have recourse to their community judges in a trial against a Muslim. Yet in both cases they could have their cases heard by their own courts, provided the two parties were Syrians. In addition, in both Cyprus and the sultanate, in marriage and dowry issues their own laws were respected. Furthermore, they enjoyed a similar tax regime for their business operations.

In 1351, the Mamluk jurist Taqī al-dīn al-Subkī wrote one of the few fatwas known dealing with the juridical status of Frankish merchants. The text continued to be used by other Mamluk muftis, and it was commented upon in the following years. Subkī's son, Abū al-Barakāt, added an analysis of the pacts underwritten with both *ḏimmīs* and *ḥarbīs*. The resulting text clearly states the different nature of pacts with both groups, and the religious duties of Muslims towards *ḏimmīs* and foreign merchants. The latter could be expelled from the *dār al-islām* when the terms of their agreement (*ʿaqd al-amān*) were broken, and their safe-conduct was subsequently revoked.[50] For eighth/fourteenth-century jurists such as the Subkīs, *dār al-ḥarb* and *dār al-islām* remained two necessary analytical categories, if only because they allowed them to differentiate local *ḏimmīs* from resident *ḥarbīs*. The possibility of being expelled from Egypt was precisely at stake in the Mamluk decree of 1421, something

48 Taqī al-dīn Aḥmad Ibn Taymiyya, *al-Siyāsa al-šarʿiyya fī iṣlāḥ al-rāʿī wa-al-raʿiyya*, ed. ʿAlī ibn Muḥammad ʿUmrān (Makka, 1429), 55–56; Antoine Fattal, *Le statut légal des non-musulmans en pays d'Islam* (Beyrouth: Imprimerie catholique, 1958), 155–56; Paul G. Forand, "Notes on ʿUšr and Maks," *Arabica* 13, no. 2 (June 1966): 137–41.

49 Richard, "La cour des Syriens de Famagouste," 386.

50 Aziz S. Atiyya, "A Fourteenth Century Fatwā on the Status of Christians in the Mamlūk Empire," in *Studien zur Geschichte und Kultur des nahen und fernen Ostens*, ed. W. Heffening, P. Kahle, and W. Kirfel (Leiden: Brill, 1935), 59–60; Taqī al-Dīn al-Subkī, *Fatāwā al-Subkī*, ed. Ḥusām al-dīn Qudsī, vol. 2, 1355, 417–21.

technically impossible for the *ḏimmī*s. The actual significance of the Mamluk-Venetian Fazolati crisis is suggested by a much later episode. In her study of the so-called "Carazo affair" (1613–1617), Tijana Krstić depicts a similar scenario for the seventeenth-century Ottoman empire. On that occasion another minority, the newly arrived Iberian *moriscos,* was involved in a bitter quarrel over extraterritoriality. Again, the expiration of the legal sojourn was used to threaten the Frankish community with being treated as *ḏimmī*s and therefore subjected to special taxation.[51]

While the normative weight of the *dār al-ḥarb* and *dār al-islām* categories remained intact in early modern times, the Fazolati dispute illustrates that not only rulers but also other social actors were aware of this theoretical divide and manipulated it to their own advantage. According to the evidence, there can be little doubt that Venetian merchants were "embracing" a Syrian Christian community, whatever that community might be. In so doing, these lower-rank Venetians were transgressing the boundaries between the two abodes, that is, they were leaving the *dār al-ḥarb* and entering the realm of Islam. In terms of agency, the strategy followed by Venetian subjects is noteworthy. By presenting themselves as followers of one of the Eastern, presumably "Syrian" churches, they were immediately accepted into the *dār al-islām* and therefore could not be expelled. Technically, it should be noted, they could not "convert" to Eastern Christianity. According to the first caliphs and subsequent jurists, conversion to religions other than Islam was not possible, as the Revelation given to Moses and Jesus had been corrupted.[52] The imprisonment of an Iberian *converso* who chose to turn back to the Jewish religion in Mamluk Syria shows the seriousness of such an offence.[53] Unfortunately, we will never know the theological arguments advanced by the Venetians—if they had any—to be recognized as *Fazolati* by the Mamluks. Yet their subtle manipulation of legal boundaries shows the ability of Mediterranean peoples to navigate through the loopholes of legal concepts and doctrines.

---

51 Tijana Krstić, "Contesting Subjecthood and Sovereignty in Ottoman Galata in the Age of Confessionalization: The *Carazo* Affair, 1613–1617," *Oriente Moderno* 93, no. 2: Minorities, Intermediaries and Middlemen in the Ottoman Empire (2013): 422–53.

52 Emon, *Religious Pluralism and Islamic Law*, 66–67; and particularly Yohanan Friedmann, "Classification of Unbelievers in Sunnī Muslim Law and Tradition," in *Tolerance and Coercion in Islam: Interfaith Relations in the Muslim Tradition*, Cambridge Studies in Islamic Civilization (New York: Cambridge University Press, 2003), 65–69.

53 Mark D. Meyerson, "Seeking the Messiah: Converso Messianism in Post-1453 Valencia," in *The Conversos and Moriscos in Late Medieval Spain and beyond*, ed. Kevin Ingram, Studies in Medieval and Reformation Traditions, v. 141, 160 (Leiden: Brill, 2009).

Assuming, then, that some individuals under Venetian jurisdiction were ready to become Fazolati, and that by so doing they transferred their allegiance from the doge to the sultan, the question remains: who were they exactly? And why would they take such a dramatic step? The answer is perhaps blurred because of how historians have thought about the medieval Mediterranean. We know that Venice was a medieval city-state where citizenship was reserved for original natives of the capital city and was never extended to its vast colonial dominion. Greeks, Jews and non-Catholics of the colonies had their trading and political rights limited. They could not engage in trade with the metropolis, nor were they admitted to merchant guilds nor could they enjoy consular protection.[54] Although historians of minorities such as David Jacoby have investigated the practical implications of these legal biases, the myth of a tolerant Venice remains strong in Mediterranean historiography, mirroring the myth of the Mamluks as intolerant despots. Yet the fact that the senators referred to these "converts" as *subditi* and *fideles* clearly indicates that the merchants in question were not full citizens but colonial subjects.[55] As for the reasons for their split with Venice, explanations have varied over time. Writing at the end of the nineteenth century, and decidedly not from a Mamluk-friendly perspective, Heyd still admitted that the *Fazolati* sought to escape from the sojourn decree.[56] A century later Ashtor discarded every

54 For a recent overview of the citizenship problem, see Reinhold C. Mueller, *Immigrazione e cittadinanza nella Venezia medievale*, Studi / Deputazione di storia patria per leVenezie 1 (Roma: Viella, 2010). For the Greek communities Jacoby, "Citoyens, sujets et protégés"; on the legal limitations imposed on the Jewish communities David Jacoby, "Venice and the Venetian Jews in the Eastern Mediterranean," in *Gli Ebrei e Venezia: secoli XIV–XVIII: atti del convegno internazionale organizzato dall'Istituto di storia della società e dello Stato veneziano della Fondazione Giorgio Cini, Venezia, Isola di San Giorgio Maggiore, 5–10 giugno 1983*, ed. Gaetano Cozzi, 1a ed. (Milano: Edizioni Comunità, 1987), 29–59; Elisabeth Santschi, "Contribution à l'étude de la communauté juive en Crète vénitienne au XIVe siècle, d'après des sources administratives et juridiques," *Studi Veneziani* 15 (1973): 177–211; A good discussion of Venetian policies of exclusion can be found in Silvano Borsari, "Ricchi e poveri nelle comunità ebraiche di Candia e Negroponte (sec. XIII–XIV)," in *Ricchi e poveri nella società dell'Oriente Grecolatino*, ed. Maltezou Chryssa, Biblioteca dell'Istituto Ellenico di Venezia 19 (Venezia: Istituto Ellenico di Studi Bizantini e Postbizantini di Venezia, 1998), 211–22.

55 Freddy Thiriet, *La Romanie Vénitienne au Moyen Age: le développement et l'exploitation du domaine colonial vénitien, XIIe–XVe siècles* (Paris: Bibliothèque des écoles françaises d'Athènes et de Rome, 1959), 269–301; Jacoby, "Citoyens, sujets et protégés"; and particularly "Les Génois dans l'Empire Byzantin: citoyens, sujets et protégés (1261–1453)," in *Trade, commodities and shipping in the medieval Mediterranean*, Variorum collected studies series CS572 (Aldershot, Hampshire, Great Britain: Variorum, 1997), 245–84.

56 Heyd, *Histoire du commerce*, 2:473.

reference to the sojourn problem.[57] While Heyd's explanation remains more realistic and respectful of the Senate discussions, both share a reluctance to admit that Venetians could voluntarily become the sultan's subjects. Both invoke a mysterious "demi-naturalisation" with no real institutional parallel in Islamic law. Perhaps it would be simpler to acknowledge that, as rank-and-file colonial subjects, they had their rights severely curtailed by Venetian regulations and were confined to a peripheral trade, that is, between the Greek islands and the Islamic lands. With the *amān* restrictions enacted, the traditional trading activities of Venetian Greeks and Jews became technically impossible. Becoming Fazolati—and therefore applying for a full *ḏimmī* status—represented the only possible way out.

Not only historians have misinterpreted the decision made by the Venetian merchants. When arguing that transgressors should be sent back to Venice and punished, the senators were lagging behind their own colonial subjects as regards their understanding of Islamic legal categories. The senators' mistake was noteworthy: for authorities in Venice, as almost everywhere in the West, status differences were the result of divine will. Status was defined by privilege and hereditary right, one of its practical manifestations being citizenship in the Italian city-states. These principles could hardly be accepted by a Muslim ruler who upheld the Islamic ideal that Revelation superseded previous beliefs by the people of the book. The existence of the *ḏimmī* status in Islamic law was a reminder of the universalist mission of the Islamic faith, and *ḏimmī*s could not be subjected to jurisdictional claims by Christian rulers. Roman legal concepts of sovereignty had been erased since the early Islamic conquests, which did away with all traces of communal jurisdiction. *Ḏimmī*s had to be granted the possibility of conversion, and therefore their right to become free Muslims could not be curtailed by any hereditary or legal principle or by any claim by Christian rulers.

References

Abou El Fadl, Khaled. "Islamic Law and Muslim Minorities: The Juristic Discourse on Muslim Minorities from the Second/Eighth to the Eleventh/Seventeenth Centuries." *Islamic Law and Society* 1, no. 2 (1994): 141–87.

Arbel, Benjamin. "L'eredità Genovese a Cipro, 1464–1571." edited by Laura Balletto, 1:21–40. Collana di fonti e studi / Università degli studi di Genova, sede di Acqui Terme 1. Genova: G. Brigati, 1997.

Ashtor, Eliyahu. *Levant Trade in the Later Middle Ages*, 1983.

57 Ashtor, *Levant Trade in the Later Middle Ages*, 400–401 and note 242.

Atiyya, Aziz S. "A Fourteenth Century Fatwā on the Status of Christians in the Mamlūk Empire." In *Studien zur Geschichte und Kultur des nahen und fernen Ostens*, edited by W. Heffening, P. Kahle, and W. Kirfel, 55–68. Leiden: Brill, 1935.

Balard, Michel. "Note sull'amministrazione Genovese di Cipro nel Quattrocento." In *La storia dei Genovesi; Atti del Convegno di studi sui ceti dirigenti nelle istituzioni della Repubblica di Genova, Genova, 11–14 Giugno 1991*, 12/2:83–93. Genova, 1994.

Balard, Michel. "La massaria génoise de Famagouste." In *Diplomatics in the eastern Mediterranean 1000–1500: aspects of cross-cultural communication*, edited by Alexander Daniel Beihammer, Maria G. Parani, and Christopher David Schabel, 235–50. The Medieval Mediterranean 74. Leiden: Brill, 2008.

Balletto, Laura. "Note sull'Isola di Cipro nel secolo XV." In *La storia dei Genovesi; Atti del Convegno di studi sui ceti dirigenti nelle istituzioni della Repubblica di Genova, Genova, 11–14 giugno 1991*, 12:119–44. Genova, 1994.

Balletto, Laura. "Ethnic Groups, Cross-Social and Cross-Cultural Contacts on Fifteenth-Century Cyprus." In *Intercultural Contacts in the Medieval Mediterranean*, edited by Benjamin Arbel and David Jacoby, 35–48. Portland, OR: F. Cass, 1996.

Borsari, Silvano. "Ricchi e poveri nelle comunità ebraiche di Candia e Negroponte (sec. XIII–XIV)." In *Ricchi e poveri nella società dell'Oriente Grecolatino*, edited by Maltezou Chryssa, 211–22. Biblioteca dell'Istituto Ellenico di Venezia 19. Venezia: Istituto Ellenico di Studi Bizantini e Postbizantini di Venezia, 1998.

Boustron, Florio. *Chronique de l'Île de Chypre. Publiée par René de Mas Latrie*. Mélanges historiques, choix de documents 5. Paris: Imprimerie Nationale, 1886.

Cahen, Claude. "Djizya I." *Encyclopaedia of Islam, Vol. II, C–G*. Leiden: Brill, 1965.

Calasso, Giovanna. "Alla ricerca di *dār al-islām*. Una ricognizione nei testi di giuristi e tradizionisti, lessicografi, geografi e viaggiatori." *Rivista degli Studi Orientali* 83 (2010): 271–96.

Coureas, Nicholas. "Losing the War but Winning the Peace: Cyprus and Mamluk Egypt and Syria in the Fifteenth Century." In *Egypt and Syria in the Fatimid, Ayyubid, and Mamluk Eras: Proceedings of the 1st, 2nd, and 3rd International Colloquium Organized at the Katholieke Universiteit Leuven in May 1992, 1993, and 1994*, edited by Urbain Vermeulen and K. d'Hulster, 7:351–62. Orientalia Lovaniensia Analecta 223. Leuven: Peeters, 2013.

Coureas, Nicholas. "The Tribute Paid to the Mamluk Sultanate, 1426–1517: The Perspective from Lusignan and Venetian Cyprus." In *Egypt and Syria in the Fatimid, Ayyubid, and Mamluk Eras: Proceedings of the 1st, 2nd, and 3rd International Colloquium Organized at the Katholieke Universiteit Leuven in May 1992, 1993, and 1994*, edited by Urbain Vermeulen and K. d'Hulster, 7:363–80. Orientalia Lovaniensia Analecta 223. Leuven: Peeters, 2013.

Darrag, Ahmad. *L'Égypte sous le règne de Barsbay, 825–841/1422–1438*. Damas: Institut français de Damas, 1961.

Emon, Anver M. *Religious Pluralism and Islamic Law: "Dhimmīs" and Others in the Empire of Law*. Oxford Islamic Legal Studies. Oxford, United Kingdom: Oxford University Press, 2012.

Fattal, Antoine. *Le statut légal des non-musulmans en pays d'Islam*. Beyrouth: Imprimerie catholique, 1958.

Forand, Paul G. "Notes on 'Ušr and Maks." *Arabica* 13, no. 2 (June 1966): 137–41.

Frantz-Murphy, Gladys. "Identity and Security in the Mediterranean World Ca. AD 640–Ca. 1517." In *Proceedings of the 25th International Congress of Papyrology: Ann Arbor, July 29–August 4, 2007*, edited by Traianos Gagos and Adam Hyatt, 253–64. American Studies in Papyrology, Special Edition. Ann Arbor: Scholarly Publishing Office, The University of Michigan Library, 2010.

Friedmann, Yohanan. "Classification of Unbelievers in Sunnī Muslim Law and Tradition." In *Tolerance and Coercion in Islam: Interfaith Relations in the Muslim Tradition*, 54–86. Cambridge Studies in Islamic Civilization. New York: Cambridge University Press, 2003.

Fuess, Albrecht. "Was Cyprus a Mamluk Protectorate? Mamluk Policies toward Cyprus between 1426 and 1517." *Journal of Cyprus Studies* 11, no. 28/29 (2005): 11–28.

Gourdin, Philippe. "Les marchands étrangers ont-ils un statut de dhimmi?" In *Migrations et diasporas méditerranéennes: Xe–XVIe siècles : actes du colloque de Conques, octobre 1999*, edited by Michel Balard and Alain Ducellier, 435–46. Paris: Publications de la Sorbonne, 2002.

Grivaud, Gilles. "Les minorités orientales à Chypre aux époques médiévale et moderne." In *Chypre et la méditerranée orientale: formations identitaires: perspectives historiques et enjeux contemporains: actes du colloque tenu à Lyon, 1997*, edited by Yannis Ioannou, F. Métral, and Marguerite Yon, 43–70. Travaux de la Maison de l'Orient méditerranéen 31. Lyon : Paris: Maison de l'Orient méditerranéen–Diffusion de Boccard, 2000.

Heyd, Wilhelm von. *Histoire du commerce du Levant au moyen âge*. 1885. Reprint, Amsterdam: A. M. Hakkert, 1967.

Hodgson, Marshall G. S. *The Classical Age of Islam*. Repr. *The Venture of Islam, conscience and history in a world civilization*; Vol. 1. Chicago: Univ. of Chicago Press, 1974.

Ibn Taymiyya, Taqī al-dīn Aḥmad. *Al-Siyāsa al-šar'iyya fī iṣlāḥ al-rā'ī wa-al-ra'iyya*. Edited by 'Alī ibn Muḥammad 'Umrān. Mecca, 1429AH.

Iorga, Nicolae [Jorga]. "Notes et extraits pour servir à l'histoire des croisades au XVe siècle. I–III. Comptes des colonies." *Revue de l'Orient Latin* 4 (1896): 25–118.

Iorga, Nicolae [Jorga]. "Notes et extraits pour servir à l'histoire des croisades au XVe siècle. IV. Documents politiques (suite)." *Revue de l'Orient Latin* 5 (1897): 108–212.

Irwin, Robert. "Under Western Eyes: A History of Mamluk Studies." *Mamluk Studies Review* 4 (2000): 27–51.

Jacoby, David. "Citoyens, sujets et protégés de Venise et de Gênes en Chypre du XIIIe au XVe siècle." In *Recherches sur la Méditerranée orientale du XIIe au XVe siécle: peuples, sociétés, économies*. London: Variorum Reprints, 1979.

Jacoby, David. "Venice and the Venetian Jews in the Eastern Mediterranean." In *Gli Ebrei e Venezia: secoli XIV–XVIII: atti del convegno internazionale organizzato dall'Istituto di storia della società e dello Stato veneziano della Fondazione Giorgio Cini, Venezia, Isola di San Giorgio Maggiore, 5–10 giugno 1983*, edited by Gaetano Cozzi, 1a ed., 29–59. Milano: Edizioni Comunità, 1987.

Jacoby, David. "Les Génois dans l'Empire Byzantin: citoyens, sujets et protégés (1261–1453)." In *Trade, commodities and shipping in the medieval Mediterranean*, 245–84. Variorum collected studies series CS572. Aldershot: Variorum, 1997.

Krstić, Tijana. "Contesting Subjecthood and Sovereignty in Ottoman Galata in the Age of Confessionalization: The *Carazo* Affair, 1613–1617." *Oriente Moderno* 93, no. 2: Minorities, Intermediaries and Middlemen in the Ottoman Empire (2013): 422–53.

Lusignano, Stefano. *Chorograffia, et breue historia vniuersale dell'isola de Cipro principiando al tempo di Noè per in fino al 1572*. Bologna, 1573.

Mas Latrie, Louis de. *Histoire de l'île de Chypre sous le règne des princes de la maison de Lusignan*. Vol. 2. 3 vols. Paris: Imprimerie impériale, 1852.

Meyerson, Mark D. "Seeking the Messiah: Converso Messianism in Post-1453 Valencia." In *The Conversos and Moriscos in Late Medieval Spain and beyond*, edited by Kevin Ingram. Studies in Medieval and Reformation Traditions, v. 141, 160. Leiden: Brill, 2009.

Mueller, Reinhold C. *Immigrazione e cittadinanza nella Venezia medievale*. Studi / Deputazione di storia patria per le Venezie 1. Roma: Viella, 2010.

Nader, Marwan. *Burgesses and Burgess Law in the Latin Kingdoms of Jerusalem and Cyprus, 1099–1325*. Aldershot: Ashgate, 2006.

Ogilvie, Sheilagh. *Institutions and European Trade: Merchant Guilds, 1000–1800*. Cambridge Studies in Economic History. Second Series. Cambridge: Cambridge University Press, 2011.

Otten, Cathérine. "Les institutions génoises et les affaires de Chypre." In *Etat et colonisation au Moyen Age et à la Renaissance*, edited by Michel Balard, 167–78. Collection L'Histoire partagée. Lyon: La Manufacture, 1989.

Otten, Cathérine. "Le registre de la Curia du capitaine Génois de Famagouste au Milieu du XV siècle: Une source pour l'étude d'une société multiculturelle." In *Diplomatics in the eastern Mediterranean 1000–1500: aspects of cross-cultural communication*, edited by Alexander Daniel Beihammer, Maria G. Parani, and Christopher David Schabel, 251–74. The Medieval Mediterranean 74. Leiden: Brill, 2008.

Prawer, Joshua. "Social Classes in the Crusader States: The 'Minorities.'" In *The Impact of the Crusades on the Near East*, edited by Kenneth M. Setton, Norman P. Zacour, and Harry W. Hazard, 59–115. A History of the Crusades, Kenneth M. Setton; [...]. Madison: the University of Wisconsin Press, 1985.

Richard, Jean. "Le peuplement latin et syrien en Chypre au XIIIe siècle." *Byzantinische Forschungen* 7 (1979): 157–73.

Richard, Jean. "Une famille de Vénitiens blancs dans le Royaume de Chypre au milieu du XV siècle: Les Audeth et la seigneurie de Marethasse." *Rivista di Studi Bizantini e Slavi* 1, no. Miscellanea Agostino Pertusi (1981): 89–131.

Richard, Jean. "La cour des Syriens de Famagouste d'après un texte de 1448." In *Croisades et états latins d'Orient: points de vue et documents*, 383–98. Collected studies series 383. Aldershot: Ashgate, 1992.

Saḥmāwī al-Qāhirī, Šams al-dīn Muḥammad b. Muḥammad al-. *Al-Ṯaġr al-bāsim fī ṣināʿat al-kātib wa'l-kātim*. Edited by Ašraf Muḥammad Anas Mursī. 2 vols. Cairo, 2009.

Santschi, Elisabeth. "Contribution à l'étude de la communauté juive en Crète vénitienne au XIVe siècle, d'après des sources administratives et juridiques." *Studi Veneziani* 15 (1973): 177–211.

Sanudo, Marino. *Le vite dei dogi (1474–1494)*. Edited by Angela Caracciolo Aricò. Vol. 1. Biblioteca veneta 8. Padova: Antenore, 2002.

Schacht, Joseph. "Amān." *Encyclopaedia of Islam, Vol. I, A–B*. Leiden: Brill, 1960.

Shatzmiller, Maya. "A misconstrued link: Europe and the economic history of Islamic trade." In *Relazioni economiche tra Europa e mondo islamico, secc. XIII–XVIII: atti della "trentottesima settimana di studi" 1–5 maggio 2006 = Europe's economic relations with the Islamic world, 13th–18th centuries*, edited by Simonetta Cavaciocchi, 387–413. Fondazione Istituto internazionale di storia economica F. Datini, Prato, Serie II—Atti delle "settimane di studi" e altri convegni 38. Grassina, Italy: Le Monnier, 2007.

Subkī, Taqī al-dīn al-. *Fatawa al-Subkī*. Edited by Ḥusām al-dīn Qudsī. Vol. 2, 1355.

Thiriet, Freddy. *La Romanie Vénitienne au Moyen Age: le développement et l'exploitation du domaine colonial vénitien, XIIe–XVe siècles*. Paris: Bibliothèque des écoles françaises d'Athènes et de Rome, 1959.

Thomas, G. M., and R. Predelli, eds. *Diplomatarium veneto-levantinum sive acta et diplomata res venetas graecas atque levantis illustrantia*. Vol. 2. 1880–1889. Reprint, Venice, 1880.

Verlinden, Charles. "Marchands chrétiens et juifs dans l'Etat mamelouk au début du XVe siècle d'après un notaire vénitien." *Bulletin de l'Institut historique belge de Rome* 51 (1981): 19–86.

Wansbrough, John. "The Safe-Conduct in Muslim Chancery Practice." *Bulletin of the School of Oriental and African Studies* 34, no. 1 (1971): 20–35.

CHAPTER 10

Some Observations on the Concept of *dār al-ʿahd* in the Ottoman Context (Sixteenth–Seventeenth Centuries)

Nicola Melis

1 Sources for the Study of Ottoman Territoriality

It happens quite often that historians of the Ottoman Empire marginalize strict Islamic law and, far from being supported by evidence, they are inclined to adopt legal concepts which are not exactly proper to Ottoman Islamic law. This study explores the Ottoman terminology about territoriality and territorial division of the world that traces back to the legal theory regarding the relationships between Islamic empires and non-Muslims (intended as individuals, groups and states). Most basically, this study seeks to present a stark empirical challenge to interpretations of classical scholarship on Ottoman institutions that portray the Ottoman world-view as uniquely based on the usual theoretical Hanafī notion of a world division into two *dār*s ("abodes," "territories"), but with an unproven Šāfiʿī influence, that provides a third category of *dār*, defined as *dār al-ʿahd* ("the Abode of the Covenant")[1] or *dār al-ṣulḥ* ("the Abode of the Reconciliation").[2]

Ottomanists and specialists in Islamic studies often ignore each other with the disappointing result that both these academic circles do not adequately

1 In Ottoman usage, the term *ʿahd* is commonly used both for civil engagements and contracts, and for political enactments. Together with the term name it refers to commercial treaties with non-Muslims outside the Ottoman lands, who are therefore called *ahl al-ʿahd*; this last term is occasionally extended, on one side to the *mustaʾmin*, and on the other to the *ḏimmis*.

2 According to *fiqh*, the term *ṣulḥ* means "amicable agreement." The records of Ottoman courts testify, during the whole Ottoman period, to this practice of dispute resolution between Muslims, drawing on the three normative systems: (*fiqh, qānūn* and *ʿurf*). See Işık Tamdoğan, "*Sulh* and the 18th Century Ottoman Courts of Üsküdar and Adana," *Islamic Law and Society* 15, no. 1 (February 1, 2008): 55–83. But *ṣulḥ* is also an amicable agreement (also termed *hudna, muhādana* or *muwādaʿa*) between the Territory of Islam and the Territory of War, stipulating the norms governing the relationship between them. According to Ottoman Hanafi law, *ṣulḥ* between the two *dārs* is not intended to exceed the obligatory dichotomist division existing between them; Majid Khadduri, "Ṣulḥ," *Encyclopaedia of Islam, Vol. IX, San-Sze* (Leiden: Brill, 1998).

 | DOI 10.1163/9789004331037_012

consider the evident divergence between the literal sense of classical *fiqh* and its practice and historical development in the Ottoman Empire. In other words, within the context of these disciplinary domains too much emphasis has been placed on a single factor, whether strictly Islamic or Ottoman oriented. Scholarship should take into consideration the theoretical Islamic view, together with its pragmatic application by means of issuing authoritative legal opinions (*iftāʾ*), secular law (*qānūn*) in all its declinations, customary law (*ʿurf*),[3] international legal and chancery practice, etc.

In the Ottoman period, the aforementioned divergence was often superseded by officials and clerks through the application of a variety of phrases, periphrases and circumlocutions that reduced and rendered acceptable non-Islamic concepts in the light of the letter and the spirit of *fiqh*. Indeed, the legal structure of the Ottoman Empire reflected its diversity.[4] Islamic law coexisted with customs, other religious legislations and *qānūn*. Thus, the Ottoman law was the result of several factors.[5]

With regard to the Ottoman conception of territoriality, we can assume an uncritical adherence by many Ottomanists to a stereotyped approach based on what Halil İnalcık, the best known Turkish historian, wrote some fifty years ago. In his article on "Dār al-ʿahd" in the second edition of the *Encyclopaedia of Islam*, İnalcık writes that the *dār al-ʿahd* "was considered as a temporary and often intermediate territory between the *dār al-islām* and the *dār al-ḥarb* by some Muslim jurists."[6] He goes further to add that "Abū Ḥanīfa, however, holds the opinion that such a land can be considered only as part of the *dār al-islām*, and there can be no other territory than the *dār al-islām* and the *dār al-ḥarb*. If people in such a land break the agreement they are to be considered as rebels." Basic to İnalcık's centralist view was the assumption that "… there existed, even in early Islam, a type of tributary lands which conformed to the theory defended by Šāfiʿī."

---

3 For a discussion of the term *ʿurf* (in Turkish, *örf*), see Uriel Heyd, *Studies in Old Ottoman Criminal Law*, ed. Victor L. Ménage (Oxford: Clarendon Press, 1973), 168–69.

4 Colin Imber, *The Ottoman Empire, 1300–1650: The Structure of Power*, 2nd ed (Houndmills, Basingstoke, Hampshire: Palgrave Macmillan, 2009), 216.

5 For a synthesis of the scholarly debate, see Evgenia Kermeli, "The Development of Ottoman Legal Studies," *Eurasian Studies* 1, no. 1 (2002): 278–301.

6 Halil İnalcık, "Dār al-ʿahd," *Encyclopaedia of Islam, Vol. II, C–G* (Leiden: Brill, 1965). See also his seminal work on the Ottoman method of gradual conquest. According to İnalcık, "[t]he Ottomans first sought to establish some sort of suzerainty over the neighbouring states. They then sought direct control over these countries by the elimination of the native dynasties." Halil İnalcık, "Ottoman Methods of Conquest," *Studia Islamica*, no. 2 (1954): 104.

With few exceptions, this description has been commonly accepted by Ottomanists in recent decades, although it is unsatisfactory and contradictory. Indeed, the scholarship since İnalcık until today has hardly rediscussed this evident incongruity, since Hanafi legal doctrine has rarely made use of Šafiʿī's categories and doesn't admit any Shafi'i idea of an intermediate territory called *dār al-ʿahd* that was nonexistent in the Hanafi discourse. This classification has been exposed by Nicolaas Biegman,[7] Daniel Goffman,[8] İlber Ortaylı and many others according to İnalcık's view and without attempting any important observation on the terminology used in Ottoman sources. Even the late Victor L. Ménage stated that Biegman, in his book on Ottoman–Ragusan relations, followed the cliché, since according to him "[t]he most interesting facet of [the] book is, without doubt, the careful description of how the juridical description of the *dār al-ṣulḥ* functioned in practice."[9] A passage from Biegman's book is given here:

> The rigid distinction between *Dār al-Islām* and *Dār al-ḥarb* soon proved impractical, and for this reason a third category emerged which consisted of countries or peoples who, though willing to pay a tribute, were not prepared to accept *dhimmī* status and could not be forced into so doing. A treaty (*ʿahd* or *ṣulḥ*) was concluded with this people ... Not all orthodox schools, however, developed a theory of a *dār al-ʿahd* or a *dār al-ṣulḥ*, existing separately between the two original categories. While the Shafi'i school did take this step—and al-Māwardī formulated the theory very clearly in his *Kitāb al-Aḥkām al-Ṣulṭāniyya*—the Hanafi doctrine, though recognizing the possibility of an armed truce, never admitted anything else but *dār al-islām* and the *dār al-ḥarb* putting into *dār al-islām* the territories which (according to Māwardī) would belong to *dār al-ʿahd*.[10]

7 Nicolaas H. Biegman, *The Turco-Ragusan Relationship According to the Firmāns of Murād III (1575–1595) Extant in the State Archives of Dubrovnik* (The Hague & Paris: Mouton, 1967).

8 Daniel Goffman, *The Ottoman Empire and Early Modern Europe*, New Approaches to European History 24 (Cambridge: Cambridge University Press, 2002), 46; "Negotiating with the Renaissance State," in *The Early Modern Ottomans: Remapping the Empire*, ed. Virginia H. Aksan and Daniel Goffman (Cambridge: Cambridge University Press, 2007), 61–74.

9 Victor L. Ménage, review of *The Turco-Ragusan Relationship According to the Firmāns of Murād III (1575–1595) Extant in the State Archives of Dubrovnik*, by Nicolaas H. Biegman, *Bulletin of the School of Oriental and African Studies* 34, no. 1 (1971): 155.

10 Biegman, *The Turco-Ragusan Relationship*, 30.

Another scholar who has dealt with *dār al-ʿahd* is Hans Theunissen.[11] When discussing the Ottoman conception of the division of the world, he writes the following words: "the *dār al-ʿahd* is a non-Muslim land, which by way of a peace treaty or more accurately an armed truce (*hudna, sulh, ʿahd*) with the Muslims, has suspended, for a fixed and specific period of time, the permanent state of war between both parties."[12] He admits also that "[n]ot all orthodox schools of Islam developed this concept of *dar al-ʿahd*.... The Hanafite doctrine, although it acknowledged the possibility of a truce between Muslims and non-Muslims, considered the *dar al-ʿahd* to be part of the *dar al-Islam* and not a separate group."[13] Both Biegman and Theunissen have based their discussion on academic secondary sources that were strictly theoretical and did not specify that the territorial dimension, in terms of *dārs*, is never mentioned in Ottoman sources when dealing with truces.[14]

Recently, with respect to Romanian lands, Cătălina Hunt painstakingly discussed the juridical status of the Romanian countries according to Ottoman law as practiced in the sixteenth century. As Hunt underlines, "there is no jurisprudential or historical support to sustain the idea of the Romanian countries as a component of the *dār al-ʿahd* territories during the 16th century or at any other time."[15]

Most likely, Alexander H. de Groot is right when he writes that "[t]he usual theoretical notion of Islamic scholars that the world was divided in two.... is not useful for our understanding of the historical development of Ottoman foreign relations,"[16] and territorial conception, I would add.

---

11 Hans Peter Alexander Theunissen, "Ottoman-Venetian Diplomatics: The *ʿAhd-Names*. The Historical Background and the Development of a Category of Political-Commercial Instruments Together with an Annotated Edition of a Corpus of Relevant Documents," *Electronic Journal of Oriental Studies* 1, no. 2 (1998): 1–698.

12 Ibid., 25.

13 Ibid.

14 See, for example, the classical Majid Khadduri, *War and Peace in the Law of Islam* (Baltimore: The Johns Hopkins Press, 1955); see also David Cook, *Understanding Jihad* (Berkeley: University of California Press, 2005).

15 Cătălina Hunt, "The Romanian Lands in the Sixteenth Century: Their Juridical Status According to Ottoman Law," in *Enjeux politiques, économiques et militaires en Mer noire (XIVe–XXIe siècles): études à la mémoire de Mihail Guboglu*, ed. Faruk Bilici, Ionel Cândea, and Anca Popescu (Braïla: Musée de Braïla–Éditions Istros, 2007), 413.

16 Alexander H. de Groot, "The Historical Development of the Capitulatory Regime in the Ottoman Middle East from the Fifteenth to the Nineteenth Centuries," ed. Maurits H. Van de Boogert and Kate Fleet, *Oriente Moderno* 22 (83), no. 3: The Ottoman Capitulations: Text and Context (2003): 576.

To sum up, therefore, this contribution aims to demonstrate that the very strict Islamic legal terminology about territoriality in Ottoman texts is contrasted with a very rich literary and administrative terminology about world division that includes several subcategories of territory. Therefore, it is intended to be a first contribution to a proper understanding of the nature of the legal cases referring to territoriality. In order to substantiate my argument, in the following pages I will try to avoid too strict a theoretical approach and I will examine the Ottoman sources relevant to the subject under discussion, seeking for more documental evidence.

2 Ottoman Sources: Islamic Tradition (*fiqh* and *iftāʾ*)

Learned jurists, in applying the norms of *fiqh* to a particular set of circumstances during their time, may interpret it in different ways. That was the case with Ottoman law, which was not abstracted from the real world but constituted an essential part of it, thanks, *inter alia*, to the flexibility of the Legal fictions upheld in order to conform to purely literal Hanafi theory.[17] This means that to be acceptable to statesmen, Ottoman legal discourse on the status of a territory had to be set in the traditional Hanafi frame. Vice versa, Hanafi categories needed to be adapted to the Ottoman context of the time. Therefore, of the official and unofficial sources which describe territoriality or refer to the Ottoman terminology about it, the richest are the jurisprudential and legal material, archival documents, the texts of international agreements, chronicles, *inşāʾ* works and miscellanies (*mecmūʿa*).[18]

Even when a Hanafi scholar accepted the principles of law articulated in Arabic by the founders of the Hanafi juridical *maḏhab*,[19] he could nonetheless

17 Ahmet Akgündüz, *Osmanlı Devleti'nde Gayrimüslimlerin Yönetimi* (İstanbul: Timaş Yayınları, 2008), 9–20, 37.

18 On the *münşeʾāt* and other miscellanies, see András J. Riedlmayer, "Ottoman Copybooks of Correspondence and Miscellanies as a Source for Political and Cultural History," *Acta Orientalia* 61, no. 1–2 (March 2008): 201–14; Michele Bernardini, "Les *Münşeʾāt* de ʿAcem Karabekir Efendi dans le fonds Kahle du Département d'Études Orientales de l'Université de Turin," ed. Michele Bernardini and Alessandro Taddei, *Eurasian Studies* 8, no. 1–2: Études en l'Honneur de Jean-Louis Bacqué-Grammont (2010): 9–26; Luca Berardi, "The Dilemmas of a Sultan: Ottoman-Safavid Relations in the Letters of the Kitāb Al-Menāmāt (Book of Dreams) of Murād III," *Eurasian Studies* 6 (2008 2007): 47–48.

19 For a brief description of the most prominent Hanafi scholars in ancient, classical and post-classical periods, see Ya'akov Meron, "The Development of Legal Thought in Ḥanafī Texts," *Studia Islamica* 30, no. 1 (1969): 73–118; see also Baber Johansen, *Contingency in a*

innovate in parts of his field of competence. Therefore, speaking of Ottomans, it is meaningless to take into consideration only the founders of this school during the classical period, such as Abū Ḥanīfa, Abū Yūsuf (d. 182/798) and Šaybānī (d. 189/805),[20] or even the second rank of learned Hanafis such as Qudūrī (d. 428/1037),[21] Saraḫsī (d. 483/1090),[22] Marġīnānī (d. 593/1197).[23] The Ottoman period had its own famous *mujtahids*,[24] such as Kamāl al-dīn

Sacred Law: Legal and Ethical Norms in the Muslim Fiqh, Studies in Islamic Law and Society, v. 7 (Leiden: Brill, 1999); Joseph Schacht, *The Origins of Muhammadan Jurisprudence* (Oxford: Clarendon Press, 1979); see also *al-Mawsūʿa al-fiqhiyya*, al-Ṭabāʿa al-ṯāniya, 45 vols. (Kuwayt: Wizārat al-awqāf al-islāmiyya, 1983).

20 John Kelsay, "Al-Shaybani and the Islamic Law of War," *Journal of Military Ethics* 2, no. 1 (March 2003): 63–75; Majid Khadduri, ed., *The Islamic Law of Nations: Shaybānī's Siyar.* Translated with an Introduction, Notes and Appendices (Baltimore: The Johns Hopkins Press, 1966).

21 Abū 'l-Ḥusayn Aḥmad al-Qudūrī, *The Mukhtaṣar of Imām Abū'l-Ḥusayn Aḥmad ibn Muḥammad ibn Aḥmad ibn Jaʿfar ibn Ḥamdān al-Qudūrī al-Baghdādī (362 AH–428 AH): a manual of Islamic law according to the Ḥanafī School*, trans. Ṭāhir Maḥmood Kiānī (London: Ta-Ha, 2010).

22 Muḥammad b. Aḥmad al-Saraḫsī, *al-Nukat wa-huwa šarḥ li-Ziyādāt al-ziyādāt li 'l-imām* [...] *Muḥammad b. al-Ḥasan al-Šaybānī wa-šarḥuhā li'l-imām Abī Naṣr Aḥmad b. Muḥammad al-ʿAttābī al-Buḫārī* (Beirut: ʿĀlam al-kutub, 1986).

23 Burhān al-dīn Abū 'l-Ḥasan al-Marġīnānī, *al-Hidāya šarḥ Bidāyat al-mubtadi'* (Cairo: Dār al-salām, 2000). Cf. also the old English translation by Charles Hamilton, *The Hedaya, or Guide: A Commentary on the Mussulman Laws* (London: W. H. Allen, 1870).

24 Here I follow the discourse about *ijtihād*, according to which Islamic scholars elaborated a theory which accounted for the realities of historical development, distinguishing between a) *ijtihād muṭlaq*, i.e. the creative act of independent interpretation of the legal sources, through which the founding imams derived from the revealed sources a systematic structure of law; b) *ijtihād al-maḏhab*, i.e. creative development of the law within the structures of the *maḏhab*, the characteristic achievement of Muslim jurists through the centuries. For further details see: Wael B. Hallaq, *Authority, Continuity, and Change in Islamic Law* (Cambridge: Cambridge University Press, 2001); Wael B. Hallaq, "Was the Gate of Ijtihad Closed?," *International Journal of Middle East Studies* 16, no. 1 (March 1984): 3–41; Baber Johansen, *The Islamic Law on Land Tax and Rent: The Peasants' Loss of Property Rights as Interpreted in the Hanafite Legal Literature of the Mamluk and Ottoman Periods*, Exeter Arabic and Islamic Series (London: Croom Helm, 1988), 1–2; Rudolph Peters, "*Idjtihād* and *Taqlīd* in 18th and 19th Century Islam," *Die Welt Des Islams* 20, no. 3–4 (1980): 131–45; Hamid Algar, "Q. 21: 78–9: A Qur'anic Basis for *ijtihad*?," *Journal of Qur'anic Studies* 4, no. 2 (2002): 1–22; Éric Chaumont, "La problématique classique de l'*ijtihâd* et la question de l'*ijtihâd* du prophète: *ijtihâd, wahy* et *ʿisma*," *Studia Islamica* 75, no. 1 (1992): 105–39; Sumbul Ali-Karamali and Fiona Dunne, "The *ijtihad* Controversy," *Arab Law Quarterly* 9 (1994): 238–57; Bernard Weiss, "Interpretation in Islamic Law: The Theory of *Ijtihad*," *American Journal of Comparative Law* 26 (1978): 199–212.

(d. 861/1457);[25] Molla Hüsrev (d. 885/1480),[26] Ibrāhīm al-Ḥalabī (d. 956/1549),[27] Ḥaṣkafī (d. 1088/1677). A work by Ḥaṣkafī, entitled *Durr al-muḫtār*[28] was to become one of the basic Hanafi references until the nineteenth century thanks to the supercommentary compiled by Ibn ʿĀbidīn (d. 1258/1842). Ottoman Hanafi scholars were also conversant with earlier Hanafi works produced in India and Central Asia: the first and foremost of these was the *Fatāwā Tātārḫānīyya*, compiled by order of Tātārḫān (d. soon after 752/1351), a nobleman at the court of Muḥammad II Ṭuġlaq (r. 725/1324–752/1351).

All these scholars are a product of their specific historical context, even though, when they discuss a single topic on the ground of pure Islamic theory, they are often likely to be detached from reality. According to Colin Imber, "most of the cases in the juristic repertory are purely hypothetical, even in areas of the law which had an application in practice." Imber goes further saying that "[t]he jurists in fact never intended large areas of the *shariʿa* to function as a practical system of law." But despite this categorical statement, even *fiqh* was not totally closed to the world outside. Indeed, works on *fiqh* could be primary sources that would provide us with historical evidence, especially in the commentaries on the margins or in treatisies (*risālas*) about specific topics.

However, as Khaled Abou El Fadl puts it, "Yet one must be careful not to confuse the views and debates of professional Muslim jurists with some grand metaphysical reality called Islam.... The juridical discourses are only a part

---

25 Kamāl al-dīn b. Humām al-Sīwāsī al-Iskandarī was born in Alexandria in Egypt. He became *qāḍī* in the town of Sivas. He wrote several works on *furūʿ al-fiqh* and *uṣūl al-fiqh* that were highly influential.

26 Muḥammad b. Farāmurz Mullā Ḫusraw [Molla Hüsrev], *Durar al-ḥukkām fī šarḥ Ġurar al-aḥkām* (İstanbul: Maṭbaʿa-i Kutubḫāna-i Meḥmed Asʿad, 1300); Ferhat Koca, *Osmanlı Şeyhülislâmı Molla Hüsrev: Hayatı, Eserleri ve Görüşleri* (Ankara: Türkiye Diyanet Vakfı Yayınları, 2011); Nicola Melis, *Trattato sulla guerra: il* Kitāb al-ǧihād *di Molla Hüsrev* (Cagliari: Aipsa, 2002); Richard Repp, "Some Observation on the Development of the Ottoman Learned Hierarchy," in *Scholars, Saints, and Sufis; Muslim Religious Institutions in the Middle East since 1500*, ed. Nikki R. Keddie (Berkeley: University of California Press, 1972), 30.

27 Ibrāhīm al-Ḥalabī, who lived in Egypt when it was conquered in 1517 by the Ottomans, then moved to the capital of the new dominating power: Constantinople. There he died in 956/1549, at the advanced age of 90 years, after having taught in his new place and raised a new generation of disciples. Ḥalabī's masterwork is *Multaqā al-abḥur*, ed. Wahbī al-Albānī, 2 vols. (Beirut: Mu'assasat al-Risāla li'l-Ṭibāʿa wa'l-Našr wa'l-Tawzīʿ, 1989).

28 There exists an English translation of this work, see Muḥammad b. ʿAlī Ḥaṣkafī, *The* Durrul Mukhtar *of Muhammad Ala-ud-Din Haskafi: Being the Well-Known Commentary of the* Tanwirul Absar *of Muhammad ibn Abdullah Tamartashi with an English Translation by Brij Mohan Dayal* (Lucknow: Anglo-Arabic Press, 1913).

of the reality of Islam."[29] This argument is also valid for the Ottoman period. Indeed, for a due understanding of the legal application in practice, one should take into consideration the major categories of Ottoman legal documents: fatwas and certificates issued by judges (on a strictly Islamic level); decrees issued by the sultan or by officials within the circle of the Palace (on an official imperial ground).

It is generally accepted that one of the most influential and incisive juridical activities in developing Ottoman Hanafi law is the *iftāʾ*, that is, handing down in the form of fatwa an authoritative opinion on a point of law.[30]. Among the many conditions required by the classical doctrine for being a mufti and delivering fatwas is a profound knowledge of the practice of *ijtihād*. In Ottoman times, the *šayḫ al-islām* Abū al-Suʿūd (Turk. Ebüssuʿūd) Efendi (d. 1574) was thought to be the most authoritative scholar to issue fatwas.[31] A famous sentence, written by the Ottoman poet ʿAṭāʾī (d. 1045/1685), claims that "the effect of [Ebüssuʿūd Efendi and Kemalpaşazade's][32] *ijtihād* is the harmonization of the *qānūn* with the noble sharia, putting religious and state affairs in the best order."[33] The legal norms regarding territoriality, according to Ottoman Islamic view, are mainly based on the issue of fatwas.[34]

The original Ottoman *iftāʾ* was written in Ottoman Turkish. On the contrary, before 1632, the most important Hanafi texts on *fiqh*, both from the Ottoman and pre-Ottoman time, were all written in Arabic. Only in 1632 was the very important text written by Molla Hüsrev in the fifteenth century (*Durar al-ḥukkām fī šarḥ Ġurar al-aḥkām*) first translated into Ottoman-Turkish by

29 Khaled Abou El Fadl, *Rebellion and Violence in Islamic Law* (Cambridge: Cambridge University Press, 2001), 21.

30 On the topic of the function of *iftāʾ*, see Muhammad Khalid Masud, Brinkley Morris Messick, and David Stephan Powers, eds., *Islamic Legal Interpretation: Muftis and Their Fatwas* (Karachi: Oxford University Press, 2005); Uriel Heyd, "Some Aspects of the Ottoman Fetvā," *Bulletin of the School of Oriental and African Studies* 32, no. 1 (February 1969): 35.

31 Colin Imber, *Ebu's-Suʿud: The Islamic Legal Tradition*, Jurists--Profiles in Legal Theory (Stanford, Calif: Stanford University Press, 1997); Engin Deniz Akarlı, review of *Ebu's-suʿud: the Islamic legal tradition*, by Colin Imber, *Islamic Law and Society*, Jurists—profiles in legal theory, 6, no. 2 (1999): 284–88; Mustafa E. Duzdağ, *Şeyhülislam Ebussu'ud Efendi Fetvâları Işığında 16. Asir Türk Hayati* (Istanbul: Enderun, 1972).

32 Kemalpaşazade [Kamāl Paşazāde] was a famous Ottoman scholar and *šayḫ al-islām* who died in the year 940/1534.

33 Nevʿīzāde ʿAṭāʾī, *Hadaʾik al-hakaʾik fī tekmilet al-šaqāʾiq* (Istanbul, 1268), 185.

34 Najwa al-Qattan, "Dhimmis in the Muslim Court: Legal Autonomy and Religious Discrimination," *International Journal of Middle Eastern Studies* 31, no. 3 (1999): 429–44.

the erudite Aḥmad b. ʿAlī al-Anqarawī. In 1640 another very important Hanafi handbook (Ḥalabī's *Multaqā al-abḥur*, written in the first half of the sixteenth century) was translated from Arabic into Ottoman-Turkish by Muḥammad Mawqufātī.[35] This shows that fatwas, as opposed to *fiqh* literature, were not limited to an inner circle of Hanafi scholars, as much as that has sometimes been maintained. Rigorous legal discourse became more available to clerks who had not received a thorough Islamic training. In fact, several bureaucrats had little or no knowledge of the Arabic language, despite the fact that clerks were usually trained in *medreses*. It was by chancery practice that Hanafi law could be applied to the context of daily life.

A good example can be found in the very well-known fatwas written in the Ottoman language by the aforementioned Ebüssuʿūd Efendi. In line with Hanafi opinion, he never takes into consideration anything but a worldview based on the division into two *dār*s, never mentioning any intermediate *dār*.[36] One of these fatwas (germane to our topic[37]), issued in June 1567 on the occasion of the renewal of the Venetian capitulation, is particularly interesting for our case.[38]

In this text Ebüssuʿūd Efendi comes out in favor of a Hanafi application of the norm and opposes those scribes who include clauses contrary to *fiqh* in

35 On the question of translation in the Ottoman Empire, cf. Mustafa Isen, "Türkçe'nin Yazı Dili Oluşumunda Çevirinin Rolü," in *Dil, Kültür ve Çağdaşlaşma*, ed. Bahaeddin Yediyıldız (Ankara: Hacettepe Üniversitesi, 2003), 137–51; Berrín Aksoy, "Translation Activities in the Ottoman Empire," *Journal Des Traducteurs/Meta: Translators' Journal* 50, no. 3 (2005): 949–56; Hilmi Ziya Ülken, *Uyanış Devirlerinde Tercümenin Rolü* (Istanbul: Ülken Yayınları, 1997).

36 For examples see Duzdağ, *Şeyhülislam Ebussu'ud Efendi Fetvâları*, n. 368 ("Mes'ele Zeyd-i zimmî İslama gelmek için Amrın gemisine binip *dâr-i İslama* gelirken, zimmî-i mezkûru, Amr-i re'is 'kulumdur' deyu beyʿ eylemek istedikte, zimmî re'is yüzüne hürriyetin isbât eylese, şerʿan halâs olur mu?"); n. 434 ("Mes'ele: Zeyd-i zimmî *dâr-i harb*den *dâr-i İslam*a gelip, Hind-i zimmiyeyi bunda alıp, mülk ev alıp, baʿdehu Hindi ev içinde koyup gidip, anda fevt olup, Zeyneb-i zimmiye, ki kız kardeşi kızıdır, *dâr-i İslam*a gelip, Hind evi beyʿ etmiş olsa, Zeyneb veraset kendine münhasır idüğünü isbat edicek evi almağa kadire olur mu? Elcevap: Eğer Zeyd bunda zimmî olup, *dâr-i harb*e ticaret üzerine gidip yine gelmek üzerine fevt olduysa, rubuʿ Hinde bakî Zeynebe değer. Eğer müste'men olup yine *dâr-i harb*e avdet ettiyse, andan zimmîler miras yemezler *dâr-i harb*deki vârisleri gelince, beyt-ül-mâlde malı durur") etc. [Italics are mine].

37 For the complete text of the fatwa, see ibid., n. 478.

38 Text in İbrahim Efendi Peçevi, *Ta'rīḫ* (Ankara: Kültür ve Turizm Bakanlığı Yayınları, 1981), 1:486–87; also in Duzdağ, *Şeyhülislam Ebussu'ud Efendi Fetvâları*, n. 478. Quoted by Victor L. Ménage, "The English Capitulation of 1580: A Review Article," *International Journal of Middle East Studies* 12, no. 2 (1980): 373–83.

the capitulations (*ʿahdnāme*s in Ottoman Turkish). Ebüssuʿūd's opinion was aimed at accommodating, but also segregating, large communities of traders coming in from the *dār al-ḥarb*, often considering them as temporary residents with a special safe-conduct (*amān*) or as people subject to *ḏimma* regulations. In brief, European consuls in the Levant should have been considered as *amanla gelen ḥarbiler* (a phrase corresponding to the Islamic category of *mustaʾmin*); the local minority groups acting as intermediaries should have been included in the category of *ḏimmī*. The distinction between resident and non-resident Genoese suggests that the status of *mustaʾmin* was linked to the temporary nature of the *amān*, and that, after a certain period of residence in the *dār al-islām*, foreign nationality was disregarded and the resident acquired the status of *ḏimmī*.[39] The status granted by the *ʿahdnāme*s did guarantee to the *mustaʾmin* certain elements of extraterritoriality and quasi-immunity that were unavailable to Ottoman non-Muslims. In other words, the discourse was focused on the group or individual status, rather than the territorial conception.

The principle of "utility" (*maṣlaḥa*) to the Islamic community (umma) is very important in Ottoman practice according to Hanafi theory. As stated in several fatwas, in fact, a long-term peace treaty, normally not acceptable according to the Hanafi view, can nonetheless be compatible with the general good or public interest (*maṣlaḥat al-ʿumūm*), as well as with an extreme pragmatism; as a corollary, there can be no peace if the peace in question is of no practical utility. The ruler has the power to direct the *qāḍī*, as his agent, to apply one doctrine and disregard another. This is exemplified in a passage from the Ebüssuʿūd's fatwa cited above:

> An agreement (*ṣulḥ*) may be made with the infidels only when it is to the interest of all the Muslims to do so. If peace, permanent or temporary, has been made, it then appears more profitable to break it, therefore it is obligatory and necessary to break it.[40]

39 Ménage, "A Review Article."

40 "Menfaʿat saymayıcak asla sulh meşruʿ değildir. Müşahede olunup müebbed yahud muvakkat sulh olunduktan sonra, menfaʿat bu zamanda bozulması enfaʾ görülse, elbette bozmak vâcîb ve lâzım olur." Duzdağ, *Şeyhülislam Ebussuʾud Efendi Fetvâları*, n. 478.

3 Ottoman Archival Documents

The Ottoman sources relevant to the question of terminology about Ottoman territoriality are predominantly archival material. The most important archival collection is called *Mühimme Defterleri* ("Registers of Important Affairs," hereafter MD) and, apart from two older Registers,[41] it is housed in the *Başbakanlık* State Archive located in Istanbul. This collection covers the period between 961/1553–54 and 1300/1882–83 and comprises 263 volumes arranged in chronological order. It is based on day-to-day records of the sultans' ongoing official correspondence with Ottoman officials and foreign representatives.

Therefore, this source includes a great deal of information on Ottoman legal and administrative tradition mainly not based on *fiqh* and is instrumental in making us understand the function of Ottoman law and administration in practice, placing our discourse on Ottoman territoriality in the historical context of its time. Unfortunately the huge amount of information is not earlier in date than the middle of the sixteenth century.

A systematic search of the innumerable documents in the edited volumes of the Registers, published by the Office of the Prime Minister, Ottoman Archives (*Başbakanlık Osmanlı Arşivi*)[42] in Istanbul, has yielded no trace of any reference to *dār al-ʿahd*. Instead, what is focused on is the legal status of communities or individuals.

Conversely, in line with Hanafi view, there are so many entries in the *Mühimme Defterleri* referring to the distinction between *dār al-islām* and *dār al-ḥarb*.[43] In the documents they are referred to also with typical Ottoman locutions, such as *Memālik-i Maḥrūse* ("the Well-Protected Domains"), *diyār-ı ḥarb* ("the Abodes of War"), *kefere vilayetleri* ("the Provinces of Disbelief"), *küffār-ı ḫāksār vilāyetleri* ("the Provinces of the Treacherous Unbelievers")[44] etc.

For example, among the many entries, in an order (*ḥüküm*) dated 979 (1571) sent to the Governor and to the Treasurer of Buda (Budun), the writer makes a

---

41 MD E-12321 (951–952/1544–45) and MD 888 are both preserved at the Museum Library of the Topkapı Palace in Istanbul (hereafter TKMS). The former has been published, see: Halil Sahillioğlu, ed., *Topkapı Sarayı Arşivi H. 951–952 Tarihli ve E-12321 Numaralı Mühimme Defteri* (Istanbul: İRCİCA, 2002); the latter has been the subject of an MA dissertation, see: Abid Yaşaroğlu, "Topkapı Sarayı Müzesi Kütüphanesi Koğuşlar 888 Numaralı Mühimme Defteri (1a-260a. Tahlil ve Transkrip)" (İstanbul Üniversitesi Sosyal Bilimler Enstitüsü Yeniçağ Tarihi Anabilim Dalı, 1995).

42 Thousand of decrees in the published Registers were surveyed (MD E-12321, 3, 5, 6, 7, 12, 82, 83, 85).

43 For instance, see MD E-12321, n. 359, 458; MD 3, n. 695; 699, 700, 701, 725, 791 etc.

44 MD 9 (977–978/1569–1570): n. 204.

reference to the territorial division between the “Abode of War” (*dār al-ḥarb*) and the “Well-Protected Domains” (*Memālik-i Maḥrūse*), saying that “a bandit living in the mountains of the People of malice (*ehl-i fesād*, i.e. trouble-making folk) came from the Abode of War to the Well-Protected Domains to cause damage” (*dārü'l-ḥarbden haydud ü ehl-i fesād Memālik-i Maḥrūse'ye zarar kasdına gelüp*).[45]

A *ḥüküm* sent to the governor (*Beylerbeyi*) of Tamesvar on the 21 *rabīʿ al-awwal* 967 (12, December 1558), mentions a specific part of *dār al-ḥarb*, the Kingdom of Austria (*Nemçe Kıralık*), that is defined as “Austria, the Kingdom and Hometown of the disbelief” (*Nemçe keferesinün memleket ve vilāyeti*).[46]

4 International Agreements

In his in-depth study on Ottoman-Polish relations, Dariusz Kołodziejczyk has published important documents that demonstrate how the terminology about territories in Ottoman international agreements (*ʿahdnāme*s and *ṣulḥnāme*s) does not necessarily refer to the real political condition of a land or to the effective sovereignty of the Ottomans there. A number of entries in *ʿahdnāme*s offer a demonstration in this respect.

For instance, in an Ottoman *ʿahdnāme* bestowed upon the Polish king, Algiers was still defined as *dār al-jihād*, even if dated 1577, that is fifty years after the Ottoman conquest. The subsequent *ʿahdnāme*s given in the period 1591 to 1667 to Poland presented an even stronger definition of Algiers, i.e. *dār al-jihād wa'l-ḥarb* (“The realm of *jihād* and war”). Here the term *dār al-jihād* is probably intended to describe the Western Mediterranean.

Here is an example of such a kind of entry from the *ʿahdnāme* sent by the Ottoman sultan, Aḥmad I (r. 1012/1603–1026/1617), to the Polish King, Sigismund III, in 1607, where the former defined himself as follows:

> the *padishah*, the sultan, and the emperor of the great dignity of the noblest of the towns and cities … and of Algiers, Western Tripoli and Tunis, [being] the area of the holy war and combat …[47]

45 İsmet Binark, ed., *12 numaralı mühimme defteri, 978–979/1570–1572*, Dîvân-ı Hümâyûn sicilleri dizisi 4 (Ankara: T. C. Başbakanlık Devlet Arşivleri Genel Müdürlüğü, 1996), n. 1139.

46 İsmet Binark, ed., *3 numaralı mühimme defteri, 966–968/1558–1560*, Dîvân-ı Hümâyûn sicilleri dizisi 1 (Ankara: T. C. Başbakanlık Devlet Arşivleri Genel Müdürlüğü, 1993), n. 600.

47 “ve darü'l-cihad ve'l-harb Cezayir-i Magrib ve Trablus-i Garb ve Tunusun […] kılaʿ-i felek-i irtifaʿın padişahı ve sultanı ve hakan-i ʿazimü […].” Dariusz Kołodziejczyk,

We can also mention the case of the agreements with the Republic of Venice, where the terms related to the concepts of the two *dār*s are not so frequently used. In the Venetian Capitulation of 1521, the Empire is possibly identified with the imperial capital and defined as the "Costantinople, the abode of the well-protected high sultanate" (*dār al-sulṭānet al-ʿaliye maḥrūse-i Qostantiniye*).[48] While the enemy territory is regularly defined as *dār al-ḥarb*, for example in the Capitulation of 1482 (*dār-i ḥarbdan zemān-i ʿadavet benim memālik-i maḥrūsemde*),[49] while the territory of Islam is defined as *dār al-islām*, there is no entry referring to any *dār al-ʿahd*. However, there is a hendiadys or even three terms, denoting the concept of peace or truce, without any emphasis on the territorial dimension, but rather in terms of the status of individuals or groups, of trade concessions, etc. Some of these hendiadys are "friendship and peace" (*dostluk ve barışlık*),[50] "peace and reconciliation" (*ṣulḥ ve ṣalāḥa*)[51] or "friendship and agreement" (*dostluk ve müʿahede*)[52] Sometimes the expression includes three terms, such as "friendship, peace and reconciliation" (*dostluk ve ṣulḥ ve ṣalāḥa*) or "friendship, love and truce" (*dostluk muḥabbet muṣālaḥa*).[53]

5 Concluding Remarks

To summarize, in the case of the Ottoman Empire, to assume the Hanafi theory of the dichotomist division between *dār al-islām* and *dār al-ḥarb*, as being the Ottoman legal practice applied to territoriality would appear to be an over-simplification. Even by assuming the existence of the third territorial category, i.e. *dār al-ʿahd*, the need to provide an accomplished description of the extreme richness and complexity of the Ottoman institutions—with a particular focus

---

Ottoman-Polish Diplomatic Relations (15th–18th Century): An Annotated Edition of ʿahdnames and Other Documents, The Ottoman Empire and Its Heritage, v. 18 (Leiden: Brill, 2000), 330 and 334; see also 270, 285, 303, 314 etc.

48 Theunissen, "Ottoman-Venetian Diplomatics: The *ʿAhd-Names*," 436. For similar definitions, see also The Venetian Capitulation of 1540 (*dār al-ḫilāfet al-ʿaliye maḥmiye-i Kostantiniyeʾde yazıldı*), Ibid., 469, and the Venetian Capitulation of 1567 (*dār al–ḫilāfet al–ʿaliye Kostantiniyeʾde yazıldı*), 469.

49 Theunissen, "Ottoman-Venetian Diplomatics: The *ʿAhd-Names*," 374.

50 See, for instance, the Venetian *ʿahdnāme* of 1619 (Ibid., 595.).

51 See, for example, the Polish *ʿahdnāme* of 1598, Kołodziejczyk, *Ottoman-Polish Diplomatic Relations (15th-18th Century)*, 314; the Venetian *ʿahdnāme* of 1625, Theunissen, "Ottoman-Venetian Diplomatics: The *ʿAhd-Names*," 620.

52 The Venetian *ʿahdnāme* of 1619, Theunissen, "Ottoman-Venetian Diplomatics: The *ʿAhd-Names*," 593.

53 It is in the Venetian *ʿahdnāme* of 1482, see ibid., 371.

on the cases of laws referring to territoriality, both within and outside the Ottoman lands—is not satisfied. As I tried to demonstrate, the classical Islamic worldview is not completely useful for our purpose of understanding.

Even in its relations with *dār al-ḥarb* the Ottoman authority considered different types of status of *ḥarbī* countries, namely, those with a *ʿahdnāme*, and those without a *ʿahdnāme*. The latter were in turn divided into states without an ambassador but represented by the ambassador of another European state with a *ʿahdnāme* and those that were not represented at all.

The same could be said for the status of territories formally part, with no distinction, of the *dār al-islām*; but, in fact, each with a different status. A case in point is the Republic of Ragusa (Dubrovnik), a tributary state of the sultan. Basically the Republic of Ragusa consisted of a small area along the western shore of the Balkans coastal strip, at the southern extremity of the Dalmatian archipelago. In Ottoman documents Ragusan people are not always termed *ḏimmī*s, but sometimes Latins. During the sixteenth century, Dubrovnik, like other local principalities in Bosnia, requested Ottoman intervention in settling their disputes. After the *ʿahdnāme* of 1442, "perhaps more unconsciously than not, Dubrovnik became an autonomous part of the Turkish Empire."[54]

Other cases in point are the southern frontier of the empire, including the Red sea coast and the "Province of Abissinia" (*Ḥabeş Eyaleti*);[55] the Black sea region,[56] in general, and the Romanian principalities,[57] Naxos (*Nakşe*) and

---

54 Biegman, *The Turco-Ragusan Relationship*, 26.

55 Cengiz Orhonlu, *Osmanlı İmparatorluğu'nun Güney Siyaseti. Habeş Eyaleti*, 2nd ed. (Ankara: Türk Tarih Kurumu Yayınları, 1996).

56 Jean-Louis Bacqué-Grammont, "Un voyageur perigourdin sur les rives de la Mer Noire au temps D'Henri IV," in *Enjeux politiques, économiques et militaires en Mer noire (XIVe–XXIe siècles): études à la mémoire de Mihail Guboglu*, ed. Faruk Bilici, Ionel Cândea, and Anca Popescu (Braïla: Musée de Braïla–Éditions Istros, 2007), 109–16; Dariusz Kołodziejczyk, "Inner lake or frontier? The Ottoman Black Sea in the Sixteenth and Seventeenth Centuries," in *Enjeux politiques, économiques et militaires en Mer noire (XIVe–XXIe siècles): études à la mémoire de Mihail Guboglu*, ed. Faruk Bilici, Ionel Cândea, and Anca Popescu (Braïla: Musée de Braïla–Éditions Istros, 2007), 125–40; Anca Popescu, "La Mer Noire ottomane: mare clausum? Mare apertum?," in *Enjeux politiques, économiques et militaires en Mer noire (XIVe–XXIe siècles): études à la mémoire de Mihail Guboglu*, ed. Faruk Bilici, Ionel Cândea, and Anca Popescu (Braïla: Musée de Braïla–Éditions Istros, 2007), 141–70.

57 Viorel Panaite, *The Ottoman Law of War and Peace: The Ottoman Empire and Tribute Payers*, East European Monographs, no. 562 (Boulder: East European Monographs, Distributed by Columbia University Press, 2000).

the Cycladies;[58] even territories on the outskirts of Istanbul, such as the Latin community of Galata-Pera.[59]

Official documents about the Province of Abissinia rarely use the *dār-al-islām* / *dār al-ḥarb* dichotomy. In place of *dār al-ḥarb*, we can find the terms "Territories of Unbelief" (*diyār-ı küfrü*)[60] or "Provinces of the Miserable Unbelievers" (*küffār-ı ḫāksār vilāyetleri*).[61] In place of *dār al-islām*, the documents constantly prefer "Well-Protected Domains" (*Memālik-i Maḥrūse*).

With respect to the Black sea region and the Romanian principalities, these lands were considered as part of either *dār al-islām* or *dār al-ḥarb,* depending on situations of peace and war. The documents on those principalities never mention either *dār al-ʿahd* or *dār al-ṣulḥ*.[62] In the province of Algier, the definition *dār al-ḥarb wa'l-jihād* remained in use for many decades, despite no longer having any literal sense.[63]

As we wrote earlier, the discourse was focused on the group or individual status, and on fiscal or commercial matters rather than the territorial issues. The Ottoman legal administrative distinction of the territory was always a legal compromise due to the fact that Ottomans were supposed to be in accordance with the prescript of Hanafi law. Rather than considering the terminology for territory, it is perhaps preferable to refer to some other legal concepts. In Ottoman documents, official and unofficial, there are two ever-recurring instances of hendiadys: "pact and safety" (*ʿahd ve-amān*)[64] and/or "security and safety" (*amn ve-amān*).[65]

---

58 B. Slot, *Archipelagus Turbatus: Les Cyclades Entre Colonisation Latine et Occupation Ottomane C. 1500–1718*, Uitgaven van Het Nederlands Historisch-Archaeologisch Instituut Te Istanbul 51 (Istanbul: Nederlands Historisch-Archaeologisch Instituut te Istanbul, 1982).

59 Galata was a "neighbourhood of the Ottoman capital with a distinct "Frankish" character, where since the Byzantine times foreign merchant communities established themselves alongside the local Greek and Jewish population." Tijana Krstić, "Contesting Subjecthood and Sovereignty in Ottoman Galata in the Age of Confessionalization: The *Carazo* Affair, 1613–1617," ed. Nicola Melis, *Oriente Moderno* 93, no. 2: Minorities, Intermediaries and Middlemen in the Ottoman Empire (2013): 427.

60 MD 47: n. 560.

61 MD 48: n. 10.

62 Hunt, "The Romanian Lands in the Sixteenth Century," 391–414; see also Panaite, *The Ottoman Law of War and Peace*, 83–86.

63 See note 47 above.

64 See, for instance, MD 3: n. 175; The Venetian *ʿahdnāme* of 1619. Theunissen, "Ottoman-Venetian Diplomatics: The *ʿAhd-Names*," 595.

65 MD 3: n. 175, 178, 180.

ʿAhd is a Qur'anic term used over the whole range of ordinary civil contracts[66] and political agreements, even between believers and unbelievers; thence: agreement, covenant, treaty.[67] *Amān* is a term that refers to the classical Islamic principle of ensuring the safety of non-Muslims coming from territories outside Islamic sovereignty; it is usually the subject of a specific chapter in the Book of jihad included in treatises on *fiqh*.[68] The *amān* is a political *ʿahd* with a religious sanction, granted to non-Muslims living for diplomatic, commercial or other purposes in lands ruled by an Islamic representative. The Ottomans, in turn, confirmed the principle of protection granted to Christian foreigners entering their territories, and gave them safe-conducts.

Based on Mamluk practice, as theorized by a famous clerk, Qalqašandī,[69] the Ottoman chanceries distinguished between the special (*ḫāṣṣ*) *amān*, granted to one or several non-Muslim foreigners, and the general (*ʿāmm*) *amān,* granted to a determinate group, or to the inhabitants of a region, exclusively by the sultan or his deputies.[70] The capitulations (*ʿahdnāmes*) should be included in the category of the *amān ʿāmm.*

There is still much to learn about the Ottoman conception of territoriality also with regard to the way the Ottoman central government interacted with the most remote frontier areas with their lack of precise and delimited borders, and with their potential for negotiation and flexibility. In conclusion, we can assume that, when at war, territories that were not part of the very core of the Empire were considered as *dār al-ḥarb*. On the contrary, if in peaceful relations they were part of *dār al-islām*. The real and effective territorial status was the result of a political, bureaucratic and administrative tradition, much more flexible than the rigid terminology of the Hanafi school.

In fact, *dār al-ḥarb* was too vast a territory for the Ottomans to be able to interact without negotiation. The idea of a perpetual jihad against all the infidels who did not accept the supremacy of Islam was eventually to become mere rhetoric.[71] In fact, the geographical limits of Ottoman commercial

66 Q 17:34; 23:8.

67 Joseph Schacht, "'Ahd," *Encyclopaedia of Islam, Vol. I, A–B* (Leiden: Brill, 1960).

68 On a Hanafi treatment of these matters in Ottoman time, cf. Nicola Melis, "Osmanlı Aracılarının Doğudaki Hukuki Statüsü, 16. Yüzyıl [The Legal Status of Ottoman Middlemen (16th Century)]," in *Harp ve Sulh. Avrupa ve Osmanlılar.* [*War and Peace. Europe and the Ottomans*], ed. Couto Dejanirah (İstanbul: Kitap Yayınevi, 2010), 203–36.

69 On the life of the eminent scholar, see Clifford E. Bosworth, "al-Ḳalḳas̲h̲andī," *Encyclopaedia of Islam, Vol. IV, Iran-Kha* (Leiden: Brill, 1978).

70 John Wansbrough, "The Safe-Conduct in Muslim Chancery Practice," *Bulletin of the School of Oriental and African Studies* 34, no. 1 (1971): 20–35.

71 Colin Imber, "The Ottoman Dynastic Myth," *Turcica* 29 (1987): 7–27.

expansion are clear: Venice, and occasionally Ancona, in the Mediterranean, and Leopolis[72] in present-day Ukraine appear to have been the westward limits of Ottoman geopolitical space in its commercial extension towards the *dār al-ḥarb*.

References

Abou El Fadl, Khaled. *Rebellion and Violence in Islamic Law*. Cambridge: Cambridge University Press, 2001.

Akarlı, Engin Deniz. Review of *Ebu's-su'ud: the Islamic legal tradition*, by Colin Imber. *Islamic Law and Society*, Jurists--profiles in legal theory, 6, no. 2 (1999): 284–88.

Akgündüz, Ahmet. *Osmanlı Devleti'nde Gayrimüslimlerin Yönetimi*. Istanbul: Timaş Yayınları, 2008.

Aksoy, Berrín. "Translation Activities in the Ottoman Empire." *Journal Des Traducteurs/ Meta: Translators' Journal* 50, no. 3 (2005): 949–56.

Algar, Hamid. "Q. 21: 78–9: A Qur'anic Basis for *ijtihad*?" *Journal of Qur'anic Studies* 4, no. 2 (2002): 1–22.

Ali-Karamali, Sumbul, and Fiona Dunne. "The *ijtihad* Controversy." *Arab Law Quarterly* 9 (1994): 238–57.

'Aṭā'ī, Nev'īzāde. *Hada'ik al-haka'ik fī tekmilet al-šaqā'iq*. Istanbul, 1268.

Bacqué-Grammont, Jean-Louis. "Un voyageur perigourdin sur les rives de la Mer Noire au temps D'Henri IV." In *Enjeux politiques, économiques et militaires en Mer noire (XIVe–XXIe siècles): études à la mémoire de Mihail Guboglu*, edited by Faruk Bilici, Ionel Cândea, and Anca Popescu, 109–16. Braïla: Musée de Braïla; Éditions Istros, 2007.

Berardi, Luca. "The Dilemmas of a Sultan: Ottoman-Safavid Relations in the Letters of the Kitāb Al-Menāmāt (Book of Dreams) of Murād III." *Eurasian Studies* 6 (2008 2007): 47–48.

Bernardini, Michele. "Les *Münşe'āt* de 'Acem Karabekir Efendi dans le fonds Kahle du Département d'Études Orientales de l'Université de Turin." Edited by Michele Bernardini and Alessandro Taddei. *Eurasian Studies* 8, no. 1–2: Études en l'Honneur de Jean-Louis Bacqué-Grammont (2010): 9–26.

Biegman, Nicolaas H. *The Turco-Ragusan Relationship According to the Firmāns of Murād III (1575–1595) Extant in the State Archives of Dubrovnik*. The Hague: Mouton, 1967.

72 The name of this old city has changed with time: it used to be called Lemberg, Leopolis, L'viv, L'vov and Lwów.

Binark, İsmet, ed. *3 numaralı mühimme defteri, 966–968/1558–1560*. Dîvân-ı Hümâyûn sicilleri dizisi 1. Ankara: T. C. Başbakanlık Devlet Arşivleri Genel Müdürlüğü, 1993.

Binark, İsmet, ed. *12 numaralı mühimme defteri, 978–979/1570–1572*. Dîvân-ı Hümâyûn sicilleri dizisi 4. Ankara: T. C. Başbakanlık Devlet Arşivleri Genel Müdürlüğü, 1996.

Bosworth, Clifford E. "al-Ḳalḳas̲h̲andī." *Encyclopaedia of Islam, Vol. IV, Iran-Kha*. Leiden: Brill, 1978.

Chaumont, Éric. "La problématique classique de l'*ijtihâd* et la question de l'*ijtihâd* du prophète: *ijtihâd, wahy* et *ʿisma*." *Studia Islamica* 75, no. 1 (1992): 105–39.

Cook, David. *Understanding Jihad*. Berkeley: University of California Press, 2005.

Duzdağ, Mustafa E. *Şeyhülislam Ebussu'ud Efendi Fetvâları Işığında 16. Asir Türk Hayati*. Istanbul: Enderun, 1972.

Goffman, Daniel. "Negotiating with the Renaissance State." In *The Early Modern Ottomans: Remapping the Empire*, edited by Virginia H. Aksan and Daniel Goffman, 61–74. Cambridge, UK: Cambridge University Press, 2007.

Goffman, Daniel. *The Ottoman Empire and Early Modern Europe*. New Approaches to European History 24. Cambridge: Cambridge University Press, 2002.

Groot, Alexander H. de. "The Historical Development of the Capitulatory Regime in the Ottoman Middle East from the Fifteenth to the Nineteenth Centuries." Edited by Maurits H. Van de Boogert and Kate Fleet. *Oriente Moderno* 22 (83), no. 3: The Ottoman Capitulations: Text and Context (2003): 575–604.

Ḥalabī, Ibrāhīm al-. *Multaqā al-abḥur*. Edited by Wahbī al-Albānī. 2 vols. Beirut: Mu'assasat al-Risāla li'l-Ṭibāʿa wa'l-Našr wa'l-Tawzīʿ, 1989.

Hallaq, Wael B. *Authority, Continuity, and Change in Islamic Law*. Cambridge: Cambridge University Press, 2001.

Hallaq, Wael B. "Was the Gate of Ijtihad Closed?" *International Journal of Middle East Studies* 16, no. 1 (March 1984): 3–41.

Hamilton, Charles. *The Hedaya, or Guide: A Commentary on the Mussulman Laws*. London: W. H. Allen, 1870.

Ḥaṣkafī, Muḥammad b. ʿAlī. *The* Durrul Mukhtar *of Muhammad Ala-ud-Din Haskafi: Being the Well-Known Commentary of the* Tanwirul Absar *of Muhammad ibn Abdullah Tamartashi with an English Translation by Brij Mohan Dayal*. Lucknow: Anglo-Arabic Press, 1913.

Heyd, Uriel. "Some Aspects of the Ottoman Fetvā." *Bulletin of the School of Oriental and African Studies* 32, no. 01 (February 1969): 35.

Heyd, Uriel. *Studies in Old Ottoman Criminal Law*. Edited by Victor L. Ménage. Oxford: Clarendon Press, 1973.

Hunt, Cătălina. "The Romanian Lands in the Sixteenth Century: Their Juridical Status According to Ottoman Law." In *Enjeux politiques, économiques et militaires en Mer noire (XIVᵉ–XXIᵉ siècles): études à la mémoire de Mihail Guboglu*, edited by Faruk

Bilici, Ionel Cândea, and Anca Popescu, 391–414. Braïla: Musée de Braïla; Éditions Istros, 2007.

Imber, Colin. *Ebu's-Suʿud: The Islamic Legal Tradition*. Jurists--Profiles in Legal Theory. Stanford, Calif: Stanford University Press, 1997.

Imber, Colin. "The Ottoman Dynastic Myth." *Turcica* 29 (1987): 7–27.

Imber, Colin. *The Ottoman Empire, 1300–1650: The Structure of Power*. 2nd ed. Houndmills, Basingstoke, Hampshire: Palgrave Macmillan, 2009.

İnalcık, Halil. "Dār al-ʿahd." *Encyclopaedia of Islam, Vol. II, C–G*. Leiden: Brill, 1965.

İnalcık, Halil. "Ottoman Methods of Conquest." *Studia Islamica*, no. 2 (1954): 103.

Isen, Mustafa. "Türkçe'nin Yazı Dili Oluşumunda Çevirinin Rolü." In *Dil, Kültür ve Çağdaşlaşma*, edited by Bahaeddin Yediyıldız, 137–51. Ankara: Hacettepe Üniversitesi, 2003.

Johansen, Baber. *Contingency in a Sacred Law: Legal and Ethical Norms in the Muslim Fiqh*. Studies in Islamic Law and Society, v. 7. Leiden: Brill, 1999.

Johansen, Baber. *The Islamic Law on Land Tax and Rent: The Peasants' Loss of Property Rights as Interpreted in the Hanafite Legal Literature of the Mamluk and Ottoman Periods*. Exeter Arabic and Islamic Series. London: Croom Helm, 1988.

Kelsay, John. "Al-Shaybani and the Islamic Law of War." *Journal of Military Ethics* 2, no. 1 (March 2003): 63–75.

Kermeli, Evgenia. "The Development of Ottoman Legal Studies." *Eurasian Studies* 1, no. 1 (2002): 278–301.

Khadduri, Majid. "Ṣulḥ." *Encyclopaedia of Islam, Vol. IX, San-Sze*. Leiden: Brill, 1998.

Khadduri, Majid, ed. *The Islamic Law of Nations: Shaybānī's Siyar.* Translated with an Introduction, Notes and Appendices. Baltimore: The Johns Hopkins Press, 1966.

Khadduri, Majid. *War and Peace in the Law of Islam*. Baltimore: The Johns Hopkins Press, 1955.

Koca, Ferhat. *Osmanlı Şeyhülislâmı Molla Hüsrev: Hayatı, Eserleri ve Görüşleri*. Ankara: Türkiye Diyanet Vakfı Yayınları, 2011.

Kołodziejczyk, Dariusz. "Inner lake or frontier? The Ottoman Black Sea in the Sixteenth and Seventeenth Centuries." In *Enjeux politiques, économiques et militaires en Mer noire (XIVe–XXIe siècles): études à la mémoire de Mihail Guboglu*, edited by Faruk Bilici, Ionel Cândea, and Anca Popescu, 125–40. Braïla: Musée de Braïla; Éditions Istros, 2007.

Kołodziejczyk, Dariusz. *Ottoman-Polish Diplomatic Relations (15th–18th Century): An Annotated Edition of ʿahdnames and Other Documents*. The Ottoman Empire and Its Heritage, v. 18. Leiden: Brill, 2000.

Krstić, Tijana. "Contesting Subjecthood and Sovereignty in Ottoman Galata in the Age of Confessionalization: The *Carazo* Affair, 1613–1617." Edited by Nicola Melis. *Oriente Moderno* 93, no. 2: Minorities, Intermediaries and Middlemen in the Ottoman Empire (2013): 422–53.

Marġīnānī, Burhān al-Dīn ʿAlī b. Abī Bakr al-. *Al-Hidāya šarḥ Bidāyat al-mubtadiʾ*. Cairo: Dār al-salām, 2000.

Masud, Muhammad Khalid, Brinkley Morris Messick, and David Stephan Powers, eds. *Islamic Legal Interpretation: Muftis and Their Fatwas*. Karachi: Oxford University Press, 2005.

Al-Mawsūʿa al-fiqhiyya. 2nd ed. 45 vols. Kuwayt: Wizārat al-awqāf al-islāmiyya, 1983.

Melis, Nicola. "Osmanlı Aracılarının Doğudaki Hukuki Statüsü, 16. Yüzyıl [The Legal Status of Ottoman Middlemen (16th Century)]." In *Harp ve Sulh. Avrupa ve Osmanlılar.* [*War and Peace. Europe and the Ottomans*], edited by Couto Dejanirah, 203–36. İstanbul: Kitap Yayınevi, 2010.

Melis, Nicola. *Trattato sulla guerra: il* Kitāb al-ǧihād *di Molla Hüsrev*. Cagliari: Aipsa, 2002.

Ménage, Victor L. "The English Capitulation of 1580: A Review Article." *International Journal of Middle East Studies* 12, no. 2 (1980): 373–83.

Ménage, Victor L. Review of *The Turco-Ragusan Relationship According to the Firmāns of Murād III (1575–1595) Extant in the State Archives of Dubrovnik*, by Nicolaas H. Biegman. *Bulletin of the School of Oriental and African Studies* 34, no. 1 (1971): 155.

Meron, Ya'akov. "The Development of Legal Thought in Ḥanafī Texts." *Studia Islamica* 30, no. 1 (1969): 73–118.

Mullā Ḫusraw [Molla Hüsrev], Muḥammad b. Faramurz. *Durar al-ḥukkām fī šarḥ Ġurar al-aḥkām*. İstanbul: Maṭbaʿa-i Kutubḫāna-i Meḥmed Asʿad, 1300.

Orhonlu, Cengiz. *Osmanlı İmparatorluğu'nun Güney Siyaseti. Habeş Eyaleti*. 2nd ed. Ankara: Türk Tarih Kurumu Yayınları, 1996.

Panaite, Viorel. *The Ottoman Law of War and Peace: The Ottoman Empire and Tribute Payers*. East European Monographs, no. 562. Boulder: East European Monographs; Distributed by Columbia University Press, 2000.

Peçevi, İbrahim Efendi. *Ta'rīḫ*. Ankara: Kültür ve Turizm Bakanlığı Yayınları, 1981.

Peters, Rudolph. "*Idjtihād* and *Taqlīd* in 18th and 19th Century Islam." *Die Welt Des Islams* 20, no. 3–4 (1980): 131–45.

Popescu, Anca. "La Mer Noire ottomane: mare clausum? Mare apertum?" In *Enjeux politiques, économiques et militaires en Mer noire (XIVe–XXIe siècles): études à la mémoire de Mihail Guboglu*, edited by Faruk Bilici, Ionel Cândea, and Anca Popescu, 141–70. Braïla: Musée de Braïla; Éditions Istros, 2007.

Qattan, Najwa al-. "Dhimmis in the Muslim Court: Legal Autonomy and Religious Discrimination." *International Journal of Middle Eastern Studies* 31, no. 3 (1999): 429–44.

Qudūrī, Abū 'l-Ḥusayn Aḥmad al-. *The Mukhtaṣar of Imām Abū'l-Ḥusayn Aḥmad ibn Muḥammad ibn Aḥmad ibn Ja'far ibn Ḥamdān al-Qudūrī al-Baghdādī (362 AH–428 AH): a manual of Islamic law according to the Ḥanafī School*. Translated by Ṭāhir Maḥmood Kiānī. London: Ta-Ha, 2010.

Repp, Richard. "Some Observation on the Development of the Ottoman Learned Hierarchy." In *Scholars, Saints, and Sufis; Muslim Religious Institutions in the Middle East since 1500*, edited by Nikki R. Keddie, 17–32. Berkeley: University of California Press, 1972.

Riedlmayer, András J. "Ottoman Copybooks of Correspondence and Miscellanies as a Source for Political and Cultural History." *Acta Orientalia* 61, no. 1–2 (March 2008): 201–14.

Sahillioğlu, Halil, ed. *Topkapı Sarayı Arşivi H. 951–952 Tarihli ve E-12321 Numaralı Mühimme Defteri*. Istanbul: IRCICA, 2002.

Saraḫsī, Muḥammad b. Aḥmad al-. *Al-Nukat wa-huwa šarḥ li-Ziyādāt al-ziyādāt li 'l-imām* [...] *Muḥammad b. al-Ḥasan al-Šaybānī wa-šarḥuhā li 'l-imām Abī Naṣr Aḥmad b. Muḥammad al-ʿAttābī al-Buḫārī*. Beirut: ʿĀlam al-kutub, 1986.

Schacht, Joseph. "ʿAhd." *Encyclopaedia of Islam, Vol. I, A–B*. Leiden: Brill, 1960.

Schacht, Joseph. *The Origins of Muhammadan Jurisprudence*. Oxford: Clarendon Press, 1979.

Slot, B. *Archipelagus Turbatus: Les Cyclades Entre Colonisation Latine et Occupation Ottomane C. 1500–1718*. Uitgaven van Het Nederlands Historisch-Archaeologisch Instituut Te Istanbul 51. Istanbul: Nederlands Historisch-Archaeologisch Instituut te Istanbul, 1982.

Tamdoğan, Işık. "*Sulh* and the 18th Century Ottoman Courts of Üsküdar and Adana." *Islamic Law and Society* 15, no. 1 (February 1, 2008): 55–83.

Theunissen, Hans Peter Alexander. "Ottoman-Venetian Diplomatics: The *ʿAhd-Names*. The Historical Background and the Development of a Category of Political-Commercial Instruments Together with an Annotated Edition of a Corpus of Relevant Documents." *Electronic Journal of Oriental Studies* 1, no. 2 (1998): 1–698.

Ülken, Hilmi Ziya. *Uyanış Devirlerinde Tercümenin Rolü*. Istanbul: Ülken Yayınları, 1997.

Wansbrough, John. "The Safe-Conduct in Muslim Chancery Practice." *Bulletin of the School of Oriental and African Studies* 34, no. 1 (1971): 20–35.

Weiss, Bernard. "Interpretation in Islamic Law: The Theory of *Ijtihad*." *American Journal of Comparative Law* 26 (1978): 199–212.

Yaşaroğlu, Abid. "Topkapı Sarayı Müzesi Kütüphanesi Koğuşlar 888 Numaralı Mühimme Defteri (1a-260a. Tahlil ve Transkrip)." İstanbul Üniversitesi Sosyal Bilimler Enstitüsü Yeniçağ Tarihi Anabilim Dalı, 1995.

PART 4

History of Specific Areas

CHAPTER 11

Some Notes on *dār al-ḥarb* in Early al-Andalus

Maribel Fierro and Luis Molina

1 Introduction

The predominant narrative regarding the history of early al-Andalus tells how the Muslims managed to conquer most of the territory of the Iberian Peninsula, whereas some Christian *nuclei* resisted in the northern area—in what is now Galicia, Asturias and the Basque country—eventually establishing kingdoms that were free of Muslim control in lands that had never been conquered or, to use the terms we are discussing, that were always *dār al-ḥarb*.[1] Also, in those northern lands that had been conquered, Muslim settlement was scarce and underwent changes. The Berbers who had initially settled in the areas of Astorga and Jillīqiya[2]—and whose degree of Islamization must have been quite low as they had recently converted—joined the Kharijite rebellion that had started on the other side of the Straits (years 122–3/740–1) and expelled the Arabs from the northern lands. Later on—from 131–136/747–754—a devastating draught forced some of them to return to North Africa.[3] The extent of this abandonment has been subject to debate,[4] a debate mostly

1 Giovanna Calasso, "Alla ricerca di *dār al-islām*. Una ricognizione nei testi di giuristi e tradizionisti, lessicografi, geografi e viaggiatori," *Rivista degli Studi Orientali* 83 (2010): 271–96.

2 This term is used in the Arabic sources to designate the lands of the kingdom of Asturias and Asturias–León: Ana María Carballeira, *Galicia y los gallegos en las fuentes árabes medievales* (Santiago de Compostela: Instituto de Estudios Gallegos Padre Sarmiento, 2007).

3 Abū ʿAbd Allāh Muḥammad al-Marrākušī Ibn ʿIḏārī, *Kitāb al-Bayān al-muġrib fī aḫbār al-Andalus wa'l-Maġrib* [=BM], ed. Georges Séraphin Colin and Évariste Lévi-Provençal (Leiden: Brill, 1948), 2:38; *Aḫbār majmūʿa* (Madrid: Rivadeneyra, 1867), 61–62.

4 Jaime Oliver Asín, *En torno a los orígenes de Castilla; su toponimia en relación con los árabes y los beréberes. Discurso leído en el acto de su recepción pública* (Madrid: Real Academia de la Historia, 1974); David Peterson, "The Men of Wavering Faith: On the Origins of Arabic Personal and Place Names in the Duero Basin," *Journal of Medieval Iberian Studies* 3, no. 2 (September 2011): 219–46; Felipe Maíllo Salgado, *Acerca de la conquista árabe de Hispania: imprecisiones, equívocos y patrañas*, Primera edición, Bibliotheca Arabo-Romanica et Islamica 7 (Gijón: Ediciones Trea, 2011).

 | DOI 10.1163/9789004331037_013

based on how to understand the presence of Arabic and North African personal and place names in the area.[5]

Regarding the Western Basque area (called Alaba in the Arabic sources), the standard narrative[6] was challenged by María Jesús Rubiera and Mikel de Epalza who—in two articles published in 1983—argued that for the Muslim conquerors this part of the Peninsula was also subject territory, as pacts of protection (*amān*) had been granted to their inhabitants and tribute was expected to be paid by them.[7]

If their proposal were accepted, what then would have been the legal status of this area? Was it *dār al-islām* as in it Muslim sovereignty—involving the payment of tribute—had been accepted, or was it *dār al-ḥarb* as there was no Muslim governor representing the Cordoban ruler and payment of tribute was often interrupted, thus having to be imposed again through military campaigns?[8] Could these lands be considered to have had an intermediate status between the "land of Islam" and the "land of war", as *dār al-ṣulḥ* or *dār al-ʿahd*? This is a category discussed by the Shafi'is: the infidels reach a pact with the Muslims according to which the infidels keep the possession of their lands and pay tribute,[9] and it is the legal situation that seems to fit the Alaba case better. But did the legal doctrines of Awzāʿī and Mālik b. Anas allow for this possibility?[10]

---

5 Juan Zozaya Stabel-Hansen, "771–856: los primeros años del Islam andalusí o una hipótesis de trabajo," *Cuadernos emeritenses* 15, no. Ruptura o continuidad: pervivencias preislámicas en El-Andalus (1998): 83–142; Victoria Aguilar Sebastián and Fernando Rodríguez Mediano, "Antroponimia de origen árabe en la documentación leonesa (siglos VIII–XIII)," in *El reino de León en la Alta Edad Media. 6*, Colección Fuentes y estudios de historia leonesa 53 (León: Centro de Estudios e Investigación "San Isidoro" [u.a.], 1994), 499–633; Victoria Aguilar Sebastián, "Onomástica de origen árabe en el Reino de León (siglo X)," *Al-Qanṭara* 15, no. 2 (1994): 351–64; and the bibliography quoted in Peterson, "The Men of Wavering Faith."

6 Standard in Spanish scholarship, not in the "Islamic" one, as shown by the title of a recent book: Aḥmad Ṭāhirī, *Fath al-Andalus y la incorporación de Occidente a Dar al-Islam* [*Fatḥ al-Andalus wa-'ltiḥāq al-ġarb bi-dār al-islām*]*: Mūsā b. Nuṣayr wa-Ṭāriq b. Ziyād*, 1st ed. (Valencia: Centro Cultural Islámico, 2011). According to this author, it was not the Iberian Peninsula that became "land of islam", but a category called "*ġarb*" which in the Spanish title is rendered as "Occidente", i.e. the West.

7 See notes 11, 23 and 70 below.

8 Eduardo Manzano Moreno, *La frontera de al-Andalus en época de los Omeyas*, Biblioteca de historia 9 (Madrid: Consejo Superior de Investigaciones Científicas, 1991), 37–44.

9 On the Shafi'i doctrine, see note 72 below.

10 The legal sources have been explored by Mathias von Bredow, Abū-Muḥammad ʿAbdallāh Ibn-Abī-Zaid al-Qairawānī, *Der Heilige Krieg (Ǧihād) aus der Sicht der mālikitischen*

In this study the first two sections will deal with the historical sources and what they have to say about the case of Alaba and the *dār al-ḥarb*. Then, in the third section, we shall examine the legal aspects according to the early sources. Finally, we shall compare the case of Alaba with that of the alleged *amān* granted to Qaštāla (old Castile) by ʿAbd al-Raḥmān I.

2 Alaba in the Arabic Sources: *dār al-širk*

According to Rubiera,[11] Andalusi sources are rich in information about the lands in the Northern regions of the Iberian Peninsula because Muslims were interested in them in connection with taxation, a crucial issue for a well-organized state. For the Cordoban Umayyads, the inhabitants of the lands facing the Cantabric Sea were fiscal subjects who tended to evade paying their taxes, hence the need periodically to organize military campaigns to force them back to payment. Those who lived in this area (such as the Basques) had not been included in the Visigothic *limes*, and this would explain why the commanders of the early Muslim army were not interested in their conquest. Muslims, in fact, would not have intended to dominate the geographical Iberian Peninsula, but to conquer the Visigothic kingdom, as shown by the fact that they did not consider the Eastern Pyrenees as a frontier and went campaigning in the Languedoc and Rosellon.[12]

What the early conquerors did occupy were the fortresses used by the Goths to protect the road leading from Bordeaux to Astorga: Amaya in the territory of the Cantabri (year 93/712), Velegia or Iruña in the lands of the people of Alaba. As regards the Eastern Basque lands, Pamplona—a Visigothic town with a bishop who attended the Toledan councils—was conquered by the Muslims in 87/718. After its brief occupation by Charlemagne, it was reconquered by ʿAbd

Rechtsschule, ed. Mathias von Bredow, Beiruter Texte und Studien 44 (Stuttgart: Steiner, 1994); Judith Loebenstein, "Legal and Historical Aspects of Jihād in Al-Andalus (2nd/8th–5th/11th Centuries)" (unpublished Ph.D. Thesis, The Hebrew University of Jerusalem, 2008). For a later period see Alejandro García Sanjuán, "Del *Dār al-Islām* al *Dār al-Ḥarb*: la cuestión mudéjar y la legalidad islámica," in *Congreso conmemorativo del 750 aniversario de la Toma de Carmona* (Carmona: Diputación de Sevilla, 1998), 177–88.

11 María Jesús Rubiera de Epalza, "Álava y los alaveses en los textos árabes medievales," in *La formación de Álava. 650 Aniversario del Pacto de Arriaga (1332–1982). Congreso de Estudios Históricos, Álava: Diputación de Álava* (Álava: Diputación de Álava, 1983), 385–93.

12 On this expansion north of the Pyrenees see Philippe Sénac, *Musulmans et sarrasins dans le sud de la Gaule: VIII*e*–XI*e *siècle* (Paris: Sycomore, 1980).

al-Raḥmān I (164/781) to be finally lost in the year 183/799.[13] In primitive or old Castille—corresponding to the area south of Cantabria and north of the Ebro river—Berber troops settled and a *madīna* (Medina de Pomar) was founded.[14]

The Berber rebellion of the year 122/740 determined, as already mentioned, that the Arabs left in unknown numbers, something the king of Asturias Alfonso I (r. 739–757) took advantage of and attacked fortresses in Muslim hands such as Velegia, but without attacking the territory outside Cantabria. Thus, most of Basque territory—by the mid-second/eighth century—was independent both from Oviedo (the capital of the kingdom of Asturias) and from Cordoba.

When in 138/756, the Umayyad prince ʿAbd al-Raḥmān I claimed possession of al-Andalus, he would have intended to dominate the whole of the Peninsula. In the year 150/767, he sent his loyal client Badr towards the frontier (*ṯaġr*) and reached Alaba, whose inhabitants submitted to him and paid him *jizya*.[15] This Badr is said to have ordered that the men in those regions be examined in order to select those who were more intelligent (*baṣāʾiruhum*), taking with him those of whom he suspected that they might cause problems in the *ṯaġr*. This means that the Umayyad military commander was trying to stop any possible "rebellion" after the submission of those lands, leaving behind those who had accepted the new situation and taking with him to Cordoba those who showed signs of disaffection.[16] Nothing is mentioned about their fate, which could have been execution, but also incorporation into the Umayyad army or perhaps treatment as hostages, as happened to some members of the Banū Qasī.[17]

13 Ibn Ḥayyān, *Muqtabis* [= M2b], ed. Maḥmūd ʿAlī Makkī (Riyadh, 2003), 115; translation: Ibn Ḥayyān, *Crónica de los emires Alḥakam I y Abdarraḥmān II entre los años 796 y 847* [*Almuqtabis II-1*], trans. Maḥmūd ʿAlī Makkī and Federico Corriente (Zaragoza: Instituto de Estudios Islámicos y de Oriente Próximo, 2001), 35.

14 Oliver Asín, *En torno a los orígenes de Castilla*, 13, 45.

15 Ibn ʿIḏārī, *BM*, 2:54 "ġazā Badr ilā l-ṯaġr wa-taqaddama ilā Alaba fa-ḥārabahā fa-aḏʿanat lahu wa-addat ilayhi ʾl-jizya…." We do not know Ibn ʿIḏārī's source.

16 The term used to describe this "selection" is *imtiḥān al-rijāl*, a practice also called *tamyīz* that has been studied by Yassir Benhima for the Almohad period ("Du *tamyīz* à l'*iʿtirāf*: usages et légitimation du massacre au début de l'époque almohade," *Annales Islamologiques* 43 [2009]: 137–53), and by Omayra Herrero for the Umayyad period (Omayra Herrero, El perdón del gobernante (al-Andalus, ss. II–V/VIII–XI). Helsinki: Academia Scientiarum Fennica, 2016).

17 Maribel Fierro, "Hostages and the dangers of cultural contact: two cases from al-Andalus," in *Acteurs des transferts culturels en Méditerranée médiévale*, ed. Rania Abdellatif et al., Ateliers des Deutschen Historischen Instituts Paris 9 (München: Oldenbourg, 2012), 73–83.

The people of Alaba were thus forced to pay the poll-tax that characterized the status of non-Muslims from the *ahl al-kitāb* (Jews and Christians) incorporated into Muslim territory, a status—that of the *ḏimma*—[18] that allowed them to preserve their internal organization, properties and religion. It is to be noted that Badr did not find among the people he fought against a clear leadership such as a *comes*, which makes sense, taking into account what is known about the social and political organization in the region, with no centralized power ruling over the local communities.[19] Note also that no mention is made of Christians or Christianity.

Rubiera links this silence to another report by Ibn ʿIḏārī, according to which in the year 179/795, king Alfonso II—whose mother was from Alaba—established an alliance with the Western and Eastern Basques (i.e., those of Alaba and those of Pamplona): "News arrived that Alfonso had gathered the troops of his country and asked for help the Basques and the *majūs* of those regions adjacent, and that his army extended from Jilliqiya to the Sakhra."[20] Rubiera understands this text as meaning that the Basques referred to are those of the eastern regions, while the *majūs* are those of Alaba.[21] Now *majūs* is a religious and political concept, not an ethnic one, first applied to the Zoroastrians and later to other peoples such as the Normans.[22] According to Rubiera and Mikel de Epalza, it is applied here because the Western Basques were pagans.[23]

18 Milka Levy-Rubin, *Non-Muslims in the Early Islamic Empire: From Surrender to Coexistence*, Cambridge Studies in Islamic Civilization (New York: Cambridge University Press, 2011).

19 Abilio Barbero de Aguilera and Marcelo Vigil Pascual, *Sobre los orígenes sociales de la reconquista*, 1. ed, Colección Ariel (Barcelona: Ed. Ariel, 1984), 75, 79, 189–90; Cf. however Agustín Azkarate and Iñaki García Camino, "El espacio circumpirenaico occidental durante los siglos VI al X d.C. según el registro arqueológico: algunos interrogantes," in *Asturias entre visigodos y mozárabes: Visigodos y Omeyas, VI–Madrid, 2010*, ed. Luis Caballero Zoreda, Pedro Mateos, and César García de Castro Valdés, Anejos de Archivo Español de Arqueología, LXIII (Madrid: Consejo Superior de Investigaciones Científicas, Instituto de Historia, Centro de Ciencias Humanas y Sociales, 2012), 331–52.

20 Rubiera de Epalza, "Álava," 388, quoting *BM*, 2:64. She identifies Saḫra with the Saḫrat Qays in Navarra.

21 Rubiera de Epalza, "Álava," 388; a report in M2b, 420/tr. 284, dated in 210/825, says that the Muslims entered Alava and reached the mountains of the Majūs.

22 M. Morony, "Madjūs," *Encyclopaedia of Islam, Vol. V, Khe-Mahi* (Leiden: Brill, 1986).

23 Mikel de Epalza Ferrer and Joaquín del Valle de Lersundi Mendizábal, "Vascos y árabes en el siglo VIII y en el XX. Historia e historias," *Hesperia, Culturas del Mediterráneo* 6 (2007): 123–53; Mikel de Epalza Ferrer, "Note about the Muslim Conquest of the 7th–8th centuries: The Basque, berber, norse Viking, Norman and Britos Magicians," *Imago Temporis: Medium Aevum* 1 (2007): 61–69; Mikel de Epalza Ferrer, "Los Māŷūs («magos»): Un hápax coránico (XXII, 17), entre lo étnico y lo jurídico, hasta su utilización en al-Andalus," in

In the campaign of the year 208/823 against Alaba and al-Qilāʿ ("the Castles"), the Muslim army is said to have entered into *dār al-širk*,[24] whereas a contemporary campaign such as that of ʿAbd Allāh al-Balansī against Barcelona in the year 213/828–9 is described as being against *dār al-ḥarb*.[25]

The second/eighth century political situation in Alaba that can be deduced from the abovementioned passage began to change in the third/ninth century. It was then that fortresses or castles (*qilāʿ*) and lords start to be mentioned in the sources. Thus, in the year 251/865, Rodrigo, count of Castille, is described as being the lord of the fortresses in al-Qilāʿ.[26] Rubiera has connected the appearance of these castles (*al-qilāʿ*) with the raids organized from Cordoba from the beginning of the third/ninth century until the reign of Alfonso III (r. 866–910). Such raids are documented during the years 185/801, 187/803, 200/816, 208/823, 210/825, 223/838, 234/848, 240/854, 249/863, 251/865 and 253/867.[27] According to Rubiera, it was this pressure that forced the people of Alaba to build fortresses such as that of Jarnīq,[28] perhaps following the example of their neighbors in old Castille. It would have been for this reason that the campaigns of 249/863 and 251/865 were directed against Castille (campaign of the Hoz de la Morcuera).[29] When Alfonso III became king of Asturias in 866, a man called Vela Jiménez is described as being count of Alaba,[30] perhaps the successor to Rodrigo, already mentioned as count of Castille. Alfonso III conquered Alaba and it is afterwards that we hear for the first time of a bishop in the area (Alvaro in Velegia) and the *majūs* disappear from the Arab sources.

El Corán ayer y hoy. Perspectivas actuales sobre el islam. Estudios en honor al profesor Julio Cortés, ed. Miguel Hernando de Larramendi and Salvador Peña Martín (Córdoba: Berenice, 2008), 399–414.

24 BM, 2:81.

25 Ibid., 2:83.

26 Ibid., 2:98.

27 Rubiera de Epalza, "Álava," 389, quoting Évariste Lévi-Provençal, *Histoire de l'Espagne musulmane*, 3 vols., París/Leiden: Maisonneuve/Brill, 1950–3 (= HEM). See now Ibn Ḥayyān, M2b, 117/tr. 37; 120/tr. 39; 139/tr. 54; 418/tr. 282; 419/tr. 283; 428/tr. 283; *Muqtabis* [= M2c], ed. Maḥmūd ʿAlī Makkī (Beirut, 1973), 2; 295; 318; 319; 320.

28 M2c, 321; M2b, 447/tr. 309. Rubiera de Epalza, "Álava," note 43, points to the difficulty of identifying this place name which appears with many variants in the Arabic sources.

29 BM, 2:98.

30 *Crónica de Albelda*: Yves Bonnaz, *Chroniques asturiennes: fin IXe siècle*, Sources d'histoire médiévale (Paris: Editions du Centre national de la recherche scientifique, 1987), 28.

3 *Dār al-ḥarb* in the Historical Sources Dealing with al-Andalus

During the third/ninth century, as these events were taking place, Alaba starts being called *balad* or *bilād al-ʿaduww* / *arḍ al-ʿaduww* or even *dār al-ḥarb* when describing the military campaigns directed there.[31] But most often chronicles and historical works just specify the geographical location which the Muslim army is aiming at, thus mentioning Alaba wa'l-Qilāʿ, as well as other specific regions such as Jillīqiya or *balad al-faranj*. When a vague specification is needed, then *arḍ al-ḥarb* is quoted: in the year 235/849–50, the emir ʿAbd al-Raḥmān II decided not to enter the land of war because it was too late in the season.[32]

Having analyzed the terminology used in Ibn Ḥayyān's (d. 469/1076) *Muqtabis*, in the volume devoted to the reign of ʿAbd al-Raḥmān II,[33] it becomes clear that *dār al-ḥarb* is used as a generic expression always accompanied by a more precise determination of the aim or aims of the campaigns. Thus, *dār al-ḥarb* appears three times in the description of the Cordoban *ġazawāt*: those of the years 208/823 and 224/839, both against *Alaba wa'l-Qilāʿ*, and that of the year 223/838, against an unspecified "Castle of the village" (*Ḥiṣn al-Qarya*).[34] As parallel expressions, employed in similar contexts and with the same function, Ibn Ḥayyan also uses *arḍ al-ʿaduww* ("land of the enemy," in the *ġazawāt* of the years 210/825 and 223/838), *balad/bilād al-ʿaduww* ("country of the enemy," also in those years and in 208/823) and *arḍ al-ḥarb* ("land of war," in the year 235/849, although it is used to specify that in that year the emir did not enter into Christian territory, as already mentioned).[35]

In the other sources analyzed, there is an occasional reference to the opposition *dār al-ḥarb* / *dār al-islām*,[36] but *dār al-ḥarb* usually appears alone, while *dār al-islām* is very rare. In any case, the expression *dār al-ḥarb* seems to be relatively rare in historical chronicles. For example, in Ibn al-Aṯīr's *Kāmil*, it appears only two times according to the search done in *Warrāq* (www.alwaraq.net) and one of them refers to al-Andalus.[37]

---

31 M2b, 418/tr. 282 (*dār al-ḥarb, balad al-ʿaduww*); 420/tr. 284 (*min balad al-ʿaduww*); 428/292 (*min balad al-ʿaduww*); 429/tr. 292 (*dār al-ḥarb*).

32 M2c, 5.

33 M2b; M2c.

34 M2b, 418/tr. 282; 429/tr. 292; 428/tr. 292.

35 Ibid., 420/tr. 284; 428/tr. 292; 418/tr. 282; M2c, 5.

36 Ibn Ḫaldūn, *Kitāb al-ʿIbar* (Būlāq, 1284/1867), 7:260.

37 Ibn al-Aṯīr, *al-Kāmil fī 'l-ta'rīḫ*, ed. C. J. Tornberg (Leiden: Brill, 1870), 5:489 (year 102).

As regards Andalusi or North African historical works, the situation is more complex. While the expression *dār al-ḥarb* can be said to be frequent in Andalusi chronicles and historical texts, the distribution of the quotations is irregular. There are sources that do not include any mention of either *dār al-islām* or *dār al-ḥarb*: the *Taʾrīḫ* by ʿAbd al-Malik Ibn Ḥabīb (d. 238/853),[38] the *Aḫbār al-fuqahāʾ wa'l-muḥaddiṯīn* by Ibn al-Ḥāriṯ al-Ḫušanī (d. 361/971),[39] the pseudo-Ibn Qutayba *al-Imāma wa'l-siyāsa* (third/ninth century or fifth/eleventh century),[40] the *Aḫbār majmūʿa* (sixth/twelfth century),[41] Ibn al-Kardabūs (sixth/twelfth century), Ibn al-Šabbāṭ (d. 681/1282),[42] the *Ḏikr bilād al-Andalus* (eighth/fourteenth-ninth/fifteenth century).[43] They appear only once in Ibn al-Qūṭiyya's (d. 367/977) *Taʾrīḫ iftitāḥ al-Andalus*[44] and in *Fatḥ al-Andalus* (sixth/twelfth century).[45] In other sources, on the contrary, *dār al-ḥarb* is quite usual such as in Ibn Ḥayyan's (377/987–469/1076) *Muqtabis*[46] or Ibn ʿIḏārī al-Marrākušī's (d. after 712/1313) *al-Bayān al-muġrib*. In this last work, having checked up to the year 300/912, there are eleven occurrences.[47] While there is no occurrence of *dār al-islām* alone in Ibn Ḫaldūn's (732/1332–808/1406) *ʿIbar*, there are forty-two passages where *dār al-ḥarb* is mentioned: five refer to the

38 ʿAbd al-Malik Ibn Ḥabīb, *Kitāb al-taʾrīj: (la historia)*, ed. Jorge Aguadé, Fuentes arábico-hispanas 1 (Madrid: Consejo Superior de Investigaciones Científicas, Instituto de Cooperación con el Mundo Arabe, 1991).

39 Muḥammad b. al-Ḥāriṯ al-Ḫušanī, *Ajbār al-fuqahāʾ wa-l-muḥaddiṯīn* (*Historia de los alfaquíes y tradicionistas de al-Andalus*), ed. María L. Ávila and Luis Molina, Fuentes arábico-hispanas 3 (Madrid: Consejo Superior de Investigaciones Científicas, 1992).

40 Pseudo-Ibn Qutayba, *al-Imāma wa'l-siyāsa*, ed. T. M. al-Zaynī (Beirut, s.d.).

41 Lafuente Alcántara, *Aḫbār Majmūʿa*.

42 ʿAbd al-Malik Ibn al-Kardabūs and Ibn al-Šabbāṭ, *Taʾrīḫ al-Andalus li-bn al-Kardabūs wa-waṣfuhu li-bn al-Šabbāṭ. Naṣṣāni jadīdāni*, ed. A. M. al-ʿAbbādī (Madrid: Instituto de estudios islàmicos, 1971).

43 Luis Molina, ed., *Una descripción anónima de al-Andalus* (Madrid: Consejo Superior de Investigaciones Científicas, Instituto "Miguel Asín," 1983).

44 Abū Bakr Ibn al-Qūṭiyya, *Taʾrīḫ iftitāḥ al-Andalus li-bn al-Qūṭiyya* (*Historia de la conquista de España*), ed. Julian Ribera, Colección de obras arábigas de historia y geografía 2 (Madrid: Tipografía de la "Revista de archivos," 1926).

45 Luis Molina, ed., *Fatḥ al-Andalus: la conquista de al-Andalus*, Fuentes arábico-hispanas 18 (Madrid: Consejo Superior de Investigaciones Científicas: Agencia Española de Cooperación Internacional, 1994), 47.

46 Ibn Ḥayyān, M2b, in the volume devoted to al-Ḥakam I and ʿAbd al-Raḥmān II: no occurrence of *dār al-islām* and only ten occurrences of *dār al-ḥarb*: 103/tr. 24; 120/tr. 39 (twice); 146/tr. 60; 153/tr. 65; 298/tr. 186; 418/tr. 282; 429/tr. 292 (twice); Ibn Ḥayyān, M2c, 43.

47 Ibn ʿIḏārī, *BM*, 2:69; 83; 85; 109; 121; 170; 172; 175; 185; 211; 221.

East, two to the Maghrib or Ifrīqiya, and thirty-five to al-Andalus.[48] Thus, in Ibn Ḫaldūn's work the use of the expression is almost as rare as in Ibn al-Aṯīr's *Kāmil*, except when dealing with al-Andalus.

In the chronicles that deal with al-Andalus the expression *dār al-ḥarb* is used mainly to describe the destination of the military campaigns directed against Christian territory, never when dealing with attacks against Muslim rebels.[49] Outside the context of military activity, *dār al-ḥarb* is seldom employed, thus its use can be said to be limited to the annalistic part of the chronicles.

In order to convey this difference, the following passage included in the volume of Ibn Ḥayyān's *Muqtabis* devoted to the reign of ʿAbd al-Raḥmān II is illuminating. In it we find one of the few references to *dār al-ḥarb* outside the annalistic sections. The jurist Aṣbaġ b. Ḫalīl (d. 272/885 or 273/886) tells how he managed to avoid joining the troops to be sent from Cordoba to help the emir who was fighting rebels in the Western districts of al-Andalus. He starts his narrative saying:[50]

خرج الأمير عبد الرحمن بن الحكم غازيا إلى بعض أهل الخلاف بالغرب الأقصى وعقده على أن لا يدخل إلى دار الحرب سنته فلم يستنفر أهل الموسطة واقتصر على مدونته

> The emir ʿAbd al-Raḥmān b. al-Ḥakam had left in campaign against certain rebels … but without any intention to enter into the *dār al-ḥarb* in that year.

A clear distinction is made here between Muslim territory—even if rebellious and therefore forcing the emir to engage in war—and the genuine *dār al-ḥarb*, a term exclusively used for infidels. The expression *balad al-ʿaduww* is used as a synonym with *dār al-ḥarb* (the emir eventually changed his mind and decided to enter into the *balad al-ʿaduww*).

Attacking the *dār al-ḥarb* is considered to be one of the virtues of the ruler, thus when describing the merits of ʿAbd al-Raḥmān II, it is highlighted that he never ceased to organize campaigns against the *dār al-ḥarb*:[51]

---

48 Examples: Ibn Ḫaldūn, *ʿIbar*, 4:118; 124; 128; 131; 132; 133.

49 The reasons for this are dealt with in Khaled Abou El Fadl, *Rebellion and Violence in Islamic Law* (Cambridge: Cambridge University Press, 2001).

50 Ibn Ḥayyān, M2c, 43.

51 Ibn Ḥayyān, M2b, 298/tr. 186.

وما إن ترك الأمير عبد الرحمن على تبنكه النعيم وحظه في اللذة الغزو
إلى دار الحرب بنفسه

The concept of jihad is explicitly linked to that of *dār al-ḥarb* as when the emir ʿAbd Allāh (r. 275/888–300/912) is said to have "interrupted the jihad against the *dār al-ḥarb*."[52]

It is worth noting that in the narratives about the conquest of al-Andalus, *dār al-ḥarb* is never mentioned. The only exception is a sentence in Ibn Ḫaldūn (copied literally by Maqqarī, d. 1041/1632) dealing with the fear felt by the Umayyad caliph Walīd (r. 86/705–96/715) when he heard of the advances made by Mūsā b. Nuṣayr when he entered the Iberian Peninsula.[53] The same report appears in numerous other sources where no mention is found of *dār al-ḥarb*, which seems to be a personal contribution by Ibn Ḫaldūn.

While there is no mention of *dār al-ḥarb* in reports on the conquest, the oldest episode in which such expression appears has to do with the death of the governor Samḥ in the year 102/721 when he was returning from fighting in the *dār al-ḥarb*:[54]

وقتل عند انصرافه من دار الحرب سنة اثنتين ومائة

Other mentions of Samḥ's death do not include any reference to *dār al-ḥarb*. Thus, in Ibn ʿIḏārī's *al-Bayān al-muġrib*, his death takes place during a campaign against the *Rūm*, while Ibn Ḥayyān identifies the enemies as "the Frankish armies."[55]

Dār al-ḥarb can also be used with a meaning that is not strictly military. Thus, after having taken part in the famous revolt of the Cordoban suburb of Secunda,[56] the Muslim Muhājir b. al-Qatīl took refuge in the year 198/813–4 in

52 Ibn ʿIḏārī, *BM*, 2:121.

53 Ibn Ḫaldūn, *ʿIbar*, 4:118; Maqqarī, *Nafḥ al-ṭīb*, ed. I. ʿAbbās (Beirut, 1968), 1:234. Cf. Ibn al-Aṯīr, *Kāmil*, 4:561; Ibn ʿIḏārī, *BM*, 2:5; *Aḫbār Majmūʿa*, 6.

54 Ibn al-Aṯīr, *Kāmil*, 5:489. Cf. *Fatḥ al-Andalus*, 47.

55 *BM*, 2:26.

56 Ibn Ḥayyān (in *Nafḥ al-ṭīb*, 3:15).

the *dār al-ḥarb*, "looking for asylum among the polytheists[57] against the sultan of the Muslim community"[58]:

وقد كان لحق بدار الحرب في سنة ثمان وتسعين ومائة بعياله ومن تبعه من أسبابه لائذا بالمشركين من سلطان الجماعة عند مخافته على نفسه وكاتبوا منها مهاجر بن القتيل الذي كان بدار الحرب هاربا من بأس الأمير الحكم أيام خالفه فيها

A Muslim can thus seek refuge in the *dār al-ḥarb* and remain a Muslim, as in the case of the Marwanid Umayya b. Isḥāq al-Qurašī who, after the execution of his rebel brother in Zaragoza, rebelled in Santarem and allied himself with the Christians. Defeated in the year 327/939, he entered the service of the king of León Ramiro II,[59] playing an important role in the battle of Simancas that saw the defeat of the Cordoban Caliph ʿAbd al-Raḥmān III at the hands of the Christians. He later returned to the obedience of his relative the caliph.[60]

Certain groups of Muslims can also ask help from the inhabitants of the *dār al-ḥarb* to fight other Muslims, as was the case with the Toledans who decided to rebel against the Umayyads asking for help to "their neighbours, the Christian inhabitants of the *dār al-ḥarb*," as shown in this report taken from ʿĪsā al-Rāzī (d. 379/989)[61] who quotes Faraj b. Sallām (third/ninth century):[62]

---

57 On the terms used in Arabic chronicles to refer to the Christians, the standard studies are those of Ron Barkai, *El enemigo en el espejo: cristianos y musulmanes en la España medieval* (Madrid: Rialp, 2007); and Eva Lapiedra Gutiérrez, *Cómo los musulmanes llamaban a los cristianos hispánicos*, Colección Textos universitaris (Alicante–Valencia: Institut de Cultura "Juan Gil-Albert"–Generalitat Valenciana, Conselleria de Cultura, Educació i Ciència, 1997).

58 Ibn Ḥayyān, M2b, 146/tr. 60; 153/tr. 65.

59 Certain circumstances may have led some Muslims to find better living conditions in the *dār al-ḥarb* than in the *dār al-islām*. For the case of some Mudéjares who emigrated to North Africa and wanted to return even if it meant living under Christian rule, see Abū 'l-ʿAbbās Aḥmad al-Wanšarīsī, *al-Miʿyār al-muġrib* (Rabat: Wizārat al-Awqāf wa'l-Šu'ūn al-Islāmiyya, 1981), 2:131.

60 Manzano Moreno, *La frontera de al-Andalus*, 191–92, 357.

61 "ʿĪsà Al-Rāzī," in *Biblioteca de Al-Andalus*, ed. Jorge Lirola Delgado, José Miguel Puerta Vílchez, and Fundación Ibn Tufayl de Estudios Árabes, vol. 7, Enciclopedia de La Cultura Andalusí 1 (Almería: Fundación Ibn Tufayl de Estudios Árabes, 2012), nº 1653.

62 M2c, 162–64.

وكانوا أول من استجاش بالمشركين جيرانهم نصارى أهل دار الحرب على المسلمين إخوا إخوانهم[63]

Another Muslim rebel, Surunbāqī, took refuge among the enemies of the *dār al-ḥarb*, in the town of Oporto:[64]

وهو [السرنباقي] يومئذ مستأمن إلى العدو من أهل دار الحرب ساكن بأصحابه بمدينة برتقال في آخر وادي دويره بين يدي بلد الإسلام وبلد العدو على مسافة ثمانين ميلا من مدينة قلمرية في ذمة الملك أذفنش بن رذمير

Seeking Christian help for Muslims is sometimes merely documented in the sources without any comment or judgment, although at other times censorship is recorded, as in the following case. In 325/937, the caliph ʿAbd al-Raḥmān III conquered Calatayud and Daroca, whose Muslim lords had rebelled. The lord of Calatayud, Muṭarrif b. Mundir al-Tujībī, had been helped by the Alabese. The caliph had censured his conduct in a message sent to him ordering him to sever any relationship with the infidels. Muṭarrif's answer was "How can I cut my right hand with the left one?,"[65] meaning that the Christians were his right hand and the caliph his left hand.[66]

How can one know where the *dār al-islām* ends and the *dār al-ḥarb* starts? This is something that seems to become clearer as time goes by. In the year 740/1339–40, the Marinid sultan Abū 'l-Ḥasan ordered his son Abū Mālik to enter into *dār al-ḥarb* in al-Andalus and to take as much booty as he could.

63 Ibid., 295.

64 Ibid., 350.

65 Ibn Ḥayyān, *al-Muqtabis (al-Juzʾ Al-ḫāmis), Ed. P. Chalmeta, F. Corriente and M. Ṣubḥ, Madrid, 1979*, ed. Pedro Chalmeta Gendrón, Federico Corriente Córdoba, and M. Ṣubḥ (Madrid: Instituto hispano-árabe de cultura, 1979), 396; Abū Marwān Ḥayyān b. Ḫalaf Ibn Ḥayyān, María Jesús Viguera, and F. Corriente, *Crónica del califa ʿAbdarraḥmān III An-Nāṣir entre los años 912 y 942 (al-Muqtabis V)*, Textos medievales 64 (Zaragoza: Anubar : Instituto Hispano-Arabe de Cultura, 1981), 296.

66 On the condemnation of having alliances with the Christians see Linda G. Jones, "The Christian Companion: A Rhetorical Trope in the Narration of Intra-Muslim Conflict during the Almohad Period," *Anuario de Estudios Medievales* 38: Actes del Col.loqui "Conflictivitat i vies de solució a la Mediterrània medieval" (2008): 793–829.

Then, he ordered him to return and, while doing so, he crossed the river that marked the border between *arḍ al-islām* and *dār al-ḥarb*:[67]

وأشار عليه الملأ بالخروج عن أرضهم وإجازة الوادي الذي كان تخما بين أرض الإسلام ودار الحرب وأن يسير إلى مدن المسلمين

In an earlier period (first half of the third/ninth century), two rebels, Ibn Marwān al-Jillīqī and Surunbāqī, had moved in the wasteland or no man's land (*qafr*) "between Muslim lands and those of the polytheists" (*bayna 'l-islām wa'l-širk*).[68] Here there is no clear border or frontier. This issue was also discussed in the legal sources, to which we now move.

4 The Legal Sources[69]

The north African jurist Saḥnūn (d. 240/854) was asked about the uninhabited area (*mafāz*) situated between the regions inhabited by Muslims (*ʿumrān al-islām*) and that inhabited by polytheists (*ʿumrān al-širk*); in that *mafāz* there are fruit trees that formerly belonged to the Muslims, but their owners had to abandon those lands that became a sort of no-man's land. The question is whether a Muslim army crossing that area can or cannot eat from those trees, i.e. if their status is the same as that of an object or animal lost, or if it can be considered booty.[70] In the answer—without going into the details—those

67 Ibn Ḫaldūn, *ʿIbar*, 7:260.

68 Reinhardt Dozy understood this passage as meaning the creation of a new religion half way between Islam and Christianity (*Histoire des Musulmans d'Espagne jusqu'a la conquête de l'Andalousie par les almoravides* (*711–1110*) [Leiden: Brill, 1861], 2:184). See also Ana Fernández Félix and Maribel Fierro, "Cristianos y conversos al islam en al-Andalus bajo los Omeyas. Una aproximación al proceso de islamización a través de una fuente legal andalusí del s. III/IX," *Anejos Archivo Español de Arqueología* 23 (2000): 417–29.

69 After this study was finished, a discussion of how *dār al-ḥarb / dār al-jihād* were used in al-Andalus appeared in Janina M. Safran, *Defining Boundaries in Al-Andalus: Muslims, Christians, and Jews in Islamic Iberia.* (Ithaca: Cornell University Press, 2013), 168–208.

70 Ana Fernández Félix, *Cuestiones legales del Islam temprano: la* ʿUtbiyya *y el proceso de formación de la sociedad islámica andalusí*, Estudios árabes e islámicos Monografías 6 (Madrid: Consejo Superior de Investigaciones Científicas, 2003), 429–31; quoting Ibn Rušd al-Jadd (d. 520/1126), *Kitāb al-Bayān wa'l-taḥṣīl*, ed. Aḥmad al-Ḥabbābī, 3rd ed., (Beirut: Dār al-ġarb al-islāmī, 1408), 3:59–60.

fruits are considered to be in the same legal category as the lost sheep that is found in the proximity of an inhabited region or in a *mawḍiʿ al-amān*.

It would thus seem that the early Malikis did consider the possibility of an intermediate status between the "land of Islam" and the "land of war," the *dār al-ṣulḥ* or *dār al-ʿahd*,[71] later much developed by the Shafi'is: the infidels reach a pact with the Muslims according to which the infidels keep the possession of their lands and pay tribute.[72]

We have seen how fighting against Muslim rebels is not considered to create a *dār al-ḥarb*. However, what happens when Muslims living outside Muslim territory participate in attacks against Muslims? This was a question asked by Yaḥyā b. Yaḥyā to the Egyptian Ibn al-Qāsim (d. 191/806): there were Muslims in Barcelona who failed to move away from them (i.e. the Christian conquerors) after the year which had been set by the Christians as the period of grace for their departure on the day the city was conquered (year 185/802).[73] Those Muslims then attacked the Muslims coming from al-Andalus, seeking

71 This is contrary to what is stated in Rudolph Peters, *Islam and Colonialism: The Doctrine of Jihad in Modern History*, Religion and Society 20 (The Hague: Mouton, 1979), 11–2: for the Hanafís and the Malikis such a territory is *dār al-Islām* because sovereignty belongs to the Muslims. See also Mikel de Epalza Ferrer, "El derecho político musulmán y su influencia en la formación de Álava (siglos VIII–XI)," in *La formación de Álava. 650 Aniversario del Pacto de Arriaga (1332–1982). Congreso de Estudios Históricos, Álava: Diputación de Álava* (Álava: Diputación de Álava, 1983), 303–13; Francisco Franco Sánchez, "Consideración jurídica y religiosa de los territorios de la Meseta y el Norte peninsular por el poder musulmán de al-Andalus," *Al-Andalus Magreb* 7 (1999): 101–33.

72 Muhammad Khalid Masud, "The Obligation to Migrate: The Doctrine of *hijra* in Islamic Law," in *Muslim Travellers: Pilgrimage, Migration, and the Religious Imagination*, ed. Dale F. Eickelman and James P. Piscatori, Comparative Studies on Muslim Societies 9 (Berkeley: University of California Press, 1990), 39; see also Peters, *Islam and Colonialism*, 12. The Hanafis have also developed rules to determine when a territory moves from one category to another. The general rule is that *dār al-ḥarb* becomes *dār al-islām* when Muslim sovereignty is imposed and when sharia is applied; according to later scholars, it is sufficient that Muslims are safe and could perform certain religious obligations, such as Friday prayer and other festivals. For the Hanafis, the *dār al-islām* becomes *dār al-ḥarb* under these conditions: a) the laws of the infidels have supremacy and Islamic law cannot be applied; b) Muslims and non Muslims stop being ruled by the original pact before non-Muslim occupation; c) the land is adjacent to the *dār al-ḥarb*.

73 The law regarding the ransoming of prisoners is the only instance other than that of jihad in which a Muslim's presence in non-Muslim territory is permitted by Maliki law: see on this Alan Verskin, *Oppressed in the Land?: Fatwas on Muslims Living under Non-Muslim Rule from the Middle Ages to the Present*, Princeton Series of Middle Eastern Sources in Translation (Princeton: Markus Wiener, 2013).

to protect themselves because they feared being killed if they were defeated by Muslims retaking the city. Ibn al-Qāsim said: "I do not see their status as any different from that of the criminal or illegitimate rebel who steals from Muslims in the *dār al-islām*; this is because he remains within the religion of Islam. If he is caught, his case is referred to the ruler, who judges in his case in the same way he would judge those involved in corruption and rebellion. As for his property, I do not see that it is permissible for anyone to take it." Ibn al-Qāsim also said: "If he was forced and commanded to do what he did, and was unable to disobey his commander out of fear for his life, then I do not see that he is a rebel, or that he should be killed if captured; nor is he punished if it is clear that he was commanded to do this and feared for his life."[74] The status of the territory does not count: even if these Muslims who fight other Muslims are outside Muslim territory, their status is the same as if they were living in the *dār al-islām*.

What about a Muslim rebel who apostatizes inside a Muslim territory? Ibn Ḥafṣūn is considered to have converted to Christianity in the year 285–6/898–9, although it is not clear what his religious status was when he died. In the historical sources, he is called "bad" and is given strong names including that of apostate,[75] but there is no clear indication that the lands under his rule were considered to be *dār al-ḥarb*, nor was fighting against him labelled jihad. However, there is a fatwa dealing with a Christian woman who belonged to Ibn Antelo. This *muwallad* (Muslim convert)[76] was initially a follower of the rebel Ibn Ḥafṣūn in Bobastro, but he eventually left him. The woman was taken by Ibn Ḥafṣūn, who married her. Later on, Ibn Antelo claimed to be given back that woman, but the jurists argued two things: 1) that possession of a slave in *dār al-ḥarb* is not acknowledged as it is in "a place of obedience" (*mawḍiʿ al-ṭāʿa*); b) that Ibn Antelo had to prove that the woman was his slave and if he could not, then the woman would be free, as Ibn Ḥafṣūn's possession had no

74 ʿUtbī in Ibn Rušd al-Jadd (d. 520/1126), *Kitāb al-Bayān wa'l-taḥṣīl*, 3:41–42. The English translation here follows that by Jocelyn N. Hendrickson, "The Islamic Obligation to Emigrate: Al-Wansharīsī's Asnā Al-Matājir Reconsidered" (Ph.D. Thesis, Emory University, 2009), 365–66; a Spanish translation in Fernández Félix, *Cuestiones legales del Islam temprano*, 427–28.

75 In Ibn Rušd al-Jadd, *Kitāb al-Bayān wa'l-taḥṣīl*, 16:427–8, the issue of an apostate who kills a Muslim is discussed and a distinction is made if the event takes place in *dār al-ḥarb* or in *dār al-islām*.

76 On another interpretation of this term see Maribel Fierro, "Cuatro preguntas en torno a Ibn Ḥafṣūn," *Al-Qanṭara* 16 (1995): 221–57; English translation in Manuela Marín, ed., *The Formation of Al-Andalus*, The Formation of the Classical Islamic World, v. 46–47 (Aldershot: Ashgate, 1998), 291–328.

legal basis for having taken place in the *dār al-ḥarb*, where the norms of Satan (*aḥkām al-šayṭān*) predominate.[77]

5 Qaštāla, *dār amān*?[78]

We have seen that the North African Maliki jurist Saḥnūn discussed the *dār amān*. We have also seen that the brief passage concerning the imposition of *jizya* payment on the inhabitants of Alaba does not mention the drafting of an *amān* document.[79] The only such document—that is, a pact granted by the Muslims to the inhabitants of lands outside their direct control—known for the period studied here is that granted to the people of Qaštāla.

This *amān* has been preserved by two late Eastern authors, Ḏahabī (d. 748/1348)[80] and Dimyāṭī (d. 814/1411).[81] Évariste Lévi-Provençal knew of its existence[82] and—following Miguel Casiri—he thought that it was included in Ibn al-Ḫaṭīb's (d. 776/1374) historical book devoted to Granada (*al-Iḥāṭa*)[83]

77 María Jesús Viguera Molins, "Cristianos, judíos y musulmanes en al-Andalus," in *Cristianos, musulmanes y judíos en la España Medieval: de la aceptación al rechazo*, ed. Julio Valdeón Baruque, 1. ed (Valladolid–Soria: Ambito Ediciones–Fundación Duques de Soria, 2004), 43–69; Virgilio Martínez Enamorado, "«Donde rigen las normas de Satán»: Ibn Antuluh, Ibn Ḥafṣūn y el asunto de la propiedad de una esclava," *Espacio, Tiempo y Forma. Serie III. Historia Medieval* 23 (2010): 97–112; (repr. in Virgilio Martínez Enamorado, *'Umar ibn Ḥafṣūn de la rebeldía a la construcción de la "Dawla": estudios en torno al rebelde de al-Andalus (880–928)* [San José (Costa Rica): Editorial UCR, 2012]).

78 What follows is based—with updates—on Maribel Fierro, "La falsificación de la historia: al-Yasaʿ b. Ḥazm y su *Kitāb al-mugrib*," *Al-Qanṭara* 16 (1995): 15–38.

79 Joseph Schacht, "Amān," *Encyclopaedia of Islam, Vol. I, A–B* (Leiden: Brill, 1960); Majid Khadduri, *The Law of War and Peace in Islam* (London: Luzac and Co., 1941), 78–81; Willi Heffening, *Das islamische Fremdenrecht bis zu den islamisch-fränkischen Staatsverträgen: eine rechtshistorische Studie zum Fiqh* (Hannover: Orient Buchh. H. Lafaire, 1925).

80 Šams al-dīn Muḥammad al-Ḏahabī, *Siyar aʿlām al-nubalā'*, ed. Šuʿayb al-Arna'ūṭ (Beirut: Mu'assasat al-Risāla, 1985), 8:250, in the biography devoted to ʿAbd al-Raḥmān I.

81 Abū Zakariyā Ibn al-Naḥḥās al-Dimyāṭī, *Mašāriʿ al-ašwāq ilā maṣāriʿ al-ʿuššāq wa-muṯīr al-ġarām ilā dār al-islām (fī faḍā'il al-jihād)*, ed. I. M. ʿAlī (Beirut, 1410AH), 2:927–28.

82 Évariste Lévi-Provençal, *Histoire de l'Espagne musulmane. 2: Le califat umaiyade de Cordoue (912–1031)* (Paris–Leiden: Maisonneuve–Brill, 1950), 103–4.

83 The same was believed by José Antonio Conde y García, *Historia de la dominación de los árabes en España, sacada de varios manuscritos y memorias arábigas* (Madrid: Marín y Compañía, 1874), 49; Francisco Javier Simonet y Baca, *Historia de los mozárabes de España: deducida de los mejores y más auténticos testimonios de los escritores cristianos y árabes* (1897–1903; repr., Amsterdam: Oriental Press, 1967), 242–43; Claudio Sánchez-Albornoz,

although he knew that there were problems with Casiri's reference.[84] Chalmeta also noted that this *amān* posed difficult problems of localization and authenticity.[85] The text in fact does not appear in Ibn al-Ḫaṭīb's work, at least not in the known manuscripts including that of El Escorial,[86] and the source used by Casiri in his quotation of the *amān* remains—up to now—without identification. Casiri states that the original source was Rāzī in his work *De Bello Hispano*, to be identified with Aḥmad b. Muḥammad b. Mūsā al-Qurṭubī (274/888–344/955) and his work *Maġāzī 'l-Andalus* (probably part of his *Ta'rīḫ al-Andalus* or *Kitāb fī aḫbār mulūk al-Andalus wa-ḫidmatihim wa-rukbānihim wa-ġazawātihim*, partially preserved).[87] However, neither Ḏahabī nor Dimyāṭī specified their sources.[88] According to these two authors, the text of the *amān* said:

> In the name of God the Merciful the Compassionate. [This is a] document of *amān*, clemency, cessation of hostilities and protection. It was granted by the most noble emir and excellent king 'Abd al-Raḥmān b. Mu'āwiya, endowed with authentic nobility and universal goodness, to

---

En torno a los orígenes del feudalismo, Colegio universitario Ediciones Istmo 12 (Mendoza: Universidad nacional de Cuyo, 1942), 209–11, note 183; *La España musulmana según los autores islamitas y cristianos medievales* (Buenos Aires: El Ateneo, 1946), 1:107–8.

84 *Histoire de l'Espagne musulmane. 1: La conquête et l'émirat hispano-umaiyade (710–912)*, vol. 1 (Paris–Leiden: Maisonneuve–Brill, 1950), 116n1.

85 Pedro Chalmeta Gendrón, "La 'sumisión de Zaragoza' del 325–937," *Anuario de Historia del Derecho Español* 46 (1976): 511.

86 Lisān al-dīn Ibn al-Ḫaṭīb, *al-Iḥāṭa fī aḫbār Ġarnāṭa*, ed. Muḥammad 'Abd Allāh 'Inān, vol. 3 (Cairo: Maktabat al-Ḫānjī, 1395), 467–71 (biography of 'Abd al-Raḥmān I); *al-Iḥāṭa fī aḫbār Ġarnāṭa*, ed. Muḥammad 'Abd Allāh 'Inān, vol. 1 (Cairo: Maktabat al-Ḫānjī, 1393), 444–45 (biography of Badr); Lisān al-dīn Ibn al-Ḫaṭīb, *al-Iḥāṭa fī aḫbār Ġarnāṭa. Nuṣūṣ jadīda lam tunšar*, ed. 'Abd al-Salām Šaqqūr (Ṭanja [Morocco]: Mu'assasat al-taġlīf wa'l-ṭibā'a wa'l-našr wa'l-tawzī' li'l-šamāl, 1988), 15.

87 Luis Molina, "Aḥmad Al-Rāzī," in *Biblioteca de Al-Andalus*, ed. Jorge Lirola Delgado, José Miguel Puerta Vílchez, and Fundación Ibn Tufayl de Estudios Árabes, vol. 7, Enciclopedia de La Cultura Andalusí 1 (Almería: Fundación Ibn Tufayl de Estudios Árabes, 2012), nº 1652.

88 Among the sources quoted by Ḏahabī in his biography of 'Abd al-Raḥmān I we find Ibn Ḥayyān, Ibn Baškuwāl, Ḥumaydī, Muḥammad b. 'Īsā Ibn Muzayn, Ibn al-Qazzāz, Ibn al-Yasa' al-Ġāfiqī and Muḥammad b. Aḥmad al-Abīwardī: Juan Castilla Brazales, "Las fuentes de al-Ḏahabī," in *Estudios onomástico-biográficos de Al-Andalus*, ed. María Luisa Ávila Navarro, vol. 3 (Madrid: Consejo Superior de Investigaciones Científicas, Instituto de Filología, Departamento de Estudios Arabes, 1988), nos. 32, 34, 41, 46, 56, 63 ("andalusíes"), no. 24 ("orientales").

> the patricians and monks (*al-baṭāriqa wa'l-ruhbān*) and those who follow them from the rest of the territory, the people of Qaštāla and its districts, as long as they remain obedient acting according to what they have committed themselves. On his part, the emir guarantees that this pact (*ʿahd*) will not be abrogated as long as they keep their yearly payment of ten thousand ounces (*ūqiyya*) in gold, ten thousand *riṭl* in silver, ten thousand of the best horses and the same number of mules, as well as one thousand coats of mail, one thousand helmets and the same number of lances made of *dardār* wood. If they would break the pact by making prisoner a Muslim or ill-treating a Muslim, this pact will be considered abrogated. The emir wrote this *amān* in their presence for a period of five years starting in ṣafar of the year 142 [June 759].

The document quoted by Casiri includes some differences such as that the *amān* is granted to the patricians, monks, notables and the Christians of al-Andalus, and that it was written in Cordoba on ṣafar 3 of the year 142 (5 June 759). We shall not take this version into account as there is no way to check Casiri's quotation.

Ḏahabī gives us the historical context for the *amān*. ʿAbd al-Raḥmān I led a military campaign against Qaštāla: he crossed the river Tajo, the Christians fled and he persecuted them until they arrived to the town of B.rnīqa of the kingdom (*mamlaka*) of Qaštāla. After putting siege, the inhabitants submitted and asked for an *amān*. The document was written by an otherwise unknown Bišr b. Saʿīd al-Ġāfiqī.[89]

José Antonio Conde was the first scholar to doubt the authenticity of the text,[90] being followed by others such as Francisco Javier Simonet[91] and Lucien Barrau Dihigo[92], as well as by Lévi-Provençal and Chalmeta.[93] Among those who accepted it, Claudio Sánchez Albornoz identified the "Qaštāla" mentioned

89 He does not appear in Manuela Marín, "Nómina de sabios de al-Andalus (93–350/711–961)," in *Estudios onomástico-biográficos de Al-Andalus*, ed. Manuela Marín, vol. 1 (Madrid: Consejo Superior de Investigaciones Científicas, Instituto de Filología, Departamento de Estudios Arabes, 1988), 23–182, nor in any chronicle.

90 José Antonio Conde y García, *Historia de la dominación de los árabes en España, sacada de varios manuscritos y memorias arábigas*, vol. 1 (Madrid: Imprenta que fue de García, 1820), 49n1.

91 Simonet y Baca, *Historia de los mozárabes de España: deducida de los mejores y más auténticos testimonios de los escritores cristianos y árabes*, 243, 813.

92 Lucien Barrau Dihigo, "Recherches sur l'histoire politique du royaume asturien (718–910)," *Revue hispanique* 52, no. 121 (1921): 149n1.

93 See note 85 above and Chalmeta Gendrón, "Sumisión," 511n57.

in the text with "Castella," capital of the district of Elvira (Granada),[94] identification that according to him solved in a positive sense the problem of authenticity. Sánchez Albornoz agrees with the scholars mentioned above that the text cannot make any reference to the area of the old Castilla: in the year 142/759—when the former emir Yūsuf al-Fihrī died—'Abd al-Raḥmān I is not known to have led any military campaign towards the north nor he could have done it as his control in the south was still too weak. It is only in the years 149–150/766–767 when his *mawlā* and general Badr led his raid against Alaba, forcing its inhabitants to pay tribute. Without going into more details of Sánchez Albornoz's identification of the area mentioned in the *amān* with Granada, it is important to note that his interest in the document was mainly motivated by his thesis that the Muslim army did not use cavalry, against Brunner's thesis that the development of cavalry in Europe was indebted to the need to confront the Muslim cavalry—a need that would have led to the birth of feudalism. For Sánchez Albornoz, the fact that 'Abd al-Raḥmān I asks in the *amān* for an elevated number of horses and mules indicates that he had realized that cavalry was important among the Christians of the Península, contrary to what happened in the East.[95]

Lévi-Provençal criticized the identification of "Qaštāla" with the capital of the district of Elvira proposed by Sánchez Albornoz,[96] a criticism to which Sánchez Albornoz reacted insisting on his position.[97] Sánchez Albornoz was followed by other authors, including M. J. Rubiera and M. de Epalza.[98] David Wasserstein discussed the *amān* in the context of Umayyad availability of gold and the interruption in the minting of gold coins until the proclamation of the caliphate.[99]

---

94 Jacinto Bosch Vilá, "Ḳasṭīliya," *Encyclopaedia of Islam, Vol. IV, Iran-Kha* (Leiden: Brill, 1978).

95 Sánchez-Albornoz, *En torno a los orígenes del feudalismo*, 245.

96 HEM, 1950, 1:116n1. This criticism does not appear in the Spanish translation made by Emilio García Gómez, *España musulmana hasta la caída del Califato de Córdoba (711–1031 de J. C.)*, trans. Emilio García Gómez, vol. 1, Historia de España 4 (Barcelona: Espasa-Calpe, 1950), 123n22, as this translation is based in the first version of the *Histoire*.

97 Claudio Sánchez Albornoz, "La saña celosa de un arabista," *Cuadernos de Historia de España* 28 (1958): 5–42.

98 Rubiera de Epalza, "Álava"; Mikel de Epalza Ferrer, "El derecho político musulmán y su influencia en la formación de Álava (siglos VIII–XI)," *Estudios de Deusto* 32, no. 73 (1984): 514.

99 David Wasserstein, *The Caliphate in the West: An Islamic Political Institution in the Iberian Peninsula* (Oxford: Clarendon Press–Oxford University Press, 1993), 9 and note 5.

While Sánchez Albornoz's identification of Qaštāla with the capital of Elvira needs to be dismissed, if Qaštāla is identified with the old Castille can the document be accepted as authentic? Objections that have been made involve the terminology used, the contents of the document and the identification of Qaštāla. The problem of terminology (use of *ʿām* instead of *sana*) is difficult to solve as we have no contemporary documentary evidence. As for the contents, the *amān* is granted to the patricians and monks,[100] without mention of any specific name indicating leadership in the area submitted—as does happen for example in the so-called pact of Tudmīr.[101] The *baṭāriqa* could be identified with local chiefs of the indigenous people—Basques—who had preserved their independence during Visigothic times,[102] also—perhaps—with Visigothic nobles or military leaders, either those who had been in charge of the few Visigothic fortresses in the area,[103] or those who may have fled there after the Muslim conquest; the same can be said about the 'monks'.[104] In any case, it fits with what is known about the area in the period: absence of any clear and centralized political or religious authority (a count or *comes*, a bishop).[105]

The *amān* is described as a document of "clemency, cessation of hostilities and protection" granted by ʿAbd al-Raḥmān I (*amīr* and king) to the people of Qaštāla, a region that may be considered to become a *dār amān*, that is, an intermediate state between *dār al-islām* and *dār al-ḥarb*. It does not seem that the people of Qaštāla became *ḏimmī*s as happened to those of Tudmīr, but only that they were safe from Muslim attacks as long as they kept the terms of the *amān*. We do not have any other similar document for the Umayyad period in al-Andalus,[106] apart from the so-called pact of Tudmīr (*ʿahd, ṣulḥ*),

100 Rubiera de Epalza, "Álava," 388, points that in the pact between Badr and the people of Álava there is no mention of any clerical authority, and that in fact there is no bishop in Álava till the end of the ninth century.

101 Joaquín Vallvé, *La división territorial de la España musulmana* (Madrid: Consejo Superior de Investigaciones Científicas, Instituto de Filología, Departamento de Estudios Arabes, 1986), 284–89; Nicola Clarke, *The Muslim Conquest of Iberia: Medieval Arabic Narratives*, Culture and Civilization in the Middle East 30 (London: Routledge, 2012), 20–21.

102 Barbero de Aguilera and Vigil Pascual, *Sobre los orígenes*, 67–68, 93, 95, 358, 361–62, 403; Manzano Moreno, *La frontera de al-Andalus*, 94, 113–15.

103 Cf. note 19 above.

104 Zacarías García Villada, *Historia eclesiástica de España*, vol. 2/1 (Madrid: Compañía Iberoamericana de Publicaciones, 1932), fig. 18 and p. 284.

105 Barbero de Aguilera and Vigil Pascual, *Sobre los orígenes*, 67–78.

106 For the case of Zaragoza see Chalmeta Gendrón, "Sumisión." O. Herrero offers now the most updated overview on the *amān*s known to have been granted in Umayyad times in al-Andalus: see note 16 above.

a region on the Levantine coast of al-Andalus where the population became *ahl al-ḏimma*, obliged to pay the *jizya*. While *jizya* is mentioned in the passage dealing with Badr and Alaba in the year 150/767,[107] no document was reported regarding that campaign and we thus have no term of comparison.

As regards the constituents of what the people of Qaštāla had to pay (gold, silver, horses, mules, military equipment),[108] they contrast with the agricultural products mentioned in the pact of Tudmīr (cereals, wine, vinegar, honey, oil). Qaštāla—as we shall see—corresponds to a mountainous area where certain products could be expected: livestock (horses, mules and leather), wood (timber) and minerals (not only gold and silver but also iron for manufacturing military equipment). The quantities of gold and silver mentioned are exaggerated: some 310 kg. of gold and 4.662 kg. of silver.[109] The Romans were interested in the Northern region of the Peninsula for its mines, but when the Muslim conquest took place the mines were already out of use.[110] It could be argued that ʿAbd al-Raḥmān I may have been interested in looking for gold and silver in order to mint coins to legitimize his rule, but the fact is that he did not mint in gold.

The reign of ʿAbd al-Raḥmān I (r. 138/756–172/788) coincided with the reign of the kings of Asturias Alfonso I (r. 739–757), Fruela I (r. 757–768), Aurelio (r. 768–774), Silo (r. 774–783) and Mauregato (r. 783–789). It was mostly during the reign of the first two (in the Arabic sources the attribution to Alfonso I or Fruela I varies) when the Asturians started a policy of expansion outside their original territory, and the military campaign commanded by Badr in the year 150/767 in the territory of Alaba is usually considered an attempt to stop such expansion. The campaign of ʿAbd al-Raḥmān I against Qaštāla could be interpreted as a precedent,[111] i.e., a campaign preceding that of Badr directed against an area located to the west of Alaba. According to Ḏahabī, the emir would have conquered a town called B.rnīqa. The ending "ica" is common

107 Rubiera de Epalza, "Álava," 387.

108 Some of these items remind us of those mentioned in the pact established by the Prophet with the people of Najrān, a pact recorded by Ibn Saʿd in his *Ṭabaqāt* and Abū Dāwūd in the *Sunan*.

109 Estimation made following Josep Pellicer i Bru, *Al-Andalus: las fuentes y la numismática (síntesis cronológico-metrológica de las acuñaciones del Califato de Córdoba)* (Barcelona: Asociación Numismática Española, 1988), 128–29.

110 Barbero de Aguilera and Vigil Pascual, *Sobre los orígenes*, 153, 155; M. Barceló, "El hiato en las acuñaciones de oro en al-Andalus, 127–316/744(5)-936(7) (Los datos fundamentales de un problema)," *Moneda y crédito* 132 (1975): especially 53–54; M. Barceló, "Monedas visigodas de Hispania," *Numisma* 27 (1977): 60.

111 So does Lévi-Provençal, HEM, 1950, 1:116.

in the toponyms of the Basque region,[112] but here most probably there is again the toponym Jarnīq that we have already encountered.

Now, the Latin term Castella was applied to the region earlier called Bardulia,[113] an area among those occupied by Alfonso I or Fruela I. Castella appears for the first time in Christian sources in a document dated in the year 800, referring to the region crossed by the tributary rivers on the left margin of the High Ebro and to part of the region called Bureba. The primitive or original Castilla extended "depuis la rive gauche de l'Ebre, à hauteur du défilé de Pancorvo, jusqu'à une petite distance au Sud de Sant Emder" (Santander).[114] For Oliver Asín, the limits of "primitive" Castille correspond to the district of Villarcayo and partially to that of Sedano. The southern limits are more difficult to establish, although the region of the tributary rivers of the Duero is to be excluded. Its capital was the *Medina Castella* or *Medina de Castella* mentioned in Medieval Christian documents and corresponding to Medina de Pomar. If the text of the *amān* were authentic, the term "Qaštāla = Castella" would be attested to before the year 800.

Now, this *amān* can be proved to be a forgery produced in the sixth/twelfth century, for which the scholar Abū Yaḥyā al-Yasaʿ b. Abī 'l-Aṣbaġ ʿĪsā b. Ḥazm b. ʿAbd Allāh b. al-Yasaʿ b. ʿAbd Allāh/ʿUmar al-Ġāfiqī al-Jayyānī (d. 575/1179 or 595/1199) was responsible. He wrote a historical work entitled *al-Muġrib fī aḫbār maḥāsin ahl al-Maġrib* while he was serving Saladin after having settled in Egypt. Ibn al-Abbār (d. 658/1260) had already questioned his reliability as a historian (*huwa muttahim fī ta'līfihi*), doubts quoted also by Ḏahabī and Ibn al-Jazarī (d. 833/1429).

Yasaʿ b. Ḥazm not only forged the alleged *amān* of Qaštāla, but also an expedition against Zamora that would have been led by Ḥakam I (r. 180/796–206/822). If in the East—where he had settled—the Crusades were still a threat, in al-Andalus the Almohad caliphs were not being successful in making substantial territorial gains against the Christians, nor were they interested in developing an activist jihad spirit among the Andalusis. Emmanuel Sivan showed a long time ago that in the sixth/twelfth century there was a

112 Such as Octaviolca, Vellica, Camarica, Moroeca: Barbero de Aguilera and Vigil Pascual, *Sobre los orígenes*, 157, 168, 170.

113 "Bardulia qui nunc vocitatur Castella": *Crónica Albendense* quoted in Oliver Asín, *En torno a los orígenes de Castilla*, 13; cf. Pedro Chalmeta Gendrón, "Ḳas̱ẖtāla," *Encyclopaedia of Islam, Vol. IV, Iran-Kha* (Leiden: Brill, 1978); Barbero de Aguilera and Vigil Pascual, *Sobre los orígenes*, 281, 282–85.

114 HEM, 1950, 1:69n4, 143 and note 1.

"réarmement moral" and a renovation of jihad ideology in the Eastern lands,[115] raising the issue of whether the Andalusis who had migrated to the East were instrumental in developing these ideological reactions against the Crusaders. This would have been contrary to what happened in al-Andalus where attempts at imposing a jihad ideology outside the state were few and not successful.[116]

The case of Yasaʿ b. Ḥazm should be put into this context. In his lost historical work written for Saladin he included the texts already mentioned that can be understood as propagandistic texts in favor of jihad (Dimyāṭī includes them in a work devoted to the merits of jihad). Because they were meant for propagandistic use, fidelity to the truth becomes unimportant. What was important was to transmit the idea that the Muslims of al-Andalus had always behaved according to the appropriate legal norms with the Christians, signing pacts that the Christians had broken, therefore making it necessary to wage jihad against them.

In the same spirit that moved Yasaʿ b. Ḥazm to volunteer to be the first to deliver a Sunni *ḫuṭba* in Cairo alter the fall of the Fatimid caliphate, he decided to write a history of the Maghrib adapted to his own times in order to make a place for himself in the new land where he had settled. By this he was trying to remedy his economic needs, but also to spread in the *dār al-islām* the need to wage jihad in al-Andalus in order to save it from the Christians. In this process, the realities of early al-Andalus vanish. The Cordoban Umayyads were not really interested in jihad, as they did not have any strictly military need to attack the Christian territories outside their direct control because they did not represent any danger for them. Their campaigns had economic implications much more relevant than military and propagandistic needs. Those campaigns could be described as having been sent against *dār al ḥarb*, but their real aim was booty, what can be called—as an invented expression—*dār al-ġanīma*. Centuries later, Yasaʿ b. Ḥazm re-imagined the Umayyads as moved by a jihad

115 Emmanuel Sivan, *L'Islam et la Croisade: idéologie et propagande dans les réactions musulmanes aux Croisades* (Paris: Maisonneuve, 1968), 23–37. See also Michael Bonner, *Jihad in Islamic History: Doctrines and Practice* (Princeton: Princeton University Press, 2006); Carole Hillenbrand, *The Crusades: Islamic Perspectives* (New York: Routledge, 2000), 89–255.

116 Dominique Urvoy, "Sur L'évolution de la notion de *Ǧihād* dans l'Espagne musulmane," *Mélanges de la Casa de Velazquez* 9 (1973): 335–71; Pierre Guichard, *Les Musulmans de Valence et la reconquête (XIe–XIIIe siècles)*, vol. 1 (Damas; Paris: Institut Français de Damas; Maisonneuve, 1990), 335–71.

spirit and when doing so he also re-imagined the legal status of the "ancestor" (Qaštāla) to the most powerful Christian state of his own times, Castille.

References

Abou El Fadl, Khaled. *Rebellion and Violence in Islamic Law*. Cambridge: Cambridge University Press, 2001.

Aguilar Sebastián, Victoria. "Onomástica de origen árabe en el Reino de León (siglo X)." *Al-Qanṭara* 15, no. 2 (1994): 351–64.

Aguilar Sebastián, Victoria, and Fernando Rodríguez Mediano. "Antroponimia de origen árabe en la documentación leonesa (siglos VIII–XIII)." In *El reino de León en la Alta Edad Media*. 6, 499–633. Colección Fuentes y estudios de historia leonesa 53. León: Centro de Estudios e Investigación "San Isidoro" [u.a.], 1994.

Azkarate, Agustín, and Iñaki García Camino. "El espacio circumpirenaico occidental durante los siglos VI al X d.C. según el registro arqueológico: algunos interrogantes." In *Asturias entre visigodos y mozárabes: Visigodos y Omeyas, VI—Madrid, 2010*, edited by Luis Caballero Zoreda, Pedro Mateos, and César García de Castro Valdés, 331–52. Anejos de Archivo Español de Arqueología, LXIII. Madrid: Consejo Superior de Investigaciones Científicas, Instituto de Historia, Centro de Ciencias Humanas y Sociales, 2012.

Barbero de Aguilera, Abilio, and Marcelo Vigil Pascual. *Sobre los orígenes sociales de la reconquista*. 1. ed. Colección Ariel. Barcelona: Ed. Ariel, 1984.

Barceló, M. "El hiato en las acuñaciones de oro en al-Andalus, 127–316/744(5)-936(7) (Los datos fundamentales de un problema)." *Moneda y crédito* 132 (1975): 33–71.

Barceló, M. "Monedas visigodas de Hispania." *Numisma* 27 (1977): 55–80.

Barkai, Ron. *El enemigo en el espejo: cristianos y musulmanes en la España medieval*. Madrid: Rialp, 2007.

Barrau Dihigo, Lucien. "Recherches sur l'histoire politique du royaume asturien (718–910)." *Revue hispanique* 52, no. 121 (1921): 1–360.

Benhima, Yassir. "Du *tamyīz* à l'*iʿtirāf*: usages et légitimation du massacre au début de l'époque almohade." *Annales Islamologiques* 43 (2009): 137–53.

Bonnaz, Yves. *Chroniques asturiennes: fin IXe siècle*. Sources d'histoire médiévale. Paris: Editions du Centre national de la recherche scientifique, 1987.

Bonner, Michael. *Jihad in Islamic History: Doctrines and Practice*. Princeton: Princeton University Press, 2006.

Bosch Vilá, Jacinto. "Ḳasṭīliya." *Encyclopaedia of Islam, Vol. IV, Iran-Kha*. Leiden: Brill, 1978.

Calasso, Giovanna. "Alla ricerca di *dār al-islām*. Una ricognizione nei testi di giuristi e tradizionisti, lessicografi, geografi e viaggiatori." *Rivista degli Studi Orientali* 83 (2010): 271–96.

Carballeira, Ana María. *Galicia y los gallegos en las fuentes árabes medievales*. Santiago de Compostela: Instituto de Estudios Gallegos Padre Sarmiento, 2007.

Castilla Brazales, Juan. "Las fuentes de al-Ḏahabī." In *Estudios onomástico-biográficos de Al-Andalus*, edited by María Luisa Ávila Navarro, 3:351–60. Madrid: Consejo Superior de Investigaciones Científicas, Instituto de Filología, Departamento de Estudios Arabes, 1988.

Chalmeta Gendrón, Pedro. "La 'sumisión de Zaragoza' del 325–937." *Anuario de Historia del Derecho Español* 46 (1976): 503–25.

Chalmeta Gendrón, Pedro. "Ḳas͟htāla." *Encyclopaedia of Islam, Vol. IV, Iran-Kha*. Leiden: Brill, 1978.

Clarke, Nicola. *The Muslim Conquest of Iberia: Medieval Arabic Narratives*. Culture and Civilization in the Middle East 30. London: Routledge, 2012.

Conde y García, José Antonio. *Historia de la dominación de los árabes en España, sacada de varios manuscritos y memorias arábigas*. Vol. 1. 3 vols. Madrid: Imprenta que fue de García, 1820.

Conde y García, José Antonio. *Historia de la dominación de los árabes en España, sacada de varios manuscritos y memorias arábigas*. Madrid: Marín y Compañía, 1874.

Ḏahabī, Šams al-dīn Muḥammad al-. *Siyar aʿlām al-nubalāʾ*. Edited by Šuʿayb al-Arnaʾūṭ. 23 vols. Beirut: Muʾassasat al-Risāla, 1985.

Dimyāṭī, Abū Zakariyā Ibn al-Naḥḥās al-. *Mašāriʿ al-ašwāq ilā maṣāriʿ al-ʿuššāq wa-muṯīr al-ġurām ilā dār al-Islām (fī faḍāʾil al-jihād)*. Edited by I. M. ʿAlī. 2 vols. Beirut, 1410AH.

Dozy, Reinhardt. *Histoire des Musulmans d'Espagne jusqu'a la conquête de l'Andalousie par les almoravides (711–1110)*. Leiden: Brill, 1861.

Epalza Ferrer, Mikel de. "El derecho político musulmán y su influencia en la formación de Álava (siglos VIII–XI)." In *La formación de Álava. 650 Aniversario del Pacto de Arriaga (1332–1982). Congreso de Estudios Históricos, Álava: Diputación de Álava*, 303–13. Álava: Diputación de Álava, 1983.

Epalza Ferrer, Mikel de. "El derecho político musulmán y su influencia en la formación de Álava (siglos VIII–XI)." *Estudios de Deusto* 32, no. 73 (1984): 505–18.

Epalza Ferrer, Mikel de. "Los Māŷūs («magos»): Un hápax coránico (XXII, 17), entre lo étnico y lo jurídico, hasta su utilización en al-Andalus." In *El Corán ayer y hoy. Perspectivas actuales sobre el islam. Estudios en honor al profesor Julio Cortés*, edited by Miguel Hernando de Larramendi and Salvador Peña Martín, 399–414. Córdoba: Berenice, 2008.

Epalza Ferrer, Mikel de. "Note about the Muslim Conquest of the 7th–8th centuries: The Basque, berber, norse Viking, Norman and Britos Magicians." *Imago Temporis: Medium Aevum* 1 (2007): 61–69.

Epalza Ferrer, Mikel de, and Joaquín del Valle de Lersundi Mendizábal. "Vascos y árabes en el siglo VIII y en el XX. Historia e historias." *Hesperia, Culturas del Mediterráneo* 6 (2007): 123–53.

Fernández Félix, Ana. *Cuestiones legales del Islam temprano: la* ʿUtbiyya *y el proceso de formación de la sociedad islámica andalusí*. Estudios árabes e islámicos Monografías 6. Madrid: Consejo Superior de Investigaciones Científicas, 2003.

Fernández Félix, Ana, and Maribel Fierro. "Cristianos y conversos al islam en al-Andalus bajo los Omeyas. Una aproximación al proceso de islamización a través de una fuente legal andalusí del s. III/IX." *Anejos Archivo Español de Arqueología* 23 (2000): 417–29.

Fierro, Maribel. "Cuatro preguntas en torno a Ibn Ḥafṣūn." *Al-Qanṭara* 16 (1995): 221–57.

Fierro, Maribel. "Hostages and the dangers of cultural contact: two cases from al-Andalus." In *Acteurs des transferts culturels en Méditerranée médiévale*, edited by Rania Abdellatif, Yassir Benhima, Daniel König, and Elisabeth Ruchaud, 73–83. Ateliers des Deutschen Historischen Instituts Paris 9. München: Oldenbourg, 2012.

Fierro, Maribel. "La falsificación de la historia: al-Yasaʿ b. Ḥazm y su *Kitāb al-mugrib*." *Al-Qanṭara* 16 (1995): 15–38.

Franco Sánchez, Francisco. "Consideración jurídica y religiosa de los territorios de la Meseta y el Norte peninsular por el poder musulmán de al-Andalus." *Al-Andalus Magreb* 7 (1999): 101–33.

García Sanjuán, Alejandro. "Del *Dār al-Islām* al *Dār al-Ḥarb*: la cuestión mudéjar y la legalidad islámica." In *Congreso conmemorativo del 750 aniversario de la Toma de Carmona*, 177–88. Carmona: Diputación de Sevilla, 1998: 177–88.

García Villada, Zacarías. *Historia eclesiástica de España*. Vol. 2/1. 3 vols. Madrid: Compañía Ibero-americana de Publicaciones, 1932.

Guichard, Pierre. *Les Musulmans de Valence et la reconquête (XIe–XIIIe siècles)*. Vol. 1. 2 vols. Damas; Paris: Institut Français de Damas; Maisonneuve, 1990.

Heffening, Willi. *Das islamische Fremdenrecht bis zu den islamisch-fränkischen Staatsverträgen: eine rechtshistorische Studie zum Fiqh*. Hannover: Orient Buchh. H. Lafaire, 1925.

Hendrickson, Jocelyn N. "The Islamic Obligation to Emigrate: Al-Wansharīsī's Asnā Al-Matājir Reconsidered." Ph.D. Thesis, Emory University, 2009.

Herrero, Omayra. El perdón del gobernante (al-Andalus, ss. II–V/VIII–XI). Helsinki: Academia Scientiarum Fennica, 2016.

Hillenbrand, Carole. *The Crusades: Islamic Perspectives*. New York: Routledge, 2000.

Ḫušanī, Muḥammad b. al-Ḥāriṯ al-. *Ajbār al-fuqahā' wa-l-muḥaddiṯīn* (*Historia de los alfaquíes y tradicionistas de al-Andalus*). Edited by María L. Ávila and Luis Molina. Fuentes arábico-hispanas 3. Madrid: Consejo Superior de Investigaciones Científicas, 1992.

Ibn-Abī-Zaid al-Qairawānī, Abū-Muḥammad ʿAbdallāh. *Der Heilige Krieg* (*Ǧihād*) *aus der Sicht der mālikitischen Rechtsschule*. Edited by Mathias von Bredow. Beiruter Texte und Studien 44. Stuttgart: Steiner, 1994.

Ibn al-Aṯīr. *Al-Kāmil fī 'l-ta'rīḫ*. Edited by C.J. Tornberg. Leiden: Brill, 1870.

Ibn al-Ḫaṭīb, Lisān al-dīn. *Al-Iḥāṭa fī aḫbār Ġarnāṭa*. Edited by Muḥammad ʿAbd Allāh ʿInān. 4 vols. Cairo: Maktabat al-Ḫānjī, 1393–95AH.

Ibn al-Ḫaṭīb, Lisān al-dīn. *Al-Iḥāṭa fī aḫbār Ġarnāṭa. Nuṣūṣ jadīda lam tunšar*. Edited by ʿAbd al-Salām Šaqqūr. Tangier: Mu'assasat al-taġlīf wa'l-ṭibāʿa wa'l-našr wa'l-tawzīʿ li'l-šamāl, 1988.

Ibn al-Kardabūs, ʿAbd al-Malik, and Ibn al-Šabbāṭ. *Ta'rīḫ al-Andalus li-bn al-Kardabūs wa-waṣfuhu li-bn al-Šabbāṭ. Naṣṣāni jadīdāni*. Edited by A. M. al-ʿAbbādī. Madrid: Instituto de estudios islàmicos, 1971.

Ibn al-Qūṭiyya, Abū Bakr. *Ta'rīḫ iftitāḥ al-Andalus li-bn al-Qūṭiyya* (*Historia de la conquista de España*). Edited by Julian Ribera. Colección de obras arábigas de historia y geografía 2. Madrid: Tipografía de la "Revista de archivos," 1926.

Ibn Ḥabīb, ʿAbd al-Malik. *Kitāb al-ta'rīj:* (*la historia*). Edited by Jorge Aguadé. Fuentes arábico-hispanas 1. Madrid: Consejo Superior de Investigaciones Científicas, Instituto de Cooperación con el Mundo Arabe, 1991.

Ibn Ḫaldūn, Walī 'l-dīn. *Kitāb al-ʿIbar*. Būlāq, 1284/1867.

Ibn Ḥayyān, Abū Marwān Ḥayyān b. Ḫalaf. *Al-Muqtabis* (*al-Juz' Al-ḫāmis*)*, Ed. P. Chalmeta, F. Corriente and M. Ṣubḥ, Madrid, 1979*. Edited by Pedro Chalmeta Gendrón, Federico Corriente Córdoba, and M. Ṣubḥ. Madrid: Instituto hispano-árabe de cultura, 1979.

Ibn Ḥayyān, Abū Marwān Ḥayyān b. Ḫalaf. *Crónica de los emires Alḥakam I y Abdarraḥmān II entre los años 796 y 847* [*Almuqtabis II-1*]. Translated by Maḥmūd ʿAlī Makkī and Federico Corriente. Zaragoza: Instituto de Estudios Islámicos y de Oriente Próximo, 2001.

Ibn Ḥayyān, Abū Marwān Ḥayyān b. Ḫalaf. *Muqtabis* [= M2b]. Edited by Maḥmūd ʿAlī Makkī. Riyadh, 2003.

Ibn Ḥayyān, Abū Marwān Ḥayyān b. Ḫalaf. *Muqtabis* [= M2c]. Edited by Maḥmūd ʿAlī Makkī. Beirut, 1973.

Ibn Ḥayyān, Abū Marwān Ḥayyān b. Ḫalaf. *Crónica del califa ʿAbdarraḥmān III An-Nāṣir entre los años 912 y 942* (*al-Muqtabis V*). Translated by María Jesús Viguera, and Federico Corriente. Textos medievales 64. Zaragoza: Anubar: Instituto Hispano-Arabe de Cultura, 1981.

Ibn ʿIḏārī, Abū ʿAbd Allāh Muḥammad al-Marrākušī. *Kitāb al-Bayān al-muġrib fī aḫbār al-Andalus wa'l-Maġrib* [=BM]. Edited by Georges Séraphin Colin and Évariste Lévi-Provençal. Leiden: Brill, 1948.

Ibn Rušd al-Jadd. *Kitāb al-Bayān wa'l-taḥṣīl*. Edited by Aḥmad al-Ḥabbābī. 3rd ed. 20 vols. Beirut: Dār al-ġarb al-islāmī, 1408AH.

Jones, Linda G. "The Christian Companion: A Rhetorical Trope in the Narration of Intra-Muslim Conflict during the Almohad Period." *Anuario de Estudios Medievales* 38: Actes del Col.loqui "Conflictivitat i vies de solució a la Mediterrània medieval" (2008): 793–829.

Khadduri, Majid. *The Law of War and Peace in Islam*. London: Luzac and Co., 1941.

Lafuente Alcántara, Emilio, ed. *Aḫbār Majmūʿa*. Madrid: Rivadeneyra, 1867.

Lapiedra Gutiérrez, Eva. *Cómo los musulmanes llamaban a los cristianos hispánicos*. Colección Textos universitaris. Alicante–Valencia: Institut de Cultura "Juan Gil-Albert"–Generalitat Valenciana, Conselleria de Cultura, Educació i Ciència, 1997.

Lévi-Provençal, Évariste. *España musulmana hasta la caída del Califato de Córdoba (711–1031 de J. C.)*. Translated by Emilio García Gómez. Vol. 1. 3 vols. Historia de España 4. Barcelona: Espasa-Calpe, 1950.

Lévi-Provençal, Évariste. *Histoire de l'Espagne musulmane. 1: La conquête et l'émirat hispano-umaiyade (710–912)*. Vol. 1. 3 vols. Paris–Leiden: Maisonneuve–Brill, 1950.

Lévi-Provençal, Évariste. *Histoire de l'Espagne musulmane. 2: Le califat umaiyade de Cordoue (912–1031)*. 3 vols. Paris–Leiden: Maisonneuve–Brill, 1950.

Levy-Rubin, Milka. *Non-Muslims in the Early Islamic Empire: From Surrender to Coexistence*. Cambridge Studies in Islamic Civilization. New York: Cambridge University Press, 2011.

Loebenstein, Judith. "Legal and Historical Aspects of Jihād in Al-Andalus (2nd/8th–5th/11th Centuries)." Unpublished Ph.D. Thesis, The Hebrew University of Jerusalem, 2008.

Maíllo Salgado, Felipe. *Acerca de la conquista árabe de Hispania: imprecisiones, equívocos y patrañas*. Primera edición. Bibliotheca Arabo-Romanica et Islamica 7. Gijón: Ediciones Trea, 2011.

Manzano Moreno, Eduardo. *La frontera de al-Andalus en época de los Omeyas*. Biblioteca de historia 9. Madrid: Consejo Superior de Investigaciones Científicas, 1991.

Maqqarī, Šihāb al-dīn Abū 'l-ʿAbbās al-. *Nafḥ al-ṭīb*. Edited by I. ʿAbbās. Beirut, 1968.

Marín, Manuela. "Nómina de sabios de al-Andalus (93–350/711–961)." In *Estudios onomástico-biográficos de Al-Andalus*, edited by Manuela Marín, 1:23–182. Madrid: Consejo Superior de Investigaciones Científicas, Instituto de Filología, Departamento de Estudios Arabes, 1988.

Marín, Manuela., ed. *The Formation of Al-Andalus*. The Formation of the Classical Islamic World, v. 46–47. Aldershot: Ashgate, 1998.

Martínez Enamorado, Virgilio. "«Donde rigen las normas de Satán»: Ibn Antuluh, Ibn Ḥafṣūn y el asunto de la propiedad de una esclava." *Espacio, Tiempo y Forma. Serie III. Historia Medieval* 23 (2010): 97–112.

Martínez Enamorado, Virgilio. *'Umar ibn Ḥafṣūn de la rebeldía a la construcción de la "Dawla": estudios en torno al rebelde de al-Andalus (880–928)*. San José (Costa Rica): Editorial UCR, 2012.

Masud, Muhammad Khalid. "The Obligation to Migrate: The Doctrine of *hijra* in Islamic Law." In *Muslim Travellers: Pilgrimage, Migration, and the Religious Imagination*, edited by Dale F. Eickelman and James P. Piscatori, 29–49. Comparative Studies on Muslim Societies 9. Berkeley: University of California Press, 1990.

Molina, Luis., ed. *Una descripción anónima de al-Andalus*. Madrid: Consejo Superior de Investigaciones Científicas, Instituto "Miguel Asín," 1983.

Molina, Luis., ed. *Fatḥ al-Andalus: la conquista de al-Andalus*. Fuentes arábico-hispanas 18. Madrid: Consejo Superior de Investigaciones Científicas : Agencia Española de Cooperación Internacional, 1994.

Molina, Luis. "Aḥmad Al-Rāzī." In *Biblioteca de Al-Andalus*, edited by Jorge Lirola Delgado, José Miguel Puerta Vílchez, and Fundación Ibn Tufayl de Estudios Árabes, 7:159–63. Enciclopedia de La Cultura Andalusí 1. Almería: Fundación Ibn Tufayl de Estudios Árabes, 2012.

Molina, Luis. "'Isà Al-Rāzı." In *Biblioteca de Al-Andalus*, edited by Jorge Lirola Delgado, José Miguel Puerta Vílchez, and Fundación Ibn Tufayl de Estudios Árabes, 7:163–68. Enciclopedia de La Cultura Andalusí 1. Almería: Fundación Ibn Tufayl de Estudios Árabes, 2012.

Morony, M. "Madjūs." *Encyclopaedia of Islam, Vol. V, Khe Mahi*. Leiden: Brill, 1986.

Oliver Asín, Jaime. *En torno a los orígenes de Castilla; su toponimia en relación con los árabes y los beréberes. Discurso leído en el acto de su recepción pública*. Madrid: Real Academia de la Historia, 1974.

Pellicer i Bru, Josep. *Al-Andalus: las fuentes y la numismática (síntesis cronológico-metrológica de las acuñaciones del Califato de Córdoba)*. Barcelona: Asociación Numismática Española, 1988.

Peters, Rudolph. *Islam and Colonialism: The Doctrine of Jihad in Modern History*. Religion and Society 20. The Hague: Mouton, 1979.

Peterson, David. "The Men of Wavering Faith: On the Origins of Arabic Personal and Place Names in the Duero Basin." *Journal of Medieval Iberian Studies* 3, no. 2 (September 2011): 219–46.

Ibn Qutayba, pseudo-. *Al-Imāma wa'l-siyāsa*. Edited by T. M. al-Zaynī. Beirut, s.d.

Rubiera de Epalza, María Jesús. "Álava y los alaveses en los textos árabes medievales." In *La formación de Álava. 650 Aniversario del Pacto de Arriaga (1332–1982). Congreso de Estudios Históricos, Álava: Diputación de Álava*, 385–93. Álava: Diputación de Álava, 1983.

Safran, Janina M. *Defining Boundaries in Al-Andalus: Muslims, Christians, and Jews in Islamic Iberia.* Ithaca: Cornell University Press, 2013.

Sánchez-Albornoz, Claudio. *En torno a los orígenes del feudalismo.* Colegio universitario Ediciones Istmo 12. Mendoza: Universidad nacional de Cuyo, 1942.

Sánchez-Albornoz, Claudio. *La España musulmana según los autores islamitas y cristianos medievales.* Buenos Aires: El Ateneo, 1946.

Sánchez-Albornoz, Claudio. "La saña celosa de un arabista." *Cuadernos de Historia de España* 28 (1958): 5–42.

Schacht, Joseph. "Amān." *Encyclopaedia of Islam, Vol. I, A–B.* Leiden: Brill, 1960.

Sénac, Philippe. *Musulmans et sarrasins dans le sud de la Gaule: VIII*[e]*–XI*[e] *siècle.* Paris: Sycomore, 1980.

Simonet y Baca, Francisco Javier. *Historia de los mozárabes de España: deducida de los mejores y más auténticos testimonios de los escritores cristianos y árabes.* 1897–1903. Reprint, Amsterdam: Oriental Press, 1967.

Sivan, Emmanuel. *L'Islam et la Croisade: idéologie et propagande dans les réactions musulmanes aux Croisades.* Paris: Maisonneuve, 1968.

Ṭāhirī, Aḥmad. *Fath al-Andalus y la incorporación de Occidente a Dar al-Islam [Fatḥ al-Andalus wa-'ltiḥāq al-ġarb bi-dār al-Islām]: Mūsā b. Nuṣayr wa-Ṭāriq b. Ziyād.* 1st ed. Valencia: Centro Cultural Islámico, 2011.

Urvoy, Dominique. "Sur L'évolution de la notion de *Ǧihād* dans l'Espagne musulmane." *Mélanges de la Casa de Velazquez* 9 (1973): 335–71.

Vallvé, Joaquín. *La división territorial de la España musulmana.* Madrid: Consejo Superior de Investigaciones Científicas, Instituto de Filología, Departamento de Estudios Arabes, 1986.

Verskin, Alan. *Oppressed in the Land?: Fatwas on Muslims Living under Non-Muslim Rule from the Middle Ages to the Present.* Princeton Series of Middle Eastern Sources in Translation. Princeton: Markus Wiener, 2013.

Viguera Molins, María Jesús. "Cristianos, judíos y musulmanes en al-Andalus." In *Cristianos, musulmanes y judíos en la España Medieval: de la aceptación al rechazo,* edited by Julio Valdeón Baruque, 1. ed., 43–69. Valladolid–Soria: Ambito Ediciones–Fundación Duques de Soria, 2004.

Wanšarīsī, Abū 'l-ʿAbbās Aḥmad al-. *Al-Miʿyār al-muġrib.* Rabat: Wizārat al-Awqāf wa'l-Šuʿūn al-Islāmiyya, 1981.

Wasserstein, David. *The Caliphate in the West: An Islamic Political Institution in the Iberian Peninsula.* Oxford: Clarendon Press–Oxford University Press, 1993.

Zozaya Stabel-Hansen, Juan. "771–856: los primeros años del Islam andalusí o una hipótesis de trabajo." *Cuadernos emeritenses* 15, no. Ruptura o continuidad: pervivencias preislámicas en El-Andalus (1998): 83–142.

CHAPTER 12

Les émirs d'Iran nord-oriental face aux steppes turques (IXe-XIe siècle) : entre légitimation, confrontation et cohabitation

Camille Rhoné

1 Introduction

En Iran nord-oriental (Khorassan et Transoxiane), comme dans le reste du monde islamique médiéval, la guerre – et le jihad en particulier, – présentée comme acte de défense de la civilisation, est un instrument primordial de légitimation politique[1]. Nous nous intéresserons à la période entre le milieu du IIIe/IXe et le milieu du Ve/XIe siècle, qui correspond à l'émancipation du pouvoir sultanien d'Iran nord-oriental à travers l'affirmation des dynasties iraniennes[2] des émirs saffarides et samanides puis des sultans ghaznévides. À cette époque, les frontières nord orientales du *dār al-islām* sont globalement fixées : après les conquêtes arabo-musulmanes du Ie/VIIe et surtout du IIe/VIIIe siècle[3], les dernières avancées territoriales d'importance ont eu lieu

1 Parmi les travaux récents, citons Philippe Sénac, *Al-Manṣūr: le fléau de l'an mil* (Paris: Perrin, 2006); Anne-Marie Eddé, *Saladin* (Paris: Flammarion, 2008); Michele Bernardini, *Mémoire et propagande à l'époque timouride* (Paris: Association pour l'avancement des études iraniennes, 2008); Annliese Nef et Élise Voguet, éd., *La légitimation du pouvoir au Maghreb médiéval. De l'orientalisation à l'émancipation politique* (Madrid: Casa de Velázquez, 2011); Denise Aigle, éd., *Le Bilād al-Šām face aux mondes extérieurs. La perception de l'Autre et la représentation du Souverain* (Damas: IFPO, 2012).

2 C'est à dessein que nous considérons les Ghaznévides comme une dynastie « iranienne » : en dépit de leurs origines turques, ses membres s'imprègnent très largement de la culture iranienne, notamment lorsqu'ils sont au service de leurs maîtres samanides. Sur ces diverses dynasties, voir Clifford E. Bosworth, *The History of the Saffarids of Sistan and Maliks of Nimruz (247/861 to 949/1542-3)* (Costa Mesa, CA: Mazda Publishers in association with Bibliotheca Persica, 1994); Deborah G. Tor, *Violent Order: Religious Warfare, Chivalry, and the ʿAyyār Phenomenon in the Medieval Islamic World*, Istanbuler Texte Und Studien 11 (Würzburg: Ergon-Verl, 2007); Luke Treadwell, « The political history of the Sāmānid state » (PhD diss., Oxford University, 1991); Clifford E. Bosworth, *The Ghaznavids. Their Empire in Afghanistan and Eastern Iran* (Edinburgh: Edinburgh University Press, 1963).

3 H. A. R. Gibb, *The Arab conquests in Central Asia* (1923; repr., New York: AMS Press, 1970).

 DOI 10.1163/9789004331037_014

lors des prises d'Isbījāb (840) et de Talas[4], dans l'actuel Kirghizistan (280/893). À l'autre extrémité de notre période d'étude, les conquêtes se produisent dans le sens inverse et sont désormais le fait des Turcs qarakhanides (à la fin du IVe/Xe siècle) et seldjoukides (dans la première moitié du Ve/XIe siècle), dont une partie sont islamisés ou en cours d'islamisation[5].

Notre objectif est d'interroger la façon dont le schéma dichotomique *dār al-islām* / *dār al-ḥarb* est transposé dans les périphéries orientales du califat, non face aux chrétiens mais face aux steppes peuplées de Turcs qui incarnent l'archétype du nomade infidèle. Comment, dans ce contexte particulier, le schéma dichotomique est-il assimilé et instrumentalisé par les dirigeants locaux, alors en train d'affirmer leur indépendance vis-à-vis de Bagdad ? Dans quelle mesure s'emparent-ils de ce discours légitimant, façonné en Irak pour les califes abbassides ?

Nous nous intéresserons d'abord au poids du système rhétorique forgé à Bagdad, qui sert de référence absolue dans les terres orientales. Il s'agira ensuite de souligner les limites de la transposition du modèle de la frontière arabo-byzantine par rapport aux spécificités de l'Iran nord-oriental. Enfin, nous analyserons les raisons qui poussent les dirigeants sultaniens et leurs historiographes à revendiquer ce modèle en dépit des particularismes orientaux et des paradoxes que cela soulève.

2 Le poids de l'imaginaire politique de Bagdad

L'imaginaire politique façonné à Bagdad au tournant des IIe/VIIIe-IIIe/IXe siècles est transposé dans les cours d'Iran nord-oriental par la circulation des hommes et des idées. Sans cesse, et bien qu'indépendants de fait, les émirs et sultans se tournent vers le calife pour appuyer leur légitimité politique et s'intégrer dans le *dār al-islām*. En matière de guerre et de jihad, l'entourage califal impose la lutte contre l'ennemi byzantin en tant que référence ultime[6] :

4 Abū Bakr Muḥammad Naršaḫī, *Ta'rīḫ-i Buḫārā*, éd. par Muḍaris Radavī (Tehran, 1387SH), 118, trans. Richard N. Frye, *The History of Bukhara, translated from a Persian Abridgment of the Arabic Original by Narshakhī* (Cambridge, Mass.: The Mediaeval Academy of America, 1954), 86-87.

5 Étienne de La Vaissière, éd., *Islamisation de l'Asie centrale. Processus locaux d'acculturation du VIIe au XIe siècle* (Paris: AAEI, 2008).

6 Michael Bonner, *Aristocratic Violence and Holy War*, Studies in the Jihad and the Arab-Byzantine Frontier, 81 (New Haven, Connecticut: American Oriental Society, 1996), 97-106; Michael Bonner, *Le jihad: origines, interprétations, combats* (Paris: Téraèdre, 2004); Paul L. Heck, « "Jihad" revisited », *The Journal of Religious Ethics* 32, nº 1 (2004): 100-113; Christophe

le combat contre les chrétiens de la péninsule Anatolienne fait office d'idéal pour les musulmans, y compris pour les souverains d'Iran nord-oriental. Ces derniers sont sensibilisés à l'idéologie califale, diffusée en particulier grâce au succès considérable que rencontrent les *maḏhab*s du Proche- et du Moyen-Orient au Khorassan et en Transoxiane : les hanafites et shafi'ites présents dans la région relaient le modèle élaboré par les ulémas au service du pouvoir central[7].

Une large partie des sources qui renseignent l'historien moderne sur l'Iran et l'Asie centrale d'époque médiévale sont elles-mêmes imprégnées par le modèle de la lutte contre les Byzantins puis les Croisés. Les textes à dimension universaliste – chroniques, histoires universelles (Ṭabarī, Ibn al-Aṯīr) et certains ouvrages des géographes classiques – insèrent l'Iran nord-oriental dans une représentation du monde souvent centrée sur Bagdad : dans ces mises en scène unitaires du califat, il est sous-entendu que les dirigeants régionaux adhèrent au modèle de lutte contre les chrétiens.

Les dictionnaires biographiques et histoires locales focalisés sur les ulémas transmettent eux aussi le modèle du jihad sur la frontière byzantine. Le tropisme occidental est marquant : à de très rares exceptions près[8], il n'y a pas dans les textes de preuve tangible que des ulémas seraient morts en martyrs et

Picard, « Regards croisés sur l'élaboration du jihad entre Occident et Orient musulman (VIIIe-XIIe siècle): perspectives et réflexion sur une origine commune », in *Regards croisés sur la guerre sainte. Guerre, religion et idéologie dans l'espace méditerranéen latin (XIe-XIIIe siècle). Actes du Colloque international tenu à la Casa de Velázquez (Madrid) du 11 au 13 avril 2005*, éd. par Daniel Baloup et Philippe Josserand (Toulouse: CNRS; Université Toulouse-II-Le Mirail, 2006), 35, 42.

7 Wilferd Madelung, *Religious Trends in Early Islamic Iran* (Oxford: Bibliotheca Persica, 1988), 26-29; Alfred Morabia, *Le Gihad dans l'Islam médiéval. Le « combat sacré » des origines au XIIe siècle* (Paris: Albin Michel, 1993), 185-91; Christopher Melchert, *The formation of the Sunni schools of law, 9th-10th centuries C.E.*, Studies in Islamic law and society, v. 4 (Leiden: Brill, 1997); Šāfiʿī, *Kitāb al-Umm*, cité dans Michael Bonner, *Aristocratic Violence and Holy War: Studies in the Jihad and the Arab-Byzantine Frontier*, American Oriental Series, 81 (New Haven, Connecticut: American Oriental Society, 1996), 40; Abū 'l-Ḥasan al-Baṣrī al-Māwardī, *Kitāb al-Aḥkām al-sulṭāniyya* (Ḥaydarābād: Jāmiʿa-yi ʿUṯmāniyya, 1931), trad. Edmond Fagnan, *Les Statuts gouvernementaux ou règles de droit public et administratif*, reproduction de l'édition d'Alger 1915 (Paris: le Sycomore, 1982); Heck, « "Jihad" revisited », 109, n. 16; Éric Chaumont, « al-Sh̲āfiʿī », *Encyclopédie de l'Islam, Vol. IX, San-Sze* (Leiden: Brill, 1997); Éric Chaumont, « al-Sh̲āfiʿiyya », *Encyclopédie de l'Islam, Vol. IX, San-Sze* (Leiden: Brill, 1997).

8 Parmi les ulémas liés à Samarcande, Ibrāhīm b. Šammās al-Ġāzī al-Samarqandī, propriétaire d'un domaine (*ḍayʿa*) à l'extérieur de Samarcande, « cavalier courageux (*fāris šujāʿ*) », est tué par les Turcs en 220 ou 221 de l'hégire. Jamāl al-dīn Abū 'l-Ḥajjāj Yūsuf al-Mizzī, *Tahḏīb al-kamāl fī asmāʾ al-rijāl* (Beyrouth: Muʾassasat al-risāla, 1994), 2:106.

en nombre sur les frontières de l'Iran nord-oriental entre le milieu du IIIe/IXe et le milieu du Ve/XIe siècle. Les très rares exemples disponibles, parmi lesquels le Khorassanien Ibrāhīm b. Adam (m. 161/777) et ʿAbd Allāh Ibn al-Mubārak (m. 181/797), concernent des hommes partis combattre à l'ouest et appartenant à la période précédente[9].

Cependant, les auteurs médiévaux s'efforcent de rattacher les confins orientaux à la tradition juridique et à l'idéal de lutte contre les infidèles en adaptant le schéma dichotomique *dār al-islām* / *dār al-ḥarb* au contexte du Khorassan et de la Transoxiane : les ennemis « orientaux » – Daylamites et Turcs – sont désignés comme autant de cibles de choix. Ainsi un récit de Masʿūdī (m. 345/956) montre que ces deux groupes ethniques incarnent l'ennemi par excellence, attribuant les paroles suivantes au calife Hādī (r. 169/785-170/786), qui venait d'apprendre la mort de Ḥusayn b. Alī, Ṣāḥib Faḫḫ (169/786), dont on lui apportait la tête : « Vous venez ici souriants [...], comme si vous m'apportiez la tête d'un Turc ou d'un Daylamite. »[10] L'objet n'est pas de rapporter des faits exacts mais de raconter une anecdote à caractère didactique. Le terme « turc » désigne ici le non musulman, avec un sens péjoratif et archétypal évident, placé sur le même plan que les Daylamites. Ces derniers, situés sur la frontière nord-ouest du Khorassan, sont souvent considérés par les autorités centrales sunnites comme des adeptes déviants de l'islam – car chiites zaydites – et des sujets remuants, en particulier du fait de leur soutien aux Bouyides[11].

---

9 Josef van Ess, *Theologie und Gesellschaft im 2. und 3. Jahrhundert Hidschra: eine Geschichte des religiösen Denkens im frühen Islam*, 6 vol. (Berlin: W. de Gruyter, 1991); Jürgen Paul, « Histories of Samarqand », *Studia Iranica* 22 (1993): 82 ff.; Jürgen Paul, *Herrscher, Gemeinwesen, Vermittler: Ostiran und Transoxanien in vormongoli*scher Zeit*, Beiruter Texte und Studien, Bd. 59 (Stuttgart: In Kommission bei F. Steiner, 1996), 108 ff.; Étienne de La Vaissière, « Le *Ribāṭ* d'Asie centrale », in *Islamisation de l'Asie Centrale: processus locaux d'acculturation du VIIe au XIe siècle*, éd. par La Vaissière, Studia Iranica Cahier 39 (Paris: Assoc. pour l'Avancement des Études Iraniennes, 2008), 83.

10 Abū 'l-Ḥasan ʿAlī al-Masʿūdī, *Kitāb murūj al-ḏahab wa-maʿādin al-jawhar. Les prairies d'or*, éd. par Charles Pellat, trad. par Barbier de Meynard et Pavet de Courteille (Paris: Société asiatique, 1962), §2475.

11 Les Daylamites, longtemps païens à l'exception peut-être de quelques chrétiens et zoroastriens, se convertissent à l'islam chiite zaydite à partir du milieu du IIIe /IXe siècle. Ibn Isfandiyār, *Taʾrīḫ-i Ṭabaristān*, trad. E. G. Browne, *An Abridged Translation of the History of Tabaristan* (Leiden: Brill; Quaritch, 1905); Wilferd Madelung, « ʿAlids », *Encyclopaedia Iranica, Vol. I, Āb-Anahid* (London: Routledge & Kegan Paul, 1985); Wilferd Madelung, « Deylamites ii. in the Islamic Period », *Encyclopaedia Iranica, Vol. VII, Dārā(b)-Ebn al-Aṯir* (London: Routledge & Kegan Paul, 1996).

Les auteurs mobilisent également un autre biais rhétorique : la citation de hadiths apocryphes permet de mentionner l'ennemi turc et d'en faire un équivalent du Byzantin en termes de menace pour le pouvoir et la civilisation islamiques. Dans le *Ṣaḥīḥ* de Buḫārī (m. 256/870), les musulmans sont enjoints à mener le jihad non seulement contre les Byzantins et les juifs – par ordre d'énumération –, mais aussi contre les Turcs, décrits par des caractéristiques physiques stéréotypées : leurs visages, larges et rouges, aux yeux petits et au nez plat, ressemblent à des boucliers de cuir[12]. Certaines sources plus tardives, au Vᵉ/XIᵉ-VIᵉ/XIIᵉ voire IXᵉ/XVᵉ siècle, attribuent d'importants mérites à la défense du territoire face aux Turcs : elles intègrent des hadiths apocryphes vantant la pratique du *ribāṭ* dans les régions orientales, comme à Samarcande[13].

Les dirigeants du Khorassan et de la Transoxiane, bien que résidant dans des zones parfois très éloignées de la frontière arabo-byzantine, s'efforcent de participer à la guerre, ne serait-ce que de manière symbolique. Les histoires locales consacrées à une dynastie, une ville ou une région, tout en étant focalisées sur l'espace irano-centre-asiatique, relaient elles aussi le modèle de lutte contre Byzance. Cela apparaît par exemple dans le *Tarīḫ-i Sīstān*, texte anonyme du Vᵉ/XIᵉ siècle pourtant considéré par certains chercheurs comme imprégné de « patriotisme » iranien et donc adhérant à un système de valeurs irano-centré : Yaʿqūb b. al-Layṯ al-Ṣaffār (r. 247/861-265/879), fondateur de la dynastie saffaride basée au Sistan et au Khorassan, aurait lancé chaque année des expéditions dans les diverses parties du *dār al-kufr* – Turkestan, Inde, Chine, Ceylan, – et en particulier à Byzance[14]. Cette mention vise à affirmer la légitimité de Yaʿqūb, accablé par une légende noire dans la plupart des autres sources en raison de la campagne qu'il lance contre le calife abbasside à la fin de sa vie : par cette référence au territoire de Rūm, le *Taʾrīḫ-i Sīstān* présente

12 Muḥammad b. Ismāʿīl al-Buḫārī, *Ṣaḥīḥ Al-Buḫārī. The Translation of the Meanings of Sahih Al-Bukhari*, trad. par Muhammad Muhsin Khan, vol. 4 (Riyadh: Darussalam Pub. & Distr., 1997), 110-111.

13 Paul, « Histories of Samarqand », 86-87, d'après la *Qandiyya* arabe.

14 Le texte est vraisemblablement une construction propagandiste visant à renforcer la légitimité de Yaʿqūb b. al-Layṯ, censé être désigné *malik al-dunyā* « maître du monde » par le frère du calife, Abū Aḥmad al-Muwaffaq. *Taʾrīḫ-i Sīstān*, éd. Muḥammad T. Bahār (Tehran: Ḫāvar, 1935), 231-32; trad. Milton Gold, *The Tarikh-i Sistan*, Serie Orientale Roma 48 (Roma: Istituto Italiano per il Medio ed Estremo Oriente, 1976), 183-184; Bosworth, *The History of the Saffarids*, 156; Julie Scott Meisami, *Persian historiography: to the end of the Twelfth century*, Islamic surveys (Edinburgh: Edinburgh University Press, 1999), 120, 135; Deborah G. Tor, « Historical Representations of Yaʿqūb b. al-Layth: A Reappraisal », *Journal of the Royal Asiatic Society* 12, nº 03 (novembre 2002): 247-75; Tor, *Violent Order*, 115.

Yaʿqūb en défenseur d'un très vaste Orient musulman allant des frontières byzantines aux confins de la Chine, et en incarnation du souverain idéal[15].

Dans les faits et dans le discours, la participation à la lutte contre les infidèles, qu'il s'agisse des Byzantins ou des Turcs, vise donc à légitimer le pouvoir sultanien d'Iran nord-oriental à l'époque où celui-ci s'émancipe de plus en plus de la tutelle califale. Les destinataires de cette propagande sur la défense du *dār al-islām* sont aussi bien le calife que les populations locales, en particulier les élites du Khorassan et de la Transoxiane, souvent réticentes à reconnaître l'autorité des dynasties émirales ou sultanales[16]. Officiellement, la légitimité des dirigeants orientaux repose sur la délégation du pouvoir par le calife à leur profit, donc sur leur adhésion à l'idéal de défense du *dār al-islām*. Les émirs se présentent en rempart protégeant le domaine de l'islam contre les hordes de Turcs infidèles[17] : ils réinterprètent à leur propre profit le schéma du souverain idéal – en particulier Ḏū 'l-Qarnayn/Alexandre le Grand, modèle du héros protecteur, défendant la civilisation contre les Gog et Magog[18]. Les Turcs sont assimilés à ces figures apocalyptiques dès l'Antiquité dans la tradition

15 Camille Rhoné, « Bilan historiographique et nouvelles perspectives sur la guerre dans l'Iran médiéval (IIIe-VIe/IXe-XIIe siècle). La représentation de l'ennemi à travers l'exemple de Yaʿqūb b. al-Layṯ al-Ṣaffār », in *La guerre dans le Proche-Orient médiéval (Xe-XVe siècle). État de la question, lieux communs, nouvelles approches*, éd. par Mathieu Eychenne et Abbès Zouache (Damas: IFPO-IFAO, 2015), 28-45.

16 Sur le manque d'obéissance (*ṭāʿat*) des élites de Boukhara face à l'arrivée au pouvoir du Samanide Ismāʿīl b. Aḥmad, en raison de leur grande richesse (*bi-sabab-i māl-i bisyār*), voir par exemple Naršaḫī, *Taʾrīḫ-i Buḫārā*, 112-113, trad. Frye, *The History of Bukhara*, 82.

17 Lorsque Ismāʿīl b. Aḥmad est confronté aux ambitions territoriales du Saffaride ʿAmr b. al-Layṯ à propos de la Transoxiane, il conseille à son rival de lui confier la tâche de protéger l'islam contre les Turcs, sur la marge orientale du monde musulman : « laisse-moi (dans) cette marche (*utruknī fī haḏā 'l-ṯaġr*) ». Ibn al-Aṯīr, *al-Kāmil fī 'l-taʾrīḫ* (Beirut: Dār al-ṣādir, 2009), 7:232.

18 David Cook, « Moral Apocalyptic in Islam », *Studia Islamica*, n° 86 (1997): 60-63; David Cook, « Muslim apocalyptic and *jihād* », *Jerusalem Studies in Arabic and Islam* 20 (1996): 96-101; David Cook, *Studies in Muslim apocalyptic*, Studies in late antiquity and early Islam 21 (Princeton, N.J: Darwin Press, 2002); Yehoshua Frenkel, « The Turks of the Eurasian Steppes in Medieval Arabic Writing », in *Mongols, Turks, and others: Eurasian nomads and the sedentary world*, éd. par Reuven Amitai, Michal Biran, Brill's Inner Asian Library, v. 11 (Leiden: Brill, 2005), 230-31; Mark Dickens, « Medieval Syriac Historians' Perceptions of the Turks » (M. Phil. diss., University of Cambridge, 2004); E. J. van Donzel et Andrea B. Schmidt, éd., *Gog and Magog in early eastern Christian and Islamic sources: Sallam's quest for Alexander's wall*, Brill's Inner Asian Library, v. 22 (Leiden: Brill, 2010).

biblique – comme en témoignent les littératures syriaques, arméniennes et latines –, puis dans la tradition coranique[19].

La dichotomie *dār al-islām* / *dār al-ḥarb* ou *dār al-kufr* apparaît dans les sources sur l'Iran nord-oriental de manière indirecte. L'emploi de ces expressions est bien moins fréquent dans les textes médiévaux que dans les ouvrages modernes, et les occurrences de qualificatifs touchant à la religion (*kufr*, *kāfir*, *mušrikūn*, etc.) sont relativement peu nombreuses. La dichotomie transparaît plutôt par des termes renvoyant à la géographie ou à des titres politico-militaires : il est question de marches (*ṯaġr* en arabe ; *marz* en persan), confiées à des gardiens ou souverains des marches (*marzbān*, *marzubān*, *mulūk al-aṭrāf*, *mulūk-i aṭrāf*), par exemple au Ṣaġāniyān (forme arabe de Čaġāniyān), au Jūzjān ou à Kāṯ, la capitale du Khwarezm[20]. L'emploi du mot *ṯaġr* ne renvoie pas à une nomenclature stricte sur le plan administratif, mais désigne au contraire des entités géographiques extrêmement variables, en particulier en termes d'échelle spatiale : sont considérés comme *ṯaġr* tantôt la Transoxiane dans son entier, tantôt des territoires frontaliers tels Isbījāb, à l'est, ou Farāwa/Afrāwa, district du sud-est de la Caspienne faisant face aux steppes occupées par les Turcs Ghuzz, ou encore des zones situées à l'intérieur du *dār al-islām* et constituant donc des marches intérieures, tels Till et Darġaš – sur le territoire de Zamīn Dawar – ou Isfizār, districts et villes situés face au Ġūr[21]. L'emploi du terme est à la discrétion des auteurs et ne semble pas renvoyer à un découpage déterminé par une quelconque autorité ou administration étatique. Il est utilisé dans un sens générique et areligieux. Une seule mention établit un

19 Les *topoi* sur les Turcs ne sont donc pas propres à l'Iran nord-oriental ni à cette période. Denise Aigle, communication personnelle.

20 *Ḥudūd al-ʿālam* (Kabul: Faculté de Lettres, 1342), 389, 395-97, 399; trans. Vladimir Minorsky, trad., *« The regions of the world ». A Persian geography, 372 A. H.-982 A. D* (Oxford: Oxford University Press, 1937), 105-106, 114-118, 121. Cette source ajoute que les dirigeants du Ferghana, de l'Īlāq et du Čāč (ar. al-Šāš) sont considérés comme ne faisant plus partie de la catégorie des *mulūk-i aṭrāf* au IVe/Xe siècle.

21 Abū 'l-Qāsim al-Naṣībī Ibn Ḥawqal, *Kitāb Ṣūrat al-arḍ*, éd. par M. J. de Goeje et J. H. Kramers (Leiden: Brill, 1967), 445, 464-68; trad. Muḥammad Ibn Hauqal [Ḥawqal], *Configuration de la terre* (Kitāb Ṣūrat al-arḍ). *Introduction et traduction, avec index, par J. H. Kramers et G. Wiet.* 2 vols. Beirut: Commission internationale pour la traduction des chefs d'oeuvre, 1964, 431, 446-450; *Ḥudūd al-ʿālam*, 392, 408, trans. *The regions of the world*, 111, 133; Muḥammad b. Aḥmad al-Muqaddasī, *Aḥsan al-taqāsīm fī maʿrifat al-aqālīm*, éd. par Michael Johan de Goeje (1877; repr., Leiden: Brill, 1967), 273-74, 305, trans. *The Best Divisions for Knowledge of the Regions: Aḥsan al-Taqāsīm fī Maʿrifat al-Aqālīm*, trad. par Basil Anthony Collins, The Great Books of Islamic Civilization (Reading: Garnet, 1994), 244, 268-69; *Taʾrīḫ-i Sīstān*, 218, trad., 244.

lien explicite entre *ṯaġr* et pratique du jihad. Il s'agit du texte de Muqaddasī, qui affirme à propos d'Isbījāb : « c'est une marche extraordinaire et [c'est] le domaine du jihad (*wa-hiya ṯaġr jalīl wa-dār jihād*) »[22].

Parallèlement à ce champ sémantique aux contours flous, l'identité de l'ennemi est décrite de manière souvent archétypale, car l'archétype est la condition qui permet l'existence du schéma dichotomique entre monde civilisé et barbarie. Sur les frontières de l'Iran nord-oriental, l'ennemi est qualifié essentiellement en termes ethniques, et se résume le plus souvent au Turc – ou à l'Indien pour les régions situées plus au sud, qui sortent de la sphère d'étude de cet article. Le recours à ce terme ethnique, alors que nous savons que les géographes classiques d'époque médiévale connaissent la diversité et la réalité des populations des steppes voisines, comme nous le verrons plus loin, confirme qu'il s'agit d'un choix volontaire, au service d'une rhétorique de légitimation. Les représentations archétypales voire stéréotypées donnent l'impression que l'ennemi est un seul peuple, uni et homogène ; pourtant, dans les faits, à cette époque, les peuples du *dār al-kufr* ne constituent en rien une menace massive, coordonnée ni structurée.

La comparaison avec la situation au Proche-Orient prouve que le modèle de l'opposition entre Arabes et Byzantins ne peut être parfaitement transposé dans le contexte de l'Iran nord-oriental.

3 Les limites de la transposition du modèle arabo-byzantin

Plusieurs éléments géomorphologiques, politiques et sociaux témoignent des limites de cette transposition.

Au Khorassan et en Transoxiane, l'État émiral – ou sultanal – fait face à un espace ouvert, steppique, dont la frontière est d'autant plus mouvante et non linéaire qu'elle évolue en fonction des comportements changeants des tribus nomades voisines : ces dernières participent à des mouvements migratoires et, surtout, contractent des alliances avec d'autres tribus ou avec les dirigeants sédentaires, formant parfois des confédérations plus ou moins lâches. Les populations turques des steppes, nomades, lancent des attaques non contre une frontière pareille au *limes* romain, mais dans des zones plus ou moins vastes. La frontière est donc mouvante et non linéaire.

L'ennemi n'est pas un empire, encore moins un empire semblable à celui des Romains d'Orient. Il s'agit plutôt d'un ensemble diffus et divisé de tribus

---

22 Muqaddasī, *Aḥsan al-taqāsīm fī maʿrifat al-aqālīm*, 273-74, trans. *The Best Divisions for Knowledge of the Regions*, 244.

en grande partie nomades, ne disposant pas, à cette époque, d'organisation étatique comparable à celle du pouvoir sultanien, en particulier depuis la scission du qaghanat turc au IIe/VIIIe siècle. Entre le milieu du IIIe/IXe et la fin du IVe/Xe siècle, l'observation des faits mentionnés par les sources montre que l'ennemi turc ne constitue pas une menace réelle pour le pouvoir des émirs et sultans, malgré quelques incursions massives au début du IVe/Xe siècle[23] : ils n'ont pas la capacité militaire d'attaquer en nombre le *dār al-islām* et leurs expéditions se limitent la plupart du temps à des raids ponctuels. À ce jour, rien dans les sources écrites et archéologiques n'indique qu'il y ait eu destruction significative – totale ou partielle – de ville par les tribus turques du *dār al-kufr* avant les invasions seldjoukides.

La confrontation du discours avec la réalité ethnique et sociale montre que l'assimilation du Turc avec la figure de l'Autre, du barbare, est largement artificielle : en Iran nord-oriental médiéval, le Turc est loin d'être un étranger et de se réduire à un archétype. La diversité et la complexité de la composition ethnique des peuples turcs sont bien connues des savants de l'époque. Ainsi les géographes du IVe/Xe siècle distinguent divers groupes – Qipchak, Oghuz, etc. – et savent les situer géographiquement, malgré, parfois, des erreurs et/ou approximations. Dès le IIIe/IXe siècle, un auteur comme Ibn al-Ḫurdāḏbih affirme par exemple :

> La contrée habitée par les Tuġuzġur est le plus vaste de tous les pays des Turcs ; elle est entourée par la Chine, le Tibet, les Ḫarluḫ [Qarluq], les Kaymāk, les Ġuzz, les Jiqir [Jiguir], les Bajānāk [Petchénègues], les Turkaš, les Aḏkaš, les Ḫifšāḫ [Qipchak], les Ḫirḫīz [Kirghizes], dans le pays de qui il y a du musc, les Ḫarluḫ et les Ḫalaj qui vivent en deçà du fleuve[24].

Les nomades et semi-nomades constituent une mosaïque de groupes ethniques, à l'extérieur comme à l'intérieur du territoire sous domination islamique : divers peuples turcs ou turquifiés, sédentaires, nomades ou

23 Plusieurs campagnes offensives d'ampleur sont lancées par les Turcs en Transoxiane voire au Khorassan pendant la décennie 291/904-301/914. Luke Treadwell, « The Account of the Samanid Dynasty in Ibn Ẓāfir al-Azdī's *Akhbār al-duwal al-munqaṭiʿa* », *Iran* 43 (2005) : éd. : 137, 139, trad. : 153-54, n. 28 ; Ibn al-Aṯīr, *Kāmil*, 7:247 ; Treadwell, « The political history of the Sāmānid state », 98, n. 124 ; 133-34, n. 139.

24 Ibn Ḫurdāḏbih, *Kitāb al-masālik wa'l-mamālik*, éd. et trad. par Michael Johan de Goeje, Bibliotheca geographorum arabicorum 6 (1889 ; repr., Leiden : Brill, 1967), éd. 31 ; trad. (modifiée) 22-23.

semi-nomades, y sont installés, parfois depuis plusieurs siècles. Dans les montagnes voisines de l'Oxus vivent par exemple les Kumījī et les Turcs K.njīna, qui sont soumis – de manière plus ou moins lâche – aux souverains des marges comme les Muhtajides et les Banijurides, dans le Ṣaġāniyān et le Ḫuttal[25]. Dès l'époque antique, les Turcs forment une main d'œuvre militaire – en tant qu'alliés ou mercenaires – au service des sédentaires (Chinois, Sogdiens) qui les considèrent comme l'incarnation du guerrier naturel[26]. Après les conquêtes arabo-musulmanes, ils se mettent au service des émirs et autres élites locales. Par ailleurs, le rôle primordial des Turcs dans le califat abbasside, en particulier à Bagdad-Samarra, est bien connu : ce n'est pas le lieu ici pour revenir sur toute l'historiographie médiévale et moderne à ce sujet. Bien loin de ne constituer qu'une masse d'hommes de troupe, les Turcs font parfois partie des élites socio-politiques locales voire régionales. En effet, certains groupes sont arrivés en Iran nord-oriental dès la deuxième moitié du VIe siècle[27]. Sédentarisés pour une bonne partie d'entre eux, ils ont contribué à mettre en valeur le territoire, à le construire et à le défendre : dans les siècles précédant l'arrivée de l'islam, s'inspirant probablement des Hephtalites, ils participent au processus d'*incastellamento*[28], qui en Orient renvoie à l'édification de forteresses sur l'ordre de chefs nomades qui imposent ainsi leur domination sur les populations et les terres environnantes. L'espace concerné par ce phénomène s'étend du Khwarezm à la Sogdiane et du Sémiretchié à l'Hindou-Kouch, tandis que le Xinjiang reste à l'écart. Lorsque l'Iran nord-oriental est intégré – nominalement

25 *Ḥudūd al-ʿālam*, 399; trad. Minorsky, *The regions of the world*, 120; Sören Stark, *Die Alttürkenzeit in Mittel- und Zentralasien: archäologische und historische Studien*, Nomaden und Sesshafte, Bd. 6 (Wiesbaden: L. Reichert, 2008), 210-17.

26 Denis Sinor, « The Inner Asian Warriors », *Journal of the American Oriental Society* 101, n° 2 (1981): 133-135; Peter Benjamin Golden, « War and Warfare in the Pre-Činggisid Western Steppes of Eurasia », in *Warfare in inner Asian history: 500-1800*, éd. par Nicola Di Cosmo, Handbook of Oriental Studies = Handbuch der Orientalistik. Section eight, Central Asia, v. 6 (Leiden: Brill, 2002), 129-30; Christopher I. Beckwith, *Empires of the Silk Road: a history of Central Eurasia from the Bronze Age to the present* (Princeton: Princeton University Press, 2009), xx-xxiii, 322; Étienne de La Vaissière, « The Turks and the other peoples of the Eurasian Steppes, to 1175 », in *Cambridge History of War*, éd. par Reuven Amitai, vol. 2 (Cambridge: Cambridge University Press, forthcoming), 3-4, 17-18.

27 Gibb, *The Arab conquests in Central Asia*, 3; Stark, *Die Alttürkenzeit*; La Vaissière, « The Turks and the other peoples », 1.

28 Pierre Toubert, *Les structures du Latium médiéval. Le Latium méridional et la Sabine du IXe à la fin du XIIe siècle* (Rome: École française de Rome, 1973), chap. 4. Étienne de La Vaissière, communication personnelle : c'est à lui qu'est empruntée l'expression « incastellamento » appliquée au contexte centre-asiatique.

du moins – dans le *dār al-islām*, les Turcs ou peuples assimilés continuent à ériger de nombreuses forteresses, comme dans les vallées secondaires de la région de Bamiyan (Afghanistan actuel) durant le IIe/VIIIe-IVe/Xe siècle et s'intègrent donc dans le paysage irano-centre-asiatique[29]. Par ailleurs, bien avant l'arrivée de l'islam et des conquérants arabes, les élites turques se lient aux élites locales, en particulier en Sogdiane[30]. On assiste

> à l'élaboration de milieux mixtes, à des intermariages et des alliances politiques, et il n'est pas rare de voire telle ou telle ville ou château d'Asie centrale contrôlés par des *condottieri* turcs, tandis que plusieurs rois de l'Asie centrale sédentaire portent alors des noms parfaitement turcs[31].

Les émirs du IIIe/IXe-Ve/XIe siècle sont eux aussi liés aux Turcs, souvent par le biais d'alliances matrimoniales : il est probable que les origines du Samanide ʿAbd al-Malik b. Nūḥ (r. 343/954-350/961), fils légitime de Nūḥ b. Naṣr (r. 331/943-343/954) et d'une princesse turque, l'aient conduit à pacifier les relations avec les nomades des steppes voisines, voire aient contribué à l'islamisation de ces derniers[32]. La diffusion de l'islam dans les steppes, qui connaît une nette accélération au IVe/Xe siècle, vient contredire plus encore l'idée d'une assimilation systématique des Turcs aux Infidèles, du *dār al-ḥarb* au *dār al-kufr*[33]. Les dirigeants sultaniens et leurs historiographes, parfaitement au fait de cette réalité métissée, perpétuent pourtant la transmission de la représentation dichotomique des confins iraniens et centre-asiatiques.

4 Un processus de légitimation de la politique sultanienne

Dès lors, pourquoi avoir recours à un schéma dichotomique aussi artificiel dans cette région ? L'opposition entre *dār al-islām* et *dār al-kufr* ou *dār al-ḥarb* semble vouée à compenser voire justifier certains aspects de la politique

---

29 Marc Le Berre, *Monuments pré-islamiques de l'Hindukush central* (Paris: Recherche sur les civilisations, 1987), 115-17.

30 Étienne de La Vaissière, *Samarcande et Samarra. Élites d'Asie centrale dans l'Empire abbasside* (Paris: AAEI, 2007), 38-44.

31 La Vaissière, « The Turks and the other peoples », 17.

32 Nūḥ épouse Qālīn bint Šaḫīr, selon l'arrangement prévu par le père de Nūḥ, Naṣr II b. Aḥmad, et par le père de la mariée, à savoir le roi des Turcs. Treadwell, « The political history of the Sāmānid state », 167, 233nn88-90. En 349/960, 200 000 « tentes » de Turcs se seraient converties à l'Islam. Ibn al-Aṯīr, *Kāmil*, 8:252.

33 La Vaissière, *Islamisation de l'Asie centrale*.

sultanienne, contestables par rapport au modèle du souverain idéal. Trois motivations expliquent ce recours rhétorique : les deux premières consistent à légitimer le pouvoir sultanien vis-à-vis, respectivement, des autorités externes et des populations internes au territoire d'Iran nord-oriental. La troisième a pour objectif de montrer l'attachement des dirigeants à la défense de l'islam en dépit de – ou parallèlement à – l'existence d'échanges transfrontaliers, commerciaux en particulier, avec celui qui est théoriquement l'incarnation de l'ennemi.

Il s'agit en premier lieu de justifier l'indépendance de fait et le tropisme occidental des dirigeants sultaniens d'Iran nord-oriental, en particulier sous les Saffarides et les Samanides. Ces deux dynasties s'efforcent d'unifier le Khorassan et la Transoxiane sous un pouvoir émiral unique plutôt que d'en agrandir les frontières face à la steppe. Elles luttent également à de nombreuses reprises pour contrôler les régions situées au sud-sud-est de la mer Caspienne et doivent résister à la pression des Bouyides. C'est vrai en particulier pour les Samanides, pendant la première moitié du IVe/Xe siècle, période pourtant considérée comme leur apogée, du moins en termes d'extension territoriale. Ismāʿīl b. Aḥmad, souvent considéré comme le fondateur de la dynastie, souverain-*ġāzī* célèbre pour ses mérites guerriers, est contraint jusqu'à la fin de son règne de lutter sur deux fronts à la fois : il mène une contre-offensive contre les Turcs de la steppe du nord-est en 293/905-906, tout en devant protéger ses intérêts dans le Daylam et le Jurjān[34]. Ses successeurs sont plus exposés encore à la concurrence sur leurs terres occidentales : les chiites zaydites et les Daylamites convoitent le Khorassan et y lancent des attaques depuis le sud de la Caspienne[35]. Puis, à partir des années 940, les Bouyides constituent l'adversaire le plus menaçant, attisant par exemple les révoltes ou mouvements indépendantistes au sein du Khorassan et du Sistan pour détourner l'effort militaire samanide des seuls environs de la Caspienne[36].

Certes, toutes les dynasties revendiquent la défense du territoire califal comme argument légitimant ; mais la défense de leurs intérêts propres contribue au morcellement interne du *dār al-islām*[37]. En effet, les dirigeants d'Iran

34 Ibn al-Aṯīr, *Kāmil*, 7:254.

35 Masʿūdī, *Les prairies d'or*, §3333; Mīrḫwānd, *Taʾrīḫ rawḍat al-ṣafāʾ fī sīrat al-anbiyāʾ wa'l-ḫulafāʾ* (Tehran: Aṣāṭīr, 1380SH/2001), 35, 38; Treadwell, « The political history of the Sāmānid state », 117-119, 150-152, 159-64.

36 Treadwell, « The political history of the Sāmānid state », 212-213 sqq., 220, 222, 227, 229, 232, 246, 256.

37 Sylvie Denoix, « Des culs-de-sacs heuristiques aux garde-fous épistémologiques ou comment aborder l'aire culturelle du « monde musulman » », *Revue des mondes musulmans et de la Méditerranée* 103-4 (2004): 7-26.

nord-oriental affrontent le plus souvent leurs coreligionnaires : il ne s'agit pas seulement de campagnes de lutte contre les hérésies chiites ou kharijites, mais aussi d'affrontements entre sunnites. Ainsi, les émirs et sultans entrent en contradiction avec le modèle du souverain idéal mobilisant ses forces pour lutter contre l'infidèle et l'hérétique et protéger tous ses sujets de l'ennemi. Les étapes successives de l'affrontement entre ʿAmr b. al-Layṯ (r. 265/879-287/900) et Ismāʿīl b. Aḥmad (r. 279/892-295/907) à la toute fin du IIIe/IXe siècle illustrent l'ampleur de ces combats – sur le terrain militaire et dans les systèmes de production propagandiste. Ismāʿīl b. Aḥmad, bien qu'incarnant le « *ġāzī* proverbial»[38], consacre la plupart de ses efforts militaires à la lutte contre son rival saffaride. En s'entourant d'ulémas et en s'attribuant une image de pieux musulmans, les Samanides consolident leur rhétorique, soulignent leur rôle d'ardents acteurs du jihad pour mieux justifier leurs campagnes militaires, en particulier contre les Bouyides et les principautés remuantes du sud de la Caspienne : Ismāʿīl b. Aḥmad est par exemple un *muḥaddiṯ* réputé, intéressé notamment par les hadiths sur le *ġazw*[39]. Par la suite, les Ghaznévides cultivent eux aussi leur image de *ġāzīs* exemplaires et de pieux souverains. Leurs campagnes indiennes participent fortement à leur aura. La mise en avant de leurs conquêtes dans le sous-continent est d'autant plus nécessaire qu'ils perdent le contrôle d'une très large partie de l'émirat des Samanides : dès la fin du IVe/Xe siècle, les Qarakhanides, certes islamisés – au moins pour certains d'entre eux – s'emparent de la Transoxiane.

Les dirigeants sultaniens normalisent et légitiment toutes leurs actions politiques et militaires en les insérant dans le schéma dichotomique *dār al-islām* / *dār al-ḥarb* inspiré de la tradition califale. Ainsi, lorsque le Saffaride ʿAmr b. al-Layṯ et le Samanide Ismāʿīl b. Aḥmad s'affrontent, à la fin du IIIe/IXe siècle, pour unifier le Khorassan et la Transoxiane sous leur pouvoir, chacun demande au calife d'arbitrer en sa faveur et cherche à justifier ses prétentions en se présentant en rempart du *dār al-islām* sur son flanc oriental[40]. Dans le *Taʾrīḫ-i*

38 Jürgen Paul, « Violence and State-Building in the Islamic East » (Mellon-Sawyer seminar, Oxford University, 2006), 14; Treadwell, « The political history of the Sāmānid state », 100-103.

39 ʿAbd al-Karīm b. Muḥammad al-Samʿānī, *Kitāb al-Ansāb*, éd. par ʿAbd al-Raḥmān Yamānī, Majlis dāʾirat al-maʿārif al-ʿuṯmāniyya (Hyderabad, 1382/1962), 7:25; Treadwell, « The political history of the Sāmānid state », 99n129.

40 *Taʾrīḫ-i Sīstān*, éd. 254-256; trad. 201-203. Gardīzī, *Taʾrīḫ-i Gardīzī* (*Zayn al-aḫbār*), éd. par ʿAbd al-Ḥayy Ḥabībī (Tehran: Dunyā-yi kitāb, 1363SH/1984); trad. Clifford E. Bosworth, *The Ornament of Histories. The History of the Eastern Islamic Lands AD 650-1041: The Persian Text of Abu Saʿid ʿAbd al-Hayy Gardizi* (London: Tauris, 2011), 50-51, 54. Treadwell, « The Account of the Samanid Dynasty », éd. 137, trad. 152-3, 152n16. Clifford E. Bosworth, « The Armies of the Ṣaffārids », *Bulletin of the School of Oriental Studies* 31 (1968): 534-35. Voir

Buḫārā, texte pro-samanide, Ismāʿīl b. Aḥmad obtient de ʿAmr b. al-Layṯ qu'il lui concède la Transoxiane, que ce dernier aurait pourtant reçue du calife, parce qu'elle est « à la frontière contre l'ennemi (*kī sar ḥadd-i dušman-ast*) »[41].

Le souverain constitue personnellement et physiquement le mur qui place la civilisation à l'abri des barbares. Il est présenté en acteur unique de la défense, seul apte à protéger ses sujets : on retrouve là l'un des attributs du souverain idéal tel qu'il apparaît également dans la tradition iranienne héritée de l'époque préislamique[42]. Les récits de bataille, en particulier dans les chroniques et histoires dynastiques, se focalisent souvent sur les gestes du seul roi guerrier, tandis que les autres combattants sont laissés dans l'ombre[43].

Le discours cible également des destinataires internes au territoire émiral. Vis-à-vis des élites locales, il s'agit pour les dynasties sultaniennes, qui ont accédé au pouvoir grâce à leur puissance militaire, de compenser l'infériorité de leurs origines sociales. Les Ghaznévides sont initialement des esclaves turcs ; les Saffarides doivent faire oublier que leur fondateur était un forgeron (Yaʿqūb b. al-Layṯ « al-Ṣaffār »). Les Samanides, issus de la strate moyenne des *dihqān*s (que nous traduirons ici par « propriétaires fonciers »), désirent s'affirmer face aux autres élites de rang égal ou supérieur, en particulier en Transoxiane, longtemps aux mains de petites dynasties seigneuriales et/ou royales indépendantes, donc peu enclines à accepter l'autorité d'une dynastie unique sur un territoire aussi vaste et désormais – théoriquement – unifié.

Par ailleurs, ces trois dynasties émirales ou sultanale sont rapidement confrontées, chacune à son tour, à la multiplication des problèmes à l'intérieur de leur territoire : querelles dynastiques, révoltes sociopolitiques, contestation religieuse ou fiscale, ambitions croissantes des généraux qui cherchent à s'emparer de fiefs considérables, etc. La rhétorique de défense du *dār al-islām* et de

---

aussi la version différente donnée dans Naršaḫī, *Taʾrīḫ-i Buḫārā*, 119-120 sqq., trad. Frye, *The History of Bukhara*, 87-88 sqq.

41 Naršaḫī, *Taʾrīḫ-i Buḫārā*, éd. 120, trad. 88.

42 Voir les travaux de Charles-Henri de Fouchécour.

43 Ainsi al-Bayhaqī (Vᵉ/XIᵉ siècle), dans sa narration des campagnes successives menées par les Ghaznévides contre les infidèles du Ġūr (Afghanistan), place Maḥmūd et Masʿūd au cœur de l'action, la mise en lumière de leurs succès héroïques contrastant avec la foule des combattants – alliés et ennemis – anonymes. Abū 'l-Faḍl Muḥammad Bayhaqī, *Taʾrīḫ-i Bayhaqī*, éd. par Ḫalīl Ḫatīb Rahbar (Tehran: Mahtāb, 1386SH); trad. Abū 'l-Fażl Beyhaqī, *The History of Beyhaqi: (the History of Sultan Masʿud of Ghazna, 1030-1041)*, éd. par Mohsen Ashtiany, trad. par Clifford E. Bosworth, Ilex Foundation Series 6 (Boston: Ilex Foundation, Center for Hellenic Studies Trustees for Harvard University, distributed by Harvard University Press, 2011). De même ʿUtbī (mort vers 431/1040), dans son *Kitāb al-Yamīnī*, accorde toute son attention aux mérites militaires de Maḥmūd.

l'orthodoxie musulmane contre les mauvais croyants ou les infidèles « de l'intérieur » est encore mobilisée. Les Saffarides se présentent en garants de la lutte contre le chiisme zaydite et le kharijisme pour mieux justifier le renversement des gouverneurs tahirides établis depuis des décennies à Nichapour par le calife[44]. Les Ghaznévides revendiquent la défense de l'orthodoxie sunnite – en particulier par leurs campagnes dans l'Inde infidèle – et le contrôle de la puissance militaire – face aux généraux ambitieux tels que les Simjurides (devenus maîtres du Khorassan) – pour légitimer leur prise du pouvoir au détriment de leurs maîtres samanides[45].

Enfin, il s'agit de perpétuer l'image des souverains menant une guerre permanente sur la frontière, en dépit de l'existence d'échanges économiques transfrontaliers. Les textes fondateurs produits par les juristes dans l'entourage du calife au tournant des IIe/VIIIe-IIIe/IXe siècles au sujet des relations avec les non musulmans, et diffusés ensuite en Orient au sein des écoles hanafite et shafi'ite, se préoccupent essentiellement d'encadrer le commerce et la fiscalité qui lui est associée. Certes, les érudits ont élaboré un schéma dichotomique divisant le monde en deux parties adverses, mais ils ont aussi prévu l'existence d'échanges commerciaux avec les habitants du *dār al-kufr*. Ils statuent sur les pratiques commerciales interdites ou autorisées : toutes les marchandises peuvent être vendues aux infidèles, à l'exception des montures, des esclaves et

44 Cet aspect du discours officiel n'empêche pas les Saffarides d'intégrer les kharijites dans leur propre armée, ce qui témoigne de l'adaptation de la politique émirale à la réalité socio-religieuse du Khorassan et du Sistan en particulier. Ya'qūb b. al-Layṯ accorde la priorité au contrôle interne et externe du territoire, et non à la lutte pour l'orthodoxie sunnite. Abū 'l-'Abbās Aḥmad al-Ya'qūbī, *Ta'rīḫ al-Ya'qūbī* (Beyrouth: Dār Ṣādir, 1379/1960), 2:495. *Ta'rīḫ-i Sīstān*, éd. 192-97, 202, 204-5, 218, trad. 153-156, 160, 162-63, 173. Ibn al-Aṯīr, *Kāmil*, 7:87-88. Aḥmad b. Muḥammad Ibn Ḫallikān, *Wafayāt al-a'yān wa-anbā' abnā' al-zamān*, éd. par Iḥsān 'Abbās (Beyrouth: Dār Ṣādir, 1977), 416; trad. Mac Guckin De Slane, *Biographical Dictionary* (1842-1871; repr., New York: Johnson Reprint Corporation, 1961), 315-16. Mīrḫwānd, *Rawḍat al-ṣafā'*, 4:11-12. Clifford E. Bosworth, « The Armies of the Ṣaffārids », 536-37, 541-44. Meisami, *Persian historiography*, 112-17. Tor, *Violent Order*, 81 sqq., 114; Tor, « Historical Representations of Ya'qūb b. al-Layth », 247.

45 Sur l'indépendance croissante des Simjurides face aux Samanides, voir par exemple al-'Utbī al-Yamīnī, *Šarḥ*: traduction persane de Jurbāḏqānī, *Tarjuma-yi Ta'rīḫ-i yamīnī*, éd. par Ja'far Ša'ār (Tehran, 1382SH), 91-92, 96-98; traduction anglaise de James Reynolds, *The Kitab-i Yamini: Historical Memoirs of the Amīr Sabaktagīn and the Sultān Mahmūd of Ghazna, Early Conquerors of Hindustan, and Founders of the Ghaznavide Dynasty. Translated from the Persian version of the contemporary Arabic chronicle of Al Utbi* (London: Oriental Translation Fund of Great Britain and Ireland, 1858), 116, 126-28.

des armes – ou du métal permettant de les fabriquer[46]. De fait, les géographes du IIIe/IXe-IVe/Xe siècle, en particulier l'auteur des *Ḥudūd al-ʿālam*, montrent que nombre des localités frontalières (Kāṯ au Khwarezm, Ṣabrān vers Isbījāb, Tirmiḏ, Nušārā près du Baḏaḫšān, Balḫ, Kaboul, Bust, Baḏaḫšān, Barwān à proximité de l'Inde, Jājarm vers le Jurjān) servent avant tout de lieu d'échange (*tijārāt, jāy-i bāzarkānān*) et accueillent de nombreux marchands, musulmans ou non, venus parfois de contrées lointaines[47]. La répartition spatiale des fortifications souligne les efforts réalisés pour protéger et contrôler les infrastructures et lieux d'échange, y compris à l'intérieur du territoire sultanien : plusieurs lieux de marché ou de foire sont protégés par des constructions fortifiées, tout comme les routes, jalonnées de *ribāṭ*s et autres *ḥiṣns*[48]. Les points de franchissement de l'Oxus, même quand les deux rives sont sous domination islamique, sont l'objet d'une surveillance accrue. C'est vrai par exemple dans le contexte de la rivalité entre Saffarides et Samanides pour le contrôle de la totalité de l'Iran nord-oriental, à la fin du IVe/Xe siècle[49]. Il en va de même lorsque l'Oxus sépare les territoires ghaznévide et qarakhanide.

L'existence de ces échanges commerciaux ou, du moins, d'une situation de cohabitation pacifique, est normalisée par la citation du célèbre hadith apocryphe : « Laissez les Turcs [tranquilles] tant qu'ils vous laissent [tranquilles] (*utrukū* [*/tārikū*] *al-turk* [*/al-atrāk*] *mā tarakūkum*). » Cette phrase apparaît dans de nombreux textes, dont les *Rasāʾil* de Jāḥiẓ (m. 255/868-869), le *Kitāb al-sunan* du hanbalite Abū Dāʾūd al-Sijistānī (m. 275/889), le *Kitāb al-buldān*

---

46 Abū Yūsuf, *Kitāb al-ḫarāj* : Abou Yousof Yaʿkoub [Abū Yūsuf], *Le livre de l'impôt foncier (Kitâb el-Kharâdj)*, trad. par Edmond Fagnan (Paris: Geuthner, 1921), 290-94. Šaybānī, *Kitāb al-aṣl* : trad. partielle Majid Khadduri, éd., *The Islamic law of nations: Shaybānī's Siyar.* Translated with an introduction, notes and appendices (Baltimore: The Johns Hopkins Press, 1966), 136, 168-69 (§428-433, 712-713, 716-720, 725, 728). Muḥammad b. Aḥmad al-Saraḫsī, *Le grand livre de la conduite de l'État: = Kitāb as-Siyar al-kabīr*, trad. par Muhammad Hamidullah, 1. éd, vol. 3 (Ankara: Türkiye Diyanet Vakfı, 1990), 164-65, 441-42.

47 *Ḥudūd al-ʿālam*, éd. 387, 390-91, 393-94, 399-400; trad. 102, 107-8, 112, 114, 121-22. Ibn Ḥawqal, *Kitāb Ṣūrat al-arḍ*, éd. 510-511, trad. 488. Muqaddasī, *Aḥsan al-taqāsīm fī maʿrifat al-aqālīm*, éd. 302, n. *d*, 319, trad. 266, 281.

48 Maxime Siroux, *Caravansérails d'Iran et petites constructions routières* (Le Caire: IFAO, 1949). Jacqueline Chabbi, « Ribāṭ 1. History and Development of the Institution », *Encyclopaedia of Islam, Vol. VIII, Ned-Sam* (Leiden: Brill, 1995). Wolfram Kleiss, *Karawanenbauten in Iran* (Berlin: Reimer, 1996/2001). Camille Rhoné, « Les *ribāṭ*-s dans l'Orient du monde musulman des origines au XIIIe siècle », *Bulletin d'Études Orientales* 55, no 2003 (s. d.): 61-76.

49 Naršaḫī, *Taʾrīḫ-i Buḫārā*, éd. 120-21, trad. 88-89.

de l'Iranien Ibn al-Faqīh al-Hamaḏānī (v. 289-290/902-903), le *Kitāb al-ḫarāj* de Qudāma b. Ja'far, fonctionnaire à Bagdad mort dans la première moitié du IVᵉ/Xᵉ siècle, ou encore le *Ḏikr aḫbār Iṣfahān* du traditionniste iranien de tendance shafi'ite Abū Nu'aym al-Iṣfahānī (336/948-430/1038)[50]. Diverses interprétations du hadith ont été proposées, le rattachant par exemple au contexte irakien[51]. Il est aussi possible de le rapprocher de la situation sur les frontières du nord-est. Ainsi, Qudāma b. Ja'far affirme : « les musulmans n'entreprennent que rarement des expéditions contre les Turcs (*laysa yakādu al-muslimūn yaġzūna al-turk*) »[52], du fait de la parole du prophète (*li-qawl al-nabī*) évoquée ci-dessus. Or, ce texte est écrit à la période de ralentissement – surtout après le milieu des années 910 – des expéditions lancées par les émirs d'Iran nord-oriental contre les Turcs des steppes.

5 Conclusion

Le schéma dichotomique forgé à la cour califale abbasside à la fin du IIᵉ/VIIIᵉ et au début du IIIᵉ/IXᵉ siècles est donc assimilé et approprié par les dirigeants de l'Iran nord-oriental pendant les siècles qui suivent. Le paradoxe est que ce schéma est utilisé face à la steppe alors que la réalité ne ressemble pas à celle de la frontière arabo-byzantine, ni en termes ethniques, sociaux, politiques ou religieux. Son exploitation rhétorique vise deux objectifs. Dans un premier temps, ce système de représentation légitime leur indépendance de fait en se présentant en défenseurs de l'orthodoxie sunnite et du *dār al-islām* contre les Turcs, réduits au statut d'ennemi infidèle et barbare. Puis son usage devient essentiellement interne : il s'agit de faire face aux lacunes du pouvoir

---

50 Abū Dā'ūd al-Sijistānī, *Kitāb al-sunan* (Le Caire: al-Cortelli, 1280/1863), livre 37, nº 4288. Ibn al-Faqīh al-Hamaḏānī, *Kitāb al-buldān* (Beyrouth: 'Ālam al-kutub, 1416/1996), 633. Qudāma b. Ja'far, *Kitāb al-ḫarāj* (extraits), in Ibn Ḫurdāḏbih, *Kitāb al-masālik wa'l-mamālik*, éd. 262-63, trad. 204. Clifford E. Bosworth, « Introduction: The coming of the Turks into the Islamic World », in *The Turks in the Early Islamic World*, par Clifford E. Bosworth (Aldershot: Ashgate Variorum, 2007), xxxii, n. 48. D'autres sources, plus tardives, reprennent également ce hadith, tels Yāqūt (m. 626/1229) dans le *Mu'jam al-buldān*, Ḏahabī (VIIᵉ/XIIIᵉ-VIIIᵉ/XIVᵉ siècle) dans le *Ta'rīḫ al-Islām* ou al-Suyūṭī dans le *Ta'rīḫ al-ḫulafā'* (IXᵉ/XVᵉ siècle).

51 Haarmann, Ulrich W., « Ideology and History, Identity and Alterity: The Arab Image of the Turk from the Abbasids to Modern Egypt », *International Journal of Middle East Studies* 20, nº 2 (1988): 180nn49-51.

52 Qudāma b. Ja'far, *Kitāb al-ḫarāj*, in *Kitāb al-masālik wa'l-mamālik*, éd. 262-63, trad. 204.

sultanien, lui-même confronté à une société composite, animée par de nombreuses forces centrifuges.

Ce qui prime, c'est la rhétorique au service de la légitimation du pouvoir, et non la description de la réalité territoriale, ethnique ou identitaire. Le fait que les Turcs soient bien connus et installés dans la région pose la question du public réellement visé et convaincu par ce discours rhétorique. Les populations locales adhèrent probablement à l'idéal du souverain protecteur de ses sujets et pieux musulman, tout en faisant la différence entre les Turcs intégrés de longue date et les tribus remuantes qui sont responsables des razzias. Les élites militaires d'ascendance turque (tels les Simjurides) ou ayant d'autres origines non iraniennes assimilent d'autant plus volontiers ce schéma qu'elles s'en emparent à leur tour pour légitimer leur pouvoir et leur emprise territoriale croissante, au détriment des dirigeants sultaniens.

Si les historiographes officiels se conforment à l'imaginaire politique inspiré de Bagdad, il serait intéressant d'étudier la diffusion d'un autre schéma dichotomique, celui qui oppose Īrān et Tūrān. Dans quelle mesure est-il utilisé pour la légitimation de la politique provinciale ? En quoi sa diffusion est-elle révélatrice des limites du schéma *dār al-islām / dār al-kufr* et d'un effort d'adaptation à la culture locale ?

References

Abou Yousof Yaʿkoub [Abū Yūsuf]. *Le livre de l'impôt foncier (Kitâb el-Kharâdj)*. Traduit par Edmond Fagnan. Paris: Geuthner, 1921.

Abū Dā'ūd al-Sijistānī. *Kitāb al-sunan*. Le Caire: al-Cortelli, 1280/1863.

Aigle, Denise, éd. *Le Bilād al-Šām face aux mondes extérieurs. La perception de l'Autre et la représentation du Souverain*. Damas: IFPO, 2012.

Bayhaqī, Abū 'l-Faḍl Muḥammad. *Ta'rīḫ-i Bayhaqī*. Édité par Ḫalīl Ḫatīb Rahbar. Tehran: Mahtāb, 1386SH.

Bayhaqī, Abū 'l-Faḍl Muḥammad. [Beyhaqī, Abū 'l-Fażl]. *The History of Beyhaqi: (the History of Sultan Masʿud of Ghazna, 1030-1041)*. Édité par Mohsen Ashtiany. Traduit par Clifford E. Bosworth. Ilex Foundation Series 6. Boston: Ilex Foundation, Center for Hellenic Studies Trustees for Harvard University, Distributed by Harvard University Press, 2011.

Beckwith, Christopher I. *Empires of the Silk Road: a history of Central Eurasia from the Bronze Age to the present*. Princeton: Princeton University Press, 2009.

Bernardini, Michele. *Mémoire et propagande à l'époque timouride*. Paris: Association pour l'avancement des études iraniennes, 2008.

Bonner, Michael. *Aristocratic Violence and Holy War*. Studies in the Jihad and the Arab-Byzantine Frontier, 81. New Haven, Connecticut: American Oriental Society, 1996.

Bonner, Michael. *Le jihad: origines, interprétations, combats*. Paris: Téraèdre, 2004.

Bosworth, Clifford E. *The Ghaznavids. Their Empire in Afghanistan and Eastern Iran*. Edinburgh: Edinburgh University Press, 1963.

Bosworth, Clifford E. « The Armies of the Ṣaffārids ». *Bulletin of the School of Oriental Studies* 31 (1968): 534-54.

Bosworth, Clifford E. *The History of the Saffarids of Sistan and Maliks of Nimruz (247/861 to 949/1542-3)*. Costa Mesa, CA: Mazda Publishers in association with Bibliotheca Persica, 1994.

Bosworth, Clifford E. *The Ornament of Histories. The History of the Eastern Islamic Lands AD 650-1041: The Persian Text of Abu Sa'id 'Abd al-Hayy Gardizi*. London: Tauris, 2011.

Bosworth, Clifford E. « Introduction: The coming of the Turks into the Islamic World ». In *The Turks in the Early Islamic World*, par Clifford E. Bosworth. Aldershot: Ashgate Variorum, 2007.

Browne, E. G. *An Abridged Translation of the History of Tabaristan*. Leiden: Brill; Quaritch, 1905.

Buḫārī, Muḥammad b. Ismāʿīl al-. *Ṣaḥīḥ Al-Buḫārī. The Translation of the Meanings of Sahih Al-Bukhari*. Traduit par Muhammad Muhsin Khan. Vol. 4. 9 vol. Riyadh: Darussalam Pub. & Distr., 1997.

Chabbi, Jacqueline. « Ribāṭ 1. History and Development of the Institution ». *Encyclopaedia of Islam, Vol. VIII, Ned-Sam*. Leiden: Brill, 1995.

Chaumont, Éric. « al-S̲h̲āfiʿī ». *Encyclopédie de l'Islam, Vol. IX, San-Sze*. Leiden: Brill, 1997.

Chaumont, Éric. « al-S̲h̲āfiʿiyya ». *Encyclopédie de l'Islam, Vol. IX, San-Sze*. Leiden: Brill, 1997.

Cook, David. « Moral Apocalyptic in Islam ». *Studia Islamica*, nº 86 (1997): 37-69.

Cook, David. « Muslim apocalyptic and *jihād* ». *Jerusalem Studies in Arabic and Islam* 20 (1996): 66-104.

Cook, David. *Studies in Muslim apocalyptic*. Studies in late antiquity and early Islam 21. Princeton, N.J.: Darwin Press, 2002.

Denoix, Sylvie. « Des culs-de-sacs heuristiques aux garde-fous épistémologiques ou comment aborder l'aire culturelle du « monde musulman » ». *Revue des mondes musulmans et de la Méditerranée* 103-4 (2004): 7-26.

De Slane, Mac Guckin. *Biographical Dictionary*. 1842-1871. Reprint, New York: Johnson Reprint Corporation, 1961.

Dickens, Mark. « Medieval Syriac Historians' Perceptions of the Turks ». M. Phil. diss., University of Cambridge, 2004.

Donzel, E. J. van, et Andrea B. Schmidt, éd. *Gog and Magog in early eastern Christian and Islamic sources: Sallam's quest for Alexander's wall*. Brill's Inner Asian Library, v. 22. Leiden: Brill, 2010.

Eddé, Anne-Marie. *Saladin*. Paris: Flammarion, 2008.

Ess, Josef van. *Theologie und Gesellschaft im 2. und 3. Jahrhundert Hidschra: eine Geschichte des religiösen Denkens im frühen Islam*. 6 vol. Berlin: W. de Gruyter, 1991.

Frenkel, Yehoshua. « The Turks of the Eurasian Steppes in Medieval Arabic Writing ». In *Mongols, Turks, and others: Eurasian nomads and the sedentary world*, éd. par Reuven Amitai, Michal Biran. 201-41. Brill's Inner Asian Library, v. 11. Leiden: Brill, 2005.

Frye, Richard N. *The History of Bukhara, translated from a Persian Abridgment of the Arabic Original by Narshakhī*. Cambridge, Mass.: The Mediaeval Academy of America, 1954.

Gardīzī, Abū Saʿīd ʿAbd al-Ḥayy (fifth/eleventh century). *Taʾrīḫ-i Gardīzī* (*Zayn al-aḫbār*). Édité par ʿAbd al-Ḥayy Ḥabībī. Tehran: Dunyā-yi kitāb, 1363SH/1984.

Gibb, H. A. R. *The Arab conquests in Central Asia*. 1923. Reprint, New York: AMS Press, 1970.

Golden, Peter Benjamin. « War and Warfare in the Pre-Činggisid Western Steppes of Eurasia ». In *Warfare in inner Asian history: 500-1800*, édité par Nicola Di Cosmo, 105-72. Handbook of Oriental Studies = Handbuch der Orientalistik. Section eight, Central Asia, v. 6. Leiden: Brill, 2002.

Haarmann, Ulrich W. « Ideology and History, Identity and Alterity: The Arab Image of the Turk from the Abbasids to Modern Egypt ». *International Journal of Middle East Studies* 20, nº 2 (1988): 175-96.

Heck, Paul L. « "Jihad" revisited ». *The Journal of Religious Ethics* 32, nº 1 (2004): 100-113.

Ḥudūd al-ʿālam. Kabul: Faculté de Lettres, 1342.

Ibn al-Aṯīr. *Al-Kāmil fī 'l-taʾrīḫ*. Beirut: Dār al-ṣādir, 2009.

Ibn al-Faqīh al-Hamaḏānī. *Kitāb al-buldān*. Beyrouth: ʿĀlam al-kutub, 1416/1996.

Ibn Ḫallikān, Aḥmad b. Muḥammad. *Wafayāt al-aʿyān wa-anbāʾ abnāʾ al-zamān*. Édité par Iḥsān ʿAbbās. Beyrouth: Dār Ṣādir, 1977.

Ibn Hauqal [Ḥawqal], Muḥammad. *Configuration de la terre* (*Kitāb Ṣūrat al-arḍ*). Introduction et traduction, avec index, par J. H. Kramers et G. Wiet. 2 vols. Beirut: Commission internationale pour la traduction des chefs d'oeuvre, 1964.

Ibn Ḥawqal, Abū 'l-Qāsim al-Naṣībī. *Kitāb Ṣūrat al-arḍ*. Édité par M. J. de Goeje et J. H. Kramers. Leiden: Brill, 1967 (réimpression de la 2ème éd. 1938-39).

Ibn Ḫurdāḏbih. *Kitāb al-masālik wa'l-mamālik*. Édité et traduit par Michael Johan de Goeje. Bibliotheca geographorum arabicorum 6. 1889. Reprint, Leiden: Brill, 1967.

Jurbāḏqānī, Abū 'l-Šaraf Nāṣiḥ. *Tarjuma-yi Taʾrīḫ-i yamīnī*. Édité par Jaʿfar Šaʿār. Tehran, 1382SH.

Khadduri, Majid, éd. *The Islamic law of nations: Shaybānī's Siyar.* Translated with an introduction, notes and appendices. Baltimore: The Johns Hopkins Press, 1966.

Kleiss, Wolfram. *Karawanenbauten in Iran*. Berlin: Reimer, 1996/2001.

La Vaissière, Étienne de, éd. *Islamisation de l'Asie centrale. Processus locaux d'acculturation du VIIe au XIe siècle*. Paris: AAEI, 2008.

La Vaissière, Étienne de, éd. « Le *Ribāṭ* d'Asie centrale ». In *Islamisation de l'Asie Centrale: processus locaux d'acculturation du VIIe au XIe siècle*, édité par La Vaissière, 71-94. Studia Iranica Cahier 39. Paris: Assoc. pour l'Avancement des Études Iraniennes, 2008.

La Vaissière, Étienne de, éd. *Samarcande et Samarra. Élites d'Asie centrale dans l'Empire abbasside*. Paris: AAEI, 2007.

La Vaissière, Étienne de. « The Turks and the other peoples of the Eurasian Steppes, to 1175 ». In *Cambridge History of War*, édité par Reuven Amitai. Vol. 2. Cambridge: Cambridge University Press, forthcoming.

Le Berre, Marc. *Monuments pré-islamiques de l'Hindukush central.* Paris: Recherche sur les civilisations, 1987.

Madelung, Wilferd. « Deylamites ii. in the Islamic Period ». *Encyclopaedia Iranica, Vol. VII, Dārā(b)-Ebn al-Aṯir.* London: Routledge & Kegan Paul, 1996.

Madelung, Wilferd. *Religious Trends in Early Islamic Iran.* Oxford: Bibliotheca Persica, 1988.

Madelung, Wilferd. « 'Alids ». *Encyclopaedia Iranica, Vol. I, Āb – Anahid.* London: Routledge & Kegan Paul, 1985.

Mas'ūdī, Abū 'l-Ḥasan 'Alī al- (m. 345/956). *Kitāb murūj al-ḏahab wa-ma'ādin al-jawhar. Les prairies d'or*. Édité par Charles Pellat. Traduit par Barbier de Meynard et Pavet de Courteille. Paris: Société asiatique, 1962.

Māwardī, Abū 'l-Ḥasan 'Alī al-. *Kitāb al-Aḥkām al-sulṭāniyya.* Ḥaydarābād: Jāmi'a-yi 'Uṯmāniyya, 1931.

Mawerdi, Abou'l-Hasan 'Ali, [Māwardī, Abū 'l-Ḥasan 'Alī al-]. *Les Statuts gouvernementaux ou règles de droit public et administratif.* Traduit par Edmond Fagnan. Reproduction de l'édition d'Alger 1915. Paris: le Sycomore, 1982.

Meisami, Julie Scott. *Persian historiography: to the end of the Twelfth century*. Islamic surveys. Edinburgh: Edinburgh University Press, 1999.

Melchert, Christopher. *The formation of the Sunni schools of law, 9th-10th centuries C.E.* Studies in Islamic law and society, v. 4. Leiden: Brill, 1997.

Minorsky, Vladimir, trad. par. *« The regions of the world ». A Persian geography, 372 A. H.-982 A. D.* Oxford: Oxford University Press, 1937.

Mīrḫwānd, Muḥammad b. Ḫwāndšāh. *Ta'rīḫ rawḍat al-ṣafā' fī sīrat al-anbiyā' wa'l-ḫulafā'*. Tehran: Aṣāṭīr, 1380SH/2001.

Mizzī, Jamāl al-dīn Abū 'l-Ḥajjāj Yūsuf al- (d. 742/1341). *Tahḏīb al-kamāl fī asmā' al-rijāl.* Beyrouth: Mu'assasat al-risāla, 1994.

Morabia, Alfred. *Le Gihad dans l'Islam médiéval. Le « combat sacré » des origines au XIIe siècle*. Paris: Albin Michel, 1993.

Muqaddasī, Muḥammad b. Aḥmad al-. *Aḥsan al-taqāsīm fī maʿrifat al-aqālīm*. Édité par Michael Johan de Goeje. 1877. Reprint, Leiden: Brill, 1967.

Muqaddasī, Muḥammad b. *The Best Divisions for Knowledge of the Regions: Aḥsan al-Taqāsīm fī Maʿrifat al-Aqālīm*. Traduit par Basil Anthony Collins. The Great Books of Islamic Civilization. Reading: Garnet, 1994.

Naršaḫī, Abū Bakr Muḥammad. *Taʾrīḫ-i Buḫārā*. Édité par Muḍaris Radavī. Tehran, 1387SH.

Nef, Annliese, et Élise Voguet, éd. *La légitimation du pouvoir au Maghreb médiéval. De l'orientalisation à l'émancipation politique*. Madrid: Casa de Velázquez, 2011.

Paul, Jürgen. *Herrscher, Gemeinwesen, Vermittler: Ostiran und Transoxanien in vormongolischer Zeit*. Beiruter Texte und Studien, Bd. 59. Stuttgart: In Kommission bei F. Steiner, 1996.

Paul, Jürgen. « Histories of Samarqand ». *Studia Iranica* 22 (1993): 69-92.

Paul, Jürgen. « Violence and State-Building in the Islamic East ». Oxford University, 2006.

Picard, Christophe. « Regards croisés sur l'élaboration du jihad entre Occident et Orient musulman (VIIIe-XIIe siècle: perspectives et réflexion sur une origine commune ». In *Regards croisés sur la guerre sainte. Guerre, religion et idéologie dans l'espace méditerranéen latin (XIe-XIIIe siècle). Actes du Colloque international tenu à la Casa de Velázquez (Madrid) du 11 au 13 avril 2005*, édité par Daniel Baloup et Philippe Josserand, 33-66. Toulouse: CNRS; Université Toulouse-II-Le Mirail, 2006.

Reynolds, James. *The Kitab-i Yamini: Historical Memoirs of the Amīr Sabaktagīn and the Sultān Mahmūd of Ghazna, Early Conquerors of Hindustan, and Founders of the Ghaznavide Dynasty. Translated from the Persian version of the contemporary Arabic chronicle of Al Utbi*. London: Oriental Translation Fund of Great Britain and Ireland, 1858.

Rhoné, Camille. « Bilan historiographique et nouvelles perspectives sur la guerre dans l'Iran médiéval (IIIe-VIe/IXe-XIIe siècle). La représentation de l'ennemi à travers l'exemple de Yaʿqūb b. al-Layṯ al-Ṣaffār ». In *La guerre dans le Proche-Orient médiéval (X[e]-XVe siècle). État de la question, lieux communs, nouvelles approches*, édité par Mathieu Eychenne et Abbès Zouache, 28-45. Damas: IFPO-IFAO, 2015.

Rhoné, Camille. « Les *ribāṭ*-s dans l'Orient du monde musulman des origines au XIIIe siècle ». *Bulletin d'Études Orientales* 55, n° 2003 (s. d.): 61-76.

Samʿānī, ʿAbd al-Karīm b. Muḥammad al-. *Kitāb al-Ansāb*. Édité par ʿAbd al-Raḥmān Yamānī. Majlis dāʾirat al-maʿārif al-ʿuṯmāniyya. Hyderabad, 1382/1962.

Saraḫsī, Muḥammad b. Aḥmad al-. *Le grand livre de la conduite de l'État: = Kitāb as-Siyar al-kabīr*. Traduit par Muhammad Hamidullah. 1. éd. Vol. 3. 4 vol. Ankara: Türkiye Diyanet Vakfı, 1990.

Sénac, Philippe. *Al-Manṣūr: le fléau de l'an mil.* Paris: Perrin, 2006.

Sinor, Denis. « The Inner Asian Warriors ». *Journal of the American Oriental Society* 101, nº 2 (1981): 133-44.

Siroux, Maxime. *Caravansérails d'Iran et petites constructions routières.* Le Caire: IFAO, 1949.

Stark, Sören. *Die Alttürkenzeit in Mittel- und Zentralasien: archäologische und historische Studien.* Nomaden und Sesshafte, Bd. 6. Wiesbaden: L. Reichert, 2008.

Ta'rīḫ-i Sīstān, éd. Muḥammad T. Bahār. Tehran: Ḫāvar, 1935.

The Tarikh-i Sistan, trad. Milton Gold. Serie Orientale Roma 48. Roma: Istituto Italiano per il Medio ed Estremo Oriente, 1976.

Tor, Deborah G. « Historical Representations of Ya'qūb b. al-Layth: A Reappraisal ». *Journal of the Royal Asiatic Society* 12, nº 03 (novembre 2002): 247-75.

Tor, Deborah G. *Violent Order: Religious Warfare, Chivalry, and the 'Ayyār Phenomenon in the Medieval Islamic World.* Istanbuler Texte Und Studien 11. Würzburg: Ergon-Verl, 2007.

Toubert, Pierre. *Les structures du Latium médiéval. Le Latium méridional et la Sabine du IXe à la fin du XIIe siècle.* Rome: École française de Rome, 1973.

Treadwell, Luke. « The Account of the Samanid Dynasty in Ibn Ẓāfir al-Azdī's *Akhbār al-duwal al-munqaṭi'a* ». *Iran* 43 (2005): 135-71.

Treadwell, Luke. « The political history of the Sāmānid state ». PhD diss., Oxford University, 1991.

Ya'qūbī, Abū 'l-'Abbās Aḥmad al-. *Ta'rīḫ al-Ya'qūbī.* Beyrouth: Dār Ṣādir, 1379/1960.

CHAPTER 13

Dār al-islām ou *bilād al-rūm* ? Le cas de l'Anatolie turque au Moyen-Âge

Michel Balivet

« Rome n'est plus dans Rome, elle est toute où je suis ». On connaît la célèbre réplique que le dramaturge français Pierre Corneille met dans la bouche du héros de la tragédie *Sertorius* (Acte III, scène 1). On sait en effet que l'idée romaine fit une longue et fructueuse carrière hors de Rome et de la latinité : à Byzance d'abord, Etat « romain » de langue grecque ; en monde « romain germanique » ensuite ; et dans la « troisième Rome moscovite » enfin, pour ne pas parler des avatars napoléoniens et allemands des deux derniers siècles ...

Ce qu'on omet parfois de mettre en relief, est le fait que certains Etats musulmans, turcs en particulier, s'affichèrent officiellement comme « romains » (*rūm*) et cela suffisamment fortement pour faire passer au deuxième plan le concept de *dār al-islām*, soit l'identité musulmane des territoires occupés par les dits Etats.

Cela est vrai pour l'Anatolie turque des Ve/XIe-VIIe/XIIIe siècles (comme ce le sera plus tard pour les Balkans ottomans connus sous le nom de *Rūm İli, Roumélie*) où chroniques et documents administratifs parlent à l'unisson de *bilād al-rūm*, de *diyār-ı rūm*, de *sulṭān-ı rūm* pour désigner l'Anatolie seldjoukide, le souverain de Konya, le territoire qu'il gouverne et les habitants qui y vivent.

L'idée « romaine » y reste si bien enracinée qu'elle remplace souvent la notion de « territoire de l'islam » (*dār al-islām*) pour les observateurs musulmans extérieurs à l'Anatolie et cela pour plusieurs raisons. La première de ces raisons réside dans le très grand nombre de Gens du Livre (*ahl al-kitāb*) qui résident dans la péninsule anatolienne sous la tutelle de dirigeants turcs encore très minoritaires aux VIIe/XIIIe et VIIIe/XIVe siècles.

Le voyageur marocain Ibn Baṭṭūṭa résume parfaitement la perception arabe de l'Anatolie, lorsqu'il débarque à Antalya en 731/1331 ; pour lui, cette région est certes « la terre de Turquie » (*barr al-Turkiyya*) mais elle est connue sous le nom de *bilād al-rūm* car, précise-t-il, c'était jadis le pays des « Romains » et des « Ioniens » (*yūnānī*). Si les musulmans la conquirent finalement et qu'elle est désormais sous la domination des Turcomans (*turkumān*), Ibn

 | DOI 10.1163/9789004331037_015

Baṭṭūṭa remarque son caractère resté largement romano-byzantin à cause de la présence d'un grand nombre de chrétiens (*naṣāra*)[1], comme l'avait constaté presque un siècle plus tôt, le frère Guillaume de Rubrouck qui, traversant la péninsule anatolienne à son retour de Mongolie, écrit : « De la Turquie, vous saurez qu'il n'y a pas un habitant sur dix qui soit sarrasin. Au contraire, tous sont Arméniens ou Grecs »[2]. De même, on lit dans *l'Histoire des patriarches d'Alexandrie*, qu'au temps du sultan de Konya Masʿūd I (r. 510/1116-551/1156), « ... la plus grande partie du territoire (de ce sultan) est occupée par des sujets grecs »[3].

Avec une telle quantité de non-musulmans en Anatolie turque, l'idée de *dār al-islām* est même, pour cette région, plusieurs fois remise en question par les sources arabo-musulmanes. Celles-ci reprochent parfois à la minorité turque qui dirige le pays de tolérer des mœurs laxistes et peu conformes aux prescriptions morales et sociales de l'islam, quand elles ne considèrent par les autorités seldjoukides elles-mêmes comme d'une orthodoxie suspecte.

Ainsi, le sultan zengide Nūr al-dīn en lutte contre le seldjoukide de Konya Kılıç Arslān II, en 568/1172-73, accepte-t-il de faire la paix avec le souverain de Rūm en imposant des conditions drastiques qui illustrent parfaitement l'opinion des sunnites non-anatoliens sur les agissements peu orthodoxes des sultans de Konya qui non seulement négligent le devoir de guerre sainte contre leurs voisins byzantins mais passent même avec eux des traités de paix, tout en professant un islam doctrinalement douteux qui rend même le Zengide soupçonneux quant à l'appartenance réelle à l'islam de Kılıç Arslān.

Voici le texte rapporté à ce sujet par Ibn al-Aṯīr dans son *Histoire des Atabegs de Mossoul* : « Dans sa lettre à Kılıç Arslān, il [Nūr al-dīn] disait : "Pour base de notre réconciliation, je vous imposerai certaines conditions (...). Primo, vous renouvellerez votre profession de foi entre les mains de mon envoyé, afin que j'aie le droit de vous laisser régner sur un pays musulman [*bilād al-islām*] car mon idée est que vous n'êtes pas un vrai croyant – on soupçonnait Kılıç Arslān

1 Muḥammad b. ʿAbd Allāh Ibn Baṭṭūṭa, *Voyages d'Ibn Batoutah*, texte arabe, accompagné d'une traduction par C. Defrémery et B. R. Sanguinetti, 2ème tirage, vol. 2 (Paris: Imprimerie Nationale, 1877), 255.

2 Guillaume de Rubrouck, *Voyage dans l'empire mongol, 1253-1255*, trad. Claire Kappler and René Kappler (Paris: Imprimerie nationale éd., 2007), 244.

3 *Siyar al-ābāʾ al-batārika*, Paris, BNF, manuscrits arabes, 301-302, 274, cité par Osman Turan, "Les souverains seldjoukides et leurs sujets non-musulmans," *Studia Islamica*, nº 1 (1953): 76, n. 2.

d'avoir adopté les opinions des philosophes [*madhab al-falāsifa*] ; secundo, quand je vous demanderai un contingent de troupes pour faire la guerre sainte, vous aurez à me le fournir ; car vous qui possédez une portion si considérable des pays où l'on professe l'islam, vous vivez en paix avec vos voisins les Grecs [*rūm*] et vous ne pensez pas à soutenir la cause de Dieu en leur faisant la guerre ; au contraire vous traitez avec eux" »[4].

Ici donc, si Nūr al-dīn considère certes les possessions de Kılıç Arslān comme *bilād al-islām*, il doute par contre de l'identité musulmane du souverain qui possède le dit territoire, souverain qui par ses agissements pacifiques semble plus proche des Byzantins que des musulmans non-anatoliens. Le chroniqueur grec Kinnamos se fait l'écho de cette mauvaise réputation de Kılıç Arslān en rapportant que même « … le calife était irrité contre Kılıç Arslān parce qu'il était lié d'amitié depuis si longtemps avec les Romains [*Rhōmaioi*= Byzantins] »[5].

Le petit-fils de Kılıç Arslān II, Kay-Kā'ūs I (r. 608/1211-616/1220) s'attire aussi les critiques de son maître en soufisme, l'Andalou Ibn 'Arabī qui lui reproche sa gestion laxiste des ses sujets chrétiens – encore majoritaires, rappelons-le, dans le sultanat de Rūm au VIIe/XIIIe siècle – ; ce qui fait ressembler l'Anatolie turque beaucoup plus à la province romano-byzantine qu'elle était avant la conquête musulmane qu'à un membre à part entière du *dār al-islām*.

Voici ce qu'écrit à Kay-Kā'ūs en 1212 Ibn 'Arabī, choqué des mœurs peu musulmanes qu'il a constaté pendant son séjour en Anatolie turque, bien que par ses origines andalouses, il soit habitué aux usages interconfessionnels relativement souples d'al-Andalus[6] : « Parmi les atteintes portées à l'islam et aux musulmans, d'autant que ces derniers sont peu nombreux (dans le sultanat de Konya), il y a la sonnerie des cloches, les démonstrations d'incroyance, la prédominance d'un enseignement polythéiste et le relâchement des contraintes imposées aux peuples protégés [*dimmī*] ». Désormais, continue l'auteur, « … qu'ils ne puissent construire ni nouvelles églises dans les villes et les terres environnantes, ni couvents ni monastères ni cellules ou autres », ce qui apparemment se passait jusque là et continua par la suite comme en témoigne

4 Ibn al-Aṯīr, "Histoire des Atabecs de Mossoul," in *Recueil des historiens des croisades. Historiens orientaux. Tome 2 / Deuxième partie / publ. par les soins de l'Académie des inscriptions et belles-lettres* (Impr. nationale (Paris), 1876), 291.

5 Jean Kinnamos, *Chronique*, trad. par Jacqueline Rosenblum, Publications de La Faculté Des Lettres et Des Sciences Humaines de Nice 10 (Paris: Les Belles Lettres, 1972), 186.

6 Ibn 'Arabî, *Les soufis d'Andalousie*, trans. R. W. J. Austin, La bibliothèque spirituelle 8 (Paris: Albin Michel, 1979), 38.

l'archéologie qui enregistre par exemple en Cappadoce des constructions d'églises financées par des notables chrétiens influents à la cour seldjoukide[7].

Comme Ibn ʿArabī, l'encyclopédiste Yāqūt (575/1179-626/1229), s'indigne de l'atmosphère bien peu musulmane qu'il constate à Erzincan et à Erzurum où consommation du vin et du porc et processions religieuses chrétiennes se font au grand jour[8].

A l'inverse les intellectuels musulmans mettent beaucoup de temps à venir, depuis les centres de savoir syriens ou irakiens, s'installer au Pays de Rūm qui reste pour beaucoup une marge très excentrée du *dār al-islām*. D'après les *ṭabaqāt*, peu de savants viennent séjourner en Anatolie avant le VIIe/XIIIe siècle. La première *madrasa* anatolienne est fondée à Kayseri en 1193, époque où il y a plus de 40 établissements de ce genre à Alep[9]. Et il faudra tous les efforts des sultans du VIIe/XIIIe siècle pour attirer des personnalités extérieures de premier plan comme le théologien Ibn ʿArabī de Murcie ou la famille de juristes de Balkh menée par Mevlānā Jalāl al-dīn, fondateur de l'ordre des « derviches tourneurs » et son père.

Les Turcs installés par vagues successives dans la Romanie byzantine depuis le Ve/XIe siècle, se sentent certes membres du *dār al-islām* en tant que musulmans implantés à demeure dans l'ancienne province-pivot de l'Empire romain d'Orient mais ils assument aussi, semble-t-il, une identité « romaine » en tant qu'occupant une portion importante du territoire bien connu depuis les origines de l'islam comme « Pays des Romains ».

Et pour reprendre la formulation de Claude Cahen, les Turcs sont « ... intégrés plus ou moins consciemment à l'entité qui s'appelle *Rūm* qu'ils peuvent aspirer à dominer, mais parce qu'ils en font partie, (ils) s'y sentent chez eux plus que dans le *dār al-islām* traditionnel »[10].

---

7 Catherine Jolivet-Lévy, *La Cappadoce: Mémoire de Byzance*, Patrimoine de La Méditerranée (Paris: Paris-Méditerranée-CNRS éditions, 1997), 104-15.

8 Yāqūt, Šihāb al-dīn b. ʿAbd Allāh al-Ḥamawī, *Muʿjam al-buldān* (*Jacut's Geographisches Wörterbuch*), herausgegeben von Ferdinand Wüstenfeld, vol. 1 (Leipzig: In Commission bei F. A. Brockhaus, 1866), 205-6; cf. Claude Cahen, *La Turquie pré-ottomane*, Varia Turcica 7 (Istanbul: Institut français d'études anatoliennes d'Istanbul : Dıvıt Matbaacılık ve Yayıncılık, 1988), 164, 212.

9 Répertoire chronologique d'épigraphie arabe, Le Caire, n° 3470, cité par Cahen, *Turquie*, 209.

10 Ibid., 171. Sur l'hésitation identitaire des Turcomans de Rūm aux XIIe-XIIIe siècles, cf. Rustam Shukurov, "Turkoman and Byzantine self-identity. Some reflections on the logic of title-making in the twelfth- and thirteenth-century Anatolia," in *Eastern approaches to Byzantium: Papers from the Thirty-third Spring Symposium of Byzantine Studies, University*

Archéologie, art, numismatique etc… rendent compte de cette identité *rūm* que partagent Turcs et Grecs d'Anatolie, à tel point que certaines sources musulmanes médiévales en utilisant le terme *rūm* pour désigner le territoire anatolien et les divers peuples qui l'habitent, laissent planer un certain flou quant à la signification ethnique ou religieuse du mot : le Rūm est-il Grec ou Turc, chrétien ou musulman et le *bilād al-rūm* désigne-t-il l'Empire byzantin ou le sultanat turc ? Des auteurs comme ʿIzz al-dīn Ibn Šaddād (613/1217-684/1285) doit dans un extrait de sa *Description de la Syrie du Nord*, préciser pour la clarté de son propos qu'il parle du « pays des *Rūms musulmans*, c'est-à-dire du sultanat seldjoukide d'Anatolie, tant « l'idée romaine » semble parfois primer l'appartenance confessionnelle musulmane ou chrétienne[11].

Cette primauté de l'identité *rūm* sur le rattachement confessionnel ou linguistique gardera toute sa force à l'époque ottomane : à côté de la stricte application du mot à la communauté grecque et slave orthodoxe (*millet-i rūm*), le terme pourra être utilisé en plein xᵉ/xviᵉ siècle (et bien au-delà) dans sa signification supraconfessionnelle et supraethnique de « sujet et habitant du territoire dominé par la dynastie d'Osmān ».

La notion de *dār al-islām* pèsera d'autant moins dans l'Empire ottoman classique (sauf peut-être au temps du pan-islamisme et du « califat ottoman » de la deuxième moitié du xixᵉ siècle) que tous dans l'Empire ont conscience que, comme le dit l'historien ʿAlī de Gallipoli à la fin du xᵉ/xviᵉ siècle : « la plupart des habitants de Rūm ont diverses origines et parmi les notables, il en est peu dont la lignée ne remonte pas à un converti »[12]. Dans un monde si cosmopolite où se côtoient religions et langues diverses, seules (1) la dépendance de tous à l'égard de la dynastie d'Osmān et (2) probablement une certaine idée universaliste d'origine romano-byzantine (entre autres traditions, islamique, persane ou turco-mongole), sont des liants socio-politiques plus forts que le lien de l'*umma* musulmane qui ne concerne qu'une partie de la population.

C'est ainsi que si, dans la langue officielle, l'Etat ottoman se présente avant tout sur une assise dynastique, *dawlat-i ʿUṯmāniyya* (turc *devlet-i Osmaniyye*), l'idée « romaine » cependant perdure dans la titulature, continuant à concurrencer la notion de *dār al-islām*: l'aire ottomane est *mamlakat-ı rūm, būm-i rūm*,

---

of Warwick, Coventry, March 1999, ed. Antony Eastmond, Publications for the society for the promotion of Byzantine studies (Burlington, VT: Ashgate, 2001), 259-76.

11 ʿIzz al-dīn Ibn Šaddād, *Description de la Syrie du Nord*, Traduction annotée de *Al-Aʿlāq al-ḫaṭīra fī ḏikr umarāʾ al-Šām wa'l-Jazīra* par Anne-Marie Eddé-Terrasse, Publications de l'Institut Français de Damas 116 (Damas: Presses de l'Ifpo, 1984), 72n1.

12 Gelibolulu Alî, *Künhü'l-Ahbar* ; cf. Michel Balivet, *Anthologie d'histoire ottomane: les deux premiers siècles, XIVᵉ-XVᵉ siècles : faits et textes* (Istanbul: Editions Isis, 2004), 81.

iqlīm-i rūm ; le sultan reste souvent appelé comme aux temps seldjoukides, *sulṭān-ı rūm*, voire *qayṣar-ı rūm* ; le *šayḫ al-islām* Abū al-Suʿūd (turc Ebüssuʿūd) au Xe/XVIe siècle est *muftī al-diyār al-rūmiyya*, etc ...[13]

Cet ancrage diachronique de l'idée « romaine » figurant en bonne place au côté de celle de *dār al-islām*, a même pu faire écrire à un auteur moderne : « The Ottoman Turks may be called the Romans of the Muslim world » ![14]

References

Balivet, Michel. *Anthologie d'histoire ottomane: les deux premiers siècles, XIVe-XVe siècles : faits et textes*. Istanbul: Editions Isis, 2004.

Cahen, Claude. *La Turquie pré-ottomane*. Varia Turcica 7. Istanbul: Institut français d'études anatoliennes d'Istanbul : Dıvıt Matbaacılık ve Yayıncılık, 1988.

Durak, Koray. "Who Are the Romans? The Definition of *Bilād al-Rūm* (Land of the Romans) in Medieval Islamic Geographies." *Journal of Intercultural Studies* 31, nº 3 (June 2010): 285-98.

Guillaume de Rubrouck. *Voyage dans l'empire mongol, 1253-1255*. Translated by Claire Kappler and René Kappler. Paris: Imprimerie nationale éd., 2007.

Hourani, Albert. "How Should We Write the History of the Middle East?" *International Journal of Middle East Studies* 23, nº 2 (1991): 125-36.

Ibn al-Aṯīr. "Histoire des Atabecs de Mossoul." In *Recueil des historiens des croisades. Historiens orientaux. Tome 2 / Deuxième partie / publ. par les soins de l'Académie des inscriptions et belles-lettres*, 291 – . Impr. nationale (Paris), 1876.

Ibn ʿArabî [Ibn ʿArabī, Muḥyī al-dīn Abū ʿAbd Allāh, al-Šayḫ al-Akbar]. *Les soufis d'Andalousie*. Trad. R. W. J. Austin. La bibliothèque spirituelle 8. Paris: Albin Michel, 1979.

Ibn Baṭṭūṭa, Muḥammad b. ʿAbd Allāh. *Voyages d'Ibn Batoutah*, texte arabe, accompagné d'une traduction par C. Defrémery et B. R. Sanguinetti. 2ème tirage. Vol. 2. Paris: Imprimerie Nationale, 1877.

Ibn Šaddād, ʿIzz al-dīn ʿAbd Allāh. *Description de la Syrie du Nord*, Traduction annotée de *Al-Aʿlāq al-ḫaṭīra fī ḏikr umarāʾ al-Šām wa'l-Jazīra* par Anne-Marie Eddé-Terrasse. Publications de l'Institut Français de Damas 116. Damas: Presses de l'Ifpo, 1984.

---

13 Salih Özbaran, "In Search of Another Identity: The 'Rumi' Perception in the Ottoman Realm," *Eurasian Studies* 1, nº 1 (2002): 115-27. Cf. aussi Koray Durak, "Who Are the Romans? The Definition of *Bilād al-Rūm* (Land of the Romans) in Medieval Islamic Geographies," *Journal of Intercultural Studies* 31, nº 3 (June 2010): 285-98.

14 Albert Hourani, "How Should We Write the History of the Middle East?," *International Journal of Middle East Studies* 23, nº 2 (1991): 130.

Jean Kinnamos. *Chronique*. trad. par Jacqueline Rosenblum. Publications de La Faculté Des Lettres et Des Sciences Humaines de Nice 10. Paris: Les Belles Lettres, 1972.

Jolivet-Lévy, Catherine. *La Cappadoce: Mémoire de Byzance*. Patrimoine de La Méditerranée. Paris : Paris: Paris-Méditerranée-CNRS éditions, 1997.

Özbaran, Salih. "In Search of Another Identity: The 'Rumi' Perception in the Ottoman Realm." *Eurasian Studies* 1, nº 1 (2002): 115-27.

Shukurov, Rustam. "Turkoman and Byzantine self-identity. Some reflections on the logic of title-making in the twelfth- and thirteenth-century Anatolia." In *Eastern approaches to Byzantium: Papers from the Thirty-third Spring Symposium of Byzantine Studies, University of Warwick, Coventry, March 1999*, edited by Antony Eastmond, 259-76. Publications for the society for the promotion of Byzantine studies. Burlington, VT: Ashgate, 2001.

Turan, Osman. "Les souverains seldjoukides et leurs sujets non-musulmans." *Studia Islamica*, nº 1 (1953): 65-100.

Yāqūt, Šihāb al-dīn b. 'Abd Allāh al-Ḥamawī. *Mu'jam al-buldān* (*Jacut's Geographisches Wörterbuch*). Herausgegeben von Ferdinand Wüstenfeld. Vol. 1. Leipzig: In Commission bei F. A. Brockhaus, 1866.

CHAPTER 14

Une appartenance controversée : trois moments dans le débat autour du statut du *bilād al-sūdān*

Francesco Zappa

Comme tous les territoires où la première expansion de l'islam n'a pas été le fruit d'une conquête militaire, l'Afrique subsaharienne occidentale (souvent appelée *bilād al-sūdān* dans les sources arabes) est une région où la délimitation de la frontière entre *dār al-islām* et *dār al-ḥarb* (ou *dār al-kufr*) n'est jamais allée de soi. Cet article se penchera sur trois moments différents de son histoire précoloniale dans lesquels cette frontière et ses enjeux ont fait l'objet d'un débat, quoique avec des motivations et des résultats bien différents. Le débat a été, bien sûr, relancé à partir de la conquête coloniale[1] sans jamais cesser complètement d'être d'actualité jusqu'à nos jours, au moins dans un cadre idéologique militant[2] ; cependant, les dynamiques enclenchées par la

1 Pour une vue d'ensemble des multiples manières dont les élites lettrées musulmanes ouest-africaines ont relevé les nouveaux défis posés par la conquête coloniale à la définition de la frontière entre *dār al-islām* et *dār al-ḥarb*, je renvoie à l'ouvrage collectif de David Robinson et Jean-Louis Triaud, éd., *Le Temps des marabouts. Itinéraires et stratégies islamiques en Afrique Occidentale Française v. 1880-1960* (Paris: Karthala, 1997). En particulier, pour un exemple tiré d'un État issu d'un jihad « endogène », voir Rowland Adevemi Adeleye, « The Dilemma of the Wazir: The Place of the *Risālat al-wazīr ilā ahl al-ʿilm wa'l-tadabbur* in the History of the Conquest of the Sokoto Caliphate », *Journal of the Historical Society of Nigeria* 4, nº 2 (juin 1968): 285-311. En revanche, pour un cas d'élites lettrées musulmanes sujettes à des autorités non-musulmanes dès la période précoloniale, cf. Robert Launay, « Des infidèles d'un autre type: Les réponses au pouvoir colonial dans une communauté musulmane de Côte d'Ivoire », in *Le Temps des marabouts: Itinéraires et stratégies islamiques en Afrique Occidentale Française v. 1880-1960*, éd. par David Robinson et Jean-Louis Triaud (Paris: Karthala, 1997), 415-30.

2 L'établissement d'un *dār al-hijra*, c'est-à-dire d'une communauté urbaine ou villageoise le plus possible autonome par rapport à l'État postcolonial et gouvernée, au moins en principe, exclusivement sur la base de la sharia, est une entreprise qui a été tentée et réalisée à plusieurs reprises dans l'histoire récente de l'Afrique de l'Ouest, aussi bien par des autorités religieuses soufies que par des mouvements d'inspiration wahhabite. Dans le cadre du soufisme confrérique, le cas le plus connu est celui de Medina Gounass dans la région sénégalaise de la Haute Casamance, sur lequel l'étude classique reste Yaya Wane, « Ceerno Muhamadu Sayid Baa. Le soufisme intégral de Madiina Gunaas (Sénégal) », *Cahiers d'Études Africaines* 14, nº 56 (1974): 671-98; sur l'assouplissement de cette expérience rigoriste depuis

 | DOI 10.1163/9789004331037_016

domination coloniale, puis par la décolonisation et ses séquelles, ont posé de nouveaux défis et de nouveaux problèmes qui me semblent déborder du cadre comparatif proposé par cet ouvrage collectif.

1 Les débuts : des enclaves musulmanes dans le *dār al-kufr*

Une première occasion de réflexion nous est offerte par la période des plus anciens contacts documentés entre marchands maghrébins et populations subsahariennes, jusqu'aux alentours du VIe/XIIe-VIIe/XIIIe siècle. À ces premiers voyageurs, l'Afrique subsaharienne apparaît d'emblée comme un territoire relevant en bloc du *dār al-kufr.* Le problème se pose donc tout d'abord en termes de licéité du commerce avec des « mécréants » n'appartenant pas aux « gens du Livre », et dont aucun élément du patrimoine religieux ne semble relever d'une « mémoire partagée » avec les musulmans.

Malgré ce sentiment d'altérité totale et le risque de contamination qu'on y associait, au fil du temps une représentation plus articulée de l'espace se dessine dès qu'on ressent l'exigence de contourner l'avis défavorable au commerce avec les mécréants du *bilād al-sūdān* émis par des juristes mālikites à l'autorité incontournable, au moins au Maghreb. En effet, dans un chapitre très hétérogène de sa célèbre *Risāla,* Ibn Abī Zayd al-Qayrawānī (m. en 386/996) avait été formel : *« Tukrahu 'l-tijāra ilā arḍ al-ʿaduww wa-balad al-sūdān »* (« il est blâmable d'aller faire du commerce en territoire ennemi et au pays des Noirs »), tout en attribuant au Prophète cette curieuse précision : *« al-safar qiṭʿa min al-ʿaḏāb »* (« le voyage, c'est une portion du châtiment »), ce qui suggère que pour avoir enduré un voyage si périlleux, on aura tout de même expié, au moins en partie, la faute de l'avoir mené *in partibus infidelium*[3]. Et encore au sixième/douzième siècle, une autorité de poids telle que le *qāḍī* ʿIyāḍ b.

---

les années 1980, voir Eduard van Hoven, « Medina Gounass: The end of a religious isolate », ISIM *Newsletter* 4 (1999): 25. Dans le cadre du militantisme wahhabite, avant la proclamation éphémère d'un État islamique indépendant dans l'ensemble du Nord du Mali en 2012, des essais plus discrets, plus localisés et moins politisés avaient été expérimentés dans plusieurs pays de la sous-région ; j'en ai illustré un exemple, tiré d'un contexte rural malien, dans Francesco Zappa, « Écrire l'islam en bambara. Lieux, réseaux et enjeux de l'entreprise d'al-Hājj Modibo Diarra », *Archives de sciences sociales des religions* 147 (juillet-septembre 2009): 174-78.

3 Ibn Abî Zayd al-Qayrawânî, *La Risâla ou Epître sur les éléments du dogme et de la loi de l'Islâm selon le rite mâlikite. Texte arabe et traduction française avec un avant-propos, des notes et trois index par Léon Bercher*, 1re éd. (1945; Alger: Editions Populaires de l'Armée, s. d.), 318 (texte arabe) /319 (trad.). Dans notre citation, la traduction de Bercher a été légèrement modifiée.

Mūsā (m. 544/1149) attribuait au fondateur même du malikisme kairouanais, Saḥnūn (m. 240/855), d'avoir refusé l'accès à sa propre maison à un marchand qui s'était enrichi par le commerce avec le *bilād al-sūdān*[4].

Quelques siècles plus tard, lorsque la conversion à l'islam de plusieurs souverains « soudanais » sera devenue une évidence, il sera assez aisé, pour les commentateurs de la *Risāla* de Qayrawānī, de neutraliser le jugement tranchant de son auteur en glosant la référence au *bilād al-sūdān* par un *« yaʿnī 'l-kuffār minhum »* (« c'est-à-dire ceux d'entre eux qui sont mécréants »), ce qui suggère l'existence de territoires du *bilād al-sūdān* ne relevant pas (ou plus) du *dār al-kufr*. C'est le cas, par exemple, d'Abū 'l-Ḥasan al-Mālikī al-Manūfī (m. 939/1532), dans son *Taḥqīq al-mabānī wa-taḥrīr al-amānī* [*min risālat Ibn Abī Zayd al-Qayrawānī*][5]. Mais dans cette première phase, tant que les souverains qui se déclarent musulmans font figure d'exceptions, il fallait des stratégies plus rusées pour contourner ces obstacles légaux et scrupules pieux : l'importance du commerce transsaharien pour l'économie du Maghreb, ainsi que de l'ensemble du bassin méditerranéen, était, en effet, trop vitale pour qu'on puisse y renoncer si facilement. Ces stratégies relèvent des ruses juridiques (*ḥiyal*) dans les écrits des juristes, et des stratagèmes narratifs dans les récits des géographes et des historiens.

Ainsi, par exemple, dans deux fatwas étudiées par Michael Brett, le *faqīh* kairouanais Qābisī (324/935-403/1012) semble partir d'un jugement aussi péremptoire que celui de son contemporain Qayrawānī[6]. En effet, interrogé, dans la première de ces deux fatwas, au sujet d'une vente par procuration (*qirāḍ* : un instrument particulièrement adapté aux transactions avec les régions éloignées)[7], il répond tout d'abord qu'« un *qirāḍ* stipulant un voyage au *bilād al-sūdān* n'est pas licite car, à son avis, il n'est pas comme un *qirāḍ* pour un voyage dans les villes de l'islam » : « le *bilād al-sūdān* n'est ni fiable ni satisfaisant pour le *qirāḍ* »[8]. Toutefois, interrogé, dans la deuxième de ces deux fatwas, au sujet d'une dispute sur l'héritage d'un marchand décédé dans une ville du

4 Cit. dans Ivor Wilks, « The Juula and the Expansion of Islam into the Forest », in *The History of Islam in Africa*, éd. par Nehemia Levtzion et Randall Lee Pouwels (Athens: Ohio University Press, 2000), 95.

5 Cit. dans ʿUṯmān Ibn Fūdī, *Bayān wujub al-hijra ʿalā l-ʿibād wa-bayān wujūb naṣb al-imām wa-iqāmat al-jihād*, éd. par F. H. El-Masri (Khartum and Oxford: Khartum University Press and Oxford University Press, 1978), 15 (ar.) / 51 (ang.).

6 V. Michael Brett, « Islam and Trade in the *Bilād al-Sūdān*, Tenth-Eleventh Century A.D. », *The Journal of African History* 24, nº 4 (octobre 1983): 431-40.

7 V. Abraham L. Udovitch, « Ḳirāḍ », *Encyclopaedia of Islam, Vol. V, Khe-Mahi* (Leiden: Brill, 1986).

8 Brett, « Islam and Trade », 433.

bilād al-sūdān, le même juriste finit par légitimer l'autorité d'un surintendant (*nāẓir*) nommé par le souverain païen local et accepté par les expatriés musulmans installés dans cette ville pour qu'il veille à leurs affaires légales selon la sharia[9]. Autrement dit, tout en ne remettant pas en question l'appartenance au *dār al-kufr* d'un territoire gouverné par un souverain mécréant, le juriste essaye de reconnaître l'existence, dans son sein, d'un espace de validité pour l'application, quoique limitée, de la sharia.

Dans ce cadre, l'autorité de ce surintendant aux affaires musulmanes est assurée non seulement par son intégrité morale et sa compétence juridique, reconnues par les expatriés musulmans qui en ont accepté le rôle, mais aussi, paradoxalement, par le fait même d'avoir été investi par un souverain qui détient un pouvoir de coercition, fût-il mécréant : on part, en effet, du principe juridique classique selon lequel tout pouvoir politique est meilleur que l'anarchie. Ainsi, la situation imparfaite et précaire de cette colonie musulmane au sein du *dār al-kufr*, soumise, faute de mieux, à l'autorité d'un *nāẓir* musulman investi par un souverain païen, finit par présenter un double avantage pour les marchands musulmans : tout en ne pouvant pas être soumis aux contraintes de toutes les obligations de la sharia, ceux-ci sont tout de même protégés au moins par ses dispositions les plus élémentaires[10].

La fortune de ces deux fatwas est par ailleurs attestée par leur inclusion, cinq siècles plus tard, dans un recueil prestigieux tel que le *Miʿyār* de Wanšarīsī (m. 914/1508)[11], et le modèle de la communauté de marchands musulmans soumise à une autorité politique païenne et, en même temps, autogouvernée dans son sein par un autorité plus ou moins formelle chargée de faire respecter la sharia, sera repris et amplifié, comme on le sait, dans les siècles suivants, par les musulmans africains subsahariens eux-mêmes, lorsqu'ils propageront plus au sud leurs réseaux marchands, sur la base d'une élaboration juridique plus articulée de ces mêmes principes. Cette élaboration est attribuée par la tradition locale au juriste malikite al-Ḥājj Sālim Suwarī, un savant d'ethnie soninké originaire de la région du Macina, ayant sans doute vécu entre la fin du IXe/XVe et le début du Xe/XVIe siècle, entre les marges méridionales de l'empire du Mali et des régions plus au Sud, où les musulmans constituaient justement une diaspora marchande et lettrée[12].

Entre-temps, cette représentation de l'espace des marchands musulmans au *bilād al-sūdān* comme une sorte de réseau d'enclaves à l'intérieur du *dār*

---

9 Ibid., 433-34.

10 Ibid., 436-37.

11 Ibid., 431.

12 Voir Wilks, « The Juula and the Expansion of Islam into the Forest », 96-98.

al-kufr devait assumer des formes plus imagées et suggestives sous la plume de géographes et d'historiens contemporains de Qābisī, ou postérieurs, n'ayant par ailleurs jamais franchi la redoutable frontière naturelle du Sahara. Deux *topoi* se dégagent, en effet, des œuvres d'auteurs tels Masʿūdī (m. 345/956), Ibn Ḥawqal (qui écrit en 378/988), Bakrī (qui écrit en 460/1068), Yāqūt (m. 629/1229), Qazwīnī (m. 682/1283) et ʿUmarī (m. 749/1349)[13].

Le premier *topos* est celui des « villes doubles », c'est-à-dire formées par la juxtaposition de deux agglomérations, séparées par un espace inhabité ou une frontière naturelle (le plus souvent un fleuve). Dans sa formulation la plus paradigmatique, celle de la ville de Ġāna décrite par Bakrī, la première agglomération est habitée exclusivement par les marchands musulmans, et compte plusieurs mosquées, écoles et juristes. La deuxième, qui rassemble la population païenne autochtone, est également le siège du palais du souverain, païen lui-aussi. Elle compte plusieurs lieux de culte de la religion traditionnelle locale, mais aussi, le plus souvent, une mosquée pour les musulmans de passage. Ce n'est d'ailleurs pas un hasard si Bakrī nous précise, au sujet de la ville de Ġāna, que cette mosquée s'y trouvait « non loin de la salle des audiences royales »[14] ; plus important encore, Bakrī distingue, dans cette même description, entre musulmans et « coreligionnaires du roi » (*ahl dīn al-mālik*) plutôt qu'entre musulmans et population locale, ce qui semble suggérer, comme l'a remarqué Nehemia Levtzion, que déjà à cette époque tous les musulmans n'étaient pas des étrangers[15].

Le deuxième *topos* évoqué par ces sources est celui du commerce muet de l'or : un système de transactions entre marchands arabo-berbères et producteurs d'or autochtones qui se serait déroulé par l'évitement de tout contact direct entre les deux parties, qui apportaient alternativement leurs marchandises à un endroit convenu en ajustant la quantité au gré d'une sorte de négociation muette. En effet, d'après les sources citées plus haut, chaque partie

---

13 Pour les passages consacrés au *bilād al-sūdān* dans l'œuvre de ces auteurs, je renvoie aux deux anthologies désormais classiques, respectivement en traduction française et anglaise : Joseph M. Cuoq, éd., *Recueil des sources arabes concernant l'Afrique Occidentale du VIIIe au XVIe siècle (Bilād al-Sūdān)* (Paris: Editions du CNRS, 1975); Nehemia Levtzion et J. F. P. Hopkins, éd., *Corpus of early Arabic sources for West African history*, trad. par J. F. P. Hopkins (Cambridge: Cambridge University Press, 1981).

14 Voir Cuoq, *Recueil des sources arabes concernant l'Afrique Occidentale du VIIIe au XVIe siècle (Bilād al-Sūdān)*, 99-100; Levtzion et Hopkins, *Corpus of early Arabic sources for West African history*, 80.

15 Nehemia Levtzion, « Islam in the Bilad al-Sudan to 1800 », in *The History of Islam in Africa*, éd. par Nehemia Levtzion et Randall Lee Pouwels (Athens: Ohio University Press, 2000), 64.

retirait, à son tour, sa marchandise, en se retirant à l'écart du lieu de la transaction, tant que la contrepartie n'était pas satisfaisante, et annonçait à chaque fois son départ par le roulement d'un tambour. Ainsi, un souci partagé d'éviter tout contact direct, signe s'il y en a d'une extrême méfiance, se serait accompagné d'une remarquable confiance réciproque, ce qui paraît assez bizarre, parce qu'il s'agissait à chaque tour de laisser sa marchandise sans surveillance[16].

Le caractère conventionnel de ces deux images fait encore l'objet de débats entre les historiens, qui ont longtemps discuté sur leur degré de crédibilité. Les sources arabes remontant à cette époque ne sont en effet qu'exceptionnellement le fruit d'une expérience directe des lieux : pour la plupart, le mélange de témoignages oraux puisés à des voyageurs et de *topoi* repris à des sources littéraires plus anciennes, y compris grecques, y apparaît presque inextricable, filtré qu'il est, le plus souvent, par une réélaboration littéraire ultérieure[17]. S'il paraît plus probable que le commerce muet relève d'un cliché littéraire, d'autant plus qu'on le trouve déjà chez Hérodote[18], l'image de la « ville double », elle, semble s'apparenter davantage au modèle d'implantation urbaine emprunté, plus tard, par les réseaux des marchands dioulas et haoussas musulmans d'inspiration « suwarienne » dans des villes animistes de la zone forestière[19]. Quoi qu'il en soit, ce qui nous intéresse ici, et qui rapproche ces deux images entre elles ainsi qu'avec la fatwa de Qābisī, c'est le fait qu'elles contribuent toutes à la représentation d'une frontière imaginaire à même de délimiter les colonies marchandes musulmanes au sein du *bilād al-sūdān* et de les protéger, ainsi, d'un contact contaminant avec un monde extérieur perçu encore comme uniformément mécréant[20]. D'autant plus que dans la représentation que nous

16 Parmi les nombreux travaux consacrés au sujet, v. notamment, pour le contexte ouest-africain, Paulo Fernando de Moraes Farias, « Silent Trade: Myth and Historical Evidence », *History in Africa* 1 (1974): 9-24.

17 Pour cet aspect de ce genre de sources, voir notamment John O. Hunwick, « A Region of the Mind: Medieval Arab Views of African Geography and Ethnography and their Legacy », *Sudanic Africa* 16 (2005): 103-36.

18 V. Moraes Farias, « Silent Trade ».

19 Cf. les considérations prudentes de Jean-Louis Triaud, « L'islam en Afrique de l'Ouest. Une histoire urbaine dans la longue durée », in *Islam et villes en Afrique au sud du Sahara: Entre soufisme et fondamentalisme*, éd. par Adriana Piga (Paris: Karthala, 2003), 134 (« sans qu'on sache exactement si cette mention est le résultat d'observations réelles ou l'effet d'un stéréotype »); sur l'analogie avec le modèle « suwarien », v. Ibid., 135-36.

20 Dans sa reconstitution d'une forme différente de commerce silencieux, pratiqué, d'après plusieurs sources, dans l'Arabie préislamique, Michael Bonner suggère justement la possibilité que le recours au silence puisse servir à préserver le statut d'une des parties en évitant ainsi toute source de honte ou de contamination. V. Michael Bonner, « The Arabian

en donnent nos sources arabes, l'échange commercial avec des populations païennes subsahariennes se situe presque constamment dans un espace liminaire, au bord d'un fleuve qui, comme l'a suggéré John Hunwick, sert aussi de frontière psychologique entre un monde subsaharien encore fréquentable par les musulmans et, dans une certaine mesure, « domestiqué » (quoique majoritairement habité et gouverné par des païens), d'où il est encore possible de « monter sur son chameau et rebrousser chemin », et un territoire plus redoutable, habité par des populations qu'on représentait volontiers comme complètement nues et s'adonnant au cannibalisme[21].

En même temps, la terminologie employée par l'ensemble de ces sources semble faire rarement recours aux expressions *dār al-islām* et *dār al-ḥarb*. Chez Qayrawānī et Qābisī, il est question plutôt de « villes de l'islam » (*mudun al-islām*)[22], « terres de l'islam » (*arḍ al-islām*) et « territoire de l'ennemi » (*arḍ al-ʿaduww*) – « inimitié » (*ʿadāwa*) étant souvent employé comme synonyme de mécréance, alors que nos sources narratives ne gardent aucune trace de ce vocabulaire juridique, qu'elles traduisent plutôt dans leur langage imagé, selon une tendance déjà observée par Giovanna Calasso dans d'autres contextes[23].

2 Des conversions des souverains à la question de l'esclavage : Aḥmad Bābā et son *Miʿrāj al-ṣuʿūd*

On connaît la suite de l'histoire : la conversion de plusieurs souverains ouest-africains à l'islam à partir sans doute du IVe/Xe siècle, puis l'expansion territoriale de certains de leurs royaumes jusqu'à en faire des empires multiethniques à partir du VIIe/XIIIe, rend vite caduc le modèle de l'enclave

---

Silent Trade: Profit and Nobility in the "Markets of the Arabs" », in *Histories of the Middle East: studies in Middle Eastern society, economy and law in honor of A.L. Udovitch*, éd. par Roxani Eleni Margariti, Adam Abdelhamid Sabra, et Petra Sijpesteijn, Islamic history and civilization, v. 79 (Leiden: Brill, 2011), 23-51.

21 V. Hunwick, « A Region of the Mind », 114. Cf. aussi Bonner, « The Arabian Silent Trade », 35, là où il parle du commerce muet en tant que « myth of the frontier: out there, where civilization and Empire come to an end, relations with the barbarians assume this reassuring form, which emphasizes our common humanity, while still furthering the interests of civilization and Empire ».

22 Une expression particulièrement intéressante en ce qu'elle suggère une identification implicite de l'espace islamique avec l'espace urbanisé ou tout au moins « civilisé ».

23 V. Giovanna Calasso, « Alla ricerca di *dār al-islām*. Una ricognizione nei testi di giuristi e tradizionisti, lessicografi, geografi e viaggiatori », *Rivista degli Studi Orientali* 83 (2010): 286-93, ainsi que sa contribution au présent ouvrage.

musulmane au sein du *dār al-ḥarb*, au moins à l'intérieur des frontières des territoires que ces souverains musulmans contrôlent. L'avantage que ceux-ci avaient à tirer de leur conversion à l'islam, à la fois dans leurs relations avec les États et les marchands d'Afrique du Nord et dans le rajout d'un élément supplémentaire, « cosmopolite » à leur prestige aux yeux de leurs sujets, a été remarqué maintes fois. De même, on insiste souvent sur le fait que dans cette longue phase, l'islam a tendance à rester l'apanage des cours royales, en plus que des milieux marchands et lettrés, ce qui se traduit parfois par un prolongement du modèle de l'enclave sous une autre forme. Certains des souverains musulmans « soudanais » de cette période iront jusqu'à légitimer leurs guerres d'expansion en les faisant cautionner comme des jihads par les oulémas, même si les dispositions légales prévues pour les *ḏimmī*s ne semblent guère avoir été systématiquement appliquées aux sujets non-musulmans. En général, la conversion de ces souverains suffit à faire considérer leurs territoires comme relevant du *dār al-islām*, et dans les rares cas où la légitimité d'un souverain est contestée par l'accusation de pratiquer un islam syncrétique ou de ne pas appliquer la sharia, ce n'est que pour légitimer après coup un renversement de son pouvoir par une nouvelle dynastie[24].

Le problème de la définition des frontières du *dār al-islām* se posera sous une nouvelle forme après plusieurs siècles d'islamisation, lors de l'effondrement de ces États impériaux régis par des dynasties locales qui se réclamaient de l'islam. C'est justement au lendemain de la chute d'une de ces grandes formations étatiques, l'empire songhaï, vaincu, paradoxalement, par une armée à la solde d'une dynastie musulmane maghrébine, celle des Saʿdiens du Maroc (999/1591), que remonte l'une des sources les plus intéressantes à cet égard. Il s'agit du *Miʿrāj al-ṣuʿūd ilā nayl ḥukm mujallab al-sūd*, connu également sous le titre *al-Kašf wa'l-bayān fī aṣnāf majlūb al-sūdān*, et rédigé en 1024/1615 par le célèbre juriste de Tombouctou Aḥmad Bābā (963/1556-1036/1627), quelques années après son retour de son exil marocain[25]. Ce traité se présente sous la

24 Sur le plus célèbre de ces cas, v. John O. Hunwick, éd., *Sharīʿa in Songhay: the replies of al-Maghīlī to the questions of Askia al-Ḥājj Muḥammad* (Oxford: Published for British Academy by Oxford University Press, 1985).

25 V. Aḥmad Bābā, *Miʿrāj al-Ṣuʿūd: Aḥmad Bābā's Replies on Slavery*, trad. par John O. Hunwick et Fatima Harrak (Rabat: Publications of the Institute of African Studies – University Mohammed V Souissi, 2000). Cette édition du traité comporte également le texte et la traduction d'une autre fatwa (ou plus précisément d'un recueil de trois *ajwiba*) sur le même sujet émise par le même auteur quelques années plus tôt, pendant sa captivité marocaine, sous demande de l'un de ses élèves marocains. Ce deuxième texte, quoiqu'un peu plus court que le *Miʿrāj* et moins disert pour ce qui est des arguments doctrinaux, est remarquablement plus riche en détails ethnographiques et géo-historiques ; loin de faire

forme d'une fatwa sollicitée par un homme (sans doute un marchand possédant des notions de *fiqh*) originaire de Tuwāt, ville relais du commerce transsaharien. L'enquêteur se renseigne sur la licéité de la réduction en esclavage des Noirs en général, et plus en particulier, sur les critères qui permettent de vérifier l'appartenance à l'islam des esclaves qui s'en réclamaient pour contester la licéité de leur statut, en prétendant qu'ils avaient été réduits en esclavage à un moment où ils étaient déjà musulmans.

Certes, le problème n'était pas entièrement nouveau, car on connaît au moins deux précédents de fatwas sur le même sujet, émises en plein essor de l'empire songhaï, et citées à leur tour par Aḥmad Bābā lui-même dans ce même traité[26]; nul besoin d'ajouter, d'ailleurs, que des abus dans la réduction en esclavage des musulmans, notamment noirs, sont attestés à toutes les époques. Reste que l'effondrement de ce grand empire et l'anarchie qui s'ensuivit doivent avoir rendu les abus encore plus fréquents, et la nécessité de disposer d'un critère de distinction encore plus pressante ; d'autant plus que le conquérant marocain n'arrivait pas à contrôler tout le territoire de l'ancien empire songhaï, dont plusieurs provinces étaient en proie à l'anarchie[27].

En outre, ce même conquérant semble avoir bien exploité les idées reçues qui circulaient à l'époque, notamment au Nord du Sahara, concernant le lien qu'on prétendait consubstantiel entre la couleur de la peau et la condition d'esclave. Parmi ces idées on trouve un récit légendaire selon lequel le *bilād al-sūdān* aurait été conquis, à une époque non précisée, par un mystérieux souverain musulman, qui aurait décidé de permettre à la population de continuer à pratiquer ses cultes ancestraux, et de la laisser provisoirement libre, tout en la réduisant dans un état d'esclavage permanent « potentiel », en ce sens que tout individu aurait pu être réclamé comme esclave par le sultan à tout moment : il s'agirait là d'une curieuse dérogation aux dispositions juridiques habituelles en matière d'esclavage, car elle ferait de celui-ci un statut social « générique » et « potentiel » plutôt qu'une relation personnelle

double emploi, il lui sert donc très utilement de complément. Sur la datation de ces deux textes et l'identité respective de leurs enquêteurs, cf. l'introduction de l'édition mais aussi John O. Hunwick, « Aḥmad Bābā on Slavery », *Sudanic Africa* 11 (2000): 131-39.

26 Il faut tout de même rappeler que ces deux avis légaux avaient été motivés par les abus commis par l'empereur songhaï Sonni ʿAlī Ber, représenté, sans doute tendancieusement, par nos sources comme le prototype du souverain apostat et persécuteur des musulmans : v. Marta García Novo, « La doctrina mālikí sobre esclavitud y el *Miʿrāŷ* de Aḥmad Bābā », *Espacio, Tiempo y Forma*, Serie III (Historia Medieval) 23 (2010): 87.

27 Voir Michel Abitbol, *Tombouctou et les Arma: De la conquête marocaine du Soudan nigérien en 1591 à l'hégémonie de l'Empire Peul du Macina en 1833* (Paris: Maisonneuve et Larose, 1979), notamment aux pp. 70-71.

d'assujettissement à un individu[28]. Une autre justification de l'idée d'un lien consubstantiel entre race et condition d'esclave se basait sur la variante musulmane, par ailleurs bien connue, du mythe de la malédiction de Cam[29]. Tout cela s'accompagnait à une tendance répandue à associer les populations noires à la mécréance et à ne pas prendre au sérieux la conversion à l'islam des Noirs, malgré le crédit dont jouissaient au Maghreb plusieurs oulémas subsahariens (dont une nombre important n'étaient pas d'origine arabo-berbère).

Comme l'a montré récemment Bruce Hall[30], ces idées reçues, qui n'avaient jamais cessé d'avoir cours au Maghreb, seront progressivement appropriées, à partir du XIe/XVIIe siècle, même à l'intérieur de la région sahélo-saharienne par des musulmans d'origine arabe et/ou berbère, au fur et à mesure que les équilibres socio-économiques et politiques entre populations sédentaires « soudanaises » et populations nomades arabo-berbères basculeront en faveur de ces dernières. Les clivages confessionnels seront alors identifiés, par un discours racial, à l'opposition entre *bīḍān* et *sūdān*, et par conséquent, pour des ethnies ou des dynasties de *sūdān* se réclamant d'un islam aussi « certifié » que celui des *bīḍān*, il deviendra encore plus vital d'insister sur la présence (évidemment fictive) d'un ancêtre arabe dans leurs généalogies, selon un mécanisme déjà rodé depuis longtemps. C'est aussi dans ce cadre que les Peuls (tout d'abord uniquement pour ce qui est de leurs lignages maraboutiques, puis dans leur ensemble) parviendront à dissocier leur identité raciale de celle des Noirs, en se faisant passer par Blancs ou, parfois, par « Rouges » sur la base d'une prétendue descendance de ʿUqba b. Nāfiʿ, bien que, encore sous la plume d'Aḥmad Bābā, ils ne soient guère représentés comme de « meilleurs musulmans » que d'autres populations soudanaises. L'intérêt du texte d'Aḥmad Bābā, lui-même un berbère *masūfa* de Tombouctou, réside donc, entre autres, aussi dans le fait qu'il témoigne d'un point de vue berbère sahélien antérieur à l'appropriation, par les *bīḍān* de la région, de ce discours alliant identité raciale et religieuse[31]. Ayant partie liée avec l'ancien régime, c'est-à-dire avec le dernier grand empire ouest-africain régi par une dynastie musulmane « noire » avant l'époque des

28 Voir Aḥmad Bābā, *Miʿrāj*, 43-44 (ar.) / 13-14 (ang.).

29 Ibid., 46-47 / 16-17.

30 V. Bruce S. Hall, *A History of Race in Muslim West Africa, 1600-1960*, African Studies 115 (Cambridge: Cambridge University Press, 2011).

31 Bruce Hall (ibid., 52), « In North Africa between 1593 and 1608, [Aḥmad Bābā] found himself confronted with a much more racialized discourse – equating blackness with slavery – than he was evidently accustomed to in Timbuktu; [...] it is, however, interesting that the first explicit discussion of race by a Sahelian writer was provoked by his exposure to North Africa » (ibid., 54).

jihads, ce juriste semble encore s'identifier tout d'abord à la communauté musulmane subsaharienne dans son ensemble, au lieu de mettre en avant les origines « blanches », nord-africaines de la lignée de lettrés dont il descend[32].

Aḥmad Bābā s'applique, en effet, à démonter ces arguments point par point, en commençant par les arguments doctrinaux et pseudo-historiques de portée générale, c'est-à-dire ceux qui impliquaient un lien quelconque entre la race et l'esclavage, et ceux qui faisaient du *bilād al-sūdān* une sorte de « réserve d'esclaves » toujours susceptible d'être exploitée[33]. Ensuite, après avoir démystifié la légende de l'ancienne conquête du *bilād al-sūdān* qu'on vient d'évoquer, et après avoir précisé que les conversions à l'islam dans cette région n'ont pas été le résultat d'un jihad[34], il procède à remplacer ces généralisations par une approche empirique[35]. Cette approche l'amène à dresser un état des lieux systématique de l'islam au *bilād al-sūdān* rangé par régions et par ethnies, ou selon une définition adoptée par plusieurs chercheurs, une « ethnographie religieuse » de l'Afrique de l'Ouest de son époque. Il faut préciser toutefois que, dans l'agencement du texte, cette reconstitution relativement précise et empirique de la réalité du terrain est souvent mêlée à la réfutation des arguments de portée générale plus qu'elle ne la suit, et l'ordre conceptuel qu'on vient d'évoquer ne correspond pas exactement à l'ordre textuel.

Au-delà des nombreux aspects déjà étudiées de ce texte, par ailleurs bien connu des spécialistes, ce qui me paraît intéressant de signaler ici c'est la manière dont il mélange, me semble-t-il, les principes de territorialité et de personnalité du droit[36]. En effet, en dressant son état des lieux de l'islam en

32 Ce qui n'empêche, par ailleurs, Aḥmad Bābā de privilégier les oulémas berbères, et notamment les membres de sa famille, dans sa reconstitution de l'histoire intellectuelle de Tombouctou telle qu'il nous l'a livrée dans ses dictionnaires biographiques. Voir Marta García Novo, « Ulemas malikíes del *bilad al-Sudan* en la obra biográfica de Ahmad Baba al-Tinbukti (963/1556-1036/1627) », in *Biografías magrebíes: identidades y grupos religiosos, sociales y políticos en el Magreb medieval*, éd. par Mohamed Meouak (Madrid: Consejo Superior de Investigaciones Científicas, 2012), 417-82.

33 Voir Aḥmad Bābā, *Miʿrāj*, 53-69 / trad. 23-39.

34 Ibid., 58 / trad. 29 : « ils se sont convertis spontanément » (*aslamū ṭawʿan*); ibid., 53 / 23: « sans que personne ne les ait soumis militairement » (*bilā ʾstīlāʾ aḥadin ʿalayhim*).

35 V. Aḥmad Bābā, *Miʿrāj*, 69-70 / trad. 39-40 et surtout l'ensemble des réponses aux questions de ʿĪsī, publiées dans le même volume par les éditeurs du *Miʿrāj*, ibid., 77-91 / trad. 41-53.

36 Cette clé de lecture des deux traités d'Aḥmad Bābā s'inspire de l'approche au binôme *dār al-islām / dār al-ḥarb* proposée par Calasso, « Alla ricerca di *dār al-islām* », (voir notamment pp. 281-6); cf. aussi sa contribution au présent ouvrage.

Afrique de l'Ouest, Aḥmad Bābā passe souvent d'un critère territorial à un critère ethnique, parfois en précisant les différentes appartenances religieuses de groupes relevant de la même ethnie mais installés dans de différents territoires (c'est le cas, par exemple, des Peuls/Fulani)[37], parfois en distinguant entre populations musulmanes et non musulmanes à l'intérieur d'un territoire donné, à partir du constat que « certains de ces groupes s'interpénètrent » (*hā'ulā' al-aṣnāf baʿḍuhā mutadāḫila*)[38]. Assez souvent, notamment dans les questions du *mustafti'*, ethnonymes et toponymes sont mélangés dans la même liste, qui est parfois elle-même définie comme une liste de « *buldān wa-qabā'il* » confondus. Dans ce cadre, la référence à l'allégeance confessionnelle de l'autorité politique à laquelle les différents groupes concernés sont soumis ne semble pas être mise en avant, ni même systématiquement évoquée. Il est question, parfois (et c'est encore plus surprenant), plutôt de l'antiquité, de la qualité ou de la « profondeur » de l'islam chez telle ou telle population à tel ou tel endroit, comme c'est le cas dans des affirmations comme « les gens de Kano, Katsina, Bornou et les Songhaï [...] sont anciens dans l'islam » (*qudamā' fī 'l-islām*)[39] ou, par opposition, « les Kunbā [=Dogon de la plaine] sont eux-aussi [mécréants], à l'exception de quelques-uns des habitants d'Hombori ou de Douentza, bien que leur islam soit superficiel (*ʿalā ḍaʿf islāmihim*), et il n'y a donc pas d'inconvénient pour toi à t'en approprier sans te poser de questions » (*fa-lā ba's ʿalayka fī tamallukihim bi-lā su'āl*)[40].

37 Cf. Aḥmad Bābā, *Miʿrāj*, 57 / trad. 27, où les Peuls sont assimilés, en majorité (*muʿẓam al-Fullān*) à une liste d'autres populations de « musulmans libres dont l'achat ne saurait être licite en aucun cas » (*fa-hum muslimūn aḥrār lā yajūzu tamallukuhum bi-wajh*), « sauf pour un groupe au-delà de Djenné au sujet duquel il nous a été rapporté qu'ils sont mécréants, sans que l'on sache s'ils le sont de souche ou bien s'ils ont apostasié » (*illā mā balaġanā ʿan ṭā'ifatin warā' Jinni yuqālu innahum kuffār wa-lā nadrī hal bi'l-aṣāla 'aw irtaddū*). Plus loin (ibid., 84-85 / trad. 46), il est plutôt question d'une évaluation qualitative : « Pour ce qui est des Peuls, ils sont eux-aussi musulmans, même si la condition de certains d'entre eux n'est pas satisfaisante, car la mauvaise conduite, les razzias et les prédations sont généralisées auprès de ce groupe, ce qui ne les prive pas pour autant du nom de musulmans » (*ammā Fullān, fa-hum ayḍan muslimūn, wa-in kāna min-hum man ḥāluhum ġayr murḍin li-kawn al-ġālib ʿalā ṣinfihim al-šarr wa'l-iġārāt wa'l-ġawra, fa-ḏālika la yaslubu ʿanhum ism al-islām*).

38 Aḥmad Bābā, *Miʿrāj*, 82 / trad. 43.

39 Ibid., 53-54 / trad. 23.

40 Ibid., 70 / trad. 40. Cette évaluation « qualitative », assez surprenante de la part d'un juriste peu enclin à des velléités de réforme religieuse, encore moins de *takfīr*, nous amène par ailleurs à nuancer l'image d'un Aḥmad Bābā prêt à cautionner systématiquement toute allégation venant des Noirs ouest-africains réduits en esclavage.

La référence au territoire semble donc finalisée à vérifier au mieux l'identité religieuse de ses ressortissants (surtout lorsque l'un de ceux-ci est réduit en esclavage et se réclame d'une identité musulmane « de souche ») plutôt qu'à délimiter les frontières du *dār al-islām* en les identifiant aux frontières des États soumis à une autorité politique musulmane chargée, au moins théoriquement, d'appliquer la sharia. La notion de *bilād* (ou parfois *buldān*) *al-islām* elle-même, bien que mentionnée à plusieurs reprises dans le texte, ne l'est pas toujours directement en lien avec le pouvoir en place : on trouve parfois aussi l'expression, à l'apparence plus nuancée, *« al-bilād al-maʿrūfa bi'l-islām »* (« les territoires connus pour leur islam »)[41], mais elle se réfère encore une fois à la religion de ses habitants plutôt que de ses souverains ; un synonyme encore plus explicite, c'est l'expression *« al-bilād allātī taqarrara islāmu ahlihā »*, qu'on peut traduire par « les territoires dont il est bien établi que les habitants sont musulmans »[42]. Cette démarche semble partir du constat que les musulmans soumis à un souverain non-musulman (ou vivant dans des sociétés « acéphales ») sont nombreux au *bilād al-sūdān*, ainsi que de la conviction que la loi doit faire valoir les droits qui découlent de leur appartenance religieuse, indépendamment des aléas d'un cadre politique changeant dont la chute de l'empire songhaï avait révélé toute la fragilité[43]. En même temps, comme cela a été relevé par Marta García Novo, les identités confessionnelles sont systématiquement attribuées en bloc à des groupes ethniquement et/ou territorialement définis, sans prévoir la possibilité de conversions individuelles de la part de membres de groupes restés païens dans leur majorité[44].

---

41 Ibid., 58 / 29.

42 Ibid., 52 / 22.

43 Parmi les éléments les plus aléatoires de ce cadre instable figure le statut des individus issus de populations païennes qui payaient la *jizya* au sultan songhaï avant la chute de celui-ci. Ce cas est évoqué en passant par Aḥmad Bābā dans la première de ses réponses à ʿĪsī (v. ibid., 83 [ar.] / 44 [ang.]); toutefois, face à l'insistance de l'enquêteur, qui évoque une pluralité d'opinions sur la question de savoir si le statut des *ḏimmī*s gardait sa validité lorsque ceux-ci sont capturés par un pouvoir musulman autre que celui qui le leur a octroyé, le juriste semble éluder la question (ibid., 89-90 / trad. 49-50). Cette ambiguïté donne l'impression que chez Aḥmad Bābā, le souci de préserver le statut des musulmans prime sur toute autre considération politique et légale, même si le caractère contraignant du contrat de *ḏimma* est affirmé ailleurs dans cet ouvrage d'une manière générale (et générique) : Ibid., 53 / trad. 23.

44 Cf. García Novo, « La doctrina mālikí », 92, où il est suggéré que cette représentation ait pu servir à cautionner implicitement l'existence bien connue de « castes serviles » dans les sociétés ouest-africaines.

Ayant fait lui-même l'expérience douloureuse de la captivité à la cour du sultan de Marrakech lors de la conquête marocaine de Tombouctou pour avoir contribué à animer la vaine opposition de l'élite savante de la ville, Aḥmad Bābā donne l'impression d'assumer en plein conscience un rôle de garant des droits des musulmans du *bilād al-sūdān*[45] ; d'autant plus qu'il n'avait jamais rétracté sa désapprobation pour une conquête motivée par l'attrait pour les mines d'or du Sahel, bien que justifiée par la propagande saʿdienne comme une entreprise visant à la réunification de l'Ouest musulman sous une seule autorité califale. On lui attribue, entre autres, d'avoir demandé ironiquement au sultan saʿdien Aḥmad al-Manṣūr pourquoi n'avait-il pas dirigé ses efforts de réunification de la umma en direction des provinces maghrébines de l'empire ottoman, plus proches de sa capitale, au lieu de viser un empire songhaï plus distant mais plus mal armé[46]. Ainsi, bien qu'enracinée dans les principes du *fiqh* malikite, l'orientation de cette œuvre se comprend mieux à la lumière du contexte de sa rédaction et de l'expérience amère de son auteur, dont la ville natale de Tombouctou, réputée pour le savoir et la piété de ses oulémas, avait été pillée et vandalisée par des armées formées essentiellement par des renégats, sous le prétexte de la ramener sous une autorité islamique dont la légitimité se voulait plus universelle[47]. Et là, au risque de l'anachronisme, il est difficile de résister à la tentation de suggérer, en passant, un rapprochement éloquent avec les tristes évènements subis tout récemment par cette ville.

45 Comme le remarque Paul E. Lovejoy, « his experience in captivity in Morocco under conditions of dubious legality made him uniquely qualified to write on matters of slavery. [...] Through captivity, Aḥmad Bābā had undoubtedly come into contact with slaves of many backgrounds, an experience which must have informed his commentary on the legal and religious issues dealing with slavery » ; Paul E. Lovejoy, « Slavery, the Bilād al-Sūdān and the Frontiers of the African Diasporas », in *Slavery on the Frontiers of Islam*, éd. par Paul E. Lovejoy (Princeton: Marcus Wiener Publishers, 2004), 11. Une lecture différente est proposée par García Novo (« La doctrina mālikí », 95), selon laquelle certains silences et ambiguïtés du texte d'Aḥmad Bābā pourraient être révélateurs, au contraire, de son intention de ne pas trop entraver un commerce d'esclaves qui pour sa classe sociale d'appartenance représentait une source de revenus non négligeable. Cette argumentation a été ultérieurement étayée par cette chercheuse dans Marta García Novo, « Islamic law and slavery in premodern West Africa », *Entremons. UPF Journal of World History* 2 (novembre 2011), http://www.upf.edu/entremons/numero2/garcia.html (dernier accès: mars 2014).

46 V. Mahmoud A. Zouber, *Ahmad Bābā de Tombouctou : sa vie et son œuvre* (Paris: Maisonneuve et Larose, 1977), 27-28.

47 Cf. aussi John O. Hunwick, « Aḥmad Bābā and the Moroccan Invasion of the Sūdān (1591) », *Journal of the Historical Society of Nigeria* 2, nº 3 (1962): 311-28; et Elias Saad, *Social History of Timbuktu* (Cambridge: Cambridge University Press, 1983), 168-84.

3 Un nouveau commencement : *takfīr, hijra* et jihad chez Usman dan Fodio

Moins de deux siècles après la rédaction du *Miʿrāj* d'Aḥmad Bābā, le débat autour de la définition de la frontière entre *dār al-islām* et *dār al-ḥarb* à l'intérieur du *bilād al-sūdān* revient à occuper le devant de la scène et à susciter une réflexion explicite et parfois systématique de la part des oulémas, cette fois-ci pour des raisons qui ne concernent qu'indirectement l'esclavage[48]. En effet, l'essor des mouvements de réforme locaux aboutissant aux grands jihads des siècles XIIe/XVIIIe-XIIIe/XIXe entraînera une remise en question radicale de l'identité musulmane des populations et des États de la région, y compris ceux qui se réclamaient de l'islam depuis plusieurs siècles[49]. Je me limiterai ici au cas le plus célèbre, voire paradigmatique, entre autres pour s'être accompagné de la plus riche production de littérature apologétique et polémique : à savoir, le jihad lancé par le *shehu* Usman dan Fodio (m. 1817) (« cheikh ʿUṯmān b. Fūdī » dans les textes arabes) au Nigeria du Nord en 1804.

Rappelons de passage que ce jihad aboutit à la fondation d'un État (ou plus précisément d'un « califat ») régi par une dynastie de *fuqahāʾ* (tout d'abord Usman dan Fodio lui-même, puis ses descendants) : une sorte de *wilāyat-i faqīh*

48 La réduction en esclavage de sujets musulmans figure cependant assez régulièrement parmi les reproches adressées par les idéologues des jihads du XIIe/XVIIIe-XIIIe/XIXe siècle, dont on va traiter dans ce chapitre, aux souverains qu'ils combattaient (mais il ne faut pas non plus oublier que la même reproche a été également adressée aux chefs militaires du jihad par leurs adversaires idéologiques). En même temps, bien que ces jihads aient été justifiés, entre autres, par l'exigence de corriger ce genre d'abus, d'un autre côté l'introduction par leurs idéologues de critères beaucoup plus stricts pour valider l'appartenance d'un individu à l'islam finissait par priver un grand nombre d'individus, considérés comme musulmans jusqu'à la veille, de l'immunité que cette identité confessionnelle leur avait naguère garantie, au moins en théorie. Au-delà de ce côté idéologique, si le poids du facteur esclavage sur les motivations « matérielles » des combattants de ces jihads est un sujet relativement peu exploré, il est certain que les conséquences de ces mouvement religieux et militaires sur la réalité de la traite des esclaves dans l'espace sahélo-saharien furent profondes et durables. Voir par exemple Paul E. Lovejoy, « Islam, slavery, and political transformation in West Africa: constraints on the trans-Atlantic slave trade », *Outre-mers* 89, n° 336-37 (2002): 247-82.

49 La littérature sur l'ensemble de ces jihads étant très riche, et les approches ne s'étant pas considérablement renouvelées depuis les années 1970-80, je renvoie, pour une synthèse d'ensemble ainsi que pour d'ultérieures références bibliographiques relativement mises à jour, à David Robinson, « Revolutions in the Western Sudan », in *The History of Islam in Africa*, éd. par Nehemia Levtzion et Randall Lee Pouwels (Athens: Ohio University Press, 2000), 131-52.

avant la lettre qui a survécu sous de différentes formes institutionnelles jusqu'à nos jours à travers la colonisation britannique, puis l'englobement dans l'État nigérian indépendant. La particularité de ce jihad est au moins double. Tout d'abord, loin d'être mené à partir d'un territoire issu, plus ou moins directement, des conquêtes de l'empire califal, donc du *dār al-islām* au sens classique du terme, il est le fait de l'initiative d'un cheikh « autochtone » d'une région d'Afrique de l'Ouest n'ayant jamais connu de véritable conquête islamique. Deuxièmement, ce jihad vise des territoires soumis à une autorité politique qui se veut musulmane depuis plusieurs siècles, les « sept cités-États haoussa », vassales, à leur tour, du sultanat de Bornou, situé sur les deux rives du lac Tchad, qui se targuait d'une tradition islamique millénaire à la fois pour la renommée de ses oulémas et pour le prestige de sa dynastie (dont la généalogie affichait des ancêtres yéménites, de toute probabilité fictifs).

Pour justifier son jihad, Usman dan Fodio se doit donc de remettre en question l'appartenance à l'islam des habitants de ces royaumes et, tout d'abord, de leurs souverains, par un véritable *takfīr* basé sur l'accusation de pratiquer un syncrétisme avec les cultes traditionnels locaux qu'il considère comme incompatible avec l'islam[50]. Plus précisément, ces souverains sont accusés d'entraver la prédication d'Usman dan Fodio jusqu'à en arriver à la persécution de ses disciples ; une persécution qui s'explique sans doute par le fait que les contenus de cette prédication ne relevaient pas uniquement de la réforme morale et religieuse (notamment de la lutte au syncrétisme), mais articulaient également dans un langage islamique des doléances plus spécifiquement politiques et sociales d'une partie de la population, par exemple vis-à-vis des exactions fiscales des États haoussas[51]. Ne reconnaissant plus les souverains haoussas comme des autorités légitimes, et considérant de ce fait leur territoire comme *dār al-kufr,* Usman dan Fodio ne dispose plus d'un territoire à partir duquel il puisse lancer son jihad, ni il ne songe à solliciter l'intervention militaire d'un souverain musulman d'un pays voisin. Il met en scène, plutôt, une véritable réactualisation consciente du modèle prophétique jusqu'à organiser une *hijra* avec la communauté de ses disciples, en s'installant sur un petit territoire (le

50 Au sujet de l'élaboration d'une notion proche de celle de syncrétisme dans le cadre de la littérature apologétique et polémique qui accompagna le jihad de Sokoto, je me permets de renvoyer à mon article « Syncrétisme ou radicalisme ? Modèles d'islamisation en conflit au Nigéria septentrional précolonial », in *Islam et villes en Afrique au sud du Sahara: Entre soufisme et fondamentalisme*, éd. par Adriana Piga (Paris: Karthala, 2003), 241-55.

51 V. par exemple Mervyn Hiskett, « *Kitāb al-Farq*: A Work on the Habe Kingdoms Attributed to 'Uthmān dan Fodio », *Bulletin of the School of Oriental and African Studies* 23, n° 3 (1960): 558-79.

dār al-hijra de Gudu, plutôt à l'écart par rapport au centre de l'émirat haoussa de Gobir) à l'intérieur duquel il se fera reconnaître comme imam à travers une véritable *bay'a*, et à partir duquel il lancera formellement son jihad.

Toute cette entreprise politico-militaire, dont l'impact symbolique est évident, s'accompagne d'une élaboration légale tout aussi systématique et explicite. Parmi les nombreuses œuvres apologétiques élaborées pendant ces années, un traité de *fiqh*, en particulier, reflète, à partir du titre, le souci de justifier et d'ériger en modèle les étapes principales de son entreprise : il s'agit du *Bayān wujūb al-hijra 'alā l-'ibād wa-bayān naṣb al-imām wa-iqāmat al-jihād*, rédigé en 1806, c'est-à-dire deux ans après avoir lancé son jihad, et deux ans avant sa victoire définitive. Ce qui de ce livre nous intéresse de plus près ici, c'est la manière dont il redessine la carte ethno-religieuse non seulement du Nord du Nigeria actuel, mais aussi de l'ensemble du *bilād al-sūdān*, qui se retrouve à être qualifié en bloc de *dār al-kufr*, malgré la présence (reconnue par l'auteur) de nombreux musulmans à l'intérieur de son territoire. Ces musulmans qui, quoique relativement nombreux, sont désormais représentés comme des individus isolés dans une mer de mécréance hostile, sont appelés, dès que les rapports de force le permettent, à rejoindre le territoire déjà soumis à l'autorité politique et militaire d'Usman dan Fodio, voire à se retrancher dans un *dār al-hijra* calqué sur le modèle de celle fondée par le *shehu* lui-même, et à lancer un jihad qui seul permettra de fonder un État légitime, dont le territoire sera digne d'être qualifié de *dār al-islām*. C'est d'ailleurs exactement de cette manière que l'État de Sokoto était en train de se constituer lors de la rédaction de cet ouvrage : non pas par une simple expansion militaire à partir d'un seul *dār al-hijra*, mais par une constellation de jihads locaux, lancés dans les différentes régions du pays haoussa (voire au-delà) chacun par un groupe différent d'oulémas peuls se réclamant de l'exemple d'Usman dan Fodio, et chacun à partir de son propre *dār al-hijra* ; l'unité d'inspiration de cet ensemble de mouvements à la fois religieux et militaires se reflètera dans le caractère fédéral de l'État, qui se voudra un véritable califat articulé en plusieurs émirats.

Le principe qui sous-tend cette redéfinition du *bilād al-sūdān* comme relevant entièrement du *dār al-kufr* est condensé dans une formule lapidaire : *ḥukm al-balad ḥukm sulṭānihi* (« le statut juridique d'un pays dépend de celui de son souverain ») ; la glose qui suit immédiatement cette formule est d'ailleurs encore plus explicite : *in kāna musliman kāna baladuhu balad (al-)islām, wa-in kāna kāfiran kāna baladu-hu balad kufr* (« si celui-ci est musulman, son pays est un pays d'islam, s'il est mécréant son pays est un pays de mécréance »)[52]. Cette formule, dont on ne connaît pas l'origine, et qui pourrait

52 'Uṯmān Ibn Fūdī, *Bayān wujub al-hijra*, 14 (texte arabe) / 50 (trad. angl.).

donc bien avoir été forgée par dan Fodio lui-même, généralement assez scrupuleux dans la citation de ses sources, a d'ailleurs été rapprochée par plusieurs chercheurs au célèbre *cuius regio, eius religio* communément associé à la paix d'Augsburg (1555) ; d'autant plus que les deux formules impliquent une obligation d'émigrer (ou de se convertir) pour les populations dont la confession ne coïncide pas avec celle du souverain, un parallèle remarquable si l'on tient compte de l'absence dans la tradition chrétienne d'une notion correspondant à celle de *hijra*[53].

L'islam dont se réclamaient depuis des siècles les souverains haoussas, ainsi que les souverains d'une large partie du *bilād al-sūdān*, est donc rejeté comme légalement nul (*bāṭil*), et ce jugement tranchant comporte, entre autres, un désaveu explicite de l'ethnographie religieuse dressée par Aḥmad Bābā, dont l'autorité était évidemment trop établie pour qu'on puisse l'ignorer. En effet, après avoir rappelé la division avancée par le plus célèbre des savants de Tombouctou entre les territoires où la mécréance prédomine et ceux où l'islam est majoritaire, Usman dan Fodio précise juste après que ces derniers sont à considérer « eux-aussi comme des *bilād kufr* sans aucun doute » (*fa-hāḏīhi ayḍan bilād kufr bilā šakk*), « parce que l'islam répandu parmi leurs habitants ne s'étend pas à leurs souverains » (*li-anna 'l-islām mustafīḍ fīhā fī ġayr salāṭīnihim*), « alors que leurs souverains sont mécréants comme ceux de la première catégorie [= celle indiquée comme relevant du *dār al-kufr* aussi par Aḥmad Bābā], même s'ils professent [extérieurement] la religion musulmane » (*wa-ammā salāṭīnuhā fa-kuffār ka'l-qism al-awwal, wa'in kānū yadīnūna bi-dīn al-islām*)[54]. Et s'il concède qu'il peut bien y avoir des exceptions, celles-ci ne sauraient infirmer, à son sens, l'extension du *takfīr* à l'ensemble du *bilād al-sūdān,* car « l'exception ne fait pas le statut légal » (*lā ḥukma li'l-nādir*)[55]. Dan Fodio rapporte ensuite scrupuleusement les avis de plusieurs oulémas, depuis le temps des fatwas kairouanaises citées au début de cet article, qui suggèrent l'appartenance d'au moins une partie du *bilād al-sūdān* aux *bilād al-islām,* pour en conclure tout de même que ces territoires lui sont inconnus et que, sur l'autorité d'un savant non nommé, on peut affirmer qu'« aucun territoire musulman n'existe au pays des Noirs » (*balad al-islām ma'dūm fī bilād*

53 Ibid., 50 (trad. angl.), note 1 (note de l'éditeur et traducteur Fathi Hasan El-Masri). La formule, introduite pour la première fois dans ce texte, a été ensuite reprise maintes fois dans de nombreuses œuvres apologétiques et polémiques par les idéologues du jihad de Sokoto.

54 Ibid., 14 / 50.

55 Ibid., 14 / 51.

al-sūdān aṣlan)[56]. Quelques années plus tard, en 1811, une fois la guerre terminée et le Califat de Sokoto bien établi, dans un traité apologétique sur son jihad intitulé *Tanbīh al-iḫwān ʿalā aḥwāl arḍ al-sūdān*, la prise de distance d'Usman dan Fodio par rapport à Aḥmad Bābā sera encore plus explicite : l'opinion de celui-ci peut bien avoir été juste à sa propre époque, mais elle ne le sera pas forcément à d'autres époques, car « chaque savant ne saurait juger que d'après ce qui est connu à son époque ; or les conditions changent avec le temps et le soin change selon la maladie »[57].

Le désaveu de l'autorité d'Aḥmad Bābā dans cette matière semble d'ailleurs avoir été facilité par l'appropriation d'un cliché de type racial qui se glisse à maintes reprises, quoique jamais d'une manière tout à fait explicite, dans les écrits des idéologues du jihad de Sokoto, ainsi que dans l'idéologie de l'ensemble des jihads ouest-africains menés par des oulémas peuls à cette époque. Le *takfīr* global des *sūdān*, parmi lesquels les musulmans font figure d'exception, est en effet rendu possible par la dissociation complète et préalable entre identité peule et identité noire, qui s'élabore sans doute dans cette même période, sur la base du mythe, évoqué plus haut, de la descendance de ʿUqba, dont les Peuls désormais se réclament, ainsi que du rôle de premiers propagateurs de l'islam au sud du Sahara qu'ils s'attribuent[58].

On peut voir là un nouvel avatar du discours racial associant « négritude » et mécréance foncière qu'Aḥmad Bābā avait rencontré dans les questions de son *mustafti*ʾ nord-africain, et qu'il avait réfuté en le considérant comme le produit d'un regard étranger déformant, mais qui avait été approprié, depuis, tout d'abord par des *bīḍān* du Sahel, puis par des Peuls jihadistes eux-mêmes. D'après Bruce Hall, « the use of the term 'blacks' in this literature is quite intentional, because it conveyed a set of meanings that invoked a range of socially inferior status positions for the people who would become the target of the jihad »[59], et on peut imaginer aisément que le renvoi à cet imaginaire ait été particulièrement stratégique à l'adresse des lecteurs *bīḍān* sahéliens qui devaient former

56 Ibid., 15 / 51.

57 V. H. Richmond Palmer, « An Early Fulani Conception of Islam (Continued) », *Journal of the Royal African Society* 14, nº 53 (octobre 1914): 53-54 (trad. angl. intégrale du *Tanbīh al-iḫwān*). Le même passage se retrouve, à quelques mots près, dans un autre traité apologétique rédigé deux ans plus tard : cf. Bradford G. Martin, « Unbelief in the Western Sudan: 'Uthman dan Fodio's *Ta'līm al-ikhwān* », *Middle Eastern Studies* 4, nº 1 (octobre 1967): 71 (texte arabe) / 88 (trad. angl.).

58 V. David Robinson, *The Holy War of Umar Tal: The Western Sudan in the Mid-Nineteenth Century* (Oxford: Clarendon Press, 1985), 81-89, ch. 2.F (« The Emergence of a Chosen People »).

59 Hall, *A history of race*, 103.

une partie non négligeable du lectorat des écrits apologétiques en arabe issus du jihad de Sokoto. En même temps, ce discours racial ne pouvait pas être poussé jusqu'à ses extrêmes conséquences, car cela aurait fini par vider de sens une entreprise militaire qui visait non seulement l'imposition d'un État islamique pleinement légitime, mais aussi l'islamisation en profondeur des populations soumises. À cela s'ajoute le constat d'une présence haoussa parmi les partisans du jihad dès sa première phase, ainsi que des efforts déployés par Usman dan Fodio et par ses successeurs pour gagner les Haoussas à leur cause, entre autres par la composition de poèmes oraux dans leur langue[60]. Toutefois, la primauté accordée à la dimension politique dans la légitimation du jihad, bien visible à travers l'énonciation du principe « *ḥukm al-balad ḥukm sulṭānihi* », renforce l'impression que dans l'idéologie qui l'a inspiré, l'objectif prioritaire était tout simplement de remplacer un pouvoir noir mécréant par un pouvoir peul authentiquement islamique.

Le *takfīr* du pays haoussa et de l'ensemble du *bilād al-sūdān* a été repris, par des arguments similaires plus ou moins développés, dans un grand nombre d'œuvres apologétiques d'Usman dan Fodio, ainsi que de son frère Abdullahi et de son fils Muḥammad Bello qui participèrent activement à tous les aspects politiques, militaires et intellectuels de son entreprise. Ce *takfīr* a fait également l'objet d'un débat polémique très serré avec Muḥammad al-Amīn al-Kānemī, un illustre représentant de la tradition intellectuelle du sultanat de Bornou, qui sur le plan doctrinal lança un sérieux défi à leurs arguments, et sur le plan militaire se montra capable de réorganiser l'armée de son sultan, jusqu'à opposer une résistance victorieuse à l'expansion vers l'Est de l'État de Sokoto[61]. Un point qui me semble important de relever ici, c'est que dans cette copieuse littérature polémique et apologétique, qui servira de référence doctrinale et de source d'inspiration aux théoriciens et chefs politico-militaires des jihads ouest-africains suivants, la présence du binôme *dār al-islām* / *dār al-ḥarb* et, plus encore, des nombreux synonymes de ces deux expressions, avec ou parfois sans article (*bilād al-islām, bilād islām, balad al-islām, mudun al-islām* ... vs. *dār ḥarb, balad ḥarb, bilād kufr, bilād al-kafara* ...) est beaucoup plus récurrente que dans les sources précédentes évoquées plus haut dans cet article.

---

60 V. Mervyn Hiskett, *A History of Hausa Islamic Verse* (London: SOAS, 1975).

61 Sur cette polémique, voir notamment Louis Brenner, « The Jihad Debate between Sokoto and Borno: an Historical Analysis of Islamic Political Discourse in Nigeria », in *Peoples and Empires in African History: Essays in Memory of Michael Crowder*, éd. par J. F. Ade Ajayi et J. D. Y. Peel (London: Longman, 1992), 21-43; cf. aussi Zappa, « Syncrétisme ou radicalisme ? ».

Nous retrouvons là, dans un contexte périphérique et à une époque très tardive, un nouvel avatar du phénomène observé par Giovanna Calasso, dans une perspective comparative, sur un échantillon de sources historiographiques et juridiques « classiques » d'époque médiévale : c'est en effet toujours en relation à une *hijra* que le binôme *dār al-islām / dār al-ḥarb* assume toute sa prégnance et, qui plus est, tout son potentiel dynamique[62]. Le *dār al-hijra* fondée par Usman dan Fodio peut alors être appréhendée, dans cette perspective, comme un prolongement non seulement de la Médine du Prophète, mais aussi des *amṣār* fondés par les premiers califes, et qualifiés eux-aussi de *dār al-hijra* dans les sources médiévales : ce n'est d'ailleurs pas un hasard si la réussite militaire du jihad s'est accompagnée de la fondation d'abord de la nouvelle capitale, Sokoto, puis de plusieurs autres nouvelles entités urbaines, dans un effort de sédentarisation des nomades peuls et de consolidation de la redéfinition de l'espace conquis en vue d'une expansion ultérieure qui s'inspirait consciemment du modèle du calife « bien dirigé » ʿUmar ibn al-Ḫaṭṭāb, tel que le représentait l'historiographie musulmane[63].

4 Conclusions

Ce qu'on peut retenir provisoirement de ce survol sur presque un millénaire d'histoire précoloniale de l'islam en Afrique de l'Ouest, c'est le caractère extrêmement flou et changeant de la frontière entre *dār al-islām* et *dār al-kufr* au *bilād al-sūdān* au gré des auteurs et des époques, loin de l'image d'une expansion lente mais constante ou d'un rétrécissement progressif. L'appartenance du *bilād al-sūdān* au *dār al-islām*, d'abord niée en bloc au moment des premiers contacts entre les deux « rives » du Sahara, est ensuite, dans une longue première phase, revendiquée petit à petit pour des territoires de plus en plus vastes, représentés au début comme des enclaves, puis identifiés à des États dont l'expansion semble constante, à tel point que lors de l'effondrement de ces États, un souci s'impose de réaffirmer cette appartenance au-delà de toute frontière politique passée ou présente. Toutefois, dans une phase ultérieure, il s'agira de remettre en question cette appartenance pour l'ensemble de la région, comme prélude nécessaire à la mise en place de formations étatiques encore plus vastes et de plus en plus consciemment structurées selon un modèle islamique légitimant. Tout au long de cette histoire, marquée aussi bien par une expansion de l'islam que par une redéfinition périodique de ses paradigmes

62 Cf. Calasso, « Alla ricerca di *dār al-islām* », 276-79.

63 Cf. Murray Last, *The Sokoto Caliphate* (London: Longman, 1967).

identitaires et territoriaux, la question de l'appartenance au *dār al-islām* fait l'objet d'un débat périodiquement relancé, et apparaît donc comme un enjeu majeur dont l'importance semble augmenter au fil du temps: on passe, ainsi, de la simple exigence pratique de cautionner un commerce légalement suspect, à celle de mettre les musulmans de la région à l'abri des abus des pilleurs d'esclaves, jusqu'à l'objectif, bien plus ambitieux, de reformer en profondeur l'islam local, dans sa dimension à la fois politique et doctrinale.

Néanmoins, au-delà de ce constat d'un surenchérissement progressif des enjeux de cette classification, l'approche aux sources proposée jusqu'ici ne me semble pas suggérer une lecture téléologique de l'islamisation de l'Afrique de l'Ouest en continuité avec le célèbre modèle évolutif articulé sur trois stades (*quarantine / mixing / reform*), qui a été introduit par Humphrey J. Fisher et repris, à quelques nuances près, par Nehemia Levtzion et par une partie importante des études désormais classiques consacrées aux grands jihads ouest-africains[64]. En effet, le fait que l'époque marquée par ces entreprises militaires et religieuses ait précédé immédiatement la conquête coloniale britannique et française de la zone sahélienne a fini, à mon avis, par contribuer à alimenter cette sorte d'illusion optique qui fait de ces jihads l'aboutissement inévitable du « cours naturel » de l'islamisation de cette région, « interrompu » ou plutôt « détourné » par la colonisation. Cependant, l'histoire des jihads ouest-africains a été suffisamment longue et complexe pour nous montrer qu'une fois établis, les États issus de ces mouvements ont tendance à devenir des États comme les autres : d'un côté, ils sont amenés par les exigences de la *Realpolitik* à nouer des relations diplomatiques avec des États musulmans locaux « non reformés », voire parfois avec des souverains non-musulmans[65] ; d'un autre côté, ils sont toujours susceptibles de faire l'objet d'un *takfīr* et d'un jihad de la part d'un nouveau réformateur armé, comme dans le cas très célèbre du conflit qui opposa l'empire oumarien à la Dīna du Macina à la moitié du XIXe siècle[66].

---

64 V. notamment Humphrey J. Fisher, « Conversion Reconsidered: Some Historical Aspects of Religious Conversion in Black Africa », *Africa* 43, nº 1 (janvier 1973): 27-40; Nehemia Levtzion, « Patterns of Islamization in West Africa », in *Conversion to Islam*, éd. par Nehemia Levtzion (New York: Holmes & Meier, 1979), 207-16.

65 V. Rowland Adevemi Adeleye, *Power and Diplomacy in Northern Nigeria, 1804-1906: The Sokoto Caliphate and its Enemies* (London: Longman, 1971).

66 Sur la dispute doctrinale qui accompagna ce conflit, v. Sidi Mohamed Mahibou et Jean-Louis Triaud, *Voilà ce qui est arrivé* / Bayān mā waqaʿa *d'al-Ḥajj ʿUmar al-Fūtī: Plaidoyer pour une guerre sainte en Afrique de l'Ouest au XIXe siècle* (Paris: Éditions du CNRS, 1983); Bintou Sanankoua, *Un empire peul au XIXe siècle: la Dina du Maasina* (Paris: Karthala / ACCT, 1990).

L'expérience du mouvement almoravide, dont le berceau se situe entre le Sahara et le Sahel, montre d'ailleurs la précocité, mais aussi la caducité du modèle de refondation du *dār al-islām* par le jihad en Afrique de l'Ouest, faute de la mise en place d'institutions capables de transformer profondément les société militairement soumises. Et même dans les cas les plus réussis, comme celui du jihad de Sokoto, la tension évoquée plus haut entre prosélytisme et sentiment d'appartenance à un « peuple élu » était toujours susceptible de limiter la portée de cette refondation du *dār al-islām* au-delà de la sphère politique et juridique *stricto sensu.*

La continuité de la tradition « suwarienne » jusqu'au seuil de la colonisation et bien au-delà dans plusieurs régions de l'Afrique de l'Ouest, et notamment dans la zone forestière, montre par ailleurs que le modèle de l'enclave musulmane était loin d'être dépassé par l'avènement des jihads. On peut également voir des variantes plus rigoristes du même modèle dans les différentes « hétérotopies maraboutiques » (pour reprendre l'heureuse définition proposée par Jean Schmitz)[67] qui ponctuent le *bilād al-sūdān* jusqu'à nos jours, et qu'on peut bien considérer comme autant d'exemples de *dār al-hijra* privées de la fonction de point de départ d'un jihad.

L'approche inclusive qu'on a vu à l'œuvre dans le recensement raisonné de *buldān wa-qabā'il* effectué par Aḥmad Bābā semble en revanche revenir périodiquement sous la plume de tout opposant d'un jihad, depuis le cas bien connu de Kānemī, redoutable adversaire doctrinal et militaire du jihad de Sokoto, jusqu'à des oulémas de l'époque coloniale comme Shaykh Muusa Kamara, auteur de précieux traités d'histoire locale commandités par des chercheurs-administrateurs français[68]. Dans ses échanges épistolaires avec les guides spirituels et politico-militaires du jihad de Sokoto, Kānemī réagit, en effet, aux prétentions d'une autorité politique islamique qui se veut plus légitime, voire la seule pleinement légitime, d'une manière qui n'est pas sans rappeler la réaction d'Aḥmad Bābā à l'invasion marocaine et à ses prétentions « califales » d'unification de la umma. Dans les deux cas, il s'agit non seulement

67 Cette notion, introduite sans doute pour la première fois dans Jean Schmitz, « Un politologue chez les marabouts », *Cahiers d'Etudes Africaines* 23, n° 91 (1983): 329-51, a été reprise par ce chercheur dans plusieurs travaux, dont notamment Jean Schmitz, « Hétérotopies maraboutiques au Sénégal: *jihad, hijra* et migrations internationales », in *Figures d'islam après le 11 septembre: Disciples et martyrs, réfugiés et migrants*, éd. par A. Mohammad-Arif et Jean Schmitz (Paris: Karthala, 2006), 169-200. Pour quelques exemples historiques d'hétérotopies maraboutiques, cf. plus haut, n. 2.

68 V. notamment Shaykh Muusa Kamara, *Florilège au jardin de l'histoire des Noirs* / Zuhūr al-basātīn. *Traduction de Saïd Bousbina, sous la direction et avec une introduction de Jean Schmitz* (Paris: CNRS Editions, 1998).

de réaffirmer son allégeance à un État islamique détruit (dans le cas de l'empire songhaï) ou survivant (dans le cas de l'empire de Bornou), ou de défendre le prestige de la tradition savante musulmane locale, mais aussi de réaffirmer l'appartenance de plein droit des populations locales à l'espace musulman global, au-delà de tout constat d'une persistance de coutumes préislamiques reprouvés[69].

Il me semble, par conséquent, plus approprié de voir ces trois moments du débat autour du statut du *bilād al-sūdān* tout simplement comme représentatifs d'une typologie d'approches et de positionnements qui ont tendance à revenir dans nos sources d'une manière périodique, parfois cyclique, mais le plus souvent imprévisible[70].

Références

Abitbol, Michel. *Tombouctou et les Arma: De la conquête marocaine du Soudan nigérien en 1591 à l'hégémonie de l'Empire Peul du Macina en 1833*. Paris: Maisonneuve et Larose, 1979.

Adeleye, Rowland Adevemi. « The Dilemma of the Wazir: The Place of the *Risālat al-wazīr ilā ahl al-ʿilm wa'l-tadabbur* in the History of the Conquest of the Sokoto Caliphate ». *Journal of the Historical Society of Nigeria* 4, nº 2 (juin 1968): 285-311.

Adeleye, Rowland Adevemi. *Power and Diplomacy in Northern Nigeria, 1804-1906: The Sokoto Caliphate and its Enemies*. London: Longman, 1971.

Aḥmad Bābā. *Miʿrāj al-Ṣuʿūd: Aḥmad Bābā's Replies on Slavery*. Traduit par John O. Hunwick et Fatima Harrak. Rabat: Publications of the Institute of African Studies – University Mohammed V Souissi, 2000.

69 Dans une lettre adressée à Usman dan Fodio, après avoir observé que certaines pratiques cultuelles préislamiques, reprochées par celui-ci aux gens de Bornou jusqu'à en faire une preuve pour les qualifier de mécréants, ressemblaient de près à des pratiques qu'il avait pu observer à Damiette (*« madīna ʿaẓīma min madāʾin al-islām »*), Kānemī en conclut : « il n'est de temps ni de pays sans son lot de péchés et désobéissances innombrables, et en cela l'Égypte et comme le Bornou, voire pire » (cit. dans Muḥammad Bello, *Infāq al-Maysūr fī taʾrīḫ bilād al-Takrūr*, publié sous le titre *Infaku'l Maisuri*, ed. from local mss by C. E. J. Whitting and the staff of the School for Arabic Studies, Kano (London: Luzac, 1951), 126-127. Pour une traduction anglaise de ce passage, v. Thomas Hodgkin, *Nigerian Perspectives : An Historical Anthology*, 2e éd. (Oxford: Oxford University Press, 1975), 263. On peut comparer ce passage avec l'extrait du *Miʿrāj al-ṣuʿūd* cité plus haut, à la fin de la note 37.

70 Cette approche typologique et « anti-téléologique » est redevable, entre autres, à Triaud, « L'islam en Afrique de l'Ouest », ainsi qu'à Louis Brenner, *Réflexions sur le savoir islamique en Afrique de l'Ouest* (Talence: Centre d'Études d'Afrique Noire, 1985).

Bello, Muḥammad. *Infāq al-Maysūr fī ta'rīḫ bilād al-Takrūr*, publié sous le titre *Infaku'l Maisuri*, ed. from local mss by C. E. J. Whitting and the staff of the School for Arabic Studies, Kano. London: Luzac, 1951.

Bonner, Michael. « The Arabian Silent Trade: Profit and Nobility in the "Markets of the Arabs" ». In *Histories of the Middle East: studies in Middle Eastern society, economy and law in honor of A. L. Udovitch*, édité par Roxani Eleni Margariti, Adam Abdelhamid Sabra, et Petra Sijpesteijn, 23-51. Islamic history and civilization, v. 79. Leiden: Brill, 2011.

Brenner, Louis. *Réflexions sur le savoir islamique en Afrique de l'Ouest*. Talence: Centre d'Études d'Afrique Noire, 1985.

Brenner, Louis. « The Jihad Debate between Sokoto and Borno: an Historical Analysis of Islamic Political Discourse in Nigeria ». In *Peoples and Empires in African History: Essays in Memory of Michael Crowder*, édité par J. F. Ade Ajayi et J. D. Y. Peel, 21-43. London: Longman, 1992.

Brett, Michael. « Islam and Trade in the *Bilād al-Sūdān*, Tenth-Eleventh Century A.D. » *The Journal of African History* 24, nº 4 (octobre 1983): 431-40.

Calasso, Giovanna. « Alla ricerca di *dār al-islām*. Una ricognizione nei testi di giuristi e tradizionisti, lessicografi, geografi e viaggiatori ». *Rivista degli Studi Orientali* 83 (2010): 271-96.

Cuoq, Joseph M., éd. *Recueil des sources arabes concernant l'Afrique Occidentale du VIIIe au XVIe siècle (Bilād al-Sūdān)*. Paris: Editions du CNRS, 1975.

Fisher, Humphrey J. « Conversion Reconsidered: Some Historical Aspects of Religious Conversion in Black Africa ». *Africa* 43, nº 1 (janvier 1973): 27-40.

García Novo, Marta. « La doctrina mālikí sobre esclavitud y el *Mi'rāŷ* de Aḥmad Bābā ». *Espacio, Tiempo y Forma*, Serie III (Historia Medieval) 23 (2010): 75-95.

García Novo, Marta. « Islamic law and slavery in premodern West Africa ». *Entremons. UPF Journal of World History* 2 (novembre 2011). http://www.upf.edu/entremons/numero2/garcia.html.

García Novo, Marta. « Ulemas malikíes del *bilad al-Sudan* en la obra biográfica de Ahmad Baba al-Tinbukti (963/1556-1036/1627) ». In *Biografías magrebíes: identidades y grupos religiosos, sociales y políticos en el Magreb medieval*, édité par Mohamed Meouak, 417-82. Madrid: Consejo Superior de Investigaciones Científicas, 2012.

Hall, Bruce S. *A History of Race in Muslim West Africa, 1600-1960*. African Studies 115. Cambridge: Cambridge University Press, 2011.

Hiskett, Mervyn. « *Kitāb al-Farq*: A Work on the Habe Kingdoms Attributed to 'Uthmān dan Fodio ». *Bulletin of the School of Oriental and African Studies* 23, nº 3 (1960): 558-79.

Hiskett, Mervyn. *A History of Hausa Islamic Verse*. London: SOAS, 1975.

Hodgkin, Thomas. *Nigerian Perspectives : An Historical Anthology*. 2e éd. Oxford: Oxford University Press, 1975.

Hoven, Eduard van. « Medina Gounass: The end of a religious isolate ». *ISIM Newsletter* 4 (1999): 25.

Hunwick, John O. « Aḥmad Bābā and the Moroccan Invasion of the Sūdān (1591) ». *Journal of the Historical Society of Nigeria* 2, n° 3 (1962): 311-28.

Hunwick, John O., éd. *Sharīʿa in Songhay: the replies of al-Maghīlī to the questions of Askia al-Ḥājj Muḥammad.* Oxford: Published for British Academy by Oxford University Press, 1985.

Hunwick, John O. « Aḥmad Bābā on Slavery ». *Sudanic Africa* 11 (2000): 131-39.

Hunwick, John O. « A Region of the Mind: Medieval Arab Views of African Geography and Ethnography and their Legacy ». *Sudanic Africa* 16 (2005): 103-36.

Ibn Abî Zayd al-Qayrawânî. *La Risâla ou Epître sur les éléments du dogme et de la loi de l'Islâm selon le rite mâlikite. Texte arabe et traduction française avec un avant-propos, des notes et trois index par Léon Bercher.* 1re éd. 1945. Alger: Editions Populaires de l'Armée, s. d.

Kamara, Shaykh Muusa. *Florilège au jardin de l'histoire des Noirs* / Zuhūr al-basātīn. *Traduction de Saïd Bousbina, sous la direction et avec une introduction de Jean Schmitz.* Paris: CNRS Editions, 1998.

Last, Murray. *The Sokoto Caliphate.* London: Longman, 1967.

Launay, Robert. « Des infidèles d'un autre type: Les réponses au pouvoir colonial dans une communauté musulmane de Côte d'Ivoire ». In *Le Temps des marabouts: Itinéraires et stratégies islamiques en Afrique Occidentale Française v. 1880-1960*, édité par David Robinson et Jean-Louis Triaud, 415-30. Paris: Karthala, 1997.

Levtzion, Nehemia. « Patterns of Islamization in West Africa ». In *Conversion to Islam*, édité par Nehemia Levtzion, 207-16. New York: Holmes & Meier, 1979.

Levtzion, Nehemia. « Islam in the Bilad al-Sudan to 1800 ». In *The History of Islam in Africa*, édité par Nehemia Levtzion et Randall Lee Pouwels, 63-91. Athens: Ohio University Press, 2000.

Levtzion, Nehemia., et J. F. P. Hopkins, éd. *Corpus of early Arabic sources for West African history*. Traduit par J. F. P. Hopkins. Cambridge: Cambridge University Press, 1981.

Lovejoy, Paul E. « Islam, slavery, and political transformation in West Africa: constraints on the trans-Atlantic slave trade ». *Outre-mers* 89, n° 336-37 (2002): 247-82.

Lovejoy, Paul E. « Slavery, the Bilād al-Sūdān and the Frontiers of the African Diasporas ». In *Slavery on the Frontiers of Islam*, édité par Paul E. Lovejoy. Princeton: Marcus Wiener Publishers, 2004.

Mahibou, Sidi Mohamed, et Jean-Louis Triaud. *Voilà ce qui est arrivé* / Bayān mā waqaʿa *d'al-Ḥajj ʿUmar al-Fūtī: Plaidoyer pour une guerre sainte en Afrique de l'Ouest au XIXe siècle.* Paris: Éditions du CNRS, 1983.

Martin, Bradford G. « Unbelief in the Western Sudan: ʿUthman dan Fodio's *Taʿlim al-ikhwān* ». *Middle Eastern Studies* 4, n° 1 (octobre 1967): 50-97.

Moraes Farias, Paulo Fernando de. « Silent Trade: Myth and Historical Evidence ». *History in Africa* 1 (1974): 9-24.

Palmer, H. Richmond. « An Early Fulani Conception of Islam ». *Journal of the Royal African Society* 13, n° 52 (juillet 1914): 407-414; 14, n° 53 (octobre 1914): 53-59; 14, n° 54 (janvier 1915): 185-92.

Robinson, David. *The Holy War of Umar Tal: The Western Sudan in the Mid-Nineteenth Century*. Oxford: Clarendon Press, 1985.

Robinson, David. « Revolutions in the Western Sudan ». In *The History of Islam in Africa*, édité par Nehemia Levtzion et Randall Lee Pouwels, 131-52. Athens: Ohio University Press, 2000.

Robinson, David., et Jean-Louis Triaud, éd. *Le Temps des marabouts: Itinéraires et stratégies islamiques en Afrique Occidentale Française v. 1880-1960*. Paris: Karthala, 1997.

Saad, Elias. *Social History of Timbuktu*. Cambridge: Cambridge University Press, 1983.

Sanankoua, Bintou. *Un empire peul au XIXe siècle: la Dina du Maasina*. Paris: Karthala / ACCT, 1990.

Schmitz, Jean. « Un politologue chez les marabouts ». *Cahiers d'Etudes Africaines* 23, n° 91 (1983): 329-51.

Schmitz, Jean. « Hétérotopies maraboutiques au Sénégal: *jihad, hijra* et migrations internationales ». In *Figures d'islam après le 11 septembre: Disciples et martyrs, réfugiés et migrants*, édité par A. Mohammad-Arif et Jean Schmitz, 169-200. Paris: Karthala, 2006.

Triaud, Jean-Louis. « L'islam en Afrique de l'Ouest. Une histoire urbaine dans la longue durée ». In *Islam et villes en Afrique au sud du Sahara: Entre soufisme et fondamentalisme*, édité par Adriana Piga, 129-48. Paris: Karthala, 2003.

Udovitch, Abraham L. « Ḳirāḍ ». *Encyclopaedia of Islam, Vol. V, Khe-Mahi*. Leiden: Brill, 1986.

'Uṯmān Ibn Fūdī. *Bayān wujub al-hijra 'alā l-'ibād wa-bayān wujūb naṣb al-imām wa-iqāmat al-jihād*. Édité par Fathi Hasan El-Masri. Khartum and Oxford: Khartum University Press and Oxford University Press, 1978.

Wane, Yaya. « Ceerno Muhamadu Sayid Baa. Le soufisme intégral de Madiina Gunaas (Sénégal) ». *Cahiers d'Études Africaines* 14, n° 56 (1974): 671-98.

Wilks, Ivor. « The Juula and the Expansion of Islam into the Forest ». In *The History of Islam in Africa*, édité par Nehemia Levtzion et Randall Lee Pouwels, 93-115. Athens: Ohio University Press, 2000.

Zappa, Francesco. « Syncrétisme ou radicalisme ? Modèles d'islamisation en conflit au Nigéria septentrional précolonial ». In *Islam et villes en Afrique au sud du Sahara: Entre soufisme et fondamentalisme*, édité par Adriana Piga, 241-55. Paris: Karthala, 2003.

Zappa, Francesco. « Écrire l'islam en bambara. Lieux, réseaux et enjeux de l'entreprise d'al-Hājj Modibo Diarra ». *Archives de sciences sociales des religions* 147 (juillet-septembre 2009): 167-86.

Zouber, Mahmoud A. *Ahmad Bābā de Tombouctou: sa vie et son œuvre*. Paris: Maisonneuve et Larose, 1977.

PART 5

Modern and Contemporary Developments

CHAPTER 15

Faith as Territory: *dār al-islām* and *dār al-ḥarb* in Modern Shi'i Sufism

Alessandro Cancian

1 Introduction

In this article I will grapple with two main obstacles, which are determined by my choice of topic. The first is that, when we talk about the concepts of *dār al-islām* and *dār al-ḥarb*, we normally and immediately think of the classical distinction between the two that has been conceptualized in Sunni Islam, that highly abstract form of Islam usually taught in introductory, general courses at universities across the globe. I agree that many of these courses have, for a long time now, been offering substantial information about minorities—often under the misleading label of "heterodox" Islam—and that primers on Islam include informative pieces on Shi'ism and its sub-categories. However, when students approach Islam they are normally taught about concepts such as the "five pillars", the "gate of *ijtihād*", and other grand categories that are indeed useful to the beginner, but do not usually highlight how these concepts have been formed at a specific time and within a specific cultural framework, and are by no means to be considered universal.

The second obstacle has to do with the fact that I am addressing a minority of a minority, i.e. Shi'i Sufism, which turns the terms of the question upside down. This is because, firstly, the Sufis themselves, as we will see, shift the coordinates of the discourse from the geographical/juridical to the spiritual/metaphysical, and, secondly, because Sufism has often been viewed as a dangerous competitor by mainstream Shi'i ulema, who have repeatedly applied the entire weight of their authority to try to displace the Sufis from the guarded domain of orthodoxy and discredit them as *ḥarbī*s, that is individuals whose blood and property are deemed to be *ḥalāl*.

2 *Dar al-islām* and *dār al-ḥarb* in Imami Hadith

As far as the classical Sunni understanding is concerned, the dichotomous division of the world has been extensively explored. Although the multiple

 | DOI 10.1163/9789004331037_017

facets of its articulations throughout history are far from being fully reflected in the academic literature, the variability of its theory as well as of its practice has been hinted at in recent literature. What emerges from a survey of this literature is that the monolithic perceptions of the vulgate should be robustly revised in favor of a more nuanced and varied outlook, one which takes into account juridical theory and practice throughout history and across the doctrinal spectrums. Sunni Hadith collections do not seem to give *dār al-islām* primary importance, and the term is absent from Buḫārī's *Ṣaḥīḥ*, for instance, as shown in a recent study by Giovanna Calasso.[1]

Be that as it may, Muslim scholars and laypersons have maintained, to some extent, a dichotomous view of the world. Whether or not this view is firmly rooted in the Qur'an and the Hadith, and in original legal practice is of little concern here. What we do know is that, at some point in the eighth century, the division of the world into *dār al-islām* and *dār al-ḥarb* was common currency among Muslims; it was not fundamentally challenged and did not seem to need much explanation. This fact holds true for Sunni and Shi'i environments alike.[2]

Implied in the divide is the notion of border. The concept of *ḥadd*, whose meaning is more generically that of "limit" rather than "border," is a very flexible one.[3] For instance, as shown by the political geography, borders and frontiers were provided, in the Medieval Islamic world as in virtually any other pre-nation state civilization, by the network of cities and the highways that interconnected them. Given the volatile nature of boundaries and frontiers, a

1 Giovanna Calasso, "Alla ricerca di *dār al-islām*. Una ricognizione nei testi di giuristi e tradizionisti, lessicografi, geografi e viaggiatori," *Rivista degli Studi Orientali* 83 (2010): 271–96.

2 On Shi'i Hadith see Gérard Lecomte, "Aspects de la littérature du *ḥadīṯ* chez les imāmites," in *Le shî'isme imamite: colloque de Strasbourg (6–9 mai 1968)* (Paris: Presses Universitaires de France, 1970), 90–103; Harald Löschner, *Die dogmatischen Grundlagen des šī'itischen Rechts: eine Untersuchung zur modernen imāmitischen Rechtsquellenlehre* (Köln: Carl Heymanns Verlag, 1971); Etan Kohlberg, "Shīʿī Ḥadīth," in *The Cambridge History of Arabic Literature, Vol. I: Arabic Literature to the End of Umayyad Period*, ed. Albert Felix Landon Beeston et al. (Cambridge: Cambridge University Press, 1983), 299–307. For earlier sources, see Mohammad Ali Amir-Moezzi, *Le Guide divin dans le shī'isme originel: aux sources de l'ésotérisme en islam* (Paris: Verdier, 1992), in particular pp. 51–56 etc. (see Mohammad Ali Amir-Moezzi, *The Spirituality of Shi'i Islam: Beliefs and Practices* [London: Tauris [u.a.], 2011], 193, n. 1).

3 See Ralph W. Brauer, "Boundaries and Frontiers in Medieval Muslim Geography," *Transactions of the American Philosophical Society* 85, no. 6 (1995): 1–73; Michael Bonner, *Aristocratic Violence and Holy War: Studies in the Jihad and the Arab-Byzantine Frontier*, American Oriental Series 81 (New Haven, Connecticut: American Oriental Society, 1996).

clear-cut distinction could not be made between what fell within the limits of a boundary and what fell outside, between Islamic and non-Islamic territories, between "ourselves" and "the other".

This situation is reflected in the juridical literature of Imamism, as well in Shi'i Hadith.[4] In Kulaynī's (d. 329/941) *Kāfī*, for example, the dyadic concept *dār al-islām / dār al-ḥarb* does appear, although not in a systematic and codified manner. Its use probably mirrored the popular understanding of the concept at the time the book was compiled, which was some decades after the notion was codified by the scholars of classical jurisprudence in the second/eighth and third/ninth centuries.[5] The concept does not seem to be used in its technical juridical sense; rather, it is accompanied by another dualism typically referred to in early Shi'ism, i.e. the dual notion of the enemies of the *ahl al-bayt* and their friends.[6] This was a central distinction in early Imamism, which kept on in Shi'i doctrine and later assumed gnostic and esoteric nuances. Overall, this second categorization seems to carry more weight, and we find it throughout many Shi'i reports and juridical literature. The "book of faith and unbelief" of the *Kāfī*[7] does not assign the label of *ḥarbī* to those who live in non-Muslim territories, but rather focuses on the internal subdivision of people based on their allegiance to the *ahl al-bayt* according to their respective good and bad qualities.

Although it is not correct to assert that the expression does not occur in the corpus of Imami traditions (the expression is well attested to in the *Kāfī*, along with the *arḍ al-ḥarb* mentioned by Algar),[8] what is in fact true is that it is not given primacy there; rather, the imams constantly remind believers that they are at war with those who are at war with the members of the family of the Prophet. Additionally, with the occultation of the twelfth imam, the concept

---

4 On jurisprudence in Shi'i Islam, see Hossein Modarressi Tabataba'i, *An Introduction to Shīʿī Law: A Bibliographical Study* (London: Ithaca Press, 1984); Yvon Linant de Bellefonds, "Le droit imâmite," in *Le shīʿisme imamite: colloque de Strasbourg (6–9 mai 1968)* (Paris: Presses Universitaires de France, 1970), 183–200; Robert Gleave, *Inevitable Doubt: Two Theories of Shīʿī Jurisprudence*, Studies in Islamic Law and Society, v. 12 (Leiden: Brill, 2000).

5 See Calasso, "Alla ricerca di *dār al-islām*."

6 On this dualism, which is a characteristic feature of early Imami Qur'anic exegesis and of exegetical material in general, see Me'ir Mikha'el Bar-Asher, *Scripture and Exegesis in Early Imāmī-Shiism*, Islamic Philosophy, Theology, and Science, v. 37 (Leiden: Brill, 1999).

7 Abū Jaʿfar Muḥammad al-Kulaynī, *al-Uṣūl min al-kāfī* (n.p., n.d.), 2:2–464.

8 Hamid Algar, "Dār al-ḥarb," *Encyclopaedia Iranica, Vol. VI, Coffeehouse–Dārā* (London: Routledge & Kegan Paul, 1993).

ceased to have juridical effect, as offensive war was no longer allowed in the absence of the *walī al-amr*.[9] According to Algar,

> The concept *of dār al-ḥarb* was not developed in any special way in Shi'ite jurisprudence. The term itself does not occur in traditions related to the imams, but only the equivalent *arḍ al-ḥarb*.... Although the imams regarded the Umayyad and Abbasid caliphs as usurpers, they permitted their followers to buy slaves captured on forays mounted into *dār al-ḥarb* under caliphal authority.... Shi'ite jurists did, however, establish a third category of territory, *dār al-īmān* (realm of faith), defined by prevailing acceptance of the imams among its people. Greater theoretical importance was given to the opposition between this realm and *dār al-islām* than to that between *dār al-islām* and *dār al-ḥarb*....

A cursory look at the Shi'i juridical literature across the centuries will show how the concept is far from being clearly and univocally treated. The *šayḫ al-ṭā'ifa* Abū Ja'far al-Ṭūsī (d. 460/1067), in his *Nihāya*, states that it is obligatory to fight all those unbelievers who oppose Islam, except those who fall into one of the following two categories: in the first are those from whom nothing can be accepted but conversion to Islam, and who may be killed or taken captive and their goods seized. This encompasses all the unbelievers who are not Jews, Christians or Zoroastrians. Into the second category fall those from whom the *jizya* is taken, i.e. the three aforementioned groups. The condition is, as usual, that the call to jihad is issued by the imam, or by his representative. It is in this context that the expressions *dār al-ḥarb* and *dār al-islām* come into play, without further explanation, which suggests that they must have had currency among Shi'is as they did among Sunnis: "who became Muslim and is afterwards in the *dār al-ḥarb*, his being Muslim protects him from being killed, and his children are equally protected from being taken captive. But, for his sons who have reached the age of maturity, a different rule is applied than that applied to the unbelievers: whatever is of dead stock (*ṣāmit*), or of commodities or of personal effects, is to be taken and it is not possible to bring it into the *dār al-islām*.... As for the lands and estates and whatever is not mobile, it must be given to the Muslims (*fay' li'l-muslimīn*)."[10] This view presented by Ṭūsī must have mirrored the one prevalent at the time in Baghdad where, prior to

---

9 Abdulaziz Abdulhussein Sachedina, *The just ruler (al-sulṭān al-'ādil) in Shi'ite Islam: the comprehensive authority of the jurist in Imamite jurisprudence* (New York: Oxford Univ. Press, 1998), 111.

10 Abū Ja'far Muḥammad al-Ṭūsī, *Al-Nihāya fī mujarrad al-fiqh wa'l-fatāwā* (Beirut: Dār al-Kitāb al-'arabī, 1390AH), 291–93.

the Saljuq conquest, both the dwellers of the *dār al-ḥarb* and the *dār al-islām* enjoyed protection and support and were free to benefit from the shared culture of a cosmopolitan capital.

Commenting on Šayḫ al-Mufīd's (d. 413/1032) *al-Muqniʿa*, Ṭūsī[11] mentions the three conditions required for a call to jihad. While the first two do not bear signs of territoriality, the third condition has a clear geographical element to it: *mušrikī al-ʿAjam, yaʿnī al-Turk, wa'l-Ḫazar wa'l-Daylam* (the pagans of ʿAjam, that is the Turks, the Khazars and the Dailamites [i.e. the inhabitants of the region south and north of the Caspian Sea]). However, the expression *dār al-ḥarb* is not mentioned. In the jurist Muḥaqqiq al-Ḥillī's (d. 726/1326) *Šarāyiʿ al-islām*,[12] the category of the *ḥarbī* is very clearly in existence. Less defined, however, is the notion of *ḥarbī*. In any case, the discussion is purely theoretical, as offensive jihad is subject to the presence of the imam, upon whose authority alone a call to war can be issued. The famous Safavid era jurist ʿAlī al-Karakī (d. 940/1534) mentions *dār al-širk* in a passage where the unlawfulness of taking residence in a domain under the unbeliever's control is established for whomever is unable to follow the laws of Islam and has the means to emigrate.[13] The expression is not detailed further, and its meaning seems to have been widely understood at the time. The juridical validity of the categories employed by Karakī, however, appears blurred by reference to the abovementioned dualism between the followers of the imams and ordinary Muslims who are not loyal to them, which confirms the complexity that the typical Shi'i dualism adds to this juridical domain.

The overall focus in the Shi'i juridical literature is not, therefore, on territoriality, although the territorial dimension does in fact play a role. When we look at how the issue of migration is treated in Shi'i Hadith collections and *fiqh* treatises, this shift in focus emerges more clearly. Adding to the voluminous literature discussing the case of the lawfulness or unlawfulness for a Muslim to migrate to, or to reside in, a non-Muslim territory,[14] Shi'i scholars, reflecting their minority position, emphasized that a Muslim's knowledge (*ʿilm*)—whose source is devotion to the imam—was more important than the place in which

11 Abū Jaʿfar Muḥammad al-Ṭūsī, *Tahḏīb al-aḥkām fī šarḥ al-Muqniʿa li'l-šayḫ al-Mufīd* (Beirut: Dār al-Taʿāruf, 1401AH), 136–37.

12 Muḥaqqiq al-Ḥillī, *Šarāyiʿ al-islām*, ed. Muḥammad Taqī Dāniš-Pažūh, trans. Abū'l-Qāsim b. Aḥmad Yazdī (Tehran: Intishārāt-i Dānishgāh-i Tihrān, 1358SH), 1:109–13.

13 Nūr al-dīn ʿAlī b. al-Ḥusayn al-Karakī, *Jāmiʿ al-maqāṣid fī šarḥ al-qawāʿid* (Qum: Mu'assisa-yi Āl al-bayt li-iḥyā' al-turāṯ, 1414), 3:384.

14 On which see Khaled Abou El Fadl, "Islamic Law and Muslim Minorities: The Juristic Discourse on Muslim Minorities from the Second/Eighth to the Eleventh/Seventeenth Centuries," *Islamic Law and Society* 1, no. 2 (1994): 141–87.

he or she chose to live. In the case, discussed also by the Hanafis and the Shafi'is, of the Prophet allowing the nomads who had converted to Islam not to join his *hijra* to Medina, reports in al-Ḥurr al-ʿĀmilī's *Wasāʾil*[15] affirm that while it is lawful for a Muslim not to migrate to a place under Islamic law, it is not desirable for him to live apart from those who have knowledge, because that is conducive to ignorance. Given the multidimensional meaning of the term *ʿilm*, which in early sources had supernatural and initiatory nuances related to the metaphysical position of the imam in Shi'i cosmology,[16] it is not difficult to see here reference to the hierarchical pre-eminence of the inner dimension of the faith over the outer dimension of the territorial and juridical divide. In fact, this is reflected in a *riwāya* attested to in Kulaynī's *Kāfī*, which says that being in the presence of the imam, who is the possessor of *ʿilm*, is equal to staying in the *dār al-ʿilm*, while being taken away from the imam is equal to living under the unbeliever's rule in the *dār al-jahl*.[17]

3 *Dār al-islām/dār al-ḥarb* in Gunābādī Literature

The Gunābādī *silsila* is an offshoot of the Niʿmat-Allāhī order. The history and vicissitudes of this branch of Persian Sufism are well known, but there are still some significant areas of shadow, particularly regarding its Indian "exile" period.[18] The order dates back to the time of Shah Niʿmat Allāh Walī

15 Muḥammad b. al-Ḥasan al-Ḥurr al-ʿĀmilī, *Wasāʾil al-Šīʿa*, ed. Aḥmad al-Rabbānī al-Šīrāzī (Beirut: Dār al-Turāṯ al-ʿarabī, 1403AH), 11:75–76.

16 See Amir-Moezzi, *Le Guide divin dans le shīʿisme originel*, 174–99. On the evolution of the term, see Mohammad Ali Amir-Moezzi, "Réflexions sur une evolution du shiʿisme duodécimain: tradition et idéologisation," in *Les retours aux Écritures: fondamentalismes présents et passés* [*actes du colloque de Paris, 27–30 janvier 1992*], ed. Evelyne Patlagean and Alain Le Boulluec (Louvain: Peeters, 1993), 63–82; see also Mohammad Ali Amir-Moezzi, "Savoir est pouvoir. Exégèses et implication du miracle dans l'imamisme ancien (Aspects de l'imamologie duodécimaine V)," in *Miracle et karāma. Hagiographies médiévales comparées* 2, ed. Denise Aigle, Bibliothèque de l'Ecole des Hautes Etudes, Sciences Religieuses, 109 (Turnhout: Brepols, 2000).

17 Quoted in Sulṭān ʿAlī Shah, *Majmaʿ al-Saʿādat* (Tehran: Ḥaqīqat, 1379), 115.

18 The modern history of the Niʿmat-Allāhīya has been made available to the Western readership in a detailed and informative article by Leonard Lewisohn, "An Introduction to the History of Modern Persian Sufism, Part I: The Niʿmatullāhī Order: Persecution, Revival and Schism," *Bulletin of the School of Oriental and African Studies* 61, no. 3 (1998): 437; while Fabrizio Speziale, "À propos du renouveau *Niʿmatullāhī*: Le centre de Hyderabad au cours de la première modernité," *Studia Iranica* 42, no. 1 (2013): 91–118, has shed light on some uncharted aspects of the obscure history of the second phase of the order in India,

(d. 834/1431), a charismatic mystic and poet of the Qādirī order and disciple of Sheikh Abū ʿAbd Allāh al-Yāfiʿī (d. 768/1367). Shah Niʿmat Allāh Walī was born in Aleppo, but eventually settled in the area of Kerman. By the time he arrived there, he had already acquired significant fame as a spiritual master. His charisma and personality allowed for his spiritual offshoot to be considered a *ṭarīqa* in its own right, which came to be known as Niʿmat-Allāhiyya.[19] When the Bahmanid ruler of the Deccan, Aḥmad Shah Bahmanī (d. 839/1436), in two subsequent letters invited first the master and then his son to provide spiritual patronage to his kingdom and to move to the Subcontinent,[20] Shah Niʿmat Allāh sent his grandson Mīr Ḍiyā' al-dīn Nūr Allāh instead. The latter became connected to the royal family when he married Ahmad Shah's daughter. Ultimately, Shah Ḫalīl Allāh (d. 859/1455), Shah Niʿmat Allāh's son and successor as the head of the order, moved to Bidar, the then Bahmanid Capital of the Deccan, actually relocating the order in India in 1431. With the head and the heart of the order permanently settled away from the motherland, Shah Niʿmat Allāh's heirs in Iran lost their edge, gradually declining into a "moribund family tradition",[21] eventually disappearing from the history of Persian Sufism by the eleventh/seventeenth century. During this time, the order now resident in the Deccan entered into a close relationship with the Bahmanids, under whose rule it completed its Twelver Shi'i turn.[22] Little is known about the doctrinal history and mystical activity of the masters of the order from this time until the second half of the eleventh/seventeenth century, to the extent that, out of the six masters between Mīr Kamāl al-dīn ʿAṭiyyat Allāh (d. after 913/1508) and Mīr Maḥmūd Dakkānī (d. 1100/1689), almost nothing

that is after the masters moved from Bidar to Hyderabad. Another recent contribution is a study on the modern Iranian Niʿmat-Allāhī orders by Matthijs Van den Bos, *Mystic Regimes: Sufism and the State in Iran, from the Late Qajar Era to the Islamic Republic*, Social, Economic, and Political Studies of the Middle East and Asia, v. 83 (Leiden: Brill, 2002).

19 On the history of the order, see Hamid Algar, "Niʿmat-Allāhiyya," *Encyclopaedia of Islam, Vol. VIII, Ned-Sam* (Leiden: Brill, 1995); Nasrollah Pourjavady and Peter Lamborn Wilson, *Kings of Love. The Poetry and History of the Niʿmatullāhī Sufi Order*, Imperial Iranian Academy of Philosophy 30 (Teheran: Imperial Iranian Academy of Philosophy, 1978).

20 Pourjavady and Wilson, *Kings of Love*, 27–29.

21 Terry Graham, "The Niʿmatu'llāhī Order under Safavid Suppression and in Indian Exile," in *The Heritage of Sufism. Vol. 3: Late Classical Persianate Sufism (1501–1750): The Safavid & Mughal Period*, ed. Leonard Lewisohn and David Morgan (Oxford: Oneworld, 1999), 178.

22 Although the order assumed a Twelver Shi'i character, in the Deccan the masters of the order continued to be known as Qādirī Sufis or Qādirī-Kirmānis (ibid., 174).

has come down to us but the names.[23] However, it does not seem that their influence had extended any further than to the royal house in the Deccan, or beyond the Persian residents of the capital.[24] In 1689 the order moved from Bidar to Hyderabad, thanks to Sheikh ʿImād al-dīn Maḥmūd Ḥusaynī, a Sufi of Iraqi descent, and a shift in the modality of transmission of the leadership, which ceased to be patrilineal,[25] seems to have occurred. From Hyderabad, the Niʿmat-Allāhī order headed back to Iran, where it spearheaded the renaissance of Sufism in the twelfth/eighteenth and thirteenth/nineteenth centuries. As Leonard Lewisohn pointed out,[26] the history of modern Sufism in Iran began with Sayyid Maʿṣūm ʿAlī Shah's mission to Persia, inspired by Mīr Maḥmūd Dakkānī and corroborated by the powerful, charismatic authority of the subsequent master, Nūr ʿAlī Shah (d. 1212/1797).[27] Despite fierce opposition at the hands of the radical and already highly politicized exoteric clerics, Nūr ʿAlī Shah, through his charisma and painstaking effort, succeeded in gathering a large following, almost as if *taṣawwuf* was just smouldering under the ashes awaiting only a spark to set it ablaze anew. This renaissance, persisting despite clerical harassment[28] and the order's wavering relationship with the Zand and Qajar rulers and local governors,[29] bred more than one generation of charismatic masters, whose influence shaped the subsequent spiritual character of the order.

After the first noteworthy schism, which occurred during the time of the *quṭbiyya* of Majḏūb ʿAlī Shah, in 1823[30] despite mounting clerical opposition,

23 These six masters were Burhān al-dīn Ḫalīl Allāh II, Šams al-dīn Muḥammad, Ḥabīb al-dīn Muḥibb Allāh II, Šams al-dīn Muḥibb Allāh II, Kamāl al-dīn ʿAṭiyyat Allāh II, Šams al-dīn Muḥammad III (Mīrzā Muḥammad Sulṭānī Gunābādī, *Rahbarān-i ṭariqat wa-ʿirfān* [Tehran: Ḥaqīqat, 1379SH], 196).

24 Muhammad Suleiman Siddiqi, *The Bahmani Ṣūfīs* (Delhi: Idarah-i Adabiyat-i Delli, 1989).

25 Speziale, "À propos du renouveau *Niʿmatullāhī*."

26 Lewisohn, "An Introduction to the History of Modern Persian Sufism, Part I," 440.

27 Asad Allāh Īzadgušasb Gulpāygānī, *Nūr al-abṣār. Dar šarḥ-i ḥāl-i yagāna-ʿārif-i kāmil wa šāʿir-i fāḍil maʿrūf wa mašhūr-i mutaʾaḫḫirīn mawlānā Muḥammad ʿAlī "Nūr ʿAli Šāh" al-awwal-i Isfahānī* (Tehran: Ḥaqīqat, 1322SH).

28 Maʿṣūm ʿAlī Shah and Nūr ʿAlī Shah were both assassinated by fanatical clerics. Maʿṣūm ʿAlī Shah was killed by Āqā Muḥammad ʿAlī Bihbahānī, infamously known by the sobriquet *ṣūfī-kūš*, "the Sufi-killer", in 1211/1795 (see Maʿṣūm ʿAlī Šāh Šīrāzī, *Ṭarāʾiq al-ḥaqāʾiq*, 2nd ed. [Tehran: Intišārāt-i Sanāʾī, 1382SH], 3:174–75).

29 This relationship fluctuated between being one of patronage and one of persecution (Lewisohn, "An Introduction to the History of Modern Persian Sufism, Part I," 442–44).

30 The order split into three branches; the two lesser branches were known as the Šamsiyya and the Kawṯariyya (Algar, "Niʿmat-Allāhiyya"). The former, despite the small following of both, produced one of the most renowned Iranian mystics of thirteenth/nineteenth–fourteenth/twentieth centuries, Sayyid Ḥusayn Šams al-ʿUrafāʾ (d. 1353/1935).

the order faced a time of relative material improvement with Muḥammad Shah's accession to the throne. The shah himself was supportive of the dervishes, and his Grand Vizier, Mīrzā Āqāsī,[31] was a Sufi who was personally involved in improving the material conditions of the Sufis in Qajar Persia, being not just the shah's spiritual master but, to some extent, a social reformer. In 1861, after Raḥmat ʿAlī Shah's death, another dispute concerning the leadership of the order led to a second schism, whereby the Niʿmat-Allāhiyya split into the following branches: Munawwar-ʿAlī-Šāhī, Ṣafīʿ-Alī-Šāhī and Gunābādī, the latter being named after Gunābād, the town in Khorasan whence the masters of the branch hailed after 1872.

The Gunābādī order is probably the most influential of the branches of the Niʿmat-Allāhiyya in today's Iran. There are no statistics supporting this claim, nor the notables of the order keep a register of the members;[32] however, given the influence of the various branches of the *ṭarīqa* at different levels,[33] the numerous historical accounts that testify to their impetuous growth and widespread influence,[34] this widely attested notion can be held true. In the following paragraphs I will assess the topic of *dār al-islām* and *dār al-ḥarb* by referring to the wealth of literature produced by the masters and the notables of this order.

Attested to in classical Shi'i religious and juridical literature, the distinction was obvious to thirteenth/nineteenth century Shi'i Sufism, as the terms were visibly in use. While there seems to have been consensus about the general meaning of *dār al-islām* and *dār al-ḥarb* in thirteenth/nineteenth and fourteenth/twentieth century Iran, as there was for the term *ḥarbī*, there seem to be no practical guidelines as to their actual application. *Fiqh* and non-*fiqh*

---

31 See Abbas Amanat, "Āqāsī," *Encyclopaedia Iranica*, (Online Edition), accessed May 27, 2013, http://www.iranicaonline.org/articles/aqasff-ujuli-mnsz-adras-ivxni-ca for details.

32 As for the Gunābādī branch, see the current master's remarks in Alessandro Cancian, "Incontro con il Maestro della Neʿmatollâhiyya Gonâbâdiyya, Nûr ʿAlî Tâbandeh ʿMajzûb ʿAlî Shâh,'" in *Con i dervisci: otto incontri sul campo*, ed. Giovanni De Zorzi (Milano: Mimesis, 2013), 155–72.

33 See for example Van den Bos, *Mystic Regimes*; Lewisohn, "An Introduction to the History of Modern Persian Sufism, Part I."

34 Writing at the beginning of the nineteenth century, Sir John Malcolm gave figures that, however much the result of guesswork they are, reflect the health of the order at the time and the consequential concern of the ulema, who reacted violently to the threat posed to their authority. According to Malcolm, Maʿṣūm ʿAlī Shah and Nūr ʿAlī Shah's disciples amounted to a total of 90,000 (*History of Persia* [London: John Murray, 1829], 295–99). William M. Miller, writing circa one century later, however, reduces the supposed number to some 10,000, of which there were only 4,000 in Gunābād ("Shi'ah Mysticism (The Sufis of Gonabad)," *The Moslem World* 13 [1923]: 352).

treatises and literature mention the terms in a way that suggests that their meaning was generally accepted. However, as it was very much the case for mainstream Shi'i thought, twelfth/eighteenth and thirteenth/nineteenth century Shi'i Sufism did not seem to give it much importance. Even though a Shi'i state with more or less defined boundaries had existed since the inception of Safavid power, the territory of the Twelver state did not seem to have ever marked a territorial divide between *īmān* and *kufr*, even though attempts had been made to turn the focus of the religious center inwards through prioritizing pilgrimages to the Persian holy centers.[35] The holy centers of Shi'ism had long been under Ottoman control; thus the Shiʿa of Iraq, while formally residing in the *dār al-islām*, lived after all under the authority of a state that was, according to religious standards, illegitimate, and to some Shi'is even less desirable than a non-Muslim state. The concept seems not to have been endowed with geographical nuances. If this was the case for the typical Shi'i ulema then, it must have been even more so for the Shi'i Sufis, who had a long history of persecution and religious hostility from anti-Sufi Shiʿa. Twelfth/nineteenth century Sufis were well acquainted with the practical implication of the concept, because they were the object of an exclusive and discriminating use of it. The Shi'i ulema saw the Sufis as dangerous rivals, not only because they were battling with them over the hearts and souls of the Iranian people, but because they were doing so at a time when there was more than enough competition from both the Baha'is and the secularists. Most ulema, therefore, sought to denounce the Sufis as unbelievers in order to undermine their influence, end even took physical action against them.

To begin with, the attacks against the Sufis in early modern Iran were normally justified through relying on a scriptural basis. One famous, controversial Hadith, attributed to the eigth imam ʿAlī al-Riḍā was typically used:

> *Man ḏukira ʿindahu al-ṣūfiyya wa lam yunkirhum bi-lisānihi wa-qalbihi fa-laysa minnā wa-man ankarahum fa-ka-annamā jāhada al-kuffār bayna yaday rasūli 'llāh* (he in front of whom the name of the Sufis is mentioned and does not disown them with tongue and heart is not one of us; and whoever disowns them is equal to the one who fought the unbelievers in the presence of the messenger of God)[36]

35 See Charles P. Melville, "Shah ʿAbbas and the Pilgrimage to Mashhad," in *Safavid Persia: The History and Politics of an Islamic Society*, ed. Charles P. Melville, Pembroke Persian Papers, v. 4 (London: I.B. Tauris, distributed by St. Martin's Press, 1996), 191–229.

36 Reported in ʿAllāma Burqaʿī, *Ḥaqīqat al-ʿirfān* (n.p., n.d.), 7. This work collects the majority of the anti-Sufi reports found throughout Imami Hadith literature.

Other *riwāyāt* along the same lines are abundant in early Shi'i literature, and some are even attributed to the authority of the Prophet, who foresaw the emergence of what many among the clergy believed to be the Sufis:

> The day of resurrection will not come to my community until a group from among them will come forth whose name will be Sufis and will not stem from me. They will gather in groups to recite the *ḏikr*, raising their voices and fooling themselves into thinking that they are treading my path, while they are in fact more astray than the unbelievers, destined to the fire and their voice is the voice of the donkey.[37]

It is clear from a survey of Gunābādī literature that if the *dār al-islām / dār al-ḥarb* divide was not of much significance to those whom the Sufis labeled the "exoteric ulema" (*ʿulamā-yi ẓāhir*) of Shi'ism, then it was even less so for modern Shi'i Sufis. The late fourteenth/twentieth century compendium of Sufi ethics, *Pand-i Ṣāliḥ*,[38] does not mention it at all. While the *Pand* is not a doctrinal treatise and it is not meant to equal the articulation of Sulṭān ʿAlī Šāh's (d. 1909) treatises, it is nonetheless the introductory booklet usually given to novices, and covers most of the ethical issues that the wayfarer might encounter. In the paragraph on jihad,[39] while the classical Sufi distinction between the greater and the smaller jihad is mentioned, no reference is made of those who are, according to juridical texts, the enemies upon which it should be waged. Jihad seems here to be limited to defense against aggressors, in preparation for which it is incumbent upon the Muslim, and particularly the Shi'a, to learn the art of fighting (*hakaḏā difāʿ az muhājim dar har zamān bā imkān wa āmuḫtan-i ādāb-i jang dar har zamān barā-yi muslimīn ʿumūman wa maḫṣūṣan šīʿa ki intiẓār i ẓuhūr-i imām wa-jihād dar rikāb-i ān buzurgwār dārand lāzim ast*).[40]

On the contrary, in Gunābādī literature *īmān* and *kufr* are modeled upon the dyadic relationship between knowledge and ignorance. We have seen how classical Imami sources emphasize the spiritual relevance of knowledge, considered as a sacred means of connection with the supernatural status of the imam. It is clear that the division between *īmān* and *kufr* mirrors the one between knowledge and ignorance. The *riwāya* on the abode of knowledge/ abode of ignorance reported above is commented upon by Sulṭān ʿAlī Šāh in

37 Ibid., 9.

38 Ṣāliḥ-ʿAlī-Šāh, *Risāla-yi šarīfa pand-i sāliḥ* (Tehran: Ḥaqīqat, 1384).

39 Ibid., 101–3.

40 Ibid., 101–3.

the *Majmaʿ al-saʿādat*,[41] the master's work devoted to the detailed analysis of the concept of knowledge. In it, Sulṭān ʿAlī Šāh explicitly associates it with the dyad of *dār al-islām / dār al kufr*. In its formulation, "abode of knowledge" has a clear metaphysical and practical pre-eminence over the "abode of Islam". The worldview represented by the Gunābādīs in their works thus produces a shift with respect to the classical dualism. The dichotomy is no longer Islam/unbelief, but rather *īmān*/unbelief, whereby Islam is merely the means through which life and property are subjected to a law capable of protecting them, while *īmān* is the true faith. In other words, Islam is the mere acceptance of the outer rulings of religion through the "general covenant" (*bayʿat-i ʿāmma*). It has no other aim than to set the rules that make an ordered society possible, while allowing those who are qualified to do so to proceed through the spiritual path. The acceptance of the outer norms (*ahkām-i qālibī*) is only propaedeutic to the acceptance of the 'inner norms' (*aḥkām-i qalbī*), which is only achieved through the connection with the *walāya* of the imam.[42] The classical categorization *ẓāhir/bāṭin* is at work in this instance, and there is no need to delve too much into it here. What is of more relevance to the topic is how this categorization is worked out with regard to *dār al-islām* and *dār al-ḥarb*: the pair is heavily de-territorialized, to be dislocated in the spiritual realm. In another work, Sulṭān ʿAlī Šāh delves more extensively into the juridical side of the concept, although his concern is far from being merely juridical. In the most important of his works, *Bayān al-saʿāda fī maqāmāt al-ʿibāda*,[43] which reenact in the form of a Qur'anic commentary the whole of the order's doctrine, he explains what really turns an unbeliever into a believer. In commenting on Q 3:151–155, in a chapter on the meanings of *širk*,[44] Sulṭān ʿAlī Šāh explains that while a man who has arrived at the age of *bulūġ* (puberty) may well be a monotheist Muslim from the point of view of creed and tenet (*ṣāra musliman muwaḥḥidan iʿtiqādan*), he is still in a state of *kufr* (*kāna kāfiran ḥālan*), for he is still trapped in the "abode of multiplicity" (*dār al-kaṯra*) and the station of the self, where nothing is seen except that very multiplicity. Later in the same passage, the commentator explains that the "abode of the self" (*dār al-nafs*) and the "abode of unbelief" are no less than the *dār al-ḥarb* that the individual

41 Sulṭān ʿAlī Šāh, *Majmaʿ al-Saʿādat*, 116.

42 Ibid. On the *walāya* for the Gunābādīs see Sulṭān ʿAlī Šāh Gunābādī, *Walāyat-nāma* (Tehran: Intišārāt-i Ḥusayniyya Amīr-Sulaymānī, 1365).

43 On this *tafsīr*, see Mahdī Kumpānī-Zāriʿ, *Gunābādī wa-tafsīr Bayān al-saʿāda* (Tehran: Ḫāna-yi Kitāb, 1390SH). I am in the process of finalizing a monograph on this work.

44 Sulṭān ʿAlī Šāh Gunābādī, *Bayān al-saʿāda fī maqāmāt al-ʿibāda* (Tehran: no publisher, 1343), 4:306–11.

only abandons when he performs the *hijra* to the "abode of the heart" or the "abode of the faith" (*dār al-qalb* and *dār al-īmān*). This is achieved through the initiation covenant (*al-bay'a al-ḫāṣṣa al-walawiyya*) that allows the initiated to enter the "city of the heart" (*madīnat al-qalb*), where safety, trust and faith rule undisturbed. The resonance here is of course with classical Sufism's emphasis on real, inwardly realized *tawḥīd*, as opposed to the mere belief in the existence of the "one God". It is only when the *basmala* becomes an ontological reality that one can attain the status of true monotheist. The degrees of *širk* are then explained, with the commentary of Q 3:151:

> As long as a man is in unbelief and *širk*, he cannot exit his associating God in matters of existence and obedience, because if he does not follow a man, he follows Satan. And if what he associates God with is God, God sends down a proof and a testimony of the righteousness of his association and the *mušrik* is a monotheist by way of his association, which is approved of and recompensed.[45]

Here, the association of God with something that has been approved of by him through a clear revelation, as the association of God with his manifestation in the person of the imams, is considered not only acceptable, but precisely the kind of association that conducts an individual to the realization of *tawḥīd*.

In commenting on the Sura of Muhammad (47: 1–11),[46] the association between those that the Qur'an calls *kāfir* to anyone who denies the *walāya* of 'Alī is made more explicit: "In this Sura the state of those who believe in 'Alī and those who rejected his authority is mentioned. Even though the literal meaning of the verse is general, the meaning is actually as follows ...: *allaḏīna kafarū* usually refers to unbelief in God, or in the Prophet, or in the afterlife, or in 'Alī and his *walāya*, but here it is specific to the *walāya* of 'Alī, as demonstrated by the rest of the verse *and bar from God's way*, as the way of God is nothing but *walāya*".[47] In this passage, the meaning of *kufr* and *īmān/islām* seems to be brought back to its historical dimension, rather than lifted up to the spiritual level. But this does not change the substance of the emphasis of the master.

However, in order to find references to the matter under scrutiny that may be of more interest, one should look at one of the less mystical works of the masters of the order. One interesting text to look at is the critique of the

45 Ibid., 4:307.

46 Ibid., 4:81–88.

47 Ibid., 4:82–83.

International Declaration of Human Rights, written by Sulṭān Ḥusayn Tābanda Gunābādī (Riḍā ʿAlī Šāh, d. 1992).[48] The work is an articulated critique of the Declaration, offered from an Islamic standpoint, with no particular Shi'i coloring and no mystical content. In it, the master affirms that the principles of brotherhood that constitute the basis of the Declaration are in fact useful, but he adds that the same principles are expressed in a more comprehensive form in Islam. This appreciation is far from being comprehensive of all aspects of the Declaration, as the master remarks that the only difference among men envisioned by Islam is the one based upon the belief in one God.[49] This belief in turn establishes a hierarchy: because belief in God corresponds to following the decrees of reason, those who do not follow reason are literally jettisoned from humanity and earth, like a gangrenous limb; they should be fought in order to protect the body.[50] While a neat divide between believers and unbelievers is established, apparently without any nuances, the discourse remains purely theoretical and nor mention of territorial discrimination is made, nor plan of action to implement the consequences of this radical position is set out. Still, this harsh and uncompromising position, where a clear divide is established between faith and unbelief, is tempered *de facto* by the absence of the only person capable of assessing the true nature of human beings—the imam, whose active presence alone can ensure the righteous implementation of religious law. In another treatise by the same author, a chapter on apostasy clarifies the point. In it, Riḍā ʿAlī Šāh expounds the classical juridical doctrine on the penalty for the apostate, only to follow it with the caveat that it is solely the ones entrusted with a supernatural discriminating power (*ṣāḥib-i quwwa-yi qiddisiyya*) who are able to assess the innermost nature of an individual's heart and thus to determine who has actually lost the intrinsic humanity of the pure monotheist and should therefore be executed.[51] The discourse remains purely theoretical and, again, no practical course of action is suggested, even in the absence of a clearly enunciated theory of the abode of Islam and the abode of unbelief.

4 Conclusion

This is but a preliminary survey of the response of modern Shi'i Sufism to the issue of *dār al-islām* and *dār al-ḥarb*. The survey is confined to post-Sulṭān

48 *Naẓar-i maḏhabī ba-iʿlāmiyya-yi ḥuqūq-i bašar* (Tehran, 1351).
49 Ibid., 38–39.
50 Ibid.
51 Riḍā ʿAlī Šāh, *Rafʿ-i šubahāt* (Tehran: Haqīqat, 1377), 123–25.

ʿAli Šāh's Gunābādī Sufism, which, as limited as it is, was nonetheless the heavy-weight of the Iranian Sufi orders from the thirteenth/nineteenth century onwards. A more detailed review of other Shi'i sources would yield a more comprehensive picture of the issues discussed in this article. Much remains to be done as far as time period, type of sources and schools of thought are concerned. Shi'i scholars responded in varied fashions according to the changing political circumstances in which they were writing. The shift of Shi'ism from a powerless minority to a state religion in Iran from the Safavid period onwards (and the previous one in the Buwayhid interlude, of course) was one important turning point brought about by political change. Another momentous turning point was no doubt the establishment of the Islamic Republic in Iran, which opened up the potential for another line of enquiry in this respect.

The parable of Shi'i Sufism spans all these historical vicissitudes, signaling a different perspective in the understanding of the Sufis' positioning within Twelver Shi'ism. If the traditional Shi'i dichotomy of *īmān/kufr* unfolds along the line of attachment to the *ahl al-bayt* (*wilāya*) and versus the dissociation (*barāʾa*) from them, resonates through Gunābādī doctrine, being a Shi'i Sufi order adds a further layer to the picture: now, it is the connection to the "tree of *walāya*" through the means of legitimate initiation by a Sufi master that establishes the boundary between Islam and *īmān*, that is to say, between faith and the mere legal protection enjoyed by anyone who accepts Islam. This awareness, tied to their having been repeatedly labeled and persecuted as *ḥarbīs* by a significant part of the clerical hierarchies[52] probably led the Shi'i Sufis to use the categories of *dār al-islām* and *dār al-ḥārb* even more vaguely than was normally the case in mainstream Shi'i discourse, where the historical state of minority and overall powerlessness had already allowed for the categories to be used at a purely theoretical level. Just as the absence of the imam from the world rules out the viability of the division of the world into the *dār al-islām* and the *dār al-ḥārb*, the presence of the imam in the inner spiritual world of the Shi'i Sufi shifts the focus of the divide from history and polities to the hierohistory of the soul. It is in this realm that the distinction gains, for the Sufis, its full meaning.

---

52 It is worth mentioning here the infamous case of Muḥammad ʿAlī Bihbahānī (d. 1216/1801), the influential *mujtahid* from Kermānšāh known by his sobriquet *ṣūfī-kuš*, the Sufi-killer. In early Qajar times he became known for his *takfīr* of the Sufis, a number of which he managed to have arrested and executed by his mob. See Hamid Algar, "Behbahānī, Moḥammad-ʿAlī," *Encyclopaedia Iranica, Vol. IV, Bāyju–Carpets* (London: Routledge & Kegan Paul, 1990).

References

Abou El Fadl, Khaled. "Islamic Law and Muslim Minorities: The Juristic Discourse on Muslim Minorities from the Second/Eighth to the Eleventh/Seventeenth Centuries." *Islamic Law and Society* 1, no. 2 (1994): 141–87.

Algar, Hamid. "Behbahānī, Moḥammad-ʿAlī." *Encyclopaedia Iranica, Vol. IV, Bāyju–Carpets*. London: Routledge & Kegan Paul, 1990.

Algar, Hamid. "Dār al-ḥarb." *Encyclopaedia Iranica, Vol. VI, Coffeehouse–Dārā*. London: Routledge & Kegan Paul, 1993.

Algar, Hamid. "Niʿmat-Allāhiyya." *Encyclopaedia of Islam, Vol. VIII, Ned-Sam*. Leiden: Brill, 1995.

Amanat, Abbas. "Āqāsī." *Encyclopaedia Iranica*. (Online Edition). Accessed May 27, 2013. http://www.iranicaonline.org/articles/aqasff-ujuli-mnsz-adras-ivxni-ca.

ʿĀmilī, al-Ḥurr al-. *Wasāʾil al-Šīʿa*. Edited by Aḥmad al-Rabbānī al-Šīrāzī. Beirut: Dār al-Turāṯ al-ʿArabī, 1403AH.

Amir-Moezzi, Mohammad Ali. *Le Guide divin dans le shīʿisme originel: aux sources de l'ésotérisme en islam*. Paris: Verdier, 1992.

Amir-Moezzi, Mohammad Ali. "Réflexions sur une evolution du shiʿisme duodécimain: tradition et idéologisation." In *Les retours aux Écritures: fondamentalismes présents et passés [actes du colloque de Paris, 27–30 janvier 1992]*, edited by Evelyne Patlagean and Alain Le Boulluec, 63–82. Louvain: Peeters, 1993.

Amir-Moezzi, Mohammad Ali. "Savoir est pouvoir. Exégèses et implication du miracle dans l'imamisme ancien (Aspects de l'imamologie duodécimaine V)." In *Miracle et karāma. Hagiographies médiévales comparées 2*, edited by Denise Aigle. Bibliothèque de l'Ecole des Hautes Etudes, Sciences Religieuses, 109. Turnhout: Brepols, 2000.

Amir-Moezzi, Mohammad Ali. *The Spirituality of Shi'i Islam: Beliefs and Practices*. London: Tauris [u.a.], 2011.

Bar-Asher, Me'ir Mikha'el. *Scripture and Exegesis in Early Imāmī-Shiism*. Islamic Philosophy, Theology, and Science, v. 37. Leiden: Brill, 1999.

Bonner, Michael. *Aristocratic Violence and Holy War. Studies in the Jihad and the Arab-Byzantine Frontier*, American Oriental Series 81. New Haven, Connecticut: American Oriental Society, 1996.

Brauer, Ralph W. "Boundaries and Frontiers in Medieval Muslim Geography." *Transactions of the American Philosophical Society* 85, no. 6 (1995): 1–73.

Burqaʿī, ʿAllāma. *Ḥaqīqat al-ʿirfān*. n.p., n.d.

Calasso, Giovanna. "Alla ricerca di *dār al-islām*. Una ricognizione nei testi di giuristi e tradizionisti, lessicografi, geografi e viaggiatori." *Rivista degli Studi Orientali* 83 (2010): 271–96.

Cancian, Alessandro. "Incontro con il Maestro della Neʿmatollâhiyya Gonâbâdiyya, Nûr ʿAlî Tâbandeh 'Majzûb ʿAlî Shâh.'" In *Con i dervisci: otto incontri sul campo*, edited by Giovanni De Zorzi, 155–72. Milano: Mimesis, 2013.

Gleave, Robert. *Inevitable Doubt: Two Theories of Shīʿī Jurisprudence*. Studies in Islamic Law and Society, v. 12. Leiden: Brill, 2000.

Graham, Terry. "The Niʿmatu'llāhī Order under Safavid Suppression and in Indian Exile." In *The Heritage of Sufism. Vol. 3: Late Classical Persianate Sufism (1501–1750): The Safavid & Mughal Period*, edited by Leonard Lewisohn and David Morgan, 165–200. Oxford: Oneworld, 1999.

Gulpāygānī, Asadullāh Īzadgušasb. *Nūr al-abṣār. Dar šarḥ-i ḥāl-i yagāna-ʿārif-i kāmil wa šāʿir-i fāḍil maʿrūf wa mašhūr-i mutaʾaḫḫirīn mawlānā Muḥammad ʿAlī "Nūr ʿAli Šāh" al-awwal-i Isfahānī*. Tehran: Ḥaqīqat, 1322SH.

Karakī, Nūr al-dīn ʿAlī b. al-Ḥusayn al- (d. 940/1534). *Jāmiʿ al-maqāṣid fī šarḥ al-qawāʿid*. Qum: Muʾassisa-yi Āl al-bayt li-iḥyāʾ al-turāṯ, 1414AH.

Kohlberg, Etan. "Shīʿī Ḥadīth." In *The Cambridge History of Arabic Literature, Vol. I: Arabic Literature to the End of Umayyad Period*, edited by Albert Felix Landon Beeston, T. M. Johnstone, R. B. Serjeant, and G. R. Smith, 299–307. Cambridge: Cambridge University Press, 1983.

Kulaynī, Abū Jaʿfar Muḥammad al-. *Al-Uṣūl min al-kāfī*. 2 vols. n.p., n.d.

Kumpānī-Zāriʿ, Mahdī. *Gunābādī wa-tafsīr Bayān al-saʿāda*. Tehran: Ḫāna-yi Kitāb, 1390SH.

Lecomte, Gérard. "Aspects de la littérature du *ḥadīṯ* chez les imāmites." In *Le shîʿisme imamite: colloque de Strasbourg (6–9 mai 1968)*, 90–103. Paris: Presses Universitaires de France, 1970.

Lewisohn, Leonard. "An Introduction to the History of Modern Persian Sufism, Part I: The Niʿmatullāhī Order: Persecution, Revival and Schism." *Bulletin of the School of Oriental and African Studies* 61, no. 3 (1998): 437.

Linant de Bellefonds, Yvon. "Le droit imâmite." In *Le shîʿisme imamite: colloque de Strasbourg (6–9 mai 1968)*, 183–200. Paris: Presses Universitaires de France, 1970.

Löschner, Harald. *Die dogmatischen Grundlagen des šīʿitischen Rechts: eine Untersuchung zur modernen imāmitischen Rechtsquellenlehre*. Köln: Carl Heymanns Verlag, 1971.

Malcolm, John. *History of Persia*. London: John Murray, 1829.

Maʿṣūm ʿAlī Šāh Šīrāzī. *Ṭarāʾiq al-ḥaqāʾiq*. 2nd ed. 3 vols. Tehrān: Intišārāt-i Sanāʾī, 1382SH.

Melville, Charles P. "Shah ʿAbbas and the Pilgrimage to Mashhad." In *Safavid Persia: The History and Politics of an Islamic Society*, edited by Charles P. Melville, 191–229. Pembroke Persian Papers, v. 4. London: I. B. Tauris, 1996.

Miller, William M. "Shi'ah Mysticism (The Sufis of Gonabad)." *The Moslem World* 13 (1923): 343–63.

Modarressi Tabatabaʾi, Hossein. *An Introduction to Shīʿī Law: A Bibliographical Study*. London: Ithaca Press, 1984.

Muḥaqqiq al-Ḥillī, Najm al-dīn Jaʿfar. *Šarāyiʿ al-islām*. Edited by Muḥammad Taqī Dāniš-Pažūh. Translated by Abū'l-Qāsim b. Aḥmad Yazdī. Tehran: Intishārāt-i Dānishgāh-i Tihrān, 1358SH.

Pourjavady, Nasrollah, and Peter Lamborn Wilson. *Kings of Love. The Poetry and History of the Niʿmatullāhī Sufi Order*. Imperial Iranian Academy of Philosophy 30. Teheran: Imperial Iranian Academy of Philosophy, 1978.

Riḍā ʿAlī Šāh. *Naẓar-i maḏhabī ba-iʿlāmiyya-yi ḥuqūq-i bašar*. Tehran, 1351SH.

Riḍā ʿAlī Šāh. *Rafʿ-i šubahāt*. Tehran: Haqīqat, 1377SH.

Sachedina, Abdulaziz Abdulhussein. *The just ruler (al-sultān al-ʿādil) in Shiʿite Islam: the comprehensive authority of the jurist in Imamite jurisprudence*. New York: Oxford Univ. Press, 1998.

Ṣāliḥ-ʿAlī Šāh. *Risāla-yi šarīfa pand-i sāliḥ*. Tehran: Ḥaqīqat, 1384SH.

Siddiqi, Muhammad Suleiman. *The Bahmani Ṣūfīs*. Delhi: Idarah-i Adabiyat-i Delli, 1989.

Speziale, Fabrizio. "À propos du renouveau *Niʿmatullāhī*: Le centre de Hyderabad au cours de la première modernité." *Studia Iranica* 42, no. 1 (2013): 91–118.

Sulṭānī Gunābādī, Mīrzā Muḥammad. *Rahbarān-i ṭariqat wa-ʿirfān*. Tehran: Ḥaqīqat, 1379.

Sulṭān ʿAlī Šāh Gunābādī. *Majmaʿ al-Saʿādat*. Tehran: Ḥaqīqat, 1379.

Sulṭān ʿAlī Šāh Gunābādī. *Bayān al-saʿāda fī maqāmāt al-ʿibāda*. Tehran, 1343SH.

Sulṭān ʿAlī Šāh Gunābādī. *Walāyat-nāma*. Tehran: Intišārāt-i Ḥusayniyya Amīr-Sulaymānī, 1365SH.

Ṭūsī, Abū Jaʿfar Muḥammad al- (d. 459–60/1066–7). *Al-Nihāya fī mujarrad al-fiqh wa'l-fatāwā*. Beirut: Dār al-kitāb al-ʿarabī, 1390.

Ṭūsī, Abū Jaʿfar Muḥammad al- (d. 459–60/1066–7). *Tahḏīb al-aḥkām fī šarḥ al-Muqniʿa li'l-šayḫ al-Mufīd*. Beirut: Dār al-Taʿāruf, 1401.

Van den Bos, Matthijs. *Mystic Regimes: Sufism and the State in Iran, from the Late Qajar Era to the Islamic Republic*. Social, Economic, and Political Studies of the Middle East and Asia, v. 83. Leiden: Brill, 2002.

CHAPTER 16

Dār al-islām and *Darul Islam*: From Political Ideal to Territorial Reality

Chiara Formichi

1 Introduction

In the 1940s, centuries after the golden ages of the Muslim Empire and thousands of miles from Damascus and Baghdad, the religious wing of the Dutch East Indies' anti-colonial movement was to pursue its project of an independent state as a political and juridical entity modeled on the ideal of a conceptual *dār al-islām*.

After a brief excursus of the usage—or lack thereof—of the *dār al-Islām* / *dār al-ḥarb* and jihad terminologies in the Indo-Malay literary traditions, this chapter examines the political currency gained by the *dār al-islām* concept in twentieth century Indonesia. Tracing the transmutations of the term's usage alongside the country's political path, I focus on the Islamic parties Sarekat Islam (est. 1912 ca.) and Masyumi (est. 1945), their leading member Sekarmadji Maridjan Kartosuwiryo (1905–1962), and the ideological-political environment in which they operated from the 1930s until 1949, when the Netherlands formally acknowledged Indonesia's independence. Besides this being a crucial period for Islamic and national politics in the Indies, it is in these two decades that Kartosuwiryo would pursue the creation of the Darul Islam as a political organization aimed at the establishment of an Islamic state.

Contributing to an emerging literature that challenges essentializations of Islam and a timeless and static understanding of these concepts, this study investigates the shaping of an anti-colonial discourse of belonging to the *dār al-islām* which does not necessarily call into question the identification of the opponent as *kāfir* or of its territory as a *dār al-ḥarb*.

2 Jihad in the Dutch East Indies

As the Portuguese and British had done in other areas of Southeast Asia, the Dutch gained control over the Indies' archipelago for the most part through agreements with local sultans and kings. Although this strategy had allowed for

 | DOI 10.1163/9789004331037_018

colonial rule to became a de facto reality even before the official "taking over," thus limiting confrontations, conflict was unavoidable (notable examples are Aceh and Bali). Evidence abounds on the clashes that took place between local rulers and the Dutch East India Company (*Vereenigde Oost-Indische Compagnie*, VOC) in the seventeenth-nineteenth centuries, often taking on the "holy war" paradigm. But were these battles a confrontation between different religious traditions? Or, more poignantly, was the European infiltration perceived and represented as an attack from the *dār al-ḥarb* onto the *dār al-islām* which required a jihad response?

In fact, a search of over 150 Indo-Malay texts dating from between the fourteenth century and the 1930s returned only three occurrences for jihad (appearing in two periodicals from the 1890s–1900s) but almost 40 instances of *ber-* or *ku- perang* (war, to be at war) *sabil* (*fī sabīlillah*) were signaled in three texts dating from the seventeenth century.[1] This overwhelming preference for the Indo-Malay term, versus its Arabic form, is confirmed in the Javanese and Acehnese literatures alike: the *Kitab Usulbiyah* (The Book *Usulbiyah*) manuscript of 1633 suggested that fighting in a *aprang sabil* had the same blessing power as going on *ḥajj* or reciting the Qur'an;[2] the *Sejarah Banten* (composed shortly after 1659, in West Java) used *perang sabil* to identify both the looting of a Portuguese ship as well as the war conducted in alliance with the sultan of Demak[3] against a *kāfir*, Hindu, ruler in Palembang, Sumatra; similarly the *Babad Kraton*, written as a foundational history of Java's first Islamic kingdom in Yogyakarta in 1777–78 (but possibly based on earlier manuscripts), presents its struggle for survival against the Dutch East Indies Company as a *prang sabil* and the Europeans (as well as their local allies) are called *kāfir*.[4] And even

1 This overview does not aspire to be an exhaustive survey of the use of jihad or *perang sabil* in Javanese manuscripts; I have here made use of the Malay Concordance Project available at www.mcp.anu.edu.au [accessed 26 October 2013]. According to the Project, only *the Hikayat Tanah Hitu* (1650 ca), *Bustan al-Salatin* (1640 ca), and *Hikayat Iskandar Zulkarnain* (1600 ca) record multiple occurrences.

2 Titiek Pudjiastuti, ed., *Kitab Yusuf*, trans. Hadipranata Hardjana (Jakarta: Departemen Pendidikan dan Kebudayaan, Proyek Penerbitan Buku Sastra Indonesia dan Daerah, 1981), 535; Merle Calvin Ricklefs, *Mystic Synthesis in Java: A History of Islamisation from the Fourteenth to the Early Nineteenth Centuries* (Norwalk, CT: Signature Books, 2006), 45–46.

3 Demak, located on the northern coast of Java, was the site of the first Islamic sultanate on the island in the ninth/fifteenth century.

4 In the 1738 manuscript of the *Babad Ing Sangkala* (part of the Babad Kraton) opposition to King Amangkurat II of Mataram is consistently referred to as *aprang sabil*. Following his acceptance of VOC patronage in 1677, King Amangkurat II had seen popular support fading away, and in an attempt to gain new ground had requested the blessing of a holy man in Giri,

the Acehnese *Hikayat Prang Sabil* (Tale of Holy War) which had been directly inspired by Palimbānī's Arabic treatise *Naṣīḥat al-muslimīn wa-taḏkirat al-mu'minīn fī faḍā'il al-jihād fī sabīl Allāh* (ca. 1788), clearly preferred the Malay to the Arabic term.[5]

In local literatures of the Indo-Malay archipelago in the eleventh/seventeenth-thirteenth/nineteenth centuries, the Arabic *jihād* was superseded by translations of "holy war" such as *aprang* or *perang sabil, perang suci,* and *sabilolah,*[6] so much so that Lance Castle has described Malay manuscripts from the seventeenth century as a "jihad-less world."[7] This peculiarity—which I only wish to present here, as any attempt at a well-rounded explanation would require much deeper delving into the literary traditions of the Muslim Indo-Malay archipelago—appears to be a necessary prologue to the terms' transformed usage in the 1920s–1940s, as well as to the fact that whilst local rulers

who was said to be a descendant of one of the *wali songo*. The *Babad* uses holy war to refer to the Panebahan Giri's defence against the King's rage and military attacks. In Ricklefs, *Mystic Synthesis*, 65. The same approach is taken by the VOC reports from the 1680s: this should be contextualized in the climate of hostility towards religion which dominated the reign of Amangkurat II; see *Babad Kraton*, 391r.–392r. in ibid., 62–66, 75; and Merle Calvin Ricklefs, "A Consideration of Three Versions of the 'Babad Tanah Djawi', with Excerpts on the Fall of Madjapahit," *Bulletin of the School of Oriental and African Studies* 35, no. 2 (1972): 290.

5 Noorhaidi Hasan, "Al-Jihad fi sabil Allah: A study on the Fatwa of 'Abd al Samad al-Palimbani Concerning Holy War for the Cause of Allah" (Master's thesis, Rijks Universiteit, 1998); and Amirul Hadi, "Exploring the Acehnese Conception of War and Peace (A Study of *Hikayat Prang Sabil*)" (First International Conference of Aceh and Indian Ocean Studies, Banda Aceh, 2007).

6 Twentieth century dictionaries show limited scope for *jihād* too. Gericke-Roorda's dictionary of 1901—which includes several Arabic words—does not include *jihād* but rather *jiyad*, classified as Javanese and meaning "to force, push, compel," see Johann Friedrich Carl Gericke et al., *Javaansch-Nederlandsch Handwoordenboek.* (Amsterdam: J. Müller, 1901); in 1939, instead, Poerwadarminta had recognized *jiyad* as an Arabic-derived word, meaning "command" as a noun, and "to force, compel" as a verb, see W. J. S Poerwadarminta, *Baoesastra Djawa,* (Batavia: J. B. Wolters, 1939); It is only the 1916 Klinkert's Malay-Dutch dictionary with Arabic characters that defined *jihād* as an Arabic root, meaning "holy war against the unbelievers", see Hillebrandus Cornelius Klinkert, *Nieuw Maleisch-Nederlandsch Woordenboek Met Arabisch Karakter, Naar de Beste En Laatste Bronnen Bewerkt* (Leiden: Brill, 1947). I am grateful to Prof. Nancy Florida for providing information on the recurrence of *jihād* in Javanese dictionaries.

7 Lance Castles, "The Jihād Motif in Indonesian Islam" (Conference on Violence in Indonesia, Melbourne: Melbourne University, 2003), 4.

saw their efforts as a holy war, the territory was hardly ever defined according to the *dār al-islām* and *dār al-ḥarb* dichotomy.[8]

3 Is This Our House?

At the turn of the twentieth century, as European powers ruled most of the Muslim peoples, the debate on whether these colonized territories were *dār al-islām* or *dār al-ḥarb* was lively; moreover, the potential implications of a declaration of jihad against the colonial authorities made it a politically sensitive one. With the start of World War I and Ottoman Turkey's alliance with Germany against Britain, the debate reached a new dimension: the determination of colonial dominions as *dār al-islām* or *dār al-ḥarb* took on an international resonance, and domestic resistance to local colonial powers was transformed into a broader jihad. Developments in British India are the most studied, but the Dutch East Indies were as involved. The "Universal Proclamation to All Peoples of Islam," or "Jihad Document," that had been issued in Istanbul in 1914 soon circulated in the Netherlands' Indies, raising much concern in colonial circles. Snouck Hurgronje, the Dutch Advisor for Native Affairs in Batavia (nowadays Jakarta), was the most invested in the debate, in 1915 requesting colonial authorities to stop the pilgrimage to Mecca for fear that the Indies' Muslims would be influenced by pan-Islamic and jihadist ideas.[9]

With the collapse of the Ottoman Empire dynamics were to change. The removal from power of sultan ʿAbd al-Majīd (Abdülmecit) II and the abrogation of the caliphate stimulated complex reactions "at the peripheries" of the Muslim world, but a sure point in the post-1924 era was the absence of a single figure that, at least formally, would unite and represent the will of all believers. One direct implication was the newly gained ability for individual "national" communities to negotiate their own relationship with the colonial authorities without the religious duty of conforming to decisions made at the "center," in Istanbul.

The question of whether or not the Dutch East Indies were *dār al-islām* came directly to the fore in the mid-1930s, and even though the sources are at

---

8 One exception could indeed exist, however corroborated only by a Dutch translation of an original now lost: in his *Mystic Synthesis* Merle Calvin Ricklefs quotes from a letter written in 1718 by a group of rebels in Surabaya who find themselves "in the land of the infidels", from which Ricklefs "presumes" a reference to the *dār al-ḥarb*; Ricklefs, *Mystic Synthesis*, 88 and personal communication.

9 Kees van Dijk, *The Netherlands Indies and the Great War, 1914–1918* (Brill, 2007), 296–99.

times at odds with each other, there is consensus that by the end of the decade the Indies were considered *dār al-islām*. The earliest source points to the 1935 annual gathering of Nahdlatul Ulama (NU), a Shafi'i traditionalist organization established in 1926 to counter the weight of the reformist Muhammadiyah (founded in 1912). In June the ulema reached the decision that Indonesia should be called a *negara Islam*—which could be interpreted either as a "Muslim" or "Islamic" state—because "it had already been fully ruled by Muslims. Even though it has been taken over by *kāfir* colonialists, the name *negara Islam* remains."[10] In his study of fatwas on jihad in 1940s Indonesia, Amiq indicates that the NU proclamation of Indonesia (here called *tanah Jawa*) as Islamic land was issued a year later, at the 1936 congress, in acceptance of a fatwa released in Hadramawt by Sheikh Muhammad SMI al-Râ'is.[11] Yet another source identifies the June 1938 NU Congress as the turning point, with the *muktamar* declaring Indonesia *dār al-islām* on the ground that the majority of the Indies' population was indeed Muslim, "the umma still ha[d] the freedom to practice sharia", and "they had in the past been ruled by Muslim kings".[12]

The 1930s were rather tense years between the Indies' Islamic leadership and the colonial government. As PSII (Partai Sarekat Islam Indonesia—Party of Islamic Association of Indonesia) grew stronger in its non-cooperation policy, the Dutch pushed for more involvement in legal religious affairs under the label of "reforms." The most ambitious project of that era was the reform of *'ādāt* and Islamic laws and courts, which peaked with the implementation of the Marriage Ordinance (initially passed in 1929). It was in reaction to these interferences that reformist and traditionalist groups joined forces in late 1937, forming the Great Islamic Council of Indonesia (MIAI—Majelis Islam A'la Indonesia) as a platform for channeling concerns shared by the colony's umma.[13] But gathering about 40 Islamic organizations nation-wide, its

---

10 Decision no. 192, Keputusan Muktamar NU ke-11, Banjarmasin, 9 June 1935. Quoted in Aziz Masyhuri, *Masalah Keagamaan Nahdlatul Ulama: Hasil Muktamar Dan Munas Ulama Kesatu-1926 S/d Kedua Puluh Sembilan 1994* (Surabaya: Dinamika press, 1997).

11 Amiq, "Two Fatwas on Jihād against the Dutch Colonisation in Indonesia: A Prosopographical Approach to the Study of Fatwa," *Studia Islamika* 5–3 (1998): 86.

12 In Ali Haidar, "Nahdlatul Ulama dan Islam di Indonesia: Pendekatan Fikih Dalam Politik" (IAIN Syarif Hidayatulah, 1993), 157; whilst Haidar makes no mention of the 1936 fatwa and *muktamar*, Masyhuri, *Masalah Keagamaan Nahdlatul Ulama* does not mention this decision when reporting the 1938 congress. I am most grateful to Robin Bush for finding these two references to Nahdlatul Ulama's decisions on *negara Islam*.

13 On MIAI and the Marriage Ordinance see Harry Jindrich Benda, *The Crescent and the Rising Sun: Indonesian Islam Under the Japanese Occupation, 1942–1945* (Dordrecht: Foris, 1985), 87–91.

formally united front was in fact highly fragmented in the way its constituencies experienced and understood colonial interference.

If in June 1938 the Nahdlatul Ulama was still so accommodating of the Dutch presence in the Indies, just a few months earlier, in February, the Sarekat Islam (PSII) had presented a motion to the MIAI congress which radically undermined the NU's position. The motion, which was approved by the congress, took a critical stance towards the colonial government's professed neutrality in religious matters and its guarantee of "full religious freedoms" for its subjects. Directly contesting the NU's statement that Muslims in the Indies could "practice" sharia law, this motion questioned the integrity of the process by pointing to the lack of conformity of the legal procedure; for Islamic law to be properly implemented—argued the motion—the law, judge and verdict had all to be "Islamic." But as the members of the religious courts were chosen by the colonial government and their decisions had to be approved by the Dutch president of the civil court, the motion complained that the colonial government undermined the principle of God's sovereignty, implicitly rejecting the idea of the Netherlands East Indies as a *dār al-islām*.[14] This sequence of events suggests that after the topic had dominated NU congresses for a few years, the MIAI motion rejecting the understanding of the Indies as *dār al-islām*, eventually pushed the NU to reaffirm its own position, exposing the deep rift between modernists and traditionalists.

It should be no surprise that the NU and PSII had such divergent understandings of the extent to which Islam could be practiced in the colony. The NU was a social organization, committed to education and poverty relief, and it was heavily dependent on colonial authorities for its survival. On the other hand, the PSII was a political party with an open anti-colonial and pro-independence agenda which, since the 1930s, had seen a steep radicalization of its religious platform. Under the leadership of Sekarmadji Maridjan Kartosuwiryo (1905–1962), author of the motion discussed above, the PSII had become a strong advocate of an Islamic state-solution for independent Indonesia and of non-cooperation with the colonial authorities, a policy usually referred to as *hijrah*.

---

14 "Preadvies tentang Raad Agama dan Mahkamat Islam Tinggi, berhoeboeng dengan pemindahan hak-waris dari Raad Agama kepada Landraad, dihidangkan pada Al-Islam-Kongres jang ke-10 di Soerabaja, pada tg. 28 Februari menghadap 1 Maart 1938" [1938], Archief van de Procureur-Generaal [hereafter APG] no. 1007, Het Nationaal Archief [hereafter NA], The Hague.

4 From Theory to Practice: *hijrah* Policy

The 1930s were a decade of great political turmoil. The appointment of conservative Bonifacius de Jonge as Governor General of the East Indies caused a dramatic narrowing of the political space, further exacerbating the internal discord over the issue of cooperation with colonial authorities, a debate which shook and weakened secular and Islamic groups alike.

With president-to-be Soekarno and his associates Mohammad Hatta and Sutan Sjahrir jailed and exiled outside Java, by the end of 1934 secular nationalist activists had *en masse* abandoned non-cooperation, embracing participation in the Dutch-created *Volksraad* as an avenue to advance demands for increased autonomy.[15] Sarekat Islam thus remained the only party committed to non-cooperation, but this came at a high cost.

By the mid-1930s members of the old guard who opposed non-cooperation were expelled, Kartosuwiryo gained the upper hand in the party cabinet (*dewan partij*) and the *hijrah* policy was sanctioned as the party's official line at the 1936 congress. Members of the PSII were no longer allowed to join the *Volksraad*, and the party was to pursue independence on its own, rejecting any offer of collaboration. Kartosuwiryo was now tasked with the writing of a pamphlet titled "PSII's *hijrah* strategy" aimed at "clarifying, explaining and expanding [Kartosuwiryo's] opinion" on the origins of such policy.[16]

Kartosuwiryo, rising star of the Sarekat Islam party, was born in a traditional Javanese family, to a father employed in the colonial administration. Because of their status Kartosuwiryo was allowed to attend western-styled schools, but in the early 1920s he abandoned his studies at the medical school in Surabaya and opted instead for a career in journalism. It is unclear why he first joined the religious Sarekat Islam party in 1927, but within a couple of years he had become vocal in the party's call for religiously-framed socio-economic justice, to the extent that Dutch observers would label him a young anti-European journalist who was fanatical in his religious views and behavior.[17] Kartosuwiryo's

---

15 For more on this see Susan Abeyasekere, "The Soetardjo Petition," *Indonesia* 15 (April 1973): 80–108. The *Volksraad* had been created by the Dutch in 1916 (effective since 1918) as a stepping stone towards self-government. Since 1931 the composition of the *Volksraad* had been half Dutch and half Indonesian, with one third of its members nominated, and the rest elected from amongst the civil servants.

16 "De PSII brochures 'Hidjrah'" [1937], Archief van het Ministerie van Kolonie, 1900–1963 [hereafter AMK]: Geheime Mailrapporten [hereafter GMr], no. 101X, NA. Kartosuwiryo, *Sikap hidjrah PSII*, 1936.

17 General Overview of the Indigenous (Malay-Chinese and Arab) Press, *Algemeen Overzicht van de Inlandsche (Maleisisch-Chineesche en Arabische) Pers*, August 1928 and

advocating for disengagement with the Dutch should thus be seen as a natural development of his views in conjunction with an evolving—increasingly repressive—political environment.

To Kartosuwiryo the 1936 congress marked the beginning of a new political era, but to several others his forced non-cooperation meant the end of their activism in the party. A year later, at the Bandung congress of 1937, several prominent members had left the party, forming new splinter organizations and taking large numbers of supporters with them. Throughout that year at least 21 branches had manifested their disagreement with the *hijrah* policy and 60 more refused to participate in the congress. Yet, at the MIAI congress he was still able to garner support for his criticism of the Dutch government's "neutral" attitude towards religion.

Moulded on the theology and history of the Prophet's migration as much as on its political implications, Kartosuwiryo contextualized the PSII's decision to engage in a political Hijra against the events surrounding Muhammad's migration from Mecca to Medina in 622. As Muhammad and his followers had left Mecca to ensure the victory of justice over evil and monotheism over polytheism by creating the first Islamic state in Medina, so Partai Sarekat Islam Indonesia had to be victorious over the Dutch by pursuing its own Hijra and starting a new era for Indonesia.

Mecca represents here a metaphorical situation of oppression and ignorance, one that could be found in any village and country of the world, and thus a situation that needed to be (figuratively, for now) abandoned in favor of a Medina–Indonesia where the law of God ruled, and the umma was happy and victorious. Indeed, at this stage of Indonesia's anti–colonial struggle, Hijra referred to a figurative migration from the "Indonesian Mecca" to the "Indonesian Medina," marking a transition from a regime of *ʿādāt* to a religious ideological framework articulated as the *dār al-islām* (or *darul Islam*, as it was often spelled in Malay–Indonesian), an ideal Islamic state.

This transformation could only be the result of jihad. The Hijra to Medina-Indonesia is clearly explained in three steps: *īmān* (faith), *tawḥīd* (unity), and jihad. Through extensive references to the Qur'an and bringing forward its practical implications for the PSII's political struggle, Kartosuwiryo pursued the argument that there is no Hijra without jihad. However, even though the Dutch authorities claimed that this policy was the outcome of Muslims'

October 1929. For a complete investigation of Sekarmadji Maridjan Kartosuwiryo see Chiara Formichi, *Islam and the Making of the Nation: Kartosuwiryo and Political Islam in Twentieth-Century Indonesia* (Leiden: KITLV, 2012).

unwillingness to cooperate with *kuffār* rule and thus seek open confrontation,[18] Kartosuwiryo was careful to explain that the "positive" struggle is the jihad of the tongue and the heart (the *jihād akbar*, led by *īmān*), and not that of the sword—the *jihād aṣġar*, defined instead as negative and destructive.

Far from equating with "war," jihad here included much broader strategies of "Islamic politics" such as, for example, the Islamization of Indonesian politics through the propagation of Islamically interpreted knowledge amongst PSII members in particular and amongst Muslims in general; the establishment of relations with Muslims across the world to work toward the realization of pan-Islamism, understood as the unity of the Islamic umma; and the dissociation of PSII actions from colonial bodies and policies.[19]

Political tensions within Sarekat Islam continued to rise, eventually leading to Kartosuwiryo's very expulsion from the party in 1939.[20] As the accommodationist wing regained control of the PSII, several leading members and entire branches across Java saw their membership revoked.[21] In January 1940 the newly established leadership declared that the party had undergone radical transformations, having moved on from Hijra to *tauhid* [*tawḥīd*], thus joining in the wider cooperative effort.[22]

Expulsion from the party gave Kartosuwiryo an opportunity to take Hijra to the "next level," from a figurative migration to a physical exit from a political system which was not enabling him to complete the transformation from Mecca–Indonesia to Medina–Indonesia. By March 1940 Kartosuwiryo had established a new party, the Komite Pertahanan Kebenaran–PSII (Committee for the Defence of the Truth–PSII). Supported by about 1,500 members originating from over 20 branches nation-wide, the KPK–PSII continued to pursue its activities as the "true Sarekat Islam" from its headquarters in Malangbong, West Java. Soon after its establishment, this splinter group printed a follow-up pamphlet to the 1936 *Sikap Hidjrah* titled *Daftar Oesaha Hidjrah*, reinforcing the need for a jihad to expand the reach of the *dār al-islām* and thus widen the constituency of Islamic society. Loyal only to God and dedicated to the implementation of sharia on an individual (*šaḫṣī*) as well as a communitarian

18 "De PSII Brochures 'Hidjrah'" [1937] AMK GMr no.101x, NA.

19 "PSII congres 1938 te Soerabaja" [1939], AMK GMr no.1170x, NA. The congress was held between 30 July and 7 August 1938.

20 See the weekly Overview of the Indigenous and Malay-Chinese Press, *Overzicht van der Inlandsche en Maleisisch-Chineesche Pers*, 17 June 1939.

21 *Politiek-politioneele overzichten van Nederlandsch-Indie*, January 1939, p. 257 and *Overzicht*, 17 June 1939.

22 *Overzicht*, 3 February 1940.

(*ijtimāʿī*) level, Sarekat Islam and this new Islamic society were committed to pursuing pan-Islamism and to achieving "the unity of Islam and oneness of God."[23]

Channeling his efforts towards creating an Islamic society, in Malangbong Kartosuwiryo established an educational institution, the Soeffah Institute, where members underwent training to develop their intellectual capacities and strengthen their character so as to be prepared to become the core of an "Islamically perfect" society.[24] Kartosuwiryo clearly intended to reconnect this experience to that of the Prophet; not only had he taken on the role of teacher, political leader and enforcer of sharia law, but also the name of the institute reminds one of the *ṣuffa* of Medina, the mosque's sheltered corner where Muhammad delivered his speeches during the day and the newly arrived *muhājirūn* spent the night.[25] The Soeffah Institute represented Kartosuwiryo's first attempt at creating a physical space for an Islamic society, a Medina–Indonesia or *darul Islam* where the embryo of an Islamic state could slowly grow to its full potential. This experiment was violently interrupted by the Japanese invasion of Java and Sumatra, begun in early 1942.

5 The House of Islam under a Japanese Roof

Upon landing on Sumatra and Java in February-March 1942, the Japanese army was seen as a liberator from European control, once again proving Asia's supremacy since Japan's victory over Russia in 1905. Yet, as World War II approached, Japanese attitudes to the occupied territories became marked by pillaging. The spirit of solidarity initially infused in the ideal of the anti-West Greater East Asia Co-Prosperity Sphere quickly turned into economic exploitation of local resources to the benefit of the Empire of the Rising Sun.

On the other hand, however, Japanese rule brought about—possibly unintentionally—the empowerment of Indonesia's political leadership, and more specifically of its Islamic wing. The restructuring of Indonesia's bureaucracy

---

23 Kartosuwiryo, *Daftar-Oesaha Hidjrah PSII bagian Muqaddima*, (Malangbong (SS W/L) Java: Poestaka Dar-oel-Islam, March 1940), in Al-Chaidar, *Pemikiran politik proklamator negara Islam Indonesia S. M. Kartosoewirjo: fakta dan data sejarah Darul Islam* ([Jakarta]: Darul Falah, 1999), 461–76.

24 "Oprichting van een nieuwe politiek-godsdienstiege partij door het KPK-PSII" [1940], AMK GMr no.529x, NA.

25 An alternative explanation could be in reference to the *Iḫwān al-ṣafāʾ*; I am grateful to Michael Laffan for pointing this out to me.

and political parties pursued in the early months of the occupation sought centralization and the merging of a multitude of small-sized groups into fewer and larger functional organizations. Upon the Japanese surrender in 1945, then, the Indonesian nationalist movement found itself strengthened throughout the territory, no longer fragmented across ethnic or regional lines, and efficiently coordinated from the grassroots through a network of local branches and military wings.

In the attempt to further strengthen social support for the new regime, the Japanese authorities had portrayed their take-over from the Dutch as an assertion of Asian power over the Europeans. Far from stopping at anti-Western propaganda, they actively co-opted Islamic scholars and ulema, instilling into them the vision that the Empire's pan-Asian ideology was in unison with pan-Islam. Kartosuwiryo, who had staunchly advocated non-cooperation with the Dutch, became an enthusiastic supporter of Japanese rule.

Having returned to his old profession, journalism, in early 1943 Kartosuwiryo publicly pledged his allegiance to Dai Nippon. Arguing that the Japanese army had expelled *Fir'aun Belanda* (the Dutch Pharaoh) and thus "opened the door to, and widened the efforts towards, Islam," the Indonesian umma now had to take advantage of this opportunity and cooperate with Japan in creating a "new world."[26] As Kartosuwiryo further explained, Japan's *dunia baru* (new world) was an embryonic Islamic state, and a bridge to *al-dar al-āḫiru,* thus deserving full cooperation.[27] To "work, help, and support [Japan] with full conviction and consciousness ... to reach common prosperity" was *wājib*, and all should join forces in an Islamic Front (*Banteng Islam*) to practice sharia law and further Islamize Indonesia.[28]

The Japanese had not given more concessions than the Dutch had, in terms of implementing Islamic law, yet Kartosuwiryo—maybe driven by hopes of a positive turn of events in the future—had readily given up his confrontational attitude towards foreign rule, becoming a supporter of the Japanese vision. Regardless, he remained committed to his goal of a fully Islamized society and continued to argue for the importance for all Muslims to follow the example of the Prophet so to ensure the establishment of the *dār al-islām* and "hopefully"

---

26 Kartosuwiryo, "Fardl-oel-'ain dan fardl-oel-kifajah," *Soeara MIAI* [hereafter SMIAI], 1 May 1943.

27 Kartosuwiryo, "Kewadjiban oemmat Islam menghadapi 'Doenia Baroe'," SMIAI, 15 May 1943.

28 Kartosuwiryo, "Benteng Islam," SMIAI, 1 September 1943.

the achievement of *dār al-salām* in the afterlife.[29] Retaining the same priorities, the difference in attitude was to affect his strategy for achieving these cherished goals: if during Dutch rule the three-fold path required *īmān, tawḥīd* and jihad, now "the keys that open the door of *dār al-islām* and *dār al-salām*" were *īmān, tawḥīd* and Islam.[30]

Kartosuwiryo's positive attitude to Japan had placed him back at the heart of political leadership: in 1943 he appeared to be mayor of Bandung,[31] then became head of the *bayt al-māl* in West Java[32] and eventually a trainer of the Banten squadron of the Barisan Pelopor (Pioneer Corps), the armed wing of the mass organization Jawa Hokokai (People's Service Association of Java).[33] A product of Japanese intervention, the Jawa Hokokai merged various ethnic constituencies with the youth and women's groups, whilst its leadership was shared between the secular-nationalist Soekarno and Masjumi's chairman Hasjim Asj'ari.[34] Despite the radical changes that had affected Indonesia in the 15 years that had passed since Kartosuwiryo's first trip to West Java, he remained deeply rooted in the region.

6 Defending the House

Jihad was only briefly out of sight, soon to return at center-stage. The discharge of the atomic bombs over Hiroshima and Nagasaki marked the sudden surrender of the Japanese Army in Southeast Asia, creating a vacuum of power in Indonesia. This is not the place to investigate the intricate sequence of events that followed from August 1945, leading to the return of Dutch authority over most of the archipelago and eventually—after four years of revolution—to the transfer of sovereignty to the Indonesian Republic in December 1949.

These years were dotted with diplomatic agreements and military confrontation between the Dutch and "Indonesian forces", but most notably within

29 Kartosuwiryo, "Menoedjoe ke arah dar-oel-Islam dan dar-oes-Salam," SMIAI, 15 March 1943.

30 Kartosuwiryo, "Kewadjiban oemmat Islam."

31 "Ketoea Dewan MIAI mengoetjapkan terima kasih," *Asia Raya*, 18 May 1943.

32 The *bayt al-māl* is an institution representing a communal treasury in which Qur'anic taxes are deposited and through which the community could support those in need of financial help, such as widows, orphans and the poor. "Gambar soesoenan baital-mal M.I.A.I.," SMIAI, 1 July 1943.

33 "Nama-nama kepala rombongan jang akan dikirimkan keloeroeh Syuu oentoek Hooshi-II," *Indonesia Merdeka*, 25 April 1945, 6.

34 Benda, *The Crescent and the Rising Sun*, 154–56.

the Indonesian front. Communist, Nationalist-Republican, and Islamist factions—which had emerged during the Japanese period—opposed each other on the plane of political ideology as well as of the battlefield, as exemplified by the fact that in this interval three "Republics" were proclaimed. Soekarno's proclamation of the Pancasila-based Indonesian Republic in August 1945 in Jakarta was followed first by the short-lived Madiun Affair, which saw Socialist and Communist forces proclaiming a counter-republic headquartered in East Java in September 1948. A year later Kartosuwiryo announced the establishment of the Islamic State of Indonesia.[35]

Focussing now on developments relevant to the Islamic faction, it ought to be noted that at the time of Japan's capitulation the secular-nationalist wing, led by Soekarno, was grouped in the Jawa Hokokai, whilst the religious political leadership had organized under the umbrella party Masyumi (Majelis Syuro Muslimin Indonesia, itself involved in the Jawa Hokokai). Even though the Islamic wing had made great gains under the Japanese, as World War II had drawn to an end the balance of power had shifted in favor of the secularists, granting them the power to shape the new state.

The fleeing Japanese authorities had granted independence to Indonesia, and Kartosuwiryo—as well as all other pro-Japan leaders—came to the fore of national politics opposing Dutch claims to the renewal of their political control. Former Sarekat Islam members carved their own space in Masyumi's post-Japan hierarchies,[36] and in 1945 Kartosuwiryo resumed his position as

35 For an approachable overview of the revolution (as well as other periods of Indonesia's history) see Merle Calvin Ricklefs, *A History of Modern Indonesia since C. 1300* (Stanford: Stanford University Press, 1993). "Proklamasi berdirinja Negara Islam Indonesia," 7 August 1949, Arsip Angkatan Bersenjata Republik Indonesia [hereafter AABRI] Darul Islam Documentation [hereafter DI], Jakarta, no. 14.

36 At the November 1945 congress, former Sarekat Islam and Partai Islam Indonesia (PII) members dominated the central board, whilst NU and Muhammadiyah leaders were only found in the Majelis Sjoero (consultative assembly). The boards of the two departments were a bit of a potpourri, with Agoes Salim and Mohammad Roem from the Penjadar Committee sitting next to Kartosuwiryo, Mohammad Natsir, Kiyai Ahmad Sanoesi, and K. H. Abdoelwahab. In the meantime Muhammad Natsir acted as vice-president of the KNIP working committee. Dewan Partij: Soekiman, from its PSII splinter Partai Islam Indonesia was the chairman, Abikoesno (PSII) and Wali Alfatah (PII) his vices, Harsono Tjokroaminoto (PSII) and Prawoto Mangkoesasmito (SIS) the secretaries. Majelis Sjoero: Kiyai Haji Hasjim Asj'ari as chairman, Ki Bagoes Hadikoesoemoe, K. Wahid Hasjim and Kasman Singodimedjo as vice-chairmen. Masjoemi, *Partai Politik Islam Indonesia* (Boekit Tinggi: Dewan Pemimpin Daerah Masjoemi Soematra Barat, n.d.): this pamphlet was most probably printed on the occasion of the 22 April 1946 Congress.

the executive committee's secretary. In the following months he found himself advancing the Islamic party's agenda at the KNIP (Komite Nasional Indonesia Pusat—Central Indonesian National Committee) Preparatory Committee for Independence (as he participated at its meetings in both 1946 and 1947), where the political elite took further steps towards consolidating the new state's structure as a functional independent nation-state. In July 1947, the apex of his recognized prominence in national politics, Kartosuwiryo was invited to represent the resuscitated PSII in Amir Sjarifuddin's first cabinet, covering the role of junior Minister of Defence.

But July 1947 was also the time when the Dutch pursued their first military campaign to re-conquer the former colony, taking control of western Java and prompting Kartosuwiryo to refuse the appointment. The Soekarno Republic's readiness to agree to a diplomatic solution which granted the re-instalment of colonial rule over West Java—so to safeguard the rest of the island—pushed Kartosuwiryo to reject any further involvement in parliamentary politics. In the following months he formally severed all ties with Soekarno's Republic, now headquartered in Yogyakarta: Kartosuwiryo declared a jihad against the Dutch and their aides, announced that the Islamic party in West Java had a different agenda and priorities from its central branch, and gave birth to a new organization committed to bringing independence and Islamic governance to West Java. This organization was to be named the Darul Islam.

The desire to see Indonesia shaped as an Islamic state implementing sharia law and molded on the model of Muhammad's Medina was not just Kartosuwiryo's vision. Japan had entrusted the secular nationalists with the task of setting up the structure of the new state because they saw Soekarno as more pragmatic, but much debate had followed his declamation of the *Pancasila*, the five principles that sanctioned Indonesia as a non-confessional state.[37] Requests for formalizing Islamic law as legal guidance for the country's Muslims were rejected on the grounds of minority rights' protection and fears that the territorial unity of the fledgling nation could be compromised,[38] in

37 *Pancasila* includes the five principles of *kebangsaan* (nationalism), *per-kemanusiaan* (humanitarianism), *permusyawaratan-perwakilan* (deliberation among representatives), *kesejahteraan* (social welfare), and *ketuhanan* (belief in One God).

38 A smaller committee was arranged to address the complaints coming from the Islamic faction and to ease emerging frictions. On 22 June the participants reached a common declaration meant to serve as the new constitution's preamble. While it did not recognize the idea of an Islamic state, this version of the constitution accepted sharia law by affirming "the obligation for adherents of Islam to practice Islamic law". This clear reference to Islam in the constitutional preamble prompted a reaction from the Christian representatives, and that sentence—later to become known as "Jakarta Charter" (*Piagam Jakarta*)—

fact it was the very exclusion of Islam from the constitution that caused a number of rebellions and attempts at secession.

As the anti-colonial revolution raged, in the months following the Allied occupation the political and military landscape of Java became increasingly fragmented. Soekarno's rejection of any formalized role for Islam, the Republic's reluctance to assert its own sovereignty against Dutch claims, and Masyumi's inability to build a political strategy and gain a more dominant position in national politics (despite its large following) led to the polarization of Republican versus Islamic ideologies as well as armed troops.

In early October 1945 the Masyumi central leadership stipulated that the party's priority was to reunite religion and state, and declared a *perang sabil* against the Japanese and the Netherlands Indies Civil Administration (NICA).[39] The decision which in the mid-1930s had sanctioned the Dutch Indies as *dār al-islām* as a strategy to prevent conflict, had now become an arrow in favor of the anti-colonial struggle. In November 1945 Kiyai Haji Hasjim Asj'ari, founder and chairman of Nahdlatul Ulama, issued a declaration of "holy war" against the Dutch.[40] Calling upon all Muslims to individually defend Indonesia from the "infidels who obstruct independence" and their NICA allies, this jihad was *farḍ ʿayn*, granting those who sacrificed their lives the status of *šahīd*. In March 1946 the Nahdlatul Ulama party congress seconded the resolution, announcing that all Muslims—men and women, adults and children, armed and unarmed—living within a 94 km radius from occupied areas had the individual religious duty to fight the Dutch.[41]

If NU had been so eager in stipulating that participating in the anti-colonial struggle was an individual religious duty, the party's central board was reluctant to endorse Asj'ari's fatwa. But as Asj'ari was also the chairman of Masyumi's Majelis Sjoero, different views about the breadth of this jihad

disappeared from the final draft presented on 13 July, replaced instead with a declaration of freedom of religion. The members of the Islamic faction had intended to further debate these changes, but as Japan was losing ground in the Pacific and would soon capitulate, Indonesian politicians felt compelled to accelerate their preparations for independence and to work with what they had. On this issue see R. E. Elson, "Another Look at the Jakarta Charter Controversy of 1945," *Indonesia* 88 (October 2009): 105–30.

39 "Overzichten van berichten betreffende het republikeinse leger in de Maleise pers van West-Java 1945 Oktober–1946 April, 34," AMK: Supplement (1664) 1826–1952 [hereafter Supp] no.78, NA.

40 *Kedaulatan Rakyat* [hereafter KR], 20 November 1945 in Amiq, "Two Fatwas on Jihād against the Dutch Colonisation in Indonesia: A Prosopographical Approach to the Study of Fatwa," 86.

41 "Resoloesi tentang djihad," *al-Djihad* no. 30, 2 April 1946.

marked a first split within the party. Understanding jihad as a duty to be pursued only by a portion of the population whilst others studied and undertook political action, the central board—after pressure was put on it from several quarters[42]—could only endorse the request for the creation of a second armed wing, the Sabilillah, in addition to the already active Hizboellah, in support of Masyumi's political pursues.[43]

To several members of Masyumi, preparation for armed confrontation bore meaning only if sided with political engagement, forging a strong connection between jihad—as war against the Dutch—and propaganda in favor of an Islamic state—the *dār al-islām*. On the occasion of the party's congress in February 1946 it was reiterated that "Indonesia is a *negeri Islam* (*Daroel Islam*)", thus making a jihad against the intruding *kuffār*, *wājib*.[44] From then on, Masyumi's dedication to establishing an independent Islamic state was constantly emphasized in the pages of its bulletin. *Al-Djihad* conducted a campaign in support of the "holy war," the establishment of an Islamic state (often referred to as *darul Islam*), and a resumption of the *hijrah* policy. In February 1946—corresponding to the month of Hijra, *rabīʿ al-awwal*—the magazine celebrated Muḥammad's migration to Medina and his defence of the Islamic city-state as models of political action, suggesting that readers should rise in an Islamic revolution as a free and independent umma "demanding freedom for its religion, people, and islands."[45]

---

42 During the *ḥuṭba* for *ʿīd al-aḍḥā* (mid-November 1945) in Bandung, Kiyai Abdoessalam had called on the large crowd to fight a holy war against the Netherlands; in "Militaire, politieke en economische gegevens uit de Maleise pers betreffende de residenties Batavia, Buitenzorg, Krawang, Bandung, Surakarta, Djokjakarta, Semarang en Kedu," 11, AMK:Supp no.76, NA.

43 "60 Miljoen kaoem Moeslimin Indonesia siap berdjihad fi sabilillah," KR, 9 November 1945 and "Barisan Sabilillah," KR, 17 November 1945. As Harun Nasution has argued, the modernists sought to create an Islamic state by first preparing its society, whilst the traditionalists believed it to be impossible to create an Islamic society without first establishing the appropriate government structures. Harun Nasution, "The Islamic State in Indonesia: The Rise of the Ideology, the Movement for Its Creation and the Theory of the MASJUMI" (Masters' thesis, McGill, 1965), 76–77.

44 *Anggaran dasar dan rentjana perdjoeangan Masjoemi, Partai Politik Islam Indonesia* (Bukit Tinggi, 1946), 36–37.

45 "Revoloesi Islam," *al-Djihād* no. 24, 13 February 1946. In addition to several articles published throughout the year 1946 (see for example "Revoloesi Islam," 13 February and "Peperangan sekarang soedah djadi fardoel ʿain," 20 April) the magazine also published boxes advertising slogans such as *SIAP sedia untuk berdjuang fiSabilillah, Djihad Sabil, Daroel Islam itoelah toedjoean kita, Berdjihadlah! FiSabilillah!*

Masyumi's vision of an Islamic state was rooted in the historical depth of the religious wing's political engagement, but also in the consciousness of the party's own evolution:

> If 33 years ago [the time of Sarekat Islam's establishment] Islam was only a final coating, considered as just enough to function as a link between organisations, now it is not like that. This Masyumi has a 100% Islamic soul, the spiritual connection among all Masyumi members is Allah's religion, Masyumi's flag is the crescent and the star on a white and red background, Masyumi's aim is the *darul Islam*, or an Indonesian Republic based on Islam.[46]

The ideological struggle between secular nationalists and the religious wing had not yet taken shape as armed confrontation, and indeed by February 1946 Masyumi appeared settled in its commitment to establish a *darul Islam*, an Islamic state, through "unity" and parliamentary engagement.[47] Masyumi accepted the Republican constitution as a "stepping stone" towards the realization of Islamic ideals in the state, it recognized *Pancasila*'s harmony with Islamic principles,[48] and it laid out its domestic and international agendas as a mixture of mild pan-Islamism, democracy and propagation of Islamic teachings in Indonesian society through education and *daʿwa*.[49] Two years later, at the 1948 Masyumi congress, held on 28 March in Madiun, prominent members of the national leadership announced their desire to see the creation of a *dār al-islām* "as soon as possible" so as to end the armed national revolution.[50]

---

46 "Masjoemi, toelang poenggoeng Republik Indonesia," *al-Djihad* no. 26, 28 February 1946. This was also worryingly reported by Dutch sources, see *ANP-Aneta Bulletin*, "Kentering in de Masoemi in Indische," *Documentatie dienst van ANP-Aneta* 10 October-27 December 1946, 423–27.

47 This commitment was further reaffirmed in the party's manifesto in June 1947 "Rencana dari Masjoemi," 20 June 1947, Arsip Kementrian Pertahanan 1946, no.1045, Arsip Nasional Republik Indonesia [hereafter ANRI], Jakarta.

48 As the *Pancasila* were never modified, this became a common exercise for Muslim intellectuals and scholars in the early 1950s.

49 Deliar Noer, "Masjumi Its Organization, Ideology, and Political Role in Indonesia" 1961, 70–75.

50 The congress had gathered after the formation of the DI-TII, and the head of the NII's information office in Tasikmalaya, Abdoelhadi Ibrahim, was present at the congress as Darul Islam's representative. However neither Wali Alfatah nor Kiyai Ahmad Sanoesi made any reference to Kartosuwiryo. "Darul Islam di Djawa Barat," Djawatan Kepolisian Negara Bagian PAM Yogyakarta, 23 July 1948, Arsip Jogja Documenten 1946–1948

Strategic differences were still rife in Masyumi, as the divide between a modernist (bottom-up) and traditionalist (top-down) approach had not been solved; yet it was evident that the party was still aiming for the same goal as in 1945.[51]

Kartosuwiryo's speech delivered in July 1946 in Garut, West Java, also followed this line of argument, and as Masyumi representative he upheld the party's commitment to parliamentary struggle, cooperation and unity. *Haloean Politik Islam* brings together a number of threads that Kartosuwiryo had developed in the past, and although it was a whole year away from his final break with formal politics and his transformation of the *dār al-islām* from ideal to political reality, the compelling need for action is evident.[52]

Having reaffirmed that the umma's concern should be for worldly matters as much as eternal salvation, with the establishment of God's will on earth—a *dār al-islām*—solely aimed at gaining admission to the *dār al-salām*, Kartosuwiryo argued that the political efforts of the Indonesian umma should be committed towards shaping the Indonesian republic as one based on Islam, where the government guaranteed the implementation of sharia law "in its widest and most complete" formulation. This he saw as a "new world" or "Islamic world," echoing the *dunia baru* of Japan's days. Such achievements were not however all a matter of military or electoral victory; the real challenge was to free the Indonesian umma of the colonial shackles that survived within society.

So it was that Kartosuwiryo differentiated between the national, social and individual revolutions. No portion of Indonesia's population was relieved of its duty and responsibility to defend the country and build national sovereignty. But the task that rested solely on the Muslims was the social revolution: a struggle aimed at deconstructing colonialism from within society. The social revolution could only be carried out by those who had already succeeded in the individual revolution having fully conformed their souls to Islam, thus the national revolution was a struggle that had to take place inside each individual before the fight could move to the broader communal and societal context.

[hereafter JogjaDoc] no.203, ANRI, states that 'the characteristics of the Darul Islam survive also amongst Masyumi circles in the Republican territory, as evidenced in the speeches of Wali Alfatah and Kjai A. Sanusi'.

51 "Kutipan Pidato2 pada tgl 28/3-'48 (Kongres Masjumi di Madiun) dari 1. Wali Alfatah 2. KA Sanoesi," JogjaDoc no.243, ANRI. Wali Alfatah would, in November, become vice-chairman of the Central Board of Masyumi; Kiyai Ahmad Sanoesi was a member of the National Majelis Sjoero.

52 Sekarmadji Maridjan Kartosoewirjo et al., *Haloean politik Islam* ([Garoet]: Dewan Penerangan Masjoemi Daerah Priangan, 1946).

To Kartosuwiryo, both the national and social revolutions—now explicitly defined as *jihād aṣġar* and *jihād akbar*, respectively—were necessary to eradicate colonialism, as they acted on two different layers of foreign domination, one external (the state and government) and the other internal (citizens' souls). Further, even though in the context experienced by Indonesia at the time these should be pursued at once, Kartosuwiryo also argued that to ensure de facto and de jure independence, initially a stronger emphasis was to be placed on the national (armed) struggle, with the general umma concentrating its efforts on supporting the physical revolution, while delegating the social revolution to the Islamic leadership.

Looking ahead, Kartosuwiryo advanced the hypothesis that the establishment of an Indonesian state based on Islam could be achieved in a top-down fashion if the umma had enough representatives in the legislature willing to comply with Islamic regulations, thus advancing the formalization of an Islamic government and coordinating laws, judiciary and rulings. But if this strategy were to fail—as Kartosuwiryo had become convinced it would, within a year from delivering this speech—the umma would still be responsible for the implementation of Islamic law at the personal level, thus creating its own *dār al-islām*. Seen as part and parcel of the individual revolution, the involvement of the umma in legal matters was the first step towards an Islamic social revolution, also called an Islamic people's revolution. It is this social dimension of the umma's organization and mobilization that Kartosuwiryo had in mind when he established the Darul Islam in 1948.

7 West Java: *dār al-islām* as *Negara Islam*

The Dutch invasion in July 1947 prompted not only the separate development of parallel paths to independence for West Java and for the Republic, but also radicalized the ideological characterization of the antagonism. In the wake of previous Masyumi calls for "holy war" to defend Indonesia as *dār al-islām* against the Dutch aggression, in mid-August Kartosuwiryo invoked a *perang sabil* for Muslims in West Java. In September this call was echoed on the national level by the Masyumi central branch. Kartosuwiryo's frustration and escalation from previous political engagements is evident: referring back to the definitions of *dār al-islām* and *dār al-salām* offered in *Haloean Politik Islam* he now "clarified" that *dār al-islām* was a *Negara Islam* where Islamic laws were implemented to administer daily life as much as to gain admission to *dār al-salām*; further, the nuanced meaning of jihad as explored in the 1936 *Brosoer Hidjrah* "is also in need of clarification" as *perang sabil* represented one specific case of jihad, which referred directly to a war aimed at defending the state's sovereignty and religion's sacredness.[53]

Kartosuwiryo's narrowing of the meaning of jihad as we see it through his writings from *Sikap Hidjrah* (1936) to *Haloean Politik Islam* (1946) and *Perang Sabil* (1947) was prompted by the changing context of West Java. As first mentioned in *Haloean Politik Islam*, the only way to establish a fully independent *darul Islam*—or Negara Islam Indonesia—that implemented *hukum Islam* (Islamic Law) was through an armed jihad that responded to an attack on the umma.[54] The Dutch aggression provided the necessary political expedient for transforming that *darul Islam* from an ideal concept to a political structure.

In an attempt to marginalize the impact of Dutch operations, in January 1948 Soekarno's Republican government agreed to recognize official colonial control over West Java (with the exception of the Banten area) and the easternmost part of Java (including Surabaya and Malang). As stipulated in the Renville agreement, signed on the homonymous US ship on January 17, Republican troops would withdraw from West Java and across the "van Mook line," the new demarcation line between Dutch- and Indonesia-controlled territory. Outraged at the readiness with which the Republican government had agreed to a diplomatic solution, many in West Java felt abandoned by the nationalist government. Coupled with the fact that Sarekat Islam and Masyumi had the strongest political grip on the population, Kartosuwiryo's declaration that the West Java branch of Masyumi was to interrupt all activities and reconstitute itself as a new organization with regionally-determined priorities and strategies garnered immediate and widespread support. Many Hizboellah and Sabilillah militias refused to withdraw, and several party sub-branches agreed to dissolve their hierarchies and become part of the new Darul Islam.

From a network of religiously-motivated activists and militias committed to defending their territory from colonial dominion, within a little over a year the Darul Islam developed into an Islamic state equipped with a constitution, a criminal code, a structured army and its own currency.

In late 1947 Kartosuwiryo, as vice-president of Masyumi for West Java, called for a conference to reorganize the party's constituency in a way that would reflect the new circumstances.[55] The transformation had its center of motion

---

53 "Keterangan ringkas tentang Perang Sabil S. M. Kartosuwiryo," JogjaDoc no. 243, ANRI.

54 "Qanun asasy Negara Islam Indonesia," AABRI DI no. 9.

55 According to "Negara Islam," Territoriaal Troepencommandant West Java, 12 June 1948, APG no.997, NA, this meeting took place in September 1947; according to "Majelis Oemat Islam," "C" Divisie "7 December," 12 August 1948, APG no. 997 NA, and CMI Publication no. 91, 29 September 1948, Archief van de Algemene Secretarie, 1944–1950 [hereafter AAS]

in Garut, where the party branch was renamed Islamic Community's Defence Council (Majelis Pertahanan Oemmat Islam, MPOI, or Dewan Pertahanan Oemmat Islam, DPOI), clearly marking the changed priorities. Parallel to the organizational restructuring, of key importance was the re-drafting of the political programme—which now stated the duty to "defend [the territory] from the attacks of the [Dutch] Royal Army"[56]—and the formation of an Islamic army, the Tentara Islam Indonesia, which merged the party's multiple armed wings, including Sabilillah, Hizboellah, and several youth groups.[57]

As the Republican TNI (Tentara Nasional Indonesia, Indonesian National Army) prepared to withdraw across the van Mook line, fighting continued. Besides the expected clashes between Indonesian soldiers and Dutch forces, much tension was arising from the internal conflict between Republican and Islamic troops, sparked by ideological as well as logistical causes. By the beginning of February 1948 roughly 22,000 republican soldiers were on their way to Yogyakarta,[58] but several thousand Hizboellah and Sabilillah militiamen remained in West Java, strengthening the bulk of the Islamic Army.[59]

---

no. 3977, NA, this instead took place in November 1947. The Islamic community of West Java was also being organized within the context of the creation of the state of Pasoendan (itself part of the scheme for a federal Republic of Indonesia, RIS), as in mid-October the Islam Conference established the *dewan agama* (religious council) and *dewan al-Islam* (Islamic council), which included a *mahkama Islam, penghulu hakim, hakim nikah* (Islamic court, Islamic judge, and marriage officer, respectively), and an educational division, thus covering all needs of the umma. "Islamic conference of West Java," 26–29 November 1947, AAS no. 3405, NA; this was followed by a similar initiative in East Java later in November 1947.

56 "Majelis Oemat Islam," "C" Divisie "7 December," 12 August 1948, APG no. 997 NA. Probably it referred to the KNIL, but the report only talks of "Nedelandse Leger" and "Tentara Keradjaan."

57 As will appear evident below, other sources claimed that the Tentara Islam Indonesia was created in February 1948. However it is possible that already by late 1947 the coordination efforts among Islamic militias in West Java had led to the formation of a unified army.

58 Abdul Haris Nasution, *Tentara Nasional Indonesia,* (Djakarta: Seruling Masa, 1968); and Ricklefs, *A History of Modern Indonesia since C. 1300*, 227.

59 Between January and mid-March the press recorded a rapid increase in Islamic militias in the Priangan. Until January the town of Maja had been hosting an average of around 300–600 Hizboellah soldiers, but in late February more than 2,000 Hizboellah soldiers, who had been stationed in the area, attacked Bandung, Maja, Majalenka, Sukahaji, and Kadipaten. In mid-March the Dutch "W" Brigade noted a "large concentration" of Tentara Islam, and by April around 3,000 Hizboellah soldiers were in the area: "Sabilillah liar bergerak di sekitar Tjamis," *Sin Po*, 1 March 1948 and "Hizbulah moendoer ke Goenoeng Tjiremei," *Keng Po*, 1 April 1948. See also Ministerie van Defensie [hereafter MD]:

Post-independence government narratives situate the emergence of the Darul Islam in a support-vacuum, suggesting that the majority of those present at the initial gatherings rejected the project of creating an Islamic state in West Java on the ground that this would create the unacceptable conditions for "a *dubbelstaat*, a state within the state."[60] According to archival sources, though, at least 500 delegates and members of five Masyumi branches from across West Java, as well as representatives of other Islamic organizations, attended the first conference held in Pangwedusan, Cisayong on 10–11 February 1948.[61] On this occasion they agreed on three points: the intent of establishing an Islamic state that would implement Islamic laws in a "special region" of the Priangan; the transformation of the Sabilillah into the Tentara Islam Indonesia (TII, Islamic Army of Indonesia); and the declaration of a holy war to defend the territory of the state.[62]

As further clarified in a second conference, held a month later in Cirebon, the Islamic army was instructed to "reach power in a tactful way, succeed in taking control of the Republic, and include it[s territory] within the Islamic state."[63] The Darul Islam was now equipped with a leadership (Imam Kartosuwiryo, Kamran and Raden Oni as heads of the military section, Sanusi Partawijaya and Toha Arsyad as leaders of the political section, and Kiyai Abdul Halim and Kiyai Haji Gozali Toesi as heads of the religious section)[64] and a legal structure

---

Archieven Strijdkrachten in Nederlands-Indie [hereafter AS], nos. 2275 and 2288, NA. By the end of the year more than 50,000 men were in the rank and file of the TII. "CMI Doc. no. 5176, Documenten betreffende de 'Daroel Islam'–beweging," 21 December 1948, AAS no.2752, NA. Among them were Zainal Abidin's group in Blubur Limbangan, Koernia's in Cicalengka, Enoks's in Wanaraja (Garut), Oni's in Mount Cupu, and Kamran's on the border between Majalengka and Tasikmalaya (Pagerageung area). Nasution, *Tentara Nasional Indonesia,* 125; Tanu Suherly, "Kekuatan gerilya di daerah Priangan pada waktu divisi Siliwangi hijrah tahun 1948" (Seminar Sejarah Nasional ke-3 di Jakarta, Jakarta, 1981), 4; the latter provides a detailed list of the various groups, ibid., 4–10.

60 Kementerian Penerangan, *Republik Indonesia: propinsi Djawa Barat* (Jakarta: Kementerian Penerangan, 1953), 215.

61 Dinas Sedjarah TNI, *Penumpasan Pemberontakan D.I./T.I.I., S. M. Kartosuwiryo Di Jawa Barat* (1974; repr., Bandung: Dinas Sejarah Tentara Nasional Indonesia Angkatan Darat, 1982), 59–65, quoting from *Sedjarah Goenoeng Tjoepoe* in Dani Wahdani, "Politik militer Angkatan Perang Negara Islam Indonesia (A.P.N.I.I.) di Jawa Barat pimpinan Imam S. M. Kartosoewirjo" (Thesis, Universitas Padjadjaran, 2003), 59.

62 "Overzicht en Ontwikkeling van de Toestand 8 April 1800 uur tot 15 April 1800 uur," Territorial ts. Tropencommandant West Java [1948], MD: AS no. 2224, NA.

63 "Dunia Masyumi," in JogjaDoc no.218h, ANRI.

64 Dinas Sedjarah TNI, *Penumpasan Pemberontakan D.I./T.I.I.*, 63. Some degree of influence was also in the hands of Dahlan Lukman (GPII-Priangan leader), Siti Murtayi'ah

(all matters related to combat were said to be determined by the Islamic government in accordance with "Islamic laws," but no details were provided at this stage),[65] and so it set out to draft a clearly defined Islamic policy. After shedding its Republican legacy by dissolving Masyumi,[66] the political agenda of the new organization focused on the preparations for a new state. This *Negara Baru* was to be a democratic Islamic state which stood as an alternative solution to a national state in case the Republican government was dissolved, or a Dutch-promoted state of West Java was created.[67]

In the early months of 1948 the Darul Islam was garnering much support, both logistically and ideologically, from the general populace and Republican politicians alike. Some of the western Javanese Masyumi branches that had initially appeared lukewarm to the idea of joining in were by mid-year issuing statements of support and establishing new TII groups.[68] Similarly, nuclei of Islamic governments, named Majelis Oemmat Islam (MOI, a variation on the Garut Islamic Community's Defence Council, MPOI, mentioned above) had been replicated across the region, creating a coordinating structure for the defence of the region.[69]

Throughout the second half of 1948 the Darul Islam underwent major changes, transitioning from a political organization-cum-army to a full-fledged

---

(GPII-*Putri* Priangan leader), Abdullah Ridwan (Hizboellah-Priangan leader), and five other *cabang*-level leaders from Garut, including Saefullah (*cabang* vice-president), who was subsequently arrested and on whose confessions the first Dutch report on the Darul Islam was based.

65 "Rencana ketenteraan oemmat Islam," in JogjaDoc no.218h, ANRI.

66 "Especially as the political negotiations between the Republican government and the Netherlands are not concluded yet, Masyumi's sub-groups GPII, Muslimat, GPII Putri, *fonds* Sabilillah, STII, SDII, Hizboellah, Sabilillah, and all the organisation's branches are to suspend their activities in the western part of Java beginning 1 March 1948 at 14.00." "Dunia Masyumi menghentikan usahanya," 1 March 1948 in "Pelaporan No.14/7/48 Perihal 'Darul Islam,'" Jawatan Kepolisian Negara Bagian PAM Yogyakarta, 17 July 1948, JogjaDoc no. 218h, ANRI.

67 "Program politik ummat Islam," in JogjaDoc no. 218h, ANRI.

68 See "Extract uit D.O.B.I. n.631 dd 10/05/48 Nefis IV dd 9-5-48 Eval A.Z.," APG no.1000, NA. on Banten and "Tentara Islam Indonesia," 17 August 1948, APG no. 1002, NA on Bogor. On Bandung see Wiranatakoesoema's participation in the formation of the Bandung MOI, "CMI Signalement: de verhouding tussen Wali Negara van Pasoendan Wiranatakoesoema en de Daroel-Islam," March 1949, AAS no. 3979, NA.

69 "Qanun Asasy Negara Islam Indonesia," AABRI, Jakarta. DI no. 9. See also "Ontstaand en ontwikkeling der 'Majelis Islam,' bezien uit militair standpunt," Territoriaal Troepencommandant West Java, 19 March 1949, APG no. 1002, NA.

state. On 27 August, Kartosuwiryo released the constitution of the Islamic state which established the Negara Islam Indonesia as a republic, led by an imam, and based on sharia law. The Darul Islam's *Qanun Asasy* remains one of very few historical attempts to formally structure an Islamic state in the Sunni Muslim world in the twentieth century, possibly only equaled by Nabhani's *Niẓām al-islām,* published in 1952 and still today used as the blueprint for Hizb ut-Tahrir's caliphal Islamic state.

8 Darul Islam: Between Community and Territoriality

Territorial gains had become a strategic and political priority for the Darul Islam, and its cadres structured their expansion from the Garut MPDOI in terms of the effective and tangible influence the Majelis Oemmat Islam held on administering the law. West Java had been divided into three areas: the *Daerah Satu* (meaning Region One and shortened in the original documents as D.I) which included villages controlled by the Darul Islam and implementing Islamic law; the *Daerah Dua* (D.II, Region Two) which included the areas where the Darul Islam, the Majelis Oemmat Islam (MOI) or the TII had freedom of movement and strong influence; and lastly, the *Daerah Tiga* (D.III, Region Three) enclosing those areas where the Darul Islam only had a limited degree of influence.[70] With Kartosuwiryo's skilful political guidance and the able military leadership of Kamran and Nur Lubis, the Darul Islam expanded widely. While strengthening its political structure, by May 1948 the Majelis Oemmat Islam-Darul Islam had established its territorial presence across the Priangan, and by September the D.I area had come to include all that back in May was part of the D.III.[71]

---

70 "Qanun Asasy Negara Islam Indonesia," AABRI DI no. 9; "Majelis Oemat Islam," 12 August 1948, APG no.997, NA, pp. 6–7; CMI Publication no. 91, 29 September 1948, AAS no. 3977, NA, pp. 8, 13. According to the latter source, in May 1948 "Region One" included the area enclosed within Tasikmalaya, Ciawi, Panumbangan, and Mount Sawal; the D.II encompassed the area between Cileungjji (Ciamis), Cisayong (Tasikmalaya), Nagrek, Darmarata, Talaga, and Mount Sawal; and the D.III stretched eastward to Majalengka and Cikijing, and southeast to Lakbok, Parigi, Cikatomas, and Tasikmalaya.

71 The D.II stretched southwest to Pameungpeuk and Mount Cupu, northwest to Tanjungsari and Tanjunkerta (Sumedang), north to the railway in Sukamelang, east to Cirebon, and then curving back in to Cikijing and Mount Sawal. And the D.III had expanded further into the Garut regency in Bungbulang, towards Bandung, Indramayu, and Cirebon in the north, and east into Central Java, with Salem under Darul Islam influence. CMI Publication no. 91, 29 September 1948, AAS no. 3977, NA.

Talks about a *dār al-islām* were then common, but at no point in time was there a description of the territory beyond Darul Islam's control, or of that under Dutch control specifically, as a *dār al-ḥarb*. Not even when throughout 1948 the Islamic Army engaged in combat with the Dutch and leftist guerrilla groups, in their attempt to expand the territorial scope of MOI-controlled areas.

Focusing the analysis on the relationship between the Darul Islam as an Islamic state and its enemies—viz. the Dutch authorities and the Indonesian Republic's army and the political establishment that supported them—it is striking that despite the status of the Negara Islam, Indonesia is often referred to as *fī waqt al-ḥarb*,[72] and the existence of a *dār al-islām* bearing the ultimate goal of ensuring its subjects' access to the *dār al-salām*[73] is devoid of a *dār al-ḥarb* counterpart. The enemy is initially identified as the Negara Belanda (Dutch state) and "those who become Dutch puppets."[74] In the months between the establishment of Darul Islam and the suppression of Kartosuwiryo's movement in 1962, the theological or ideological framing of the Islamic army's approach to "other forces" withered, and it was developed case-by-case, more often than not on the basis of military-strategic considerations.

Following political-military developments between the Islamic, Republican and Dutch armies, it is possible to trace how the enemies of the Islamic state were defined through the years. By the end of the 1950s, as the Dutch had been fully removed from Indonesia, Soekarno had started to implement the "Guided Democracy," and the Army had succeeded in imposing a heavier repression of the rebellion, the Darul Islam / *dār al-islām* terminology disappeared altogether. In 1948 the enemies of NII included Republican "wild militias."[75] In 1949, following the Roem–von Royem agreement, the Federal State of Indonesia (Republik Indonesia Serikat, RIS) was described as a "puppet state" whose sovereignty was "fake" because granted by the Dutch.[76] In the NII's criminal code "those who fight [the NII]" were targets of jihad and were called *muḥarrib*, or *kāfir ḥarbī*.[77] By the early 1950s the NII was set to fight all "enemies of God's religion, and enemies of the Islamic State."[78] Soon afterwards they came to be identified through the lens of *jāhiliyya*: the Republican TNI was a "*jāhiliyya* Army"[79] and *Pancasila* was

72 See *Qanun Asasy* but also *Ma'lumat Imam* no. 7, 23 December 1948.

73 Among other, see *Ma'lumat Imam* no. 6, 21 December 1948.

74 *Ma'lumat Imam* no. 7.

75 *Maklumat Militer NII* no. 1, 25 January 1949.

76 *Manifesto Politik* 1/7, 26 August 1949.

77 *Hukum Pidana*, Chapter X (25) on *Jihad*.

78 *Ma'lumat Komandemen Tertinggi* no. 7, 7 February 1951.

79 *Ma'lumat Komandemen Tertinggi* no. 10, 21 October 1952.

"an ideology of ignorance."[80] But after a decade of ideological Islamist framing of the struggle, the group entered a new phase, one focussed on a political and military confrontation against Soekarno's Republic, and thus far removed from Islamic ideals. The Political Manifesto issued by the NII in 1959, while deeply engaged with military matters, had abandoned the concept of a *dār al-islām* concerned with otherworldly salvation.

9 Concluding Remarks

The historical trajectory of the *dār al-islām* ideal in colonial and independent Indonesia, and its relation to *dār al-ḥarb* and jihad, as delineated in this article, sets itself aside from studies of these concepts in their classical or theoretical manifestations. Thus, it offers a window on its lived experience and contextualized understanding as an encounter of religious ideology and political-military circumstances in the modern era of nation-states' formation. The analysis of *dār al-islām* as a societal, community-based structure—or even as an individual's behavior—aimed at eternal salvation while under *kāfir* rule, and its transformation into a territorially defined (and expanding) political entity ruled through a set of Islamic laws in order to defy colonial authorities, aims at highlighting how enmeshed in the surrounding political and historical context the implementation of religiously-based strategies is.

References

Abeyasekere, Susan. "The Soetardjo Petition." *Indonesia* 15 (April 1973): 80–108.

Al-Chaidar. *Pemikiran politik proklamator negara Islam Indonesia S. M. Kartosoewirjo: fakta dan data sejarah Darul Islam*. Jakarta: Darul Falah, 1999.

Amiq, Amiq. "Two Fatwas on Jihād against the Dutch Colonisation in Indonesia: A Prosopographical Approach to the Study of Fatwa." *Studia Islamika* 5–3 (1998): 81–124.

Benda, Harry Jindrich. *The Crescent and the Rising Sun: Indonesian Islam Under the Japanese Occupation, 1942–1945*. Dordrecht: Foris, 1985.

Castles, Lance. "The Jihād Motif in Indonesian Islam." Melbourne: Melbourne University, 2003.

Dijk, Kees van. *The Netherlands Indies and the Great War, 1914–1918*. Leiden: Brill, 2007.

80 Statement Pemerintah NII no. VI/7, 3 September 1953, point 2.

Dinas Sedjarah TNI. *Penumpasan Pemberontakan D.I./T.I.I., S. M. Kartosuwiryo Di Jawa Barat*. 1974. Reprint, Bandung: Dinas Sejarah Tentara Nasional Indonesia Angkatan Darat, 1982.

Elson, R. E. "Another Look at the Jakarta Charter Controversy of 1945." *Indonesia* 88 (October 2009): 105–30.

Formichi, Chiara. *Islam and the Making of the Nation: Kartosuwiryo and Political Islam in Twentieth-Century Indonesia*. Leiden: KITLV, 2012.

Gericke, Johann Friedrich Carl, Johannes Gerhardus Hermanus Gunning, Albert Cornelis Vreede, and Taco Roorda. *Javaansch-Nederlandsch Handwoordenboek*. Amsterdam: J. Müller, 1901.

Hadi, Amirul. "Exploring the Acehnese Conception of War and Peace (A Study of *Hikayat Prang Sabil*)." Banda Aceh, 2007.

Haidar, Ali. "Nahdlatul Ulama dan Islam di Indonesia: Pendekatan Fikih Dalam Politik." IAIN Syarif Hidayatulah, 1993.

Hasan, Noorhaidi. "Al-Jihād fī sabīl Allah: A study on the Fatwa of 'Abd al-Samad al-Palimbani Concerning Holy War for the Cause of Allah." Master's thesis, Rijks Universiteit, 1998.

Kartosoewirjo, Sekarmadji Maridjan. *Haloean politik Islam*. [Garoet]: Dewan Penerangan Masjoemi Daerah Priangan, 1946.

Kementerian Penerangan. *Republik Indonesia: propinsi Djawa Barat*. Jakarta: Kementerian Penerangan, 1953.

Klinkert, Hillebrandus Cornelius. *Nieuw Maleisch-Nederlandsch Woordenboek Met Arabisch Karakter, Naar de Beste En Laatste Bronnen Bewerkt*. Leiden: Brill, 1947.

Masjoemi. *Partai Politik Islam Indonesia*. Boekit Tinggi: Dewan Pemimpin Daerah Masjoemi Soematra Barat, n.d.

Masyhuri, Aziz. *Masalah Keagamaan Nahdlatul Ulama: Hasil Muktamar Dan Munas Ulama Kesatu-1926 S/d Kedua Puluh Sembilan 1994*. Surabaya: Dinamika press, 1997.

Nasution, Abdul Haris. *Tentara Nasional Indonesia*. Djakarta: Seruling Masa, 1968.

Nasution, Harun. "The Islamic State in Indonesia: The Rise of the Ideology, the Movement for Its Creation and the Theory of the MASJUMI." Masters' thesis, McGill, 1965.

Noer, Deliar. "Masjumi: Its Organization, Ideology, and Political Role in Indonesia," 1961.

Poerwadarminta, W. J. S. *Baoesastra Djawa,*. Batavia: J. B. Wolters, 1939.

Pudjiastuti, Titiek, ed. *Kitab Yusuf*. Translated by Hadipranata Hardjana. Jakarta: Departemen Pendidikan dan Kebudayaan, Proyek Penerbitan Buku Sastra Indonesia dan Daerah, 1981.

Ricklefs, Merle Calvin. "A Consideration of Three Versions of the 'Babad Tanah Djawi', with Excerpts on the Fall of Madjapahit." *Bulletin of the School of Oriental and African Studies* 35, no. 2 (1972): 285–315.

Ricklefs, Merle Calvin. *A History of Modern Indonesia since C. 1300*. Stanford: Stanford University Press, 1993.

Ricklefs, Merle Calvin. *Mystic Synthesis in Java: A History of Islamisation from the Fourteenth to the Early Nineteenth Centuries*. Norwalk, CT: Signature Books, 2006.

Suherly, Tanu. "Kekuatan gerilya di daerah Priangan pada waktu divisi Siliwangi hijrah tahun 1948." Jakarta, 1981.

Wahdani, Dani. "Politik militer Angkatan Perang Negara Islam Indonesia (A.P.N.I.I.) di Jawa Barat pimpinan Imam S. M. Kartosoewirjo." Thesis, Universitas Padjadjaran, 2003.

Periodical Publications

al-Djihad

Algemeen overzicht van de Inlandsche (Maleisisch-Chineesche en Arabische) Pers

ANP-Aneta Bulletin

Asia Raya

Indonesia Merdeka

Keng Po

Overzicht van der Inlandsche en Maleisisch-Chineesche Pers

Politiek-politioneele overzichten van Nederlandsch-Indie

Sin Po

Soeara MIAI

Archives and Collections

Het Nationaal Archief, The Hague.

Archief van de Algemene Secretarie, 1944–1950

Archief van de Procureur-Generaal

Archief van het Ministerie van Kolonie, 1900–1963 Geheime Mailrapporten

Arsip Angkatan Bersenjata Republik Indonesia, Jakarta

Arsip Nasional Republik Indonesia Jakarta

Arsip Jogja Documenten 1946–1948

Arsip Kementrian Pertahanan 1946

DI-NII Pamphlets and Documents (in chronological order)

Sikap hidjrah PSII, 10 September 1936

Daftar oesaha hidjrah PSII, March 1940

Haloean politik Islam, 16 August 1946

Perang sabil, 27 Ramadhan 1366/15 August 1947

Qanun asasy Negara Islam Indonesia, 22 Syawal 1367/27 August 1948

Proklamasi Negara Islam Indonesia, 12 Syawal 1368/18 August 1949

Manifesto politik 1/7, 1 Dzulqa'idah 1368/26 August 1949

CHAPTER 17

Dār al-islām and *dār al-ḥarb* in Modern Indian Muslim Thought

Yohanan Friedmann

In memory of my ham-pīrah *and friend,*
the late Professor Mušīr al-Ḥaqq

1

Classical Muslim religious literature reflects an inclination to classify religions, human beings and geographical areas. The Qur'an divides humanity into believers, "The People of the Book" (*ahl al-kitāb*), infidels and polytheists; it also mentions Sabeans and Zoroastrians. The jurisprudents expand and refine this classification: they speak about believers, infidels, polytheists (Arab and non-Arab), Arab Christians and Arab Jews (*naṣārā al-ʿarab wa yahūduhum*), "the protected communities" (*ahl al-ḏimma*), "the people of war" (*ahl al-ḥarb*), "the people of contract" (*ahl al-ʿahd*) and "the people who have been given safe conduct (*ahl al-amān*)" and reside temporarily in the Muslim world.[1] There is no classification of geographical areas in the Qur'an. In the *Ṣaḥīḥ* of Buḫārī, the expressions *dār al-islām* and *dār al-ḥarb* appear only in the Hadith headlines, not in the *matn* of the Hadith.[2] The situation is different in the classical geographical literature. In an important article, Giovanna Calasso analyzed the

1 Yohanan Friedmann, *Tolerance and Coercion in Islam. Interfaith Relations in the Muslim Tradition* (Cambridge: Cambridge University Press, 2003), 54–86; (=Yohanan Friedmann, "Classification of Unbelievers in Sunnī Muslim Law and Tradition," *Jerusalem Studies in Arabic and Islam* 22 [1998]: 163–95).

2 Giovanna Calasso, "Alla ricerca di *dār al-islām*. Una ricognizione nei testi di giuristi e tradizionisti, lessicografi, geografi e viaggiatori," *Rivista degli Studi Orientali* 83 (2010): 280; cf. Muḥammad b. Ismāʿīl al-Buḫārī, *Le recueil des traditions mahométanes par el-Bokhâri (al-Ṣaḥīḥ)*, ed. M. Ludolf Krehl, vol. 1 (Leiden: Brill, 1862), vol. 2, 260, 262.

 | DOI 10.1163/9789004331037_019

ways in which geographers describe the various parts of the world.[3] They use for non-Muslim areas terms such as *bilād al-kufr, bilād al-širk, mulk al-naṣārā, diyār Fāris wa'l-rūm,* or *Ifranja.* The regions inhabited by Muslims are usually called *mamlakat al-islām, bilād al-islām,* or *diyār al-ʿarab. Dār al-islām* and *dār al-ḥarb* are less frequent.[4] When Iṣṭaḫrī describes Ethiopia, he says that "they are peaceful people and [their country] is not an abode of war" (*wa-hum ahl silm laysū bi-dār ḥarb*).[5] This means that a region which has peaceful relations with the Muslims is not *dār al-ḥarb* even if it is not under Muslim rule. It is also significant to note that a substantial collection of Muslim maps from the fifth/eleventh century does not use the term *dār al-ḥarb* or *dār al-islām.*[6] It seems that the juristic discourse which is the mainstay of the present study spread into other branches of Muslim literature only partially, but this requires further research.[7]

The jurisprudents speak about "the abode of Islam" (*dār al-islām*), "the abode of war" (*dār al-ḥarb*), "the abode of truce" (*dār al-hudna*), "the abode of safety" (*dār al-amān*) and "the abode of treaty" (*dār al-ʿahd*).[8] However, we do not find in their works a general statement defining the desirable relationship between them. In modern research the situation is different. Majid Khadduri maintains in his influential *War and peace in the law of Islam* that

> on the assumption that the ultimate aim of islam was world-wide, the *dār al-islām* was always, in theory, at war with the *dār al-ḥarb*.... Failure by non-Muslims to accept Islam or pay the poll-tax made it incumbent on the Muslim state to declare *jihād* ... upon the recalcitrant individuals and communities.[9]

---

3 Calasso, "Alla ricerca di *dār al-islām,*" 286–90.

4 Abū Isḥāq Ibrāhīm al-Iṣṭaḫrī, *Kitāb Masālik al-mamālik* (Leiden: Brill, 1927), 281 ll. 10–11; 290 ll. 3–4 from bottom; 291 ll. 2–3; Abū 'l-Qāsim al-Naṣībī Ibn Ḥawqal, *Kitāb Ṣūrat al-arḍ* (Leiden: Brill, 1948), 14, l. 17; p. 340 *supra*; p. 449, l. 4 (*dūr al-kufr,* in the plural form).

5 Calasso, "Alla ricerca di *dār al-islām,*" 288n60; cf. Iṣṭaḫrī, *Kitāb Masālik al-mamālik,* 35 *infra,* 36 l. 1.

6 See Yossef Rapoport and Emilie Savage-Smith, eds., *An Eleventh-Century Egyptian Guide to the Universe: The Book of Curiosities,* Islamic Philosophy, Theology and Science, v. 87 (Leiden: Brill, 2014) and a personal communication by Yossef Rapoport, January 31, 2014.

7 Calasso, "Alla ricerca di *dār al-islām,*" 289 *infra.*

8 For further terms, see the path-breaking article of Khaled Abou El Fadl, "Islamic Law and Muslim Minorities: The Juristic Discourse on Muslim Minorities from the Second/Eighth to the Eleventh/Seventeenth Centuries," *Islamic Law and Society* 1, no. 2 (1994): 161.

9 Majid Khadduri, *War and Peace in the Law of Islam* (Baltimore: The Johns Hopkins Press, 1955), 55; cf. idem *The Islamic Law of Nations: Shaybānī's Siyar.* Translated with an Introduction,

Bernard Lewis maintains that between *dār al-islām* and *dār al-ḥarb* "there is a morally necessary, legally and religiously obligatory state of war, until the final and inevitable triumph of Islam over unbelief."[10] Patricia Crone writes that "Muslims were legally obliged to wage holy war against *dār al-ḥarb* until it ceased to exist ..."[11] Armand Abel seems to concur with this opinion[12] and the Pakistani version of the *Encyclopaedia of Islam* mentions the view that it is not permissible to wage war against a non-Muslim area without reason, but if the inhabitants refuse to embrace islam or accept *ḏimmī* status, jihad becomes obligatory.[13] It is easy to substantiate this interpretation by referring to various Qur'anic verses, such as Q 9:29,[14] and the idea that the imam should wage jihad against the infidels as frequently as possible is pervasive in the books of law.[15] It is, nevertheless, noteworthy that a general definition of *dār al-ḥarb* along these lines cannot easily be found in the works of the classical Muslim jurisprudents. This does not mean that these jurisprudents opposed it; it seems, rather, that the two concepts and their interpretation were so well known that the jurisprudents did not deem it necessary to elaborate on their meaning. The basic and prevalent understanding of the classical jurists is that *dār al-islām* is an area in which a Muslim is the sovereign, Islamic law is enforced, and Muslims and *ḏimmīs* enjoy security. *Dār al-ḥarb* is under the sovereignty of non-Muslims who enforce non-Muslim laws in the area under their jurisdiction. The classical Muslim sources seem to assume that the non-Muslim rulers deny religious

---

Notes and Appendices (Baltimore: The Johns Hopkins Press, 1966), 11–12; numerous articles in Marie-Luisa Frick and Andreas Th. Müller, eds., *Islam and International Law: Engaging Self-Centrism from a Plurality of Perspectives*, Brill's Arab and Islamic Law Series, volume 7 (Leiden: Brill–Nijhoff, 2013) are relevant to the modern discussions of the issue.

10 Bernard Lewis, *The Political Language of Islam*, 4th ed. (Chicago: Univ. of Chicago Press, 1991), 73 and index, s.v. *dār al–ḥarb*.

11 Patricia Crone, *Medieval Islamic Political Thought* (Edinburgh: Edinburgh Univ. Press, 2004), 362.

12 Armand Abel, "Dār al-ḥarb," *Encyclopaedia of Islam, Vol. II, C-G* (Leiden: Brill, 1965).

13 Ẓahūr Aḥmad Aẓhar, "Dār al-ḥarb," *Urdū Dā'ira-yi Ma'ārif-i Islāmiyya* (Lahore: University of the Panjab, 1972); see also Mohammad-Reza Djalili, "Dār al-ḥarb," *The Oxford Encyclopedia of the Islamic world*, ed. John L. Esposito (New York, N.Y.: Oxford University Press, 2009).

14 "Fight those who believe not in God and the Last Day and do not forbid what God and His messenger have forbidden – such men as practice not the religion of truth, being of those who have been given the Book – until they pay the tribute out of hand and have been humbled." Translation by Arthur John Arberry, ed., *The Koran Interpreted: A Translation*, A Touchstone Book (New York: Simon & Schuster, 1996).

15 See, for instance, Abū 'Abd Allāh Muḥammad al-Šāfi'ī, *Kitāb al-Umm* (Beirut: Dār al-kutub al-'ilmiyya, 1993), vol. 4, 235–37.

freedom to the Muslim inhabitants of *dār al-ḥarb*. The term *ḥarbī* is used in the sense of an inhabitant of the *dār al-ḥarb*. In the classical legal sources I have not come across an explicit statement according to which *dār al-ḥarb* is so called because it should be incorporated into *dār al-islām* by means of war. Abū al-Aʿlā Mawdūdī has interpreted *dār al-ḥarb* as a political entity at war with the Muslims,[16] but I have not seen this interpretation in the classical books of law. Arab dictionaries, on the other hand, routinely define *dār al-ḥarb* as "the land of the idolaters who do not have a peace agreement with the Muslims" (*dār al-ḥarb bilād al-mušrikīn allaḏīna lā ṣulḥa baynahum wa-bayna 'l-muslimīn*).[17] This is also not very clear: areas which have no peace agreement with the Muslims are *dār al-ḥarb*, but we are not told what are the conclusions which the Muslims should draw from this legal assertion. Tahānawī defines the *dār al-ḥarb* as "an area in which the writ of the infidel ruler runs" (*wa-dār al-ḥarb ʿindahum mā yajrī fīhi amr raʾīs al-kuffār min al-bilād*) or "an area in which (the Muslims) live in fear of the infidels (*wa-dār al-ḥarb mā ḫāfū fīhi min al-kāfirīn*).[18] Mushtaq Muhammad Ahmad maintains that the division of the world into *dār al-islām* and *dār al-ḥarb* or *dār al-kufr* is "an affirmation of the principle of territorial jurisdiction," meaning that Muslim courts have no jurisdiction over transgressions committed beyond the borders of the Muslim state, and this nomenclature does not have a necessary link with the idea that the Islamic state should perennially be locked in hostilities with the rest of the world.[19] This is a reasonable explanation of the division of the world into two areas, but it does not take into account the terms used, especially not the term *dār al-ḥarb*.

As noted above, in the classical Muslim books of law I have not come across an explicit statement according to which the *dār al-ḥarb* is so called because it is to be conquered by the Muslims by force of arms. The jurisprudents are mainly interested in the behavior expected of Muslims in *dār al-ḥarb* or of

---

16 Mawdūdī maintains that the early jurists used this term because in their days the *dār al-kufr* was also *dār al-ḥarb*; this is to say, all countries beyond the border of Islam were at war with the Muslims. In later periods, this situation no longer obtains and a distinction between the two concepts must be made. See Abū al-Aʿlā Mawdūdī, *Sūd*, 25th ed. (1st ed. 1961) (Lahore: Islamic Publications Limited, 2005), 312.

17 Giuliano Lancioni, "The Missing *dār*: On Collocations in Classical Arabic Dictionaries," this volume; Calasso, "Alla ricerca di *dār al-islām*," 294.

18 Muḥammad Aʿlā b. ʿAlī al-Tahānawī, *Kaššāf iṣṭilāḥāt al-funūn*, ed. Aḥmad Jawdat (Istanbul: Dār al-Ḫilāfa al-ʿaliyya, 1317), vol. 1, p. 512.

19 Mushtaq Muhammad Ahmad, "The notions of *dār al-ḥarb* and *dār al-Islām* in Islamic jurisprudence with special reference to the Ḥanafī school," *Islamic Studies* 47 (2008): passim; conclusions on p. 36.

non-Muslim *musta'mins* in *dār al-islām*. For example, Dabbūsī (d. 430/1039)[20] maintains in his work on the differences between the schools of law that in the Hanafi school the world is divided into *dār al-islām* and *dār al-ḥarb,* while according to Šāfiʿī the whole world is "one abode" (*dār wāḥida*). He says nothing about the meaning of these terms and about the desired relationship between the two abodes. Instead, he moves immediately to discuss questions such as the laws concerning married couples who live in different abodes or the applicability of *lex talionis* in *dār al-ḥarb*.[21]

The pertinent chapters in the books of law usually speak about the rights and obligations of Muslims in *dār al-ḥarb* and of non-Muslims in *dār al-islām.* An excellent example of this approach is the *Kitāb al-Siyar al-kabīr* by Muḥammad b. al-Ḥasan al-Šaybānī (d. 189/805). It includes ample material about laws which should be followed in both areas, but no meaningful definition of the areas themselves can be found there. The impression which one gains from the legal questions adduced by Šaybānī is that there are intermittent battles on the border between *dār al-islām* and *dār al-ḥarb,* but at the same time there are also economic transactions and other relationships between the two areas. This can be gauged from the extensive discussion of types of merchandise which may or may not be exported into *dār al-ḥarb*.[22]

In the debates which are analyzed in the main part of the present study, the issue of *dār al-islām* and *dār al-ḥarb* is frequently discussed together with the question of the legality or otherwise of interest[23] transactions. As is well known, the Qur'an prohibited interest. Responding to those who say that "trading is like interest", the Qur'an asserts that "God has permitted trading and has forbidden interest" (*qālū innamā al-bayʿu miṯlu al-ribā wa-aḥalla 'llāh al-bayʿa wa-ḥarrama al-ribā*).[24] Of particular significance for our purpose is the verse which urges Muslims: "do not consume your goods between you unjustly, unless if it is mutually agreed trading" (... *lā ta'kulū amwālakum baynakum bi'l-bāṭil illā an takūna tijāratan ʿan tarāḍin minkum ...*).[25] On the face of it, the verse does not speak of interest, but if "consuming your goods

20 See Brockelmann, *Geschichte der arabischen Litteratur*, vol. 1 (Leiden: Brill, 1937), 296–297; 1. Supplementband. (Leiden: Brill, 1938); 296–97.

21 Abū Zayd ʿUbayd Allāh b. ʿUmar b. ʿĪsā Dabbūsī, *Kitāb ta'sīs al-naẓar* (Cairo, n.d.), 58–59.

22 Muḥammad b. al-Ḥasan al-Šaybānī, *Šarḥ al-Siyar al-kabīr*, ed. al-Munajjid (Cairo, 1957), vol. 4, pp. 1567ff.

23 When discussing the question of interest transactions, several scholars use the term "usury" for Arabic *ribā* or Persian and Urdu *sūd.* This is misleading: the Qur'an prohibited any interest, not only exorbitant one.

24 Q 2:275. Cf. Q 2:276, 278; 3:130; 4:160; 30:39.

25 Q 4:28. Cf. Q 2:188.

between you unjustly" could be interpreted as relating to interest transactions, then "between you" could mean that these transactions are forbidden only between Muslims and could be understood as legalizing such transactions if they are between Muslims and non-Muslims. There are also prophetic traditions which can be understood in a similar way. A tradition which has been used several times in the thirteenth/nineteenth century debate reads: "There is no interest between the master and his slave and between a Muslim and a *ḥarbī* in *dār al-ḥarb*" (*lā ribā bayna al-mawlā wa ʿabdihi wa-lā bayna al-muslim wa'l-ḥarbī fī dār al-ḥarb*). This tradition, which is not included in the canonical books of Hadith but appears in numerous other collections and in books of law,[26] has been interpreted by Abū Ḥanīfa as allowing interest transactions in *dār al-ḥarb*. Abū Ḥanīfa opined that when a Muslim takes interest from a *ḥarbī*, he does not commit a transgression because the property of a *ḥarbī* is not protected, and as long as the *ḥarbī* agrees to the transaction and the Muslim's actions do not involve treachery, the Muslim can appropriate a *ḥarbī*'s property in any way. In other words, the prohibition of interest is not of universal validity; it is applicable only in *dār al-islām*. Abū Ḥanīfa's interpretation has no support in the other schools of law, which maintain that the Qur'anic injunction against interest is valid everywhere.[27] Another formulation of Abū Ḥanīfa's view also allows the taking of interest from the inhabitants of *dār al-ḥarb*, but it describes it as a deferred sale transaction rather than interest:

> If a (Muslim) *musta'min* among them (i.e. among the people of *dār al-ḥarb*) sold them a dirham for two dirhams (to be paid) after a year, then came to our abode, then returned to them or set out after a year (*min ʿāmihi*), then returned to them after the date (agreed upon) and took the dirhams, there is nothing wrong in it
>
> (law anna al-musta'min fīhim bāʿahum dirhaman bi-dirhamayn ilā sana ṯumma ḫaraja ilā dārinā ṯumma rajaʿa ilayhim aw ḫaraja min ʿāmihi

---

26 Muḥammad b. Aḥmad al-Saraḫsī, *Kitāb al-Mabṣūṭ fī 'l-fiqh al-Ḥanafī*, (Beirut: Dār al-Maʿrifa, n.d.), vol. 14, 56–57; Burhān al-dīn Abū 'l-Ḥasan al-Marġīnānī, *al-Hidāya šarḥ Bidāyat al-mubtadi'* (Cairo: Dār al-salām, 2000), vol. 3, 1011.

27 Marġīnānī, *Hidāya*, vol. 3, 1011; for a summary of the contradictory views of Šāfiʿī, Awzāʿī and even Abū Yūsuf (Abū Ḥanīfa's disciple), see Saraḫsī, *al-Mabṣūṭ*, vol. 14, 56–57; Šāfiʿī, *al-Umm*, vol. 3, 37, 38n5.

> ṯumma raja'a ilayhim fa-aḫaḏa al-darāhim ba'da ḥulūl al-ajal lam yakun bihi ba's).[28]

The circumlocution is telling: it allows for a manifest interest transaction while calling it a "deferred sale" of one dirham for two.[29] It is significant to observe that the connection between the legal status of an area as *dār al-ḥarb* and interest transactions, which is crucial in the relevant discussions in British India in the thirteenth/nineteenth century, can be found in the Hanafi sources of the second/eighth century.

Later scholars relate to the question under what conditions *dār al-ḥarb* becomes *dār al-islām* and vice versa. However, one should be aware of the fact that this rather schematic division does not allow for complex situations which developed after the classical law crystallized. The classical jurisprudents assume that non-Muslim authorities deny Muslims living under their jurisdiction freedom of religious belief and observance. However, this was not always the case. For instance, Transoxania in the sixth/twelfth century came under the rule of the Qara Khitai dynasty which did not embrace Islam, but allowed unrestricted freedom of worship to the predominantly Muslim population. Local Muslim rulers were retained under the overall authority of their non-Muslim overlords.[30] Michal Biran asserted that "the Qara Khitai policies created a situation in which at least Transoxania ... considered itself part of *dār al-islām* despite its infidel overlords."[31] Her assertion can be substantiated by a significant passage found in *Fatāwā fuṣūl al-iḥkām fī uṣūl al-aḥkām* by

28 Šaybānī, *Siyar*, vol. 4, 1486 (no. 2899); cf. ibid., 1493–94 (no. 2919). The opinion of Abū Ḥanīfa is not shared by Abū Yūsuf, Awzā'ī and Šāfi'ī who maintain that interest is prohibited everywhere (*al-ribā 'alayhi ḥarām fī dār al-ḥarb wa ġayrihā*). See Abū Bakr Aḥmad b. al-Ḥusayn b. 'Alī al-Bayhaqī, *Ma'rifat al-Sunan wa'l-āṯār*, ed. Sayyid Kisrawī Ḥasan (Beirut: Dār al-kutub al-'ilmiyya, 1991), vol. 7, 47–48 (no. 1148); see also Saraḫsī, *al-Mabṣūṭ*, vol. 14, p. 56.

29 Cf. Gīlānī's suggestion to take interest in *dār al-ḥarb*, but consider it spoils (*fay'*) or call it "a small quantity given above the quantity purchased" (*phā'ō*); cf. note 100 below.

30 This is somewhat similar to the situation of India under British rule and the similarity was not lost on the Indian Muslim scholars who argued in the nineteenth century that India continues to be *dār al-islām* despite the British takeover. See Karāmat 'Alī, *Lecture*, p. 3, where the *Fatāwā* by Marġīnānī, also known as *al-Fuṣūl al-'imādiyya* (or *Fuṣūl-i 'imādī*), is quoted in support of the idea that India under the British is *dār al-islām*. For similar views of Ṣiddīq Ḥasan Ḫān, see note 81 below.

31 Michal Biran, *The Empire of the Qara Khitai in Eurasian History: Between China and the Islamic World*, Cambridge Studies in Islamic Civilization (Cambridge: Cambridge University Press, 2005), 171–201 (the quotation is on p. 191).

Marġīnānī, a Hanafi scholar who flourished in Central Asia during the Qara Khitai takeover.[32] In a clear reference to the events of his time and place, he says at the beginning of the first chapter of his book:

> I have begun [the book] with [the question in what way] an Abode of Islam becomes an Abode of War since we need to know it in our time because of the infidel takeover of these parts. May God give them what will make them fortunate in this world and in the next
>
> (bada'tu awwalan bimā taṣīru bihi dāru 'l-islām dāra 'l-ḥarb li-'ftiqārinā ilayhi fī zamāninā bi-sabab istīlā'i al-kuffār ʿalā hāḏihi al-diyār. atāhum Allāh mā yusʿiduhum bihi fī 'l-dārayn).[33]

While the idea that *dār al-islām* which was taken over by infidels remains *dār al-islām* exists elsewhere in the Hanafi school,[34] it is not a common matter for a mediaeval Muslim scholar to felicitate in this manner infidels who took over a part of *dār al-islām*. It is also not common to start a book on jurisprudence with this question, and there seems to be a clear intent to accord it as much prominence and visibility as possible. Marġīnānī then goes on to marshal arguments supporting the proposition that Central Asia under the Qara Khitai remained *dār al-islām*. Quoting several Hanafi scholars, he asserts that *dār al-islām* does not become *dār al-ḥarb* if any Islamic law remains in effect "even if the dominance of the Muslims ceased to exist" (*wa-in zāla* [sic] *ġalabat ahl al-islām*).[35] The lands which are in the hands of the infidels—presumably he means Transoxania—are undoubtedly Lands of Islam, not Lands of War—because they are not contiguous with the Lands of War and because the infidels did not publicly introduce into them the laws of infidelity; rather, the judges are Muslims and the governors who obey them (i.e. the infidels) under duress are Muslims; (the situation would be the same) even if they did not act under duress. Similarly, in every city in which there is a

32 This is not the famous author of the *Hidāya*, but his son (or grandson), Abū al-Fatḥ b. Abī Bakr b. ʿAbd al-Jalīl who died in 1271. Willi Heffening, "al-Marghinānī," *Encyclopaedia of Islam, Vol. VI, Mahk-Mid* (Leiden: Brill, 1991); Carl Brockelmann, *Geschichte der arabischen Litteratur*, vol. 1 (Leiden: Brill, 1937), 382; ʿAbd al-Ḥayy Laḥnawī, *al-Fawā'id al-bahiyya fī tarājim al-ḥanafiyya* (Cairo: Maṭbaʿat al-Saʿāda, 1334), 146–47.

33 Burhān al-dīn Abū 'l-Ḥasan al-Marġīnānī, *Fatāwā fuṣūl al-iḥkām fī uṣūl al-aḥkām al-maʿrūf bi-Fuṣūl-i ʿimādī* (Calcutta: Asiatic Lithographic Press, 1827), 18 supra.

34 See Abou El Fadl, "Islamic Law and Muslim Minorities," 156.

35 Marġīnānī, *Fuṣūl al-iḥkām*, 17–18 (the quotation is on p. 18, l. 2).

governor (who rules) on the infidels' behalf, it is permissible for the Muslims to perform the congregational prayers on Fridays and the festival days (i.e. on *ʿīd al-fiṭr* and *ʿīd al-aḍḥā*), to levy the land tax (*ḫarāj*), to appoint judges, and to marry off widows—because a Muslim is in charge of these matters. As for the obedience to the infidels, this is (merely) truce (*muwādaʿa*)[36] or deception (*muḫādaʿa*). Even in areas which are under (direct?) rule of infidel governors, the Muslims are permitted to perform congregational prayers, and the juridical functions are exercised by the consent of the Muslims, (even if the judge was not appointed by a Muslim *amīr*). If such situations develop, the Muslims should request to appoint a Muslim governor;[37] in other words, if sovereignty is out of reach, Muslims should strive at least for autonomy. The thrust of the argument is that *dār al-ḥarb* is transformed into *dār al-islām* by the application of Muslim laws in it, and *dār al-islām* will retain its status as long as even one Muslim law is in effect—even under non-Muslim sovereignty.

2

India has been propitious for vibrant intellectual debate on many central issues in Islamic thought. There are several reasons for this. Immediately after the first Muslim incursions into India, the Muslims had to deal with the question of how to treat the local population which could easily be perceived as similar to the polytheists of the Arabian peninsula. Second, since the seventh/thirteenth century and until the formal incorporation of the Indian subcontinent into the British empire in 1858, the Muslims were the ruling power in most areas of India, but they ruled over a population of which only one quarter embraced Islam, while the rest adhered to religious traditions which went unmentioned in the sacred sources of Islam. Third, the Indian subcontinent came under European domination at the beginning of the thirteenth/nineteenth century, earlier than most other regions of the Muslim world.

It is quite clear that in the view of Muslim jurists, India was part of *dār al-islām* for six centuries, roughly between 1200 and 1800 CE. But it was a

36 The text has *muwāʿada*, but this is a slip of the pen.

37 Marġīnānī, *Fuṣūl al-iḥkām*, 18. A similar idea was suggested by Shah ʿAbd al-ʿAzīz in the thirteenth/nineteenth century. He says that if there is a governor appointed by the infidels, Friday prayer is legal by his consent; if there is none, the Muslims should appoint a pious person who will organize it and perform other essential services, such as marrying off girls who have no guardian, dividing inheritance according to the portions specified in the Qur'an, etc. See his *Fatāwā-yi ʿAzīzī* (Delhi: Maṭbaʿ-i Mujtabāʾī, 1311), vol. 1, 34 supra.

dār al-islām of a special kind. Some areas were under autonomous non-Muslim rulers who accepted, in various ways, the suzerainty of the Delhi Sultanate and later of the Mughul empire in Delhi. India is probably also the only part of medieval *dār al-islām* in which one emperor, Jalāl al-dīn Akbar (r. 963/1556–1013/1605), behaved in a way which could easily be interpreted as incompatible with the hallowed Muslim tradition and abolished the *jizya* tax on the non-Muslims. The tax remained in abeyance for a century (1564 or 1579–1679).[38]

The earliest legal work written in India in which I was able to find a reference to *dār al-islām* and *dār al-ḥarb* is the *Fatāwā-yi ʿĀlamgīrī,* a compendium of Hanafi law prepared according to the instructions of Emperor Awrangzēb in the second half of the eleventh/seventeenth century.[39] The passage is quoted from the *Ziyādāt* of Muḥammad b. al-Ḥasan al-Šaybānī,[40] appears in other standard Hanafi compendia and says obviously nothing specific about India, but since it has become a foundational text used later in order to rule on a specific Indian situation, it is helpful to adduce it at this point.

> Know that *dār al-ḥarb* becomes *dār al-islām* when one condition is fulfilled: the manifestation of Islamic rule in it. Muḥammad (b. al-Ḥasan al-Šaybānī) said in (his) *Ziyādāt: dār al-islām* becomes *dār al-ḥarb,* according to Abū Ḥanīfa, only when three conditions are fulfilled: 1. public introduction of infidel laws and non-implementation of the law of Islam in it; 2. (the area in question) is contiguous with *dār al-ḥarb* and no Muslim country is located between them; 3. no believer or *ḏimmī* who remains in it is safe according to his original *amān* which was in effect before the seizure of power by the infidels; the Muslim had the *amān* because of his conversion to Islam, and the *ḏimmī* because of the *ḏimma* contract.
>
> This question can emerge in three ways: 1. If the people of war capture an abode of our abodes; 2. If the people of a city apostatize, take power and introduce the laws of infidelity; 3. If the *ḏimmī*s break the contract and seize their abode. In all these cases, (the area) will not become

38 See Peter Hardy, "D̲jizya III–India", *EI²*, s.v.

39 A. S. Bazmee Ansari, "al-Fatāwā al-ʿĀlamgīriyya," *Encyclopaedia of Islam, Vol. II, C-G* (Leiden: Brill, 1965).

40 The only edition of the *Ziyādāt* which I was able to locate is Muḥammad b. Aḥmad al-Saraḫsī, *al-Nukat wa-huwa šarḥ li-Ziyādāt al-ziyādāt li-'l-imām* [...] *Muḥammad b. al-Ḥasan al-Šaybānī wa šarḥuhā li-'l-imām Abī Naṣr Aḥmad b. Muḥammad al-ʿAttābī al-Buḫārī* (Beirut: ʿĀlam al-kutub, 1986). The issue under consideration is not included in this edition.

> *dār ḥarb*, unless three conditions are fulfilled. Abū Yūsuf and Muḥammad (b. al-Ḥasan al-Šaybānī) say: (the area will become *dār al-ḥarb*) when one condition is fulfilled and nothing else: the manifestation of the laws of infidelity and this is the *qiyās*.[41]

In contradistinction to his two students, Abū Ḥanīfa is clearly reluctant to allow an easy transformation of *dār al-islām* into *dār al-ḥarb*. We shall see later that this reluctance got even stronger in the writings of many later jurists.

The first instance in which the question of the legal status of India was referred to in the early modern period can be found in Mawlānā Muḥammad Ismāʿīl al-Šahīd's *Ṣirāṭ-i mustaqīm*. The reference is very brief and only says that at the time of writing in 1232/1816–7, when the area of Delhi had already been under British rule, most of India has become *dār al-ḥarb*.[42] No conclusions are drawn from this assertion. A much more extensive discussion can be found in the *Fatāwā-yi ʿAzīzī* by Shah ʿAbd al-ʿAzīz al-Dihlawī (1159/1746–1239/1824). One of the fatwas deals with the question whether a *dār al-islām* can become a *dār al-ḥarb*. After quoting the three conditions which need to be fulfilled for *dār al-islām* to become *dār al-ḥarb*, he continues with a description of the situation in Delhi and says:

> In this city the rule of the Muslim imam is not in force at all and the Christians rule without fear. What is meant by the implementation of the infidel laws is that the infidels are acting as rulers in the affairs of state, in the management of the affairs of the subjects, in the collection of land revenue, tolls, customs and taxes on commerce, in punishing robbers and thieves, in deciding on disputes and in punishing crimes. The infidels govern in their own ways. Indeed, if some of them do not oppose (the implementation of) Muslim laws such the prayers on Friday and on the two festivals (*īd al-fiṭr* and *ʿīd al-aḍḥā*), the call to prayer and the sacrifice of the cow—the basis of this is that these things have no value in their eyes (*īn čīz-hā nazd-i īšān habāʾ o hadar ast*) because they destroy

41 Niẓām Burhānpūrī, *Fatāwā-yi ʿĀlamgīrī* (Kānpūr: Al-Maṭbaʿa al-Majīdī, 1350), 2:269, ult.–270, l. 4; See also ʿAlāʾ al-Dīn Abū Bakr al-Kāsānī, *Badāʾiʿ al-ṣanāʾiʿ fī tartīb al-šarāʾiʿ*, ed. Muḥammad Ḫayr Ṭuʿma Ḥalabī (Beirut: Dār al-Maʿrifa, 2000), vol. 7, 211 infra.

42 Muḥammad Ismāʿīl al-Šahīd, *Sirāṭ al-Mustaqīm* [sic] (Calcutta: Šayḫ Hidāyat Allāh, 1238), 237; cf. Rajarshi Ghose, "Politics for Faith: Karamat Ali Jaunpuri and Islamic Revivalist Movements in British India circa 1800–73." (Ph.D. Dissertation, University of Chicago, 2012), 61; Rudolph Peters, *Islam and Colonialism: The Doctrine of Jihad in Modern History*, Religion and Society 20 (The Hague: Mouton, 1979), 47–48.

> mosques without any hesitation. No Muslim or *ḏimmī* can come to the city or its environs without their permission.[43]

Though the fatwa does not say so explicitly, it can easily be inferred from it that he considered Delhi (probably after the British takeover in 1803) to be *dār al-ḥarb.* In most modern scholarship the conclusion was drawn that ʿAbd al-ʿAzīz implied that the Muslims must strive for the restoration of Islamic authority in India or migrate to a Muslim area.[44] This interpretation was prevalent until the seminal work of the late Professor Mušīr al-Ḥaqq who convincingly argued that this conclusion was wrong, that the real intention of Shah ʿAbd al-ʿAzīz was completely different and was related to economic problems which the Indian Muslims encountered as a result of the British takeover. In more specific terms, the declaration of India as *dār al-ḥarb* was intended to allow the Muslims to widen their economic activities by engaging in interest transactions with the Hindus and the British.[45] This conclusion is supported by the *Fatāwā* themselves and is also compatible with parts of the Hanafi tradition which consider interest transactions in *dār al-ḥarb* permissible.[46] That

---

43 ʿAbd al-ʿAzīz, *Fatāwā-yi ʿAzīzī,* 1:17; translation by Mushiru-l-Haqq [Mušīr al-Ḥaqq], "Indian Muslim Attitude to the British in the Early Nineteenth Century: A Case Study of Shāh ʿAbdul ʿAzīz." (Unpublished M.A. thesis, McGill, 1964), 39–40 (modified in numerous places); Mushiru-l-Haqq [Mušīr al-Ḥaqq], "Unnīswīn ṣadī kē Hindūstān kī hay'at-i šarʿī: Šāh ʿAbd al-ʿAzīz kē fatāwā-yi *dār al-ḥarb* kā ēk ʿilmī tajzi'a," *Burhān* 63 (1969): passim.

44 See Ishtiaq Husain Qureshi, *The Muslim Community in the Indo-Pakistan Subcontinent (610–1947). A Brief Historical Analysis* (The Hague: Mouton & Co., 1962), 194–95; Aziz Ahmad, *Studies in Islamic Culture in the Indian Environment* (Oxford: Clarendon Press, 1964), 215. For a list of Urdu authors who hold the same opinion, see Muhammad Khalid Masud, "The World of Shah ʿAbd Al-ʿAziz (1746–1824)," in *Perspectives of Mutual Encounters in South Asian History, 1760–1860,* ed. Jamal Malik, Social, Economic and Political Studies of the Middle East and Asia, v. 73 (Leiden: Brill, 2000), 298n4. The same view is maintained by Mushtaq Muhammad Ahmad who is apparently unaware of Mushiru-l-Haqq's work; see his "Notions of *dār al-ḥarb* and *dār al-Islām,*" 15n31.

45 Mushiru-l-Haqq [Mušīr al-Ḥaqq], "Indian Muslim Attitude to the British," 45; Ayesha Jalal, *Partisans of Allah: Jihad in South Asia* (Cambridge, Mass.: Harvard University Press, 2008), 68. Mušīr al-Ḥaqq was preceded in this interpretation by Sir Sayyid Aḥmad Ḫān, in his *Review of Dr. Hunter's* Indian Musalmans: Are They Bound in Conscience to Rebel against the Queen? (Benares: The Medical Hall Press, 1872), Appendices:XI.

46 Šaybānī, *Siyar,* 4:1486 (no. 2899). See also Kāsānī, *Badāʾiʿ al-ṣanāʾiʿ,* 7:214. According to him, Abū Ḥanīfa and Šaybānī allowed a Muslim in *dār al-ḥarb* to contract an interest transaction or other transactions invalid in Islam with the *ḥarbīs,* but Abū Yūsuf maintained that "a Muslim may not do in *dār al-ḥarb* what is not permissible to him in *dār al-islām* (*lā yajūzu li'l-muslim fī dār al-ḥarb illā mā yajūzu lahu fī dār al-Islām*).

the declaration of India as *dār al-ḥarb* was not intended to declare jihad can also be supported by ʿAbd al-ʿAzīz's discussion of the question whether it is permissble for the Muslims to serve in the British administration and the permission which he gave to do this under certain conditions.[47]

The connection between the legal status of India and the legality of interest transactions continued to be discussed in Indo-Muslim literature during British rule. The first scholar who dealt with this issue after Shah ʿAbd al-ʿAzīz was Muḥammad ʿAbd al-Ḥayy Lakhnawī (1264/1848–1304/1886).[48] His treatment of the subject is indirect and I could not find in his *Fatāwā* an explicit statement about the legal status of India. Nevertheless, he uses expressions from which we can gauge his attitude to the question. It seems that he considers parts of India, probably those which were still under the nominal rule of the Mughul emperor, to be *dār al-islām*, and considers the British to be *ḥarbīs*. When asked whether it is permissible to take interest from the Hindūs, he answers by saying that it is not "because taking or paying interest in *dār al-islām* is forbidden (… *kyūnkih dār al-islām mēñ sūd lēnā awr dēnā ḥarām hay*), since *ahl al-ḏimma* are equal to Muslims in such transactions." The existence of *ahl al-ḏimma* is, of course, an indication that the area is *dār al-islām*.[49] The question whether it is legal to take interest from the British is left without an explicit answer with regard to the British, but the ruling according to which it is forbidden to take interest from a *ḥarbī* who enters *dār al-islām* can easily be understood as applicable to them. The ruling remains the same even if thousands of Muslims "eat" interest because widespread practice cannot influence questions of permissibility (*ḥalāl*) or prohibition (*ḥarām*).[50] On the other hand, areas under "Christian jurisdiction" (*naṣārā kī ʿamaldārī*)—possibly those which entered into "the Subsidiary Alliance" with the British at the turn of the nineteenth century[51]—conceded much of their sovereignty to the British and therefore ʿAbd al-Ḥayy Lakhnawī chose to consider them as *dār al-ḥarb* and the taking of interest in these areas legal. There is no discussion of the question whether interest transactions between Muslims in these areas

47 Mushiru-l-Haqq [Mušīr al-Ḥaqq], "Indian Muslim Attitude to the British," 54–56.

48 Sh. Inayatullah, "ʿAbd al-Ḥayy," *Encyclopaedia of Islam, Vol. I, A–B* (Leiden: Brill, 1960); for a list of ʿAbd al-Ḥayy's books and students, see Raḥmān ʿAlī, *Taḏkira-yi ʿulamāʾ-i Hind* (Lucknow: Naval Kishōr, 1294AH), 114–17.

49 ʿAbd al-Ḥayy Lakhnawī, *Majmūʿat al-fatāwā* (Lahore: Shahzād Publishers, n.d.), 2:173 *infra*.

50 Ibid., 2:175, l. 20 – 176, l. 1.

51 For this type of relationship between the British and various Indian states, see C. A. Bayly, *Indian Society and the Making of the British Empire*, The New Cambridge History of India, II, 1 (Cambridge: Cambridge University Press, 1987), 79–105.

are legal or not; the reason for this omission may be that the negative answer to this is obvious.[52]

The next scholar whose views deserve to be discussed is Muḥammad Qāsim Nānawtawī (1248/1832–1297/1880), who established the *dār al-ʿulūm* of Deoband together with Rašīd Aḥmad Gangōhī.[53] The context of his discussion of the legal status of India is also the question of interest transactions. His attitude is based on a selection of Hanafi views which make the transformation of *dār al-islām* into *dār al-ḥarb* next to impossible. According to one view, *dār al-islām* becomes *dār al-ḥarb* only if all elements because of which it became *dār al-islām* disappear. According to another, *dār al-islām* remains *dār al-islām* even if only one Muslim law remains in effect. As long as one element of Islam (*ʿulqa min ʿalāʾiq al-islām*) remains, Islam prevails. All these quotations indicate that India is *dār al-islām.*[54] This analysis is another example of the pronounced unwillingness of Hanafi scholars to allow for the transformation of *dār al-islām* into *dār al-ḥarb*.

Rašīd Aḥmad Gangōhī (1244/1829–1323/1905),[55] Muḥammad Qāsim Nānawtawī's associate in the establishment of the Deoband *madrasa,* speaks with two voices and I have not yet been able to explain the divergence of his views. In one place in his *Fatāwā,* he is asked whether

> the country of India which is governed by the Christians, and the protected kingdoms of the Indian *nawwāb*s and *rāja*s—are they *dār ḥarb*

---

52 Lakhnawī, *Fatāwā*, 2:170, 173–174.Cf. Peter Hardy, *The Muslims of British India* (Cambridge: Cambridge University Press, 1972), 114. Hardy is not aware of the distinction between the various areas of India. Hunter (*Our Indian Musalmans: Are They Bound in Conscience to Rebel against the Queen?* [London: Trübner and Company, 1871], 123) refers to the fatwa of ʿAbd al-Ḥayy and says that he affirms that India is *dār al-islām*, but avoids drawing the inference that rebellion is unlawful. This is true, but a reference to rebellion is not to be expected because the fatwa deals with the question of the legality of interest transactions in India rather than with the question whether the Muslims should rebel against the British or not. See also ibid., 149, where he quotes an opposite view of ʿAbd al-Ḥayy concerning the area "from Calcutta to Delhi" which he declares *dār al-ḥarb*.. Cf. Muin-ud-din Ahmad Khan, *History of the Fara'idi Movement in Bengal, 1818–1906* (Karachi: Pakistan Historical Society, 1965), 71.

53 Hardy, *The Muslims of British India*, 170; Sayyid Maḥbūb Riḍwī, *Taʾrīḫ-i Dēoband: Dēoband awr Dār al-ʿulūm ke ḥālāt* (Dēoband: ʿIlmī Markaz, 1972), 120–35.

54 Muḥammad Qāsim Nānawtawī, *Qāsim al-ʿulūm maʿa Urdū tarjuma Anwār al-nujūm*, ed. Muḥammad Anwār al-Ḥasan Shērkoṭī (Lahore: Nāshirān-i Qurʾān Limited, 1974), 360–62.

55 Nasīm Aḥmad Farīdī, "Rashīd Aḥmad Gangōhī," *Urdū Dāʾira-yi maʿārif-i islāmiyya* (Lahore: University of the Panjab, 1972).

> or *dār islām*? And the infidels – are they the rulers of the kingdoms or the ruled? Are they *ḥarbīs* or *ḏimmīs*, whether they are Hindus or non-Hindus? … The female infidels of Hindustan—should they be considered *ḥarbiyyāt* or *ḏimmiyyāt*?

In this place, Gangōhī answers the question in the affirmative: he says that in his view all of India is *dār al-ḥarb* and the female infidels residing in it are *ḥarbiyyāt* (and a Muslim woman must therefore veil herself from their gaze).[56] Elsewhere, however, when asked the same question, he says that most ulema consider India *dār al-islām*; some consider it *dār al-ḥarb* and he himself refrains from making a decision.[57]

In Bengal, the discussion about the legal status of India went in a different direction. There the question was not the permissibility of interest transactions, but rather the legality of congregational prayer in areas under non-Muslim rule. The debate in Bengal was started in the first half of the nineteenth century by the Farā'iḍīs, one of the first radical Muslim movements in India, founded by Ḥājjī Šarī'at Allāh.[58] On the basis of views expressed by various Hanafi scholars,[59] the Farā'iḍīs insisted that Friday prayers cannot be held in Bengal because there are no *amīrs* and judges appointed by a Muslim

---

56 Rašīd Aḥmad Gangōhī, *Fatāwā Rašīdiyya*, vol. 3 (Murādābād: 'Azīz al al-Dīn and 'Alī Naẓar, 1910), 14–15.

57 Rašīd Aḥmad Gangōhī, *Fatāwā Rašīdiyya*, vol. 1 (Murādābād: 'Azīz al al-Dīn and 'Alī Naẓar, 1906), 76; *Fatāwā Rašīdiyya* (Delhi: Hindustan Electric Printing Works, 1924), 73. Hardy (*The Muslims of British India*, 115) is aware only of this last view.

58 Alessandro Bausani, "Farā'iḍiyya," *Encyclopaedia of Islam, Vol. II, C-G* (Leiden: Brill, 1965).

59 For an extensive study of *miṣr jāmi'* in Islamic law, see Baber Johansen, "The All-Embracing Town and Its Mosques: *al-miṣr al-jāmi'*," in *Contingency in a Sacred Law: Legal and Ethical Norms in the Muslim Fiqh*, Studies in Islamic Law and Society, v. 7 (Leiden: Brill, 1999), especially 86. My thanks go to Nurit Tsafrir who drew my attention to this work. The classical Hanafi definition of localities in which the Friday prayer may be performed can be found in Marġīnānī, *Hidāya*, 1:204: "*Miṣr jāmi'* is a place where there is an *amīr* and a judge who implements the laws and imposes the Qur'anic punishments" (*wa'l-miṣr al-jāmi': kullu mawḍi' lahu amīr wa-qāḍin yunaffiḏu al-aḥkām wa-yuqīmu al-ḥudūd*). Other schools of law have different views on this issue. The Shafi'is, for instance, maintain that Friday prayers may be held in any place where there are (at least) forty free male permanent residents; no other conditions are mentioned. An unidentified scholar suggests that the minimum number is ten thousand inhabitants or ten thousand warriors. For a convenient survey of the various views on this issue in Muslim law, see Abū Muḥammad Badr al-dīn al-'Aynī, *'Umdat al-qārī' šarḥ Ṣaḥīḥ al-Buḫārī* (Beirut: Dār Iḥyā' al-turāṯ al-'arabī, n.d.), 6:187–188; Abū 'l-'Abbās Šihāb al-dīn al-Qasṭallānī, *Iršād al-sārī šarḥ Ṣaḥīḥ al-Buḫārī* (Beirut: Dār al-Kutub al-'ilmiyya, 1996), 2:562–63; Šāfi'ī, *al-Umm*, 3:328–29.

sovereign, and therefore the Muslim localities in Bengal cannot be considered an "all-embracing town" (*miṣr jāmiʿ*) which is a prerequisite for holding congregational prayers.[60] Though the Farāʾiḍīs do not say so explicitly—probably because of their fear of the British power—their refusal to hold congregational prayer is close to declaring India to be *dār al-ḥarb*.[61]

The main opponent of the Farāʾiḍīs on this issue was Karāmat ʿAlī Jawnpūrī (d. 1290/1873).[62] The criticism of Farāʾiḍī religious principles is the main subject of Karāmat ʿAlī's *Ḥujjat-i qāṭiʿa* ("The decisive proof") and *Ištihār–nāma* ("The announcement").[63] The vehemence of his criticsm can be gauged from the fact that he calls the Farāʾiḍīs "the Kharijis of Bengal" (*Bangālē kē ḫārijī*). He accuses them of adopting the Khariji view according to which acts (in the sense of commandments) are indispensable for belief and a person who believes but does not perform the commandments is not a believer. In view of this principle, they refuse to perform the funeral prayers for people who expressed their belief by pronouncing the *šahāda* (*kalima-gū*), but neglected their prayers. He also accuses them of using the religious ignorance of the Bengali Muslims, especially of those who live in remote villages and on the sea shore, to teach them numerous deviations from Islamic law. The Farāʾiḍīs use alms money for

60 Ahmad Khan, *History of the Fara'idi Movement*, 67; Muhammad Ahsanullah Faisal, *Haji Shariatullah's Faraizi Movement: History, Da'wah & Political Ideology* (Dhaka [Bangladesh]: Shariatia Library, 2010), 124–26; Narahari Kaviraj, *Wahabi and Farazi* [sic] *Rebels of Bengal* (New Delhi: People's Publishing House, 1982), 64. For British ethnographers' description of the Farāʾiḍīs, see James Taylor, *A Sketch of the Topography & Statistics of Dacca* (Calcutta: G. H. Huttmann, Military Orphan Press, 1840), 247–50 (does not mention the issue of congregational prayers) and; James Wise, *Notes on the Races, Castes and Trades of Eastern Bengal* (London: Harrison and sons, 1883), 21–27. Only Wise mentions (on p. 22) the non-observance of the Friday prayers by Sharīʿatullāh, considers it a Wahhābī innovation, and does not connect it to the question of India's legal status as *dār al-islām* or *dār al-ḥarb*. See also "Farāʾiḍī firqa", *Urdu dāʾira-yi maʿārif-i islāmiyya*, s.v.

61 Cf. Ahmad Khan, *History of the Fara'idi Movement*, 80.

62 See A. Yusuf Ali, "Karāmat ʿAlī," *Encyclopaedia of Islam, Vol. IV, Iran-Kha* (Leiden: Brill, 1978). See also a few details in Wise, *Eastern Bengal*, 27–32. He mentions Karāmat ʿAlī's view that India is not *dār al-ḥarb* (p. 28) and his insistence on performing the Friday prayers by his Taʿayyunī followers (p. 32), but is not aware of the connection between the two issues. Modern research in Karāmat ʿAlī is scanty. For a standard biography, see Shaykh Muḥammad Ikrām, *Mawj-i Kawṯar, yaʿnī Musalmānōñ kī maḏhabī awr ʿilmī taʾrīḫ* (Lahore: Fīrōz Sons Ltd., 1968), 60; M. Imamul Hoque, "Jaunpuri, Karamat Ali," *Banglapedia, The National Encyclopedia of Bangladesh*, ed. Sirajul Islam, (Dhaka: Asiatic Society of Bangladesh, 2003).

63 I am immensely grateful to Dr. Rajarshi Ghose for putting a copy of this very rare book at my disposal.

private purposes, levy illegal fines from their followers and use this money for their leaders' livelihood. They impose discretionary punishments (*taʿzīr*) without having the authority to do this. Quoting the *Fatāwā-yi ʿĀlamgīrī,* Karāmat ʿAlī asserts that if there was a Muslim ruler in Bengal, he would punish those who act in this way.[64] In his view, all this amounts to establishing a new sharia (*naʾī šarīʿat*). The Farāʾiḍīs disregard the views of the ulema from the whole Muslim world and consider all those who do not belong to their group as non-Muslims. Thus, the Farāʾiḍīs cannot be considered *ahl al-sunna waʾl-jamāʿa.*[65]

As Ghose has recently shown, Karāmat ʿAlī started his religious and reformist activities in the *Ṭarīqa Muḥammadiyya* of Sayyid Aḥmad *šahīd*, and in the 1830s seems to have considered India as *dār al-ḥarb*. However, in the 1850s he changed his mind—possibly because of his involvement in the sectarian struggle against the Farāʾiḍīs—[66] and started supporting the idea that India under the British is an "Abode of Safety" (*dār al-amān*) and also continues to be "Abode of Islam" (*dār al-islām*).[67] This is not discussed directly in the *Ḥujjat-i qāṭiʿa*. However, the issue of the legality of congregational prayers which is a corollary of an area being *dār al-islām* is a main point of contention in Karāmat ʿAlī's polemics with the Farāʾiḍīs. He maintains that "all *fuqahāʾ*" have ruled that when a non-Muslim group takes over a country, as happened in India, including Bengal, the prayers on Fridays and on the two festivals (i.e. the *ʿīd al-fiṭr* and *ʿīd al-aḍḥā*) are legally valid (*durust*) and obligatory. After these ulema gave proper considerations to these issues, no one has the right to open the issue again. This is especially true in Bengal where the religious knowledge of the population is woefully insufficient. Therefore congregational prayers, which are a very important institution in Islam, must be held.[68] Elsewhere, Karāmat ʿAlī approvingly quotes a passage from the *Fatāwā-yi ʿĀlamgīrī*, which maintains that if the king of a city is an infidel, the Muslims should appoint a *qāḍī* and a prayer leader (imam) from amongst themselves and perform the prayer under his guidance.[69]

---

64 The relevant passage in *Fatāwā-yi ʿĀlamgīrī* is in volume 2, p. 236.

65 Karāmat ʿAlī, "Ḥujjat-i Qāṭiʿa," in *Ḏaḫīra-yi Karāmat*, vol. 1 (Kānpūr: Maṭbaʿ-i Majīdī, 1929), 88–89, 94, ll. 13ff; Karāmat ʿAlī, "Ištihār Nāma," in *Ḏaḫīra-yi Karāmat*, vol. 1 (Kānpūr: Maṭbaʿ-i Majīdī, 1929), 120–21.

66 See Rajarshi Ghose, "Islamic Law and Imperial Space: British India as 'domain of Islam' circa 1803–1870," *Journal of Colonialism and Colonial History* 15, no. 1 (2014): 5.

67 Ghose, "Politics for Faith," 189–191; and Ahmad Khan, *History of the Fara'idi Movement*, 98–99.

68 Karāmat ʿAlī, "Ḥujjat-i Qāṭiʿa," 103, ll. 5–14; 105, ll. 11–15.

69 Karāmat ʿAlī, *Miftāḥ al-janna* (Kānpūr: Naval Kishōr, 1877), 86; Burhānpūrī, *Fatāwā-yi ʿĀlamgīrī*, 1:75, l. 25. For earlier instances of such an idea, see note 37 above.

The issue of the legal status of the country had implications beyond the question of ritual prayers: a declaration that India was *dār al-ḥarb* could easily be interpreted as a call for jihad against the British. The connection between the status of India as *dār al-ḥarb* and the waging of jihad is extensively discussed in a lecture delivered by Karāmat ʿAlī in November 1870 at the meeting of "The Mahomedan Literary Society of Calcutta." At the beginning of the lecture, Karāmat ʿAlī refers to the passage from *Fatāwā-yi ʿĀlamgīrī* quoted above,[70] as well as to similar passages from other Hanafi works which reflect the reticence of Hanafi scholars to allow for the transformation of an area which had been *dār al-islām* into *dār al-ḥarb*.[71] He then asserts that the three conditions necessary to transform *dār al-islām* into *dār al-ḥarb* do not exist in India. Though the government is in the hands of the Christians, most of the injunctions of Islam remain in effect and the rulers do not impede the performance of Muslim commandments in any way. The contiguity between India and *dār al-ḥarb* also does not exist: countries to the West and the North-West are certainly *dār al-islām* and in India itself there are also numerous principalities which may also be considered as belonging to the same category. As for the question of the safety (*amān*) enjoyed by Muslims and Hindu *ḏimmīs*, none of these communities is worse off than it was before. All this clearly indicates that India is *dār al-islām* and there is no obligation on the part of the Muslims to emigrate from it and there is certainly no permission to wage jihad against its British rulers.[72] These views were given some prominence by the British administrator and ethnographer W. W. Hunter, though he did not consider them as widespread and maintained that "it would be a political blunder for us to accept without inquiry the views of the Muhammadan Literary Society of Calcutta as those of the Indian Musalmans."[73] It is also noteworthy that Hunter writes as if he were a Muslim scholar, weighing the various views in Muslim jurisprudence and reaching the conclusion that India is *dār al-ḥarb*, despite

---

70 See above, at note 41.

71 Karāmat ʿAlī, *Lecture by Moulvie Karamat Ali on a Question of Mahomedan Law, Involving the Duty of Mahomedans in British India towards the Ruling Power. Abstract of Proceedings of the Mahomedan Literary Sociey of Calcutta* (Calcutta: Erasmus Jones, Cambrian Press, 1871), 3–5.

72 Ibid., 5–6. For a similar ruling by the Shafiʿi scholar al-Ramlī (d. 1595–1596), see Abou El Fadl, "Islamic Law and Muslim Minorities," 159–60.

73 Hunter, *Our Indian Musalmans*, 120–21. For a criticism of Hunter's views, see Sayyid Aḥmad Ḫān, *Review*, passim. For a self laudatory description of the Muhammadan Literary Society of Calcutta, see Enamul Haque, *Nawab Bahadur Abdul Latif: His Writings and Related Documents* (Dacca: Samudra Prokashani, 1968), 139–55.

the views expressed by Karāmat 'Alī and his associates.[74] On the other hand, Karāmat 'Alī and his supporters were able to use in their support several fatwas allegedly issued by Meccan ulema who ruled that "as long as even some of the peculiar observances of Islam prevail in it, it is *dār al-islām*."[75]

Other scholars who were present at the meeting spoke in a similar vein. Faḍl-i 'Alī stressed that if India were *dār al-ḥarb*, it would be incumbent on its Muslim inhabitants to migrate from it. Yet thousands of pious Muslims, who are well aware of the principles of Islam, remained in the country for decades after the British takeover. Furthermore, there was even immigration of Muslims from Mecca and Medina to India. Disregarding the famous fatwa of Shah 'Abd al-'Azīz,[76] Faḍl-i 'Alī asserted that since the British takeover, Muslims had considered interest transactions as illegal; this is a clear indication that they considered India as *dār al-islām* because such transactions would be legal if India were *dār al-ḥarb*. Of similar significance is the regular performance of public prayers which is forbidden in *dār al-ḥarb*. The alliance of the British with the Ottoman empire in the Crimean war is an indication of Britain's friendliness with Muslims and an additional consideration supporting India's status as *dār al-islām*.[77] It is fascinating to observe that while the support given by the British to the Ottoman sultan in the Crimean war is lavishly praised in several pages of our proceedings, the war of 1857–1858 in India is not mentioned at all. No historical events which could lead the participants in an anti-British direction were allowed to bear on the issue.

Nawwāb Ṣiddīq Ḥasan Ḫān (1248/1832–1307/1890), a prolific writer, statesman and supporter of the *ahl-i ḥadīṯ*,[78] devoted to the question of *dār al-ḥarb* a chapter in his book on fighting, martyrdom and emigration (*al-'Ibra mimmā*

74 Hunter, *Our Indian Musalmans*, 124–28.

75 These fatwas were published in an English translation in Ibid., 213–14; Karāmat 'Alī, *Lecture*, 22; (Aḥmad Ḫān) Sayyid Aḥmad Ḫān, *Review*, Appendices:1–2. Unfortunately, I have not been able to locate the Arabic originals of these decisions.

76 One of the participants in the debate even misrepresents the view of 'Abd al-'Azīz by saying that he "read in some manuscript" that 'Abd al-'Azīz declared India to be *dār al-islām*. See Karāmat 'Alī, *Lecture*, 13.

77 Ibid., 7–8. For a favorable reaction of the British administration to Karāmat 'Alī's views, see Hunter, *Our Indian Musalmans*, 114, 120–21.

78 Ẓafarul-Islām Khān, "Nawwāb Sayyid Ṣiddīq Ḥasan K͟hān," *Encyclopaedia of Islam, Vol. VII, Mif-Naz* (Leiden: Brill, 1993). This article deals mainly with his biography and political activities. In Aziz Ahmad, *Islamic Modernism in India and Pakistan, 1857–1964* (Oxford: Oxford University Press, 1967), there is a brief description of his religious views, but nothing on the subject of our inquiry. An extensive list of his works can be found in Raḥmān 'Alī, *Taḏkira*, 94–96. See also Ikrām, *Mawj-i Kawṯar*, 65–68.

jāʾa fī ʾl-ġazw waʾl-šahāda waʾl-hijra). *Dār al-ḥarb* is defined by him as *dār ibāḥa*; this means that "God ordered us to fight the polytheists and made their blood, their property an their women licit to us" (*inna ʾllāh ... amaranā bi-qitāl ahl al-širk wa-abāḥa lanā dimāʾahum wa-amwālahum wa-nisāʾahum*).[79] On the question of the legal status of India, there is enough evidence to suggest that Ṣiddīq Ḥasan Ḫān maintained that India under the British was *dār al-ḥarb*. But he did not express himself in an unequivocal manner, probably out of the desire not to incur the ire of the British administration. In *ʿIbra*, first he approvingly quotes a passage from *Majālis al-abrār wa masālik al-aḫyār*[80] in which it is said that the countries under Mongol rule were *dār al-islām* because they did not border on *dār al-ḥarb* and the non-Muslim rulers did not publicly introduce there the laws of infidelity (*li-ʿadami ʾttiṣālihā bi-dār al-ḥarb wa-lam yuẓhirū fīhā aḥkām al-kufr*).[81] He surveys the various views concerning the definiton of *dār al-islām* and *dār al-ḥarb*. According to one view, *dār al-Islām* is an area in which the two declarations of faith are pronounced, prayers are performed in public and "infidel features" (*ḫaṣla kufriyya*) are in evidence only by permission of the Muslims, such as manifestations of Judaism and Christianity in Muslim cities. Abū Ḥanīfa, al-Muʾayyad bi-ʾllāh[82] and other Shiʾi scholars say that an area is *dār al-islām* if the two declarations of faith are pronounced and prayers are performed, even if the infidel features are visible without Muslim permission. Still others maintain that the decisive criterion should be power: if power is in the hands of an infidel ruler or an infidel population, it is *dār kufr*. If it is in the hands of Muslims, it is *dār al-islām*. Some say that the definiton depends on the majority of the population: a place where Muslims hold the majority is *dār al-islām* and a place where the majority is infidel is *dār kufr*.[83] Having surveyed these views, Ṣiddīq Ḥasan Ḫān lends his support to Abū Ḥanīfa and al-Muʾayyad bi-ʾllāh and asserts that India and Aden are *dār*

---

79 Ṣiddīq Ḥasan Ḫān, *al-ʿIbra mimmā jāʾa fī ʾl-ġazw waʾl-šahāda wa al-hijra* (Beirut: Dār al-Kutub al-ʿilmiyya, 1988), 228.

80 A book with an identical title by Aḥmad b. ʿAbd al-Qāhir al-Rūmī (d. 1631) is listed by Carl Brockelmann, *Geschichte der arabischen Litteratur*, 2. Supplementband (Leiden: Brill, 1938), 661–662. It was not available to the present writer.

81 Ṣiddīq Ḥasan Ḫān, *al-ʿIbra*, 232. He probably means the policies of the Qara Khitai dynasty, for which see notes 30–36 above.

82 There are two Shiʾi Zaydi scholars bearing this name. See J. R. Blackburn, "al-Muʾayyad bi-ʾllāh Muḥammad," *Encyclopaedia of Islam, Vol. VII, Mif-Naz* (Leiden: Brill, 1993).

83 Ṣiddīq Ḥasan Ḫān, *al-ʿIbra*, 234. This is in stark contradiction to medieval attitudes according to which the decisive factor in determining the legal status of an area is the identity of the ruler rather than the majority of the population. No medieval jurist would consider Mughul India or Egypt before it became a Muslim majority country as anything but *dār al-islām*.

al-islām despite the visibility of infidel features and the power wielded in them by the Europeans (*Ifranj*).[84] Nevertheless, in a later passage in the same work, he gives preference to the idea that India is *dār al-ḥarb*; he maintains, however, that the issue is doubtful (*min al-muštabihāt*) and has no satisfactory solution. Therefore, he continues:

> you will see that I wrote about it in *Hidāyat al-sā'il ilā adillat al-masā'il*[85] according to the Hanafi *maḏhab* which asserts that India is part of *dār al-islām*. Elsewhere I wrote about it according to the views of the *ahl al-ḥadīṯ* who assert that it is part of *dār al-kufr*. Here (i.e. in *al-ʿIbra*) I combined the lizard and the whale and did not express a firm opinion on it. It is possible to say that there are two equally strong opinions on this issue, though its being an abode of infidelity is preferable in view of manifest proofs and clear (requirements of) piety. The Messenger of God, may Allah bless him and grant him peace, said: He who bewares of doubtful things, heals his religion and his honour. He also said: Leave what fills you with misgivings for what does not. And God, may He be extolled, knows better and His knowledge is more complete and firmer
>
> (wa-li-ḏā tarānī ḥarrartuhā fī Hidāyat al-sā'il ilā adillat al-masā'il muqayyadan bi'l-maḏhab al-ḥanafī al-dāll ʿalā anna bilād al-Hind diyār al–islām wa–katabtuhā fī mawḍiʿin āḫar ʿalā ṭarīqat ahl al-ḥadīṯ al-dālla ʿalā annahā diyār al-kufr wa jamaʿtu hunā bayna al-ḍabb wa'l-nūn wa-lam aqṭaʿ bi-šay'in min ḏālika wa yumkinu an yuqāl anna fī 'l-mas'ala qawlayni wa humā qawiyyāni mutasāwiyāni wa-in kāna kawnuhā dāra kufr aẓhara naẓaran ilā ẓāhir al-adilla wa wāḍiḥ al-taqwā. Wa-qad qāla rasūl Allāh ṣallā Allah ʿalayhi wa-sallam: fa-man ittaqā al-šubuhāt fa-qad istabra'a li-dīnihi wa ʿirḍihi. Wa-qāla: daʿ mā yurībuka ilā mā lā yurībuka. Wa'llāh subḥānahu aʿlam wa-ʿilmuhu atamm wa-aḥkam).[86]

Then he quotes opinions according to which if infidels take over an area which is part of *dār al-islām* it remains *dār al-islām* and the Muslims must exert themselves in order to take it back from the infidels.[87]

84 Ibid., 235–36; 237 *infra*.

85 This work was not available to the present writer.

86 Ṣiddīq Ḥasan Ḫān, *al-ʿIbra*, 238–39.

87 Ibid., 240, 241–42. This opinion is contradictory to that of Karāmat ʿAlī who drew from the characterization of India as *dār al-islām* the opposite conclusion: he asserted that since India is *dār al-islām*, Muslims are not allowed to wage jihad against the British.

In his *Ḥujaj al-karāma li-ašrāṭ al-sāʿa,*[88] Ṣiddīq Ḥasan Ḫān also refrains from making a clear judgment, and marshals evidence for both positions. On the one hand, the infidel laws of Britain are applied in India; on the other hand, though Islamic law in general is not applied, Muslim prayers are performed, and Muslims are allowed to perform ritual slaughter and similar things. Concerning such situations, the author quotes Ibn ʿĀbidīn[89] who says that if both Muslim laws and infidel laws are applied, the area is not *dār al-ḥarb*. India does not border on *dār al-ḥarb*, but the safety which Muslims and *ḏimmī*s should enjoy in *dār al-islām* does not exist. This analysis includes evidence pointing in opposite directions and Ṣiddīq Ḥasan Ḫān does not explicitly state his position. He only describes the differences of opinion among scholars: one group allowed interest transactions with the *ḥarbī*s while the other supported the obligation to migrate to *dār al-islām*. In his view the first view is to be rejected, while the second prevails. Both views are possible only if India is considered *dār al-ḥarb,* and this seems to be the implied opinion of Ṣiddīq Ḥasan Ḫān in this passage.[90] As we have already seen, his circumspection is probably caused by his fear of raising the anger of the British government who suspected him of entertaining "seditious" opinions.

The question whether India is *dār al-islām* or *dār al-ḥarb* came to the fore again in the context of the Ḫilāfat and non-cooperation movement. The leaders of the movement were not unanimous on this theoretical question nor on the question whether it is advisable to leave the country because of the

88 Also known as *Ḥujaj al-karāma fī āṯār al-qiyāma.* See Raḥmān ʿAlī, *Taḏkira*, 95.

89 He is the Syrian Hanafi scholar Muḥammad Amīn b. ʿUmar b. ʿAbd al-ʿAzīz Ibn ʿĀbidīn (1198/1784–1258/1842). See "Ibn ʿĀbidīn," *Encyclopaedia of Islam, Vol. III, H-Iram* (Leiden: Brill, 1971). Cf. Muḥammad Amīn Ibn ʿĀbidīn, *Ḥāšiyat radd al-Muḥtār* (Cairo: Muṣṭafā al-Bābī al-Ḥalabī, 1966), 4:175: "… if both Muslim and polytheist laws are applied, (the area in question) does not become *dār ḥarb* (*… law ujriyat aḥkām al-muslimīn wa-aḥkām ahl al-širk lā takūnu dār ḥarb*).

90 Ṣiddīq Ḥasan Ḫān, *Ḥujaj al-karāma li-ašrāṭ al-sāʿa* (Bhopal, n.d.), 91–92. The author says at the end of this discussion that he investigated this matter further at the end of his *Ifādat al-šuyūḫ.* I have checked two editions of this work (Kānpūr 1297AH, and Kānpūr 1288AH), but could not find a discussion of this topic. The book deals with abrogating and abrogated verses and traditions (*Ifādat al-šuyūḫ bi-miqdār al-nāsiḫ wa'l-mansūḫ*) and a discussion of *dār al-islām* and *dār al-ḥarb* would be out of place there. In view of this discussion, it is not easy to accept Qureshi's position that "the *ahl-i ḥadīṯ ʿulamāʾ*, in the tradition of Ṣiddīq Ḥasan Ḫān, firmly decided to repudiate the concept of British India as *dār al-ḥarb …*" (M. Naeem Qureshi, *Pan-Islam in British Indian Politics: A Study of the Khilafat Movement, 1918–1924*, Social, Economic, and Political Studies of the Middle East and Asia, v. 66 [Leiden: Brill, 1999], 178).

conditions in which the Muslims find themeselves there, but some of the most prominent of them, such as Abū al-Kalām Āzād and the Ali brothers, recommended migration (*hijra*) from India. In a speech delivered in February 1920, Amanullah Khan, the *amīr* of Afghanistan, undertook to welcome all those who wanted to migrate from India to his country. The sincerity of this undertaking has been doubted, but by August 1920 about 40.000 Indian Muslims had migrated to Afghanistan. This strained the resources of Afghanistan to such an extent that on August 9 the *amīr* stopped further migration until the migrants who had already come had been absorbed. The movement collapsed. Many migrants died of privation and disease, while others returned to India in destitution. The *hijra* movement of 1920 seems to be the only case in which concrete conclusions were drawn from relevant legal discussions—and with disastrous consequences.[91]

In the late 1930s, the question of the legal status of India was extensively debated by Munāẓir Aḥsan Gīlānī and Abū al-Aʿlā Mawdūdī. Munāẓir Aḥsan Gīlānī (1892–1956)[92] wrote a treatise entitled *The question of interest and the abode of war* (*Masʾala-yi sūd awr dār al-ḥarb*).[93] He divides the areas in non-Muslim possession into two types: areas which were never under Muslim rule, and those which had been under Muslim rule at some time, but were later captured by non-Muslims. As for the first type, nobody says that they may be considered a Muslim area. The situation is much more complicated regarding the second type. The question here is under what conditions such an area can cease to be *dār al-islām* and be transformed into *dār al-kufr*. To phrase it in more specific terms in our context, the question is whether Abū Ḥanīfa's conditions have materialized in pre-partition India.

91 The *hijra* movement has been extensively treated by Qureshi, *Pan-Islam in British Indian Politics*, 174–231. This richly documented work allows us to be very brief on this topic. See also Muhammad Khalid Masud, "The Obligation to Migrate: The Doctrine of *hijra* in Islamic Law," in *Muslim Travellers: Pilgrimage, Migration, and the Religious Imagination*, ed. Dale F. Eickelman and James P. Piscatori, Comparative Studies on Muslim Societies 9 (Berkeley: University of California Press, 1990), 40–41.

92 Gīlānī studied at Deoband and served as a Professor of Religious Studies at the ʿUṯmāniyya University in Ḥaydarābād. For his biography and scholarly contributions, see Muḥammad Ikrām Čuġtāʾī, *Mawlānā Munāẓir Aḥsan Gīlanī: ʿĀlim-e bē-badal* (Lahore: Sang-e-Meel Publications, 2009), passim.

93 I have not been able to locate a stand-alone version of this work, but it has been printed as an appendix to Mawdūdī's *Sūd*, on pp. 228–80. Mawdūdī seems to have written his own book in order to refute Gīlānī's work, added his critical notes in numerous places on the margins and written a systematic refutation of it on pp. 281–351.

It is clear that India is ruled by British law and not by the sharia; the first of Abū Ḥanīfa's conditions has therefore been fulfilled. The second condition also applies: most countries adjacent to India are infidel countries.[94] As for the sea, it is dominated by non-Muslims to such an extent that nobody can sail there without their permission.[95] Therefore, the second of Abū Ḥanīfa's conditions also applies. As for the third condition, it is clear that the British government completely disregards the *amān* which the Muslims acquired by their conversion and the *ḏimmīs* by their treaty of protection. It is clear that no attention is given to the question whether the various punishments imposed on Muslims are compatible with Islamic law. Property is transferred from Muslims to non-Muslims without asking whether this was legal according to Islamic law or not. Muslims are being arrested, flogged and expelled. There is no safety (*amān*) of life, property or honor. A country in which this situation exists is to be considered *dār al-kufr*, though some ulema used the term *dār al-ḥarb* and this caused considerable misunderstanding.[96] A Muslim who finds himself living in such an area is defined by Gīlānī as a Muslim *musta'min* (*musta'min*

94 Pre-partition India had a common boundary with Afghanistan which was governed by a Muslim ruler. This could be the reason why Gīlānī says that "most of the boundaries of India are with non-Muslim states" (... *Hindūstān kē akṯar ḥudūd ġayr islāmī mamālik awr ḥukūmatōñ sē muttaṣil hayñ*), rather than "all." See Mawdūdī, *Sūd*, 230 (Gīlānī). The existence of India's boundary with Afghanistan could undermine Gīlānī's argument and it is understandable that he disregards it. On the other hand, it is surprising that Mawdūdī did not use the existence of a common boundary with Afghanistan in order to weaken Gīlānī's analysis. It is noteworthy that W. W. Hunter—who writes substantial parts of his *Our Indian Musalmans* as if he were a Muslim sage who analyzes the various traditional views on the legal status of India and reaches his own conclusions concerning the "correct" one—asserts that Afghanistan is not relevant to this discussion because the way from India to England does not pass through Afghanistan, but rather through the sea which is considered *dār al-ḥarb* by numerous jurists. See Hunter, *Our Indian Musalmans*, 125–26. In Gīlānī's view, areas which are surrounded by Muslim countries are not considered *dār al-ḥarb*. He gives the example of Jabal al-Durūz in Syria, which is governed by Druze and Christians who are judged by their own judges and at times curse Islam and Muslims, but they are surrounded by Muslim areas from all sides and if the adjacent Muslim rulers wanted, they would be able to impose Muslim rule on the area. This is approvingly quoted from Ibn ʿĀbidīn, *Ḥāšiyat radd al-Muḫtār*, 4:175; cf. Ṣiddīq Ḥasan Ḫān, *al-ʿIbra*, 231; See Mawdūdī, *Sūd*, 261 (Gīlānī).

95 For various views on the legal status of the sea, see Ibn ʿĀbidīn, *Ḥāšiyat radd al-Muḫtār*, 4:160. The views mentioned here are expressed without reference to the power which rules the sea. See also Ṣiddīq Ḥasan Ḫān *al-ʿIbra*, 231.

96 Mawdūdī, *Sūd*, 231–33 (Gīlānī). Gīlānī does not spell out what the misunderstanding is. He probably means that the use of the term *dār al-ḥarb* could indicate that it is the duty

musalmān), a Muslim who has received protection from a non-Muslim government in power and is bound to obey the laws of the country in which he lives. Quoting Q 9:4 and 23:8[97], Gīlānī concludes that a Muslim who does not behave in this way is not only in breach of the law of the land, but also in breach of his contract and in breach of Islamic law (*islām kā, Qur'ān kā, ḫudā kā mujrim hōgā, gunāh-gār hōgā, ēk aysē fi'l kā murtakib hōgā jis kī ḥurmat Qur'ān o ḥadīṯ awr ijmā' sē ṯābit hay*). Some ulema issued a fatwa according to which a Muslim who does not pay full postage or takes on the train luggage in excess of the permitted weight is not only in breach of the law of the land, but also in breach of his religious law.[98] Yet the situation is not without dilemmas: for instance, taking interest is permissible in the laws of the infidels, but forbidden in Islam. On the other hand, taking money or other property from *ḥarbīs* is permissible. It is not possible to legalize interest which is prohibited by the Qur'an, but it is possible to achieve the same purpose by calling various types of Muslim revenue in *dār al-ḥarb* as spoils (*fay'*), or, in Hindī, *phā'ō* "a small quantity given above the quantity purchased."[99] Like Šaybānī before him, Gīlānī uses a legal stratagem to legitimize interest transactions and enables Muslims to obtain an economic advantage. It is also a fascinating example of an ingenious use of nomenclature in order to solve an economic and legal predicament.

It is noteworthy that in private conversations Gīlānī was less circumspect. His biographer Ẓafīr al-dīn Miftāḥī reports that Gīlānī was particularly concerned about the economic losses which the Muslims incurred because of their negative approach to interest transactions. Non-Muslims take interest from Muslims, but Muslims do not take interest from non-Muslims. The result is a lack of economic equilibrium and the unjustified transfer of Muslim property to non-Muslims. Miftāḥī reports that Gīlānī explicitly allowed Muslims to take interest from non-Muslims in order to restore that equilibrium and arrest the economic decline of the Muslim community.[100]

---

of the Muslims to wage jihad in order to reunite the area with *dār al-islām*. This is not his intention.

97 "And give good tidings to the unbelievers of a painful chastisement) excepting those of the idolaters with whom you made covenant ..." (9:4); "(Prosperous are the believers) ... who preserve their trusts and their covenant ..." (23:8).

98 Mawdūdī, *Sūd*, 233–34, 243 (Gīlānī).

99 Ibid., 248–53 (Gīlānī); for *phā'ō*, see John Thompson Platts, *A Dictionary of Urdu, Classical Hindi, and English* (London: W. H. Allen & Co., 1884), s.v.

100 Ẓafīr al-dīn Miftāḥī, *Ḥayāt-i Mawlānā Gīlānī* (Benares: Mawlana Yūsuf Academy, 1989), 322–24. Gīlānī published an article on the interest problem in the June 1944 issue of *Ma'ārif*, but this article was not available to the present writer. See ibid., 323 supra.

Summing up, Gīlānī says that India is *dār al-kufr* and "in *dār al-kufr* it is permissible to take hold of unprotected property by means of contracts which are invalid in Islam" (*dār al-kufr mēñ ʿuqūd-i fāsida fī ʾl-islām kē ḏariʿē sē amwāl-i ġayr maʿṣūma kā lēnā mubāḥ hay*). This means that a Muslim who lives there may engage in interest transactions or make a profit from gambling.

It is common for Muslim scholars to find support for their views in traditions about the early, ideal period of Islam. In our case, Gīlānī finds support for his views in the traditions concerning the Prophet's uncle al-ʿAbbās b. ʿAbd al-Muṭṭalib. In classical Islamic biographies, ʿAbbās is described as a rich man whose money "was spread among his people" (*kāna lahu māl mutafarriq fī qawmihi*). This is understood to mean that he was a money lender in Mecca. He engaged in this trade—and presumably received interest—until the conquest of Mecca by the Muslims despite the fact that according to several traditions he embraced Islam secretly much earlier, even before the battle of Badr.[101] He was ordered to stop interest transactions only in the Prophet's sermon at the "Farewell Pilgrimage" (*ḥijjat al-wadāʿ*) in 632. Since Mecca was considered *dār al-ḥarb* before its conquest by the Muslims, Šaybānī draws from these details in the biography of al-ʿAbbās the conclusion that "interest transactions between a Muslim and a *ḥarbī* are permissible in *dār al-ḥarb*" (*fa-tabayyana annahu yajūzu ʿaqd al-ribā bayn al-muslim wa al-ḥarbī fī dār al-ḥarb*).[102]

Gīlānī mentions these and similar traditions in order to create an analogy between Mecca before its conquest by the Muslims in 630 and India under the British rule.[103] He relates that after al-ʿAbbās converted to Islam, he went from Medina to Mecca before its conquest by the Muslims in order to engage in interest transactions. Of similar import are traditions about a wager which Abū Bakr is said to have made in Mecca. When Q 30:2–5 was revealed before the *hijra* and predicted the victory of the Byzantines over the Persians within a few years,[104] Abū Bakr wagered with Ubayy b. Ḫalaf, a Meccan *mušrik*, that this prediction would come true. The Prophet not only approved of what Abū Bakr did, but also instructed him to raise the stake from ten camels to one hundred and, at the same time, to postpone the date by which the Byzantine victory had to take place. The wager was made in Mecca when the city was still under polytheistic rule; the conclusion drawn from this is that wagering, which

101 Ibn Saʿd, *Ṭabaqāt*, ed. Julius Lippert, vol. 4/1 (Leiden: Brill, 1906), 5, ll. 15–18; 20, l. 28.

102 Šaybānī, *Siyar*, 4:1488 (no. 2903).

103 Mawdūdī, *Sūd*, 271–73 (Gīlānī).

104 "The Byzantines have been vanquished in the nearer part of the land; and after their vanquishing, they shall be the victors in a few years …"

is forbidden in *dār al-islām*, is permissible in *dār al-ḥarb*.[105] According to this, Muslim law applies only in territory under Muslim rule. The tradition is used to strengthen the idea that interest taking also is legal in *dār al-ḥarb*.

Abū al-Aʿlā Mawdūdī responded extensively to these arguments in his book entitled *Sūd* ("Interest"), adopting a substantially different stance. The book was completed in 1937 and reflects the conditions in British India in that period. According to Mawdūdī's criteria, it is next to impossible for an area to be transformed from *dār al-islām* to *dār al-ḥarb* or *dār al-kufr*. Quoting from several Hanafi scholars, he maintains that such a transformation does not take place as long as some manifestations of Islam are in evidence in that area. As long as one element of Islam (*ulqiyya* (sc. *ʿulqa*) *min ʿalāʾiq al-islām*) remains, Islam prevails. Only when all elements because of which an area became *dār al-islām* disappear does the area stop being *dār al-islām*. It is impossible to maintain that principalities such as Ḥaydarābād or Bhopal became *dār al-ḥarb* after losing their independence by entering into the "Subsidiary Alliance" with the British at the turn of the thirteenth/nineteenth century. Had the ulema declared Hyderabad as *dār al-ḥarb* at that time, Islam would have been corrupted in that area beyond recognition. In Mawdūdī's view, declaring an area as *dār al ḥarb* is a kind of self-fulfilling prophecy.[106]

In addition to his intense unwillingness to declare areas which were part of *dār al-islām* as *dār al-ḥarb*, Mawdūdī also contributes various refinements to the general debate concerning this issue. His view on the distinction between *dār al-kufr* and *dār al-ḥarb* is particularly noteworthy. He maintains that *dār al-kufr* is merely "foreign territory" (*ʿalāqa-yi ġayr*) and the term has nothing to do with matters of war and peace. The classical jurists used the term *dār al-ḥarb* because in their day countries adjacent to *dār al-islām* were at war with the Muslims and therefore they used the term for all countries under non-Muslim

105 Mawdūdī, *Sūd*, 273–74 (Gīlānī). For these traditions in Hanafi legal literature, see Saraḫsī, *al-Mabṣūṭ*, 14:56–57. The story appears in a slightly different version in Abū Jaʿfar Muḥammad b. Jarīr b. Yazīd al-Ṭabarī, *Jāmiʿ al-bayān ʿan tafsīr āy al-Qurʾān* (1954; repr., Beirut: Dār al-Fikr, 1988), 21:17, 19. and in other Qur'anic commentaries, but there Abū Bakr's action is justified by saying that the episode took place before the prohibition of wagering (*qabla an yunhā ʿan al-qimār*). This is well in line with the traditional dating of the Qur'an, because Q 5:90, which prohibited the *maysir* game and, by extension, any hazard game or wagering, is traditionally considered a late Medinan verse.

For a short account of the Perso- Byzantine wars in the beginning of the seventh century, which are the background of Q 30:2–5, see Josef Wiesehöfer, "The Late Sasanian Near East," in *The New Cambridge History of Islam*, ed. Chase F. Robinson, vol. 1 (Cambridge: Cambridge University Press, 2010), 98–152.

106 Mawdūdī, *Sūd*, 261–62, note.

rule.[107] Mawdūdī maintains that Gīlānī is wrong when he declares all non-*ḏimmī* infidels as *ḥarbī*s (enemies) and all non-Muslim possessions as *dār al-ḥarb* (enemy country). In Muslim international law, this is a wrong interpretation: only countries at war with the Muslims are *dār al-ḥarb*.[108]

These are the principles which Mawdūdī established concerning the transformation of *dār al-islām* into *dār al-ḥarb* or *dār al-kufr*. The question is how does he apply them to the modern history of India. There is no doubt in his mind that India was *dār al-islām* before the British entered the subcontinent and gradually expanded the areas under their effective rule. At the beginning of the thirteenth/nineteenth century, when Shah ʿAbd al-ʿAzīz wrote the fatwa which we have seen, India became *dār al-ḥarb* because the British were fighting against the Muslim government of the country. At that time, Muslims were obliged to fight for the preservation of the Muslim government; if they failed, they were obliged to perform *hijra*. When the British takeover became complete and the Muslims accepted subjugation while having the freedom to apply their law of personal status, India ceased to be *dār al-ḥarb* for them. It became a *dār al-kufr* in which Muslims lived as subjects (*ēk aysā dār al-kufr hō gayā jis mēñ musalmān raʿiyyat kī ḥayṯiyyat sē rehtē hayñ*) and enjoyed religious freedom within limits specified by the law of the land. To declare such a country to be *dār al-ḥarb* is against the principles of Islamic law. It is also dangerous: if this is done, Muslims will abandon the few options which they have in this country to apply Islamic laws. Even the few laws of the sharia which helped to preserve their distinct existence will not remain in effect and Muslims will be drawn into the non-Muslim system. Islam relaxed some of its rules and allowed some concessions for Muslims who are scattered individuals living among enemies, without any social power. Islam made these concessions only in cases of dire necessity. Even in these cases, Muslims were encouraged not to remain in these conditions and move to *dār al-islām* as soon as possible. Gīlānī accords these concessions to hundreds of thousands of people who live in India permanently. The rules of *dār al-ḥarb* are never applicable to such people. Not only must they make an effort to apply Islamic laws to the extent possible; they also must exert themselves to transform the *dār al-kufr* into *dār al-islām*.[109]

Mawdūdī concedes that India may have been *dār al-ḥarb* in the eyes of some Afghan tribal groups in the North Western Frontier Province—probably during the several wars waged by the British during the thirteenth/nineteenth

107 Ibid., 312.
108 Ibid., 245, note.
109 Ibid., 248–50, note.

century; this being so, they may have contracted in India invalid transactions (*ʿuqūd-i fāsida*) which could be considered legal in Hanafi law. Yet this permissibility is merely legal (*maḥḍ qānūnī jawāz*); these Muslims can never be accepted by God because they demean Islam in the eyes of non-Muslims by "eating" interest, selling wine, gambling and consuming pork. Similarly, India could have been considered *dār al-ḥarb* by the Turks, probably during World War I. But, Mawdūdī maintains, at the time of writing his treatise in the 1930s India should be considered *dār al-ṣulḥ* for all the Muslim governments. At the same time it is also *dār al-kufr*. There is no contradiction between these two terms: it is *dār al-kufr* because Muslim laws are not in effect, and it is *dār al-ṣulḥ* because it is not at war with a Muslim country.[110]

Mawdūdī revisited the subject in 1946. An unnamed "religious grandee" (*mutadayyin buzurg*)—who was also a professor of religious studies at a university—expressed the opinion that

> a merchant or a landowner who pays tax or rent to the government, if he deposits money at the Post Office or the Imperial Bank and receives interest, it is permissible for him to take interest in the amount of the tax or the rent which he paid.

Another well-known religious scholar went further, blamed the economic misfortunes of the Indian Muslims on the prohibiton of interest and challenged anybody to produce a Qur'anic verse or a Hadith to prove that the property of a *ḥarbī* is protected (and it is therefore forbidden to take interest from him). He bemoans the fact that the ulema have never considered in a dispassionate manner the economic difficulties suffered by the Muslims for a century and a half—since the beginning of British rule—during which one part of the population took interest and the other paid interest. It is not Islam that is responsible for "the lack of economic equilibrium" (*maʿāšī ʿadam-i tawāzun*) which developed in the country, but rather the ulema who had the tools to treat the economic system, yet took care of one part of it and neglected the other.[111]

Responding to these arguments, Mawdūdī suggests disregarding the complexities of the law and concentrating on the duty of the Muslims to raise the flag of religion, morality and civilization which were proclaimed as true in the Qur'an and the prophetic Sunna, and remove from the world thoughts and deeds which were declared false. In a country where falsehood has the upper

110 Ibid., 349.

111 He seems to mean that the ulema declared India to be *dār al-ḥarb* but did not draw the conclusion that interest is permissible. As we already know, this is only partially true.

hand and infidel laws are in effect, it is not the task of the Muslims to abide by them; they should strive instead for the establishment of an Islamic system. Mawdūdī maintains that if the Muslims break their own laws when in *dār al-kufr*, they will lose the high moral ground and will not be able to strive for the attainment of this goal. It is totally against the true religion to make Muslims spend their lives in happiness and tranquility under an infidel government.

> Now consider this: if we take interest, how will we be able to raise our voice against the infidels who do the same? If the infidels take our property in illegitimate ways, or if the infidel government takes part of our property without being entitled to do it (this is to say, without right based on divine authority), then how can it be right for us to start engaging in similarly forbidden activities and use illegal gain in order to take it back? In such a way, the door will be open for all kinds of forbidden activities, in addition to the taking of interest, such as wine drinking, producing musical instruments, production of obscene films, prostitution, dancing and singing, carving of idols, painting obscenities, engaging in speculative transactions in the money market (*saṭa bāzī*)[112], and gambling. In that case, tell me, what moral difference is there between us and the infidels on the strength of which we will make the effort to transform the *dār al-kufr* into *dār al-islām*?[113]

A few general observations on this analysis are now in order. There is a certain contradiction between Mawdūdī's general analysis which makes the transformation from *dār al-islām* to *dār al-ḥarb* next to impossible, and the determination that India under the British is *dār al-kufr*. The clear distinction between *dār al-ḥarb* and *dār al-kufr* is also novel; the classical jurists use these terms interchangeably, and I have not seen a precise definiton of them in the classical sources. The possible convergence of *dār al-kufr* and *dār al-ṣulḥ* is also not found in the classical sources. The most surprising element in Mawdūdī's analysis is the idea that a given area can be *dār al-islām* for one Muslim group and *dār al-ḥarb* for another. This is hardly compatible with the classical idea asserting the unity and the common destiny of the Muslim umma.

Mawdūdī has additional reasons to reject the idea that British India was *dār al-ḥarb*. Basing himself on various views in Hanafi jurisprudence, Gīlānī argued that transactions prohibited in *dār al-islām* are permissible in *dār al-ḥarb* or

112 I am indebted to Professor Muzaffar Alam who clarified this term to me.

113 Abū al-Aʿlā Mawdūdī, *Rasāʾil o Masāʾil* (Lahore: Islamic Publications Limited, 2006), 1:84–87 (quotation on pp. 85–86).

dār al-kufr. In contradistinction to him, Mawdūdī maintains that Islamic law is of universal validity and things which are forbidden in one place cannot be permissible in another. In a similar vein, nobody ever said that transactions forbidden between Muslims are permissible between Muslims and infidels. In Mawdūdī's view, permitting forbidden things outside *dār al-islām*, or permitting them in transactions with non-Muslims, would undermine the moral basis of Islam.[114]

In contradistinction to Gīlānī, Mawdūdī rejects the idea that the Muslim inhabitants of India can be considered as *musta'mins*. The first condition of a *musta'min* is to be a citizen of *dār al-islām*. The second condition is to stay in *dār al-ḥarb* for a short period of time; in Hanafi law, a year or slightly more. By analogy, this would mean that a Muslim *musta'min* can also not stay in *dār al-ḥarb* more than one or two years. Islamic sharia insists that Muslims live in *dār al-islām*, make the infidels into *d̲immī*s and never give permission (to Muslims) to make *dār al-ḥarb* their permanent homeland, to procreate there and live as *musta'mins* (for a protracted period). If this is not permissible for a single individual, how can it be permissible for millions of *Muslims* to live as *musta'mins* for centuries (*ābādī*) in a large country, to enjoy the permissions given to a *musta'min* only for a limited period of time, and, at the same time, to be free of Islamic law and abide by the laws of the infidels?[115] The true legal position of Indian Muslims is that they are a people who were taken over by (*istīlā'*) infidels. Their country became *dār al-ḥarb* when the British fought against its Muslim government; after the British takeover was completed, it became *dār al-kufr* in which some elements of *dār al-islām* remain. The question is what should the Indian Muslims do in this situation. Their obligation is either to migrate to a *dār al-islām*, and if they are not able to do this they have to do their utmost to preserve the manifestations of Islam (*islāmī āt̲ār*) in India. They also must do whatever is possible to restore India to being *dār al-islām*, because the lives which they live under infidel laws—every breath of them is a sin.[116]

As for Mawdūdī's perception of the situation of Muslims in independent India, it requires much further research. There are, however, some indications that in his opinion their situation is no better than it was under the British. Responding to Madanī's assertion that a country such as India should be considered *dār al-islām*,[117] Mawdūdī maintains that the participation of Muslims

114 Mawdūdī, *Sūd*, 289–90.

115 Mawdūdī, *Sūd*.

116 Ibid., 350.

117 See notes 122–123 below.

in the British administration was larger than in independent India. In a manifest attempt to denigrate the Indian government's attitude to Muslims, he asserts that the situation of the Muslims in independent India is no better than under the British and, therefore, if independent India is *dār al-islām*, the same should apply to the British *rāj*. With biting sarcasm Mawdūdī asks: "If present day India is *dār al-islām*, can there be any *dār al-kufr* in the world? (*mawjūda Bhārat bhī agar dār al-islām hay to phir dunyā mēñ ko'ī mulk dār al-kufr hō bhī saktā hay yā nahiñ?*).[118]

During the last years of the Indian struggle for independence, India's legal status was discussed in the works of Ḥusayn Aḥmad Madanī (1879–1957), the President of the *Jam'iyyat al-'ulamā'-i Hind*. This organization of Indian Muslim religious scholars was intensely anti-British, demanded the elimination of the *rāj* and supported the idea of "composite nationalism" (*muttaḥida qawmiyyat*) of Hindus and Muslims who together constitute one Indian nation. This ideology stood against the "two nations theory" (*dō qawmī naẓariyya*) of the Muslim League which held that Muslims and Hindus constitute two distinct nations, and therefore supported the partition of India and the establishment of Pakistan. The *Jam'iyya* maintained that after the removal of British rule a united, independent India should come into being.[119] Like other members of his organization, Madanī adopted a stringent anti-British stance, described India under British rule as *dār al-ḥarb* and asserted that it will so remain as long as infidelity is preponderant in it. All the definitions given to *dār al-ḥarb* apply to India under the British. Madanī invokes the fatwas of Shah 'Abd al-'Azīz, Rašīd Aḥmad Gangōhī and Faḍl al-Ḥaqq Ḫayrābādī in support of his views. He also deals with the question of interest, uses the standard Hanafi argument according to which the property of a *ḥarbī* in *dār al-ḥarb* is not protected, the Muslims can appropriate it if treachery is not involved and therefore taking interest from a non-Muslim in India is permissible. However, he clarifies that it is not permissible to give interest to a non-Muslim or to take interest from a Muslim. He also has reservations about saving money in a bank whose proprietor is a non-Muslim because he may use the money in a way detrimental to Islam and the Muslims. If however such an investment was made and interest accumulated in the account, it is not permissible to leave the interest in

118 Mawdūdī, *Rasā'il o Masā'il*, 4:117–18.

119 For the ideology of the *Jam'iyya*, see Yohanan Friedmann, "The attitude of the *Jam'iyyat al-'ulamā-i Hind* to the Indian national movement and the establishment of Pakistan," *Asian and African Studies* 7 (1971): 157–80. For an excellent analysis of Madanī's life and thought, see Barbara Daly Metcalf, *Husain Ahmad Madani: The Jihad for Islam and India's Freedom*, The Makers of the Muslim World Series (Oxford: Oneworld, 2009), passim.

the bank but rather to use it for Muslim social purposes.[120] The fact that the Muslims enjoy religious freedom under British rule—which was mentioned time and again by the nineteenth century scholars who held that India under the British remained *dār al-islām*—is not mentioned; on the contrary, Madanī accuses the British of systematic destruction of Islamic values in India.[121]

As for Madanī's views on the *šarʿī st*atus of independent India, I have so far located only one relevant quotation in Mawdūdī's *Rasāʾil o Masāʾil*.[122] An anonymous questioner brought to Mawdūdī's attention a passage quoted from Madanī's autobiography. In this passage, Madanī asserts that a country which is governed by non-Muslims, but in which the Muslims have a share in the government and their religious rights are respected—should be considered *dār al-islām*. The Muslims should consider it as their own and wish it well. Madanī thought that even Shah ʿAbd al-ʿAzīz—who declared India to be *dār al-ḥarb* at the beginning of the thirteenth/nineteenth century—would concur with this opinion.[123] Like Karāmat ʿAlī in the thirteenth/nineteenth century, Madanī asserts that the legal status of an area is not determined by the religious affiliation of its ruler, but by the extent to which its Muslims inhabitants enjoy religious freedom.

A comprehensive analysis of the *šarʿī* status of India after partition has been attempted by Saʿīd Aḥmad Akbarābādī, a prolific Deobandī *ʿālim* who served as the head of the Department of Sunni religious studies in Aligarh Muslim University in the 1950s and 1960s. In 1968 he published a book entitled "The *Šarʿī* Status of India (*Hindūstān kī šarʿī ḥayṯiyyat*). His book is an attempt to define the *šarʿī st*atus of India since the British takeover and, most importantly, after the establishment of independent India. In order to understand his position, we must remember that Akbarābādī was a member of the *Jamʿiyyat al-ʿulamāʾ-i Hind*, a representative organization of Indian Muslim ulema, who opposed partition, maintained that all Indians belong to the same nation despite their religious differences and supported the Indian National

120 Ḥusayn Aḥmad Madanī, *Maktūbāt-i Šaykh al-Islām*, ed. Najm al-Dīn Iṣlāḥī (Deoband: National Printing Press, 1963), 2:123–24.

121 Friedmann, "The attitude of the *Jamʿiyyat al-ʿulamā-i Hind*," 160–61.

122 Madanī, *Maktūbāt-i Šaykh al-Islām*, 4:117–18.

123 The questioner quotes Madanī, *Naqš-i ḥayāt*, 2:1. I have not found this passage in the edition at my disposal (Deoband: National Printing Press, 1954 (?)), but it is likely that Madanī did indeed hold this opinion. He was intensely anti-British and maintained that the British transformed India into *dār al-kufr*. The theory of "composite nationalism" (*muttaḥida qawmiyyat*) espoused by Madanī can hardly be compatible with the perception of independent India as *dār al-ḥarb*. For the "composite nationalism" theory, Friedmann, "The attitude of the *Jamʿiyyat al-ʿulamā-i Hind*," passim.

Congress in the independence struggle. In view of this background, we can easily understand that when Akbarābādī analyses the legal status of independent India from the point of view of its Muslim minority, he uses the most restrictive conditions for the definition of a country as *dār al-ḥarb*. Discussing the definition of "domination" (*istīlā'*) used by Muslim jurisprudents for a non-Muslim takeover of a Muslim area, he says that this domination takes effect only when the Muslims have no say in the government of the country and enjoy no religious freedom. If they are debarred from government but do enjoy religious freedom, the country still does not become *dār al-ḥarb*. India cannot be considered *dār al-ḥarb* according to these criteria. It is a secular, democratic (*secular jumhūrī*) state, the government is not in the hands of any one religious group and one cannot claim that it is dominated by infidels. The equality of civil rights guaranted by the constitution means that Muslims have a share in the government. They enjoy full religious freedom. Neither India nor any other democratic country can today be considered *dār al-ḥarb*.[124] India is also not *dār al-islām* because it declared itself secular and non-religious (*secular awr lā dīnī*). It is not *dār al-ʿahd* or *dār al-amān* either, because the relationship of *muʿāhid, āmin* or *musta'min* do not exist in modern times.[125]

In this way, Akbarābādī reaches the conclusion that the *šarʿī* classification of countries is not applicable to the circumstances which prevail in moden India; moreover, it is not suitable in modern times at all. It is therefore essential to define the Indian situation in a new way. India has to be considered by its Muslim inhabitants as their national home (*Hindūstān kī šarʿī ḥayṯiyyat yahān kē musalmānōn kē li'ē yih hay kih yih unkā al-waṭan al-qawmī* national home *hay*).[126] This is a definition which is totally removed from traditonal *šarʿī* thought, but Akbarābādī does not hesitate to describe the concept of "national home" as a *šarʿī* category.

It is now time to make some concluding observations. Shah ʿAbd al-ʿAzīz, ʿAbd al-Ḥayy Laḫnawī, Muḥammad Qāsim Nānawtawī, Rašīd Aḥmad Gangōhī and Munāẓir Aḥsan Gīlānī operate within the Hanafi legal tradition, though their conclusions are not identical. All of them give much weight to the

---

124 Saʿīd Aḥmad Akbarābādī, *Nafthat al-maṣdūr awr Hindūstān kī šarʿī ḥayṯiyyat* (Aligarh: Aligarh Muslim University Press, 1968), 72; Yohanan Friedmann, "The Jamʿiyyat al-ʿulamā'-i Hind in the wake of partition," *Asian and African Studies* 11 (1976): 196.

125 Akbarābādī, *Hindūstān kī šarʿī ḥayṯiyyat*, 96–97; Friedmann, "The Jamʿiyyat al-ʿulamā'-i Hind in the wake of partition," 196.

126 Akbarābādī, *Hindūstān kī šarʿī ḥayṯiyyat*, 103; Friedmann, "The Jamʿiyyat al-ʿulamā'-i Hind in the wake of partition," 196–97.

political situation in India in their times. The analysis of Mawdūdī is much more complex. He is not bound by the Hanafi legal tradition. Except for his reluctance to allow for the transformation of *dār al-islām* into *dār al-ḥarb,* he does not base his analysis of the legal status of India on the standard material found in the Hanafi books of law, certainly not to the extent that this is done by the other scholars whose views have been described above. As he is devoted to describing Islam as an exemplary civilization which is destined to change the world order, he is averse to rulings which conflict with this major goal. He is extremely sensitive to the possibility that certain aspects of the laws concerning interest—especially the ruling according to which Muslims in *dār al-ḥarb* are allowed to take interest from non-Muslims but are forbidden to take interest from Muslims or pay interest to non-Muslims—may place Islam in a morally inferior position and undermine its presentation as an exemplary civilization. As a thinker who is deeply involved in civilizational polemics against the West, the preservation of the high moral ground for Islam is for him of crucial importance.

The most significant deviation from the classical norms can be found in the work of Saʿīd Aḥmad Akbarābādī. In his discussion of the issue he uses the classical concepts only in order to show that they are outdated and inapplicable to modern situations. The concept of "national home" by which he describes the status of modern India from the point of view of its Muslim citizens is taken from modern secular political thought and is totally removed from that of the classical jurists. This is of particular significance because the idea is propounded by an *ʿālim* of traditional upbringing. It is an example indicating that when historical realities require it, Muslim law may develop in rather unexpected directions.

References

ʿAbd al-ʿAzīz al-Dihlawī, Shah. *Fatāwā-yi ʿAzīzī.* Delhi: Maṭbaʿ-i Mujtabāʾī, 1311AH.

ʿAbd al-Ḥayy Muḥammad Abū ʾl-Ḥasanāt Lakhnawī. *Al-Fawāʾid al-bahiyya fī tarājim al-ḥanafiyya.* Cairo: Maṭbaʿat al-Saʿāda, 1334AH.

ʿAbd al-Ḥayy Muḥammad Abū ʾl-Ḥasanāt Lakhnawī. *Majmūʿat al-fatāwā.* Lahore: Shahzād Publishers, n.d.

Abel, Armand. "Dār al-ḥarb." *Encyclopaedia of Islam, Vol. II, C-G.* Leiden: Brill, 1965.

Abou El Fadl, Khaled. "Islamic Law and Muslim Minorities: The Juristic Discourse on Muslim Minorities from the Second/Eighth to the Eleventh/Seventeenth Centuries." *Islamic Law and Society* 1, no. 2 (1994): 141–87.

Ahmad, Aziz. *Islamic Modernism in India and Pakistan, 1857–1964*. Oxford: Oxford University Press, 1967.

Ahmad, Aziz. *Studies in Islamic Culture in the Indian Environment*. Oxford: Clarendon Press, 1964.

Ahmad, Mushtaq Muhammad. "The notions of *dār al-ḥarb* and *dār al-Islām* in Islamic jurisprudence with special reference to the Ḥanafī school." *Islamic Studies* 47 (2008): 5–37.

Ahmad Khan, Muin-ud-din. *History of the Fara'idi Movement in Bengal, 1818–1906*. Karachi: Pakistan Historical Society, 1965.

Akbarābādī, Saʿīd Aḥmad. *Nafthat al-maṣdūr awr Hindūstān kī šarʿī ḥayṯiyyat*. Aligarh: Aligarh Muslim University Press, 1968.

Arberry, Arthur John, ed. *The Koran Interpreted: A Translation*. A Touchstone Book. New York: Simon & Schuster, 1996.

ʿAynī, Abū Muḥammad Badr al-dīn al-. *ʿUmdat al-qārī' šarḥ Ṣaḥīḥ al-Buḫārī*. Beirut: Dār Iḥyā' al-turāth al-ʿarabī, n.d.

Aẓhar, Ẓahūr Aḥmad. "Dār al-ḥarb." *Urdū Dā'ira-yi Maʿārif-i Islāmiyya*. Lahore: University of the Panjab, 1972.

Bausani, Alessandro. "Farā'iḍiyya." *Encyclopaedia of Islam, Vol. II, C-G*. Leiden: Brill, 1965.

Bayhaqī, Abū Bakr Aḥmad b. al-Ḥusayn b. ʿAlī al-. *Maʿrifat al-Sunan wa'l-āṯār*. Edited by Sayyid Kisrawī Ḥasan. Beirut: Dār al-Kutub al-ʿilmiyya, 1991.

Bayly, C. A. *Indian Society and the Making of the British Empire*. The New Cambridge History of India, II, 1. Cambridge: Cambridge University Press, 1987.

Bazmee Ansari, A.S. "al-Fatāwā al-ʿĀlamgīriyya." *Encyclopaedia of Islam, Vol. II, C-G*. Leiden: Brill, 1965.

Biran, Michal. *The Empire of the Qara Khitai in Eurasian History: Between China and the Islamic World*. Cambridge Studies in Islamic Civilization. Cambridge: Cambridge University Press, 2005.

Blackburn, J. R. "al-Mu'ayyad bi-'llāh Muḥammad." *Encyclopaedia of Islam, Vol. VII, Mif-Naz*. Leiden: Brill, 1993.

Brockelmann, Carl. *Geschichte der arabischen Litteratur*. Vol. 1. Leiden: Brill, 1937.

Brockelmann, Carl. *Geschichte der arabischen Litteratur*, Supplementband. Leiden: Brill, 1938.

Buḫārī, Muḥammad b. Ismāʿīl al-. *Le recueil des traditions mahométanes par el-Bokhâri (al-Ṣaḥīḥ)*. Edited by M. Ludolf Krehl. Vol. 1. 4 vols. Leiden: Brill, 1862.

Burhānpūrī, Niẓām. *Fatāwā-yi ʿĀlamgīrī*. Kānpūr: Al-Maṭbaʿa al-Majīdī, 1350.

Calasso, Giovanna. "Alla ricerca di *dār al-islām*. Una ricognizione nei testi di giuristi e tradizionisti, lessicografi, geografi e viaggiatori." *Rivista degli Studi Orientali* 83 (2010): 271–96.

Crone, Patricia. *Medieval Islamic Political Thought*. Edinburgh: Edinburgh Univ. Press, 2004.

Čuġtā'ī, Muḥammad Ikrām. *Mawlānā Munāẓir Aḥsan Gīlanī: 'Ālim-e bē-badal*. Lahore: Sang-e-Meel Publications, 2009.

Dabbūsī, Abū Zayd 'Ubayd Allāh b. 'Umar b. 'Īsā. *Kitāb ta'sīs al-naẓar*. Cairo, n.d.

Djalili, Mohammad-Reza. "Dār al-ḥarb." In *The Oxford Encyclopedia of the Islamic world*, edited by John L. Esposito. New York: Oxford University Press, 2009.

Faisal, Muhammad Ahsanullah. *Haji Shariatullah's Faraizi Movement: History, Da'wah & Political Ideology*. Dhaka [Bangladesh]: Shariatia Library, 2010.

Farīdī, Nasīm Aḥmad. "Rashīd Aḥmad Gangōhī." *Urdū Dā'ira-yi ma'ārif-i islāmiyya*. Lahore: University of the Panjab, 1972.

Frick, Marie-Luisa, and Andreas Th. Müller, eds. *Islam and International Law: Engaging Self-Centrism from a Plurality of Perspectives*. Brill's Arab and Islamic Law Series, volume 7. Leiden: Brill–Nijhoff, 2013.

Friedmann, Yohanan. "Classification of Unbelievers in Sunnī Muslim Law and Tradition." *Jerusalem Studies in Arabic and Islam* 22 (1998): 163–95.

Friedmann, Yohanan. "The attitude of the *Jam'iyyat al-'ulamā-i Hind* to the Indian national movement and the establishment of Pakistan." *Asian and African Studies* 7 (1971): 157–80.

Friedmann, Yohanan. "The Jam'iyyat al-'ulamā'-i Hind in the wake of partition." *Asian and African Studies* 11 (1976): 181–211.

Friedmann, Yohanan. *Tolerance and Coercion in Islam. Interfaith Relations in the Muslim Tradition*. Cambridge: Cambridge University Press, 2003.

Gangōhī, Rašīd Aḥmad. *Fatāwā Rašīdiyya*. Vol. 1. Murādābād: 'Azīz al al-Dīn and 'Alī Naẓar, 1906.

Gangōhī, Rašīd Aḥmad. *Fatāwā Rašīdiyya*. Vol. 3. Murādābād: 'Azīz al al-Dīn and 'Alī Naẓar, 1910.

Gangōhī, Rašīd Aḥmad. *Fatāwā Rašīdiyya*. Delhi: Hindustan Electric Printing Works, 1924.

Ghose, Rajarshi. "Islamic Law and Imperial Space: British India as 'domain of Islam' circa 1803–1870." *Journal of Colonialism and Colonial History* 15, no. 1 (2014).

Ghose, Rajarshi. "Politics for Faith: Karamat Ali Jaunpuri and Islamic Revivalist Movements in British India circa 1800–73." Ph.D. Dissertation, University of Chicago, 2012.

Haque, Enamul. *Nawab Bahadur Abdul Latif: His Writings and Related Documents*. Dacca: Samudra Prokashani, 1968.

Hardy, Peter. *The Muslims of British India*. Cambridge: Cambridge University Press, 1972.

Heffening, Willi. "al-Marghinānī." *Encyclopaedia of Islam, Vol. VI, Mahk-Mid*. Leiden: Brill, 1991.

Hunter, W. W. *Our Indian Musalmans: Are They Bound in Conscience to Rebel against the Queen?* London: Trübner and Company, 1871.

Ibn Ḥawqal, Abū 'l-Qāsim al-Naṣībī. *Kitāb Ṣūrat al-arḍ*. Leiden: Brill, 1948.

Ibn Saʿd, Abū ʿAbd Allāh Muḥammad. *Ṭabaqāt*. Edited by Julius Lippert. Vol. 4/1. Leiden: Brill, 1906.

"Ibn ʿĀbidīn." *Encyclopaedia of Islam, Vol. III, H-Iram*. Leiden: Brill, 1971.

Ibn ʿĀbidīn, Muḥammad Amīn. *Ḥāšiyat radd al-Muḫtār*. Cairo: Muṣṭafā al-Bābī al-Ḥalabī, 1966.

Ikrām, Shaykh Muḥammad. *Mawj-i Kawṯar, yaʿnī Musalmānōñ kī maḏhabī awr ʿilmī taʾrīḫ*. Lahore: Fīrōz Sons Ltd., 1968.

Imamul Hoque, M. "Jaunpuri, Karamat Ali." In *Banglapedia, The National Encyclopedia of Bangladesh*, edited by Sirajul Islam. Dhaka: Asiatic Society of Bangladesh, 2003.

Inayatullah, Sh. "ʿAbd al-Ḥayy." *Encyclopaedia of Islam, Vol. I, A–B*. Leiden: Brill, 1960.

Ismāʿīl al-Šahīd, Mawlānā Muḥammad. *Sirāṭ al-Mustaqīm* [sic]. Calcutta: Šayḫ Hidāyat Allāh, 1238AH.

Iṣṭaḫrī, Abū Isḥāq Ibrāhīm al-. *Kitāb Masālik al-mamālik*. Leiden: Brill, 1927.

Jalal, Ayesha. *Partisans of Allah: Jihad in South Asia*. Cambridge, Mass.: Harvard University Press, 2008.

Johansen, Baber. "The All-Embracing Town and Its Mosques: *Al-Miṣr Al-Jāmiʿ*." In *Contingency in a Sacred Law: Legal and Ethical Norms in the Muslim Fiqh*, 77–106. Studies in Islamic Law and Society, v. 7. Leiden Brill, 1999.

Karāmat ʿAlī Jawnpūrī. "Ḥujjat-i Qāṭiʿa." In *Ḏaḫīra-yi Karāmat*, 1:85–119. Kānpūr: Maṭbaʿ-i Majīdī, 1929.

Karāmat ʿAlī Jawnpūrī. "Ištihār Nāma." In *Ḏaḫīra-yi Karāmat*, 1:119–24. Kānpūr: Maṭbaʿ-i Majīdī, 1929.

Karāmat ʿAlī Jawnpūrī. *Lecture by Moulvie Karamat Ali on a Question of Mahomedan Law, Involving the Duty of Mahomedans in British India towards the Ruling Power. Abstract of Proceedings of the Mahomedan Literary Sociey of Calcutta*. Calcutta: Erasmus Jones, Cambrian Press, 1871.

Karāmat ʿAlī Jawnpūrī. *Miftāḥ al-janna*. Kānpūr: Naval Kishōr, 1877.

Kāsānī, ʿAlāʾ al-Dīn Abū Bakr al-. *Badāʾiʿ al-ṣanāʾiʿ fī tartīb al-šarāʾiʿ*. Edited by Muḥammad Ḫayr Ṭuʿma Ḥalabī. Beirut: Dār al-Maʿrifa, 2000.

Kaviraj, Narahari. *Wahabi and Farazi* [sic] *Rebels of Bengal*. New Delhi: People's Publishing House, 1982.

Khadduri, Majid, ed. *The Islamic Law of Nations: Shaybānī's Siyar*. Translated with an Introduction, Notes and Appendices. Baltimore: The Johns Hopkins Press, 1966.

Khadduri, Majid, ed. *War and Peace in the Law of Islam*. Baltimore: The Johns Hopkins Press, 1955.

Lewis, Bernard. *The Political Language of Islam*. Paperback 4th ed., Chicago: Univ. of Chicago Press, 1991.

Madanī, Ḥusayn Aḥmad. *Maktūbāt-i Šaykh al-Islām*. Edited by Najm al-Dīn Iṣlāḥī. Deoband: National Printing Press, 1963.

Marġīnānī, Burhān al-Dīn ʿAlī b. Abī Bakr al-. *Al-Hidāya šarḥ Bidāyat al-mubtadiʾ*. Cairo: Dār al-salām, 2000.

Marġīnānī, Burhān al-Dīn ʿAlī b. *Fatāwā fuṣūl al-iḥkām fī uṣūl al-aḥkām al-maʿrūf bi-Fuṣūl-i ʿimādī*. Calcutta: Asiatic Lithographic Press, 1827.

Masud, Muhammad Khalid. "The Obligation to Migrate: The Doctrine of *hijra* in Islamic Law." In *Muslim Travellers: Pilgrimage, Migration, and the Religious Imagination*, edited by Dale F. Eickelman and James P. Piscatori, 29–49. Comparative Studies on Muslim Societies 9. Berkeley: University of California Press, 1990.

Masud, Muhammad Khalid. "The World of Shah ʿAbd Al-ʿAziz (1746–1824)." In *Perspectives of Mutual Encounters in South Asian History, 1760–1860*, edited by Jamal Malik, 298–314. Social, Economic and Political Studies of the Middle East and Asia, v. 73. Leiden: Brill, 2000.

Mawdūdī, Abū al-Aʿlā. *Rasāʾil o Masāʾil*. Lahore: Islamic Publications Limited, 2006.

Mawdūdī, Abū al-Aʿlā. *Sūd*. 25th ed. (1st ed. 1961). Lahore: Islamic Publications Limited, 2005.

Metcalf, Barbara Daly. *Husain Ahmad Madani: The Jihad for Islam and India's Freedom*. The Makers of the Muslim World Series. Oxford: Oneworld, 2009.

Miftāḥī, Ẓafīr al-dīn. *Ḥayāt-i Mawlānā Gīlānī*. Benares: Mawlana Yūsuf Academy, 1989.

Mushiru-l-Haqq [Mušīr al-Ḥaqq]. "Indian Muslim Attitude to the British in the Early Nineteenth Century: A Case Study of Shāh ʿAbdul ʿAzīz." Unpublished M.A. thesis, McGill, 1964.

Mushiru-l-Haqq [Mušīr al-Ḥaqq]. "Unnīswīn ṣadī kē Hindūstān kī hayʾat-i šarʿī: Šāh ʿAbd al-ʿAzīz kē fatāwā-yi *dār al-ḥarb* kā ēk ʿilmī tajziʾa." *Burhān* 63 (1969): 221–43.

Nānawtawī, Muḥammad Qāsim. *Qāsim al-ʿulūm maʿa Urdū tarjuma Anwār al-nujūm*. Edited by Muḥammad Anwār al-Ḥasan Shērkoṫī. Lahore: Nāshirān-i Qurʾān Limited, 1974.

Peters, Rudolph. *Islam and Colonialism: The Doctrine of Jihad in Modern History*. Religion and Society 20. The Hague: Mouton, 1979.

Platts, John Thompson. *A Dictionary of Urdu, Classical Hindi, and English*. London: W. H. Allen & Co., 1884.

Qasṭallānī, Abū 'l-ʿAbbās Šihāb al-dīn al- (d. 923/1517). *Iršād al-sārī šarḥ Ṣaḥīḥ al-Buḫārī*. Bayrūt: Dār al-kutub al-ʿilmiyya, 1996.

Qureshi, Ishtiaq Husain. *The Muslim Community in the Indo-Pakistan Subcontinent (610–1947). A Brief Historical Analysis*. The Hague: Mouton & Co., 1962.

Qureshi, M. Naeem. *Pan-Islam in British Indian Politics: A Study of the Khilafat Movement, 1918–1924*. Social, Economic, and Political Studies of the Middle East and Asia, v. 66. Leiden: Brill, 1999.

Raḥmān ʿAlī. *Tadkira-yi ʿulamaʾ-i Hind*. Lucknow: Naval Kishōr, 1294 AH.

Rapoport, Yossef, and Emilie Savage-Smith, eds. *An Eleventh-Century Egyptian Guide to the Universe: The Book of Curiosities*. Islamic Philosophy, Theology and Science, v. 87. Leiden: Brill, 2014.

Riḍwī, Sayyid Maḥbūb. *Ta'rīḫ-i Dēoband: Dēoband awr Dār al-ʿulūm ke ḥālāt*. Dēoband: ʿIlmī Markaz, 1972.

Šāfiʿī, Abū ʿAbd Allāh Muḥammad al-. *Kitāb al-Umm*. Bayrūt: Dār al-kutub al-ʿilmiyya, 1993.

Saraḫsī, Muḥammad b. Aḥmad al-. *Al-Nukat wa-huwa šarḥ li-Ziyādāt al-ziyādāt li-'l-imām* [...] *Muḥammad b. al-Ḥasan al-Šaybānī wa šarḥuhā li-'l-imām Abī Naṣr Aḥmad b. Muḥammad al-ʿAttābī al-Buḫārī*. Bayrūt: ʿĀlam al-kutub, 1986.

Saraḫsī, Muḥammad b. *Kitāb al-Mabṣūṭ fī 'l-fiqh al-Ḥanafī*. Beirūt: Dār al-Maʿrifa, n.d.

Šaybānī, Muḥammad b. al-Ḥasan al-. *Šarḥ al-Siyar al-kabīr*. Edited by al-Munajjid. Cairo, 1957.

Sayyid Aḥmad Ḫān. *Review of Dr. Hunter's* Indian Musalmans: Are They Bound in Conscience to Rebel against the Queen? Benares: The Medical Hall Press, 1872.

Ṣiddīq Ḥasan Ḫān. *Al-ʿIbra mimmā jā'a fī 'l-ġazw wa'l-šahāda wa al-hijra*. Beirut: Dār al-Kutub al-ʿilmiyya, 1988.

Ṣiddīq Ḥasan Ḫān. *Ḥujaj al-karāma li-ašrāṭ al-sāʿa*. Bhopal, n.d.

Ṭabarī, Abū Jaʿfar Muḥammad b. Jarīr al-. *Jāmiʿ al-bayān ʿan tafsīr āy al-Qur'ān*. 1954. Reprint, Beirut: Dār al-Fikr, 1988.

Tahānawī, Muḥammad Aʿlā b. ʿAlī al-. *Kaššāf iṣṭilāḥāt al-funūn*. Edited by Aḥmad Jawdat. Istanbul: Dār al-Ḫilāfa al-ʿaliyya, 1317AH.

Taylor, James. *A Sketch of the Topography & Statistics of Dacca*. Calcutta: G. H. Huttmann, Military Orphan Press, 1840.

Wiesehöfer, Josef. "The Late Sasanian Near East." In *The New Cambridge History of Islam*, edited by Chase F. Robinson, 1:98–152. Cambridge: Cambridge University Press, 2010.

Wise, James. *Notes on the Races, Castes and Trades of Eastern Bengal*. London: Harrison and sons, 1883.

Yusuf Ali, A. "Karāmat ʿAlī." *Encyclopaedia of Islam, Vol. IV, Iran-Kha*. Leiden: Brill, 1978.

Ẓafarul-Islām Khān. "Nawwāb Sayyid Ṣiddīq Ḥasan K͟hān." *Encyclopaedia of Islam, Vol. VII, Mif-Naz*. Leiden: Brill, 1993.

CHAPTER 18

Better *barr al-ʿaduww* Than *dār al-ḥarb*

Some Considerations about Eighteenth-Century Maghribi Chronicles

Antonino Pellitteri

1 Introduction

The topic of the *dār al-islām* / *dār al-ḥarb* dichotomy which is at the center of this volume can be dealt with from several points of view. I shall limit myself mainly to analyzing the matter starting with the reading of a number of essays by two Maghribi historians from the Ottoman period, the Libyan Ibn Ġalbūn (Abū ʿAbd Allāh Muḥammad Ibn Ḫalīl Ġalbūn al-Ṭarābulusī al-Miṣrātī, twelfth/eighteenth century) and the Tunisian Maḥmūd al-Maqdīš al-Safāqusī (d. 1226/1811), with some reference to other authors from different historical periods and geographical contexts.

Ibn Ġalbūn and al-Maqdīš are representatives of an as yet little studied local historiography. They both studied *fiqh*, *tafsīr* and Hadith according to the tradition of that period. In the chronicles that we take into account, the two historians and *fuqahāʾ* seem to be more interested in describing the Other as representing similarity and diversity at the same time. This orientation should be approached, in my view, taking into account what my colleague and friend Gianroberto Scarcia wrote about the dichotomies *islām*/*ḥarb* and *ʿarab*/*ʿajam*:

> What is not Islam, then, is not what is located beyond clear—although controversial and variable—territorial boundaries but a merely historical "flaw" of the human soul. A flaw which is behavioral, superficial, political and not a way of being (a "diversity") of an anthropological order: a moral flaw indeed, which is, in Islam, juridical.[1]

It is sufficient to consider the use of the term *ṯaġr* (pl. *ṯuġūr*) in Arabic sources to realize that Scarcia's observations are very insightful. According to the *Lisān*

1 Gianroberto Scarcia, "*Islām* e *Ḥarb, ʿArab* e *ʿAjam*: nota a due celeberrime dicotomie islamiche," in *Azhàr: studi arabo-islamici in memoria di Umberto Rizzitano (1913–1980)*, ed. Antonino Pellitteri and Giovanni Montaina, Annali della Facoltà di lettere e filosofia dell'Università di Palermo. Studi e ricerche 23 (Palermo: Facoltà di lettere e filosofia dell'Università di Palermo, 1995), 205–6 (my translation).

 | DOI 10.1163/9789004331037_020

al-ʿarab by Ibn Manẓūr, the meaning of *ṯaġr* is "breach," an open and fluctuating passage. The territory beyond the breach is not necessarily a grey zone between white and black; it represents what is contiguous to the world of Islam, a place of apprehension.[2] In this regard, it can be useful to look at the Fatimid period and the role of Sicily in that historical and ideological context, even though at first sight this reference may appear inappropriate.

Indeed, if we examine the case of Calabria in particular—although this region wasn't actually part of the Islamic territories, in the tenth century its population used to pay the *jizya* to the Fatimid *ʿāmil* of Sicily—or more generally the case of Southern Italy at the time of the first Banū Abī 'l-Ḥusayn, or Kalbids—governors of Muslim Sicily on behalf of the Fatimids—we can better understand the complexity of the matter.[3] In this context, an important document concerning Sicily at the time of the victory of the *daʿwa fāṭimiyya* in North Africa is very revealing. The document expresses a coherent—if we consider the time and place in which it was drafted—definition of the Other as a reflection of the Self. It is a message dated 296/909 and addressed to the Muslim Sicilians by the *dāʿī* Abū ʿAbd Allāh al-Ṣanʿānī after the Fatimid victory over the Aghlabids in the same year. According to *qāḍī* al-Nuʿmān, the message was part of a more comprehensive document sent to all the territories administered by the Aghlabids, promising *amān* to everyone who had shown obedience and loyalty towards the *daʿwa fāṭimiyya*. There is no explicit mention of the *dār al-islām* / *dār al-ḥarb* dichotomy in the document, but only a reference—appropriate to the history of that time—to *dārikum* and *dār al-mušrikīn*, a sort of problematic invitation to the *ḥaqq al-jihād* and an even more problematic appeal "*li-jihādikum al-kafara al-ẓālimīn*." The latter should be intended—in my opinion—as a fight against the usurpers, the Bānū al-Aġlāb, who persist in error, as clarified by the above-mentioned *qāḍī* al-Nuʿmān in his *Iftitāḥ al-daʿwa* which contains the aforesaid document.[4]

وأنتم معشر أهل جزيرة صقلية أحق بما أوليته من المعروف والإحسان
واسديته، وأولى به وأقرب إليه لقرب داركم من دار المشركين ولجهادكم

---

2 See Antonino Pellitteri, *I Fatimiti e la Sicilia (sec. X): materiali per uno studio sulla Sicilia* thaghr *e terra di* gihâd *con particolare riferimento a fonti ismailite dell'epoca* (Palermo: Centro Culturale al-Farabi, 1997), 15.

3 Abū ʿAbd Allāh Muḥammad al-Marrākušī Ibn ʿIḏārī, *Kitāb al-Bayān al-muġrib fī aḫbār al-Andalus wa'l-Maġrib* [= BM], ed. Georges Séraphin Colin and Évariste Lévi-Provençal (Leiden: Brill, 1948), 1:130–32.

4 Pellitteri, *I Fatimiti e la Sicilia*, 46–49.

الكفرة الظالمين وسوف أملأ إن شاء الله جزيرتكم خيلاً ورجالاً من المؤمنين الذين يجاهدون في الله حق جهاده فيعز الله بهم الدين والمسلمين ويذل بهم الشرك والمشركين والحول والقوة لله العلي العظيم وهو حسبنا ونعم الوكيل

A) And you, the people of the island of Sicily have a greater right and are (even) more deserving of the benevolence that I have awarded to you; all the more so, since **your land is closer to that of the godless (*al-mušrikīn*), and because of your jihad against the unbelieving sinners.** I will fill your island, if God be willing, with horsemen and foot soldiers, who are believers **and will have the task of fighting the just cause of the jihad in the name of God.** And God will consolidate, through these, the hold of religion and the strength of the Muslims, and through these, will humiliate the idolatry of the godless. The power and strength are with God Almighty and Omnipotent; He suffices, for our needs, and is our most excellent Defender.

B) And when what was written was read out in the country, its people felt safe and confident, calm and grateful. Their fears were appeased, and delegations reached him from every corner of the land to thank him, to rejoice with him and to acknowledge his justice, goodness and successful running of public affairs. This increased their exultation and joy for him.[5]

There is no doubt that this letter to the Sicilians should be analyzed also by taking into account the specific terminology and framework of the fourth/tenth–century *daʿwa fāṭimiyya* both from a historical-political and a juridical–theoretical point of view, but that is beyond the scope of the present study. Nevertheless, we can affirm that in *qāḍī* al-Nuʿmān's text one can find references to the fact that Islam urges all humankind to know one another, according to the Qur'an: "And (We) have made you nations and tribes that you may know one another (*sūrat al-ḥujurāt*, Q 49:13)." On the other hand, the idea of geographical divisions along religious lines is mentioned neither in the Qur'an nor in the sayings of the Prophet. The notion of "houses" or "divisions" of the

5 See Antonino Pellitteri, "The Historical-Ideological Framework of Islamic Fatimid Sicily (Fourth/Tenth Century) with the Reference to Works of the Qāḍī Al-Nuʿmān," *Al-Masāq* 7 (1994): 148.

world such as *dār al-islām* and *dār al-ḥarb* does not appear in the Qur'an or in the Hadith. Early Islamic jurists devised these terms to denote the legal rulings in connection with the Islamic expansion.

Since Islam is not necessarily intended as "a physical space," the *dār al-islām* / *dār al-ḥarb* dichotomy is not applicable to real history. The Arab historians themselves, although they were often *fuqahā'*, coined different terms for different regions according to the actual situations prevailing therein, like *dār al-amān* (territory of security), *dār al-silm* (territory of peace) and *dār al-muwādaʿa* (territory of mutual peace). As an example that is closer to the historical period which is the main focus of this article, I would like to mention the case of the Yemeni historian and Shafi'i *faqīh* Zayn al-dīn b. ʿAbd al-ʿAzīz al-Maʿbarī, who noted in his *Tuḥfat al-mujāhidīn fī baʿḍ aḫbār al-burtuġāliyyīn* (ca. 985/1577):

> In Mulaybar, Muslims had no authoritative chief. Their unfaithful lord used to govern them according to the regional laws … Nevertheless, Muslims used to enjoy respect and consideration. They were allowed to pray, to celebrate their festivities; judges and muezzins regulated their duties and cared about the application of the laws among Muslims. People were not allowed to interrupt their activities on Friday, and whoever did not respect the rules was fined. If a Muslim committed a crime punishable by death, the penalty was applied only by the consent of the notables of the Muslim community. In the same way, when a Muslim transgressed the Law, he was not arrested without the notables' authorization. And when a member belonging to a lower social class converted to Islam, he was respected as a Muslim even if he came from the lowest caste."[6]

What ʿAbd al-ʿAzīz al-Maʿbarī adds is therefore important:

> *al-muslimūn daḫalū fī banādir Mulaybar wa-tawaṭṭanū fīhā* wa-daḫala ahluhā fī dīn al-Islām yawman fa-yawman *wa-ẓahara fīhā al-Islām ẓuhūran bāliġan ḥattā kaṯṯara al-muslimūn fīhā wa-ʿumira bihim buldānuhā maʿa qillat ẓulm ruʿātihā al-kaffāra.*[7]

6 Zayn al-dīn b. ʿAbd al-ʿAzīz al-Maʿbarī, *Tuḥfat al-mujāhidīn fī baʿḍ aḫbār al-burtuġāliyyīn*, ed. Amīn Tawfīq al-Ṭībī (Tripoli, 1987), 75.

7 "Muslims entered the ports of Mulaybar, settled there and local people *entered Islam day after day*, so that Islam appeared more and more prominent until Muslim multiplied there and the country was inhabited by them, since the infidel subjects showed little enmity": ibid., 46.

Conversely, with regard to the coming of the Portuguese (*ahl Burtuqāl min al-ifranj*), Maʿbarī underlined: "*fa-ẓalamūhum wa-afsadū wa-ʿtadū ʿalayhim min aṣnāf al-ẓulm wa'l-fasād al-ẓāhira bayna ahl al-bilād*."[8]

It is useful to point out that the Yemeni author describes elsewhere the modalitics of the Islamization of the Mulaybar local population by using the expression: "*daḫala ahluhā fī 'l-dīn qalīlan qalīlan*," (their people entered into the religion little by little) as if he intended to denote a condition that was continuously redefining itself: that of *dār al-ʿahd*, or the "land of the pact," which, according to Šāfiʿī, whose school the Yemeni historian belonged to, would be a temporary juridical status of a territory, between *dār al-islām* and *dār al-ḥarb*.[9]

2 Al-Maqdīš al-Safāqusī and Ibn Ġalbūn al-Ṭarābulusī

Having considered these precedents, what is more interesting to us is the representation of the *barr al-ʿaduww* in the works of Ibn Ġalbūn and Maqdīš al-Safāqusī.

Little is known about the life of Abū ʿAbd Allāh Muḥammad Ibn Ḫalīl Ġalbūn al-Ṭarābulusī al-Miṣrātī, who is better known as *al-ustāḏ al-fāḍil al-muʾarriḫ al-ʿallāma*, apart from the fact that he belonged to a family of well-known ulema who were active in the Miṣrāta and Misillāta areas, then in Tripoli, and that he lived at the time of the governor Aḥmad Pasha Qaramanli.[10]

In 1133/1721 he must have come back to Misrāta, in Libya, his hometown, from Cairo, where he had studied at al-Azhar under the sheikh Raʾūf al-Bišbīšī and *al-ustāḏ* Muḥammad ʿAbd Allāh b. Yaḥyā al-Sūsī.[11]

In Miṣrāta, he used to teach *tafsīr*, *fiqh*—he belonged to the Maliki *maḏhab*—and Hadith. In the course of his teachings, he seems to have asked the governor for the suspension of the fees which were due from the students, and the request was accepted by Aḥmad Pasha. According to another anecdote which refers to him, he acted as a governor's spokesman in order to inhibit the spread of the alcoholic beverages deriving from the fermentation of dates.[12]

8 "They [scil. the Portuguese] oppressed them, spread corruption and showed hostility towards them with several acts of oppression and corruption among the people of the country": ibid., 46–47.

9 Ibid., 74.

10 See al-Ṭāhir Aḥmad al-Zāwī, *Aʿlām Lībiyā*, 3rd ed. (Tripoli: Dār al-madār al-islāmī, 2004), 331–32.

11 See al-Ṭāhir Aḥmad al-Zāwī al-Ṭarabulusī, "Tarjamat al-muʾallif," in *Al-Tiḏkār fī-man malaka Ṭarābulus wa-mā kāna bihā min al-aḫbār*, by Ibn Ġalbūn, ed. al-Ṭāhir Aḥmad al-Zāwī al-Ṭarabulusī (Cairo: al-Maktaba al-salafiyya, 1349), rāʾ–zāʾ.

12 Zāwī, *Aʿlām Lībiyā*, 332.

The only extant work of the historian of Miṣrāta is the *History of Tripoli in Libya*, or *al-Tiḏkār fī man malaka Ṭarābulus wa-mā kāna bihā min al-aḫbār*.

Better known are the biography and work of the Tunisian Maḥmūd Maqdīš al-Safāqusī, who was a man of wide culture, an expert in law, science and specifically the science of *tawḥīd*.

His work *Nuzhat al-anẓār fī ʿajāʾib al-tawārīḫ wa'l-aḫbār*, written in the second half of the twelfth/eighteenth century, is typologically meaningful with regard to the succession of its chapters: the geographical introduction—largely dedicated to Sicily—in which the historian borrows from his predecessors such as Idrīsī and Ibn Jubayr; some notes on medieval history; the closing chapter concerning the city of Sfax, its territory and the history of the events at the end of the eighteenth century, with regard to relations in the Mediterranean and the policy of Venice.

Carlo Alfonso Nallino provided a partial translation into Italian of al-Maqdīš's work, and in particular the appendix—or final chapter—published under the title "Della guerra santa che gli abitanti di Sfax ebbero a sostenere in questi ultimi tempi."[13]

This translation prompts us to return to the original text in Arabic in order to consider the point of view of "mirroring." From this perspective, we can affirm that his re-reading of the traditional topics of the great Muslim geographers, travelers and historians of the past should not be considered as a sterile imitation, but as the establishing of the representation of the *ʿaduww* as a reflection of the Self.

Nallino's translation, although valuable, has a limit (but the same could apply to other great orientalists): it does not take into due account, even in the title, the connection between representation, perception and memory, image and its meaning. In fact, when al-Maqdīš wrote that there were many islands "between al-Andalus and the land of the enemies," he intended representation as an active process inscribed in a complex cognitive apparatus, as congruently expressed by the Arabic: "*bayna al-Andalus wa-barr al-ʿudwa*."

Both in this and in Ibn Ġalbūn's work, we do not come across the *dār al-islām / dār al-ḥarb* dichotomy. Moreover, in accordance with the Muslim historiographical tradition Ibn Ġalbūn never uses the term *ṣalībiyyūn*, or Crusaders, to indicate the non-Muslim Other, either when he refers to the past or when he narrates contemporary events. In this respect, the aforemen-

13 Carlo Alfonso Nallino, "Venezia e Sfax nel secolo XVIII secondo il cronista arabo Maqdîsh," in *Centenario della nascita di Michele Amari*, vol. 1 (Palermo: Stabilimento Tipografico Virzì, 1910), 329–56.

tioned Maʿbarī, in the course of the first chapter of his work dedicated to jihad, refers to non-Muslims, especially the Portuguese, by calling them generically *kuffār*. He also distinguishes them into two kinds: those who are *mustaqirrīn fī bilādihim* (i.e. those who permanently live in their countries)—in this case the jihad is *farḍ kifāya*—and those who are aggressive towards the Muslim countries, in which case the jihad is *farḍ ʿayn ʿalā kull muslim mukallaf*.[14]

The terminology used by the two Maghribi authors has ethnic and geographical connotations (*ifranj*, *rūm* and *bilād al-rūm*); political connotations (*al-ʿaduww*); and juridical-ideological connotations (*ahl al-kufr*, *naṣāra* and *naṣrānī*) as it appears in Ibn Ġalbūn. As far as this aspect is concerned, the eleventh/seventeenth-century Maghribi historian Ibn Abī Dīnār might have had some influence. In fact, with regard to the Sicilians and Roger II, he wrote that the Norman king, in order to conquer the isle of Djerba, sent a fleet including "*muslimīn min ahl Ṣiqilliyya wa-naṣāra min al-Ifranjiyyīn*" (Muslims from the people of Sicily and Christian Franks), making almost no distinction within the enemy group, which is remarkable if we consider that the author was a highly regarded *qāḍī*.[15]

In turn, to designate Roger, Ibn Ġalbūn used the expressions *malik al-Ifranj ṣāḥib Ṣiqilliyya* (king of the Franks, master of Sicily).[16] Both authors considered that the policy of Roger II towards Muslim north Africa represented a historical watershed and a crucial moment of trespassing from a political point of view, not only for the loss of Sicily but also for the changes it produced in the whole system of relationships in the Mediterranean area. Ibn Ġalbūn recalled that *Rūjār al-rūmī ṣāḥib Ṣiqilliyya malik al-Ifranj* persisted in *ṭuġyān*, and it is known that according to the Qur'an the term *ṭuġyān* means "rebellious trespassing" as it occurs in Sura of the Cow (Q 2:15). In this regard, the historian of Tripoli added:

التذكار—ولاية الحسن بن علي

كان سن الحسن بن علي يوم ولايته اثنتي عشرة سنة، ولما تولى أمره صندل، راسل أمير المؤمنين علي بن يوسف بن تاشفين الملثم بمراكش

14 Maʿbarī, *Tuḥfat al-mujāhidīn*, 51.

15 Ibn Abī Dīnār al-Qayrawānī, *al-Muʾnis fī aḫbār Ifrīqiyya wa-Tūnis*, 3rd ed. (Beirut: Dār al-Masīra, 1993), 113.

16 Ibn Ġalbūn, *Al-Tiḏkār fī man malaka Ṭarābulus wa-mā kāna bihā min al-aḫbār*, ed. al-Ṭāhir Aḥmad al-Zāwī al-Ṭarabulusī (Cairo: al-Maktaba al-salafiyya, 1349/1930), 48.

لما كان بينه وبين والده من المودة لما وقعت الوحشة بينه وبين رجار صاحب صقلية بسبب الأسطول الذي كان قد صنعه عامله مكنى بن كامل الدهمائي والي قابس من قبله لحمل التجارة، واستعانة مكنى بن كامل برجار واتفق أن وصل بأثر توليته أسطول أمير المؤمنين علي بن يوسف مع قائده علي بن ميمون إلى بلاد رجار فافتتح منها حصونًا وسبي منها سبايا كثيرة فلم يشك النصراني أن الباعث لعلي بن يوسف علي ذلك إنما هو الحسن فاستجاش وحشد أجناده ومقاتلته وبالغ في كتم أمره بمنع السفن من سواحل المسلمين فلم يخف على الحسن مقصده وخشي أن يطرق بلاده دون أهبه له فأمر باتخاذ الأسلحة وتشييد الأسوار واستقدام القبائل من الأعراب وغيرهم للجهاد، فوصلت الحشود إليه من كل جهة، ونزلت الأعراب بظاهر المهدية، فلما كان يوم السبت لخمس بقين من جمادي الأولى سنة سبع عشرة وخمسمائة، وصل أسطول رجار إلى المهدية فرسى بالجزيرة المعروفة بجزيرة الاحاسي وهي على عشرة أميال من المهدية، ونزل قائداه عبد الرحمن وجورجي إلى الجزيرة وضربت لهما ولمقدمي الإفرنج مضارب هناك وكان وصولهم آخر النهار فخرج منهم إلى البر تلك الليلة خلق كثير وانبسطا حتى تعدوا عن البحر أميالاً ثم عادوا إلى الجزيرة، ووصل القائدان في اليوم في البحر إلى المهدية في بعض قطع ، فأطافا بها وانتهيا إلى ساحل زويلة فهالهما ما رأيا بالأسوار والسواحل من الناس وانصرفا عائدين إلى الجزيرة فوجدا طائفة من العرب والأجناد قد حطوا حواليها وكشفوا من كان بها من الروم عن مواضعهم، وقتلوا

منهم قوماً ونهبوا بعض أسلحتهم، فلما كان اليوم الثالث تمكن النصارى من القصر المعروف بقصر الديماس وحصل به زهاء مائة بإعانة بعض الأعراب لهم على ذلك لما مناهم به عبد الرحمن وصاحبه.

وقد كان رجار أمرهما بالنزول بجزيرة الأحامي والتحيل على أخذ قصر الديماس بمباطنة العرب، ثم الزحف من هناك في البر بالرجال والخيل إلى المهدية، فلما كان في اليوم الرابع اجتمع المسلمون وخرجوا من المدينة وكبروا تكبيرة راعت من في الجزيرة فظنوا أنهم داخلون إليهم فانهزموا إلى مراكبهم وقتلوا بأيديهم كثيراً من خيلهم، ودخل المسلمون الجزيرة وليس بها أحد منهم فوجدوا بأيديهم كثيراً من خيلهم وآلات وأسلحة أعجلهم الهرب عنها، وأحاطوا الديماس يقاتلونه والأسطول في البحر يعاين ذلك ولا يستطيع إغاثة من في القصر لكثرة ما اجتمع في البر من عساكر المسلمين. فلما عاينوا أنهم غير قادرين على إنقاذ من بالقصر أقلعوا عائدين إلى صقلية، وأقام المسلمون يقاتلون من حصر بقصر الديماس منهم إلى أن اشتد الحصار عليهم، وفني ماؤهم وطعامهم فخرجوا منه ليلة الأربعاء الرابع عشر من جمادي الآخرة، فتخلفتهم سيوف الأعراب فقتلوهم عن أخرهم، وهنيء الحسن بهذا الفتح.

The author here refers to the battle of Cape Dīmās which is considered a crucial moment in the first Norman aggressive attempt against Ifrīqiya (July 1123). The fleet, coming from Sicily, arrived on July 21 at the island of Aḥāsī, off Cape Dīmās, about 10 kilometers from al-Mahdiyya, the political center of the Zīrids. The island was inhabited by Arabs, while most of the army that rushed to defend al-Mahdiyya was formed by Berbers. Roger's assault was doomed to fail.

Ibn Ġalbūn employs an interesting terminology:

1. Roger is *ṣāḥib Ṣiqilliyya*, which is also called *bilād Rūjār*. Roger is *al-naṣrānī*, while his men are called *al-ifranj* and *al-rūm*. This last definition probably refers to a specific Greek Byzantine unit bound to Roger's admiral Jīrjī al-Anṭākī and headed by the very chief of the Norman expedition, Christodoulos, who was a Muslim converted to oriental Christianity.
2. Even with regard to the defense of al-Mahdiyya, Ibn Ġalbūn specifies that the battlefields are *sawāḥil al-muslimīn*; the inhabitants of the island of Aḥāsī are *ṭā'ifa min al-ʿarab*; the Zīrids' troops, whose main part is formed by Berbers as we have already remarked, are called *ʿasākir al-muslimīn*. They had gathered for jihad and a part of them was made up by *qabā'il min al-aʿrāb*.

As for Ibn Abī Dīnār, he says that, during the battle of Djerba, *al-fransīs* killed several men, raped the women of the island and captured children and young men who were later sold in Sicily.[17]

We can therefore affirm that both Ibn Abī Dīnār first, and later Ibn Ġalbūn, dealing with the historical facts related to the *ifranj* expansion in North Africa, aimed to appeal to the Muslim governors to restore justice as an antidote to the system of *ẓulm*. This can easily be noted in the context of the narrative of the rise of the Almohads, some of whom were depicted as courageous and able to restore justice, *ʿādil bi'l-kitāb wa'l-sunna*: the emir Abū Fāris ʿAbd al-ʿAzīz—as recorded by Ibn Abī Dīnār—was a pious man who did justice to the oppressed (*al-maẓlūm*) against his oppressor (*al-ẓālim*). More importantly, the Tunisian historian put the governor's doings in an international context, underlining that the Almohad emir had shown an ability to react to the European expansionism.

In this regard, the way Ibn Abī Dīnār explains the term *imbirāṭūr* in the context of sixteenth-century Mediterranean history, is revealing: "*al-imbirāṭūr fī ḏālika al-zaman huwa ṣāḥib Isbāniya* (…) *wa'l-imbirāṭūr min asmā' mulūk al-Almān li-anna mulkahum qadīm wa'l-imbirāṭūr ʿindahum ka'l-ḫalīfa ʿinda 'l-muslimīn*."[18] With regard to the policy of Charles v, the author defined precisely the idea and the practice of *mujāhadat al-kafara*, which he used as a device to oppose the alliance between the Sicilian Christians and the Hafsid

17 Ibn Abī Dīnār al-Qayrawānī, *Mu'nis*, 114.

18 "At that time, the emperor was the master of Spain … 'emperor' was among the names of the kings of Germany, because their regality was ancient and the emperor among them was like the caliph among the Muslims": ibid., 185.

power of Tunis, stressing his sympathy for the Ottoman conquest defined as *al-fatḥ al-mubārak*, despite the reticence expressed elsewhere in his work.[19]

3 Conclusions

The Arabic terminology which we here refer to, and which has been employed by Ottoman North African historians as well as *fuqahāʾ*—even if this could well concern in general the Arabic historiography of the same period—is meaningful with regard to the representation of a *dār al-ḥarb* which is not "territory of war or chaos," and to the fact that the *dār al-islām / dār al-ḥarb* dichotomy is not relevant to the reality of *barr al-ʿaduww*. The Arabic historians whom we have taken into account—as one can see—propose an analysis of *barr al-ʿaduww*, in which the system of *ẓulm*, *ẓālim* and *maẓlūm* is much more significant, as unquestionably attested to by the historian and *faqīh* Ibn Abī Dīnār al-Qayrawānī. Even Ibn Ġalbūn and al-Maqdīš al-Safāqusī use the above-mentioned terminology to represent the Other according to a concept connected to an idea of "mirroring." This kind of Alterity, even though at an unconscious level, proves to be similarity or, in other words, resemblance of "he who represents" to "whom is represented," so that *barr al-ʿaduww* is to be preferred to *dār al-ḥarb*.

References

Ibn Abī Dīnār al-Qayrawānī. *Al-Muʾnis fī aḫbār Ifrīqiyya wa-Tūnis*. 3rd ed. Beirut: Dār al-Masīra, 1993.

Ibn Ġalbūn, Muḥammad b. Ḫalīl al-Ṭarābulusī. *Al-Tiḏkār fī man malaka Ṭarābulus wa-mā kāna bihā min al-aḫbār*. Edited by al-Ṭāhir Aḥmad al-Zāwī al-Ṭarabulusī. Cairo: al-Maktaba al-salafiyya, 1349/1930.

Ibn ʿIḏārī, Abū ʿAbd Allāh Muḥammad al-Marrākušī. *Kitāb al-Bayān al-muġrib fī aḫbār al-Andalus wa'l-Maġrib* [=BM]. Edited by Georges Séraphin Colin and Évariste Lévi-Provençal. Leiden: Brill, 1948.

Maʿbarī, Zayn al-dīn b. ʿAbd al-ʿAzīz al-. *Tuḥfat al-mujāhidīn fī baʿḍ aḫbār al-burtuġāliyyīn*. Edited by Amīn Tawfīq al-Ṭībī. Tripoli, 1987.

Nallino, Carlo Alfonso. "Venezia e Sfax nel secolo XVIII secondo il cronista arabo Maqdîsh." In *Centenario della nascita di Michele Amari*, 1:306–56. Palermo: Stabilimento Tipografico Virzì, 1910.

19 Ibid., 220.

Pellitteri, Antonino. *I Fatimiti e la Sicilia* (*sec. X*)*: materiali per uno studio sulla Sicilia* thaghr *e terra di* gihâd *con particolare riferimento a fonti ismailite dell'epoca*. Palermo: Centro Culturale al-Farabi, 1997.

Pellitteri, Antonino. "The Historical-Ideological Framework of Islamic Fatimid Sicily (Fourth/Tenth Century) with the Reference to Works of the Qāḍī Al-Nu'mān." *Al-Masāq* 7 (1994): 111–63.

Scarcia, Gianroberto. "*Islām* e *Ḥarb, 'Arab* e *'Ajam*: nota a due celeberrime dicotomie islamiche." In *Azhàr: studi arabo-islamici in memoria di Umberto Rizzitano* (*1913–1980*), edited by Antonino Pellitteri and Giovanni Montaina, 205–10. Annali della Facoltà di lettere e filosofia dell'Università di Palermo. Studi e ricerche 23. Palermo: Facoltà di lettere e filosofia dell'Università di Palermo, 1995.

Zāwī, al-Ṭāhir Aḥmad al-. *A'lām Lībiyā*. 3rd ed. Tripoli: Dār al-madār al-islāmī, 2004.

Zāwī, al-Ṭāhir Aḥmad al-. "Tarjamat al-mu'allif." In *Tiḏkār fī-man malaka Ṭarābulus wa-mā kāna bihā min al-aḫbār*, by Ibn Ġalbūn, edited by al-Ṭāhir Aḥmad al-Zāwī al-Ṭarabulusī. Cairo: al-Maktaba al-salafiyya, 1349.

CHAPTER 19

Muḥammad Bayram's *Risāla fī dār al-ḥarb wa-suknāhā*

A Modern Reinterpretation of Living in dār al-ḥarb

*Francesca Romana Romani and Eleonora Di Vincenzo**

1 Biographical Information: The Life of Muḥammad Bayram

Muḥammad Bayram al-Ḫāmis is a remarkable representative of the *Nahḍa*, more specifically of its Islamic reformist component. Born in March 1256/1840 in Tunis, he died in 1307/1889 in Egypt, where he was buried. This sheikh, reformer, journalist and traveler stemmed from a prominent Tunisian family of Turkish origin, whose eponym was an officer in the Ottoman army that took Tunis in 981/1573 under the lead of Sinān Pasha.

Starting with Muḥammad Bayram I (1140/1727–1214/1800), the family distinguished itself in the religious-juridical establishment by occupying in an almost dynastic fashion the office of Hanafi chief *muftī* of Tunis.[1] The qualification *al-Ḫāmis*, "the fifth," refers exactly to this dynastic sequence (see the genealogical tree in Figure 1). The first to obtain the title of *šayḫ al-islām* was Muḥammad's uncle, the fourth of the series (Muḥammad's father chose not to be a jurist). Stemming from a Turkish family—as partly shown by his own adherence to the Hanafi rite—Muḥammad was a relative of the beylical family.[2]

Muḥammad's father, Muṣṭafā, was charged by the reform-minded sovereign Muḥammad al-Ṣādiq Bey (1855–82), who enacted the first Tunisian constitution

---

* The present paper has been written jointly by the two authors. As far as academic responsibility is concerned, section 1 is to be attributed to Francesca Romana Romani, sections 2 and 3 to Eleonora Di Vincenzo.

1 On Muḥammad Bayram's biography, see G. S. van Krieken, "Muḥammad Bayram al-Khāmis," *Encyclopaedia of Islam, Vol. VII, Mif-Naz* (Leiden: Brill, 1993); Kenneth J. Perkins, *Historical Dictionary of Tunisia*, African Historical Dictionaries 45 (Lanham, MD: Scarecrow Press, 1997), 28–29.

2 Among Muḥammad Bayram V's family, an important role is played by Muḥammad Bayram II, whom Arnold H. Green, "A Comparative Historical Analysis of the Ulama and the State in Egypt and Tunisia", *Revue de l'Occident Musulman et de la Méditerranée*. 29 (1980): 35–36, identifies as one of the partisans of the ideal of *siyāsa šarʿiyya*, a subject on which Muḥammad Bayram I had already composed a treatise; see Jamil M. Abun-Nasr, "The Tunisian State in the Eighteenth Century," *Revue de l'Occident Musulman et de la Méditerranée*, 33 (1982): 53–54.

 | DOI 10.1163/9789004331037_021

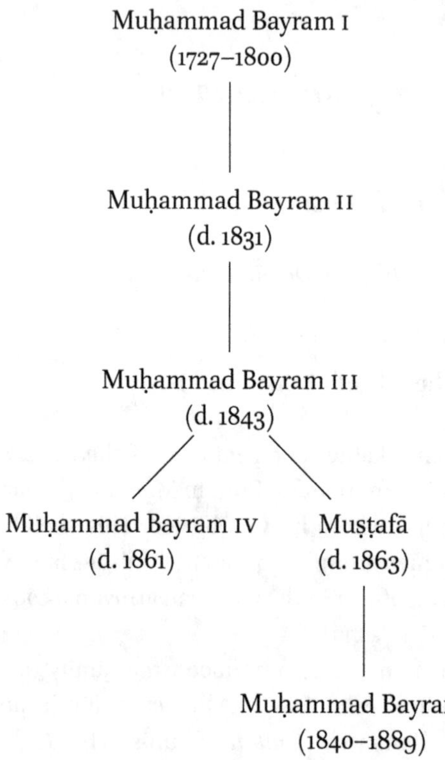

FIGURE 19.1 *Genealogy of the Bayram family.*

in 1861, with the management of the *awqāf,* and then he left his son a big inheritance that allowed him to live comfortably and to dedicate himself to studying and achieving a deep knowledge of traditional sciences and history. He studied at the Zaytūna Mosque, where he started to teach in 1861.

From his formative years, Muḥammad Bayram V showed a keen interest in questions related to the conciliation of traditional Islamic teaching and the issues raised by the contemporary world.

Besides his academic career, which blossomed when he became the headmaster of the *Madrasa ʿUnuqiyya* in the same year 1861, Muḥammad Bayram started to work regularly as a consultant and a collaborator with the well-known Ottoman administrator, Ḫayr al-dīn Pasha (d. 1307/1890),[3] after the latter was appointed to the title of *wazīr akbar*, roughly equivalent to a Prime Minister, by the Tunisian ruler Muḥammad al-Ṣādiq Bey in 1873–1877, and

3 Cf. Mohamed Haddad, *Le réformisme musulman: une histoire critique* (Mimesis: Paris, 2013), 88–91, 100–104.

regularly involved him in his reform projects, by appointing him also to some high-ranking positions, such as the office of president of the *jam'iyyat al-awqāf* founded in 1874 to centralize the administration of *waqf* properties, an office which allowed Muḥammad Bayram to control a relatively large source of revenue and power. He served as well as the editor of the progressive newspaper, *al-Rā'id al-tūnusī* "the Tunisian pioneer," perhaps the most *Nahḍa*-friendly title possible,[4] and as the chairman of the commission charged in 1875 to establish the teaching programs of the newly founded Sadiki college, also known as the *Madrasa Ṣādiqiyya*, an important institution of the Tunisian reformist government where the teaching of the traditional disciplines of the Islamic curriculum was accompanied by "modern" sciences, such as Western-styled mathematics and chemistry and foreign languages, French and Italian, alongside Turkish.

This choice that Muḥammad Bayram shared with the other members of the commission shows the author's typical ambivalence: while he never learned foreign languages himself, despite traveling extensively through the Islamic world and Europe, and always used Classical Arabic to spread his ideas (by advocating also the need to use Arabic in scientific writing, an attitude that would be shared by Arab nationalism), he was nevertheless convinced that the assimilation of foreign knowledge, including languages, was a necessary prerequisite for young students of his own age.

In fact, a characteristic Muḥammad Bayram shared with most representatives of the *Nahḍa* was his deep interest in education. In particular, he showed a deep concern for the renewal of the traditional learning system, where he favored the establishment of a mixed type of higher education institution, well exemplified by the Sadiki college itself.

This period is the exact time frame in which Muḥammad Bayram himself declared he had conceived his treatise, more specifically during a short exile he had to undergo in 1290/1873, immediately before joining Ḫayr al-dīn's staff.

1873 was indeed a crucial year in Ḫayr al-dīn's, and by extension in Muḥammad Bayram's, political career, since at the end of the year he was able to replace his long-time rival Muṣṭafā Ḫaznadār, the first minister, in whose cabinet he had been sitting since 1869 and who had been his first political sponsor.

Ḫayr al-dīn's program was characterized by a strong reformist agenda, which he tried to pursue for several years, until his dismissal in 1877 and his final

4 Muḥammad Bayram v himself was a contributor to *al-Rā'id al-tunusī* and to the other reform-minded Tunisian journal, *Aqwam al-masālik*, founded by Ḫayr al-dīn: see Béchir Tlili, "Contribution à l'étude de la pensée sociale et politique de Bayram V (1840–1889)," *Revue de l'Occident Musulman et de la Méditerranée* 15–16 (1973): 327–28, 329.

disgrace, partly delayed by a short term (eight months) served as the Great Vizier of the Ottoman Empire in 1878.

It was under Ḫayr al-dīn's rule, 1873 through 1877, that Muḥammad Bayram took part in an enlightened reform program, directed at modernizing and rationalizing the muddled, corrupted administrative system in its different areas, whose different areas—the judiciary, religious and financial sectors, the last linked with the *waqf* management—were strictly connected in the Tunisia of that time.

Other works by Muḥammad Bayram reveal the same mindset that frames the treatise at issue. In particular Tlili[5] mentions another text, comparatively less known, which contains Muḥammad Bayram V's general framework for reforms: the *Mulāḥaẓāt* (Observations) he addressed in 1881 to the Ottoman caliph, immediately before the beginning of the French Protectorate in Tunisia. It is a critical period in Muḥammad Bayram's life: after the fall of Ḫayr al-dīn, he endeavored—after several refusals by the authorities to allow him to leave—to make a long journey abroad on the occasion of the Pilgrimage, during which he learned he had been subjected to an official inquiry for misappropriation of public funds and consequently removed from all his remaining official charges, which prompted him to spend the rest of his life in exile.[6]

As in the case of many actors of this historical period, Muḥammad Bayram's life and career didn't have a happy end. While he managed to survive a few years after the fall of his own protector Ḫayr al-dīn Pasha, he had to leave Tunisia definitively in the wake of the establishment of the French protectorate and, after wandering in the Muslim world, including an unfortunate sojourn in Istanbul where he discovered that his views were quite removed from those of the new Ottoman rulers, he settled in Cairo and died there in 1889.

The *Mulāḥaẓāt* represents, according to Tlili,[7] a true watershed in Muḥammad Bayram V's political thinking: here he states for the first time his position in favor of a true liberal, representative government instead of the enlightened-despotism style of Ottoman *tanẓimāt* and, by consequence, in favor of Tunisian reformism.

This aspect is also shown by the proposals Muḥammad Bayram made about the reform of Islamic law, a subject which had interested him since he was a student. On the one hand, he was deeply entrenched in the tradition of Islamic law, which he always considered the main source of juridical reasoning; on the other hand, however, he felt very deeply the need to come to terms with

5 Ibid., 328.

6 See ibid., 329–30.

7 Ibid., 331ff.

modernity in order to allow social and political changes to make their way into the foundations of Islamic law.

Examples of this attitude can be found in a variety of Muḥammad Bayram's writings: ranging from relatively tiny details such as the *ḥalāl* character of the flesh of animals killed with firearms—a case where the *qiyās* extension of traditional rulings about the licit character of game killed in hunting is matched with the acceptance of modern weapons—to more substantial cases such as an important treatise, yet to be edited, on slavery (*al-taḥqīq fī mas'alat al-raqīq* "Elucidation on the issue of slaves") where explicit support for the abolitionary efforts of the Ottoman governments is obtained through arguments exclusively drawn from sharia; or, again, the demonstration of the non-*ribā* character of bonds issued by Muslim governments, which believers would therefore be free to subscribe to, a strongly debated issue to this day.

From this point of view, Muḥammad Bayram and Ḫayr al-dīn shared a common fate, not unusual among Muslim modernists: desperately trying to keep a *via media* between the adoption of Western-style politics and law and the adherence to the Islamic tradition, they fell victim to the growing paramountcy of European countries, France in the case of Tunisia, in the Arab world.

Disillusion towards the West was common to many actors of the *Nahḍa* after becoming open to modern ideas appeared to be the passepartout for the colonization of the Arab world, but this feeling was perhaps even stronger among moderate Islamic reformists such as Muḥammad Bayram and Ḫayr al-dīn, since their critical attitude towards some aspects of the Western model made it a more difficult choice, to strive for modernization of law, education and ethics, which made the final disappointment even worse.

Of course, the special role played by Tunisia in the modernization process is hard to overstate.[8] This is widely shown in Muḥammad Bayram V's main work, the chronicle *Ṣafwat al-i'tibār bi-mustawda' al-amṣār wa'l-aqṭār*,[9] which continues the work of another Tunisian reformist, Abū al-'Abbās Aḥmad Ibn Abī Ḍiyāf (1291/1802–3–1291/1874), author of the *Itḥāf ahl al-zamān bi-aḫbār mulūk Tūnus wa-'ahd al-amān*.[10]

---

8 See Jean-Marie Miossec, "Identité tunisienne: de la personnalité géographique d'un pays du Maghreb, du monde arabo-islamique et de la Méditerranée," *Annales de Géographie* 108, no. 607 (1999): 255–76 on the "geographic personality" of Tunisia.

9 Muḥammad Bayram al-Ḫāmis al-Tūnisī, *Ṣafwat al-i'tibār bi-mustawda' al-amṣār wa'l-aqṭār*, 5 vols. (Beirut: Dār Sādir, 2001–3).

10 Ibn Abī Ḍiyāf, *Itḥāf ahl al-zamān bi-aḫbār mulūk Tūnus wa-'ahd al-amān*, 8 vols. (Tunis: Sécretariat d'État aux Affaires Culturelles, 1963–68); cf. Béchir Tlili, "Note sur la notion d'Etat dans la pensée de Ah'mad Ibn Abi Ad'-d'Iyaf, réformateur tunisien du XIXe siècle

2 *Al-Risāla fī dār al-ḥarb wa suknāhā*[11]

2.1 *Some Notes about the Manuscript*

As far as we know, Muḥammad Bayram's *Risāla* exists in only one manuscript copy kept in excellent conditions in the library of King Saud University in Riyadh.[12] It numbers 12 folios. Its measurements are approximately 20.5×16.5 cm. (for the written area) and about 20 lines per page (some contain 19 and a few others 21). It is written in an elegant hand, which can be characterized as *ruqʿa*, a simple style with essential curves, known and used throughout the Arab world for the normal purposes of handwriting.[13]

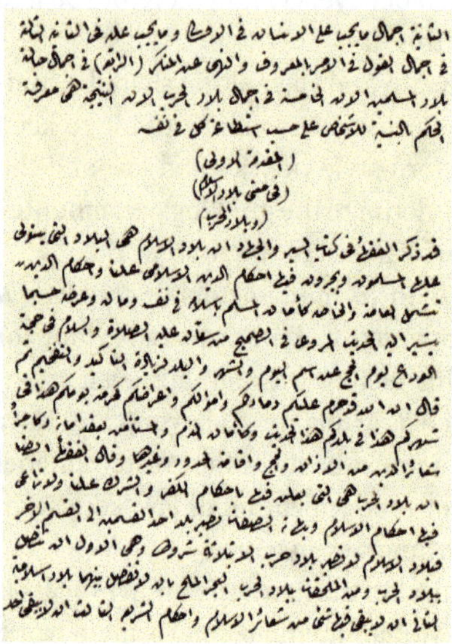

FIGURE 19.2
The manuscript of Muḥammad Bayram Al-Risāla, *f.* 2r.

(1804/5–1874)," *Revue de l'Occident musulman et de la Méditerranée* 8, no. 1 (1970): 141–70; Miossec, "Identité tunisienne," 264–65.

11 Treatise on *dār al-ḥarb* and living in it.

12 Manuscript Nr. 3456. Since I have not seen the book personally, I will report here only some information on its physical aspect provided by the cataloguer's description. A digitized copy of the manuscript is available on the website of the King Saud University Library (http://makhtota.ksu.edu.sa/makhtota/3739/1#.UqGtMFRd7IU, accessed March 20, 2016).

13 Cf. Terence Frederick Mitchell, *Writing Arabic: A Practical Introduction to the Ruqʿah Script* (1953; repr., Oxford: Oxford University Press, 1990), 5; also Salah Moussawy, *Cahier de calligraphie arabe: style roquʿa* (Paris: Bachari, 2002), 12.

The colophon is completely missing. According to the cataloguer at the King Saud University Library, this document could have been written by the author himself.[14]

2.2 *Content Overview*

The purpose of the *Risāla fī dār al-ḥarb wa-suknāhā* ('Treatise on *dār al-ḥarb* and living in it) is to provide behavioral guidelines from both a juridical and a religious point of view to the Muslims who face the necessity of residing in *dār al-ḥarb*. This can be clearly deduced from Muḥammad Bayram's words of introduction to the *Risāla*:

> When the French occupied my homeland in AH 1290 because of our sins and our well-known weaknesses, I was living by myself in solitude in Constantinople whereas my family was still in Tunis. I had left for the same reasons that would have eventually led to that occupation, but I thought that I would be able to come back before the situation would become alarming. Nevertheless, even if things remained as they were and the administration had been reformed as far as possible, my supposition [to be able to be back before everything happened] would not have prevented what was destined from happening. As a matter of fact, predictions that try to evaluate the future condition of a country are easily wrong because of the defectiveness of the analogical method that, being based on postulates, does not ensure that one will actually see what he has predicted.
>
> At this point, it is my duty to consider how and where my sons and I should live, since the believer must undertake something only after having known the will of God about it. For this reason, I have collected in these leaves a summary of what is related to this topic, so that it could be a guide for myself and for any of my compatriots according to how God wills.

Aiming to act in accordance with Islamic law during an indefinite stay outside Muslim territory, the author of this brief treatise gathered all the juridical material at his disposal regarding the dichotomous division of the inhabited world into *dār al-islām* and *dār al-ḥarb*, and organized it in five broad sections (*muqaddimāt*), dealing with the following topics:

---

14 This hypothesis is not substantiated by any explanation. I can only assume that the physical analysis of the code and the handwritten style gave evidences to the cataloguer.

1. Definitions of *bilād al-islām* and *bilād al-ḥarb*;
2. Summary of the duties of the *mukallaf* when living in *bilād al-islām* and when in *bilād al-ḥarb*;
3. Summary of sayings about "commanding good and forbidding evil";
4. Situation of *bilād al-muslimīn* in Muḥammad Bayram's time;
5. Situation of *bilād al-ḥarb* in Muḥammad Bayram's time.

2.3 Al-Muqaddima al-ʾūla*: Definition of* bilād al-islām *and* bilād al-ḥarb

Taking up a classical definition of the Hanafi doctrine in regard to the bipartition of the inhabited earth,[15] Muḥammad Bayram explains that the expression *bilād al-islām* identifies the countries conquered by the Muslims, where the rules of the Islamic religion are overtly in force. He then specifies that the religious law governs both the public and the private spheres in the lives of people residing there, and aims to achieve the following specific goals:

1. Safety of the Muslim, his property, and his honor. The foundation of this point lies in the saying uttered by Muḥammad during his Farewell Pilgrimage on the day of Sacrifice at the Valley of Mina:

   Fa-inna dimāʾakum wa-amwālakum wa-aʿrāḍakum ḥarāmun ʿalaykum ka-ḥurmati yawmikum haḏā fī šahrikum haḏā fī baladikum haḏā

   No doubt, Allah made your blood, your properties, and your honor sacred to one another like the sanctity of this day of yours in this month of yours in this town of yours.[16]

2. Safety of the *ḏimmī* and the *mustaʾmin*;
3. Fulfillment of religious duties, such as *aḏān* (call to prayer), the Pilgrimage, the implementation of *ḥudūd*.

15 On the views of the Hanafi school on the division of the world into two political entities with different territorial jurisdiction, see Mushtaq Muhammad Ahmad, "The notions of *dār al-ḥarb* and *dār al-Islām* in Islamic jurisprudence with special reference to the Ḥanafī school," *Islamic Studies* 47 (2008): 7–15, 18. Further discussion about what is technically called *iḫtilāf al-dārayn* "the difference between the two realms" is in Carlo Alfonso Nallino, "Delle assicurazioni in diritto musulmano hanafita," *Oriente moderno* 7 (1927): 447–452.

16 Muḥammad b. Ismāʿīl al-Buḫārī, *Le recueil des traditions mahométanes par el-Bokhâri (al-Ṣaḥīḥ)*, ed. M. Ludolf Krehl, vol. 1 (Leiden: Brill, 1862), 236; Id., *Ṣaḥīḥ al-Buḫārī. The Translation of the Meanings of Sahih al-Bukhari*, trans. Muhammad Muhsin Khan, vol. 2 (Riyadh: Darussalam, 1997), 452.

Conversely, according to Bayram's report, the expression *bilād al-ḥarb* identifies the countries where *aḥkām al-kufr wa'l-širk* (rules of unbelief and polytheism) are enforced overtly, while the Islamic law is ignored.

Since the circumstances that make a state belong to *bilād al-islām* or *bilād al-ḥarb* are subject to change over time, a country can switch from one side to the other. However, Bayram clarifies two points. First, a country of *bilād al-ḥarb* does not turn into *bilād al-islām* as soon as Islamic Law comes into force. Second, an Islamic country turns into *bilād al-ḥarb* if the following three conditions are met: (1) if it borders a *bilād al-ḥarb* country which, in turn, is washed by a sea and the two (the sea and *bilād al-ḥarb*) are not separated by any Islamic country; (2) if there remains no trace of Islamic requirements or sharia rules; (3) if its inhabitants lose their original protection provided by their being Muslim, *ḏimmī* or *musta'min*.

A further clarification is provided by the citation of an excerpt from Bazzāzī's *Fatāwā*, where it is stated that "it has already been established by unanimous consensus that if any of these three conditions does not occur, the rule is not applied".[17] In fact, although the Tartar sovereigns permitted the wine trade, enacted laws, levied taxes and customs duties, the conquered territories remained, without doubt, *dār al-islām*. That was because, with the approval of their rulers, people continued to practice a number of rules of worship and to follow some Islamic principles, such as *aḏān*, Friday as a day of rest, collective prayer, the application of the sharia rules, and the teaching of sharia, encouraging the spread of knowledge.

2.4 Al-Muqaddima al-ṯāniya: *Duties of* mukallaf *in* dār al-islām *and* dār al-ḥarb

The *mukallaf* who lives in an Islamic country must fulfill all the individual and collective duties (*al-furūḍ al-ʿayniyya wa'l-furūḍ al-kifāya*) imposed by his religion. The latter are mandatory only for a few members of the community who, unlike others, have the opportunity and the ability to carry them out. The duties of man are steered by the idea which Bayram discusses in detail in the third section of the *Risāla* (see below, § 2.5). The *mukallaf*'s duties in *dār al-islām* include: the manifest performance of religious rites; the application of Islamic rules and the implementation of penalties laid down in the Qur'an (*ḥudūd*); the distribution of benefits from state coffers to those who are entitled to them; the proclamation of the duty of obedience and the prohibition of

17 *Al-Fatāwā al-bazzāziyya*, in margin of volumes IV–VI of *al-Fatāwā al-hindiyya* (Būlāq: Al-Maṭbaʿa al-kubrā al-amīriyya, 1310/1912–3). The author is the Hanafi jurist Muḥammad b. Muḥammad al-Kardarī, known as al-Bazzāzī (d. 827/1424).

disobedience (*al-iʿlān bi-ījāb al-ṭāʿāt wa al-manʿ ʿan al-maʿāṣī*), since obedience is a cardinal point of faith.

The acts of disobedience to God's law are made public in *bilād al-islām* and the *mukallaf* who does not have the ability to prevent them has to move to another place, where such acts do not happen or occur to a lesser extent.

The obligation to emigrate under certain conditions has its foundation in the following verse:

> *a-lam takun arḍu 'llāhi wāsiʿatan fa-tuhājirū fīhā*
>
> But was not the God's earth wide, so that you might have emigrated in it? (Q 4:97).[18]

According to some commentators, this verse indicates that if a person is prevented from practicing religion as he should in the place where he lives, he has to emigrate. This obligation is also reiterated by Abū al-Suʿūd (d. 982/1574)[19] who mentioned in this regard the Prophet's saying "he who escapes from land to land in the name of religion and forsakes even one span of the land he owned will have deserved heaven".

Bayram goes on to quote some other passages that confirm the obligation to emigrate for the Muslim who is prevented from fulfilling his duties. Since this specific subject was not dealt with in a satisfactory way in Hanafi sources, he refers to the regulations of other juridical schools. Thus, for example, he quotes a brief excerpt from Maliki jurisprudence, where it is stated that it is one's duty to emigrate from a land in which acts of disobedience to God's law are perpetuated. Specifically, the inability to "command the good and forbid the evil" in the place where someone lives makes it obligatory for them to get out and move on to a safer place. Otherwise, it appears from unnamed sources that the obligation to leave a place is imposed only when immorality closely involves

18 The English translation of all the Qur'anic verses mentioned in this contribution has been taken from Arthur John Arberry, ed., *The Koran Interpreted: A Translation*, A Touchstone Book (New York: Simon & Schuster, 1996).

19 He refers to the Ottoman jurist Abū al-Suʿūd Efendi (d. 982/1574), author of the Qur'anic commentary *Tafsīr Abī al-Suʿūd aw Iršād al-ʿaql al-salīm ilā mazāyā 'l-kitāb al-karīm*, 5 vols. (Cairo, 1971). For a detailed biography, see Joseph Schacht, "Abū 'l-Suʿūd," *Encyclopaedia of Islam, Vol. I, A-B* (Leiden: Brill, 1960). For further details on the Qur'anic commentary, see also Shuruq Naguib, "Guiding the Sound Mind: Ebū's-Suʿūd's *Tafsīr* and Rhetorical Interpretation of the Qur'an in the Post-Classical Period," *The Journal of Ottoman Studies* 42 (2013): 1–52.

the life of a Muslim. This is explained by the fact that if he is not present during such acts, he does not fail in his religious duties.

Discussing the duties of the *mukallaf* in *bilād al-ḥarb*, Bayram considers two aspects: (1) the cases in which he is allowed to enter and reside; (2) the *mukallaf*'s duties.

As to the first point, according to Islamic law the *mukallaf* is allowed to enter and reside in *bilād al-ḥarb* only in the event that he hailed from that place and he had embraced Islam there. Furthermore, other concurrent conditions must be met, lest he should be subject to the obligation to emigrate. These conditions are: that his safety be protected; that the inhabitants do not prevent him from fulfilling his religious duties, nor restrict him, his goods and his religious ties; that they be respectful of the agreements; that, in such place, he have the chance to acquire knowledge, because Islam requires it.

Nevertheless, if we consider a series of cases reported in the decisions of the ulema, we will see that it is licit to enter and reside in *bilād al-ḥarb* also in the event that a Muslim aims to satisfy an interest of a public or private nature. For example, in a fatwa by Bayram II (d. 1247/1831), he answered the question "is the person who sails in direction of *dār al-ḥarb* breaking the law?" by saying that "it depends on why he does it". Giving a further clarification, Muḥammad Bayram V added that a sick person who cannot be cured in *dār al-islām* does not break the law if he enters *dār al-ḥarb* in order to receive adequate treatment. There is also the case, discussed in *Fatāwā hindiyya*, of a man who had to go to *dār al-ḥarb* for jihad and asked the jurist (*faqīh*) whether he needed his parents' approval. The answer was that "even if he wanted to enter *dār al-ḥarb* for trading without his parents' approval, he would be allowed to do so, in the absence of reasons to fear for his safety, if local people had been respectful of agreements and if he had benefited". Therefore, the action would have been considered lawful, despite the fact that it entailed a reprehensible act of disobedience to the parents. Nevertheless, it would be better if one's aim were not mere economic profit. Another proof of lawfulness for a Muslim to enter, and stay in, *dār al-ḥarb* comes from an unspecified chapter of *Ḏaḫīra*, where it is reported that an imam sent a few people at a time to *dār al-ḥarb* in order to spy on enemies, without defining the period of their stay in that place. According to Bayram's interpretation, the lack of an explicit indication of the length of their stay corresponds to the possibility of extending it. He adds that the rule authorizing Muslim ambassadors to travel to and reside in foreign countries falls into the same category, since their office is aimed at a public utility for Muslims.

The clarification about taking women and a copy of the Qur'an into *dār al-ḥarb* is also interesting. In this regard, Bayram adds that an aversion is expressed in *Ḏaḫīra* and elsewhere to taking the Qur'an into *dār al-ḥarb* where only a few Muslim soldiers are deployed, because they cannot guarantee its protection from vilification. This aversion has no reason to exist if a larger Islamic military presence ensures an adequate level of protection and if the inhabitants of that place are respectful of pacts. The same rule is applied with regard to women in order to protect them from being taken prisoner.

Having established that there is no difference between the Muslim native of a country of *dār al-ḥarb* (*al-aṣlī*) and the Muslim coming from *dār al-islām* (*al-wārid*) and that both are allowed to enter and reside in *dār al-ḥarb*, Muḥammad Bayram reiterates that this is not allowed to the Muslim who aims to fulfil worldly interests and obtain benefits not legitimated by the sharia. Indeed, as Ibn al-Šiḥna states in *Šarḥ al-Wahbāniyya*, the Muslim who lives in *dār al-ḥarb* risks being integrated with the locals and, behaving as they do, even breaking Islamic Law. For example, many times it is said in the Qur'an that the Muslim who makes himself to look like infidels (*kuffār*) to win their benevolence or to obtain their approval commits a prohibited act (*ḥarām*).

The *mukallaf*'s duties in *bilād al-ḥarb*, namely the second point of the discussion of Muḥammad Bayram, are summarized in the following verse:

> *Lā yanhākumu 'llāhu ʿan allaḏīna lam yuqātilukum fī 'l-dīni wa-lam yuḫrijukum min diyārikum an tabarrūhum wa-tuqsiṭū ilayhim*
>
> God forbids you not, as regards those who have not fought you in religion's cause, nor expelled you from your habitations, that you should be kindly to them, and act justly towards them (Q 60:8).

Therefore, the *mukallaf* who resides in *arḍ al-ḥarb* in addition to the obligation to perform the acts of worship (*ʿibādāt*) must in no way injure the locals and must not impose anything on them, because they are not subject to Islamic Law.

It is in this sense that the rule of the Hanafi jurisprudence that forbids interest on loaned capital (*ribā*)[20] between a Muslim and a *ḥarbī* in *dār al-ḥarb* should be interpreted: indeed, it imposes on the Muslim honest behavior towards the people of *dār al-ḥarb* and does not imply any obligation for Muslims to enter into contracts with them according to the sharia. Rather, Bayram adds, it is recommended to please them in every possible way, so that

20 On this subject, see Muḥammad b. Aḥmad al-Saraḫsī, *Kitāb al-Mabṣūṭ fī 'l-fiqh al-Ḥanafī*, vol. 14 (Cairo, 1324–31AH), 56–59.

the Muslim be an example to others in *dār al-ḥarb* and lead people to the right path. Moreover, he should show such behavior towards everyone, without distinguishing between natives and people coming from outside. This last point is set out in the following verse:

> *Illā 'lladīna yaṣilūna ilā qawmin baynakum wa-baynahum mīṯāqun*
>
> Except those that betake themselves to a people who are joined with you by a compact (Q 4:90).

2.5 Al-Muqaddima al-ṯāliṯa: *About "Commanding Good and Forbidding Evil"*

Several times in Qur'an and Sunna it is reiterated that "commanding the good and forbidding the evil" is an obligation for everyone. For example:

> *Wa'l-takun minkum ummatun yad'ūna ilā 'l-ḫayri wa ya'murūna bi'l-ma'rūfi wa-yanhawna 'an al-munkari wa-ula'ika humu 'l-mufliḥūna*
>
> Let there be one nation of you, calling to good, and bidding to honour, and forbidding dishonour; those are the prosperers (Q 3:104).
>
> *Wa 'ttaqū fitnatan lā tuṣibanna alladīna ẓalamū minkum ḫāṣṣatan*
>
> And fear a trial which will not strike those who have wronged among you exclusively (Q 8:25).
>
> *Lā taqifanna 'inda rajulin yuqtalu maẓlūman fa-inna al-la'nata tanzilu 'alā man ḥaḍarahu wa-lam yarfa'u 'anhu wa lā taqifanna 'inda rajulin yuḍrabu maẓlūman fa-inna al-la'nata tanzilu 'alā man ḥaḍarahu wa-lam yarfa'u 'anhu*
>
> Do not stand motionless in front of a man who is killed unjustly, because God's curse falls on people who were there and did nothing; and do not stand motionless in front of a man who is beaten unjustly, because God's curse falls on those who were there and did nothing.[21]

---

21 Abū 'l-Qāsim al-Ṭabarānī, *al-Mu'jam al-kabīr* (Cairo: Maktabat Ibn Taymiyya, 1415/1994), 11:260.

According to Ġazālī (d. 505/1111),[22] the Hadith mentioned above shows that it is not permitted to be present in places where one can passively witness evil deeds, on the pretext that one is unable to prevent them. If one cannot do anything to prevent them, one is not allowed to be present in that place.

Similarly, in *Kitāb al-Karāhiyya wa 'l-istiḥsān* it is written that if a person is invited to a reception and on that occasion he witnesses an evil deed, he has the duty to take action to prevent or stop it, if he is close enough to be able to do this. Otherwise, he has to leave that house by virtue of the following verse:

> *Fa-lā taqʿud baʿda al-ḏikrā maʿa al-qawmi al-ẓālimīna*
>
> Do not sit, after the reminding, with the people of the evildoers (Q 6:68).

Even in the event that one was at a greater distance from the people involved in the evil act, one must try to dissuade the wrongdoer. If he does not accept one's invitation and continues, it is necessary for the upright Muslim to leave that house and those people as a sign of disapproval. If, before setting out, one is already informed that such acts are being perpetrated in that house, one should avoid going at all.

This brings us back to the second chapter of the *Risāla* or, to be more precise, to the duties of the *mukallaf* who resides in a territory where crimes are perpetrated, because, according to Muḥammad Bayram V, rules about the house may also be applied to countries. After all, the equivalence between "house" and "country" has already been established by Bayram II in his *Ḥasan al-nabaʾ fī jawāz al-taḥaffuẓ min al-wabaʾ* (The good announcement, on the lawfulness to protect oneself from infectious diseases), where it is said: "it is forbidden to go to a house where it is known that there is a danger of contracting an infectious disease, as well as it is forbidden to travel to a country where reprehensible actions take place, especially if that is well known before traveling".

2.6 Al-Muqaddima al-rābiʿa*: Situation of* bilād al-muslimīn *in Muḥammad Bayram's Time*

Bayram informs us that according to news he had, there was no country among *bilād al-muslimīn* (Muslims' countries) in his time in which sharia was applied as it should have been. Specifying that the non-compliance with the religious regulations varied from place to place, he offered a long and detailed description of the most degenerate reality of which he had become aware. Here is an excerpt:

22 Abū Ḥāmid Muḥammad al-Ġazālī, *Iḥyāʾ ʿulūm al-dīn*, vol. 2 (Cairo, 1957), 309.

> In some of these countries they hide [their weaknesses by maintaining] some fundamental [Islamic laws] while they behave as those who betray Muslims and do not know the acts of worship. They pay attention to detractors and wicked people, and care [only] to achieve their own purposes. In those places, acts of disbelief—such as the exhibition of the [Christian] cross, the ringing of the [churches'] bells, the closure of offices and schools on Sunday, the soldiers' refusal to [participate in] the Friday prayer—are openly displayed.
>
> Similar things happen for the sale of wine, the places for loaning for interests (*ribā*), the immoral contracts and the fornication (*zinā*) with Muslim women, who stay in public places, show their faces uncovered and address men by assuming a mawkish attitude ...
>
> And in addition to [all that]: the clear compliance with the infidels' laws (*qawānīn al-kuffār*) rather than the Islamic Law; the granting of judiciary power to the infidel; the end of the application of Qur'anic penalties (*ḥudūd*); the collection of taxes; the misappropriation of money; the inadequate payment of tithe (*'ušr*) and alms (*zakāt*); corruption in courts; corruption and favoritism in the allocation of high offices; deliberate defamation; overt cessation of fast in [the month of] Ramadan ...
>
> Therefore, only a few religious things remain, e.g.: the name *islām*, the call to prayer from minarets (*aḏān*), prayer and religious officials, i.e. *qāḍī*, *muftī* and imam.

As discussed above (§ 2.3), the safety of the individual, whether Muslim, *ḏimmī* or *musta'min*, is an essential condition in order to consider a country part of *dār al-islām*. On this point, Bayram informs us that such safety was no more guaranteed in these countries in his time:

> Regarding personal safety, [you should be aware that] road bandits kidnap people at the walls of the city, assail them in the houses at night to steal their wealth and occasionally they kill them. In other cities, gangs of thieves sneak into the houses, take everything they find and kill the people who are sleeping there. Other times, they steal in the street from passers-by even in broad daylight and they do not come across [any] rescuer, nor [guards] protecting the royal castles. Rather, they offend wives and daughters [of the unfortunate] by selling them to our eminent rulers who hold powers and lie with virtuous and free women.

Later, Bayram lists further examples showing a diverse reality, a reality which is still far from the ideal of *dār al-islām*:

> In some Islamic countries, you find religious sciences, the prayer and the fast, but some influential people ignore them. You'll find there the names of some authoritative offices but there is no trace of Qur'anic penalties. There is [still] something of what I mentioned before, but the implementation of sentences and individual rights have disappeared, since the authorities are mainly Christians and foreign people who govern according to their laws alongside [a few] isolated Muslims ...
>
> In other countries, sharia law exists almost without restrictions, but sentences pronounced against some authorities are never actually enforced and are (indefinitely) postponed. These people govern following policies which are sometimes fair, sometimes unfair.

2.7 Al-Muqaddima al-ḫāmisa*: The Situation of* bilād al-ḥarb *in Muḥammad Bayram's Time*

The *Risāla*'s author classifies *bilād al-ḥarb* into three categories. Into the first he puts those countries whose governments protect the safety of people and respect the individual freedoms of both practicing religion (*ʿibādāt*) and dealing with people (*muʿāmalāt*) as is proper for a Muslim. In these countries—Bayram explains—a person who slanders the government or its members' policies is judged according to the law in a manner that is very close to justice. This first category includes the United States of America and most of Europe, except for France. The second category differs from the first in only one respect: under their authority these countries prevent Muslims from fulfilling their duties: France belongs to this category. The third category groups those countries where people, religion and goods are not safe: Russia and all the remaining "realms of war" (*mamālik al-ḥarb*) are part of this category.

This brief description of country types existing in *dār al-ḥarb* is clearly aimed at guiding the Muslim in choosing where he might live and it is preliminary to an interesting discussion on the different ways *fiqh* perceives the act of emigrating to *bilād al-ḥarb*. This means that leaving *dār al-islām* to go to *dār al-ḥarb* may be considered as prohibited, reprehensible, recommended or even obligatory, depending on the perspective. As is stated in the following excerpts:

> [A Muslim] who thinks that he cannot be of help to other Muslims by leading them and commanding the good, because in that country [of war] it is forbidden or he is unable to do so, it is preferable that he remain in Islamic countries. Conversely, [as regards a Muslim] who thinks that he can help other Muslims by showing them the rules of sharia that they

> did not know or by spreading the positive aspects of religion, explaining its tenets, and attracting locals to him, we cannot say that he has the duty to go [to *dār al-ḥarb*], but at least that he is [the person] most qualified [to do that] … However, if there is no impediment, the action is mandatory for him, because most of the people living in the territory of war ascribe to the Islamic religion things that do not actually correspond to reality. Moreover, their lack of tenacity and zeal strengthens the hope that they may be guided. This is valid for those countries of war that allow the spreading of [Islam] in safety …
>
> We know that to reside in territory of war without a reasonable cause is reprehensible and that to expose oneself to injustice is prohibited. Therefore, if it were necessary to choose between committing a reprehensible act and a prohibited act, [you should consider that] it is essential to avoid what is prohibited …
>
> If we had to give a legal evaluation about emigrating to territory of war, we should say that it fluctuates between: a due and a recommendable act, i.e. entering for a benefit that you will get by being there; a reprehensible act, i.e. giving up commanding the good in Islamic countries fearing for oneself; a prohibited act, i.e. exposing oneself to injustice. But, [when all is pondered], we are more apt to consider it recommended and dutiful.

In this passage, as in many others, the legitimacy of emigrating to *bilād al-ḥarb*, presented mainly as a dutiful and recommended act, is to be interpreted as an invitation for those who are able to go. The references to the Prophet's life and the Qur'an verses inviting emigration form the foundation of the rule and are also applicable to the modern realities through the use of the analogical reasoning (*qiyās*):

> It is said that when the Prophet saw what happened to his companions because of the strife with the Qurayš in the fifth year of the mission, he ordered them to go to Ethiopia telling them that there they would find a righteous king who prevents anyone from committing injustices in his kingdom. They went until God gave them comfort … Eleven men and four women had left including ʿUṯmān b. ʿAffān and his wife Ruqayya, daughter of the Prophet …
>
> Let no one say that [the emigration was a due act only] when Muslims were forbidden to profess the Islamic religion and that Islamic countries today do not reach this point, because we have already mentioned what are the duties to be fulfilled in Islamic countries …

> Abū 'l-Suʿūd, commenting on the verse "and those the angels take, while still they are wronging themselves" (Q 4:97), said: "emigrate to another region where you are able to fulfill religious duties, as those who have emigrated to Medina and Ethiopia".

A further reason that makes emigration to *bilād al-ḥarb* a mandatory action is that the Muslim is closely committed to jihad and the spread of Islam among the people who live there.

> That which authorizes unequivocally and with no restriction [the Muslim] to move [to *bilād al-ḥarb*] is the statement that jihad—which aims at guiding people to Islam and not at damaging them—is necessary ...
>
> All jurists explained that we [the Muslims] fight only after having invited them [to embrace Islam], because we already know that starting the fight is difficult (if only we were able to preserve our kingdoms, that would be in itself the biggest booty!). Since starting all that is difficult, it is better to start [doing] what is easier, namely to invite [people] to the evidence, especially now that the states have opened their doors, allow freedom of worship and do not forbid to invite and to preach in their territory.
>
> This is undoubtedly something that is ordered to all those who can do it, if they act in accordance to the rules. If no one does it, all of them are sinners.
>
> Let no one say that this duty can be fulfilled starting [by doing it] in an Islamic country, since what is essential is to inform [people] directly by means of spreading and discussing. Sending words from far away is not the same thing.

The *Risāla fī dār al-ḥarb wa suknāhā* by Muḥammad Bayram V represents a successful attempt to adapt the rules of classical Hanafi jurisprudence to the changing needs of a new international scenario. Its value is unquestionable in both historical and legal terms. Indeed, if, on the one hand, it testifies to the social, political and religious realities of its time, on the other hand, it shows the flexibility—at least on a theoretical level—of a legal system apparently rigid but actually open to modernization through the application of analogical reasoning (*qiyās*).

The author's sensitivity to the reality around him and his critical spirit stand out implicitly most of the time while sometimes being hidden in the details. An example of this is the use of terminology: starting from the fourth chapter of the *Risāla* (§ 2.6), where a rather harsh description is offered of the situation of Islamic countries in the author's time, the phrase indicating the Islamic sphere is no longer *dār al-islām, arḍ al-islām* or *bilād al-islām* as in classical juridical literature and in the previous chapters of the treatise, but it becomes *bilād al-muslimīn* (lands of Muslims), which gives us a much better idea of the change that had occurred at government level in Islamic countries. A change, precisely, that resulted in confining Islam to the sole religious sphere of Muslims.

From the methodological point of view, the *Risāla* of Muḥammad Bayram V gives us an example of a masterful ability in the use of analogical reasoning, a valuable instrument for the Hanafi doctrine. Indeed, we have seen how the author, by connecting a number of passages taken from sources and fatwas belonging mainly to the Hanafi school, has succeeded in identifying some conditions that made permissible, and in some cases even mandatory, something that was originally presented as forbidden.

Such is the case with the emigration of Muslim to the "territory of war," which at first is said to be licit only for people born and converted in that territory. It was stated that staying there was allowed only if some specific conditions existed (§ 2.4), but according to a fatwa of Bayram II this action also becomes permitted for Muslims born in Islamic lands if they emigrate pursuing an interest of a public or private nature; an interest that can be obtained only by going there. Obviously, if the interests pursued are not valid according to sharia, the action is considered reprehensible.

On the other hand, with reference to the Qur'anic verse which forbids remaining in a place where there is a danger for oneself, the action of emigrating becomes mandatory for the Muslim who, in that place, can be exposed to criminal and unfair deeds, even if that place is his own country. This point is of particular importance if we consider the conditions of the Islamic countries described by the author, although he emphasizes that living in *bilād al-muslimīn* is always preferable.

A further reason that makes emigration to the "territory of war" mandatory is possessing the requirements and the ability to convert people of other nations to Islam or to be a leader for the Muslims who are already there.

3 Conclusions

The *Risāla fī dār al-ḥarb wa suknāhā* by Muḥammad Bayram V is an example of a successful attempt to adapt Islamic law to changed international relationships, dictated by the global evolution of societies. Part of its value is undoubtedly attributable to the keen awareness of the author of unprecedented social and juridical changes in the legal system of each individual state, which clearly emerges from numerous passages of the fourth and the fifth *muqaddima,* and even from his use of terminology. For example, in the two aforementioned chapters, the notion of "Islamic countries" is no longer expressed by *bilād al-islām, dār al-islām,* or *arḍ al-islām,* as in classical sources and in the three previous chapters, but rather by *bilād al-muslimīn* (Muslims' countries), in order to emphasize the relevant changes that occurred in these places in modern times, first of all in the method of governing and consequently in social manners and security.

Another interesting point of the *Risāla* consists in the use of analogical reasoning, which is at the basis of the whole process of modernization of Islamic law. A source of primary importance for Hanafi *fiqh* after Qur'an and Sunna, analogical reasoning is here cleverly used by the Tunisian jurist to face a number of issues. One of these concerns the qualification of the act of traveling and staying in a non-Islamic country by a Muslim in possession of his own juridical capacity. As clearly stated in the fifth chapter, depending on the conformity of the motivation that drives a Muslim to move to a non-Islamic territory with the principles of sharia, the act can be qualified as reprehensible, prohibited, dutiful or recommendable. Each one of these degrees of permissibility is derived by analogy from parallel situations because sources dealing with the matter in a specific way apparently do not exist. Thus, the act is qualified as reprehensible by virtue of the fatwa by Bayram II that states, "when it is asked whether sailing in the direction of *dār al-ḥarb* contravenes justice, the answer is that it depends on the reason why it is done"; it is prohibited by virtue of the equivalence established, again by Bayram II, between the "house" and the "country," saying "as it is forbidden to go to a house where someone is aware there is danger of contracting an infectious disease, it is equally forbidden to travel to a country where reprehensible actions take place, especially when that is well known before traveling"; it is dutiful in order to protect oneself from injustices suffered in one's own Islamic country and for those who are moved by public interests; it is recommended because "commanding the good" includes preservation of oneself and others from injustice.

References

Abū al-Suʿūd Efendi. *Tafsīr Abī al-Suʿūd aw Iršād al-ʿaql al-salīm ilā mazāyā 'l-kitāb al-karīm*, edited by ʿAbd al-Qādir Aḥmad ʿAṭā. 5 vols. Cairo, 1971.

Abun-Nasr, Jamil M. "The Tunisian State in the Eighteenth Century." *Revue de l'Occident Musulman et de la Méditerranée*, 33 (1982): 33–66.

Ahmad, Mushtaq Muhammad. "The notions of *dār al-ḥarb* and *dār al-Islām* in Islamic jurisprudence with special reference to the Ḥanafī school." *Islamic Studies* 47 (2008): 5–37.

Arberry, Arthur John, ed. *The Koran Interpreted: A Translation*. A Touchstone Book. New York: Simon & Schuster, 1996.

Buḫārī, Muḥammad b. Ismāʿīl al-. *Le recueil des traditions mahométanes par el-Bokhâri (al-Ṣaḥīḥ)*. Edited by M. Ludolf Krehl. Vol. 1. 4 vols. Leiden: Brill, 1862.

Buḫārī, Muḥammad b. Ismāʿīl al-. Ismāʿīl al-. *Ṣaḥīḥ al-Buḫārī. The Translation of the Meanings of Sahih Al-Bukhari*. Translated by Muhammad Muhsin Khan. Vol. 2. 9 vols. Riyadh: Darussalam, 1997.

Al-Fatāwā al-hindiyya. Būlāq: Al-Maṭbaʿa al-kubrā al-amīriyya, 1310/1912–13.

Ġazālī, Abū Ḥāmid Muḥammad al-. *Iḥyāʾ ʿulūm al-dīn*. Vol. 2. Cairo, 1957.

Green, Arnold H. "A Comparative Historical Analysis of the Ulama and the State in Egypt and Tunisia", *Revue de l'Occident Musulman et de la Méditerranée*. 29 (1980): 31–54.

Haddad, Mohamed. *Le réformisme musulman: une histoire critique*. Mimesis: Paris, 2013.

Ibn Abī Ḍiyāf. *Itḥāf ahl al-zamān bi-aḫbār mulūk Tūnus wa-ʿahd al-amān*. 8 vols. Tunis: Sécretariat d'État aux Affaires Culturelles, 1963–68.

Krieken, G. S. van. "Muḥammad Bayram al-Khāmis." *Encyclopaedia of Islam, Vol. VII, Mif-Naz*. Leiden: Brill, 1993.

Miossec, Jean-Marie. "Identité tunisienne: de la personnalité géographique d'un pays du Maghreb, du monde arabo-islamique et de la Méditerranée." *Annales de Géographie* 108, no. 607 (1999): 255–76.

Mitchell, Terence Frederick. *Writing Arabic: A Practical Introduction to the Ruqʿuh Script*. 1953. Reprint, Oxford: Oxford University Press, 1990.

Moussawy, Salah. *Cahier de calligraphie arabe: style roqu'a*. Paris: Bachari, 2002.

Muḥammad Bayram al-Ḫāmis al-Tūnisī. *Ṣafwat al-iʿtibār bi-mustawdaʿ al-amṣār wa'l-aqṭār*. 5 vols. Beirut: Dār Sādir, 2001–3.

Naguib, Shuruq. "Guiding the Sound Mind: Ebū's-Suʿūd's *Tafsīr* and Rhetorical Interpretation of the Qur'an in the Post-Classical Period." *The Journal of Ottoman Studies* 42 (2013): 1–52.

Nallino, Carlo Alfonso. "Delle assicurazioni in diritto musulmano hanafita." *Oriente moderno* 7 (1927): 446–61.

Perkins, Kenneth J. *Historical Dictionary of Tunisia*. African Historical Dictionaries 45. Lanham, MD: Scarecrow Press, 1997.

Saraḫsī, Muḥammad b. Aḥmad al-. *Kitāb al-Mabṣūṭ fī 'l-fiqh al-Ḥanafī*. Vol. 14. Cairo, 1324–31AH.

Schacht, Joseph. "Abū 'l-Su'ūd." *Encyclopaedia of Islam, Vol. I, A-B.* Leiden: Brill, 1960.

Ṭabarānī, Abū 'l-Qāsim al-. *Al-Mu'jam al-kabīr.* Cairo: Maktabat Ibn Taymiyya, 1415/1994.

Tlili, Béchir. "Contribution à l'étude de la pensée sociale et politique de Bayram V (1840–1889)." *Revue de l'Occident Musulman et de la Méditerranée* 15–16 (1973): 327–43.

Tlili, Béchir. "Note sur la notion d'Etat dans la pensée de Ah'mad Ibn Abi Ad'-d'Iyaf, réformateur tunisien du XIXe siècle (1804/5–1874)." *Revue de l'Occident musulman et de la Méditerranée* 8, no. 1 (1970): 141–70.

Concluding Remarks: The Terminological Array

Giuliano Lancioni

1 General Issues

In the analysis of the *dār al-ḥarb* / *dār al-islām* dichotomy, terminology clearly plays a paramount role. Contributions in this volume cope with, and try to explain and reconcile, the relatively large variation in words and their combinations found in sources to refer to the concepts and the subjects involved in this dichotomy. Some observations are in order to try to sort out this variation, without any ambition to achieve exhaustiveness, and to identify what factors trigger the choice between possible alternatives.

An important source of variation lies in the different denotata that each term refers to: the dichotomy may refer (1) to a territory (in what is perhaps the original stage of the dichotomy, at least according to the *communis opinio*), (2) to people living in that territory, or (3) to the specific religious community that prevails in the same territory.

The territorial dimension (1) is clearly expressed in the standard form of the dichotomy: both entities are marked as *dār* "abode," a choice that might seem natural enough but which should perhaps require some additional reflection. In particular, it is not obvious why *dār* came to be selected over other possible synonyms or quasi-synonyms (*bayt* comes immediately to mind, an alternative possibly excluded by its early adoption in such collocations as *ahl al-bayt*),[1] nor is it clear why this specific metonymy—a dwelling for a territory—came to become standard.

Alternatives do indeed occur in sources, as several papers in this volume show. First, the more literal *arḍ* "land" (a frequent occurrence in Ibn al-Mubārak's *Kitāb al-jihād*, as Roberta Denaro's list of loci shows), coupled with a variety of nouns. These nouns in most cases do not refer to a general juridical concept, but rather to a more specific geographical entity: this is hardly surprising in sources that do not aim at a strictly juridical discussion.

The same holds for *bilād*, a noun whose original plural denotation suggests a distributional, opposite to holistic, view of a territory: a "country" as a set of places (*balad*) rather than a unity (*arḍ*). This term is usually preferred by authors—such as geographers, travelers, as well as historians—who are more interested in describing territories or events than in establishing abstract

1 See the discussion on *dār*/*bayt* synonymy in section 4 below.

 | DOI 10.1163/9789004331037_022

categories, as shown, in different contexts, by Giovanna Calasso, Camille Rhoné and Francesco Zappa.

The plural of *dār*, quite frequent elsewhere in similar contexts (*diyār Miṣr*, but also place names as *diyār Bakīr* = Diarbakir), doesn't seem to be used frequently, perhaps because of the lexicalization of the singular metonymy *dār* ≅ territory.[2]

The second possible denotatum (2) is people living in a specific territory which is outside *dār al-islām* (or, perhaps, outside what would have come to be so called).

In this regard, an interesting point in terminology, which reflects a difference in categorization, is the lack of superposition between the *dār al-islām / dār al-ḥarb* dichotomy and the familiar binary opposition Roman (or, for such a matter, Greek) vs Barbarian evoked at the beginning of Roberta Denaro's chapter. We do find the *ʿarab* vs *ʿajam* opposition in sources, as my own discussion of dictionary definitions shows, but this opposition basically does not overlap with the *dār al-islām / dār al-ḥarb* dichotomy because of the early conquest of the prototypical non-Arab lands, the former Persian empire, and the subsequent integration of *bilād al-ʿajam* in *dār al-islām*. Instead, it is *arḍ/bilād al-rūm* "the country/ies of the Romans/Byzantines" to become the prototypical other to Islam, with later alternatives, in different historical circumstances, as *Ifranja* "Franks" (see remarks by Michel Balivet and discussion in Yaacov Lev's paper).

This way, *dār al-ḥarb* becomes a kind of hypernym with several hyponyms, from the more general/prototypical *arḍ al-rūm* to more specific territorial denominations of individual countries outside *dār al-islām*. In this case, reference to peoples living in these countries can quite naturally be replaced by the geographical name of the area, so that, e.g., Šām "(Greater) Syria" at the time of the conquest refers to a territory which later juridical categories would have included in the concept of *dār al-ḥarb*.

Coming down to the second shift of reference, the term used to refer to the religious community (3) living in a territory brings us closer to the basis of the *dār al-islām / dār al-ḥarb* dichotomy. However, from a conceptual point of view the polar opposite to *dār al-islām* is not *dār al-ḥarb*: it is rather *dār al-kufr* (the abode of unbelief), *ḥarb* being the juridical consequence of *kufr*. In many contexts *dār al-ḥarb* / *dār* (or *bilād*) *al-kufr* seem to be used inter-

2 However, see the discussion on the use of the alternative plural form *dūr* in Giovanna Calasso's *Introduction*, p. 15. Some examples of the use of these alternative plurals in geographical texts are referred to in Giovanna Calasso's article in the present volume, p. 25.

changeably, and a double denomination—such as Yaacov Lev employs in his contribution—would perhaps be more accurate, if cumbersome.

However, this interchangeability is put into question by Hanafi authors—as shown by some hypothetical cases considered by medieval jurists (Calasso) as well as in actual political debate in modern India (Friedmann)—who make a clear-cut distinction between *dār al-kufr* and *dār al-ḥarb*.

The word *ʿaduww* "enemy" in this context is the natural consequence, or perhaps even the source, of the concept of *dār al-ḥarb*: if a territory is legally entitled to war, who lives there is best qualified as an enemy.

2 Issues in the History of the Arabic Lexicon

In some cases, we do not find in sources what we might expect because of an anachronistic projection of a later state of affairs. This is the case with the lack of such *nisbas* (nouns/adjectives of relation) as *ḥarbī* in the early literature: as Roberta Denaro remarks, they cannot e.g. be found in Ibn al-Mubārak's *Kitāb al-jihād*.

However, this is hardly surprising in a text from the second half of the second/eighth century, since a well-known feature in the history of the Arabic language is that the adoption of *nisba* into a universal word-formation mechanism happens within the frame of the translation movement in early Abbasid Baghdad: as Gérard Troupeau noted in the introduction to his *Léxique-Index*,[3] in Sībawayhi's *Kitāb* (a text roughly contemporary to the *Kitāb al-jihād*) all *nisbas* have the original toponymic/demonymic source, with the sole exception of the highly debated term *naḥwī*: we find metaphorical collocations as *banāt al-ṯālāṯa* lit. "the daughters of three (letters)" instead of the later normative *ṯulāṯī* (triliteral), already found at the beginning of the fourth/tenth century in Ibn al-Sarrāj's *Kitāb al-uṣūl*. This feature is so characteristic that it can be used quite confidently to date quotations, as I showed in trying to date grammatical references in some passages of alchemic texts attributed to the (pseudo-)Jābir b. Ḥayyān.[4] Therefore, we cannot be surprised that Ibn al-Mubārak does not use *ḥarbī*: the opposite would be a striking feature indeed.

More generally, adjectives and nouns of relation did not gain general—opposite to toponymic/demonymic—use before the translation movement

---

3 Gérard Troupeau, *Lexique-index du "Kitāb" de Sībawayhi*, Études arabes et islamiques : série 3, Études et documents; 7 (Paris: Klincksieck, 1976).

4 Giuliano Lancioni, "La terminologia grammaticale del corpus giabiriano," *Rivista degli Studi Orientali* 71 (1997): 83–97.

of the late second/eighth–early third/ninth centuries, when the employ, and coinage, of *nisba* forms became a general translational strategy to cope with the abundance of abstract concepts in Greek philosophical and scientific texts which did not have an immediate Arabic equivalent.

As a consequence, *nisba* forms with an *-ī* desinence[5] (together with their feminine counterparts in *-iyya*, often used for abstracts) were not generally available in the formative age of the Arabic–Islamic juridical terminology and we find just a few of them, mainly as a variant of and a shortcut for older and longer denominations: apart from *ḥarbī*, the most widespread example is perhaps *ḏimmī* "(non-Muslim) protected person."

The late emergence of *-ī* forms as a general word-formation strategy is reflected in the presence of gaps in the paradigm: no *nisba* form is found when a previous one-word alternative exists, mostly in the form of participles. Therefore, we found *mušrik, kāfir* and *muslim*, but not **širkī*, **kufrī* or **islāmī* (the availability of the latter is exploited in its contemporary employ to refer to militants of political Islam).

The reason why such forms as *ḥarbī* and *ḏimmī* do enter the lexicon is likely the unavailability of a previous shorter definition: in the first case, perhaps for the opaque relation between *ḥarb* and *dār al-ḥarb*—which may lend support to Gianroberto Scarcia's hypothesis,[6] adopted in Raoul Villano's paper, of the original meaning of the collocation as the "abode of those who wage war against God"—which prevented the emergence of a participle such as *muḥārib*, which does exist in the general meaning of "fighter," as a designation for people belonging to the "abode of war."

In the case of *ḏimmī*, the lack of an older short form is perhaps linked to the nature of the source word and the concept it designates: while *islām, širk*, and *kufr* are verbal nouns that denote an activity, or a permanent status—which lends itself naturally to the employ of a participle to denote people prototypically involved in that activity—*ḏimma* denotes a non-active status, and no verb is directly related to it—lexicons register only a II-form causative *ḏammama* in the meaning of "to grant" or "demand protection," according to the argument structure. Therefore, a more general derivation mechanism is

5 According to general practice, we quote the *–iyy* desinence of the *nisba* in its pausal form (*-ī*).

6 Gianroberto Scarcia, "*Islām* e *Ḥarb*, *ʿArab* e *ʿAjam*: nota a due celeberrime dicotomie islamiche," in *Azhàr: studi arabo-islamici in memoria di Umberto Rizzitano (1913–1980)*, ed. Antonino Pellitteri and Giovanni Montaina, Annali della Facoltà di lettere e filosofia dell'Università di Palermo. Studi e ricerche 23 (Palermo: Facoltà di lettere e filosofia dell'Università di Palermo, 1995), 205–10.

needed to build a single-word concept, and here is where the *nisba*-strategy, once available, fits best.

3 Shifting Meanings

Relabeling of concepts according to a shifted terminology is a very common feature in the process that led to the definition of classical Arabic-Islamic sciences in the fourth/tenth century: as Roberto Tottoli remarks, Ṭabarī's commentary freely reinterprets the Qur'anic text in the framework of the *dār al-islām / dār al-ḥarb* dichotomy, which is notoriously lacking in the original.

This relabeling process can be found quite often in the choice of editorial titles for book sections: Hadith collections do have sections about *dār al-ḥarb*, while the term itself never occurs in actual traditions; analogously, editors of early grammatical texts consistently label sections with standardized terms that are rare, or outright absent, in the original wording (e.g., *taṣġīr* "diminutive" in editorial titles of Sībawayhi's *Kitāb* instead than *taḥqīr*, absolutely prevailing in the text).[7]

Another source of shift in meanings, and words that denote them, comes from new theological/juridical needs: when the rationale for the original opposition becomes less relevant, a new opposition is partially superposed on the original one and a more or less perfect overlap arises between couples of opposites.

A very clear example of this phenomenon is shown in a specific Shi'i reinterpretation of the dichotomy, according to the primacy of knowledge, analyzed in Alessandro Cancian's paper: *dār al-ʿilm* (abode of knowledge), bound to the classical Shi'i association of knowledge with the imam, is opposed to *dār al-jahl* (abode of ignorance), with a mirrored opposition between *dār al-īmān* (abode of faith) and *dār al-kufr* (abode of unbelief). This is a most interesting feature of the Shi'i/Sunni divide: the lack of an association between faith and territory that characterizes Shi'ism—especially before the tenth/sixteenth century Safavid declaration of Twelver Shi'a as the official religion of Iran (but, of course, even later outside Iran)—transfers the *dār* opposition from the domain of countries and territories into the more abstract domain of knowledge and faith (see also discussion in Biancamaria Scarcia Amoretti's paper in this regard).

7 See Giuliano Lancioni, *Diminutives in Sībawayhi's* Kitāb*: An Inquiry into the History of Linguistic Theories* (Roma: Sapienza Università di Roma, Istituto Italiano di Studi Orientali, 2011).

Shifts can be less substantial in nature and give rise to new designations which match better a changed social and geographic landscape: this is the case for the employ of *barr* "(open) land" as an equivalent for *bilād* or similar, more entrenched terms in such different contexts as Anatolia—as shown in a short hint in Michel Balivet's paper—and Libya (see the discussion in Antonino Pellitteri's contribution). In both cases, the perception of a specific landscape seems to be the base for a new phrasing, if not a new conceptualization.

4 Why Synonyms are Not Exactly Alike

Synonymy is a battered question in lexicography, linguistics and philosophy of language: what "having the same meaning" amounts to is difficult, and perhaps impossible, to say; in any case, a definition of synonymy requires the preliminary definition of a number of issues about meaning, lexical relations and other theoretical points, for which little, if any, agreement exists in language-related studies.

While this is not the best place to tackle such complex theoretical issues, a sensible approach to synonymy is possible, and indeed needed, if a meaningful discussion of technical terminology is in order.

A classical, relatively undemanding definition of synonymy is linked to interchangeability: if a word (or a phrase) can be substituted for another in a given context without significantly altering the sentence's meaning, the two words/phrases can be considered to be equivalent, and therefore synonyms, at least in the given context. While seemingly oversimplified and even naïve, this definition is working enough to become the cornerstone of the concept of synset (synonym set) in the largest, most cited electronic dictionary/thesaurus currently available, Wordnet.[8]

However, historical shifts in meaning are common in the slippery world of words: interchangeability evolves across times, and terms may become virtual synonyms when an original distinction becomes blurred or less relevant.

Such a case in our context is the *dār*/*bayt* synonymy. In Modern Standard Arabic these words can be regarded as interchangeable in most contexts—equivalent clauses with *dār* and *bayt* are routinely employed in language teaching to show students the difference between masculine and feminine

8 See the discussion in Christiane Fellbaum, "Introduction," in *WordNet: an electronic lexical database*, ed. Christiane Fellbaum, Language, speech, and communication (Cambridge, Mass: MIT Press, 1998), 1–19.

forms, since *dār* happens to be feminine and *bayt* masculine. However, these expressions are not strictly synonyms in Classical Arabic.

Bayt originally designates a dwelling, typically in the form of a tent; its strict association with the idea of "living" or "dwelling" somewhere is clearly shown by the denominative verb *bāta* "to spend the night." *Dār*, in its turn, is originally a "courtyard," the space between tents or other dwellings, and comes to mean "house" by metonymy, referring first to the group of houses that share a courtyard or a common area. In this case, the I-form verb *dāra* means "to go around:" the primary association is with an area to encircle, rather than a place to live in.

This distinction is clear to classical Arab lexicographers: Fīrūzābādī in the *Qāmūs*, while not defining *bayt* explicitly—an implicit admission that he does not find a perfect synonym for this word—helps readers identify the word by adding *min al-šaʿar wa'l-madar* "(made) of hair or mud," referring by this means to a "tent" or a more stable "house."[9] In the case of *dār*, however, the *Qāmūs* does have a definition: *al-maḥall yajmaʿu 'l-bināʾ wa'l-ʿarṣa* "a place which gathers a building and a courtyard."[10]

Of course, the inclusion of a dwelling in both cases produced an amount of overlap between two originally clearly distinguished meanings. This overlap, which over time produced a near synonymy, was clearly not wide enough to allow these terms to be exchanged freely in the period when the core of the juridical lexicon was formed. Therefore, while the existence of such early set expressions as *ahl al-bayt* was likely to reduce the "usability" of *bayt* for other purposes, a more substantial difference between the two words is likely to have played a major role in the choice of *dār* for territorial designations.

We can try to express this distinction in basic, somewhat abstract, terms. *Bayt* primarily denotes a closed area conceptualized as a point: while its meaning can be extended, it still refers to something relatively small and localized, a "house:" this readily explains metaphorical uses such as *ahl al-bayt* "people of the House (the family of the Prophet)", *bayt al-māl* "the house (administration) of budget," *bayt al-ḥikma* "the house of wisdom" (how the palatial library of the Abbasid caliphs came to be called).

On the contrary, *dār* refers to an area, perhaps a small area, but nevertheless a non-punctual space surrounding, and possibly including, a building. When reference must be made to a territory linked to a religious/juridical belonging, *dār* is a much more logical choice than *bayt*.

---

9 Fīrūzābādī, *al-Qāmūs al-muḥīṭ*, ed. Muḥammad Naʿīm al-ʿIrqsūsī, 8th ed. (Beirut: Mu'assasat al-Risāla, 1426/2005), 148, s.v. *byt*.

10 Ibid., 393, s.v. *dwr*.

A striking phenomenon in *dār*-related lexicon is the virtual absence of construct state forms where *dār* is constructed with a plural form designating a group, and the strong preference for phrases where *dār* is constructed with a verbal or an abstract noun designating belief or unbelief: we routinely have *dār al-islām, dār al-kufr, dār al-ḥarb*, but not **dār al-muslimīn, *dār al-kuffār, *dār al-ḥarbiyyīn, *dār al-muʾminīn.*[11] In all these cases, we have regular couples where *bilād* is used with group designations and *dār* with abstract, such as *bilād al-muslimīn* vs *dār al-islām*.

Such a regular alternation can be explained again by the lack of perfect overlap between seemingly similar concept such as *dār* and *bilād*: while *dār* denotes a territory *around* a center (and therefore does not easily match a group designation), *bilād* is a much more distributed, centerless designation, and fits well with a plural noun. This could help explain why the term *dār* came to be preferred through time by jurists as a designation for abstract categories.

5 The General Picture: The Lexicographical Array

As it is shown in my own paper, a major point in the lack of definition for some terms (strikingly, *dār al-islām*) lies in the word/collocation distinction: lexicographers do not give the same status to a word and to concepts expressed by a sequence of words. Dictionary users generally regard the lack of a word in a lexicon as a fault, while the lack of a collocation is much less important. This point is particularly significant in a language such as Arabic, where there are virtually no compounds and collocations (especially construct states) play a key role in lexical formation processes.

This attitude can be seen most clearly in specialized dictionaries. While the tradition of *kutub al-ḥudūd* (books of definitions), started in grammar by Rummānī's *Kitāb al-ḥudūd* (fourth/tenth century), reached juridical disciplines strikingly late (especially if we think of the constant association of grammatical and juridical studies throughout the history of classical Islamic societies), it is even more striking that juridical dictionaries usually lack an explicit definition of the collocations of this key dichotomy.

While speakers can employ collocations and phrases as technical terms without an explicit definition in general or technical dictionaries, lack of formal technical status can contribute to making them less stable and more shifting: if speakers/writers cannot find a collocation explicitly defined they will naturally tend to feel less normative pressure to use them and will tend to replace them more liberally with more or less equivalent expressions and phrases.

11 An exception is *dār al-širk*, which alternates with *dār al-mušrikīn*.

This aspect leads us to try a general systematization of technical and less technical collocations discussed in the essays gathered in the present volume. This systematization is based on multiword expressions (that is, collocations that can be regarded as fully lexicalized terms), regular collocations, and gaps in theoretically possible combinations of territory/place words and nouns designating beliefs (or lack thereof)/groups.

Modeling (and, by the nature of a modeling process, simplifying somewhat) a rather complex picture, we can build a two-dimensional array that gives a graphic picture of the core terminology found in this collection of papers.

TABLE 20.1 *The lexicographical array*

	ahl	***arḍ***	***balad***	***barr***	***bilād***	***dār/diyār/dūr***
ʿaduww		*arḍ al-ʿaduww* (expression)	*balad al-ʿaduww* (regular)	*barr al-ʿaduww* (regular)	*bilād al-ʿaduww* (regular)	
ʿahd	*ahl al-ʿahd* (regular)					*dār al-ʿahd* (regular)
ʿajam					*bilād al-ʿajam* (regular)	
amān	*ahl al-amān*					*dār (al-)amān* (regular)
ḏimma	*ahl al-ḏimma* (regular)					
faranj			*balad al-faranj*			
Fāris		*arḍ Fāris*				*diyār Fāris*
fāsiqūn						*dār al-fāsiqīn*
ġanīma						*dār al-ġanīma*
ḥarb	*ahl al-ḥarb* (expression)	*arḍ al-ḥarb* (expression)	*balad (al-) ḥarb*		*bilād al-ḥarb* (regular)	*dār (al-)ḥarb* / *dūr al-ḥarb* (expression)
hijra						*dār al-hijra* (expression)
hudna						*dār al-hudna*
ʿilm						*dār al-ʿilm* (expression)
īmān	*ahl al-īmān*					*dār al-īmān*

TABLE 20.1 *The lexicographical array* (cont.)

	ahl	***arḍ***	***balad***	***barr***	***bilād***	***dār/diyār/dūr***
islām	*ahl al-islām* (regular)	*arḍ al-islām* (expression)	*balad al-islām*		*bilād al-islām* (regular)	*dār (al-)islām / diyār al-islām* (expression)
jahl						*dār al-jahl*
jihād						*dār al-jihād* (regular)
kitāb	*ahl al-kitāb* (expression)					
kuffār			*balad al-kuffār*			
kufr	*ahl al-kufr* (regular)	*arḍ al-kufr*	*balad kufr*		*bilād (al-) kufr*	*dār (al-)kufr / diyār al-kufr / dūr al-kufr* (expression)
muslimūn		*arḍ al-muslimīn* (regular)	*balad al-muslimīn*		*bilād al-muslimīn* (expression)	
mušrikūn					*bilād al-mušrikīn* (expression)	*dār al-mušrikīn*
muwādaʿa						*dār al-muwādaʿa*
qarār						*dār al-qarār*
rūm		*arḍ al-rūm* (expression)			*bilād al-rūm* (expression)	
salām						*dār al-salām* (expression)
silm						*dār al-silm*
širk	*ahl al-širk* (expression)	*arḍ al-širk* (regular)			*bilād al-širk* (expression)	*dār al-širk* (expression)
sūdān		*arḍ al-sūdān*	*balad al-sūdān*		*bilād al-sūdān*	
ṣulḥ		*arḍ al-ṣulḥ*				*dār al-ṣulḥ*
turk		*arḍ al-turk*		*barr al-Turkiyya*		

While labels in this array are somewhat tentative—the difference between a multiword expression, a regular collocation and a casual one is blurred, while gaps cannot be definitely asserted without a fuller corpus research—the general picture is clear, and interesting: not everything possible is attested to, and neat asymmetries are present in the array.

While the previous discussion tries to elicit some general trends and rationales behind these asymmetries, it is only the deep, informed and nuanced discussion of terminology in the papers of the present volume that may shed light on, validate (or partially invalidate) this schema. To these discussions the reader is referred.

As a final remark, this survey of structural features and gaps in theoretically possible designations for notions related to the *dār al-islām* / *dār al-ḥarb* dichotomy recalls the need for "investigating absences" raised by Giovanna Calasso in the book's introduction as one of the major challenges in this domain of research.

References

Fellbaum, Christiane. "Introduction." In *WordNet: an electronic lexical database*, edited by Christiane Fellbaum, 1–19. Language, speech, and communication. Cambridge, Mass: MIT Press, 1998.

Fīrūzābādī, Abū 'l-Ṭāhir Muḥammad al-. *Al-Qāmūs al-muḥīṭ*. Edited by Muḥammad Naʿīm al-ʿIrqsūsī. 8th ed. Beirut: Muʾassasat al-Risāla, 1426/2005.

Lancioni, Giuliano. "La terminologia grammaticale del corpus giabiriano." *Rivista degli Studi Orientali* 71 (1997): 83–97.

Lancioni, Giuliano. *Diminutives in Sībawayhi's* Kitāb*: An Inquiry into the History of Linguistic Theories*. Roma: Sapienza Università di Roma, Istituto Italiano di Studi Orientali, 2011.

Scarcia, Gianroberto. "*Islām* e *Ḥarb*, *ʿArab* e *ʿAjam*: nota a due celeberrime dicotomie islamiche." In *Azhàr: studi arabo-islamici in memoria di Umberto Rizzitano (1913–1980)*, edited by Antonino Pellitteri and Giovanni Montaina, 205–10. Annali della Facoltà di lettere e filosofia dell'Università di Palermo. Studi e ricerche 23. Palermo: Facoltà di lettere e filosofia dell'Università di Palermo, 1995.

Troupeau, Gérard. *Lexique-index du "Kitāb" de Sībawayhi*. Études arabes et islamiques : série 3, Études et documents; 7. Paris: Klincksieck, 1976.

Index of Arabic and Other Technical Terms

Index of Names

www.ingramcontent.com/pod-product-compliance
Lightning Source LLC
LaVergne TN
LVHW010541300926
849162LV00002B/195
9789004328686